REPRESENTATIVE ONE–ACT PLAYS
BY AMERICAN AUTHORS

Representative
ONE-ACT PLAYS
BY AMERICAN AUTHORS

Selected, with Biographical Notes by

MARGARET MAYORGA
*Author of "A Short History of the American
Drama"*

REVISED EDITION

BOSTON
LITTLE, BROWN AND COMPANY
1937

Published October 1937

DEDICATED
TO MY SON
ERIC

FOREWORD

When the first edition of *Representative One-Act Plays by American Authors* appeared in 1919, it was acknowledged as a pioneer in a new field, for there was no other anthology of one-act plays. Percival Wilde, whose "A Question of Morality" was included in that volume, now writes me: "It may interest you to know that your 1919 anthology was the first volume of the kind in which I was included. Your new one will be the fiftieth."

If I was enthusiastic about American one-act plays eighteen years ago, — some of the reviewers did hint that mine was the optimism of youth, — evidently I was not alone.

Many of us at the time were beguiled by the novelties, it is true, and failed to observe the form beneath the artistic covering. But even when our perception was astigmatic, we did feel that something new and vital was happening in the American theatre. Had some seer told us that the vitality and progress of the new playwriting lay in the direction of democracy, perhaps we might have sneered, might even have felt robbed of something exquisite.

For when the one-act drama first became conscious of itself, it was the plaything of the choosey few, of the set which know about the *Théâtre Libre* in Paris and the *Freie Bühne* in Berlin, and yearned to bring similar artistic refinements to the streets of New York.

There were, of course, those who knew also about the People's Theatres of Russia and the German *Volksbühne*, psychologically interesting ventures which lacked the charm of the Moscow Art Theatre or the Abbey Theatre in Dublin, and were, in fact, largely imitative in their cultural ideals. It took a while for the People's Theatres to discover their destiny.

But about 1910 organized audiences first began to appear in the American theatre, about the time that the Theatre Syndicate — which had controlled all first-class theatres in the country for much too long — gave way before theatrical and motion-picture competition and left a clear field for Little Theatre developments.

As Ibsen's influence in the creation of plays of ideas was then at its height, and *théâtres intimes* were needed to observe dramatic action in close-up, groups everywhere looked to regular patrons for financial support for Little Theatre ventures. The early sponsors of the art theatres in this country were people of wealth, like Mr. MacDowell of the famed galleries, Mr. Joseph I. C. Clarke, and the Lewisohn sisters, all of New York; and societies of leisure-time culture-bearers, such as the Women's Clubs and the Drama Leagues.

Within the decade from 1910 to 1920, thousands of art ventures were established. Most of them fell short of the ideals of their founders, and others learned that even non-professional theatres may fail in quite professional ways. But in proportion as they served their localities and forgot about Paris and Berlin, they sometimes succeeded in their artistic endeavors, and became established as important centers in their communities. The Pasadena and Cleveland Playhouses, the Seattle Repertory Playhouse, and the theatres of Santa Barbara, Boston, Buffalo, Dallas, New Orleans, Birmingham, Mobile, Duluth, Omaha, and the Hedgerow Theatre are only a few of those which have merged their artistic aims with their community needs.

In New York, art for art's sake is usually taken quite seriously; it is the town's own local pattern. And so it happens that here several of the original members of the Provincetown Players, who trod the boards of an old wharf on Cape Cod for a few summers and of a stable in a back alley of New York's Greenwich Village for a few winters, were ultimately taken over by the Washington Square Players. They first convened in a bookshop but now successfully translate European glamour at a profit to the handsome Guild Theatre. The Theatre Guild is the one art project which has done beautifully what every Little Theatre in the country aspired to do not very long ago.

Did the Guild, after achieving financial freedom, toss aside the one-act play that the struggling players had been so tender of? It is no matter: Broadway likes long plays, not short ones; that also is a piece of the local pattern. And it was Henrik Ibsen rather than Eugene O'Neill or any other American dramatist who really set the stage for the establishment of the one-act play as a democratic institution.

For the drama of a democracy must present various points of view, some of which may not be welcomed on a commercial stage, or else may be welcomed in New York, disputed in Washington, and banned in Boston. But no one, in any city, has ever seriously objected to the type of short play which can be traced directly back to the *Commedia dell'arte;* nor has anyone objected even to the offspring of the farces, travesties, extravaganzas, burlesques, and burlettas that deluged the English stage as curtain raisers during most of the nineteenth century.

It is the progeny of Nora Helmer who speak in many tongues to confound the keepers of the *status quo.* And it was Ibsen's dramas of ideas which proved that short plays need not be either slapstick dramas or abbreviated playlets, but may have dynamic conflicts that can be presented as effectively in one act as in several.

Such plays have helped some of our best dramatists to express themselves and the American scene. It was the serious one-act plays, written by such men as Percy MacKaye, George Middleton, Percival Wilde, and Eugene O'Neill, which provided the first steps in the approach of American drama to the status of a lively social institution.

There may have been some lone pioneering sponsor of dramatics in some public high school at the beginning of the twentieth century, but I know that only the very large high schools in the principal cities boasted them in 1910. And Barrett H. Clark has recorded how Robert Herrick and

Percy Boynton ran the risk of losing caste with the faculty
of the University of Chicago because they encouraged drama
discourse there.

It was in 1910 that Charles Coburn realized the need for
a university theatre association which would visit the colleges
with plays carefully selected for their cultural value, and so
he organized his own professional company for that purpose,
and played the college circuit successfully for several years.
In 1915, Stuart Walker's Portmanteau Company carried
the drama still further, into country clubs and civic groups.

By this time the Carnegie Institute of Technology in
Pittsburgh was ready to train play directors and students in
its workshop courses; and at Harvard, George Pierce Baker
had inaugurated what was to become the most famous of
all the workshop groups. Wisconsin, Minnesota, North
Dakota, Washington, North Carolina followed; it is esti-
mated that to-day more than seven hundred colleges and
universities regularly enroll thirty-five thousand to forty
thousand students in their dramatic departments. Most
of these students have no wish to enter the professional field,
but return to their home towns to popularize community
play-making with their neighbors and friends.

Recently, in the colleges, another trend is evident: the
interest in folk drama, which has been most successfully
inspired by Frederick Henry Koch. In the plays of Paul
Green and the Carolina Playmakers, new and revealing
conceptions of the drama of a democracy become apparent.

But there are many angles of approach to the American
scene, for ours is still a "melting pot" civilization; Americans are not yet a homogeneous people. Apart from the
art interests, the educational aspects, the folklore of our
plays, is the proletarian purpose. The plays for the workers'
groups and for federal theatre projects constitute a mighty
force which is advancing primarily toward social rather than
aesthetic ideals.

Yet beneath the varied aspects, the native enthusiasm
grows strong and deep, and the popularity of one-act play-

making in general creates a favorable milieu for the spread
of American genius. I suspect that social democracy and
the appreciation of plays by the laity may prove to be our
necessary prelude to dramatic beauty and maturity.

The twenty-five plays in this revised edition are offered
as representative of the play spirit that has spread significantly among us during the last twenty-five years, and as
representative of some authors who have contributed notably
to its development and prevalence. The bibliography contains detailed lists of the one-act plays of these authors, as
well as of some two hundred others.

I am indebted to the writings of Barrett H. Clark and
Ben Blake, and also to the assistance of Walter Prichard
Eaton, Ben Irwin, the Librarian of Harvard University,
and Jack Walsh of Samuel French for certain factual material which I have included. To play agents — especially
Mr. Sheil of Samuel French — and to thousands of friendly
readers whose approval of the original volume has inspired
the revised edition, my gratitude extends.

MARGARET MAYORGA

Long Island, 1937.

CONTENTS

The Body Politic

REPRESENTATIVE ONE-ACT PLAYS

*A survey of the product of American
authors in the one-act form
during twenty-five years*

SAM AVERAGE

PERCY MACKAYE

It is fitting to begin this collection of *Representative One-Act Plays by American Authors* with Percy MacKaye's "Sam Average", for the play is an interpretation of the birth of our symbolic Uncle Sam and the author is one of the pioneers among our one-act playwrights.

Mr. MacKaye was born in New York City on March 16, 1875, of a family which had already won laurels for itself in drama. His father, Steele MacKaye, wrote some twenty-five plays, the last of his work merging with his son's in a series of productions which affected the history and development of American drama for sixty years.

Percy MacKaye was educated at Harvard University and at the University of Leipzig. He has received honorary degrees from Dartmouth College (M.A., 1914) and from Miami University (Litt.D., 1924); and he held the first creative fellowship in poetry and drama at Miami from 1920 to 1924.

He is a member of the National Institute of Arts and Letters, the Dramatists' Guild, P.E.N., the MacDowell Colony Association, and a charter member of the Poetry Society of America. In 1936, the International Mark Twain Society conferred upon him honorary membership in recognition of his American biography: *Epoch — The Life of Steele MacKaye*, a two-volume memoir of his father.

Percy MacKaye has been a pioneer in several dramatic fields. His *Yankee Fantasies* was one of the first published collections of one-act plays (1912), some of them written as early as 1901. His *Kentucky Mountain Fantasies* (plays written from 1921 to 1923) was the first collection of American folk-plays by one author. His *The Civic Theatre*, comprising addresses delivered from 1908 to 1912, set forth at an early date an idea for the nation-wide establishment of noncommercial community and university theatres. His "Gloucester Pageant" (1909) was the first large-scale festival drama. His ballad play, "Washington" (1918), produced by Walter Hampden, introduced a new dramatic form. His "Wakefield" (1932), a folk-masque of America, was the first dramatic work commissioned, published, and produced by the United States Federal Government.

His operas have been produced both by the New York Metropolitan Opera House and by the Chicago Opera Company, and the festival productions of his masques have enlisted the largest audiences and numbers of acting participants in American dramatic history. Thousands of people participated in "Caliban"; hundreds of thousands were seated in the audiences.

In the field of folklore, Percy MacKaye's APPALACHIAN FOLK CYCLE (plays, poems, and tales, in five volumes written from 1921 to 1929) preserves the ancient folk-speech of our mountain people.

Several of his plays have been produced abroad and in translation; in London, by E. H. Sothern and Julia Marlowe; in Berlin, by Reinhardt; in Moscow, by Stanislavsky; in France, by Copeau.

Percy MacKaye is author of some fifty volumes: poems, plays, masques, operas, tales, essays, and a biography. Among the most important of these works are: PLAYS IN VERSE, "A Garland to Sylvia", "The Canterbury Pilgrims", "Fenris the Wolf", "Jeanne d'Arc", "Sappho and Phaon", "A Thousand Years Ago"; PLAYS IN PROSE, "The Scarecrow", "Mater", "Anti-Matrimony", *Yankee Fantasies* (four one-act plays), *Kentucky Mountain Fantasies* (three short plays), "The Sphinx", "This Fine-Pretty World"; MASQUES, "Gloucester Pageant", "Sanctuary" (a Bird Masque), "Saint Louis", "Caliban", "The Evergreen Tree", "The Roll Call" (Red Cross Masque), "The Will of

Song", "The Pilgrim and the Book", "Wakefield"; OPERAS, "The Canterbury Pilgrims", "The Immigrants", "Sinbad and the Peacock Lady", "Rip Van Winkle"; ESSAYS, *The Playhouse and the Play*, *The Civic Theatre*, *Community Drama*, "A Substitute for War"; BIOGRAPHY, *Epoch — The Life of Steele MacKaye*.

SAM AVERAGE

A SILHOUETTE

By PERCY MACKAYE

"Sam Average" was originally produced at the Toy Theatre, Boston, on February 26, 1912.

Original Cast

ANDREW . . . . Mr. Freedley
JOEL . . . . Mr. Bunker
ELLEN . . . . Miss Lingard
SAM AVERAGE . . . . Mr. Menard

SAM AVERAGE

SCENE. *An intrenchment in Canada, near Niagara Falls, in the year 1814. Night, shortly before dawn.*

On the right, the dull glow of a smouldering wood-fire ruddies the earthen embankment, the low-stretched outline of which forms, with darkness, the scenic background.

Near the centre, left, against the dark, a flag with stars floats from its standard.

Beside the fire, ANDREW, *reclined, gazes at a small frame in his hand; near him is a knapsack, with contents emptied beside it.*

On the embankment, JOEL, *with a gun, paces back and forth, a blanket thrown about his shoulders.*

JOEL (*with a singing call*). Four o'clock! — All 's well!

[*Jumping down from the embankment, he approaches the fire,*

ANDREW. By God, Joel, it 's bitter.

JOEL (*rubbing his hands over the coals*). A mite sharpish.

ANDREW (*looks up eagerly*). What?

JOEL. Cuts sharp, for Thanksgivin'.

ANDREW (*sinks back, gloomily*). Oh! (*A pause*) I wondered you should agree with me. You meant the weather. I meant —

[*A pause again.*

JOEL. Well, Andy: what 'd you mean?

ANDREW. Life.

JOEL. Shucks!

ANDREW (*to himself*). Living!

JOEL (*sauntering over left, listens*). Hear a rooster crow?

ANDREW. No. What are you doing?

JOEL. Tiltin' the flag over crooked in the dirt. That 's our signal.

ANDREW. Nothing could be more appropriate, unless we buried it — buried it in the dirt!

JOEL. She 's to find us where the flag 's turned down. I fixed that with the sergeant all right. The rooster crowin' 's *her* watch-word for us.

ANDREW. An eagle screaming, Joel: that would have been better. (*Rising*) — Ah!

[*He laughs painfully.*

JOEL. Hush up, Andy! The nearest men ain't two rods away. You 'll wake 'em. Pitch it low.

ANDREW. Don't be alarmed. I 'm coward enough.

JOEL. 'Course, though, there ain't much danger. I 'm sentinel this end, and the sergeant has the tip at t'other. Besides, you may call it the reg'lar thing. There 's been two thousand deserters already in this tuppenny-ha'penny war, and none on 'em the worse off. When a man don't get his pay for nine months — well, he ups and takes his vacation: why not? When Nell joins us, we 'll hike up the Niagara, cross over to Tonawanda and take our breakfast in Buffalo. By that time, the boys here will be marchin' away toward Lundy's Lane.

ANDREW (*walks back and forth, shivering*). I 'm afraid.

JOEL. 'Fraid? Bosh!

ANDREW. I 'm afraid to face —

JOEL. Face what? — We won't get caught.

ANDREW. Your sister — my wife.

JOEL. Nell! — Why, ain't she comin' here just a-purpose to get you? Ain't there reason enough, Lord knows? Ain't you made up your mind to light out home anyhow?

ANDREW. Yes; that 's just what she 'll never forgive me for. In her heart she 'll never think of me the same. For she knows as well as I what pledge I 'll be breaking — what sacred pledge.

JOEL. What you mean?

ANDREW. No matter, no matter: this is gush.

[*He returns to the fire and begins to fumble over the contents of his knapsack. Joel watches him idly.*

JOEL. One of *her* curls?

ANDREW (*looking at a lock of hair, in the firelight*). No; the baby's, little Andy's. Some day they'll tell him how his father —

[*He winces, and puts the lock away.*

JOEL (*going toward the embankment*). Listen!

ANDREW (*ties up the package, muttering*). Son of a traitor!

JOEL (*tiptoeing back*). It's crowed. — That's her.

[*Leaping to his feet, Andrew stares toward the embankment where the flag is dipped; then turns his back to it, closing his eyes and gripping his hands.*

After a pause, silently the figure of a YOUNG WOMAN *emerges from the dark and stands on the embankment. She is bareheaded and ill-clad.*

Joel touches Andrew, who turns and looks toward her.

Silently, she steals down to him and they embrace.

ANDREW. My Nell!

ELLEN. Nearly a year —

ANDREW. Now, at last!

ELLEN. Hold me close, Andy.

ANDREW. You're better?

ELLEN. Let's forget — just for now.

ANDREW. Is he grown much?

ELLEN. Grown? — You should see him! But so ill: What could I do? You see —

ANDREW. I know, I know.

ELLEN. The money was all gone. They turned me out at the old place, and then —

ANDREW. I know, dear.

ELLEN. I got sewing, but when the smallpox —

ANDREW. I have all your letters, Nell. Come, help me to pack.

ELLEN. What! You're really decided —

JOEL (*approaching*). Hello, Sis!

ELLEN (*absently*). Ah, Joel: that you?

(*Eagerly, following Andrew to the knapsack*)
But my dear —

ANDREW.   Just these few things, and we 're off.

ELLEN (*agitated*).   Wait; wait!   You don't know yet why I 've come — instead of writing.

ANDREW.   I can guess.

ELLEN.   But you can't: that 's — what 's so hard.   I have to tell you something, and then — (*Slowly*)   I must know from your own eyes, from yourself, that you wish to do this, Andrew : that you think it is *right*.

ANDREW (*gently*).   I guessed that.

ELLEN.   This is what I must tell you. — It 's not just the sickness, it 's not only the baby, not the money gone — and all that; it 's — it 's —

ANDREW (*murmurs*).   My God!

ELLEN.   It 's what all that brings — the helplessness : I 've been insulted.   Andy —

(*Her voice breaks*)

— I want a protector.

ANDREW (*taking her in his arms, where she sobs*).   There, dear !

ELLEN (*with a low moan*).   You know.

ANDREW.   I know. — Come, now : we 'll go.

ELLEN (*her face lighting up*).   Oh ! — and you *dare?*   It 's *right?*

ANDREW (*moving from her, with a hoarse laugh*).   *Dare?*   Dare I be damned by God and all His angels?   Ha ! — Come, we 're slow.

JOEL.   Time enough.

ELLEN (*sinking upon Joel's knapsack as a seat, leans her head on her hands, and looks strangely at Andrew*).   I 'd better have written, I 'm afraid.

ANDREW (*controlling his emotion*).   Now don't take it that way.   I 've considered it all.

ELLEN (*with deep quiet*).   Blasphemously?

ANDREW.   Reasonably, my brave wife.   When I enlisted, I did so in a dream.   I dreamed I was called to love and serve our country.   But that dream is shattered.   This sordid war, this political murder, has not one single prin-

ciple of humanity to excuse its bloody sacrilege. It does-
n't deserve my loyalty — our loyalty.

ELLEN. Are you saying this — for my sake? What of
"God and His angels"?

ANDREW (*not looking at her*). If we had a just cause — a
cause of liberty like that in Seventy-six; if to serve one's
country meant to serve God and His angels — then, yes:
a man might put away wife and child. He might say:
"I will not be a husband, a father; I will be a patriot."
But now — like this — tangled in a web of spiders — caught
in a grab-net of politicians — and you, you and our baby-
boy, like this — hell let in on our home — no, Country
be cursed!

ELLEN (*slowly*). So, then, when little Andy grows up —

ANDREW (*groaning*). I say that the only thing —

ELLEN. I am to tell him —

ANDREW (*defiantly*). Tell him his father deserted his country, and thanked God for the chance.

(*Looking about him passionately*)

Here!

(*He tears a part of the flag from its standard, and reaches it
toward her*)

You're cold; put this round you.

⌐*As he is putting the strip of colored silk about her shoulders,
there rises, faint yet close by, a sound of fifes and flutes, playing the merry march-strains of "Yankee Doodle."*

*At the same time, there enters along the embankment, dimly,
enveloped in a great cloak, a tall* FIGURE, *which pauses beside
the standard of the torn flag, silhouetted against the first pale
streaks of the dawn.*

ELLEN (*gazing at Andrew*). What's the matter?

ANDREW (*listening*). Who are they? Where is it?

JOEL (*starts, alertly*). He hears something.

ANDREW. Why should they play before daybreak?

ELLEN. Andy —

JOEL (*whispers*). Ssh! Look out: we're spied on.

[*He points to the embankment. Andrew and Ellen draw back.*

THE FIGURE (*straightening the flag-standard, and leaning on it*).
Desartin'?

ANDREW (*puts Eller behind him*). Who's there? The
watchword!

THE FIGURE. God save the smart folks!

JOEL (*to Andrew*). He's on to us. Pickle him quiet, or it's
court-martial!
(*Showing a long knife*)
Shall I give him this?

ANDREW (*taking it from him*). No; *I* will.

ELLEN (*seizing his arm*). Andrew!

ANDREW. Let go.
(*The Figure, descending into the entrenchment, approaches
with face muffled. Joel draws Ellen away. Andrew moves
toward the Figure slowly. They meet and pause*)
You're a spy!
[*With a quick flash, Andrew raises the knife to strike, but
pauses, staring. The Figure, throwing up one arm toward
the blow, reveals — through the parted cloak — a glint of stars
in the firelight.*[1]

THE FIGURE. Steady boys : I'm one of ye. The sergeant
told me to drop round.

JOEL. Oh, the sergeant! That's all right, then.

ANDREW (*dropping the knife*). Who are you?

THE FIGURE. Who be *I*? My name, ye mean? — My name's
Average : Sam Average : Univarsal Sam, some o' my
prophetic friends calls me.

ANDREW. What are you doing here — now?

THE FIGURE. Oh, tendin' to business.

JOEL. Tendin' to *other* folks' business, eh?

THE FIGURE (*with a touch of weariness*). Ye-es; reckon that
is my business. Some other folks is me.

JOEL (*grimacing to Ellen*). Cracked!

---

[1] The head and face of the Figure are partly hidden by a beak-shaped
cowl. Momentarily, however, when his head is turned toward the fire,
enough of the face is discernible to reveal his narrow iron-gray beard,
shaven upper lip, aquiline nose, and eyes that twinkle in the dimness.

THE FIGURE (*to Andrew*).   You're a mite back'ard in wages, ain't ye?

ANDREW.   Nine months.   What of that?

THE FIGURE.   That's what I dropped round for.   Seems like when a man's endoored and fit, like you have, for his country, and calc'lates he 'll quit, he ought to be takin' a little suthin' hom' for Thanksgivin'.   So I fetched round your pay.

ANDREW.   My pay!   You?

THE FIGURE.   Yes; I'm the paymaster.

ELLEN (*coming forward, eagerly*).   Andy!   The money, is it?

THE FIGURE (*bows with a grave, old-fashioned stateliness*). Your sarvent, Ma'am!

ANDREW (*speaking low*).   Keep back, Nell.

(*To the Figure*)

You — you were saying —

THE FIGURE.   I were about to say how gold bein' scarce down to the Treasury, I fetched ye some s'curities instead: some national I.O.U's, as ye might say.

(*He takes out an old powder horn, and rattles it quietly*)

That's them.

(*Pouring from the horn into his palm some glistening, golden grains*)

Here they be.

ELLEN (*peering, with Joel*).   Gold, Andy!

JOEL (*with a snigger*).   Gold — nothin'!   That's corn — just Injun corn: ha!

THE FIGURE (*bowing gravely*).   It's the quality, Ma'am, what counts, as ye might say.

JOEL (*behind his hand*).   His top-loft leaks!

THE FIGURE.   These here karnels, now, were give' me down Plymouth way, in Massachusetts, the fust Thanksgivin' seems like I can remember.   'T wa'n't long after the famine we had thar.   Me bein' some hungry, the red folks fetched a hull-lot o' this round, with the compliments of their capting — what were his name now? —

Massasoit. This here 's the last handful on 't left.
Thought ye might like some, bein' Thanksgivin'.

JOEL (*in a low voice to Ellen*). His screws are droppin' out.
Come and pack. We 've got to mark time and skip.

THE FIGURE (*without looking at Joel*). Eight or ten minutes
still to spare, boys. The sergeant said — wait till ye
hear his jew's-harp playin' of that new war tune: *The
Star Spangled Banner*. Then ye 'll know the coast 's
clear.

JOEL. Gad, that 's right. I remember now.

[*He draws Ellen away to the knapsack, which they begin to
pack. Andrew has never removed his eyes from the tall form
in the cloak.*

*Now, as the Figure pours back the yellow grains from his
palm into the powder horn, he speaks, hesitatingly.*

ANDREW. I think — I 'd like some.

THE FIGURE. Some o' what?

ANDREW. Those — my pay.

THE FIGURE (*cheerfully*). So; would ye?

(*Handing him the horn*)

Reckon that 's enough?

ANDREW (*not taking it*). That 's what I want to make sure
of — first.

THE FIGURE. Oh! So ye 're hesitatin'!

ANDREW. Yes; but I want you to help me decide. Pardon
me, Sir; you 're a stranger; yet somehow I feel I may ask
your help. You 've come just in time.

THE FIGURE. Queer I should a-dropped round jest now,
wa'n't it? S'posin' we take a turn.

[*Together they walk toward the embankment.*

By the knapsack, Ellen finds the little frame.

ELLEN (*to herself*). My picture!

[*She looks toward Andrew affectionately.*

Joel, lifting the knapsack, beckons to her.

JOEL. There 's more stuff over here.

[*He goes off, right; Ellen follows him.*

ANDREW (*to the Figure*). I should like the judgment of your experience, Sir. I can't quite see your face, yet you appear to be one who has had a great deal of experience.

THE FIGURE. Why, consid'able some.

ANDREW. Did you — happen to fight in the late war for independence?

THE FIGURE. Happen to?

(*Laughing quietly*)

N-no, not fight: ye see — I was paymaster.

ANDREW. But you went through the war?

THE FIGURE. Ye-es, oh yes; I went through it. I took out my fust reg'lar papers down to Philadelphie, in '76, seems like 't was the fourth day o' July. But I was paymaster afore that.

ANDREW. Tell me: I 've heard it said there were deserters even in those days, even from the roll-call of Washington. Is it true?

THE FIGURE. True, boy? — Have ye ever watched a prairie fire rollin' towards ye, billowin' with flame and smoke, and seed all the midget cowerin' prairie-dogs scootin' for their holes? Wall, that 's the way I watched Howe's army sweepin' crosst the Jarsey marshes, and seed the desartin' little patriots, with their chins over their shoulders skedaddlin' home'ards.

ANDREW. What — the Americans!

THE FIGURE. All but a handful on 'em — them as weren't canines, ye might say, but men. *They* set a back-fire goin' at Valley Forge. Most on 'em burnt their toes and fingers off, lightin' on 't thar in the white frost, but they stuck it through and saved — wall, the prairie-dogs.

ANDREW. But they — those others: What reason did they give to God and their own souls for deserting?

THE FIGURE. To who?

ANDREW. To their consciences: What was their reason? It must have been a noble one in Seventy-six. *Their* reason *then:* don't you see, I must have it. I must know what reason real heroes gave for their acts. You were there. You can tell me.

THE FIGURE. *Real* heroes, eh? Look around ye, then: To-day 's the heroic age, and the true brand o' hero is al'ays in the market. Look around ye!

ANDREW. What, here — in this war of jobsters, this petty campaign of monstrous boodle?

THE FIGURE. Thar we be!

ANDREW. Why, here are only a lot of cowardly half-men, like me — lovers of their own folks — their wives and babies at home. They 'll make sacrifices for them. But real men like our fathers in Seventy-six: they looked in the beautiful face of Liberty, and sacrificed to *her!*

THE FIGURE. Our fathers, my boy, was jest as fond o' poetry as you be. They talked about the beautiful face o' Liberty same 's you; but when the hom'-made eyes and cheeks of their sweethearts and young uns took to cryin ', they desarted their beautiful goddess and skun out hom'.

ANDREW. But there were some —

THE FIGURE. Thar was some as didn't — yes; and thar 's some as don't to-day. Those be the folks on my pay-roll. Why, look a-here: I calc'late I wouldn't fetch much on the beauty counter. My talk ain't rhyme stuff, nor the Muse o' Grammar wa'n't my schoolma'am. Th' ain't painter nor clay-sculptor would pictur' me jest like I stand. For the axe has hewed me, and the plough has furrered; and the arnin' of gold by my own elbow-grease has give' me the shrewd eye at a bargain. I manure my crops this side o'Jordan, and as for t'other shore, I'd ruther swap jokes with the Lord than listen to his sarmons. And yet for the likes o' me, jest for to arn my wages — ha, the many, many boys and gals that 's gone to their grave-beds, and when I a-closed their eyes, the love-light was shinin' thar.

ANDREW (*who has listened, with awe*). What *are* you? What *are* you?

THE FIGURE. Me? I'm the pay-master.

ANDREW. I want to serve you — like those others.

THE FIGURE. Slow, slow, boy! Nobody sarves *me*.

ANDREW. But they died for you — the others.

THE FIGURE. No, 't wa'n't for me: 't was for him as pays the wages: the one as works through me — the one higher up. I'm only the pay-master: kind of a needful make-shift — his obedient sarvent.

ANDREW (*with increasing curiosity, seeks to peer in the Figure's face*). But the one up higher — who is he?

THE FIGURE (*turning his head away*). Would ye sarve him, think, if ye heerd his voice?

ANDREW (*ardently, drawing closer*). And saw his face!

[*Drawing his cowl lower and taking Andrew's arm, the Figure leads him up on the embankment, where they stand together.*

THE FIGURE. Hark a-yonder!

ANDREW (*listening*). Is it thunder?

THE FIGURE. Have ye forgot?

ANDREW. The voice! I remember now: — Niagara!

[*With awe, Andrew looks toward the Figure, who stands shrouded and still, facing the dawn. From far off comes a sound as of falling waters, and with that — a deep, murmurous voice, which seems to issue from the Figure's cowl.*

THE VOICE. I am the Voice that was heard of your fathers, and your fathers' fathers. Mightier — mightier, I shall be heard of your sons. I am the Million in whom the one is lost, and I am the One in whom the millions are saved. Their ears shall be shut to my thunders, their eyes to my blinding stars. In shallow streams they shall tap my life-blood for gold. With dregs of coal and of copper they shall pollute me. In the mystery of my mountains they shall assail me; in the majesty of my forests, strike me down; with engine and derrick and mill-stone, bind me their slave. Some for a lust, some for a love, shall desert me. One and one, for his own, shall fall away. Yet one and one and one shall return to me for life; the deserter and the destroyer shall re-create me. Primeval, their life-blood is mine. My pouring waters are passion, my lightnings are laughter of man. I am the One in whom

the millions are saved, and I am the Million in whom the
one is lost.

ANDREW (*yearningly, to the Figure*).   Your face!

(*The Figure turns majestically away.   Andrew clings to
him*)

Your face!

[*In the shadow of the flag, the Figure unmuffles for an instant.
Peering, dazzled, Andrew staggers back, with a low cry, and,
covering his eyes, falls upon the embankment.
From away, left, the thrumming of a jew's-harp is heard,
playing " The Star Spangled Banner."
From the right, enter Joel and Ellen.
Descending from the embankment, the Figure stands apart.*

JOEL.   Well, Colonel Average, time's up.

ELLEN (*seeing Andrew's prostrate form, hastens to him*).   Andy!
What's happened?

ANDREW (*rising slowly*).   Come here.   I'll whisper it.

[*He leads her beside the embankment, beyond which the dawn
is beginning to redden.*

JOEL.   Yonder's the sergeant's jew's-harp.   That's our signal, Nell.   So long, Colonel.

THE FIGURE (*nodding*).   So long, sonny.

ANDREW (*holding Ellen's hands, passionately*).   You understand?   You *do*?

ELLEN (*looking in his eyes*).   I understand, dear.

[*They kiss each other.*

JOEL (*calls low*).   Come, you married turtles.   The road's
clear.   Follow me now.   Sneak.

[*Carrying his knapsack, Joel climbs over the embankment,
and disappears.
The thrumming of the jew's-harp continues.
Ellen, taking the strip of silk flag from her shoulders, ties it
to the standard.*

ANDREW (*faintly*).   God bless you!

ELLEN (*as they part hands*).   Good-bye!

[*The Figure has remounted the embankment, where — in the
distincter glow of the red dawn — the grey folds of his cloak,*

hanging from his shoulders, resemble the half-closed wings of an eagle, the beaked cowl falling, as a kind of visor, before his face, concealing it.

THE FIGURE. Come, little gal.

(Ellen goes to him, and hides her face in the great cloak. As she does so, he draws from it a paper, writes on it, and hands it to Andrew, with the powder horn)

By the bye, Andy, here 's that s'curity. Them here 's my initials : they 're all what 's needful. Jest file this in the right pigeonhole, and you 'll draw your pay. — Keep your upper lip, boy. I 'll meet ye later, mebbe, at Lundy's Lane.

ANDREW *(wistfully)*. You 'll take her home?

THE FIGURE. Yes : reckon she 'll housekeep for your uncle, till you get back; won't ye, Nellie? Come, don't cry, little gal. We 'll soon git 'quainted. 'T aint the fust time sweethearts has called me *Uncle*.

[Flinging back his great cloak, he throws one wing of it, with his arm, about her shoulders, thus with half its reverse side draping her with shining stripes and stars. By the same action, his own figure is made partly visible — the legs clad in the tight, instep-strapped trousers [blue and white] of the Napoleonic era. Holding the girl gently to him — while her face turns back toward Andrew — he leads her, silhouetted against the sunrise, along the embankment, and disappears. Meantime the thrumming twang of the jew's-harp grows sweeter, mellower, modulated with harmonies that, filling now the air with elusive strains of the American war-hymn, mingle with the faint dawn-twitterings of birds.

Andrew stares silently after the departed forms; then, slowly coming down into the entrenchment, lifts from the ground his gun and ramrod, leans on the gun, and — reading the paper in his hand by the growing light — mutters it aloud:

U. S. A.

Smiling sternly, he crumples the paper in his fist, makes a wad of it, and rams it into his gun-barrel.

CURTAIN

A GOOD WOMAN

GEORGE MIDDLETON

READERS of to-day may find it difficult to realize that publication of play texts is a very modern pursuit; but George Middleton was one of the first to advocate its practice, about 1910. In 1911 he published a collection of one-act plays of his own, all on contemporary problems of American life; and thereafter he was influential in writing short plays of ideas for Little Theatre audiences. At one time he lectured widely to encourage the Little Theatre movement, and contributed interesting articles on the subject to the magazines.

Mr. Middleton was born in Paterson, New Jersey, on October 27, 1880, and received his B.A. at Columbia University in 1902. From 1912 to 1925 he was Literary Editor of *La Follette's Weekly*.

He had his first play produced by Julia Marlowe immediately after he was graduated from Columbia University. Since then, he has been author or co-author of more than twenty plays, three of which were produced by David Belasco. His original works have been acted in both London and Paris, and he has made adaptations from the French of Brieux, Edouard Bourdet, and Sacha Guitry.

George Middleton has been President of the Dramatists' Guild, Honorary Vice President of the Authors' League, and Honorary Vice President of the International Confederation of Authors and Composers, before whose Congress, in Berlin in 1928, he represented American playwrights.

He spent three years in Hollywood, writing and producing talking pictures.

Among his best-known plays are "Hiss! Boom!! Blah!!!", "Polly with a Past", "Adam and Eva", "The Big Pond", "The Road Together", "The Cavalier", "Nowadays", "The Cave Girl", "The Sinner", "Blood Money", "Accused" (from Brieux), "The Wife's Strategy", "The Other Rose" (from Bourdet), "The Light of the World", "The Prodigal Judge" (dramatization), "The Bride", "Hit-the-Trail-Holliday", "The House of a Thousand Candles" (dramatization). His four collections of one-act plays are entitled: *Embers, Tradition, Possession,* and *Masks.* "That Was Balzac" is his newest play; although unproduced as yet, its publication has been ardently received.

A GOOD WOMAN

By GEORGE MIDDLETON

"A Good Woman" was originally produced by the North-ampton Municipal Theatre Company at the private theatre in the home of Mr. George B. McCallum, Northampton, Massachusetts, January 6, 1916.

Original Cast

CORA WARREN . . . . Gertrude Workman
HAL MERRILL . . . . William H. Powell

A GOOD WOMAN

SCENE. *At Cora Warren's flat. A large city in New York State. Late one winter evening.*

A small room in what is a modest but comfortable flat, up several flights of stairs. In back, a door opens on the landing. A snow-lined window may be seen at the right through the pretty lace curtains. Opposite this a door leads off into the other rooms. The furnishings are simple but adequate; wicker chairs, a couch, a small table, carefully selected pictures, some bookshelves, and a large warm rug upon the hardwood floor are conspicuous. A house telephone is on the left wall near the door. There is something seclusive, personal, and intimate about the little room, softly lighted by several shaded wicker-lamps which blend in color with the one-toned patternless wall-paper.

Outside the wind is heard howling as it drives the snow and sleet against the window. After some moments, a bell is heard. Cora Warren enters quickly and opens the outer door, admitting Hal Merrill. She closes the door and kisses him.

Cora Warren is a woman of thirty, full of rich feeling, sensitive, impulsive, yet withal clear-visioned and courageous. There is every mark of refinement, culture, and distinction in speech, with nothing exotic or abnormal in her manner. She is in a pretty negligée.

Hal Merrill is older, beginning to settle, in fact, but full of mental and physical vigor, in spite of features which, when relaxed, betray a certain careworn expression. He, too, is evidently well-born, and has had, no doubt, many advantages. His heavy overcoat, rubbers, and soft felt hat are wet with the snow.

CORA. I'm so glad you've come. Why, you're all wet.

HAL (*taking off his overcoat*). I walked uptown.

CORA (*playfully admonishing him throughout*). In this storm?
And you knew I was waiting?

HAL. You are always waiting.

CORA. You'll get your death, dear. Give me the coat.
I'll hang it over a chair before the gas stove. And your
feet — my — my! Soaked?

HAL. No, rubbers.

CORA. So you *did* mind me and wear them.

HAL. Yes.

[*Kicking them off.*

CORA. You must take more care of yourself. What would
I do if you were ill? You should have ridden.

HAL. It clears your thoughts to walk with the snow beating in your face.

CORA (*detecting a hidden meaning*). Hal?

HAL. It's good to be here with you again, Cora.

CORA (*cheerfully again*). Yes: it's been so long since yesterday. (*They laugh*) Now sit down and rest. I've a hot
toddy all ready for you.

HAL. Just what I wanted.

CORA. Here's your pipe — old and strong as ever. Did you
forget the tobacco?

HAL. No. (*Taking the pipe*) You always make it seem
like home, dearest.

CORA (*hurt*). "Seem?"

HAL (*holding her hand during a slight pause*). You know
what I mean.

CORA (*as she strikes a match and lights the pipe which he has
filled*). How worn and tired you are, dear. I'll be glad
when this lawsuit is over. Just relax. Let go. (*She kisses
him*) Dearest. (*Cora takes up the coat and rubbers, going
out quickly in back. Hal stops smoking, the smile disappears, and his head lowers, as he seems overcome with the
mood he has been trying to fight back. Cora comes in unobserved with the toddy. She looks at him, shakes her head and
then comes, placing her hand on his arm. He starts up from
his reverie*) What is it, Hal?

HAL. Nothing.

CORA (*not believing him*). Take this, dear.

HAL. Thanks. (*He sips it*) Um! it's hot, Cora. Just the right amount of sugar, too. (*Cora watches him questioningly as he sips it slowly. She picks up a couple of sofa cushions and comes over to him, placing them by him, on the floor. She sits on them, waiting for him to speak*) That tastes good.

CORA. You're sure you didn't get chilled?

HAL. I walked rapidly.

CORA. Did anything go wrong with the case?

HAL (*patting her*). What makes you think that?

CORA. Something's worrying you.

HAL. Something did: but it's all settled now.

CORA. So that's why you walked in the storm?

HAL. Yes.

CORA. I'm glad it's settled; only I should like to have helped settle it.

HAL. Cora?

CORA (*she turns and looks up into his face*). Yes?

HAL. I wonder how great a test your love for me would stand?

CORA. Could I have given more?

HAL. There *is* something more I must ask.

CORA (*puzzled*). Something more? Tell me, Hal.

HAL (*holding her head between his hands*). Is your love strong enough to accept a silence?

CORA. Aren't there silent places in every love?

HAL (*with some slight hesitation*). I mean if — if I should *do* something which I thought best not to explain.

CORA (*simply*). I should accept everything so long as you were honest with me. Only —

HAL. Only what, dear?

CORA (*thoughtfully*). Silence itself is not always honest.

HAL. In this particular matter will you let me be the judge of that?

CORA. A woman in my position must accept.

HAL. Cora!

CORA (*quickly*). Oh, I didn't mean that, Hal; *that* was unworthy of me.

HAL You know how I love you.

CORA. Yes, yes, dear. Of course I know. I am ashamed of nothing. I'm proud of all we have here in the quiet. But the snow beating against the window has been reminding me all day of the world outside.

HAL. The snow is so free!

CORA. Yes; and you and I are bound by secrecy. That's what hurts; the secrecy.

HAL (*stroking her hair*). If you could only be my wife.

CORA (*smiling*). Just for the freedom it would give me to share everything in the open with you. That's all. Just for the freedom we can't have now.

HAL. But, Cora, even in marriage itself only the happy are free.

CORA (*intimating a hidden thought*). I suppose the most difficult thing for some people is to *give* freedom. (*He nods in understanding*) Poor Hal! How you have suffered, too, with this tangle we are in. (*The 'phone rings. They are surprised*) Who could that be?

HAL (*nervously*). No one knows your number?

CORA. No.

[*The ring is repeated.*

HAL (*dismissing it*). Central's made a mistake. Don't answer it.

CORA. Everything startles me so these days. (*Dismissing it too*) Have another toddy?

HAL. Not now.

CORA. Tell me about the case. Is "Boss" McQuinn still going to take his libel suit into court?

HAL. It's called for to-morrow at ten.

CORA (*pleased*). To-morrow! It's come at last, then, after all your months of work. To-morrow. (*With a sigh*) And I can't be there in court to hear you when you testify, or to follow, in the open, each step we've talked over here. That's where my position hurts.

HAL (*with apparent difficulty throughout*). Perhaps I sha'n't take the stand against McQuinn, after all.

CORA. You mean it won't be necessary?

HAL. Not exactly that.

CORA. But what you wrote about McQuinn in the Monthly —— ?

HAL. Every word of my exposure was true.

CORA. But you've said so often the whole defense of the magazine in McQuinn's libel suit against it rests on *your* testimony alone.

HAL. Yes, yes.

CORA (*disappointed*). I see. You mean the Monthly has decided to retract?

HAL. No.

CORA (*not quite grasping the significance*). Is this why you walked with the snow beating in your face?

HAL (*with feeling*). This is the silent place! I'm not going to testify in this suit, after all. Please don't question me about it, dear.

CORA (*startled*). Not going to testify?

HAL (*earnestly*). Just trust me, Cora; and let me be silent as to the reason.

CORA (*restraining her instinctive impulse to question and placing her hands on his shoulders*). Whatever is the reason, I know you must have suffered. It is not like you to give up. (*He lowers his eyes*) You've never asked anything greater of me than this silence.

HAL (*deeply moved*). Perhaps I've never given anything greater, Cora.

[*The 'phone rings again : they look toward it.*

CORA (*slowly*). Did you give our number to any one?

HAL (*nervously*). No.

[*It rings again.*

CORA. Nobody ever rings here but you. (*She goes apprehensively to the 'phone in spite of his movement to restrain her*) Yes, this is Cora Warren. . . . Who? . . . Mr. McQuinn! (*They look at each other. She quickly controls herself and*

speaks casually) Mr. Merrill? . . . You're mistaken —
why should *he* be here? . . . There's no need of ringing
me up later. (*She hangs up the receiver*) He laughed,
Hal. He *laughed!* (*She goes to him*) He has found out
about you and me!!

HAL. No, no.

CORA (*shaken*). That's what it is. It was the *way* he laughed!

HAL (*confused*). Nonsense.

CORA (*slowly grasping the situation*). For months you've
told me McQuinn has been fighting for his political life,
desperate over your exposures. He's been doing everything to "get" your witnesses — to "get" something on
you. Why, he offered you money — enough to make you
independent for life. You refused all that; but, *now*,
you're going to do what he wants.

HAL. I'm doing what I want, I tell you; what *I* want.

CORA. That's not so. This investigation has been your
absorbing passion for months. You've seen what it means
to the hundreds of women and children who have suffered
by his exploitations. He's got something on you, something you had to give in to.

HAL. No, no!

CORA. It's you and me, Hal. You ask silence of me because
you didn't want to hurt me. It's you and me; you and
me.

HAL. No, no!

CORA (*slowly*). Hal, it is that. Answer me, boy. It *is* that
—isn't it?

HAL (*admitting it, after a futile denial*). And I didn't want
you to know.

CORA. He threatened to tell about our relations together if
you testified against him?

HAL. Yes: the blackguard.

CORA (*moved*). And you love me more than —

HAL (*tenderly*). I only did what any man would. (*She
lowers her head*) Dearest, don't take it so hard. I'm glad
a chance came to show you how I loved you.

CORA. I knew without this proof, Hal; I knew. [*She sits with her face buried in her hands. He stands beside her.*

HAL. McQuinn met me to-night, on the street, alone. He said he knew about our three years — our summer abroad — this place — all. He said he hated to hit a woman, but he knew he was beaten and had to use any weapon he could find. All he asked of me was silence and he would give the same about us — or for me to forget a bit on the stand or muddle my testimony. Of course, I saw what it would mean to the case: but it was the only way to save you. (*He shrugs his shoulders*) He must have guessed I'd come straight to you. He has ways of finding out 'phone numbers. I suppose he wanted to frighten you and thus make sure I wouldn't change my mind.

CORA (*slowly*). Did he mention your wife?

HAL. Yes.

CORA (*desperately*). Did you tell him you and she had been separated before you met me? That she didn't love you, that she hated you, yet clung to your name because she knew you wanted freedom to marry me? Did you tell him she wouldn't give you that freedom, because of a few words mumbled over her by an official, and because she said she was "a good woman"?

HAL. I did not discuss the matter. It was my wife who told him about us.

CORA. Your wife!

HAL. Yes. That act describes her, doesn't it?

CORA (*bitterly*). And the law gives a woman like that the right to keep you — a woman whose body is dry and her love cold — and it discards me who — oh!

HAL (*sarcastically*). It was my wife's way of disentangling me. She thought I'd rather give you up than this case. She thought I'd sacrifice you. But she didn't know me: she never knew me.

CORA. And she knew me!

HAL. It's done. Now we must forget and go on.

CORA (*gazing dully before her*). What are you going to do now?

HAL. That's what we must think of.

CORA. It will mean you will have to leave the Monthly.

HAL. Yes. They're tired of the suit, anyway. Their advertising has fallen off. (*Putting his arm about her*) We have each other.

CORA (*ominously*). And always we'd fear McQuinn knocking at our door.

HAL (*trying to cheer her*). Nonsense, dear. He'll never bother to come up our stairs.

CORA. How we women hamper you men. (*He protests*) Yes, we do. Your wife's "respectability" — and my —

HAL. Hush, dear. It's not our fault.

CORA. That we love? No. But because we've spoken the whole language of love the world blames us. (*With growing emotion*) If I'd kept my love hidden, worn myself sapless, wasted without expression, then I'd have been "a good woman"! If I'd seen you casually, or if I'd let you come near me, with the flames smoldering, burning us both inside so that there was nothing in our thoughts but fire; nothing of comradeship and beauty that we now have — then I'd still have been "a good woman." But because I let you see my love, because I wasn't a contemptible tease, because I knew all things were equally important in love, because I gave myself to you, I'm *not* "a good woman"! [*She laughs ironically.*

HAL. We live in the world, dear.

CORA. And we must go on living. (*With a quick resolution*) But there is no need of our being cowards!

HAL. Cowards!

CORA. Yes. Up to now, Hal, as I see it, we have not been that. We did what we believed was right, no matter what others may say. But now you and I are thinking of doing what we *know* is wrong; and that is the test of our courage.

HAL. You mean?

CORA. That now we're asking somebody else to pay the price: the hundreds of women and children in this city whom McQuinn would still go on exploiting if you did not go on the stand and drive him out of power.

HAL (*losing momentary control*). It's true; it's true. But how could I ask that of *you?*

CORA. Why not?

HAL. No, no. We must think of ourselves now — ourselves.

CORA (*putting her hand on his arm*). You and I cannot do as many others. We've got to keep right, in each other's eyes, or the world will beat us.

HAL. I've done the hardest thing for you I could, Cora.

CORA. It's not always easy to be a coward, Hal. And that's what I'd also be if I accepted. Somebody else would be paying. Somebody else. That can never be right. (*She bows her head. There is a long pause. He rises, goes to the window, then paces up and down. The snow is heard freely beating against the pane. Her mind slowly gains control of her emotions and she looks up at him*) Hal?

HAL. Yes.

CORA. If you went on the stand to-morrow and told the truth about McQuinn, would your relations with me hurt your statement about him?

HAL (*bitterly*). No. It's only a *woman* whose sex morals can be taken that advantage of in our courts.

CORA (*with determination*). Then you must tell the truth.

HAL (*desperately*). And have you hurt? Never!

CORA. I would be hurt far worse if you did not love me enough to do what I ask.

HAL. Cora! (*Comes to her*) You don't realize what it means.

CORA (*calmly*). I realize that your public usefulness would be destroyed because you wished to protect my reputation. What people think of me matters little now.

HAL. What people think of you means everything to me.

CORA. You fear to have them think me a bad woman?

HAL. Cora!

CORA. Then what difference what they think so long as *we* understand each other?

HAL. They'd forgive a man. But you're a woman. They'd never forgive you — never.

CORA. Nothing will be harder than cowardice.

HAL (*going to her*). I can't do this — I can't. They'd think me a *cad* to sacrifice you like this.

CORA. That thought has made liars and cowards of many men!

HAL. We mustn't be foolish. There's nothing greater in life than what two people feel for each other.

CORA (*desperately*). That's why I am asking this of you. Don't make it harder for me — don't!

HAL. You are thinking of those out in the city; I am thinking only of you.

CORA. But you mustn't.

HAL. You're worth more to me than all of them.

CORA. But you must think of the people.

HAL. The people? That mob any fool can lead with a few catch phrases? That ignorant mass that cheers one day and crucifies the next? What do they really give anybody? I'll tell you. Nothing but ingratitude and scars while you live with immortelles and a monument when you're dead. Why should I sacrifice you for them?

CORA. Hal! You don't know them —

HAL. Oh, yes, I do. They can't sustain their moral attitudes. It's all a periodic fit with them. They shout a lot while the brass band plays and they cheer any fool in the red light. Then they settle back into their old self-righteousness while the McQuinns are always on the job.

CORA. You're unjust. You don't know what you're saying. It's because they *are* ignorant that strong leaders like you should go to them. (*He laughs*) You must not forget those others who are working with you against McQuinn.

HAL. The Reformers? Huh. I know them, too. I'm sick to death of political reforms and reformers who plant together but reap their fruits separately.

CORA (*trying to stop him*). They're human and —

HAL. Yes; that's it. Damn human! Why, even now they're squabbling over who shall run for Mayor once they put McQuinn out of power. They're fighting, just like the grafters, with all the same petty jealous personalities. Reformers! Would they put *you* on their visiting list even if they knew you sacrificed your reputation for them? With all their political morality do you think they'd dare go against public opinion on private morals? No! They couldn't run for office themselves if they did. They'd think you unclean —

CORA. No, no!

HAL. Yes: just as they think McQuinn unclean. They'd accept your sacrifice. But they'd use it as they use their causes: to ride into power themselves. Reformers! I sha'n't sacrifice you for them. What do they care for you and me?

CORA. But it's not a sacrifice to do what is right.

HAL. Others will try to do what I have failed in. There are always plenty of reformers. I don't want the glory. I've seen the graves of martyrs. No, no. I'll go through with what McQuinn demands just because it's you and me who matter — you and me.

CORA. With McQuinn always waiting at the door. (*The 'phone rings sharply again*) You see?

HAL. Damn him! Why doesn't he leave us alone?

CORA. We'll never be alone again.

HAL. I'll fix him.

CORA (*with calm strength*). He must be answered now as well as later.

HAL (*as she starts to the 'phone*). You sha'n't do this.

CORA. I'll not let your work be ruined by my cowardice.

HAL. I tell you I'm through with that work.

CORA. But you're not through with my love! It's my love speaking now for *our* love, which I must keep clean in my own eyes. Our love which the law punishes by denying it freedom to live in the open! Our love which keeps me from being "a good woman" — like your wife! (*She *goes to the 'phone. Hal, seeing the futility of further words, sinks back into his chair overcome by what the future holds)* Yes. This is Cora Warren. . . . Who wishes to talk to Mr. Merrill? . . . Is this Mr. McQuinn talking? . . . Mr. McQuinn, I'm glad you rang up. . . . I'm fully acquainted with the particulars of the case. . . . Yes, of course, we're going to be sensible. . . . What are you going to do? . . . Thanks for putting it so clearly. I wanted you to say that to *me* also. We're not at all anxious to have this story come out. . . . No. But Mr. Merrill is going on the stand to-morrow to tell the truth. . . . Yes. . . . And . . . if the story is subsequently published . . . or if he is cross-examined by your lawyers about our relations, *I* shall go on the stand, produce a record that you 'phoned me twice, and corroborate his statement that you tried to blackmail him into silence. . . . You are quite sure you understand? . . . You're sorry for me? . . . Oh, that's all right, Mr. McQuinn. . . . What's that? (*Her voice trails off*) Yes, I know I'm "a hell of a fine woman." (*She hangs up the receiver and goes slowly to Hal*) You did what you thought best for me. I did what *is* best for you.

HAL (*holding her close as she kneels beside him*). Poor dear, brave girl. He'll publish it. I know him. And then — oh!

CORA. Yes, dearest. But he didn't *laugh* this time! [*There is a triumphant smile upon her face.*

The curtain falls.

PAWNS

PERCIVAL WILDE

BECAUSE of Percival Wilde's versatile use of the different moods in short play form, and the popularity of his work, his contribution to the general development of the American one-act play has been outstanding. He has written more one-act plays than any other American playwright. Over one hundred of them have been produced, some many times, and one was acted by two hundred and sixty-one different organizations in a single calendar month. "Pawns" has been entered in tournaments in various countries, and has received a number of prizes.

Mr. Wilde was born March 1, 1887, and was graduated from Columbia University in 1906. After being in the banking business for four years, he commenced writing, but was interrupted by the World War, during which he was an officer in active Navy service. Most of his plays have been written since then.

His collected volumes of one-act plays are: *Dawn, and Other One-Act Plays of Life Today; Confessional and Other American Plays; The Unseen Host and Other War Plays; Eight Comedies for Little Theatres; The Inn of Discontent, and Other Fantastic Plays; Three-Minute Plays; Ten Plays for Little Theatres; Comrades in Arms and Other Plays for Little Theatres.*

In addition to these he has written *The Craftsmanship of the One-Act Play, Rogues in Clover* (short stories), *The Devil's Booth* (a novel), *There is a Tide* (a novel), and has edited *Contemporary One-Act Plays from Nine Countries.* His one-act plays which do not appear in his collections are: "The

Line of No Resistance", "The Reckoning", "The Toy-Shop", "Reverie", "The Enchanted Christmas Tree", "Kings in Nomania", "Alias Santa Claus", "To Kill a Man", "Nanny."

PAWNS

By PERCIVAL WILDE

"Pawns" was originally produced by the East-West Players on February 21, 1918, at the Lenox Little Theatre, New York, N. Y.

Original Cast

GRIGOR, a Russian peasant	Mark Hoffman
STEPAN ⎫ his sons	⎧ Max Lieberman
ILIA ⎭	⎩ Irving Zechnoff
MICHAEL, an Austrian peasant . . .	George Goldberg
PETER, his man	Milton J. Bernd
A SERGEANT, of the Russian Army . .	Gustav Blum
A VOICE	William Hirscher

Stage Setting by John Wenger.

PAWNS

The lights are extinguished. The prologue is spoken by a male voice.

Frontier! What images the mere word suggests! Barbed wire, and sentries, and eternal vigilance, even in times of peace. To the traveler, a place where certain necessary inconveniences must be encountered. To the native, the end of the world. To the statesman, an irksome demarcation, painfully cramping, encroaching, which, some day, for no reason now apparent, must be moved farther off, as a result of which various colored ribbons, jeweled badges, and sonorous titles will accrue to the said statesman, until his alien confrères, in turn, find pretexts to move the line back to the precise degree of longitude which originally marked it, or perhaps, even beyond that point. Then the whole process will commence again, and statesmen will invent new pretexts, and monarchs new color combinations for their ribbons. And in the cloistered seclusion of the colleges, anæmic professors will compile learned histories, immortalizing the statesmen, and only incidentally celebrating the rôle that their countrymen have played, these same countrymen now sepultured in battleground, cemeteries, and so forth, under long-winded inscriptions which nine tenths of them, lately become heroes, would not have been able to decipher in life.

In accordance with treaties of peace, new frontiers will come into existence, with new sentries, new barbed wire, new vigilance.

But there are frontiers where no human sentries are needed — or possible; where, in the impenetrable depths of the marshes, bullfrogs swim across the invisible line a thousand

times in the course of a day, without troubling themselves
to decide whether they are German bullfrogs — or French
bullfrogs — or Austrian bullfrogs — or Russian bullfrogs.
And such places there are in plenty along the southwestern
Russian border, where alternating hill and valley, precipice
and abyss, virgin forest and unlit swampland have seen
no sentries, save only those whom Nature placed there,
since time began.

It is near one of these natural barriers that the scene is
laid; a barrier almost impassable to the stranger, but an
easy and accustomed path to the native, who threads its
tortuous windings without fear. Indeed, he looks upon
it as a most useful friend; but for it, townspeople, not so
far away, would have reached out cunning hands for the
few acres he cultivates with so much labor; because of it
they leave him alone, him, and his similarly situated
neighbors.

In the neighborhood of such places men are denational-
ized; are neither Russian nor Austrian, but are Volhynian
— or Galician — or Podolian, without having a clear idea,
in their isolation, of what the terms mean, until war comes
and the Volhynian is told that the Podolian is his ally and
the Galician his enemy, is given a gun, and told to glorify
God and his country by shooting straight and.wasting no
ammunition. . . .

[The voice ceases.
Chimes.
The curtain rises in darkness.
Night: near the end of night, before morning. A forest of
swampy nature. Here and there, little irregular hummocks
of ground. Frogs croaking. Near the center, a small fire,
with a thin, straight flame, casting but little light, so that ten
feet away from it there is darkness.
Three men are grouped about the fire: Grigor, a Russian
peasant in his fifties, bearded, grave, with something of the
peculiar dignity which his class acquires as it ages; Stepan,
his older son, enormous, powerful, bearded, stretched out full

length on the ground, and the younger son, Ilia, hardly more than a boy.

[A pause.

ILIA. An hour more, and it will be light. I can tell by the croaking of the frogs. It is as if they were afraid of the light. Their croaking is different. Listen!

[A pause.

GRIGOR. Thirty versts more to Zawichost.

ILIA. Is it so far? That is farther than I have ever been.

GRIGOR. What of that? By nightfall we will be there.

STEPAN (*moving his huge frame lazily*). And then, God willing, one more day, and we return home!

GRIGOR. God willing!

ILIA. Is it a large city? Will there be many people?

STEPAN (*with an indulgent smile*). More than you have ever seen before.

ILIA. That will be wonderful!

STEPAN. There are streets; more streets than you can count, and shops, where they sell beautiful things, and great houses all built of stone.

ILIA. I shall love to see that!

GRIGOR. Not I! (*He shakes his head*) I am afraid of the cities! Oh, I am afraid of the cities! (*He addresses Stepan*) Had you not gone to the city, they would have left us alone.

STEPAN. No.

GRIGOR. They have always left us alone. Here are the marshes, and the quicksands. Who knows his way through them? Not the city people. They are far too comfortable in their stone houses.

STEPAN. Nevertheless they would have sent for us. So the police said.

GRIGOR. The police? Since when do we talk with the police? Have I not said that when an honest moujik sees a policeman on one side of the street he crosses to the other?

STEPAN. It was no use. There were too many of them. There were police at every corner. There were signs in the street, and crowds reading the signs.

GRIGOR. Signs! Ah, yes! Signs telling you what to do! Signs telling you what not to do! But read? How should a moujik read? How to plow a straight furrow in the earth, when to sow, when to reap, how to feed his hen, his cow, that he knows, and that is far better than reading signs! Pah! Because you could not read, they told you what they pleased!

STEPAN. So I thought at first.

GRIGOR. Well?

STEPAN. Then I asked others. They all said the same.

GRIGOR. Hm! We must go to Zawichost.

STEPAN. Yes; to Zawichost.

GRIGOR. And lose three days in harvest time.

STEPAN. So they said; all of us.

GRIGOR. While Michael and lame Peter work in their field undisturbed, on the other side of the marsh! When we return, when we ask them to help us, they will refuse; we have not helped them. (*He pauses in disgust*) If there were only a reason it would be otherwise, but for mobilization? (*With crowning contempt*) What *is* mobilization?

STEPAN. When I asked they pointed me out to each other; said I was a fine hulk of a man to be asking what was mobilization. They laughed at me. They threw stones at me. (*He is getting angry at the recollection*) Then I took the biggest of them by the arm — so — and I pressed a little, so that his face went white beneath the dirt, and the sweat stood out in drops on his forehead, and he begged for mercy, and the others, they stopped laughing!

ILIA (*who is listening with breathless interest*). And then?

STEPAN. Then I came away.

[*There is a pause. Then the younger brother, who has been much impressed, takes up the conversation.*

ILIA. You took him by the arm?

STEPAN (*smiling*). Yes, little brother.

ILIA. With one hand only?

STEPAN. This selfsame hand. (*The boy feels the horny palm with interest*) Shall I show you?

ILIA (*darting out of his reach*). No, no! I do not doubt you!

STEPAN (*laughing*). For that, thanks!

ILIA. Still, if you *must* show me —

STEPAN (*with the growl of a good-natured bear*). What?

ILIA. Wait until we come to the city to-day.

STEPAN. And then?

ILIA. Perhaps they will laugh at us —

STEPAN (*with understanding*). Yes, little brother!

ILIA. Oh, I hope I shall see that!

[*There is a pause.*

GRIGOR. For fifty years I have been a good Christian. I know every holiday of the orthodox church. But mobilization? That I have never heard of.

STEPAN. Perhaps the Metropolitan has decreed a new festival.

GRIGOR. In harvest time? Pah!

STEPAN. Harvest time is nothing to the people who live in cities. They know nothing of harvests.

ILIA (*suddenly*). I hear steps.

GRIGOR. What?

ILIA. Listen!

[*They listen. There is no sound.*

GRIGOR. I hear nothing.

STEPAN. The boy has quicker ears than you or I. Listen.

[*Still there is no sound.*

STEPAN (*addressing Ilia*). What do you hear?

ILIA. Two men.

STEPAN. Which way?

ILIA. From there.

[*He points towards the right.*

GRIGOR. But who should come that way? That is the way we have come. The city is in the other direction.

[*A crackling of branches becomes audible.*

STEPAN. Now I hear them! Hullo! Hullo!

VOICES. Hullo! Hullo!

ILIA. Michael and lame Peter. I know their voices.

STEPAN. Hullo! This way!

GRIGOR. They will not know where we are. Guide them.

[*Stepan starts off.*

ILIA. Here! A burning faggot!

STEPAN. Since when do I need a light, little brother?

[*He disappears.*

GRIGOR. Michael and lame Peter? Are you sure?

ILIA (*listening*). I hear them speaking . . . Now he has found them . . . They are coming this way.

GRIGOR. Why should they follow us?

[*Stepan reappears, followed by two more peasants who carry packs, Peter, a farmhand of twenty-two, who walks with a pronounced limp, and Michael, his employer, a robust man near Grigor's age.*

GRIGOR (*rising ceremoniously*). Christ be with you!

MICHAEL. Grigor Ignátievitch, Christ be with you!

GRIGOR (*as the others drop their packs and draw near to the fire*). What brings you to the swamp at this time of night?

MICHAEL. We asked at the farm. They said you had gone this way.

PETER. We too, we go to the mobilization.

GRIGOR. You also?

ILIA. You go to Zawichost?

PETER. No; to Sandomierz.

GRIGOR. Oh! So there is mobilization in more than one place at once?

ILIA. It must be a great festival indeed.

PETER (*eagerly*). A festival, is it then?

GRIGOR. Who knows?

MICHAEL. But that is why we followed you. We do not know what mobilization may be. But Anna Petrovna said you had gone there. We thought you would know.

GRIGOR (*shrugging his shoulders*). Whatever it is, we will know to-day.

PETER. But now, you cannot tell us?

GRIGOR. No. (*He pauses*) Why do you go to the mobilization in Sandomierz while we go to that in Zawichost?

MICHAEL. A soldier said we were to go to Sandomierz.

STEPAN. A soldier here? In these swamps?

MICHAEL. All the way to the farm he came. We must go, he said. We were afraid to disobey.

GRIGOR. He did not tell you why you must go?

MICHAEL. He had no time. He had to tell many others.

STEPAN. And you asked him nothing?

MICHAEL. We asked. He swore, and said that if we were not gone when he passed again on his way back, we should be beaten.

[*There is a pause.*

ILIA. And lame Peter, must he go too?

MICHAEL. I and all my men, he said. I have only the one.

ILIA. But he is lame.

PETER (*good-naturedly*). Lame Peter will travel as far and as fast as any of them! And if there is to be a festival, why should not lame Peter be there with the others?

GRIGOR. But the harvest?

MICHAEL. Yes, the harvest!

STEPAN. When we return we will reap our fields together, and then lame Peter will have a chance to show what a worker he is!

ILIA (*abruptly*). A sound!

[*They stop talking.*

STEPAN. What is it?

ILIA (*listening*). A horse.

STEPAN (*incredulously*). A horse? This time you are wrong!

GRIGOR. What fool would try to ride a horse through the swamp?

ILIA. Now I hear it more plainly.

PETER. Perhaps it is a riderless horse.

ILIA. No. A rider is using the whip.

[*He is looking off left.*

GRIGOR (*following his glance*). A rider from the city?

[*The peasants look at each other. The crackling of branches becomes audible. Stepan rises silently, and goes out at the left.*

MICHAEL. As if there were no better use for a good animal than that! To ride through the swamp, where the ground is hardly firm enough to carry a man!

PETER. And quicksands, quicksands to right and left of him! The horse knows better than his master.

[*There is the sound of a drunken voice raised in anger.*

ILIA. Listen to him!

PETER. Swearing at his horse, as if the poor beast could do any more!

ILIA. He's afraid! I know he's afraid! He feels the earth crumbling under his hoofs! How he must tremble!

[*The sound of a whip being used unmercifully.*

ILIA. Now he's beating him! I hope he throws him! Oh, I hope he throws him!

[*There is a loud crash.*

GRIGOR. He *has* thrown him!

ILIA. I knew he would!

PETER. It serves him right! To treat a good horse like that!

ILIA. And into the mud! The rider from the city in the mud! I should love to see that!

[*There is the report of a revolver. The peasants rise; look at each other in terrified inquiry.*

GRIGOR. What was that?

MICHAEL. A shot!

ILIA. And Stepan!

PETER. Perhaps Stepan said something!

ILIA. Something the rider didn't like!

MICHAEL. He was always quick-tempered, your Stepan. He was not the man to stand there and see the horse beaten for no fault of its own.

GRIGOR (*in horror*). Christ!

[*Stepan reënters.*

ILIA (*with a shout of relief*). Here he comes!

GRIGOR. Stepan!

MICHAEL. What happened?

STEPAN (*briefly*). His horse fell. It wouldn't rise again. He shot it.

ILIA. Oh!

PETER. Shot his horse!

[*At the left there enters a Russian sergeant, booted, spurred, carrying a whip. He is very muddy and very drunk.*

PETER (*repeats in horror*). He shot his horse!

THE SERGEANT. Well, what of it? It was *my* horse, wasn't it? I could do what I wanted with it.

MICHAEL (*more mildly*). It must have been worth many roubles.

THE SERGEANT. The rich government will pay for it. (*He stumbles nearer the fire*) Give me something to drink.

MICHAEL. What would we be doing with drink?

GRIGOR. We are only honest moujiks.

THE SERGEANT. You have nothing? Well, then —

[*He pulls a flask from a pocket, and applies it to his lips.*

STEPAN (*to Grigor, as the sergeant drinks*). He has had too much to drink already.

GRIGOR (*shrugging his shoulders*). A Christian is a Christian.

THE SERGEANT (*wiping his lips on his sleeve, and replacing his bottle without offering it elsewhere*). Ah! That puts the heart in you! Make place for me at your fire, you! (*He elbows his way to a seat. The peasants edge away, so that he is alone at one side, and they together at the other*) There! That's something like.

[*There is a pause.*

GRIGOR (*courteously*). May I ask your name?

THE SERGEANT (*warming his hands at the fire*). What?

GRIGOR. Your name and surnames?

THE SERGEANT. Alexei Ivanovitch Liboff, Sergeant.

GRIGOR (*inclining his head*). I am Grigor Ignátievitch Arshin. This is my son Stepan. This is my son Ilia. This is my good neighbor —

THE SERGEANT (*interrupts rudely with a drinking song*).

It isn't sleep that bows my head,
But the drink, the drink that's in it!

GRIGOR (*in amazement*). What?

STEPAN (*starting to rise angrily*). The boor!

GRIGOR (*laying a hand on his arm*). A Christian is a Christian.

THE SERGEANT.

> I'll up and away to a distant glade!
> Where the wild red raspberries grow,
> And I'll meet a little Cossack girl,
> A little Cossack girl from the Don!

(*He stops suddenly*) Well, why don't you say something?

GRIGOR. It is not for us to speak in the presence of your excellency.

THE SERGEANT. Then my excellency graciously grants you permission. (*He rises, bows grotesquely, stumbles, falls*)

> I'll meet a little Cossack girl,
> A little Cossack girl from the Don!

(*He stops; points at Ilia*) You, speak! (*Ilia remains silent. He points at Stepan*) You! (*Stepan folds his arms and glares. He points at Grigor*) You, old man! Are you all a pack of fools?

GRIGOR. Your excellency has traveled far?

THE SERGEANT. My excellency has traveled far. Through these cursed swamps on a stumbling horse all the way from Zawichost.

STEPAN (*involuntarily*). From Zawichost?

THE SERGEANT. Have I not said so? All the way from Zawichost, since eleven o'clock this morning.

STEPAN (*starting to put the question which is uppermost in all their minds*). Perhaps, then —

[*He breaks off.*

THE SERGEANT. Perhaps what?

GRIGOR. Perhaps your excellency can tell us something of the mobilization?

THE SERGEANT (*yawning*). The mobilization, oh, yes.

ILIA. It is a festival, is it not?

THE SERGEANT (*shutting his mouth with a surprised snap*). What?

GRIGOR. A festival of the holy church?

THE SERGEANT. Who told you that? (*He laughs loudly*) A festival of the church!

MICHAEL (*somewhat nettled*). What, then, is the mobilization?

THE SERGEANT. You don't know?

PETER. How should we? We live far from the cities.

THE SERGEANT. Then why do you go there?

MICHAEL. We do as we are told.

THE SERGEANT (*very drunkenly*). Quite right! Do as you are told! Obey orders! That's the way for a moujik!

GRIGOR. But what is mobilization?

THE SERGEANT (*turning on him*). Mobilization is this: they stand you up in rows, the big men in back, and the little men in front. Then they put guns in your hands, and you shoot.

ILIA. I should love to shoot.

MICHAEL. But we don't know how.

THE SERGEANT. That doesn't matter. They teach you.

STEPAN. We shoot. Very well, what then? When we have shot do we go home?

THE SERGEANT. Oh, no! It only begins so. When you have shot, you march. Then they stand you up in rows again, and you shoot some more.

MICHAEL. What do you shoot at?

ILIA. Targets?

THE SERGEANT. Better than that!

PETER. Animals?

THE SERGEANT. Still better than that! (*He pauses for his effect*) How would you like to shoot at men?

ILIA. Shoot at men?

MICHAEL. What have they done that they should be shot at?

GRIGOR. What have we done that we should shoot at them?

THE SERGEANT (*amused*). You don't believe me?

[*He laughs; produces his bottle, drinks again.*

STEPAN (*to Grigor*). He is very drunk. He doesn't know what he is saying.

PETER (*with a sudden laugh*). I have found it!

THE SERGEANT. What have you found?

PETER. I have found the trick! You shoot at men, yes, but not with real bullets!

THE SERGEANT (*laughing, as the others laugh, but for a different reason*). Not with real bullets? Wait a minute. (*He fumbles in his bandolier*) Here's one of them!

[*He tosses them a loaded cartridge.*

MICHAEL (*while they all examine it with curiosity*). What is it?

THE SERGEANT. Give it to me. (*He demonstrates*) This is full of powder. The hammer strikes here, and the powder explodes. And this — this — (*he bites it out*) — is the bullet.

[*He passes it to them.*

ILIA. What a cruel thing!

PETER. How heavy it is!

GRIGOR. And is this what we shoot at men?

THE SERGEANT. Bullets like this — and bigger.

GRIGOR. But if we hit them?

THE SERGEANT. What?

GRIGOR (*repeating his question*). If we hit them?

THE SERGEANT. You want to hit them.

GRIGOR. And hurt them?

THE SERGEANT. You want to hurt them.

GRIGOR. Or even — kill them?

THE SERGEANT (*reaching his climax*). You want to kill them!

[*The peasants look at one another blankly. The sergeant is immensely pleased with the impression he has produced.*

STEPAN. We are peaceable moujiks.

MICHAEL. We want to kill nobody.

PETER. They must have sent for the wrong men. They could not have wanted us.

GRIGOR (*voicing the general opinion*). We, we want to kill no man. For fifty years I have been a good Christian. I have killed nothing except that which I was to eat; I and my children. We do not eat men; we do not kill men.

THE SERGEANT. All right, then. You will learn how.

GRIGOR. I do not wish to learn how.

THE SERGEANT. So they say in the beginning. So was I in the beginning. The first time you pull your trigger, the first time you see a strong man fall, you are afraid, oh, you are afraid! But then the lust of killing sweeps over you, and you shoot, and shoot, while the metal of your gun burns the flesh of your hands, and you scream with joy, and are glad, and you kill! You kill!

GRIGOR. Far rather would I be killed myself!

THE SERGEANT. That may happen also!

[*He drinks.*

STEPAN (*to Grigor*). He lies.

MICHAEL. He is a soldier. Soldiers always lie.

ILIA. And he is drunk! Pah!

GRIGOR (*to the sergeant, as he corks his bottle*). These men, whom we shoot at —

[*He stops.*

THE SERGEANT. Yes?

GRIGOR. They have stolen? They have murdered?

[*The sergeant laughs.*

GRIGOR (*patiently*). They must be great criminals. What crime have they done?

THE SERGEANT. No crime.

GRIGOR. Then why do they let us shoot at them?

THE SERGEANT. They do not *let* you.

GRIGOR. No?

THE SERGEANT. You shoot.

GRIGOR. And what do they do?

THE SERGEANT. They shoot also.

GRIGOR. At us?

THE SERGEANT. Where else, then? They are the enemy.

GRIGOR. But we, we have no enemy.

THE SERGEANT. You will learn otherwise. These men, these men whom you shoot at and who shoot at you, they are your enemy.

[*There is a pause. The peasants exchange signs of incredulity.*

ILIA (*reflectively*). To shoot, that is not so bad. But to be shot at, that I should not like at all!

GRIGOR (*silencing him*). And who are these men?

PETER (*sarcastically*). Yes, our enemies, who are they?

THE SERGEANT (*waving his hand*). Prussians. Germans. Austrians.

GRIGOR. And what are Prussians? — Germans? — Austrians?

THE SERGEANT. Men who live on the other side of the border. Men who live on the other side of the swamps.

GRIGOR. On the other side of the swamps? (*He glances meaningly at Michael and Peter*) What do you mean?

THE SERGEANT (*growing drunkenly expansive*). Well, you see, here is Russia, (*a gesture to the left*) here are the swamps, (*a gesture in front*) that is, the border, and there is Austria. (*A gesture to the right*) Here we are. There is the enemy.

[*Rather unaccountably the peasants begin to laugh, a hearty laugh of relief, as if the sergeant has finally exposed the falsehood of everything that he has said by venturing upon a glaringly untrue statement.*

THE SERGEANT (*irritated*). Well, what are you laughing at?

MICHAEL. A good joke!

PETER. Yes, a fine joke!

MICHAEL. A liar! Such a liar as there never was!

STEPAN. When a man has had too much to drink he should stay home!

GRIGOR (*relaxing his dignity*). And for a time we believed him! We believed him!

THE SERGEANT. What?

STEPAN. Instead of telling lies to honest moujiks —

THE SERGEANT (*interrupting*). What do you mean?

PETER. We (*indicating Michael*), we live on the other side of the swamps!

THE SERGEANT. Well, what of it?

MICHAEL. We are going to the mobilization also!

THE SERGEANT (*with superiority*). Here is the border line. But the line bends.

PETER. You said they shot at us! Because we lived on the other side of the swamps! Old Grigor, and Stepan, and Ilia! They shoot at us!

STEPAN (*laughing*). Rather would we shoot at you, Alexei Ivanovitch!

THE SERGEANT (*growing angry*). Laugh, if you like! Laugh, but to-morrow, when you reach Zawichost, when you find that I am your superior officer, then *I* laugh!

PETER. To Zawichost? But we do not go there!

MICHAEL. We go to Sandomierz!

THE SERGEANT (*thunderstruck*). To Sandomierz!

PETER (*snapping his fingers at him*). Where you are *not* my superior officer!

THE SERGEANT (*with sudden awakening*). No, that I am not! But you, you are the enemy!

PETER. What?

ILIA. Did you hear what he said?

STEPAN (*laughing scornfully*). The enemy?

MICHAEL. When we have tilled our fields together?

THE SERGEANT (*balancing himself with difficulty*). Sandomierz, that is in Austria!

GRIGOR (*disregarding him*). Enemies! When we live a single verst apart from each other!

MICHAEL. When we have helped each other with the harvest, aye, since we were children!

THE SERGEANT (*shouting*). We are Russians! You are Austrians! There is war between us! (*He draws his revolver*) I command you to surrender.

PETER (*mimicking him, dancing up and down in front of him*). I command you to surrender!

THE SERGEANT. Surrender!

PETER. Listen to the drunken fool! Surrender!

[*The Sergeant shoots. Peter falls. There is a sudden and dreadful pause.*

STEPAN (*laying his hand over Peter's heart*). Dead! Dead as his horse!

GRIGOR (*rising to his feet like a prophet of old*). Are we men or are we beasts of the field?

THE SERGEANT (*turning triumphantly on Michael*). Now, you Austrian swine, will you surrender?

[*But Stepan is already advancing upon him, breathing deep, slowly, massively, like some awful engine of destruction. At first the Sergeant does not see him, but something in the expression of the others warns him. He wheels.*

THE SERGEANT. Back! Stop where you are!

[*Stepan continues grimly, his great hands rising slowly from his sides.*

THE SERGEANT (*in an ecstasy of fear*). Back, I say!

[*He fires.*

Stepan shakes himself, as if stung by a hornet, and throws his towering bulk upon the Sergeant. There is a sigh of satisfaction from the moujik as his fingers lock about his adversary's throat. And there is a scream from the Sergeant, a scream ending in a choke. . . . The struggling figures fall outside of the circle of light. For a moment there is a threshing, as when some small animal is caught in a trap. Then quiet.

GRIGOR (*almost sobbing*). And not so long ago I thought it was easier to be killed than to kill!

MICHAEL (*with staring eyes*). Murder! That I have lived to see a murder!

ILIA. Lame Peter! Poor lame Peter!

[*There is a pause. Then Stepan rises, holding the Sergeant's revolver between two fingers.*

STEPAN. What shall I do with this?

GRIGOR (*raising his head*). What?

[*Stepan hands him the revolver.*

GRIGOR. Pah!

[*He flings it away. A pause.*

ILIA (*in a trembling voice*).   I so wanted to see you use your strength, and now that I have seen it — how horrible it is, how horrible!

[*Stepan does not reply.   Instead, he turns to Grigor.*

STEPAN.   The bodies?

GRIGOR.   The swamp will swallow them up.

[*Stepan beckons to Ilia.   Silently they raise Peter's body, carry it out at the back.   They return.*

GRIGOR (*rises, bows his head, folds his hands.   The others follow his example*).   May we all be happy.   May the dead reach God's kingdom.   May we all be preserved in good health.   Amen.

[*The others repeat the Amen.   He makes the sign of the cross. The others follow his example.   A little light begins to filter through the trees.*

GRIGOR (*turning to Michael*).   And now, you on your way, we on ours.

MICHAEL.   Farewell, brother.

GRIGOR.   Brother, farewell!

[*Michael takes up two packs, his own, and Peter's; goes out at the back.*

Grigor, Stepan, Ilia, take up their own packs, go out at the left.

THE CURTAIN FALLS

THE MERRY MERRY CUCKOO

JEANNETTE MARKS

JEANNETTE MARKS, at Mt. Holyoke College, was among
the first of the collegiate group to become interested in one-
act plays. On a homeward voyage from England one year,
Edward Knoblock discussed with her the dramatic possi-
bilities of some of her short stories. *Three Welsh Plays*, of
which "The Merry Merry Cuckoo" is one, were the result.
Two of the three plays were entered by an acquaintance,
without the author's knowledge, in the competition for Lord
Howard DeWalden's prize for the best Welsh plays, in 1911,
and were awarded first place by the Welsh National Theatre,
although the prize had been planned for a three-act play.

Miss Marks was born in 1875 in Chattanooga, Tennessee,
but spent her early life in Philadelphia. Her father, the late
William Dennis Marks, was Professor of Dynamics at the
University of Pennsylvania, and President of the Edison
Electric Light Company, besides being the author of several
scientific books.

Jeannette Marks attended school at Dresden and in this
country before entering Wellesley College, where she was
graduated in 1900. After a year of graduate work at
Wellesley, she became instructress in the Department of
English Literature at Mt. Holyoke College, where she is now
chairman of the Department of English Literature and
Drama, and Director of the Laboratory Theatre. There she
has instituted the Play and Poetry Shop Talks, where poets
and writers speak to the students on authors of the day.

Jeannette Marks' interest in Wales was the result of
several summers spent among the northern Welsh moun-

tains, where she walked over the hills and through the valleys, knapsack on back, and became intimately acquainted with Welsh peasant life. The result of her observations is to be found in her books and in her many short stories published in magazines.

Her published works are: *The Cheerful Cricket* (1907); *The English Pastoral* (1908); *Through Welsh Doorways* (1909); *The End of a Song* (1911); *A Girl's School Days and After* (1911); *Gallant Little Wales* (1912); *Vacation Camping for Girls* (1913); *Leviathan* (1913); *Early English Hero Tales* (1915); "The Sun Chaser" (in O'Brien's *Best Short Stories* for 1916); *Three Welsh Plays* (1917); *Madame France*, and *Courage* (1919); *Children in the Wood Stories* (1919); *Geoffrey's Window* (1921); *Willow Pollen* (verse, 1921); "The Sun Chaser" (as a full-length play, 1922); *Genius and Disaster* (1925–1926); *Thirteen Days* (1929).

THE MERRY MERRY CUCKOO

By JEANNETTE MARKS

"The Merry Merry Cuckoo" was originally produced at the Toy Theatre, Boston, in 1911.

Original Cast

DAVID	Mr. MacGregor Jenkins
ANNIE	Ruth B. Delano
PASTOR MORRIS	Mr. Pettis
LOWRY PRICHARD	Mary Kellogg
GUTO PRICHARD	Mr. Clarke

Reprinted from "Three Welsh Plays" by permission of, and special arrangement with, Miss Jeannette Marks and Little, Brown and Company.

Application for the right of performing "The Merry Merry Cuckoo" must be made to Jeannette Marks, South Hadley, Mass.

THE MERRY MERRY CUCKOO

SCENE. *A garden. Cottage at back running from right to center. A group of three windows in the shape of a bay, showing a bed inside and an old man lying on it. A door leads into cottage. A gate in fence on the right side leads to the road and village beyond. All of the left side of stage a garden and orchard, with a path through it to a gate in wall at back; garden wall to left, at back over it village chapel from which the church music comes.*

A thatched cottage with whitewashed walls. Ivy is growing about the doorway, and hanging from the thatch above the door; fuchsia bushes on either side of door; trees to the left in garden, including holly and yew; green grass; mountains beyond cottage and garden and chapel. In the foreground, to right by cottage door, is a washtub.

It is about six o'clock, the first Monday in April. Towards end of act the sun sets.

At rise of curtain, windows of the cottage closed, and Annie, old, very plump, with sparse gray hair escaping from under her white cap and damp on her forehead from work, and wearing a short skirt, apron, fichu over shoulders, clogs on her feet, is washing. Church music off left continues a minute after rise of curtain. David calls out. Annie leaves the tub and hurries to the windows to open them from the outside. David, a very old man, with white hair and thin face, is seen lying in bed.

DAVID (*calling*). Annie, Annie!

ANNIE (*opening windows*). Aye, lad dear, I was listenin' for ye; yiss, yiss, an' expectin' ye to call.

DAVID (*sleepily*). I was dreamin' an' — dear, dear, what a dream! It seemed like fifty years ago when we were married, an', you remember, we stood out there in the garden that first night. Are there any violets bloomin' yet?

ANNIE. Not yet, Davy lad.

DAVID. An' the marsh marigolds?

ANNIE. I'm thinkin' they're sure to be out.

DAVID. An' that same night, Annie, do ye remember we heard the cuckoo singin'?

ANNIE. Aye, lad darlin', fifty years ago this comin' week, an' a cuckoo singin' to us every spring since then. (*Annie takes a tumbler from the sill and gives him a spoonful of medicine*) Take this, dear; there, 'twill be makin' ye better.

DAVID (*taking medicine*). An' well?

ANNIE. Yiss, yiss, better.

DAVID. But the cuckoo, will the cuckoo be singin' soon?

ANNIE (*words inconclusive*). Lad, dear, no more, or ye'll be havin' an attack an' — Dear people, chapel is out, an' I hear them on the road!

DAVID (*plaintively*). The Monday meetin'. Why have ye not been?

ANNIE. Work is keepin' me home, lad.

DAVID. But, Annie, ye've not said a word of the cuckoo.

ANNIE (*sending her voice up as cheerfully as she can*). Aye, the cuckoo; yiss, the cuckoo —

DAVID (*clasping and unclasping his hands*). Has it come? Did ye hear it?

ANNIE (*gulping*). David, dear, if ye'd but listen to what I was a-goin' to say. I was a-goin' to say that I've not heard the cuckoo yet, but that everthin's over-early this spring in Wales, an' I'm expectin' to hear one any time now. 'Tis so warm there might be one singin' at dusk to-day — there might be!

DAVID (*brightening*). Might there be, Annie?

ANNIE (*smoothing his head with her hand*). Aye, lad. Hush. lad, they're singin' in the chapel!

[*She stands there with one hand resting on his forehead, listen-*

*ing to the singing of Penlan, a hymn by David Jenkins.
When the music stops, she moves away.*

DAVID. 'Tis over-early, an', Annie —

ANNIE. Davy dear, be still! Pastor Morris says — Tut,
tut, I'll close the window, for there comes that Lowry
Prichard and her man.

[*Annie closes windows hastily and goes back to her washing.
Enter from right Lowry and her husband Guto, coming from
the Monday prayer meeting and carrying hymnals. Lowry
dressed in Welsh costume, clogs, short full skirt, striped apron,
white sleeves from elbow to wrist, tight bodice, shawl over her
shoulders, white cap, and tall, Welsh beaver hat. Guto, Welsh
beaver hat on like his wife's, striped vest, brass buttons on lapels
of black cloth coat, long, somewhat tight trousers. At sight
of washtub and Annie busy over it, Lowry and Guto make
gestures of shocked dismay to each other.*

LOWRY. Good evenin', Annie Dalben.

ANNIE (*wiping her wet hand on her apron*). Good evenin',
Lowry Prichard, an' to you, Guto.

GUTO. Good evenin', mum.

LOWRY. How is your man?

ANNIE. He's no better.

LOWRY. Is he worse?

ANNIE. Nay.

LOWRY. We missed ye, Annie Dalben.

GUTO. Aye, we did. Why were ye not at meetin'?

ANNIE. I've my man to mind these days.

LOWRY (*triumphantly*). But ye said he was no worse, ye
did.

ANNIE. Aye, I did, but I cannot leave him alone.

GUTO. But ye're neglectin' chapel an' forgettin' the Lord
Annie Dalben. Ye'll go quite on the downfall, like
this.

LOWRY. Aye, ye've not been to meetin's, an' 'tis bad when
he's dyin' for ye to forget your Lord. Is he in there?

ANNIE (*moving protectingly nearer the closed window*). Yiss.

LOWRY. Why were ye washin'?

ANNIE. Ye've no cause to ask that — ye know. Except I did the washin', what would there be for me to care for David with — now that he needs me?

GUTO. Yiss, but ye could do it on some other day.

ANNIE. Nay, for the ladies are waitin' now for what they've given me to do — an' they so kind.

LOWRY. I see Pastor Morris comin' in.

ANNIE. Aye, he's comin' every day an' some days bringin' me the food from his own table for my man.

[*Enter Pastor Morris, young, earnest and rather severe because of his youth.*

LOWRY (*the inquisitional look on her face deepening, and her voice growing more shrill, pointing to Annie*). Ye see, sir, what Annie Dalben's been doin' while we were in meetin'. She's needin' a sermon, aye, that she is.

GUTO. She's goin' quite on the downfall, sir.

ANNIE. Lowry Prichard, ye've no cause to speak so about me. When was I ever absent when my man was well? But now, sir, (*turning to Morris*) as ye know, he's ill an' needin' me an' all the s'illin's I can earn. I cannot go away from him.

LOWRY (*speaking to Pastor Morris*). She's needin' your advice, sir. 'Tis that she is needin' whatever. Warn her well.

GUTO. Yiss, an' rebuke her.

LOWRY. Ye're young, sir, but ye're the instrument of the Lord whatever. 'Tis your duty to bring her back to her conscience.

GUTO. Amen.

[*Lowry and Guto go off very self-righteous and looking triumphantly at Annie, who, quiet, her face pale and weary, turns to her washing and rubs and rinses diligently, while the minister is talking.*

MORRIS (*gently*). I've been troubled, for I knew that it would come to this, Annie. I should have spoken with you before about going to chapel. Some one could be found to stay with David while you were at meeting. You have not been to chapel for a month, Annie.

ANNIE (*continuing her work, but in her voice the attitude of the older woman towards the young man*). Ye're very kind, sir, to take the interest, but I'm thinkin' ye cannot understand. There's been no occasion, sir, for ye to understand through what I've been goin' these days.

[*She rubs her sleeve across her tear-filled eyes and continues washing sturdily.*

MORRIS. Yes, but, Annie, what is David thinking? Does he want you to stay away from the meetings where you have always been together?

ANNIE. Nay, sir.

MORRIS. Has he spoken of your staying away?

ANNIE (*reluctantly*). Aye, sir, he asked this evenin' why I was not in meetin'.

MORRIS (*reflectively*). He did. Well, I am thinking that —

ANNIE (*dropping her work and speaking as if worried*). Nay, sir, I've no cause to excuse myself to ye — ye're naught but a lad. 'Tis past your knowledge how my man is everythin' to me — everythin', he is. He's been such a husband as no one but myself can know, thinkin' of me all the time, livin' for me, as gentle an' tender to me as if I had been a child, an' now, sir, he's ill — he may be dyin', an' I can think of nothin' but doin' everythin' for — (*David taps on window and Annie turns to open it*) Aye, lad dear. 'Tis the Pastor comin' to see ye again.

DAVID (*smiling and holding out one weak old hand*). Good evenin', sir, such a grand day, with spring everywhere. We've been expectin' the cuckoo, sir — the wife and I. Have ye heard the cuckoo, yet, Annie?

MORRIS (*starting to speak*). 'Twill be a fortnight be —

ANNIE (*interrupting hurriedly*). Nay, lad dear, I've been busy, but I'm thinkin' I'm likely to hear it now any moment — aye, any moment.

MORRIS. But, Annie, the cuckoo doesn't —

ANNIE. Tut, sir, I could almost promise the cuckoo would be singin' at sundown whatever — aye, indeed, lad darlin'. Now I'll —

DAVID (*interrupting*).   Annie, ye mind that baby cuckoo we
saw the sky-lark a-feedin' that first spring in Blaen Cwm?
It all comes back so clear now an' clearer every moment
I'd not once thought of it, sir, since then.

MORRIS.   But, David, the —

ANNIE (*speaking to David and closing the windows*).   Lie down,
lad darlin', an' be quiet.   I'll call ye, if the cuckoo sings.

[*In the distance the choir can be heard practising Cariad, a
revival hymn, in the chapel.   Continues until Annie is alone
and talking to herself.*

MORRIS (*severely*).   But, Annie, you know the cuckoo will
not sing at least for another fortnight.   It is mid-April
before the cuckoo sings.

ANNIE (*wearily*).   Aye, sir.

MORRIS.   Why did you say that to David?

ANNIE.   He's achin', sir, to hear the cuckoo sing, an' I'm
wantin' to comfort him.

MORRIS.   But, Annie, it is a lie to say what you did to
him.

ANNIE (*vigorously*).   Aye, sir, but I'm not carin' whatever.

MORRIS (*severely*).   Not caring about telling a lie?

ANNIE.   Nay, sir, I'm not carin' about anythin' but makin'
him happy.

MORRIS (*rebukingly*).   Annie!   (*Annie continues washing and
does not reply*)   Annie!   Well, indeed, Annie, if there is
nothing I can do for you, and you will not listen to me, I
must be going to choir practice.   I promised to be there
this evening.

ANNIE (*without turning from the tub*).   Aye, sir.   (*Pastor
Morris off through garden path to choir practice.   Goes to
left.   Annie continues washing until he is well out of sight.
She stands up straight and looks about the garden*)   He's
wantin' to hear the cuckoo more nor anythin' else, dear,
dear!   Everywhere 'tis green now, an' the lilies will be
here before long — but lad, lad, the cuckoo, will it come?
(*She goes to left into garden, the wet clothes in a basket under
her arm and stands there, looking about*)   'Twas over there

it laid its egg in the robin's nest this year ago in May —
aye, an' one poor little bird pushed the other out, an' ye
picked it up, lad dear, an' were so tender with it.   An'
they're not wantin' ye, Davy, my old lad darlin', to think
the cuckoo will be singin' soon.   Dear God, is there to be
no cuckoo singin' for the lad again?   Just once more,
dear God, to sing to him and comfort him?   Aye! just
the one song?   No cuckoo?   Aye, there will be a cuckoo
singin', there shall be a cuckoo singin'!   (*She looks towards
the closed windows behind which David lies, and puts down
her basket of clothes*) He's asleep! Hush, I'll be the
cuckoo! He'll wake an' think the spring has really come.
Here by this tree.   They're in the chapel, an' they'll never
know.   (*Throughout this scene, until Lowry speaks, a cuckoo
song is being played very softly.   And it is into a few notes
of this, several times repeated, that Annie swings when she
actually sings her cuckoo song.   She opens her mouth to begin, a look of appealing misery on her face*) 'Twas somethin' like this: Coo-o.   Coo-o! Tut, that sounds like a
hen.   I know, it goes over an' over again, sing-song,
sing-song, like this: cu-cu, cu-cu.   Aye, that's better.
(*She rocks herself backwards and forwards practising it and
repeating cu-cu, cu-cu*) 'Tis growin' better, but lad, lad,
I'm plannin' to deceive ye whatever!   (*Brushes tears away
impatiently and begins song again*) Cucu-cu, cucu-cu,
cucucu-cu, cu! Aye, that's fair; aye, 'tis fine! He'll not
know me from a real cuckoo.   I'll try it loud now, for
ye've no long, dearie.
[*She holds eagerly on to tree beside her, so lost in the cuckoo
music that she is not aware of a head popping up behind the
garden wall and down again.   She draws a long breath and
begins, softly, slowly, the song sounding as if it came from a
distance.   She waits a moment, — the heads are well above the
wall now in amazement, — and then sings more loudly,
making the song sound as if it came from the garden where she
is standing.*
DAVID (*calling*).   Annie!

ANNIE (*hurrying to open his windows*). Aye, lad dear, I'm comin'.

DAVID (*ecstatically*). Annie, Annie, dear, I heard the cuckoo singin'; I was dreamin' again, an' all at once I heard the cuckoo singin' in the garden, loud and clear. It sang three times; first, it sounded like somethin' else, 'twas so breathless; then it sang quiet an' sweet like a cuckoo; an' the third time it seemed comin' from the old mill wheel.

ANNIE. But, lad darlin', ye've heard it, an' I'm that glad! Three times; yiss, yiss, 'tis a real fine cuckoo. Now ye're happy, darlin', an' ye'll sleep well upon it.

DAVID (*disappointedly*). Did ye no hear it?

ANNIE. I'm thinkin' I did an' thinkin' I didn't.

DAVID. Where were ye?

ANNIE. Out in the garden, hangin' out the clothes.

DAVID (*still more disappointedly*). An' ye didn't hear it?

ANNIE. I'm no certain, darlin'; I heard somethin' — I did, indeed.

DAVID (*proudly*). 'Twas the cuckoo, Annie dear; I'm hearin' it first every year; ye must be growin' deaf.

ANNIE. Yiss, yiss. Now go to sleep, an' I'll call ye if I hear the cuckoo sing.

DAVID. Will it sing again?

ANNIE. Aye, darlin', if ye heard it once, 'tis sure to sing again.

DAVID. I'll be gettin' well, Annie, is it not so?

ANNIE (*turning away suddenly*). Indeed, lad dear, ye'll be about among the heather 'fore long.

DAVID (*speaking quietly, almost to himself*). To think the cuckoo's singin' — singin' for me!

ANNIE. Aye, aye; now go to sleep.

[*He lies back and closes his eyes obediently. Annie, drying her eyes on her apron, goes to left towards her basket of clothes. She stands by the tree where she had sung the cuckoo song for David, unconscious that two people are head and shoulders above the garden wall, looking at her.*

LOWRY (*in a loud voice*). So ye've come back, Annie Dalben, to sing the cuckoo again.

GUTO. Aye, we heard ye singin' the cuckoo.

LOWRY. Pooh, 'tis a pretty cuckoo ye make, an old woman like you, an' a pretty song!

ANNIE. Lowry Prichard, have a care!

GUTO. 'Tis over-early for the cuckoo, is it not?

ANNIE. Yiss.

GUTO. An' what are ye singin' in your garden for, an' David dyin'?

[*Annie does not reply but stoops to her basket of clothes and begins to hang them out.*

LOWRY. So ye'll give no answer? Well, indeed, maybe ye'll answer Pastor Morris. Aye, Guto, go fetch the Pastor.

[*Guto goes off to left, through garden gate in garden wall.*

LOWRY (*going towards the windows behind which David lies*). 'Tis a godly song ye've sung, Annie, an' a tale for the chapel, eh?

ANNIE (*following and stepping in front of Lowry*). Ye may go out of this garden, an' that this minute!

LOWRY (*making her way nearer and nearer the window*). Nay, nay, I'm a-goin' to speak with David an' tell him he's a cuckoo for a wife. Tut, ye look fair crazy, Annie, crazy with wrath! Your hair is all rumpled, an' your smock is dirty. David, bein' a cuckoo is —

[*But the taunt is left unfinished, for at that moment young Morris comes in hastily, Guto following.*

MORRIS (*authoritatively*). Annie! Lowry! Annie, is this I hear true? Have you been imitating the cuckoo?

ANNIE. Aye, sir.

MORRIS (*turning to Lowry and Guto*). You may go. Leave this to me.

[*Guto and Lowry go off right, through front gate, staring in at David as they pass.*

MORRIS (*sternly*). So, Annie, you have been acting the cuckoo — acting a lie. With this lie upon you, how will it be with salvation?

ANNIE (*hotly*). Salvation, sir? I've no mind to your salvation; no, nor to heaven's, if the Lord makes this singin'

a lie! I'm thinkin' of David as I've thought of him
these fifty years, years before ye were born, sir, an' if a
lie will make him happy when he's dyin', then I'm willin'
to lie, an' do it every minute of the day.

MORRIS.   That means you are willing to sin?

ANNIE.   Aye, sir, to sin. I'm a willin' sinner!

MORRIS (*more gently*).   You are overwrought, Annie.

ANNIE (*wearily*).   Ye're all against me, sir.

MORRIS.   Nay, nay, but wouldn't it be better if I were to
tell David about the cuckoo?

ANNIE (*sobbing*).   Oh, no, no, no, sir!   Not that!

MORRIS (*stretching out his hand to comfort her*).   Annie, there,
there, you mustn't cry so.

ANNIE.   'Tis all the happiness he's got, an' he's goin'.   Oh,
my lad, my lad!

MORRIS.   There, there, Annie!

ANNIE.   We've been married fifty years this spring, an'
every spring we've listened for the cuckoo an' not one
missed.   An' now he's a-dyin' an' a-wantin' to hear it so,
an' 'twas over-early, an' then I thought of bein' the cuckoo
myself.   Oh, Davy, Davy darlin'!

MORRIS (*altogether forgetting his pastoral severity*).   There,
Annie, there, dear, tell me about it!   We'll see, Annie.

ANNIE.   There's no more.   Only he kept askin' about the
spring, the violets an' marsh marigolds, an' I knew all the
time he was thinkin' of the cuckoo an' not askin' because
he was goin' an' mightn't hear it.   An' then he did.   An'
I said I thought he'd hear one this evenin', that everythin'
was over-early whatever.   After that he seemed happier
than I'd seen him, an' I closed his windows an' went off
into the garden to practise it.   I worked at it till I could
do it fair.   Oh, Davy, Davy lad!

MORRIS.   Now, Annie dear, don't cry, just tell me more.

ANNIE.   Then, sir, I sang the song here by this tree, an'
when he called me to him, there was such a look of joy on
his face as has not been there this long time.   'Tis the
last happiness I can give him, sir.

DAVID (*calling*). Annie, Annie!

ANNIE. · He's callin'. Aye, lad dear, I'm comin'.

[*She goes into cottage and, after opening all the windows, stands by the foot of David's bed.*

DAVID. Have ye heard the cuckoo singin'?

ANNIE. No, not yet. It must be singin' again soon.

DAVID (*anxiously*). Ye're sure 'tis *goin'* to sing?

ANNIE (*gathering him up and turning his pillow*). Indeed, yiss, an' with the windows all open, ye'll be hearin' it fine an' clear, ye will. I'll go back up into the garden to see is the cuckoo there.

DAVID. Will it be singin' over an' over again, the way it did that first time?

ANNIE. Aye, I'm thinkin' so, lad darlin'. Ye must listen quietly.

DAVID. 'Twas so beautiful singin'. I'd like hearin' it with ye here beside me.

ANNIE (*kissing him*). I'll come back, lad.

DAVID. Aye, I'll be waitin' for ye.

[*Annie goes out of the cottage door and back into garden where Pastor Morris is standing, his hat off, while Annie and David are talking together. He can see them both, but David cannot see him. Annie and Morris converse in whispers. The cuckoo song begins to be played softly.*

MORRIS. Is he worse?

ANNIE (*looking at Morris beseechingly*). I cannot tell, sir, but he's longin' to hear the cuckoo sing again.

MORRIS. I see, and you are wishing to do it again?

ANNIE. Yiss, an' with the lad dyin', can ye tell me not to do what Davy is askin' for? Each time might be his last, sir.

MORRIS (*after a moment's hesitation*). Nay, go sing for him. I will stand guard for you, and no one shall disturb you.

ANNIE (*a deep sigh of relief*). Oh, sir, thank you! 'Tis sure to be a comfort. But ye're harmin' your conscience for me, sir, are ye?

MORRIS (*humbly*). I'm not saying, Annie; I'm over-young to have a conscience in some things.

ANNIE (*taking his hand to kiss it*). May God bless ye, sir, for bein' kind to an old woman!

[*The sun has set behind the chapel, and it is rapidly growing dark as the music grows louder. Morris steps back to the garden gate to keep watch. Annie stands by the tree and, dropping her hands by her side, lifting her head, and swaying her old body to and fro, sings the cuckoo song over and over again three times. David has risen in bed, an expression of rapturous delight upon his face as he leans against the casement listening. The lights are being lighted in the chapel, and the chapel bell begins to ring.*

DAVID (*calling faintly*). Annie, Annie darlin', come quickly, the cuckoo's singin'!

ANNIE (*hastening towards him*). Yiss, lad, I'm comin'.

DAVID (*stretching out his hands towards her*). Annie, sweetheart, did ye *hear* the cuckoo singin'?

ANNIE. Yiss, dearie, loud and clear.

DAVID (*trying to imitate its song while his voice grows fainter*). It sang over an' over like this —

ANNIE (*within the cottage and beside David*). Yiss, dear, I see.

DAVID (*sinking back into her arms*). An' — it — was — quiet — but — Annie —

ANNIE (*holding him to her and crying out*). Lad, lad dear. Davy, can ye not speak to me?

[*The bell for chapel stops ringing. The organ playing "Jesus, Lover of my Soul" is heard. Morris is standing by the gate, facing towards the old people, his hat off, his head bowed.*

CURTAIN

RYLAND

THOMAS WOOD STEVENS

THE CARNEGIE INSTITUTE OF TECHNOLOGY in Pittsburgh was the first college to grant the degree of Bachelor of Arts at the completion of a four years' course in its department of drama, a department with a complete curriculum, theatre auditorium, and workshops, which Thomas Wood Stevens inaugurated in 1913. Prior to that, he had been influential in organizing one of the first art theatre groups in Chicago, and in popularizing the one-act play there. "Ryland" is one of several plays which were written in collaboration with Kenneth Sawyer Goodman for production by the Chicago Stage Guild.

Mr. Stevens was born in Daysville, Illinois, on January 26, 1880. He graduated from Armour Scientific Academy in 1897 and then undertook a three years' course in mechanical engineering at Armour Institute of Technology, Chicago. In 1903 he took charge of the Department of Illustration at the Art Institute of Chicago, and in 1912 he became lecturer in art history at the University of Wisconsin. In 1913 he was appointed head of the department of drama at the Carnegie Institute of Technology, but left Pittsburgh in 1925 to direct the Goodman Memorial Theatre, Chicago, in connection with the Chicago Art Institute. Since 1934 he has directed Globe Theatre Productions, Ltd.

Thomas Wood Stevens, like Percy MacKaye, was one of the first in America to undertake the work of community pageantry professionally, and he has been author and director of many successful pageants.

His Globe Theatre versions of Shakespeare, which have been produced with great success by the players of the Globe

Theatre at the Century of Progress, the San Diego Exposition, the Texas Centennial, and the Great Lakes Exposition, are special arrangements of the texts that play from thirty minutes to about an hour each.

Thomas Wood Stevens is the author of *The Etching of Cities* (1913) and *Lettering* (1916). His most important dramatic works are: "The Chaplet of Pan" (in collaboration with Wallace Rice, produced by Donald Robertson in 1908); "A Pageant of the Italian Renaissance" (1909); "Independence Day Pageant" (with K. S. Goodman, 1911); *Masques of East and West* (with K. S. Goodman, 1915); "The Pageant of Saint Louis" (1914); "The Drawing of the Sword" (Red Cross Pageant, 1917); "Joan of Arc" (1918); *The Nursery Maid of Heaven and Other Plays* (1927); *Yorktown Pageants* (1931); *The Theatre, from Athens to Broadway* (1932).

KENNETH SAWYER GOODMAN

LIEUTENANT KENNETH SAWYER GOODMAN was born in 1883, and died very suddenly of pneumonia on November 29, 1918. At the time of his death he was chief aid to Captain Moffett at the Great Lakes Naval Station.

In coöperating with B. Iden Payne during the Chicago Theatre Society's season at the Fine Arts Theatre in 1913, he helped to give the city one of its most interesting repertory engagements. He was an officer of the Chicago Theatre Society during its three years of life, and contributed to the repertory of its Drama Players in 1911 a translation of Hervieu's "La Course en Flambeau", which was successfully acted at the Lyric Theatre under the title of "The Passing of the Torch." By the study of playwriting, of stage decoration, and of theatre management, he was preparing himself for important work in dramatic art.

He is the author of: *Quick Curtains*, which contains "Dust of the Road", "The Game of Chess", "Barbara", "Ephraim and the Winged Bear", "Back of the Yards", "Dancing

Dolls", and "A Man Can Only Do His Best"; co-author of "An Idyl of the Shops", "The Hero of Santa Maria", and "The Wonder Hat" (these three in collaboration with Ben Hecht); and "Holbein in Blackfriars", "Ryland", "Rainald and the Red Wolf", *Masques of East and West* (in collaboration with Thomas Wood Stevens).

In 1925, the friends of Kenneth Sawyer Goodman erected the Goodman Memorial Theatre to give dramatic arts representation in the Chicago Art Institute, and to create a repertory company.

RYLAND

A COMEDY

By THOMAS WOOD STEVENS AND KENNETH
SAWYER GOODMAN

"Ryland" was originally produced by The Stage Guild for the Chicago Society of Etchers, February 22, 1912, at the Art Institute, Chicago.

Original Cast

WILLIAM WYNNE RYLAND, Engraver	Frederick K. Cowley
THE GAOLER	Ralph Holmes
HENRY FIELDING, Ryland's Pupil	Roy S. Hambleton
HADDRILL, a print-seller . . .	Thomas Wood Stevens
SIR JOSHUA REYNOLDS . . .	Kenneth Sawyer Goodman
MARY RYLAND	Gertrude Spaller
ANGELICA KAUFFMAN . . .	Elaine Hyman

RYLAND

Scene. *Ryland's cell in Newgate. Right, window, with an engraving screen; a table and stool; engraving tools, etc.; on the wall a composition by Angelica Kauffman. Left, a bench and a barred door, leading to the corridor. Right Center, a small table with breakfast tray.*

Ryland and the Gaoler discovered.

THE GAOLER. Your breakfast, Mr. Ryland. Your last breakfast, God help us all! Many's the good man I've seen go out of here to Tyburn, housebreakers and murderers and thieves, but never a great artist, Mr. Ryland — never till you.

RYLAND. So I'm to be hanged to-morrow morning, eh?

GAOLER. Yes, sir. To-morrow at six.

RYLAND. Well . . . No more of this (*indicating the engraving*) and good-bye to that, eh?

[*With a gesture at the composition.*

GAOLER (*gloomily*). To-morrow at six, sir.

RYLAND. Buck up, man. It's I, not you. You will breakfast to-morrow.

GAOLER. It has been very pleasant, having you here, sir. And profitable, too.

RYLAND. I dare say.

GAOLER. Yes, Mr. Ryland, I've had a tidy bit from the gentlemen who have come in to see you. Some bacon, sir — I can recommend it — none of the prison fare, that. And you've been most comfortable to deal with. No howling, no shaking the bars, no cursing at night.

RYLAND. No, none of that, I hope.

GAOLER. It's because you've been busy with the plate, there. The picture-making has been a blessing to you. Then, you've never given up hope —

RYLAND. I find myself hungry. That's strange.

GAOLER. Not at all, sir. Many of them are so. (*Pause*) Mr. Ryland, might I make so bold as to say, it would be a great service to me, if you would get another reprieve; work a week longer on the plate. It can't be anything to you, sir, so near the end, or I wouldn't be asking it.

RYLAND. It would be a service to you, would it?

GAOLER. You could work at your engraving —

RYLAND. I've overworked it now.

GAOLER. Oh, I'm sorry to hear that, sir.

[*A knock outside. Enter Fielding outside the grating.*

FIELDING. May I speak with Mr. Ryland?

GAOLER. I don't know; it's against the rules. (*Fielding gives him money*) Who shall I say, sir?

FIELDING. Mr. Fielding. You've seen me often enough.

GAOLER. To be sure, Mr. Fielding, but I likes to observe the formalities. It'll be five shillings, sir.

FIELDING. Yesterday it was only two.

GAOLER. He'll be leaving me soon — I've got to make the best of him while he lasts, God help him.

[*He takes the money, unlocks the grating, and calls to Ryland.*

GAOLER. Mr. Fielding's compliments to Mr. Ryland.

[*Exit Gaoler.*

RYLAND. My dear Henry, this is kind of you.

FIELDING. Oh, Mr. Ryland, I came directly I could get word of Lord Wycombe's decision on your appeal —

RYLAND. Oh, the pardon?

FIELDING. Yes, sir —

RYLAND. You'll forgive me if I finish my breakfast. I can't offer you a chair —

FIELDING. Oh, Mr. Ryland!

RYLAND. Well — well?

FIELDING. I went to Lord Wycombe's secretary as soon as he was out of his bed. . . . Oh, Mr. Ryland!

RYLAND. Out with it! Am I pardoned, or only reprieved for another week?

FIELDING. Neither.

RYLAND. Come, come —

FIELDING. Neither, sir. Lord Wycombe denies both your appeals.

RYLAND. I've lost my appetite. . . .

FIELDING (*leaning over him; Ryland looking over his breakfast*). He said you had been three times reprieved, that you might finish this plate; that his lordship had been more than merciful, considering the nature of your crime —

RYLAND. I beg you not to mention it, Henry. I had committed no crime.

FIELDING. Never before, he said, had the statute in so grave a matter as forgery been stayed, and in your case only that your wife might not be left unprovided for.

RYLAND. I understand his lordship's mercy. . . .

FIELDING. And now, he says, if the plate is still unfinished, it must be carried on by another hand.

RYLAND. That will not be necessary

FIELDING. He said that your wife — Oh, Mr. Ryland! . . . where else shall I go? What other appeal is there?

RYLAND (*gets up and puts his hand on Fielding's shoulder*). My poor boy! You have been more than faithful. I can't be altogether worthless, to have you stick to me like this. Tell me — you will take care of her? You will be as devoted to her as you have been to me?

FIELDING. My life, Mr. Ryland, shall be spent in her service.

RYLAND. I dare say. (*Moving up stage*) Well, after all, there's a satisfaction in knowing the next day's work. It might have ended three week's ago. . . . The ride in the cart will be pleasant. The air, man! I've not had a full breath since — since the minions of the law broke in upon my seclusion. . . . But for these reprieves, I should have had it over and done with, and you and my wife would be already half comforted . . . shall I say? It's a miserable business, this shrinking back from the verge.

FIELDING. Oh, sir, you must see that we are on the verge —

RYLAND. I am on the verge, Fielding.

FIELDING. For God's sake, sir, drop this pretense. It's one thing to jest at death when you're safe at home. It's another when you're — . . . Until to-day I never dreamed that you . . . that you could not escape. We must make some last effort.

RYLAND. So you actually expect to see me kicking my heels at the end of a rope?

FIELDING. Oh, sir, you must see it, too. You must think. You must give me orders. If you sit and jest, I am helpless. It will all be over —

RYLAND. My dear boy, what is there you can do? You tell me to drop the pretense. . . . What have I left? I admit I never thought it would come to this. I still believed in my destiny. It's an ignominious end, it seems, . . . and I must meet it with what grace I may. In faith, it matters little : a wasted life gone out : a slender ghost of a talent strangled. . . . (*Moves over to the table where the plate is*) I'm not sorry I've had this respite, Fielding. I've made a good plate here, and in this have paid a last courtesy to Mistress Angelica. I hope she will like it . . . if she ever comes back to see it. She's a dem'd fine woman, Angelica Kauffman, and this is as good a thing as ever she painted. I hope she likes it. . . .

FIELDING. Could Mistress Kauffman do nothing to save you, sir?

RYLAND. She's a white moon, lad! She rides high on the winds of fame these days. It takes a long time for a cry of pain to mount that far, Fielding. . . .

FIELDING. But have you tried? Have you written?

RYLAND. I can be proud on occasion . . . even with a rope around my neck. Once she wasn't so far, so cold. . . . But that's another matter, a matter that's closed. To-morrow . . . tush, I'm content. I'm tired. I'm ready to step off.

FIELDING. But, sir, she might —

RYLAND. No. I had it from Sir Joshua at the trial. She's in Italy.

FIELDING. She's here in London! I saw her only this morning.

RYLAND. Say that again!

FIELDING. She's here in London.

RYLAND. You fool! Why didn't you tell me? You stand there and blither about Lord Wycombe's secretary, when Angelica Kauffman's in London. . . . In London! Why didn't I know it? I did know it. I felt it through these stifling walls. I was a dolt . . . I thought it was only Spring in the air, April in my blood. It was hope, it was life. A moment ago you had me seeing myself on Tyburn Hill! And all the time I knew it could never come to that.

FIELDING. What am I to do?

RYLAND. Bring her here. Hunt her from one end of the town to the other. Bring her here, lad; I must talk to her. She can twist the Queen around her little finger. Through the Queen she can get me a royal pardon.

FIELDING. The time is short.

RYLAND. Time enough if she still cares!

[*The Gaoler knocks at the door.*

GAOLER. A lady to see you, sir.

FIELDING. Ah!

RYLAND. Who is she?

GAOLER. Your wife, sir.

RYLAND. Show her in.

[*Fielding goes to the door and pays the Gaoler; Mary Ryland comes in, and runs across to Ryland.*

MARY RYLAND. William — . . .

RYLAND. Good morning, my dear.

MARY RYLAND. Aren't you glad to see me?

RYLAND. Why shouldn't I be glad to see you?

MARY RYLAND. You look disappointed. You haven't kissed me.

RYLAND. I beg your pardon! (*He kisses her hand, and turns to Fielding*) Well, why don't you go?

FIELDING. Where shall I look for her?

RYLAND. Her house is in Golden Street. If you fail there, go to Sir Joshua. Spend what you need, but lose no time.

MARY RYLAND. Has something happened? Where is he to go?

RYLAND. He is to bring Angelica Kauffman here. He has my orders.

MARY RYLAND. No, I say. I'll not have her here. I'll not have you see her. I'll not allow — . . .

RYLAND. Pardon me, my dear. He shall bring her.

MARY RYLAND (*weeping*). And I've come day after day, and you've treated me like a stranger . . . and now you're sending for her.

FIELDING (*taking a step toward her*). It's all as it should be, Mistress Ryland.

MARY RYLAND. You tell me that, Henry. Do you know? . . .

FIELDING. I know there is need for her.

MARY RYLAND. Then do as you think right.

FIELDING. It's not that, Mistress Ryland. It's necessary, now that Lord Wycombe —

RYLAND. Sst! Go. (*Fielding goes out*) My dear, I'm not flattered by your jealousy, I assure you. There is no need for you to question me — and Mistress Kauffman is a great artist. I must have her see this plate — to-day. That should be enough.

MARY RYLAND. But, William, you knew her before you ever saw me, and it hurts me to think — . . .

RYLAND. There, there, my dear.

[*The Gaoler knocks at the door.*

GAOLER. Mr. Haddrill, on important business with Mr. Ryland.

RYLAND. Ask Mr. Haddrill to sit down outside. You can squeeze an extra shilling out of him for a chair.

MARY RYLAND. But, William, you can't keep Mr. Haddrill waiting.

RYLAND. To-day it is my privilege to keep anybody waiting.

MARY RYLAND. But Mr. Haddrill's your publisher.

RYLAND. He's a tradesman to whom I'm doing a favor. A favor by which you are to profit, not I.

MARY RYLAND. Don't make it harder for me.

RYLAND. Mary, I want a few moments alone with you.

MARY RYLAND. I thought you'd rather be rid of me . . . that you'd rather —

RYLAND. My poor child. You seem to forget that my last plate, the thing I've let them stretch out my life, week by week, to finish — for your benefit; the only profitable thing I can leave you, in this world, is a copper mirror fashioned to reflect the genius of Angelica Kauffman.

MARY RYLAND. It's for her pleasure, her fame, you've been working, not for me. You've sent Fielding to fetch her. . . .

RYLAND. The plate's finished. It must have her approval before . . . I go.

MARY RYLAND. Don't! Don't speak of the end. . . . I can't bear it. I'm your wife.

RYLAND. Poor child. Poor little creature. I think you pity yourself more than you pity me.

MARY RYLAND. How can you? How can you?

RYLAND. Why all this snivelling about so simple a thing as death? A little jaunt from here to somewhere else . . . a step off into the empty air. My dear, it's I that take the step, not you.

MARY RYLAND. Oh! Oh, how can you go on about it this way?

RYLAND. Because I want to see you smile again. Because you're young. Because I've wasted a year of your life, and I'm sorry for it. . . . Because I want you to understand that if it happens I've come to the end of my lane, you are only turning into yours. . . and the hedgerows are white with hawthorn bloom. You'll see the green trees in the Mall, the red sun over the chimney pots, the silver river when you walk on the embankment at night.

MARY RYLAND. But the loneliness, the separation!

RYLAND (*losing patience a little*). Tush! Such separations are only terrible when two people love each other.

MARY RYLAND. But I love you.

RYLAND. No, I dazzled you. . . . And now I want to make it easy for you.

HADDRILL (*heard outside*). I won't wait any longer, Ryland. This business is urgent. (*He comes in, stops on seeing Mistress Ryland, and bows to her rather curtly*) Your servant, madam.

RYLAND. To what am I indebted, Mr. Haddrill?

HADDRILL. In Mistress Ryland's presence — . . .

MARY RYLAND. I pray you not to consider my feelings, Mr. Haddrill.

HADDRILL. Egad, madam, it's for you to say. (*Turns to Ryland*) Here you've put me in a fix! They say you've no more reprieve, no chance of pardon. That you hang at sunrise to-morrow. You should have considered my interest. You should have given me more time.

MARY RYLAND. No reprieve . . . no pardon!

HADDRILL (*paying no attention to her*). Is the plate done, signed, ready to print? Don't you see I've only the day for the edition, and the advertisement and all, or I'll miss the big sale at the stalls along the Tyburn road?

RYLAND. Ah, that would be a pity. It's ready, you see. [*Holds up plate.*

HADDRILL. Ready! . . . But the ink won't be dry before they have the halter on you. And I'd planned to make it a great day in the trade, — a great day, sir, for the art of England. It's a wonderful opportunity for a pushing man — the last plate and the artist hanged to-day . . . I had made some very striking preparations, Ryland.

RYLAND. Hadn't you forgotten something, Mr. Haddrill?

HADDRILL. Not a thing. . . . But you give me so little time. I plan to sell the prints at my shop, in Saint Paul's Churchyard, at Temple Bar, at stalls along the way to Tyburn; and I have six most lugubrious-looking fellows — picked them out for their woebegone faces — all with crepe on their hats, sir, to sell them at Tyburn. Then I've got out broadsides, sir; and I've had a ballad written to sell at the hanging — all about you and your crime, and the prints for sale at my shop. Here it is, sir — like to look at it? (*He hands Ryland a ballad*) And now there's so little chance to get 'em out. I take it very hard, Ryland.

RYLAND. This is miserable stuff.

HADDRILL. I'd have you know, sir, the same author wrote one last month for the celebrated highwayman, Jack Sparrow. It took the town by storm.

RYLAND. My name will go down in illustrious company. . . .

HADDRILL. Perhaps a little revision, with our help?

RYLAND. No, let it serve as it is. I've a bargain to strike with you, Haddrill.

HADDRILL. I thought you'd struck a pretty stiff bargain already, Ryland. I'm to pay your wife five shillings to the pound more than I'd give any living engraver. I've even advanced you ten pounds. I call it sharp practice — . . .

RYLAND. These are my final conditions, Mr. Haddrill. You offer five shillings. That won't do. You must double it.

HADDRILL. Double it!

RYLAND. All proofs must be numbered in the presence of Mr. Fielding.

HADDRILL. You mean you don't trust me, Ryland?

RYLAND. Remember, I shan't be here. I trust Fielding. You've advanced ten pounds. Before the plate leaves my hands she must have fifty.

HADDRILL. Egad, you're driving it altogether too hard.

RYLAND. No, Haddrill, but I understand my position. I'm a public figure to-day. London will stand tiptoe all night to see me hanged in the morning. Another condition. I must see the contract you sign with my relict widow, Mary Ryland here. I must see you sign it in the presence of Fielding and Sir Joshua. They'll hold you to it.

HADDRILL. Look you, Mr. Ryland, I agree to the double royalty. But this goes too far, too dem'd far! I'm a man of my word, sir. I'll not be treated like a shuffling huckster, like a cheating fishmonger, like a dem'd criminal. I'm a communicant of the Church of England, sir! I won't be bound hand and foot.

RYLAND. I thought not.

HADDRILL. Deuce take you, sir! Blast your eyes, sir! What do you mean by that, sir?

RYLAND. Only this. You promise quickly enough, but I mean to see that you perform.

HADDRILL (*taking up his hat*). Very well, sir. Very well. I'm sorry you're so headstrong.

RYLAND. You know how many printsellers there are in London. . . . All waiting for this chance.

HADDRILL. You won't abate your conditions?

RYLAND. Not a penny.

HADDRILL. I'm sorry I can't take you. . . . And I had it all planned.

RYLAND. You had it planned! A clumsy, niggardly plan you had. I know what the town will think. I know how the town will buy. Six hang-dog hucksters with crepe on their hats! That's like you, Haddrill; no taste whatever. Twelve young gentlemen, dressed in the height of fashion — veritable macaronis, — that's what you should have, and them selling the prints like mad, and all for the sake of charity to a pretty widow. . . . Flowers! My cart to be loaded with violets when it stops at St. Sepulchre's. It's an occasion, sir, when the King's Engraver rides to Tyburn! At Holborn Bar you will have them fetch me a flagon of old port —

HADDRILL. But think of the expense, man, the expense!

RYLAND. Will you stick at a few pounds at a time like this? I wouldn't deal in sixpences on a great day for the art of England.

HADDRILL. You dealt in thousands, and see where it brought you. Think of me.

RYLAND. Why should I think of you! I'm the one to be hanged, Haddrill, not you. Broadsides, and a ballad! I

can make a speech from the scaffold that'll ring through the
town until this plate's worn thin as paper. Where will
your ballad and your broadsides be then?

HADDRILL. You'll make a speech?

RYLAND. Aye, that I will. But it depends on you, Haddrill, what sort of speech.

HADDRILL. You're a genius, Ryland.

RYLAND. The speech will cost you twenty pounds extra to
Mistress Ryland — mentioned in the contract.

HADDRILL (*writing*). Mentioned in the contract. Violets
at Saint Sepulchre's; a flagon of port at Holborn Bar:
twenty pounds extra for a speech on the scaffold; twelve
young gentlemen — no crepe on their hats. You're a
genius, Ryland — but you bargain like a Jew.

RYLAND. I must protect Mistress Ryland's interests.

MARY RYLAND. Oh, oh!

HADDRILL. You'll give me the plate immediately?

RYLAND. When you bring me the contract.

HADDRILL. I give you my oath I'll treat your wife handsomely. I had something else in mind. . . . A very
pretty idea, and quite genteel, too; quite up to your tone.
If Mistress Ryland would sit in my shop for a week after
the hanging and sell the prints herself — . . .

MARY RYLAND. Oh! the shame of it.

RYLAND. How much will you pay her?

MARY RYLAND. William, William, how can you? . . .

RYLAND. Hush, my dear. Mr. Haddrill will think you are
over-sensitive. This is a matter of business.

HADDRILL. It would have a great effect. You might mention it in your speech. . . .

MARY RYLAND. This is monstrous. . . . This is terrible.
I'll have nothing to do with it. I won't listen. I —

RYLAND. You see, Haddrill, there is still some delicacy of
feeling left in England.

HADDRILL. I thought it most genteel, most suitable. Very
— well, touching. But it's for Mistress Ryland to say.

RYLAND. She appears to object.

HADDRILL. At least she'll be at Tyburn . . . dressed in black, when the young gentlemen sell the prints. She'll be where the crowd can see her? It would help amazingly.

RYLAND. Surely, my dear, you can't refuse him that much. It's only what any dutiful wife would be expected to do, under the circumstances. . . . You'll have everyone's sympathy.

HADDRILL. Very fitting, very proper, I'm sure. Have you a black dress, Mistress Ryland?

MARY RYLAND. William, this is a nightmare. . . . Tell me I'm not awake, William.

RYLAND. There, there, child! Go with Mr. Haddrill. He'll take you to a draper's. Be sure you get a becoming frock — he has no taste.

MARY RYLAND. No, no!

HADDRILL. Come, madam. I'll bring you back when I fetch the contract.

RYLAND. Yes, child, go. I'm expecting other visitors. . . . Go on with your preparations, Mr. Haddrill.

[*Haddrill and Mistress Ryland start to go out; as they turn away, Ryland laughs aloud, and Haddrill faces about.*

RYLAND. But what if I shouldn't be hanged?

HADDRILL. Good Lord!

RYLAND. Do you think there's a reasonable doubt?

HADDRILL (*thinking it over and smiling grimly*). No, Ryland, I don't. . . . But I confess you gave me a turn.

RYLAND. Au revoir, Mr. Haddrill.

[*Haddrill again turns toward the door, finds it barred, the Gaoler with his hand on the lock. Haddrill steps toward the door, but the Gaoler makes no move to open it.*

HADDRILL. Den of thieves.

[*He pays the Gaoler and goes out. Ryland hums a line of song, and moves about the table, putting his proofs and materials in order. Fielding's voice is heard outside the door.*

FIELDING. Mr. Ryland, Mr. Ryland. I've seen her. . . .

RYLAND. She's coming?

FIELDING. Yes.

RYLAND. Alone?

FIELDING. No. . . . She's bringing Sir Joshua.

RYLAND. The devil!

GAOLER. I don't call this fair to me, Mr. Ryland.

RYLAND. My dear man, you've spoken yourself of the generous treatment you've had from me and my friends. Let this pass, don't be grasping. . . . Besides, there's a lady coming — and a gentleman. They'll pay handsomely. In fact, it would be worth your while to bring in another chair.

GAOLER. I've no wish to be hard with you, Mr. Ryland, but there are rules.

RYLAND. I know. You make them yourself.

FIELDING (*outside*). Am I to come in, Mr. Ryland?

RYLAND (*putting on his coat*). No. You've done your share. Wait and see that this . . . butler welcomes them properly. [*The Gaoler brings in the chair, and goes out. Ryland moves the chair so that Angelica and Sir Joshua must sit far apart, and hums the song again. The door opens.*

GAOLER. Sir Joshua Reynolds. Mistress Angelica Kauffman.

[*The Gaoler goes out, smiling broadly, as the visitors have been generous.*

SIR JOSHUA REYNOLDS. I trust you'll pardon my intrusion, Mr. Ryland. But ladies of fashion . . . gentleman's apartment . . . you understand. Even in so irreproachable a place as Newgate.

ANGELICA KAUFFMAN (*crossing Sir Joshua*). It grieves me deeply, Mr. Ryland — . . .

RYLAND (*to Angelica*). Couldn't you have trusted me enough to come alone?

SIR JOSHUA (*adjusting his ear trumpet*). Eh, what's that?

ANGELICA. Mr. Ryland spoke of his sense of the honour you do him in coming, Sir Joshua.

SIR JOSHUA. Ah, did he say that? Well, well, where's the plate? We came to see the plate you've engraved from Mistress Kauffman's picture.

[*Ryland holds up the plate, bows Sir Joshua to the chair, extreme right, and goes over to Angelica, handing her the plate.*

RYLAND (*to Angelica*). It was more, much more than the plate. . . .

SIR JOSHUA. Eh, what's that? A little more distinctly, sir.

RYLAND (*to Angelica*). Confound your dragon. (*To Sir Joshua*) I wish to consult Mistress Kauffman about the drawing of the arm.

SIR JOSHUA. Eh? Oh. . . . Ah, the drawing. I shouldn't examine it. Better let it pass.

ANGELICA. Oh, lud, sir, I scarcely know how to take you.

SIR JOSHUA. Always said, dear lady, your art . . . transcends mere drawing.

ANGELICA. Ah, the kind lies he tosses to the vanity of his friends. Dear Sir Joshua.

SIR JOSHUA. Well, sir, have you nothing to show? No trial proofs? Let me see the work, sir, and I'll toss you no kind lies. I've an engagement.

RYLAND. Give it to him, madam, and for God's sake grant me a moment's speech with you apart.

SIR JOSHUA. If you desire my criticism, Mr. Ryland, you must speak more distinctly.

ANGELICA (*hands a proof to Sir Joshua*). Do me the honor, sir. (*Referring to the plate*) This is all my intention in the cartoon, Mr. Ryland. You have a wonderful gift of patience.

RYLAND. Not patience, Mistress, but an exquisite pleasure. . . . to follow your fancy, your sentiment. . . .

SIR JOSHUA. It does you credit, sir — and the lady as well. Admirable. . . . Though I see nothing in it to stay the course of justice.

RYLAND (*with lofty resignation*). So you believe it to be justice, sir?

SIR JOSHUA. My belief has no weight, Ryland. . . . But now that this is done, and the legal pother over with, what are you going to do with it?

RYLAND. If it has Mistress Kauffman's approval, what do I care — what they do with it?

SIR JOSHUA. You take it too lightly. The plate must be worth money, and your obligations to your —

RYLAND (*glancing toward Angelica*). Spare me that, Sir Joshua, I beg you. What is money, to a man who lodges here for the last night?

SIR JOSHUA. Rubbish! Your affairs should be left in order. . . . That is the least you can do for —

RYLAND. Do you not understand, sir, that this pains me deeply. Money has been the shadow, the strain of discord, the flaw in the metal. . . . Money has been my ruin . . . and you ask me to spend my last hours haggling —

SIR JOSHUA. Calm yourself, sir. Haddrill, I suppose, brings it out. I'll look to this for you.

RYLAND. That is more than I have a right to ask of you, Sir Joshua.

SIR JOSHUA. Tush, tush. I'm not speaking of your rights, but in the interest of your —

RYLAND. Haddrill will attend to everything. He's bringing me a contract. He's a very generous fellow, Haddrill. I shall sign it, Sir Joshua, without reading.

SIR JOSHUA. Not without *my* reading. . . . Must take care of you, even if you choose to hang yourself.

ANGELICA (*protesting at the word*). Oh, Sir Joshua.

RYLAND. I thank you for that, Mistress.

GAOLER (*at the door*). Mr. Haddrill is back. Says he's forgotten something. Shall I admit him, Mr. Ryland?

SIR JOSHUA. Very fortunate. . . . Show him in. I'll arrange this matter now . . . take care of all the quibbles before they come up.

RYLAND. Sir Joshua, I beg you not to afflict me. I have only a few hours . . . and this is torture. If you are inflexible in your kindness toward me, go to Haddrill and do what you can in my behalf. It's more than I ought to ask . . . and I hope you will not find I have been too heedless.

SIR JOSHUA. It should be done in your presence, but you're so dem'd improvident.

RYLAND. I am not so improvident as to be ungrateful, sir. (*He bows Sir Joshua out and turns to face Angelica*) You at least have a sympathy for me, Mistress; you who understand so well the delicacy of my feelings in an hour like this.

ANGELICA. I hardly know. This is all so shocking, so terrible. I am . . .

RYLAND. Dear lady, I have been a brute to drag you here, you, who live in the glow and the music . . . to see a man in this hopeless gloomy cell, a poor devil who is about to die —

ANGELICA. Please don't . . . . I shall faint.

RYLAND. I beg you not to faint. I will speak of other days, and you shall listen — out of charity. It doesn't so much matter to me now; I've done with it all. But it was hard to face the end without seeing you again. Now I can go. . . . I'm not unready.

ANGELICA. What difference can seeing me make?

RYLAND. What difference? . . . I ride to Tyburn with a vision of you in my eyes, the sound of your voice in my ears, the touch of your pity on my defeated heart. . . . What difference? . . . If you had not come, I should have gone out of here with the gallows swinging before me, and my misspent years blowing in my face.

ANGELICA. This is very sentimental, Ryland. I hardly imagined that you . . . that I —

RYLAND. That it meant so much to me, when you last refused me?

ANGELICA. There, there, Ryland. You knew it was impossible.

RYLAND. I know. . . . You thought you loved —

ANGELICA. I beg you not to speak of him. He was unworthy, and he is gone . . . out of my life.

RYLAND (*suddenly hilarious*). And out of England! Egad, why shouldn't I speak of him. The town talked on nothing else : The distinguished Count de Horn shows an interest in the incomparable Mistress Kauffman ; he is accepted ; he isn't ; he is. . . . They are married ; they are not ; they are. . . . He is an impostor ; he is a prince in disguise ; he is the son of his father's cook ! and then . . . pouf ! He's gone.

ANGELICA. You can not imagine, sir, this is pleasant to me.

RYLAND. Nor was it pleasant to me. The Count de Horn . . . the son of his father's cook . . . and a bigamist ! Mistress Kauffman will prosecute ; she will not ; she will. . . . He was a criminal. He had imposed upon your faith, your heart, your honour. You could have let him hang. . . . But instead of that you gave him his freedom and five hundred pounds.

ANGELICA. Three hundred.

RYLAND. Generous soul !

ANGELICA. I will not remain here, sir, to be taunted with my past misfortunes.

RYLAND. Nothing was further from my intention.

ANGELICA. Then why do you recall this ?

RYLAND. I'm sure I don't know. . . . It's my whim to marvel, just for the moment, at the charity which gives a scoundrel, who had wronged you, his freedom and three hundred pounds, while you see a man who has devoted his life to the spreading of your fame, a man who has loved you, and who still loves you, go to the gallows without the compliment of a tear.

ANGELICA. This is most unjust. You have given me neither time nor proper occasion for weeping, Ryland.

RYLAND (*coming close to her*). And it does not occur to you, now that you see me again ? . . .

ANGELICA (*she backs toward the door*). Nothing occurs to me ; I'm all upset by your impudence.

RYLAND. Unkind, unkind ! When this is my last living day, and you could, if you chose . . .

ANGELICA. If you come a step nearer, I shall call Sir Joshua.

RYLAND (*stops and looks at her, his eyes filled with admiration*). The winter in Italy has agreed with you. . . . I've never seen you look so . . . dangerous, Angelica.

ANGELICA. You mustn't call me that. . . . My name —

RYLAND. That was what I called you when we danced together at Tunbridge, the night you laughed with me over Fuseli's proposal; Angelica I called you when we sat together on Richmond Hi'l, and watched the moon trace out the Thames with silver fingers; Angelica I called you that divine day in Windsor Forest, — the day I first told you I loved you; — Angelica —

ANGELICA. You play upon the word, Ryland, as though it were a refrain.

RYLAND. The refrain of a living love, dearest . . . in the song of a dead life.

ANGELICA. Is it a dead life, William? . . .

RYLAND. It dies at sunrise . . . and all for a few pounds unwisely borrowed, a few creditors inhumanly clamorous, and the lies of a paper-maker who hated me.

ANGELICA. What is it they accuse you of?

RYLAND. Forgery.

ANGELICA. And you are not guilty.

RYLAND. Guilty? . . . I have borrowed unwisely, I tell you. I was hungry for the sight of . . . Italy. Is that guilt? There was a matter of a note — an India company note. Thirty men had signed it, and not one of them at the trial could say the hand was not his own. (*She makes a gesture of inquiry*) This paper-maker . . . he swore he had made the paper on which it was written a year after the date of the note. Guilty? . . . That would have been criminally stupid, and of stupidity no one has ever accused me. . . . For all that, the court passed sentence.

ANGELICA. And is there no appeal?

RYLAND. What need of appeal, if it no longer touches you?

ANGELICA. But if it does touch me?

RYLAND. We have tried what we could. . . . I have been three times reprieved, to finish this plate. It is done. His Majesty is inexorable. But with you in England, with the lure of you —

ANGELICA. Don't tell me you would not make the effort except as I inspired it.

RYLAND. Why?

ANGELICA. I could not believe you.

RYLAND. The truth, then: you can reach the Queen. Through her, King George. Till you came, I had no voice to reach him. You can have what you ask. Let it be . . . my life.

ANGELICA. You want me to go to the Queen?

RYLAND. Yes!

ANGELICA. This would compromise me more deeply than you can imagine.

RYLAND (*sardonically*). You have not imagined how high it will hang me . . . if you refuse.

ANGELICA. And if I fail?

RYLAND. I shall not murmur. . . . But I do not believe you can fail.

ANGELICA. Willliam. William. . . . No, don't come near me. I will go. This must be secret —

RYLAND. You can trust me.

ANGELICA. And there must be no more talk of love . . . no notes, messages, flowers, tokens. You are to be merely a man — an artist — in whose work I take a great interest . . . an innocent man whom I endeavor to deliver from an unjust death —

RYLAND. Stop. I agree to the secrecy, but I do not pledge myself not to love you.

ANGELICA. You must.

RYLAND. I will not take life on these terms. Secrecy — discretion — yes. . . . You can not require that I forget you.

ANGELICA. It cuts me . . . you have been faithful to a memory so long. Perhaps, when this is over, I may permit you to remember again.

RYLAND (*seizing her hand and kissing it*). Better to blot out
my life than the memories of Richmond Hill!

ANGELICA. You must keep them deep hidden, William. . . .
These are perilous things, these memories.

RYLAND. They have been my stay, my comfort, since these
ungentle days came upon me. A faith like mine, Angelica,
a love that endures unshaken . . . it must be something,
even to you. Tell me you go to the Queen because you
too remember —

ANGELICA. It is enough that I go.

RYLAND. No. . . . That you go out of love for me.

ANGELICA. You must content yourself, William. . . . For
you I go to the Queen.

[*She starts toward the bars, when the Gaoler opens them quietly
and Mary Ryland comes in. Mistress Ryland pauses,
glances at Angelica, and goes over to Ryland, who waves her
away and sinks back against the table. Mary comes down,
Left, hesitates a moment, then comes down above Angelica,
Left Center, and falls on her knees, clasping Angelica's
hand.*

MARY RYLAND. Oh madam, madam!

ANGELICA. What's this? . . . Let go my hand, girl.

RYLAND. What brings you back? . . .

MARY RYLAND. Mr. Haddrill says . . . Oh, Madam, you
could do something, you could help us —

ANGELICA. Help us? Who are you, child?

MARY RYLAND. I'm the unhappiest woman . . . I've been a
jealous fool . . . But I know he's too proud, too hon-
ourable. He would die rather than be too heavily beholden
to you. But I have no pride: I can beg you to plead for
him; I can beseech you on my knees. If you are not moved
to do your utmost for him, at least you must look with
pity on me. . . .

ANGELICA. Is this lady your wife, Mr. Ryland?

RYLAND. Yes.

ANGELICA (*with menace*). I regret that you omitted to
mention her.

[*Mary Ryland moves away from her, and Ryland sinks back in despair.*

SIR JOSHUA (*heard outside*). Well, I must say, Haddrill, he's driven a sharp bargain with you.

HADDRILL. Sharp bargain! Dem'd close to robbery, I call it.

[*Enter Sir Joshua and Haddrill, Fielding following them.*

ANGELICA (*to Sir Joshua*). So *you've* not found him so simple?

SIR JOSHUA. Simple! He has bound this poor fellow to support *his* wife for the rest of her days.

HADDRILL. I'm a man of my word, Ryland. If you're satisfied, I'll trouble you for the plate. (*Ryland hands over the plate, bowing*) I shall live up to my part of the contract.

RYLAND. You may rest assured as to my part of it.

SIR JOSHUA. I'm sorry, Ryland. I tell you frankly, I wished to think well of you. But this contract . . . a man capable of such a document, sir — I spare you my opinion, in your wife's presence.

ANGELICA (*joining Haddrill and Sir Joshua*). Your presumption, sir; your lack of candour — . . .

RYLAND. My best friends . . . it grieves me exceedingly that the confidence of one's best friends should be turned aside by a man's natural efforts to save his neck and to provide for his family.

MARY RYLAND (*to Angelica*). Madam, is there nothing you can do?

ANGELICA. Nothing I care to do.

FIELDING. Oh, Mr. Ryland, if you would only —

RYLAND. Let me alone. You won't grieve long. You'll get your reward.

MARY RYLAND. Oh, William, William!

RYLAND. Tush, child, go with Fielding. He'll take care of you. You've done enough . . . for me.

ANGELICA. For shame, Ryland! (*She gathers Mary Ryland under her arm*) When you need to see her, Mr. Haddrill, come to me.

HADDRILL (*from the door, where he and Sir Joshua are about to go out*). Your servant, madam.

SIR JOSHUA. Come, Mistress Angelica. Remember, Ryland, I wished to think well of you.

RYLAND. I have not long to remember. Sir, your very humble servant.

[*Exeunt Sir Joshua, Haddrill, and Fielding. Angelica stops at the door and turns back, Mary Ryland with her.*

ANGELICA. She goes under my protection, Ryland.

[*Mistress Ryland leaves Angelica for a moment, and goes slowly over to Ryland, who kisses her forehead and leads her back to Angelica.*

RYLAND. I am filled with gratitude, Mistress. Mary, you will find it most pleasant I am sure. . . . A gay household, Mary — you'll like that.

ANGELICA. Not so gay as it has been, Ryland. You see, I have my husband to consider.

[*Ryland draws himself up, swiftly.*

RYLAND. Your husband? . . . I'm sorry you omitted to mention him. My compliments, madam. (*Exeunt Angelica and Mistress Ryland. Ryland speaks to the Gaoler, who is about to close the door*) It won't be necessary to admit any more visitors.

GAOLER. No, sir. But there's the chaplain to see you, sir.

RYLAND. What's that?

GAOLER. The chaplain of the prison, Mr. Ryland, to see you.

RYLAND (*rising and fumbling with his cravat*). The chaplain. . . . Oh, God, yes! . . . Yes, yes, yes! I suppose I shall have to see the chaplain.

CURTAIN

THE CLOD

LEWIS BEACH

THE INAUGURATION of the Harvard 47 Workshop by George Pierce Baker, which took its name from the course English 47, marked an epoch in the coming-of-age of American drama. It was there that Lewis Beach received his early training in theatre art, like many other aspirants who were guided to success through their experiments in this congenial environment. To name only a few of the writers of one-act plays who studied there, the names of Eugene O'Neill, Josephine Preston Peabody, Elizabeth McFadden, Doris Halman come quickly to mind; among the directors and scene designers were Winthrop Ames, Robert Edmond Jones, Kenneth Macgowan, Arthur Hopkins, and Lee Simonson, all of whom have contributed greatly to the advance of the American theatre.

It was at Harvard that "The Clod" was first produced. Mr. Beach's other published one-act plays are: "A Guest for Dinner", "Love among the Lions", and "Brothers." His published longer plays are: "A Square Peg", "Ann Vroome", "The Goose Hangs High", and "Merry Andrew."

THE CLOD

By LEWIS BEACH

"The Clod" was originally produced by the Harvard Dramatic Club on March 31, 1914.

Original Cast

THADDEUS TRASK . . . . N. B. Clark
MARY TRASK . . . . Christine Hayes
A NORTHERN SOLDIER . . . . . . D. L. Kennedy
A SOUTHERN SERGEANT . . . . . . J. W. D. Seymour
DICK . . . . R. B. Southgate

THE CLOD

SCENE. *The kitchen of a farmhouse on the borderline between the Northern and Southern states. It is ten o'clock in the
evening, September, 1863.*

*The back wall is broken at stage Left by the projection at right
angles of a partially enclosed staircase; the four steps leading
to the landing cut into the room. Underneath the enclosed part
of the stairway, a cubby-hole; in front of it a small table which
partially hides the door. To the Left of the table a kitchen
chair. A door, leading to the yard, is the centre of the unbroken
wall, Back. To the Right of the door, a cupboard; to the Left,
a small cooking-stove. Two windows in the Right wall. Between them a bench on which a pail and a tin dipper stand.
Above the bench a towel hanging on a nail, and above the towel
a double-barrelled shotgun suspended on two pegs. Well
downstage Left, a closed door leading to a second room. In the
Centre of the kitchen a large table; straight-backed chairs to
the Right and Left of it. A lighted candle on this table.
("Right" and "Left" are the actors' "Right" and "Left.")*

*The moon shines into the room through the windows, but at
no time is the kitchen brightly lighted. The characters appear
as silhouettes except when they stand near the candle or the lantern, and then the lights throw huge shadows on the roughly
plastered walls. When the door, Back, is opened one sees a bit
of the farmyard, desolate even in the moonlight.*

[*As the curtain rises, Thaddeus Trask, a man of sixty odd
years, short and thick-set, slow in speech and action, yet in perfect health, sits at the Left of the Centre table. He is pressing
tobacco into his corncob pipe. He lights it with the candle.
After a moment, Mary Trask, a tired, emaciated woman,
whose years equal her husband's, enters from the yard carrying a heavy pail of water and a lighted lantern. She puts*

*the pail on the bench and hangs the lantern above it; then
crosses to the stove.*

MARY. Ain't got wood 'nough fer breakfast, Thad.

THADDEUS. I'm too tired t' go out now. Wait 'til mornin'.
(*Pause. Mary lays the fire in the stove*) Did I tell yuh
that old man Reed saw three Southern troopers pass his
house this mornin'?

MARY (*takes coffee-pot from stove, crosses to bench, fills pot with
water*). I wish them soldiers would git out o' the neighborhood. Whenever I see 'em passin', I have t' steady
myself 'gainst somethin' or I'd fall. I couldn't hardly
breathe yesterday when them Southerners came after
fodder. I'd died if they'd spoke t' me.

THADDEUS. Yuh needn't be afraid o' Northern soldiers.

MARY (*carries coffee-pot to stove*). I hate 'em all — Union or
Southern. I can't make head or tail t' what all this fight-
in's 'bout. An' I don't care who wins, so long as they git
through, an' them soldiers stop stealin' our corn an'
potatoes.

THADDEUS. Yuh can't hardly blame 'em if they're hungry,
ken yuh?

MARY. It ain't right that they should steal from us poor
folk. (*Lifts a huge gunny sack of potatoes from the table,
and begins setting the table for breakfast, getting knives, forks,
spoons, plates, cups and saucers — two of each — from the
cupboard*) We have hard 'nough times t' make things
meet now. I ain't set down onct to-day 'cept fer meals.
An' when I think o' the work I got t' do t'morrow, I ought
t' been in bed hours ago.

THADDEUS. I'd help if I could, but it ain't my fault if
the Lord seed fit t' lay me up so I'm always ailin' . . .
(*Rises lazily*) . . . Yuh better try an' take things easy
t'morrow.

MARY. It's well enough t' say, but them apples is got t' be
picked an' the rest o' the potatoes sorted. If I could sleep
at night it'd be all right, but with them soldiers 'bout, I
can't.

THADDEUS (*crosses Right; fondly handles his gun*). Golly, wish I'd see a flock o' birds.

MARY (*nervously*). I'd rather go without than hear yuh fire. I wish yuh didn't keep it loaded.

THADDEUS. Yuh know I ain't got time t' stop an' load when I see the birds. They don't wait fer yuh. (*Hangs gun on wall, drops into his chair; dejectedly*) Them pigs has got t' be butchered.

MARY. Wait 'til I git a chance t' go t' sister's. I can't stand it t' hear 'em squeal.

THADDEUS (*pulling off his boots — grunting meanwhile*). Best go soon then, 'cause they's fat as they'll ever be, an' there ain't no use in wastin' feed on 'em. (*Pause; rises*) Ain't yuh 'most ready fer bed?

MARY. Go on up. (*Thaddeus takes the candle in one hand, his boots in the other, and climbs the stairs. Mary speaks when he reaches the landing*) An' Thad, try not t' snore t'night.

THADDEUS. Poke me if I do. (*Disappears*)

[*Mary fills the kettle with water and puts it on the stove; closes the door, Back; takes the lantern from the wall and tries twice before she succeeds in blowing it out. Puts the lantern on the table before the cubby-hole. Slowly drags herself up the stairs, pausing a moment on the top step for breath before she disappears. There is a silence. Then the door, Back, is opened a trifle and a man's hand is seen. Cautiously the door is opened wide and a young Northern Private stands silhouetted on the threshold. He wears a dirty uniform, and a bloody bandage is tied about his head. He is wounded, sick, and exhausted. He stands at the door a moment, listening intently; then hastily moves to the Centre table looking for food. He bumps against a chair and mutters an oath. Finding nothing on the table, he hurries to the cupboard. Suddenly the galloping of horses is heard in the distance. The Northerner starts, then rushes to the window nearer the audience. For a moment the sound ceases, then it begins again, growing gradually louder and louder. The Northerner hurries into the room at the Left. Horses and voices are heard in the yard, and almost immediately heavy, thundering knocks sound on the door, Back. The men at the door grow impatient and push the door open. A large, powerfully built Southern Sergeant, and a smaller, younger Trooper of the same army enter. Thaddeus appears on the stairs, carrying a candle.*

SERGEANT (*to Thaddeus; not unkindly*). Sorry, my friend, but you were so darn slow 'bout openin' the door that we had to walk in. Has there been a Northern soldier round here to-day?

THADDEUS (*timidly*). I ain't seed one.
[*Comes down the stairs.*

SERGEANT. Have you been here all day?

THADDEUS. I ain't stirred from the place.

SERGEANT. Call the rest of your family down.

THADDEUS. My wife's all there is. (*Goes to foot of stairs, and calls loudly and excitedly*) Mary! Mary! Come down. Right off!

SERGEANT. You better not lie to me or it'll go tough with you.

THADDEUS. I swear I ain't seed no one. (*Mary comes downstairs slowly. She is all atremble*) Say, Mary, you was here —

SERGEANT. Keep still, man. I'll do the talkin'. (*To Mary*) You were here at the house all day? (*Mary is very frightened and embarrassed, but after a moment manages to nod her head slowly*) You didn't take a trip down to the store? (*Mary shakes her head slowly*) Haven't you got a tongue?

MARY (*with difficulty*). Y-e-s.

SERGEANT. Then use it. The Northern soldier who came here a while ago was pretty badly wounded, wasn't he?

MARY. I — I — no one's been here.

SERGEANT. Come, come, woman, don't lie. (*Mary shows a slight sign of anger*) He had a bad cut in his forehead, and you felt sorry for him, and gave him a bite to eat.

MARY (*haltingly*). No one's been near the house t'day.

SERGEANT (*trying a different tone*). We're not going to hurt him, woman. He's a friend of ours. We want to find him, and put him in a hospital, don't we, Dick?
[*Turning to his companion.*
DICK. He's sick and needs to go to bed for a while.
MARY. He ain't here.
SERGEANT. What do you want to lie for?
MARY (*quickly*). I ain't lyin'. I ain't seed no soldier. [*She stands rooted to the spot where she stopped when she came downstairs. Her eyes are still fixed on the Sergeant.*
SERGEANT. I reckon you know what'll happen to you if you are hidin' the spy.
THADDEUS. There ain't no one here. We both been here all day, an' there couldn't no one come without our knowin' it. What would they want round here anyway?
SERGEANT. We'll search the place, Dick.
MARY (*quickly*). Yuh ain't got no —
SERGEANT (*sharply*). What's that, woman?
MARY. There ain't no one here, an' yer keepin' us from our sleep.
SERGEANT. Your sleep? This is an affair of life and death. Get us a lantern. (*Thaddeus moves to the small table and lights the lantern with the candle which he holds in his hand. He gives the lantern to the Sergeant. The Sergeant notices the door to the cubby-hole*) Ha! Tryin' to hide the door, are you, by puttin' a table in front of it? You can't fool me. (*To Thaddeus*) Pull the table away and let's see what's behind the door.
THADDEUS. It's a cubby-hole an' ain't been opened in years.
SERGEANT (*sternly and emphatically*). I said to open the door. (*Thaddeus sets the candle on the larger table, moves the smaller table to the Right, and opens the door to the cubby-hole. Mary is angry. The Sergeant takes a long-barrelled revolver from his belt and peers into the cubby-hole. Returning his revolver to his belt*) We're goin' to tear

this place to pieces 'til we find him. You might just as
well hand him over now.

MARY.   There ain't no one here.

SERGEANT.   All right. Now we'll see. Dick, you stand
guard at the door. (*Dick goes to the door, Back, and stands
gazing out into the night, — his back to the audience. To
Thaddeus*) Come along, man. I'll have to look at the
upstairs. (*To Mary*) You sit down in that chair.
(*Points to chair at Right of Centre table, and feels for a sufficiently strong threat*) Don't you stir or I'll — I'll set fire
to your house. (*To Thaddeus*) Go on ahead.

[*Thaddeus and the Sergeant go upstairs. Mary sinks life-
lessly into the chair. She is the picture of fear. She sits
facing Left. Suddenly she leans forward. She opens her
eyes wide, and draws her breath sharply. She opens her
mouth as though she would scream, but makes no sound. The
Northerner has opened the door. He enters slowly and cautiously, his gun pointed at Mary. Dick cannot see him
because of the jog in the wall. Mary only stares in bewilderment at the Northerner, as he, with eyes fixed appealingly on
her, opens the door to the cubby-hole and crawls inside.*

DICK.   Woman!

MARY (*almost with a cry, thinking that Dick has seen the Northerner*). Yes.

DICK.   Have you got an apple handy? I'm starved.

[*Mary rises and moves to the cupboard. The Sergeant and
Thaddeus come downstairs. The Sergeant, seeing that Mary
is not where he left her, looks about rapidly and discovers her
at the cupboard.*

SERGEANT.   Here, what did I tell you I'd do if you moved
from that chair?

MARY (*terrified*). Oh, I didn't — I only — he wanted —

DICK.   It's all right, Sergeant. I asked her to get me an
apple.

SERGEANT.   Take this lantern and search the barn. (*Dick
takes the lantern from the Sergeant and goes out, Back. To
Thaddeus*) Come in here with me. (*The Sergeant picks*

up the candle. He and Thaddeus move toward the door, Left. As though in a stupor, Mary starts to follow) Sit down! (*Mary drops into the chair at the Right of the table. The Sergeant and Thaddeus go into the room, Left. They can be heard moving furniture about. Mary sees a pin on the floor. She stoops, picks it up, and fastens it in her belt. The Sergeant and Thaddeus return)* If I find him now after all the trouble you've given me, you know what'll happen. There's likely to be two dead men and a woman, instead of only the Yankee.

DICK (*bounding into the room*). Sergeant!

SERGEANT. What is it? (*Dick hurries to the Sergeant and says something to him in a low voice. The Sergeant smiles)* Now, my good people, how did that horse get here?

THADDEUS. What horse?

DICK. There's a horse in the barn with a saddle on his back. I swear he's been ridden lately.

THADDEUS (*amazed*). There is?

SERGEANT. You know it. (*To Mary*) Come, woman, who drove that horse here?

MARY (*silent for a moment, her eyes on the floor*). I don't know. I didn't hear nothin'.

THADDEUS (*moving toward the door*). Let me go an' see.

SERGEANT (*pushing Thaddeus back*). No, you don't. You two have done enough to justify the harshest measures. Show us the man's hiding place.

THADDEUS. If there's anybody here, he's come in the night without our knowin' it. I tell yuh I didn't see anybody, an' she didn't, an' —

SERGEANT (*has been watching Mary*). Where is he?

[*His tone makes Thaddeus jump. There is a pause, during which Mary seems trying to compose herself. Then slowly she lifts her eyes and looks at the Sergeant.*

MARY. There ain't nobody in the house 'cept us two.

SERGEANT (*to Dick*). Did you search all the out-buildings?

DICK. Yes. There's not a trace of him except the horse.

SERGEANT (*wiping the perspiration from his face; speaks with apparent deliberation at first, but becomes very emphatic).* He didn't have much of a start of us, and I think he was wounded. A farmer down the road said he heard hoof-beats. The man the other side of you heard nothin', *and the horse is in your barn. (Slowly draws his revolver and points it at Thaddeus)* There are ways of making people confess.

THADDEUS *(covering his face with his hands).* For God's sake, don't. I know that horse looks bad, but, as I live, I ain't heard a sound, or seen anybody. I'd give the man up in a minute if he was here.

SERGEANT *(lowering his gun).* Yes, I guess you would. You wouldn't want me to hand you and your wife over to our army to be shot down like dogs. *(Mary shivers. Sergeant swings round sharply and points the gun at Mary)* Your wife knows where he's hid.

MARY *(breaking out in irritating, rasping voice).* I'm sure I wish I did. I'd tell yuh quick an' git yuh out o' here. 'T ain't no fun fer me t' have yuh prowlin' all over my house, trackin' it up with yer dirty boots. Yuh ain't got no right t' torment me like this. Lord knows how I'll git my day's work done, if I can't have my sleep out.

SERGEANT *(has been gazing at her in astonishment; lowers his gun).* Good God! Nothing but her own petty exist-ence. *(In different voice to Mary)* I'll have to ask you to get us some breakfast. We're famished. *(With relief but showing some anger, Mary turns to the stove. She lights the fire and puts more coffee in the pot)* Come, Dick, we better give our horses some water. They're all tired out. *(In lower voice)* The man isn't here. If he were he couldn't get away while we're in the yard. *(To Thaddeus)* Get us a pail to give the horses some water in. *[Sees the pails on the bench. Picks one of them up and moves toward the door.*

MARY. That ain't the horses' pail.

SERGEANT *(to Thaddeus).* Come along. You can help.

MARY (*louder*). That's the drinkin' water pail.

SERGEANT. That's all right.

[*The Sergeant, Thaddeus, and Dick — carrying the lantern — go out back. Mary needs more wood for the fire, so she follows in a moment. When she has disappeared, the Northerner drags himself from the cubby-hole. Mary returns with an armful of wood.*

MARY (*sees the Northerner. Shows no sympathy for him in this speech nor during the entire scene*). Yuh git back! Them soldiers 'll see yuh.

NORTHERNER. Some water. Quick. (*Falls into chair at Left of table*) It was so hot in there.

MARY (*gives him water in the dipper*). Don't yuh faint here! If them soldiers git yuh, they 'll kill me an' Thad. Hustle an' git back in that cubby-hole. (*Turns quickly to the stove*)

[*The Northerner drinks the water, puts the dipper on the table. Then, summoning all his strength, rises and crosses to Mary. He touches her on the sleeve. Mary is so startled that she jumps and utters a faint cry.*

NORTHERNER. Be still or they 'll hear you. How are you going to get me out of here?

MARY. Yuh git out! Why did yuh come here, a-bringin' me all this extra work, an' maybe death?

NORTHERNER. I couldn't go any farther. My horse and I were ready to drop. Won't you help me?

MARY. No, I won't. I don't know who yuh are or nothin' 'bout yuh, 'cept that them men want t' ketch yuh. (*In a changed tone of curiosity*) Did yuh steal somethin' from 'em?

NORTHERNER. Don't you understand? Those men belong to the Confederacy, and I 'm a Northerner. They 've been chasing me all day. (*Pulling a bit of crumpled paper from his breast*) They want this paper. If they get it before to-morrow morning it will mean the greatest disaster that 's ever come to the Union army.

MARY (*with frank curiosity*). Was it yuh rode by yesterday?

NORTHERNER. Don't you see what you can do? Get me out of here and away from those men, and you'll have done more than any soldier could do for the country, — for *your* country.

MARY. I ain't got no country. Me an' Thad's only got this farm. Thad's ailin', an' I do most the work, an' —

NORTHERNER. The lives of thirty thousand men hang by a thread. I must save them. And you must help me!

MARY. I don't know nothin' 'bout yuh, an' I don't know what yer talkin' 'bout.

NORTHERNER. Only help me get away.

MARY (*angrily*). No one ever helped me or Thad. I lift no finger in this business. Why yuh come here in the first place is beyond me — sneakin' in our house, spoilin' our well-earned sleep. If them soldiers ketch yuh, they'll kill me an' Thad. Maybe you didn't know that.

NORTHERNER. What's your life and your husband's compared to thirty thousand? I haven't any money or I'd give it to you.

MARY. I don't want yer money.

NORTHERNER. What do you want?

MARY. I want yuh t' git out. I don't care what happens t' yuh. Only git out o' here.

NORTHERNER. I can't with the Southerners in the yard. They'd shoot me like a dog. Besides, I've got to have my horse.

MARY (*with naïve curiosity*). What kind o' lookin' horse is it?

NORTHERNER (*dropping into the chair at Left of Centre table in disgust and despair*). Oh, God! If I'd only turned in at the other farm. I might have found people with red blood.

[*Pulls out his gun and hopelessly opens the empty chamber.*

MARY (*alarmed*). What yuh goin' t' do with that gun?

NORTHERNER. Don't be afraid.

MARY. I'd call 'em if I wasn't —

NORTHERNER (*leaping to the wall, Left, and bracing himself against it*). Go call them in. Save your poor skin and your husband's if you can. Call them in. You can't save yourself. (*Laughs hysterically*) You can't save your miserable skin. 'Cause if they get me, and don't shoot you, *I will*.

MARY (*leaning against the Left side of the table for support; in agony*). Oh!

NORTHERNER. You see? You've got to help me whether you want to or not.

MARY (*feeling absolutely caught*). I ain't done nothin'. I don't see why yuh an' them others come here a-threatenin' t' shoot me. I don't want nothin'. I don't want t' do nothin'. I jest want yuh all t' git out o' here an' leave me an' Thad t' go t' sleep. Oh, I don't know what t' do. Yuh got me in a corner where I can't move.

[*Passes her hand back along the table. Touches the dipper accidentally, and it falls to the floor. Screams at the sound.*

NORTHERNER (*leaping toward her*). Now you've done it. They'll be here in a minute. You can't give me up. They'll shoot me if you do. THEY'LL *shoot*. (*Hurries up the stairs and disappears*)

[*Mary stands beside the table, trembling terribly. The Sergeant, Dick, and Thaddeus come running in.*

SERGEANT. What did you yell for? (*Mary does not answer. He seizes her by the arm*) Answer!

MARY. I knocked the dipper off the table. It scared me.

SERGEANT (*dropping wearily into chair at Left of Centre table*). Well, don't drop our breakfast. Put it on the table. We're ready.

MARY (*stands looking at the Sergeant*). It ain't finished.

SERGEANT (*worn out by his day's work and Mary's stupidity, from now on absolutely brutish*). You've had time to cook a dozen meals. What did you do all the time we were in the yard?

MARY. I didn't do nothin'.

SERGEANT. You good-for-nothin' — Get a move on and give us something fit to eat. Don't try to get rid of any left-overs on us. If you do, you'll suffer for it. (*Mary stands looking at him*) Don't you know anything, you brainless farm-drudge? *Hurry*, I said.

[*Mary picks up the dipper and turns to the stove. Thaddeus sits in the chair at Left of smaller table.*

DICK. What a night! My stomach's as hollow as these people's heads.

[*Takes towel which hangs above the bench, and wipes the barrel of his gun with it.*

MARY. That's one of my best towels.

DICK. Can't help it.

SERGEANT. 'Tend to the breakfast. That's enough for you to do at one time. (*Dick puts his gun on the smaller table, and sits at the Right of the larger. Then the Sergeant speaks, quietly*) I don't see how he gave us the slip.

DICK. He knew we were after him, drove his horse in here, and went on afoot. Clever scheme, I must admit.

THADDEUS (*endeavoring to get them into conversation*). Have yuh rid far t'night, Misters?

DICK (*shortly*). Far enough.

THADDEUS. Twenty miles or so?

DICK. Perhaps.

THADDEUS. How long yuh been chasin' the critter?

SERGEANT. Oh, shut up! Don't you see we don't want to talk to you? Take hold and hurry, woman. My patience's at an end.

[*Mary puts a loaf of bread, some fried eggs, and a coffee-pot on the table.*

MARY. There! I hope yer satisfied.

[*Dick and the Sergeant pull up their chairs and begin to eat.*

SERGEANT. Is this all we get? Come, it won't do you any good to be stingy.

MARY. It's all I got.

SERGEANT. It isn't a mouthful for a chickadee! Give us some butter.

MARY. There ain't none.

SERGEANT. No butter on a farm? God, the way you lie.

MARY. I —

SERGEANT. Shut up!

DICK. Have you got any cider?

SERGEANT. Don't ask. She and the man probably drank themselves stupid on it. (*Throws fork on floor*) I never struck such a place in my life. Get me another fork. How do you expect me to eat with that bent thing? (*Mary stoops with difficulty and picks up the fork. Gets another from the cupboard and gives it to the Sergeant*) Now give me some salt. Don't you know that folks eat it on eggs? (*Mary crosses to the cupboard; mistakes the pepper for the salt and puts it on the table. Sergeant sprinkles pepper on his food*) I said salt, woman. (*Spelling*) S-a-l-t. Salt! Salt! (*Mary gets the salt and gives it to the Sergeant. Almost ready to drop, she drags herself to the window nearer the back and leans against it, watching the Southerners like a hunted animal. Thaddeus is nodding in the corner. The Sergeant and Dick go on devouring the food. The former pours the coffee, puts his cup to his lips, takes one swallow; then, jumping to his feet and upsetting his chair as he does so, he hurls his cup to the floor. Bellowing and pointing to the fluid trickling on the floor*) Have you tried to poison us, you God damn hag?

[*Mary screams and the faces of the men turn white. It is the cry of an animal goaded beyond endurance.*

MARY (*screeching*). Break my cup? Call my coffee poison? Call me a hag, will yuh? I'll learn yuh! I'm a woman, but yer drivin' me crazy. (*She has snatched the gun from the wall and pointed it at the Sergeant. Fires*)

[*The Sergeant falls to the floor. Mary keeps on screeching. Dick rushes for his gun.*

THADDEUS. Mary! Mary!

MARY (*aiming at Dick and firing*). I ain't a hag. I'm a woman, but yer killin' me.

[*Dick falls just as he reaches his gun. Thaddeus is in the corner with his hands over his ears. The Northerner stands on the stairs. Mary continues to pull the trigger of the empty gun. The Northerner is motionless for a moment; then he goes to Thaddeus and shakes him.*

NORTHERNER. Go get my horse. Quick! (*Thaddeus hurries out. The Northerner turns to Mary and speaks with great fervor. She gazes at him but does not understand a word he says*) I'm ashamed of what I said. The whole country will hear of this, and you.

[*He takes her hand and presses it to his lips; then turns and hurries out of the house.*

Mary still holds the gun in her hand. She pushes a strand of grey hair back from her face, and begins to pick up the fragments of the broken cup.

MARY (*in dead, flat tone*). I'll have t' drink out the tin cup now.

[*The hoof-beats of the Northerner's horse are heard.*

CURTAIN

WILL O' THE WISP

DORIS F. HALMAN

WHILE a student at Radcliffe College, Doris Halman was a member of the 47 Workshop group. Her impressionistic drama, "Will O' the Wisp", first produced there, has been popular for twenty years, and has been published in several anthologies since its first appearance in this collection.

Miss Halman was born in Ellsworth, Maine, October 28, 1895. She was educated in Boston, and graduated from Radcliffe in 1916. For a while she was play reader for the American Play Company of New York City, and now is reader for RKO Pictures.

She has published "The Land Where Lost Things Go", which received a prize from the Drama League, and "It Behooves Us", a play written for the World War; *Set the Stage for Eight*, a collection of one-act plays; "The Voice of the Snake"; "Lenna Looks Down"; "How Not to Write a Play"; and one novel, *Honk! A Motor Romance*.

WILL O' THE WISP

By DORIS F. HALMAN

"Will O' the Wisp" was originally produced under the direction of Professor George P. Baker in his 47 Workshop at Cambridge, Massachusetts, on December 8, 1916.

Original Cast

THE WHITE-FACED GIRL . . .	Miss Vianna Knowlton
THE COUNTRYWOMAN	Miss Eleanor Hinkley
THE POET'S WIFE	Miss Frederica Gilbert
THE SERVING-MAID	Miss Mary Ellis

WILL O' THE WISP

SCENE. *Interior of a farmhouse at the end of things. A plain, gray room, with black furniture and a smoke-blackened fireplace. Door to outside, left back. Door to stairs, right. Fireplace in upper right-hand corner; armchair in lower right-hand corner. Below the door, left, a square table with a chair at either side. The whole center of the wall, back, is taken up by a huge window, through which one can glimpse the black spaces of a moor, rising in the distance to a sharp cliff-head silhouetted against the intense blue of an early evening sky. With the passage of the action, this blue fades into a starless night. There are two candles burning in the room, one on the table, the other on a shelf above the armchair.*

When the curtain rises, the countrywoman, an old and withered dame, is lighting the candle on the table. Crouching by the fireplace at the other side of the room, is the ragged figure of a girl with a white face and big wistful eyes, a strange little figure wearing a tight-fitting gray cap which covers all her hair, a silent figure, never speaking. Until she lifts her head, she is little more than a dim gray heap in the shadows.

THE COUNTRYWOMAN. So I don't know what's to become of me any more, with my one boarder gone. A poet he was, to be sure, but a good one; and he paid me enough every summer to keep my soul and body together through the rest of the long year. Seven summers he came that way, and now the time's gone by, and I hear never no word. How I'm to keep myself alive, I don't know; and since I've took you in, bless you, there's the two of us. It may be you'll have to go again, the way you came, out of the

night, though you're a great comfort bein' here to talk
to, and a help to me in my work. Not but what there'd
be more comfort yet, if your poor tongue weren't cursed
with dumbness! (*She turns away, sighing, and a queer
smile flickers over the stray's face*)
Dear sake, yes, I'm growin' used to you. But a stray who
comes to the land's end is as welcome as any other. Nor
are those likely to reach here at all, who aren't vagabonds
— or poets. By which I think that my poet is gone for
good, and you must follow after, and then I'll be left to
dwell for the rest of my days alone with the spirits of the
moor and of the sea beyond. Oh, alack! (*She sits down,
wiping her eyes*)
I'll not forget the night you came. A month ago it was;
the second of June; and the day before was the time the
poet always come, himself. When I see your white face
peerin' through the window there, I thought 'twas him,
late, and lookin' in for the joke of it, to see if I'd given
him up. Then in another minute you was standin' in the
door, poor white creature that you were. And behind you
was the wind sweepin' over the moor, and the waves sighin'
up the cliffhead from the sea. God knows where you come
from, and you couldn't tell. But you're not troublesome.
(*The creature smiles at her, as the old woman goes over to her,
and pats her shoulder*)
No, you're not. Neither was he. Off all the time he was,
with the will-o'-the-wisps of the field and the mermaids of
the deep, learnin' their sweet songs. No trouble at all,
either of you, — only, *he* paid. (*A knock at the door. The
old woman starts and cries out joyfully. As she hurries to
open, she does not notice that the girl's face grows illumined
as she stretches forth her thin arms in a gesture of infinite
grace*)
He's come! After four weeks, at last! He'll pay again!
[*The door, opened by her, reveals a woman in her thirty-fifth
year, dressed in the extreme of style. She enters, followed by a
black-clad maid, who carries a traveling bag. Disappointed,*

*but amazed, the old woman falls back before her. By this
time, the figure near the fireplace is crouching expressionless
as before.*

THE STYLISH LADY. Is this the farmhouse at the land's end?

THE COUNTRYWOMAN. Yes, so please you.

[*She curtsies as well as her bent back will permit. The stray's
eyes have gone from the lady to the maid, and are fixed on the
servant when the lady speaks.*

THE LADY. Ah! — You may set down the bag, Nora.

THE MAID (*with a soft brogue*). Yes, ma'am.

[*She gazes nervously about the dusky room.*

THE LADY (*to the countrywoman*). My husband sent me to
you.

[*Quick as a flash, the stray's big eyes are fastened on the lady.
They never waver till the end of the scene.*

THE COUNTRYWOMAN. Your husband? How? There are
no husbands at the land's end. Nobody but me.

THE LADY. My husband has been here. He used to board
with you, in the summer time.

THE COUNTRYWOMAN. Oh! The poet?

THE LADY. Yes. I am the poet's wife.

THE COUNTRYWOMAN. But —

THE LADY. We've not been married very long. (*She hastens
to add, with a forced sigh*) Of course, it pained me to leave
him! But I was so wearied from social pleasures that he
wanted me to rest; and what was I to do? I was even
growing bored, not being as fresh as he to such fulness of
life. But you can know nothing of that, here at the end
of things. You've never seen the world?

THE COUNTRYWOMAN (*glancing through the window*). I've
seen how big it is, and how — queer.

[*Her voice grows hushed with awe. Follows a slight pause.
The serving-maid becomes aware of the crouching stray, and
moves farther away, crossing herself. The lady's stare at the
old woman ends in a burst of laughter.*

THE LADY. Oh, how amusing! I think I shall enjoy my stay
with you. Will you take me in for a while?

THE COUNTRYWOMAN (*cackling with pleasure*). Now, by all the clouds in the sky to-night, I will!

THE LADY. I shall require a room for myself and another for my maid.

THE COUNTRYWOMAN. And your husband, good ma'am? Doesn't he come?

THE LADY. No. I thought better not. . . . There seemed to be some influence here that was not good for him.

THE COUNTRYWOMAN. Here, ma'am? At the land's end he loved so much?

THE LADY (*laughing unpleasantly*). Oh, I don't deny he found his inspiration in this neighborhood. Summer brought his best work, every one knows that. . . . Tell me, how did he use to spend his time?

THE COUNTRYWOMAN. Why, most of it, out there.
[*She waves her hand toward the darkening scene beyond the windows.*

THE LADY (*sitting at the right of the table*). Ah? You see, he never told me about it in detail, for fear I — couldn't understand. But you think I can understand, don't you?

THE COUNTRYWOMAN. Good ma'am, are you acquainted with the spirits?

THE LADY. Certainly not! What spirits?

THE COUNTRYWOMAN. Those he knew.

THE LADY. Oh! So he did have other friends — beside yourself?

THE COUNTRYWOMAN. They was all his friends, good ma'am. He's the only person I ever knew could walk on the moor by night, without the will-o'-the-wisp should dance him over the cliff. Instead o' that, it taught him the tune it dances to, and he made a song out of it. My own man ventured into the darkness years ago, and never came back more. But the poet and It was friends.

THE LADY. A will-o'-the-wisp, what is that?

THE COUNTRYWOMAN (*in a voice of awe*). It's what keeps you in the house o' nights. It's a wavin' light that beckons you to follow it. And when you've been for miles and miles,

always behind, why, then it leaves you; and the morning
finds you dead in a ravine, or floatin' under the cliff-head
in the sea.

THE LADY (*laughing*). Oh, really! What a pleasant companion for my husband! (*The crouching figure creeps forward a bit from its place by the fireside. Again the maid,
flattened against the wall, crosses herself*) But pray tell
me, whom else did he know?

THE COUNTRYWOMAN. Poor Will, a goblin who cries through
the land's end, under the curse of an old, old sin. And
the mermaids with green hair, that sing when a ship goes
down.

THE LADY. Did my husband tell you all this?

THE COUNTRYWOMAN. Yes, good ma'am, and more; whenever for hunger he come home, he had a tale for me.

THE LADY. And you believed it?

THE COUNTRYWOMAN. He was a dear young man, I'm not
even blamin' the spirits, that they loved him.

THE LADY (*laughing*). But, I mean, do you believe in *spirits?*

THE COUNTRYWOMAN. How could I choose? I see them, I
hear them. The night your husband should have come —
that was the first of June — I saw the will-o'-the-wisp out
yonder on the moor, as plain as I see my candles. Not
dancin' it was, but goin' quite slow and steady-like, with
its lantern lit, as if it was seekin' him. And I'm not
wonderin' if, sooner or later, it didn't come peepin' and
lookin' through this very window into my house, to find
the friend it missed.

THE LADY. Oh, what nonsense! What utter, silly bosh!
*The serving-maid comes down to the left of the table, speaking
in a worried whisper.*

THE MAID. I'd not be sayin' the like, ma'am, if I was you.
It's offering the goblins temptation.

THE LADY (*turning, astonished*). What You, too, Nora?
I thought you had more sense!

THE MAID. In the old country, ma'am, it's the way with us
all, to believe.

THE LADY. Oh, dear me! Well, I can't grow superstitious, Nora, just to oblige you. That will do.

THE MAID. Yes, ma'am. . . . But I think I'll be leaving you.

THE LADY. What?

THE MAID. Oh, it's afraid I am, what with the old woman's talk, and the look of the moor outside. We'd better be going, ma'am, the both of us. There's no good waits for us here.

THE LADY. You may go when you please. For myself, I prefer to stay and meet — some of my husband's friends. I shall certainly not be frightened away by the tales my husband — left behind for me.

[*She laughs again unpleasantly; and the creeping figure comes very near her chair. Across the table, the maid bursts into tears, and sinks down in the chair opposite.*

THE MAID (*sobbing*). How shall I take me way back, alone? Oh, the Lord pity me!

THE COUNTRYWOMAN. There, there, good soul, the spirits wish you no harm, they'll not hurt you.

THE LADY (*impatiently*). Oh, both of you, be still!

THE COUNTRYWOMAN. Now, you see, your husband should have come.

THE LADY. My good woman, I told you, I preferred not; he is so contented where he is — among *my* friends.

THE COUNTRYWOMAN. Alack! Is he then never to come again?

THE LADY. Don't expect him.

THE COUNTRYWOMAN. But the songs? The tunes he made, and paid for with his heart?

THE LADY. Fortunately, it's no longer a question of that.

[*The stray's white face peers round at her. Its eyes seem to burn the woman in the chair.*

THE COUNTRYWOMAN. Good ma'am, pretty ma'am, you don't mean he's give up — singin'?

THE LADY. Oh, yes. Poets usually do, you know, when they marry rich women. Weak, the lot of them.

[The crouching figure half starts up; its teeth are bared; then it sinks back again. The countrywoman, covering her head with her apron, begins to sway in her chair.

THE COUNTRYWOMAN. Alack! Alack the day! Alack the winter time!

THE LADY. Indeed? I didn't know people like you cared for poetry.

THE COUNTRYWOMAN. He'll sing no more, he'll pay no more. The land's end will be poor and still.

THE LADY. Ah, now I understand you. You have a point of view; well, so have the wives of poets. Just as he gave you comfort in return for his inspiration, we give them ease in which to love us. Why shouldn't we? Why should they play at their little toy battle with life, when we can put all existence into their very hands? That is our mission; and it makes them very comfortable, I assure you.

[The stray springs up with clawing hands behind the lady. The countrywoman sees her.

THE COUNTRYWOMAN. Here, girl, here!

[At the cry, the stray sinks back on the floor. But her eyes never cease to burn the woman's face. The poet's wife, looking down, has now become aware of her. Her silly suspicion seems assured.

THE LADY (*sharply*). Who is this?

THE COUNTRYWOMAN (*moving the stray back*). A poor waif, ma'am. A harmless, dumb waif, who helps me in the house.

THE LADY. Oho! Did you mention her among my husband's friends?

THE COUNTRYWOMAN. Why, no. He never saw her. Been here only a month, she has, the poor creature.

THE LADY. Where did she come from?

THE COUNTRYWOMAN. The good Lord knows! Not I.

THE LADY. Ah. Well, from the looks of her, I should say it didn't matter, how long she was with you. . . . Come here, girl.

THE COUNTRYWOMAN. Mind what the lady bids you.

[*The figure on the floor lifts a face, now expressionless, to the poet's wife. For the third time, the maid crosses herself.*

THE LADY. Hm! The total effect of you is not — dangerous. (*She takes the stray's face between her hands. A violent shudder shakes the latter from head to foot, as she shrinks back with a gliding motion; but this does not discourage the poet's wife*) Don't be afraid of me, silly thing! (*She turns to the countrywoman*) Funny how fashion impresses them, isn't it? This girl turned clammy cold.

THE COUNTRYWOMAN (*nodding*). It's the feel of her.

[*The poet's wife returns to her scrutiny of the girl's face.*

THE LADY. Yet, you know, your features aren't so bad. If you only had a little color. . . . You should never wear gray with that white face of yours. (*She addresses the room in general, and the maid in particular*) Country people invariably have no idea how to dress. Eh, Nora?

THE MAID. Ma'am, for the love of God, be careful! I'm not liking the eyes of herself!

THE LADY (*laughing lightly*). Oh, her eyes are so much better than her clothes! But I forgot; you're not fit to talk to to-night, are you? Well, that will do. (*She turns back to the countrywoman*) Why do you let your servant wear that awful cap? Doesn't she ever take it off?

THE COUNTRYWOMAN. Many's the time I've spoke of it; but it's a stubborn habit with her. So I lets her have her way, for peace.

THE LADY (*to the stray*). But, my poor girl, that cap is awful! If only your hair showed, you'd be so much better looking. What makes you wear it?

[*For answer, the stray, rising, shuffles past the poet's wife to the table. It is the first time during the scene that she has looked away from her. As she nears the table, the maid on the other side shrinks back. Once there, the stray turns on the woman, and, watching her instead of what she herself does, she reaches for the candle. She lifts the metal extinguisher from the candlestick, holds it out so that the poet's wife may see it, then with a quick motion places it over the flame. The candle goes out, leaving the room dim with one light. In her nervousness, the serving-maid sobs once aloud.*

THE COUNTRYWOMAN. What would this be?

THE LADY. Do you know what she meant?

THE COUNTRYWOMAN. I don't see — I don't see. . . .

THE LADY. She's probably mad, poor soul.

THE MAID. Oh, Mother of God! Mother of God! The magic!

THE LADY. I fail to find any magic in a candle going out, when I've just watched the process. Really, I prefer bed to such gloomy companionship. (*She rises, and speaks to the countrywoman*) Will you light us upstairs, please. I'm quite sorry I came.

THE COUNTRYWOMAN (*re-lighting the second candle*). There, there, good ma'am. It'll all be more cheerful in the morning.

THE LADY. I feel as if morning would never come, with this whole night dragging at me.

[*The countrywoman gives the candle to Nora, who has picked up her mistress' bag. Then the old dame crosses toward the candle on the shelf.*

THE COUNTRYWOMAN. Now, if you and your woman will follow me. . . . The poet's room was ready for him. . . . [*This mention of the poet brings another convulsive motion from the stray. The lady's attention is thereby arrested.*

THE LADY. Where does that creature sleep?

THE COUNTRYWOMAN. Oh, down here, on a mat by the fireside. She'll not trouble you more, good ma'am. She'll not trouble you more.

[*She opens the door to the stairs.*

THE LADY (*after a brief hesitation*). Come, Nora.

[*She goes out. The countrywoman pauses to speak to the stray.*

THE COUNTRYWOMAN. Good night, girl. Go to sleep quietly. (*She disappears, and we hear her voice*) Now, good ma'am. Now, so please you. . . .

[*The room, lighted only by Nora's candle, is dim again. Outside, the night is very black. The serving-maid crosses the room silently. In its center, she passes close to the stray, who has crept there to look after the poet's wife. The maid, making a quick detour, gasps with terror. When she reaches the fireplace, she rushes for the stairs with a little scream that puts her candle out; we hear the door bang behind her. The room is completely black.*

A silence. Then the motion of some one springing upright; and the place is suffused with a dim glow of orange light. The light shines from the orange-red hair of the white-faced girl, a burning mass of quivering, gleaming strands. And the girl herself stands revealed, a spirit-creature, red and white and clad in fluttering gray, her body slim and swaying with infinite grace. Not even the poet's wife could question the beauty of her wild white face, lit into a fierce exaltation by the glow of that tumbling hair. In her fingers is the ugly cap, held mockingly toward the door; and then she drops it.

Now a faint music sounds from somewhere, a langorous melody; and the spirit begins to sway to it. Not quite a dance yet nothing else, this moving through the room.

The door to the stairs opens, and the poet's wife appears, trailing a white room-robe about her. The white-faced girl smiles at her, smiles quite close to her, with a demon behind her smile.

THE LADY. Who are you? — Why do you smile at me, — unless — you're *glad* that I came down? — You knew I would answer to that music — *he* used to sing me a song to it, when he courted me. — Was it out of his love for you, he made that song? — Oh, it might well have been, you with your long white arms and your strange white face! — But he sang it to me, do you hear? To me, to me, to me, it is my song!

You smile. — You are so sure it isn't mine. — But you aren't singing it now, any more than I am! — Where does that music come from? — What *are* you?

Oh, I knew there was something here that held him.— I

had all the right to him. — I took his life, and made of it what I would, — but I couldn't reach his soul. It was bound up to something else, his soul. — I wanted to see. — I see now. — But I don't understand! What are you? Can you talk? You can, you can, you devil! You called me down to tell your story, didn't you? Well, triumph over me, — triumph! — only *speak!* (*The white-faced girl, in her dance, is moving toward the outer door, ever eluding the poet's wife, who takes a few steps after her*) No, you're not going away without it, you and your magic hair! (*She reaches desperately for the waving hand, which glides from under her grasp*) You burned him with that hair — you burned the soul out of him. — But now I've come in his place, and you can't burn me, and I *will* learn why you smile! (*Again the reach, and the white hand slips away*) Do you mean you can't talk? — Or do you want me alone? (*The white-faced girl, near the door, has raised a beckoning hand. There is now a teasing invitation in her smile*) Oh, I'm not afraid to go with you, out there! — Wait! Wait!

[*For the white-faced girl has opened the door. As the poet's wife crosses the room, the countrywoman comes, drawn by the talk, down the stairs. She gives a sudden shriek.*

THE COUNTRYWOMAN. Oh, God!

THE LADY (*briefly turning, annoyed*). What, you?

THE COUNTRYWOMAN. I heard. I came. (*The poet's wife takes another step*) Don't follow, don't follow, for the love of Heaven! It's the Will-O'-The-Wisp!

[*In the doorway, the white-faced girl stoops, and smiles her smile, and beckons.*

THE LADY (*with authority*). Let be! — I am going after her! — I am going to learn the truth!

[*She nears the door, just as the serving-maid appears at the foot of the stairs. With a scream, Nora rushes to the poet's wife, and clings to her.*

THE MAID. Stay back! Stay back! It's to your death you go!

THE LADY (*pushing her to the floor*). Take your hands off me. — There are no such things as spirits! — It's a trick they made for me! — my husband and her! WAIT! —
[*For the white-faced girl has passed outside. Only the glow of her hair, quite near, shines in through the open door.*

THE COUNTRYWOMAN. The Will-O'-The-Wisp! — It's her! — It's her!

THE MAID (*crying out at the same time*). Stop, I tell ye! — Stop, stop, stop!
[*The poet's wife is on the threshold. The orange light recedes, and the room darkens.*

THE LADY (*almost majestic*). Wait! — I'm not afraid! — WAIT FOR ME! —
[*She, too, passes outside the door. The serving-maid breaks into a torrent of sobs. After a moment, in which the country-woman reaches the window, the room is black again. And the music has died away.*

THE COUNTRYWOMAN. Hush! — (*The sobs of the serving-maid die down to a low moan*) Come here by me at the window. Ah, see!

THE MAID (*whispering*). What is it?
[*Now through door and window, there can be seen in the distance a moving light, growing smaller and smaller, making straight for where one saw the cliff-head over the sea.*

THE COUNTRYWOMAN. The light! The Will-O'-The-Wisp! And something white behind it.

THE MAID (*whispering*). Is it — me mistress?

THE COUNTRYWOMAN (*turning away*). Yes. God have mercy upon her.
[*The maid has dragged herself over to the window, and kneels on the floor, looking out.*

THE MAID. A shadow in the dark, lit up by that thing ahead! Oh, it is! It is!

THE COUNTRYWOMAN (*nerving herself for the sight*). Ah, the spirit! — it's *out beyond* the cliff-head! And the cold sea lies beneath! Woe to one who follows the Will-O'-The-Wisp! Woe!

[*Then a slight pause, in which the light no longer moves.*

THE MAID (*crying out*).   Look, where the light is after standing still! And not a sign of *her!* — Oh, she's gone over! Gone, she is! And she'll never come back! —

[*She starts to keen — three long ochones — as the curtain falls.*

SIX WHO PASS WHILE THE LENTILS BOIL

STUART WALKER

THE year 1915 was an epoch-making one in Little Theatre history. In that year three different groups organized workshop activities that were destined to broaden the entire field of American drama, both on Broadway and in the communities. Stuart Walker's Portmanteau Theatre, which could be packed up and carried from one city to another, was one of these groups, and "Six Who Pass While the Lentils Boil" was one of the most popular plays in its repertory. It is still being played throughout the country, by both adult and children's theatres.

Mr. Walker was born in Augusta, Kentucky; and moved to Cincinnati in 1890. There he received his degree in 1902, but later came to New York for a course at the American Academy of Dramatic Arts. He was associated with David Belasco from 1909 to 1914, and became his General Director. In 1914 he was associated with Jessie Bonstelle, and in 1915 began a career of independent management which lasted until 1931. In addition to the Portmanteau Theatre, Stuart Walker organized repertory companies in New York, Chicago, Cincinnati, Indianapolis, Dayton, Baltimore, Louisville, and a junior company in Huntington, West Virginia.

In 1930 he joined Columbia Pictures as a director, from 1931 to 1933 he was with Paramount, and in 1934 and 1935 with Universal, where he directed "Great Expectations" and "The Mystery of Edwin Drood", among others. In 1936, he rejoined Paramount as an Associate Producer.

In his theatre work, he is particularly happy to have done the first professional production of "The Book of Job" (King James version), which was played many hundreds of times between 1918 and 1930; and to have popularized the plays of Lord Dunsany and other imaginative writers.

Some of his plays are: "The Moon Lady"; "The Seven Gifts" (a pantomime); a dramatization of Booth Tarkington's *Seventeen;* and three collections of one-act plays, *Portmanteau Plays, More Portmanteau Plays,* and *Portmanteau Adaptations.*

SIX WHO PASS WHILE THE LENTILS BOIL

By STUART WALKER

"Six Who Pass While the Lentils Boil" was originally produced at an invitation performance at Christodora House, New York City, July 14, 1915. The first public performance was at Jordan Hall, Boston, February 14, 1916. Both performances were given under the auspices of the Portmanteau Theatre.

Original Cast

	1915	1916
THE PROLOGUE . .	Henry Kiefer	Lew Medbury
THE DEVICE-BEARER	Edmond Crenshaw	Edmond Crenshaw
BOY	James W. Morrison	Gregory Kelly
QUEEN	Judith Lowry	Judith Lowry
MIME	William Farrell	Wilmot Heitland
MILKMAID . . .	Nancy Winston	Nancy Winston
BLINDMAN	Joseph Graham	Edgar Stehli
BALLAD SINGER . .	Tom Powers	Stuart Walker
HEADSMAN . . .	McKay Morris	McKay Morris

SIX WHO PASS WHILE THE LENTILS BOIL

THE SCENE *is a kitchen.*

THE PERIOD *is when you will.*

Before the opening of the curtains the Prologue enters upon the forestage and summons the Device-Bearer who carries a large copper pot.

PROLOGUE. This is a copper pot. (*The Device-Bearer shows it to the audience carefully*) It is filled with boiling water. (*The Device-Bearer makes the sound of bubbling water*) It is on the fire. See the flames. (*The Device-Bearer sets the pot in the center of the forestage and blows under it with a pair of bellows*) And see the water boiling over. (*The Device-Bearer again makes the sound of bubbling water and then withdraws to where he can see the play from the side of the forestage*) We are looking into the kitchen of the Boy whose mother left him alone. I do not know where she has gone but I do know that he is gathering lentils now.

YOU. What are lentils?

PROLOGUE. A lentil? Why a lentil, don't you see, is not a bean nor yet a pea; but it is kin to both . . . You must imagine that the boy has built the fire and set the water boiling. He is very industrious but you need not feel sorry for him. His mother is very good to him and he is safe. Are you ready now? . . . Very well. Be quiet.

[*The Prologue claps his hands twice.*

The curtains open and a kitchen is disclosed. There are a bench, a stool and a cupboard. A great door at the back opens into a corridor. There are also two windows — one higher than the other — looking upon the corridor. At the right a door opens into the bedroom of the Boy's mother. A great pewter spoon lies upon the shelf in the cupboard.

A large Butterfly comes in through the doorway, flits about and looks off stage.

The song of the Boy is heard from the garden.

The Butterfly goes to the door, poises a moment, then alights on the cupboard.

The Boy enters with a great bowl filled with lentils.

The Butterfly flies to the bowl and satisfied returns to the cupboard.

The Boy smiles at the Butterfly but he does not touch him. Then he empties the lentils into the pot and water splashes on his careless hand.

A moan is heard in the distance. The Boy and the Butterfly go to the door.

The Queen's voice is heard calling:

Butterfly, Butterfly, where shall I hide?

[*Enter the Queen.*

QUEEN. Boy, Boy — oh, I am distraught!

YOU. What is distraught?

PROLOGUE. Distraught means distracted, perplexed, beset with doubt, worried by some fear.

BOY (*pityingly*). Why are you distraught?

QUEEN. Oh — Oh — Oh — They are going to behead me!

BOY. When?

QUEEN. Before mid-day.

BOY. Why are they going to behead you? Is it a story? Tell it to me.

QUEEN. I was guilty of a breach of etiquette.

BOY. What is that?

QUEEN. I did something that was considered bad manners and the law says the punishment is decapitation.

YOU. What is decapitation?

PROLOGUE. Decapitation is beheading; cutting off one's head.

BOY. Why, only kings and queens can be decapitated.

QUEEN. Oh, I know — I know —

BOY (*disappointed*). Are you a queen?

QUEEN. Yes.

BOY. I thought all queens were big. My mother says they are always regal. And my mother knows.

QUEEN. Oh, I *am* the queen. *I am* the queen; but I am so unhappy.

BOY. My mother told me kings and queens knew no fear? Why, you're afraid.

QUEEN. Oh, Boy, Boy, I *am* your queen and I *am* afraid and unhappy. And queens are just like other people when they are afraid and unhappy.

BOY (*disappointed*). Aren't they always regal?

QUEEN. No — no. Oh, little boy, hide me, hide me from the Dreadful Headsman!

BOY. I haven't any place to hide you. You couldn't get under the bench and you couldn't get into the cupboard.

QUEEN. Little boy, can't you see that I shall lose my head if I am found?

BOY. You might have hidden in the pot if I hadn't put it on the fire.

QUEEN. Oh — Oh — Oh —

BOY. I'm sorry.

QUEEN. I am distraught.

BOY. Well, I'll hide you, because you are distraught; but — I am not sure you are a queen. . . . Where's your crown? You can't be a queen without a crown!
[*She reaches up to her head.*

QUEEN. Oh, I was running so fast that it must have slipped from my head. (*Sees the Butterfly*) Butterfly, tell him I am your Queen.
[*The Butterfly flies to her head and lights on her disheveled locks like a diadem.*

BOY. Oh, I have talked to the Queen! . . . You can hide in my mother's bedroom in there; but first please tell me a story.

QUEEN. They will find me here. I'll tell you a story afterward.

BOY. I want you to tell me now.

QUEEN. Well, you watch at the door and warn me when

you see some one coming.   (*The Butterfly brushes her ear*)
But stay, the Butterfly says he'll watch.

[*The Butterfly goes to the door.*

BOY.   Will he know?

QUEEN.   Oh, yes.   He is a wonderful butterfly — wise beyond his years.

BOY.   Sit down and tell me your story.

[*He places a black pillow for the Queen on the step and an orange pillow for himself.*

QUEEN.   Last night we celebrated the second year of peace with the neighboring kingdom.   We were dancing the minuet just after the banquet, when I stepped on the ring-toe of my husband the King's great aunt.

BOY.   Didn't you say excuse me?

QUEEN.   It was useless.   The law says that if a queen steps on the ring-toe of the King's great aunt or any member of her family the Queen must be beheaded while the King's four clocks are striking twelve at mid-day.

BOY.   Oh, that means to-day?

QUEEN.   Yes.

BOY.   Why, it's almost mid-day now.   See, I've just set the lentils boiling.

QUEEN.   If you can hide me until after the King's four clocks strike twelve I shall be safe.

BOY.   Why are there four clocks?

QUEEN.   Because the law allows only one clock for each tower in the castle.

BOY.   Then I hear all the King's clocks every day!   There's a big clock, and two clocks not so big, and a tiny little clock.

QUEEN.   Yes, those are the four.

BOY.   Why will you be safe *after* the four clocks strike twelve?

QUEEN.   Because that is the law.

BOY.   Aren't laws funny?

QUEEN.   Funny?   This one is very sad, I think.

BOY.   Mightn't it be twelve any mid-day?

QUEEN. No; the Prime Minister of my grandfather who passed the law decided that it meant only the following mid-day.

BOY (*rising and rushing to the door*). They'll find you here.

QUEEN (*rising calmly*). Oh, no, this is the short cut to the beheading block. Through that corridor.

BOY. Why didn't you run the other way?

QUEEN. Because they always search for escaped people in that direction. So I ran through your garden and into this room. They'll never search for me so close to the castle.

BOY. How did you escape?

QUEEN. I —

[*The Butterfly seems agitated.*

BOY. You —

QUEEN. Some one is coming. Hide me!

BOY. In here — in my mother's room. 'Sh! 'Sh!

[*The Queen goes out.*

Enter the Mime.

He pokes his head in the lower window and peeps around the door.

The boy turns.

BOY (*weakly*). Are you the Dreadful Headsman?

MIME. *What?*

BOY. Are you the Dreadful Headsman?

MIME. Do I look like a headsman?

BOY. I don't know; I've never seen one.

MIME. Well, suppose I am.

BOY. Are you?

MIME. Maybe I am.

BOY. Oh!

MIME. Booh!

BOY. I'm — I'm — not afraid.

MIME. Bah!

BOY. And my mother isn't here.

MIME. Br — r — r — r!

[*The Boy reaches for his knife.*

MIME. Bing!

BOY. I wasn't going to hurt you!

MIME. 'Sh . . . 'Sh! . . . 'Sh! . . .

BOY. I'll give you my knife if you'll go 'way.

MIME. Ah, — ha!

BOY. It's nearly mid-day and you'd better go.

MIME. Well, give me the knife.

BOY. Promise me to go.

MIME (*laughs, turning away*). Aren't you going to the be-heading?

BOY. No. I have to boil the lentils for our mid-day meal.

MIME. May I come back and eat some?

BOY. You'll have to ask my mother.

MIME. Where is she?

BOY. She's over that way. She went to the market to buy a bobbin.

YOU. What is a bobbin?

PROLOGUE. A bobbin is a spool upon which thread is wound, and it is sharp at one end so that it can be easily passed backward and forward, to and fro, through the other threads in making lace.

MIME (*starting off*). Well, I'll be back to eat some lentils.

BOY (*too eagerly*). You'd better hurry.

MIME. You seem to want to get rid of me.

BOY (*allaying suspicion*). Well, I think you'd better go or you'll be late — and it's very wrong to be late.

MIME (*going toward the door*). I think I'll (*changing his mind*) sit down.

BOY (*disappointed*). Oh!

MIME. What would you say if I wasn't the Headsman?

BOY. But you said you were.

MIME. I said *maybe* I was.

BOY. Aren't you?

MIME. Maybe I'm not.

BOY. Honest?

MIME. Um, hum.

BOY (*relieved*). Oh! . . .

MIME. You *were* afraid.

BOY. No . . . I wasn't.

MIME. Would you fight?

BOY. You bet I would.

MIME. It wouldn't take me a minute to lick you.

BOY. Maybe it wouldn't, but I wouldn't give up right away. That would be cowardly. . . . Who are you?

MIME. I'm a mime —

BOY. What's a mime?

MIME. A mime's a mime.

BOY. Go on and tell me.

MIME. A mime's a mountebank.

BOY. What's a mountebank?

MIME. A mountebank's a strolling player.

BOY. Are you going to perform for me?

MIME. Not to-day — I'm on my way to the decapitation.

BOY. Do you want to see the decapitation?

MIME. Well, yes. But most of all I want to pick up a few coins.

BOY. How?

MIME. Why, I'll perform after the Queen has lost her head.

BOY. Won't you be too sorry?

MIME. No. You see, I'll be thinking mostly about what I'm going to do. I have to do my best because it is hard to be more interesting than a decapitation. And after it's all over the crowd will begin to talk and to move about: and I'll have to rush up to the front of them and cry out at the top of my lungs, "Stop — Ho, for Jack the Juggler! Would you miss him? In London where the king of kings lives, all the knights and ladies of the Court would leave a crowning to watch Jack the Juggler toss three golden balls with one hand or balance a weathervane upon his nose." Then a silence will come upon the crowd and they will all turn to me. Some one will say, "Where is this Jack the Juggler?" And I shall answer, "Jack the Juggler, the greatest of the great, the pet of kings, entertainer to the Pope and the joy of Cathay stands before you." And

I'll throw back my cloak and stand revealed. So! Some one will then shout, "Let us have it, Jack." So I'll draw my three golden balls from my pouch — like this — and then begin.

[*The Boy is watching breathlessly and the Butterfly is interested too. Their disappointment is keen when Jack does nothing.*

BOY. Aren't you going to show me?

MIME. No, I must be off.

BOY. Aren't you ever coming back?

MIME. Maybe, yes; perhaps, no.

BOY. I'll give you some lentils if you'll juggle the balls for me.

MIME (*sniffs the pot*). They aren't cooked yet.

BOY. Let me hold your golden balls.

MIME (*takes a gold ball from his pouch and lets the Boy hold it*). Here's one.

BOY. And do they pay you well?

MIME (*taking the ball from the Boy*). Ay, that they do. If I am as interesting as the beheading I'll get perhaps fifteen farthings in money and other things that I can exchange for food and raiment.

BOY. I'm going to be a mime and buy a castle and a sword.

MIME. Maybe so and maybe not. Who knows? . . . Good-by.

[*He goes out.*

BOY (*to the Butterfly*). If he had been the Dreadful Headsman I would have slain him. So! . . . "Ah, wicked headsman, you shall not behead the Queen! . . . Cross not that threshold or I'll run you through."

[*Throughout this the Butterfly shows great interest and enters into the spirit of it, being absorbed at times and frightened at others.*

Enter the Milkmaid at door.

MILKMAID. Pst! . . . Pst!

BOY (*startled*). Oh!

MILKMAID. Are you going to the decapitation?

BOY. No. Are you?

MILKMAID. That I am.

BOY. Will your mother let you go?

MILKMAID. She doesn't know.

BOY. Did you run away?

MILKMAID. No. I went out to milk the cow.

BOY. And did you do it?

MILKMAID. Yes.

BOY. Why didn't you wait until you came back?

MILKMAID. My mother was looking and I had to let her see me doing something.

BOY. How did you get away when you took the milk pails into the house?

MILKMAID. I didn't take them in. As soon as my mother turned her back I hid the pails and I ran through here to take a short cut.

BOY. Where did you hide the milk?

MILKMAID. In the hollow tree.

BOY. Won't it sour?

MILKMAID. Maybe.

BOY. Won't your mother scold you?

MILKMAID. Yes, of course, but I couldn't miss the beheading.

BOY. Will you take the sour milk home?

MILKMAID. Yes, and after my mother scolds me I'll make it into nice cheese and sell it to the King's Cook and then mother will forgive me.

BOY (*sniffing the pot*). You'd better hurry. It's nearly midday. Don't you smell the lentils?

MILKMAID. The headsman hasn't started yet

BOY (*giggling*). He'd better hurry.

MILKMAID. They can't find the Queen.

BOY (*so innocently*). Did she escape?

MILKMAID. Yes.

BOY. Are they hunting for her?

MILKMAID. Yes, and they've offered a big reward to the person who finds her.

BOY. How much?

MILKMAID. A pail of gold and a pair of finger rings.

BOY. That's a good deal . . . with a pail of gold I could buy my mother a velvet dress and a silken kerchief and a bonnet made of cloth of gold — and I could buy myself a milk-white palfrey.

MILKMAID. And you'd never have to work again.

BOY. But she's such a gentle queen. Where are they hunting her?

MILKMAID. Everywhere.

BOY. Everywhere! . . . Maybe she's waiting at the be-heading block.

MILKMAID. Silly goose! She wouldn't try to escape this way. She'd go in the opposite direction.

BOY. Do people always run in the opposite direction?

MILKMAID. Of course, everybody knows that.

BOY. I wish I could go.

MILKMAID. Come on.

BOY. Um — uh. The lentils might burn.

MILKMAID. Pour some cold water on them.

BOY. Um — uh. I promised I wouldn't leave the house.

MILKMAID. Oh, it will be wonderful!

BOY. The Mime will be there.

MILKMAID. The one with the long cloak and the golden balls?

BOY. Um — uh.

MILKMAID. Ooh!

BOY. How did you know?

MILKMAID. I saw him on the way to the market one day — and when my mother wasn't looking at me I gave him a farthing.

BOY. Is he a good juggler?

MILKMAID. He's magic! Why, he can throw three golden balls in the air and catch them with one hand and then keep them floating in the air in a circle.

BOY. And can he balance a weathervane on his nose while it's turning?

MILKMAID. Yes, and he can balance an egg on the end of a long stick that is balanced on his chin !

BOY. Oh — I wish I could see him.

[*Looks at the pot to see if the lentils are done.*

MILKMAID. Come on !

BOY. Well —

[*Begins to weaken and just as he is about to start, the Butterfly flits past him into the Queen's room.*

MILKMAID. Oh — what a lovely butterfly !

BOY. No — No — I can't go. But you had better hurry.

MILKMAID. Well, I'll try to catch the butterfly first.

BOY. Oh, no, you mustn't touch that butterfly.

MILKMAID. Why ?

BOY. Because — because he's my friend.

MILKMAID. Silly !

BOY. He *is* a good friend and he's the wisest butterfly in the world.

MILKMAID. What can he do ?

BOY. He can almost talk.

MILKMAID. Almost ? . . . Oh, I know. I'm a goose. You want to play a trick on me so I'll miss the beheading.

BOY. You'd better hurry.

MILKMAID. I wish you'd come.

BOY (*sadly*). I can't. I've a duty to perform.

MILKMAID. Aren't duties always hard ? [*Both sigh.*

She takes up her milk pail.

BOY. What are you going to do with that pail ?

MILKMAID. I'm going to stand on it. . . . Good-by.

[*She goes out.*

BOY. Good-by. (*He watches for a moment, then goes to the pot and tries the lentils; then whispers through door to the Queen*) The lentils are getting soft.

[*There is a fumbling in the passage and a voice is heard,* "Help the blind. Help the blind."

[*The Butterfly returns to the top of the cupboard.*

The Blind man appears at the door.

PROLOGUE. He's blind, but he'll show you how the blind can see.

BLIND MAN (*sniffing*). Cooking lentils?

BOY. Yes.

BLIND MAN. Cook, which way to the beheading?

BOY. Keep straight ahead — the way you are going, old man.

BLIND MAN. Don't you want to take me with you?

BOY. I'm not going.

BLIND MAN. Not going to the beheading?

BOY. No, I have to cook the lentils.

BLIND MAN. Come on and go with me and maybe I'll give you a farthing.

BOY. I can't.

BLIND MAN. Yes, you can. Who else is here?

BOY (*swallowing: it's hard to fib*). No one.

BLIND MAN. Can't you run away? Your mother won't know you've gone.

BOY. It's my duty to stay here.

BLIND MAN. It's your duty to help a poor blind man, little boy.

BOY. Are you stone blind?

BLIND MAN. Yes.

BOY. Then how did you know I was a *little* boy?

BLIND MAN. Because you *sound* like a little boy.

BOY. Well, if you're stone blind why do you want to go to the beheading?

BLIND MAN. I can see with my ears.

BOY. Aw —

BLIND MAN. Didn't I know you were a little boy?

BOY. Yes, but you had to guess twice. First you thought I was a cook.

BLIND MAN. Well, aren't you cooking lentils?

BOY. Yes; but you can smell them.

BLIND MAN. Well, I see with my nose, too.

BOY. Aw — how can you see with your nose?

BLIND MAN. If you give me some bread I'll show you.

BOY. I can't give you any bread, but I'll give you some raw lentils.

BLIND MAN. All right. Give me lentils.

BOY. . . . I'll put them by the pot — Ready.

BLIND MAN. All right. (*Sniffs. Walks to the pot and gets lentils and puts them in an old pouch*) Isn't that seeing with my nose?

BOY. H'm! (*In wonder*) Now see with your ears and I'll give you some more lentils.

BLIND MAN. All right. Speak.

[*The Boy gets behind the stool and speaks.*
The Blind man goes toward him. The Boy moves around stealthily.

BLIND MAN. You're cheating. You've moved.

BOY (*jumping up on the bench*). Well, where am I?

BLIND MAN. You're standing on something.

BOY. How did you guess it?

BLIND MAN. I didn't guess it. I know it.

BOY. Why can't I do that?

BLIND MAN. You can if you try; but it takes practice.

BOY. Can you see the door now?

BLIND MAN. No. I've turned around too many times. Besides there is more than one door.

BOY. Oh — m-m. . . You aren't really blind!

BLIND MAN. Blind people learn to use what they have. Once I too could see with my eyes.

BOY. Just like me?

BLIND MAN. Yes. And then I didn't take the trouble to see with my ears and my nose and my fingers — after I became blind I had to learn . . . Why, I can tell whether a man who passes me at the palace gate is a poor man or a noble or a merchant.

BOY. How can you do that?

BLIND MAN. By sound of the step

BOY. Aw — how can you do that?

BLIND MAN. Shut your eyes and try it.

BOY. Well, I know what you are. That would be easy.

BLIND MAN. I'll pretend I'm somebody else.

[Feels with his stick; touches bench. Feels around again.

BOY. Why are you doing that?

BLIND MAN. To see how far I can walk without bumping into something.

BOY. Um —

BLIND MAN. Ready.

BOY (*hides face in hands*). Yes.

BLIND MAN. Don't peep.

[The Boy tries hard not to.

BOY. I won't.

BLIND MAN. All ready. (*Shuffles like a commoner*) Who was it?

BOY. A poor man.

BLIND MAN. See how easy?

BOY. I could see him as plain as if I had my eyes open. . . . Now try me again.

BLIND MAN. Ready.

BOY. All right.

[The Blind Man seems to grow in height. His face is filled with a rare brightness. He steadies himself a moment and then walks magnificently down the room.

BOY (*in beautiful wonder*). A noble! I could see him.

BLIND MAN. All you have to do is try.

BOY. I always thought it was terrible to be blind.

BLIND MAN. Sometimes it is.

BOY. But I thought everything was black.

BLIND MAN. It used to be until I taught myself how to see.

BOY. Why is it terrible sometimes?

BLIND MAN. Because I cannot help the poor who need help. If I had money I could feed the hungry and clothe the poor little beggar children in winter!

BOY. Would a pail of gold and a pair of finger rings help you feed the hungry and clothe the poor little beggar children in winter?

BLIND MAN. A pail of gold! I have dreamed of what I might do with so much wealth!

BOY. I can get a pail of gold if I break a promise.

BLIND MAN. Would *you* break a promise?

BOY . . . No — but — No!

BLIND MAN. Of course you wouldn't.

BOY. I couldn't break a promise for *two* pails of gold.

BLIND MAN. Nor twenty-two, little boy.

BOY. When you walked like a noble I saw a beautiful man behind my eyes with a crown of gold.

BLIND MAN. If you broke a promise for a pail of gold and two finger rings you would never see a beautiful noble with a crown of gold when you closed your eyes . . .

BOY. Can blind men see beautiful things even when it's rainy?

BLIND MAN. Blind men can always see beautiful things if they try. Clouds and rain are beautiful to me — and when I get wet I think of the sunshine. I saw sunshine with my eyes when I was a little boy. Now I see it with my whole body when it warms me. I saw rain with my eyes when I was a little boy. Now I see it with my hands when it falls on them — drop — drop — drop — dropity — dropity — and I love it because it makes the lentils grow.

BOY. I never thought of that. Rain makes me stay indoors and I never like it except in June.

BLIND MAN. You don't have to stay in for long.

BOY. Can blind men see beautiful things in a beheading?

BLIND MAN. No. But I must be there with the crowd. I shall tell stories to the people and perhaps they will give me food or money.

BOY. Can't you stay and tell me stories?

BLIND MAN. No. I must be on my way . . . If I do not see the beheading I cannot tell about it when I meet some one who was not there. Oh, I shall make a thrilling tale of it.

BOY. Tell it to me when you come back.

BLIND MAN. If you give me some cooked lentils.

BOY. I'll save you some.

BLIND MAN. Are the lentils nearly done?

BOY. Half.

BLIND MAN. I must be on my way then. . . . Good-by.

[*Starting to go in the wrong direction.*

BOY. Here's the door.

BLIND MAN. Thank you, little boy. . . . Don't forget to see with your ears and nose and fingers.

[*The Blind Man goes out.*

BOY. I won't.

BLIND MAN. Good-by.

BOY. Good-by. (*The Boy covers his eyes and tries to see with his ears and his nose*) It's easier with the ears.

[*Singing is heard.*

Enter the Ballad-Singer.

SINGER. Hello!

BOY. Hello!

SINGER. How are you?

BOY. I'm very well.

SINGER. That's good.

BOY. Thank you.

SINGER. Cooking?

BOY. Yes.

SINGER (*coming into the room*). Something good?

BOY. Lentils.

SINGER. Give me some?

BOY. They aren't done.

SINGER. Nearly. I can smell them.

BOY. Do you like them?

SINGER. When I'm hungry.

BOY. Are you hungry now?

SINGER. I'm always hungry.

[*They laugh.*

BOY. Were you singing?

SINGER. Yes.

BOY. Do you like to sing?

SINGER. When I get something for my ballads.

BOY. Are you a ballad-singer?

SINGER. Yes.

BOY. Sing one for me?

SINGER. Give me some lentils?

BOY. I'll give you some raw lentils.

SINGER. I want some of the cooked ones.

BOY. They aren't done.

SINGER. Are they nearly done?

BOY. More than half.

SINGER. I like them that way.

BOY. All right. Sing me a ballad.

SINGER. Well, give me the lentils first.

BOY. Oh, no, sing the ballad first.

SINGER. No, sir, give me the lentils first.

BOY. That isn't fair.

SINGER. Why not? After I sing to you maybe you won't pay me.

BOY. Yes, I will.

SINGER. Then why not pay me first?

BOY. You might not sing.

SINGER (*laughing*). Yes, I will.

BOY (*laughing*). Well, I'll give you some lentils at the end of each verse.

SINGER. That's a bargain.

BOY. Sing.

SINGER (*sings one line*).

Six stalwart sons the miller had —
Give me the lentils.

BOY. Finish that verse.

SINGER. I did finish it.

BOY. Now that's not fair. You only sang a line.

SINGER. Well, a line's a verse.

BOY (*with a gesture that indicates how long a verse ought to be*). I meant a whole verse.

SINGER (*mimicking the gesture*). A line's a whole verse.

BOY. Oh, now, be fair, I mean a *whole*, whole verse.

SINGER. You mean a *stanza*.

BOY. I always heard it called a verse.

SINGER. Well, keep the bargain. I sang a verse. Give me some lentils.

BOY (*rising and taking a very few lentils on his spoon*). Next time I mean a stanza. . . . Here are some lentils.

[*The Ballad-Singer eyes the meager portion, cools it and eats.*

SINGER. Stingy.

BOY. Isn't that *some* lentils?

SINGER (*laughs*). Well —

BOY. Now begin again.

SINGER. At the end of every stanza a spoonful of lentils.

BOY. I didn't say a spoonful.

SINGER (*starts to go*). Very well, I won't sing a ballad.

BOY. All right. I'll give you a spoonful at the end of each — stanza.

[*He sits on the floor by the pot of lentils.*

SINGER (*sings*).

The Ballad of the Miller and His Six Sons

Six stalwart sons the miller had
All brave and fair to see —
He taught them each a worthy trade —
And they grew gallantly.
Tara — da — da — da-da-da — da-da-da
Tara — da — da — da-de — da-dee.

Give me some lentils.

BOY. Here . . . Hurry up.

SINGER (*sings*).

The first was John of the dimpled chin
And a fist of iron had he —
He learned to wield the broadsword well
And turned to soldiery.
Tara — da — da, etc.

BOY. Please! Please don't stop.

SINGER. Keep to the bargain.

BOY. Here, take two spoonfuls and finish without stopping.

SINGER (*sings rest of ballad*).

> The second son was christened Hugh
> And curly locks had he —
> He learned to use the tabor and lute
> And turned to minstrelsy.
> Tara — da — da, etc.
>
> The third was James of the gentle ways
> And speech of gold had he —
> He learned his psalms and learned his creed
> And turned to simony.
> Tara — da — da, etc.
>
> The fourth was Dick of the hazel eye,
> And a steady hand had he —
> With a hammer and saw and a chest of tools
> He turned to carpentry.
> Tara — da — da, etc.
>
> The fifth was Ned of the velvet tread
> And feather fingers had he.
> He used his gifts in a naughty way
> And turned to burglary.
> Tara — da — da, etc.
>
> The sixth was Robin, surnamed the Rare,
> For always young was he —
> He learned the joy of this sunny world
> And turned to poetry.
> Tara — da — da, etc.
>
> The Miller approached three score and ten,
> A happy man was he,
> His five good sons and the one who was bad
> All turned to gallantry.
> Tara — da — da, etc.

BOY. Sing me another.

SINGER. A spoonful at the end of every stanza.

BOY. Don't stop after you begin.

SINGER. Pay me in advance.

BOY. I suppose I'll have to.

[*He feeds the Ballad-Singer.*

SINGER (*sings second ballad*).

The Ballad of the Three Little Pigs

Two little pigs were pink — pink — pink —
And one little pig was black — black —
The three little pigs were very good friends,
But one little pig was black — black.

Three little pigs would play — play — play —
But one little pig was black — black —
And three little pigs would have a jolly time
Though one little pig was black — black.

Three little pigs soon grew — grew — grew —
And one little pig was black — black.
The three little pigs became fat hogs —
And one fat hog was black — black.

The two fat hogs were pink — pink — pink —
And one fat hog was black — black.
The three fat hogs all made good ham,
Though one fat hog was black — black.

BOY. Sing me another.

SINGER. I can't. I'm tired.

BOY. Are you going to sing those at the beheading?

SINGER. What beheading?

BOY. At the Queen's beheading.

SINGER. Where?

BOY. Over there.

SINGER. When?

BOY. To-day.

SINGER. I must be going. Certainly I'll sing there and I'll take up a collection.

BOY. It's going to be before the King's four clocks strike twelve.

SINGER. It's nearly time now. If I can collect a piece of gold I can buy a vermilion robe and sing at the King's court.

BOY. I could collect a pail of gold and two finger rings and sit at the feet of the King if I'd break a promise.

SINGER. Perhaps you will.

BOY. Would you?

SINGER. I'd rather sing along the highway all my life. It is better to dream of a vermilion robe than to have one that is not honestly got.

BOY. The Blind Man said something like that.

SINGER. Who said what?

BOY. The Blind Man said if I broke a promise I'd never again see a beautiful noble with a golden crown when I closed my eyes.

SINGER. He was right.

BOY. When you get your vermilion robe will you let me see it?

SINGER. That I will. . . . Good-by.

BOY. Good-by.

[*Singer goes out.*

BOY (*hums a snatch of the ballads*).

[*The Headsman steps into the door and plants his axe beside him for an impressive picture. The Boy turns and starts in terror.*

HEADSMAN. Have you seen the Queen?

BOY. Sir?

HEADSMAN. Have you seen the Queen?

BOY. How should I, sir? I've been cooking the lentils.

HEADSMAN. She is here!

BOY. How — could — she — be — here, sir?

HEADSMAN. Well, if she isn't here, where is she?

BOY (*relieved*). I don't know where she is if she isn't here, sir.

HEADSMAN. She has too much sense to hide so near the castle and on the short cut to the headsman's block . . . Do you know who I am?

BOY. I think so — sir.

HEADSMAN. Think? Don't you *know?*

BOY. Yes, sir.

HEADSMAN. Who am I then?

BOY. You're the Dreadful Headsman.

HEADSMAN. I am the winder of the king's four clocks *and* when I am needed I am the best headsman in three kingdoms. And *this* is my axe.

BOY. Is it sharp?

HEADSMAN. It will split a hair in two.

[*Runs finger near blade meaningly.*

BOY. Oh!

HEADSMAN. A hair in two!

BOY. Would you really cut off the Queen's head?

HEADSMAN. That's my business: to cut off heads and the nobler the head the better my business.

BOY. She's such a nice queen.

HEADSMAN. Have you seen her?

BOY. Y — es, sir.

HEADSMAN. When?

BOY. One day — when I was boiling some lentils.

HEADSMAN. Did you see her neck?

BOY. Yes, sir.

HEADSMAN. Not much bigger than a hair.

BOY (*desperately friendly*). Have you seen my knife?

HEADSMAN (*sharply*). *I'm* talking about the Queen and I'm going to talk about myself until I hear the King's trumpeter calling me to the beheading.

BOY. Yes, sir.

[*Edging between the bench and door of the room where the Queen is hidden.*

HEADSMAN. Sit down.

BOY. I'd rather stand, sir.

HEADSMAN. *Sit down!* And I'll tell you how I'm going to behead the Queen.

BOY. You can't behead her after the King's four clocks have struck twelve.

HEADSMAN. How did you know that?

BOY (*realizing his blunder*). Well —

HEADSMAN. Nobody knows that except the royal family and people of the court.

BOY. A little — bird told — me.

HEADSMAN. Where is the little bird that I may cut its head off?

BOY. Don't hurt the little bird, but tell me how you are going to behead the Queen.

HEADSMAN. Well — (*At the stool*) This is the block. There's the Queen behind the iron gate. We'll say that door is the gate.

(*The Boy starts*)

And out there is the crowd. Now, I appear like this and walk up the steps. The crowd cheers, so I bow and show myself and my axe. Then I walk over to the gate —

BOY. Don't go in there. That's my mother's room and you might frighten *her*.

HEADSMAN. Who's in your mother's room?

BOY. *She* is.

HEADSMAN. Well, if she's in there, maybe she'd like to hear my story.

BOY. She's in bed.

HEADSMAN. Sick? (*The Boy nods vigorously*) All right. . . . Well, I've bowed to the crowd and I start for the Queen. — If you won't open the door, you pretend you're the Queen.

BOY. I don't want to be the Queen.

HEADSMAN. Come on and pretend. I walk up to the gate — so, and open it and then I say "Your Majesty, I'm going to cut off you head" and she bows — *bow* — (*The Boy bows*) And then I say "Are you ready?" and she says, "I am ready." Then I blindfold her —

BOY. Now, don't blindfold me, sir!

HEADSMAN. I'm showing you how it's done.

BOY. But if you blindfold me I can't see when you do it.

HEADSMAN (*admitting the point*). All right. . . . Then I blindfold her and I lead her to the block and I say, "Have you made your peace with Heaven?" and she says, "Yes." . . .

BOY. If you won't tell me any more I'll give you my knife.

HEADSMAN. Aren't you interested?

BOY. Yes, but your axe is so sharp and it might slip.

HEADSMAN. Sharp? It will cut a hair in two, but I know how to handle it. . . . Come on . . . (*The Boy reluctantly falls into the picture again*) And then . . . (*Raising his axe*) And then . . . (*Headsman sees the Butterfly*) And then . . . How-d'-ye-do, Butterfly?

[*The Boy runs to the pot unnoticed by the Headsman.*

BOY. Lentils, lentils, boil the time away

That my good queen may live to-day.

[*The Headsman and the Butterfly are having quite a game. Suddenly the great clock begins to strike and the two next larger follow slowly.*

The Headsman rushes to the back door with his axe.

HEADSMAN. Why doesn't the trumpeter blow his call!

[*The Boy counts the strokes of the clock and as the third clock strikes twelve he rushes to the door of the bedroom.*

BOY. Queen! Queen! It's mid-day.

HEADSMAN. Queen — queen — (*He strides to the bedroom and drags the Queen out*) The little clock hasn't struck yet! (*He pulls the Queen toward the rear door and shouts*) Here! Here! don't let the little clock strike! I've won the pail of gold!*

[*The Boy has set the bench in the doorway so that the Headsman stumbles. The Butterfly keeps flying against the Headsman's nose, which makes him sneeze.*

BOY. No one heard you!

QUEEN. Let me go! Let me go!

HEADSMAN (*sneezing as only a headsman can*). The Queen! The Queen!

(*The little clock begins to strike.*

The Boy counts eagerly, one, two, three, etc.

Between strokes the Headsman sneezes and shouts) **The Queen ! The Queen !**

[*At the fifth stroke the Headsman falls on his knees. The Queen becomes regal, her foot on his neck. The Boy kneels at her side.*

QUEEN. Base villain ! According to the law I am saved ! But you are doomed. As Winder of the King's four clocks the law commands that you be decapitated because the four clocks did not strike together. Do you know that law ?

HEADSMAN. Oh, Lady, I do, but I did but do my duty. I was sharpening my axe this morning and I couldn't wind the clocks. Intercede for me.

QUEEN. It is useless.

BOY. Is there any other headsman ?

QUEEN. The law says the Chief Headsman must behead the Chief Winder of the King's four clocks.

BOY. Can the Dreadful Headsman behead himself ?

QUEEN. Aye, there's the difficulty.

HEADSMAN. Oh, your Majesty, pardon me !

BOY. Yes, pardon him.

QUEEN. On one condition : He is to give his axe to the museum and devote all his old age to the care of the King's four clocks. . . . For myself, I shall pass a law requiring the ladies of the court to wear no jewels. So, if the King's aunt can wear no rings, she assuredly cannot have a ring-toe, and hereafter I may step where I please. . . . Sir Headsman, lead the way. . . . And now, my little boy, to you I grant every Friday afternoon an hour's sport with the Mime, a spotted cow for the little Milkmaid, a cushion and a canopy at the palace gate for the Blind Man, a ver-milion cloak for the Ballad-Singer, a velvet gown, a silken kerchief and a cloth-of-gold bonnet for your mother, and for yourself a milk-white palfrey, two pails of gold, two finger rings, a castle and a sword. . . . Arise, Sir Little Boy. . . . Your arm.

BOY. May I take my knife, your Majesty ?

QUEEN. That you may. (*He gets the knife and returns to her. She lays her hand on his arm*) Sir Headsman, announce our coming.

HEADSMAN. Make way — make way — for her Majesty the Queen.

QUEEN (*correcting*). *And* Sir Little Boy.

HEADSMAN. What's his other name, your Majesty?

BOY (*whispering with the wonder of it all*). Davie.

QUEEN (*to the Headsman*). Davie.

HEADSMAN. Make way — make way for her Majesty the Queen and Sir Davie Little Boy.

[*They go out.*

Immediately the Boy returns and gets the pot of lentils and runs after the Queen as

The Curtains Close.

IN THE ZONE

EUGENE O'NEILL

EUGENE O'NEILL was among those who studied in the 47 Workshop at Harvard, where personal association with Professor Baker and his group gave him encouragement to go ahead with his work. But it was his association with the Provincetown Players, which began in 1915, which determined the course of his career.

The Provincetown Players, who played on an old wharf at Provincetown, Massachusetts, in the summer, and in New York City's Greenwich Village during the winter, produced all of the early plays of O'Neill. The dramatic episode, "In the Zone", one of a group of sea plays which O'Neill wrote about the lives of the sailors aboard the *S.S. Glencairn*, was an outstanding success. In fact, the general approval given to all of O'Neill's early plays was undoubtedly the greatest single factor in the subsequent popularity and development of one-act play production in America.

The boy O'Neill was born October 16, 1888, in New York City, the son of James O'Neill, a popular American actor. His first seven years were spent accompanying his father and mother on road tours throughout the United States, after which he attended Catholic and other boarding schools for six years, and in 1902 was sent to Betts Academy in Stamford, Connecticut.

He spent one year at Princeton University (Class of 1910), and then became secretary of a small mail-order house in New York City. In 1909 he joined a gold prospecting expedition to Spanish Honduras, but found no gold. After a short season as assistant manager of a theatrical company which toured the Middle West, he shipped as a sailor on a

Norwegian bark which took sixty-five days to make the trip
from Boston to Buenos Aires. '

In the Argentine he found work first in the drafting
department of the Westinghouse Electrical Company in
Buenos Aires, and then in the Swift Packing Company's plant
at La Plata. Later he worked for the Singer Sewing Machine Company in Buenos Aires.

He made his second trip to sea on a British tramp, from
Buenos Aires to Durban, South Africa, and return, finally
shipping on another British steamer back to New York.
He did not stay in New York long, however, but signed as
an able seaman for service first on the S.S. *New York* and
then on the S.S. *Philadelphia*, both of the American Line.

The following winter, Eugene O'Neill played a part in his
father's tabloid version of "Monte Cristo" on the Orpheum
vaudeville circuit in the Far West. The next summer and
fall he worked as a reporter on the New London, Connecticut,
Telegraph.

In December, 1912, his health broke down, and for a while
he rested in a sanatorium for the cure of tuberculosis. Since
then, he has devoted himself exclusively to writing.

His published works are the one-act plays, *Thirst and
Other One-Act Plays, The Moon of the Caribbees and Six Other
Plays of the Sea;* "Before Breakfast" and "The Dreamy
Kid"; and the longer plays, "Beyond the Horizon",
"Gold", "The Emperor Jones", "Diff'rent", "The Straw",
"The Hairy Ape", "Anna Christie", "The First Man",
"All God's Chillun Got Wings", "Welded", "Desire Under
the Elms", "The Great God Brown", "The Fountain",
"Marco Millions", "Lazarus Laughed", "Strange Inter-
lude", "Dynamo", "Mourning Becomes Electra", "Ah,
Wilderness!", "Days Without End."

He has received the Pulitzer Prize three times, was awarded
a medal for artistic achievement by the American Academy
of Arts and Science, received the honorary degree of Doctor
of Literature from Yale in 1926, and received the Nobel Prize
for Literature in 1936.

His plays are produced and read in England, France, Germany, Russia, Czechoslovakia, the Scandinavian countries, China, and Japan.

Although, since 1924, O'Neill has felt that the one-act form is a limited one for his uses, he still thinks it "a fine vehicle for something poetical, for something spiritual in feeling that cannot be carried through a long play."

IN THE ZONE

By EUGENE G. O'NEILL

"In the Zone" was originally produced by the Washington Square Players, October 31, 1917, at the Comedy Theatre, New York.

Original Cast

Seamen of the tramp steamer (British) *Glencairn*

SMITTY, the "Duke." Twenty-five — slender — his face is refined, and handsome in a weak way. He wears a short blond mustache . . . . . Frederick Roland

DAVIS. Middle-aged — thin face with a black mustache. . . . . Robert Strange

OLSON. Middle-aged — short stocky Swede with a bushy blond mustache . . . . William Gillette

SCOTTY. Just past twenty — thin and wiry — sandy hair . . . . Eugene Lincoln

IVAN. In the thirties — hulking and awkward, with a broad, stupid, swarthy face . . . . Edward Balzerit

YANK. Twenty-eight — tall, well-built, dark, and rather good-looking in a tough sort of way . . . Gay Strong

DRISCOLL. Thirty — a powerfully-built Irishman with a battered, good-natured face . . . . . Arthur Hohl

COCKY. Fifty — a wizened runt of a man with a straggling wisp of gray mustache . . . . . Rienzi de Cordova

IN THE ZONE

SCENE. *The seamen's forecastle of the British tramp steamer Glencairn, an irregular-shaped compartment, the sides of which almost meet at the far end to form a triangle. Sleeping bunks about six feet long, ranged three deep, with a space of two feet separating the upper from the lower, are built against the sides. On the right, above the bunks, three or four portholes covered with black cloth can be seen. In front of the bunks, rough wooden benches. Over the bunks on the left, a lamp in a bracket. In the left foreground, a doorway. On the floor near it, a pail with a tin dipper. Oilskins are hanging from hooks near the doorway.*

The far side of the forecastle is so narrow that it contains only one series of bunks. In under the bunks a glimpse can be had of sea chests, suitcases, sea boots, etc., jammed in indiscriminately.

The lamp is not lit. A lantern in the middle of the floor, turned down very low, throws a dim light around the place. Five men — Scotty, Ivan, Olson, Smitty, and the Norwegian, Paul—are in their bunks, apparently asleep. There is no sound but the deep breathing of the sleepers and the rustling of the oilskins against each other as the ship rolls. It is about ten minutes of twelve in the night. The time is the spring of 1915.

Smitty turns slowly in his bunk, and, leaning out over the side, looks from one to another of the men as if he were assuring himself they were asleep. Then he climbs carefully out of his bunk and stands in the middle of the forecastle, fully dressed, but in his stocking feet, glancing around him suspiciously. Reassured, he leans down and cautiously pulls out a suitcase from under the bunks in front of him. •

Just at that moment Davis appears in the doorway, carrying a large steaming coffee pot in his hand. He stops short when he sees Smitty. A puzzled expression comes over his face, followed by one of suspicion, and he retreats farther back in the alleyway, where he can watch Smitty without being seen.

All of the latter's movements indicate a fear of discovery. He takes out a small bunch of keys and unlocks the suitcase, making a slight noise as he does so. Scotty wakes up and peers at him over the side of his bunk. Smitty opens the suitcase and takes out a small black tin box. Scotty's eyes nearly pop out of his head with fright when he sees this, but he shuts them tight as Smitty turns around, and opens them again in time to see him place the black box carefully under his mattress. Smitty then climbs back into his bunk, taking great care to make no noise, closes his eyes, and commences to snore loudly.

Davis enters the forecastle, places the coffee pot beside the lantern, and goes from one to the other of the sleepers — with the exception of Paul, who is day man — and shakes them vigorously, saying to each in a low voice, "Near eight bells, Scotty. Arise and shine, Ollie. Eight bells, Ivan." *He stops before Smitty's bunk and looks at him with a keen glance of mistrust which is both curious and timid. He reaches out his hand to grab Smitty's shoulder, hesitates, and finally ends up by saying gruffly:* "Eight bells, Smitty." *Upon which he sits down on a bench as far away from Smitty as the narrow forecastle will permit, glancing at him every moment out of the corner of his eye.*

Smitty yawns loudly with a great pretence of having been dead asleep. All the rest of the men tumble out of their bunks, stretching and gaping, and commence to pull on their shoes. Except for these, they are fully dressed. Scotty betrays great inward uneasiness, staring suspiciously at Smitty whenever the latter's back is turned.

They go one by one to the cupboard which is near the open doorway, front, and take out their cups and spoons, put sugar in the cups, grab a couple of sea-biscuits, and sit down together on the benches. The coffee pot is passed around and placed

*back again beside the lantern.   They munch their biscuits and
sip their coffee in a dull silence.*

DAVIS (*suddenly jumping to his feet — nervously*).   Where's
that air comin' from?

[*All are startled and look at him wonderingly.*

OLSON (*grumpily*).   What air?   I don't feel not'ing.

DAVIS (*excitedly*).   I kin feel it — a draft.   (*He stands on
the bench and looks around — suddenly exploding*)   Damn
fool square-head!   (*He leans over the upper bunk in which
Paul is sleeping and slams the porthole shut*)   I got a good
notion to report him.   Serve him bloody well right!
What's the use o' blindin' the ports when that thick-head
goes an' leaves 'em open?

OLSON (*yawning — too sleepy to be aroused by anything —
carelessly*).   Dey don't see what little light go out yust
one port.

SCOTTY (*protestingly*).   Dinna be a loon, Ollie!   D'ye no ken
the dangerr o' showin' a licht wi' a pack o' submarrines
lyin' aboot?

IVAN (*shaking his shaggy ox-like head in an emphatic affirmative*).   Dot's right, Scotty.   I don' li-ike blow up, no, by
devil!

SMITTY (*his manner slightly contemptuous*).   I don't think
there's much danger of meeting any of their submarines,
not until we get into the war zone, at any rate.

DAVIS (*he and Scotty look at Smitty suspiciously — harshly*).
You don't, eh?   (*He lowers his voice and speaks slowly*)
Well, we're in the war zone right this minit if you wants to
know.

[*The effect of this speech is instantaneous.   All sit bolt upright on their benches and stare at Davis.*

SMITTY.   How do you know, Davis?

DAVIS (*angrily*).   'Cos Drisc heard the First send the Third
below to wake the skipper when we fetched the zone —
bout five bells, it was.   Now whata y' got to say?

SMITTY (*conciliatingly*).   Oh, I wasn't doubting your word,
Davis; but you know they're not pasting up bulletins to

let the crew know when the zone is reached — especially on ammunition ships like this.

IVAN (*decidedly*). I don' li-ike dees voyage. Next time I ship on windjammer Boston to River Plate, load with wood only so it float, by golly!

OLSON (*fretfully*). I hope British navy blow 'em to hell, those submarines, py damn!

SCOTTY (*looking at Smitty, who is staring at the doorway in a dream, his chin on his hands. Meaningly*). It's no the submarrines only we've to fear, I'm thinkin', Ollie.

DAVIS (*assenting eagerly*). That's no lie, Scotty.

OLSON. You mean the mines?

SCOTTY. I wasna thinkin' o' mines eitherr.

DAVIS. There's many a good ship blown up and at the bottom of the sea, Ollie, what never hit no mine or torpedo.

SCOTTY. Did ye neverr read of the Gerrman spies and the dirrty work they're doin' all the war?

[*He and Davis both glance at Smitty, who is deep in thought and is not listening to the conversation.*

DAVIS. An' the clever way they fool you!

OLSON. Sure; I read it in paper many time.

DAVIS. Well — (*He is about to speak, but hesitates and finishes lamely*) You got to watch out, that's all I says.

IVAN (*drinking the last of his coffee and slamming his fist on the bench — explosively*). I tell you dis rotten coffee give me belly-ache, yes!

[*They all look at him in amused disgust.*

SCOTTY (*sardonically*). Dinna fret aboot it, Ivan. If we blow up ye'll no be mindin' the pain in your middle.

[*Yank enters. He wears dungarees and a heavy jersey.*

YANK. Eight bells, fellers.

IVAN (*stupidly*). I don' hear bell ring.

YANK. No, and yuh won't hear any ring, yuh boob — (*lowering his voice unconsciously*) now we're in the war zone.

OLSON (*anxiously*). Is the boats all ready?

YANK. Sure; we can lower 'em in a second.

DAVIS. A lot o' good the boats'll do, with us loaded deep with all kinds o' dynamite and stuff the like o' that! If a torpedo hits this hooker we'll all be in hell b'fore you could wink your eye.

YANK. They ain't goin' to hit us, see? That's my dope. Whose wheel is it?

IVAN (*sullenly*). My wheel.

[*He lumbers out.*

YANK. And whose lookout?

OLSON. Mine, I tink.

[*He follows Ivan.*

YANK (*scornfully*). A hell of a lot of use keepin' a lookout! We couldn't run away or fight if we wanted to. (*To Scotty and Smitty*) Better look up the bo'sun or the Fourth, you two, and let 'em see you're awake. (*Scotty goes to the doorway and turns to wait for Smitty, who is still in the same position, head on hands, seemingly unconscious of everything. Yank slaps him roughly on the shoulder and he comes to with a start*) Aft and report, Duke! What's the matter with yuh — in a dope dream? (*Smitty goes out after Scotty without answering. Yank looks after him with a frown*) He's a queer guy. I can't figger him out.

DAVIS. Nor no one else. (*Lowering his voice — meaningly*) An' he's liable to turn out queerer than any of us think, if we ain't careful.

YANK (*suspiciously*). What d'yuh mean?

[*They are interrupted by the entrance of Driscoll and Cocky.*

COCKY (*protestingly*). Blimey if I don't fink I'll put in this 'ere watch ahtside on deck. (*He and Driscoll go over and get their cups*) I down't want to be caught in this 'ole if they 'its us.

[*He pours out coffee.*

DRISCOLL (*pouring his*). Divil a bit ut wud matther where ye arre. Ye'd be blown to smithereens b'fore ye cud say your name. (*He sits down, overturning as he does so the untouched cup of coffee which Smitty had forgotten and left on the bench. They all jump nervously as the tin cup hits the*

floor with a bang. Driscoll flies into an unreasoning rage)
Who's the dirty scut left this cup where a man 'ud sit on ut?

DAVIS. It's Smitty's.

DRISCOLL (*kicking the cup across the forecastle*). Does he think
he's too much av a bloody gentleman to put his own away
loike the rist av us? If he does, I'm the bye'll beat that
noshun out av his head.

COCKY. Be the airs 'e puts on you'd think 'e was the Prince
of Wales. Wot's 'e doin' on a ship, I arsks yer? 'E
ain't now good as a sailor, is 'e? — dawdlin' abaht on deck
like a chicken wiv 'is 'ead cut orf!

YANK (*good-naturedly*). Aw, the Duke's all right. S'posin'
he did ferget his cup — what's the dif? (*He picks up the
cup and puts it away — with a grin*) This war zone stuff's
got yer goat, Drisc — and yours too, Cocky — and I
ain't cheerin' much fur it myself neither.

COCKY (*with a sigh*). Blimey, it ain't no bleedin' joke, it
ain't, yer first trip, to know as there's a ship full of shells
li'ble to go 'orf in under your bloomin' feet, as you might
say, if we gets 'it be a torpedo or mine. (*With sudden
savagery*) Calls theyselves 'uman bein's, too! Blarsted
'Uns!

DRISCOLL (*gloomily*). 'Tis me last trip in the bloody Zone,
God help me. The divil take their twenty-foive per cent
bonus — and be drowned like a rat in a trap in the bargain, maybe.

DAVIS. Wouldn't be so bad if she wasn't carryin' ammunition.
Them's the kind the subs is layin' for.

DRISCOLL (*irritably*). Fur the love av hivin, don't be talkin'
about ut. I'm sick wid thinkin' and jumpin' at iviry bit
av a noise.

[*There is a pause during which they all stare gloomily at the
floor.*

YANK. Hey, Davis, what was you sayin' about Smitty when
they come in?

DAVIS (*with a great air of mystery*). I'll tell you in a minit.
I want to wait an' see if he's comin' back. (*Impressively*)

You won't be callin' him all right when you hears what
I seen with my own eyes. (*He adds with an air of satisfaction*) An' you won't be feelin' no safer, neither.
[*They all look at him with puzzled glances full of a vague
apprehension.*

DRISCOLL (*fiercely*). God blarst ut!
[*He fills his pipe and lights it. The others, with an air of
remembering something they had forgotten, do the same.
Scotty enters.*

SCOTTY (*in awed tones*). Mon, but it's clear ootside the
nicht! Like day.

DAVIS (*in low tones*). Where's Smitty, Scotty?

SCOTTY. Out on the hatch starin' at the moon like a
mon half-daft.

DAVIS. Kin you see him from the doorway?

DAVIS (*goes to doorway and carefully peeks out*). Aye; he's
still there.

DAVIS. Keep your eyes on him for a moment. I've got
something I wants to tell the boys and I don't want him
walkin' in in the middle of it. Give a shout if he starts
this way.

SCOTTY (*with suppressed excitement*). Aye, I'll watch him.
And I've somethin' myself to tell aboot his Lordship.

DRISCOLL (*impatiently*). Out wid ut! You're talkin' more
than a pair av auld women wud be, standin' in the road,
and gettin' no further along.

DAVIS. Listen! You 'member when I went to git the coffee,
Yank?

YANK. Sure, I do.

DAVIS. Well, I brings it down here same as usual and got as
far as the door there when I sees him.

YANK. Smitty?

DAVIS. Yes, Smitty! He was standin' in the middle of the
fo'c's'tle there (*pointing*) lookin' around sneakin'-like at
Ivan and Ollie and the rest, 'sif he wants to make certain
they're asleep.

[*He pauses significantly, looking from one to the other of his listeners. Scotty is nervously dividing his attention between Smitty on the hatch outside and Davis' story, fairly bursting to break in with his own revelations.*

YANK (*impatiently*). What of it?

DAVIS. Listen! He was standin' right there — (*pointing again*) in his stockin' feet — no shoes on, mind, so he wouldn't make no noise!

YANK (*spitting disgustedly*). Aw!

DAVIS (*not heeding the interruption*). I seen right away somethin' on the queer was up, so I slides back into the alleyway where I kin see him but he can't see me. After he makes sure they're all asleep he goes in under the bunks there — bein' careful not to raise a noise, mind! — an' takes out his bag there. (*By this time every one, Yank included, is listening breathlessly to his story*) Then he fishes in his pocket an' takes out a bunch o' keys an' kneels down beside the bag an' opens it.

SCOTTY (*unable to keep silent longer*). Mon, didn't I see him do that same thing wi' these two eyes. 'Twas just that moment I woke and spied him.

DAVIS (*surprised, and a bit nettled to have to share his story with any one*). Oh, you seen him too, eh? (*To the others*) Then Scotty kin tell you if I'm lyin' or not.

DRISCOLL. An' what did he do whin he'd the bag opened?

DAVIS. He bends down and reaches out his hand sort o' scared-like, like it was somethin' dang'rous he was after, an' feels round in under his duds — hidden in under his duds an' wrapped up in 'em, it was — an' he brings out a black iron box!

COCKY (*looking around him with a frightened glance*). Gawd blimey!

[*The others likewise betray their uneasiness, shuffling their feet nervously.*

DAVIS. Ain't that right, Scotty?

SCOTTY. Right as rain, I'm tellin' ye!

DAVIS (*to the others with an air of satisfaction*). There you are! (*Lowering his voice*) An' then what d'you suppose he did? Sneaks to his bunk an' slips the black box in under his mattress — in under his mattress, mind! —

YANK. And it's there now?

DAVIS. Corse it is!

[*Yank starts toward Smitty's bunk. Driscoll grabs him by the arm.*

DRISCOLL. Don't be touchin' ut, Yank!

YANK. Yuh needn't worry. I ain't goin' to touch it. (*He pulls up Smitty's mattress and looks down. The others stare at him, holding their breaths. He turns to them, trying hard to assume a careless tone*) It's there, aw right.

COCKY (*miserably upset*). I'm gointer 'op it aht on deck. (*He gets up, but Driscoll pulls him down again. Cocky protests*) It fair guvs me the trembles sittin' still in 'ere.

DRISCOLL (*scornfully*). Are ye frightened, ye toad? 'Tis a hell av a thing fur grown men to be shiverin' loike childer at a bit av a black box. (*Scratching his head in uneasy perplexity*) Still, ut's damn queer, the looks av ut.

DAVIS (*sarcastically*). A bit of a black box, eh? How big d'you think them — (*he hesitates*) — things has to be — big as this fo'c's'le?

YANK (*in a voice meant to be reassuring*). Aw, hell! I'll bet it ain't nothin' but some coin he's saved he's got locked up in there.

DAVIS (*scornfully*). That's likely, ain't it? Then why does he act so s'picious? He's been on ship near a year, ain't he? He knows damn well there ain't no thiefs in this fo'c's'le, don't he? An' you know 'swell 's I do he didn't have no money when he came on board an' he ain't saved none since. Don't you? (*Yank doesn't answer*) Listen! D'you know what he done after he put that thing in under his mattress? — an' Scotty'll tell you if I ain't speakin' truth. He looks round to see if any one's woke up.

SCOTTY. I clapped my eyes shut when he turned round.

DAVIS. An' then he crawls into his bunk an' shuts his eyes, an' starts in *snorin'*, *pretendin'* he was asleep, mind!

SCOTTY. Aye, I could hear him.

DAVIS. An' when I goes to call him I don't even shake him. I just says: "Eight bells, Smitty" in a'most a whisper-like, an' up he gets yawnin' an' stretchin' fit to kill hisself 'sif he'd been dead asleep.

COCKY. Gawd blimey!

DRISCOLL (*shaking his head*). Ut looks bad, divil a doubt av ut.

DAVIS (*excitedly*). An' now I come to think of it, there's the porthole. How'd it come to git open, tell me that? I know'd well Paul never opened it. Ain't he grumblin' about bein' cold all the time?

SCOTTY. The mon that opened it meant no good to this ship, whoever he was.

YANK (*sourly*). What porthole? What're yuh talkin' about?

DAVIS (*pointing over Paul's bunk*). There. It was open when I come in. I felt the cold air on my neck an' shut it. It would'a been clear's a lighthouse to any sub that was watchin' — an' we s'posed to have all the ports blinded! Who'd do a dirty trick like that? It wasn't none of us, nor Scotty here, nor Olson, nor Ivan. Who would it be, then?

COCKY (*angrily*). Must'a been 'is bloody Lordship.

DAVIS. For all's we know he might'a been signallin' with it. They does it like that by winkin' a light. Ain't you read how they gets caught doin' it in London an' on the coast?

COCKY (*firmly convinced now*). An' wots 'e doin' aht alone on the 'atch — keepin' 'isself clear of us like 'e was afraid?

DRISCOLL. Kape your eye on him, Scotty.

SCOTTY. There's no a move oot o' him.

YANK (*in irritated perplexity*). But, hell, ain't he an Eng-lishman? What'd he want a —

DAVIS. English? How d'we know he's English? Cos he talks it? That ain't no proof. Ain't you read in the papers how all them German spies they been catchin' in England has been livin' there for ten, often as not twenty years, an' talks English as good's any one? An' look here,

ain't you noticed he don't talk natural? He talks it too
damn good, that's what I mean. He don't talk exactly
like a toff, does he, Cocky?

COCKY. Not like any toff as I ever met up wiv.

DAVIS. No; an' he don't talk it like us, that's certain.
An' he don't look English. An' what d'we know about
him when you come to look at it? Nothin'! He ain't
ever said where he comes from or why. All we knows is
he ships on here in London six months b'fore the war starts,
as an A.B. — stole his papers most lik'ly — when he don't
know how to box the compass, hardly. Ain't that queer
in itself? An' was he ever open with us like a good ship-
mate? No; he's always had that sly air about him 's if
he was hidin' somethin'.

DRISCOLL (*slapping his thigh — angrily*). Divil take me if
I don't think ye have the truth av ut, Davis.

COCKY (*scornfully*). Lettin' on be 'is silly airs, and all, 'e's
the son of a blarsted earl or somethink!

DAVIS. An' the name he calls hisself — Smith! I'd risk a
quid of my next pay day that his real name is Schmidt, if
the truth was known.

YANK (*evidently fighting against his own conviction*). Aw,
say, you guys give me a pain! What'd they want puttin'
a spy on this old tub for?

DAVIS (*shaking his head sagely*). They're deep ones, an'
there's a lot o' things a sailor'll see in the ports he puts in
ought to be useful to 'em. An' if he kin signal to 'em an'
they blows us up it's one ship less, ain't it? (*Lowering
his voice and indicating Smitty's bunk*) Or if he blows us
up hisself.

SCOTTY (*in alarmed tones*). Hush, mon! Here he comes!

[*Scotty hurries over to a bench and sits down. A thick silence
settles over the forecastle. The men look from one to another
with uneasy glances. Smitty enters and sits down beside his
bunk. He is seemingly unaware of the dark glances of suspicion directed at him from all sides. He slides his hand back
stealthily over his mattress and his fingers move, evidently feel-*

ing to make sure the box is still there.   The others follow this movement carefully with quick looks out of the corners of their eyes.   Their attitudes grow tense as if they were about to spring at him.   Satisfied the box is safe, Smitty draws his hand away slowly and utters a sigh of relief.

SMITTY (*in a casual tone which to them sounds sinister*). It's a good light night for the subs if there's any about.

[*For a moment he sits staring in front of him.   Finally he seems to sense the hostile atmosphere of the forecastle and looks from one to the other of the men in surprise.   All of them avoid his eyes.   He sighs with a puzzled expression and gets up and walks out of the doorway.   There is silence for a moment after his departure and then a storm of excited talk breaks loose.*

DAVIS.   Did you see him feelin' if it was there?

COCKY.   'E ain't arf a sly one wiv 'is talk of submarines, Gawd blind 'im!

SCOTTY.   Did ye see the sneekin' looks he gave us?

DRISCOLL.   If ivir I saw black shame on a man's face 'twas on his whin he sat there!

YANK (*thoroughly convinced at last*).   He looked bad to me. He's a crook, aw right.

DAVIS (*excitedly*).   What'll we do?   We gotter do somethin' quick or —

[*He is interrupted by the sound of something hitting against the port side of the forecastle with a dull, heavy thud.   The men start to their feet in wild-eyed terror and turn as if they were going to rush for the deck.   They stand that way for a strained moment, scarcely breathing, and listening intently.*

YANK (*with a sickly smile*).   Hell!   It's on'y a piece of driftwood or a floatin' log.

[*He sits down again.*

DAVIS (*sarcastically*).   Or a mine that didn't go of — that time — or a piece o' wreckage from some ship they've sent to Davy Jones.

COCKY (*mopping his brow with a trembling hand*).   Blimey!

[*He sinks back weakly on a bench.*

DRISCOLL (*furiously*). God blarst ut! No man at all cud be puttin' up wid the loike av this — an' I'm not wan to be fearin' anything or any man in the worrld'll stand up to me face to face; but this divil's thrickery in the darrk — (*he starts for Smitty's bunk*) I'll throw ut out wan av the portholes an' be done wid ut.

[*He reaches toward the mattress.*

SCOTTY (*grabbing his arm — wildly*). Arre ye daft, mon?

DAVIS. Don't monkey with it, Drisc. I knows what to do. Bring the bucket o' water here, Yank, will you? (*Yank gets it and brings it over to Davis*) An' you, Scotty, see if he's back on the hatch.

SCOTTY (*cautiously peering out*). Aye, he's sittin' there the noo.

DAVIS. Sing out if he makes a move. Lift up the mattress, Drisc, — careful now! (*Driscoll does so with infinite caution*) Take it out, Yank — careful — don't shake it now, for Christ's sake! Here — put it in the water — easy! There, that's fixed it! (*They all sit down with great sighs of relief*) The water'll git in and spoil it.

DRISCOLL (*slapping Davis on the back*). Good wurrk for ye, Davis, ye scut! (*He spits on his hands aggressively*) An' now what's to be done wid that blackhearted thraitor?

COCKY (*belligerently*). Guv 'im a shove in the marf and 'eave 'im over the side!

DAVIS. An' serve him right!

YANK. Aw say, give him a chance. Yuh can't prove nothin' till yuh find out what's in there.

DRISCOLL (*heatedly*). Is ut more proof ye'd be needin' afther what we've seen an' heard? Then listen to me — an' ut's Driscoll talkin' — if there's divilmint in that box an' we see plain 'twas his plan to murrdher his own shipmates that have served him fair — (*he raises his fist*) I'll choke his rotten hearrt out wid me own hands, an' over the side wid him, and one man missin' in the mornin'.

DAVIS. An' noone the wiser. He's the balmy kind what commits suicide.

COCKY. They 'angs spies ashore.

YANK (*resentfully*). If he's done what yuh think I'll croak him myself. Is that good enough for yuh?

DRISCOLL (*looking down at the box*). How'll we be openin' this, I wonder?

SCOTTY (*from the doorway — warningly*). He's standin' up.

DAVIS. We'll take his keys away from him when he comes in. Quick, Drisc! You an' Yank get beside the door and grab him. (*They get on either side of the door. Davis snatches a small coil of rope from one of the upper bunks*) This'll do for me an' Scotty to tie him.

SCOTTY. He's turrnin' this way — he's comin'!

[*He moves away from door.*

DAVIS. Stand by to lend a hand, Cocky.

COCKY. Righto.

[*As Smitty enters the forecastle he is seized roughly from both sides and his arms pinned behind him. At first he struggles fiercely, but seeing the uselessness of this, he finally stands calmly and allows Davis and Scotty to tie up his arms.*

SMITTY (*when they have finished — with cold contempt*). If this is your idea of a joke I'll have to confess it's a bit too thick for me to enjoy.

COCKY (*angrily*). Shut yer marf, 'ear!

DRISCOLL (*roughly*). Ye'll find ut's no joke, me bucko, b'fore we're done wid you. (*To Scotty*) Kape your eye peeled, Scotty, and sing out if any one's comin'.

[*Scotty resumes his post at the door.*

SMITTY (*with the same icy contempt*). If you'd be good enough to explain —

DRISCOLL (*furiously*). Explain, is ut? 'Tis you'll do the explainin' — an' damn quick, or we'll know the reason why. (*To Yank and Davis*) Bring him here, now. (*They push Smitty over to the bucket*) Look here, ye murrdherin' swab. D'you see ut?

[*Smitty looks down with an expression of amazement which rapidly changes to one of anguish.*

DAVIS (*with a sneer*). Look at him! S'prised, ain't you? If you wants to try your dirty spyin' tricks on us you've gotter git up earlier in the mornin'.

COCKY. Thorght yer weren't 'arf a fox, didn't yer?

SMITTY (*trying to restrain his growing rage*). What — what do you mean? That's only — How dare — What are you doing with my private belongings?

COCKY (*sarcastically*). Ho yus! Private b'longings!

DRISCOLL (*shouting*). What is ut, ye swine? Will you tell us to our faces? What's in ut?

SMITTY (*biting his lips — holding himself in check with a great effort*). Nothing but — That's my business. You'll please attend to your own.

DRISCOLL. Oho, ut is, is ut? (*Shaking his fist in Smitty's face*) Talk aisy now if ye know what's best for you. Your business, indade! Then we'll be makin' ut our's, I'm thinkin'. (*To Yank and Davis*) Take his keys away from him an' we'll see if there's one'll open ut, maybe. (*They start in searching Smitty, who tries to resist and kicks out at the bucket. Driscoll leaps forward and helps them push him away*) Try to kick ut over, wud ye? Did ye see him then? Tryin' to murrdher us all, the scut! Take that pail out av his way, Cocky.

[*Smitty struggles with all of his strength and keeps them busy for a few seconds. As Cocky grabs the pail Smitty makes a final effort and, lunging forward, kicks again at the bucket, but only succeeds in hitting Cocky on the shin. Cocky immediately sets down the pail with a bang and, clutching his knee in both hands, starts hopping around the forecastle, groaning and swearing.*

COCKY. Ooow! Gawd strike me pink! Kicked me, 'e did! Bloody, bleedin', rotten Dutch 'og! (*Approaching Smitty, who has given up the fight and is pushed back against the wall near the doorway with Yank and Davis holding him on either side — wrathfully, at the top of his lungs*) Kick me, will yer? I'll show yer what for, yer bleedin' sneak! !*He draws back his fist. Driscoll pushes him to one side.*

DRISCOLL. Shut your mouth! D'you want to wake the whole ship?

[*Cocky grumbles and retires to a bench, nursing his sore shin.*

YANK (*taking a small bunch of keys from Smitty's pocket*). Here yuh are, Drisc.

DRISCOLL (*taking them*). We'll soon be knowin'.

[*He takes the pail and sits down, placing it on the floor between his feet. Smitty again tries to break loose, but he is too tired and is easily held back against the wall.*

SMITTY (*breathing heavily and very pale*). Cowards!

YANK (*with a growl*). Nix on the rough talk, see! That don't git yuh nothin.'

DRISCOLL (*looking at the lock on the box in the water and then scrutinizing the keys in his hand*). This'll be ut, I'm thinkin'.

[*He selects one and gingerly reaches his hand in the water.*

SMITTY (*his face grown livid — chokingly*). Don't you open that box, Driscoll. If you do, so help me God, I'll kill you if I have to hang for it.

DRISCOLL (*pausing — his hand in the water*). Whin I open this box I'll not be the wan to be kilt, me sonny bye! I'm no dirty spy.

SMITTY (*his voice trembling with rage. His eyes are fixed on Driscoll's hand*). Spy? What are you talking about? I only put that box there so I could get it quick in case we were torpedoed. Are you all mad? Do you think I'm — (*chokingly*) You stupid curs! You cowardly dolts!

[*Davis claps his hand over Smitty's mouth.*

DAVIS. That'll be enough from you!

[*Driscoll takes the dripping box from the water and starts to fit in the key. Smitty springs forward furiously, almost escaping from their grasp, and drags them after him half-way across the forecastle.*

DRISCOLL. Hold him, ye divils!

[*He puts the box back in the water and jumps to their aid. Cocky hovers on the outskirts of the battle, mindful of the kick he received.*

SMITTY (*raging*). Cowards! Damn you! Rotten curs! (*He is thrown to the floor and held there*) Cowards! Cowards!

DRISCOLL. I'll shut your dirty mouth for you. [*He goes to his bunk and pulls out a big wad of waste and comes back to Smitty.*

SMITTY. Cowards! Cowards!

DRISCOLL (*with no gentle hand slaps the waste over Smitty's mouth*). That'll teach you to be misnamin' a man, ye sneak. Have ye a handkerchief, Yank? (*Yank hands him one and he ties it tightly around Smitty's head over the waste*) That'll fix your gab. Stand him up, now, and tie his feet, too, so he'll not be movin'. (*They do so and leave him with his back against the wall near Scotty. Then they all sit down beside Driscoll, who again lifts the box out of the water and sets it carefully on his knees. He picks out the key, then hesitates, looking from one to the other uncertainly*) We'd best be takin' this to the skipper, d'you think, maybe?

YANK (*irritably*). To hell with the old man. This is our game and we c'n play it without no help.

COCKY. No bleedin' horficers, I says!

DAVIS. They'd only be takin' all the credit and makin' heroes of theyselves.

DRISCOLL (*boldly*). Here goes thin. (*He slowly turns the key in the lock. The others instinctively back away. He carefully pushes the cover back on its hinges and looks at what he sees inside with an expression of puzzled astonishment. The others crowd up close. Even Scotty leaves his post to take a look*) What is ut, Davis?

DAVIS (*mystified*). Looks funny, don't it? Somethin' square tied up in a rubber bag. Maybe it's dynamite — or somethin' — you can't never tell.

YANK. Aw, it ain't got no works, so it ain't no bomb, I'll bet.

DAVIS (*dubiously*). They makes them all kinds, they do.

YANK. Open it up, Drisc.

DAVIS. Careful now!

[*Driscoll takes a black rubber bag resembling a large tobacco pouch from the box and unties the string which is wound tightly around the top. He opens it and takes out a small packet of letters also tied up with string. He turns these over in his hands and looks at the others questioningly.*

YANK (*with a broad grin*). On'y letters! (*Slapping Davis on the back*) Yuh're a hell of a Sherlock Holmes, ain't yuh? Letters from his best girl too, I'll bet. Let's turn the Duke loose, what d'yuh say?

[*He starts to get up.*

DAVIS (*fixing him with a withering look*). Don't be so damned smart, Yank. Letters, you says, 's if there never was no harm in 'em. How d'you s'pose spies gets their orders and sends back what they finds out if it ain't by letters and such things? There's many a letter is worser'n any bomb.

COCKY. Righto! They ain't as innercent as they looks, I'll take me oath, when you read 'em. (*Pointing at Smitty*) Not 'is Lordship's letters; not be no means!

YANK (*sitting down again*). Well, read 'em and find out.

[*Driscoll commences untying the packet. There is a muffled groan of rage and protest from Smitty.*

DAVIS (*triumphantly*). There! Listen to him! Look at him tryin' to git loose! Ain't that proof enough? He knows well we're findin' him out. Listen to me! Love letters, you says, Yank, 's if they couldn't harm nothin'. Listen! I was readin' in some magazine in New York on'y two weeks back how some German spy in Paris was writin' love letters to some woman spy in Switzerland who sent 'em on to Berlin, Germany. To read 'em you wouldn't s'pect nothin' — just mush and all. (*Impressively*) But they had a way o' doin' it — a damn sneakin' way. They had a piece o' plain paper with pieces cut out of it an when they puts it on top o' the letter they sees on'y the words what tells them what they wants to know. An' the Frenchies gets beat in a fight all on account o' that letter.

COCKY (*awed*). Gawd blimey! They ain't 'arf smart bleeders!

DAVIS (*seeing his audience is again all with him*). An' even if these letters of his do sound all right they may have what they calls a code. You can't never tell. (*To Driscoll who has finished untying the packet*) Read one of 'em, Drisc. My eyes is weak.

DRISCOLL (*takes the first one out of its envelope and bends down to the lantern with it. He turns up the wick to give him a better light*). I'm no hand to be readin', but I'll try ut.
[*Again there is a muffled groan from Smitty as he strains at his bonds.*

DAVIS (*gloatingly*). Listen to him! He knows. Go ahead, Drisc!

DRISCOLL (*his brow furrowed with concentration*). Ut begins: "Dearest Man — (*His eyes travel down the page*) An' thin there's a lot av blarney tellin' him how much she misses him now she's gone away to singin' school — an' how she hopes he'll settle down to rale worrk an' not be skylarkin' around now that she's away, loike he used to before she met up wid him — and ut ends: "I love you betther than anythin' in the worrld. You know that, don't you, dear? But b'fore I can agree to live out my life wid you, you must prove to me that the black shadow — I won't menshun its hateful name, but you know what I mean — which might wreck both our lives, does not exist for you. You can do that, can't you, dear? Don't you see you must, for my sake?" (*He pauses for a moment — then adds gruffly*) Ut's signed: Edith.
[*At the sound of the name Smitty, who has stood tensely with his eyes shut as if he were undergoing torture during the reading, makes a muffled sound like a sob and half turns his face to the wall.*

YANK (*sympathetically*). Hell! What's the use of readin' that stuff even if —

DAVIS (*interrupting him sharply*). Wait! Where's that letter from, Drisc?

DRISCOLL. There's no address on the top av ut.

DAVIS (*meaningly*). What'd I tell you? Look at the post-mark, Drisc, — on the envelope.

DRISCOLL. The name that's written is Sidney Davidson, wan hunderd an' —

DAVIS. Never mind that. O' corse it's a false name. Look at the postmark.

DRISCOLL. There's a furrin' stamp on ut by the looks av ut. The mark's blurred so it's hard to read. (*He spells it out laboriously*) B-e-r-, the nixt is an l, I think, —i— an' an n.

DAVIS (*excitedly*). Berlin! What did I tell you? I knew them letters was from Germany.

COCKY (*shaking his fist in Smitty's direction*). Rotten 'ound! [*The others look at Smitty as if this last fact had utterly con-demned him in their eyes.*

DAVIS. Give me the letter, Drisc. Maybe I kin make some-thin' out of it. (*Driscoll hands the letter to him*) You go through the others, Drisc, and sing out if you sees anythin' queer.

[*He bends over the first letter as if he were determined to figure out its secret meaning. Yank, Cocky, and Scotty look over his shoulder with eager curiosity. Driscoll takes out some of the other letters, running his eyes quickly down the pages. He looks curiously over at Smitty from time to time, and sighs frequently with a puzzled frown.*

DAVIS (*disappointedly*). I gotter give it up. It's too deep for me, but we'll turn 'em over to the perlice when we docks at Liverpool, to look through. This one I got was written a year before the war started, anyway. Find anythin' in yours, Drisc?

DRISCOLL. They're all the same as the first — lovin' blarney, an' how her singin' is doin', an' the grreat things the Dutch teacher says about her voice, an' how glad she is that her Sidney bye is worrkin' harrd an' makin' a man av himself for her sake.

[*Smitty turns his face completely to the wall.*

DAVIS (*disgustedly*). If we on'y had the code!

DRISCOLL (*taking up the bottom letter*). Hullo! Here's wan addressed to this ship — S.S. *Glencairn*, ut says — whin we was in Cape Town sivin months ago. (*Looking at the postmark*) Ut's from London.

DAVIS (*eagerly*). Read it!

[*There is another choking groan from Smitty.*

DRISCOLL (*reads slowly — his voice becomes lower and lower as he goes on*). Ut begins wid simply the name Sidney Davidson — no dearest or swaetheart to this wan. "Ut is only from your chance meetin' wid Harry — whin you were drunk — that I happen to know where to reach you. So you have run away to sea loike the coward you are, because you knew I had found out the truth — the truth you have covered over wid your mean little lies all the time I was away in Berlin and blindly trusted you. Very well, you have chosen. You have shown that your drunkenness means more to you than any love or faith av mine. I am sorry — for I loved you, Sidney Davidson — but this is the end. I lave you — the mem'ries; an' if ut is any satisfaction to you I lave you the real-i-zation that you have wrecked my loife as you have wrecked your own. My one remainin' hope is that nivir in God's worrld will I ivir see your face again. Good-by, Edith."

[*As he finishes there is a deep silence, broken only by Smitty's muffled sobbing. The men cannot look at each other. Driscoll holds the rubber bag limply in his hand and some small white object falls out of it and drops noiselessly on the floor. Mechanically Driscoll leans over and picks it up, and looks at it wonderingly.*

DAVIS (*in a dull voice*). What's that?

DRISCOLL (*slowly*). A bit av a dried-up flower, — a rose, maybe.

[*He drops it into the bag and gathers up the letters and puts them back. He replaces the bag in the box, and locks it and puts it back in under Smitty's mattress. The others follow him with their eyes. He steps softly over to Smitty and cuts the ropes about his arms and ankles with his sheath knife,*

*and unties the handkerchief over the gag. Smitty does not
turn around, but covers his face with his hands and leans his
head against the wall. His shoulders continue to heave
spasmodically, but he makes no further sound.*

DRISCOLL (*stalks back to the others — there is a moment of silence
in which each man is in agony with the hopelessness of finding
a word he can say — then Driscoll explodes*).　God stiffen us,
are we never goin' to turn in fur a wink av sleep?

[*They all start as if awakening from a bad dream and grate-
fully crawl into their bunks, shoes and all, turning their faces
to the wall, and pulling their blankets up over their shoulders.
Scotty tiptoes past Smitty out into the darkness. Driscoll
turns down the lights and crawls into his bunk as*

THE CURTAIN FALLS

SUPPRESSED DESIRES

GEORGE CRAM COOK

GEORGE CRAM COOK was one of the leaders of the Province-town Players, and directed their productions from 1915 to 1923. "Suppressed Desires", written in collaboration with Susan Glaspell, has been very popular ever since it was first played by the Provincetown group.

Mr. Cook was born in Davenport, Iowa, in 1873. He studied at the University of Iowa, Harvard, Heidelberg, and the University of Geneva. He was professor at the University of Iowa from 1895 to 1899, and at Leland Stanford University from 1902 to 1903. In 1911 he was Associate Literary Editor of the *Chicago Evening Post*.

Mr. Cook and his wife went to Greece in 1920. He died in Delphi in 1923, and was buried there. In recognition of his love of Greece, evidenced in his poems and a play, "The Athenian Woman", which he himself translated into modern Greek and which was published in Athens, the Greek Government had one of the ancient stones from the temple of Apollo used as his headstone. After his death, his poems were collected and published under the title, *Greek Coins*. Susan Glaspell's biography of him, called *The Road to the Temple*, includes a full story of the Provincetown Players.

In addition to the Greek writings, George Cram Cook was the author of : *In Hampton Roads* (novel) ; *Roderick Talia-ferro; Evolution and the Superman* ; *The Chasm* (novel) ; *Battle Hymn of the Workers; An American Hero; The Third American Sex; The W.C.T.U.;* "The Breath of War" (a play) ; "The Spring" (a play) ; and two plays in collaboration with Susan Glaspell : "Suppressed Desires" and "Tickless Time."

SUSAN GLASPELL

AFTER Eugene O'Neill, the Provincetown Players have inspired another Pulitzer prize winner, Susan Glaspell, now Mrs. Norman Matson. She was one of the founders of the Provincetown group, and all of her early plays were produced by them.

Born in Davenport, Iowa, in 1882, she studied at Drake University, Iowa, and there received the degree of Ph.B. After taking post-graduate work at the University of Chicago, she became State House and Legislative Reporter of the *News and the Capital*, Des Moines, Iowa.

She is the author of *Brook Evans*, *Fugitive's Return*, *Ambrose Holt and Family* (all novels); her principal one-act plays are "Trifles", of which she is sole author, and "Tickless Time" and "Suppressed Desires", of which she is co-author. Her full-length plays are "Bernice", "Inheritors", "The Verge", and "Allison's House" (which won the Pulitzer prize of 1932). She has written one long play in collaboration with Norman Matson, — "The Comic Artist", — and a biography of George Cram Cook — *The Road to the Temple*.

SUPPRESSED DESIRES

A FREUDIAN COMEDY

By GEORGE CRAM COOK AND SUSAN GLASPELL

"Suppressed Desires" was originally produced by the Provincetown Players, New York City.

Original Cast

HENRIETTA BREWSTER . . . . . Susan Glaspell
STEPHEN BREWSTER . . . . . . George Cram Cook
MABEL . . . . Mary Pyne

SUPPRESSED DESIRES

Scene I

The stage represents a studio, used as living and dining room in an upper story, Washington Square South. Through an immense north window in the back wall appear tree tops and the upper part of the Washington Arch. Beyond it you look up Fifth Avenue. There are rugs, bookcases, a divan. Near the window is a big table, loaded at one end with serious-looking books and austere scientific periodicals. At the other end are architect's drawings, blue prints, dividing compasses, square, ruler, etc. There is a door in each side wall. Near the one to the spectator's right stands a costumer with hats and coats, masculine and feminine. There is a breakfast table set for three, but only two seated at it — namely Henrietta and Stephen Brewster. As the curtains withdraw Steve pushes back his coffee cup and sits dejected.

HENRIETTA. It isn't the coffee, Steve dear. There's nothing the matter with the coffee. There's something the matter with *you.*

STEVE (*doggedly*). There may be something the matter with my stomach.

HENRIETTA (*scornfully*). Your stomach! The trouble is not with your stomach but in your subconscious mind.

STEVE. Subconscious piffle!

[*Takes morning paper and tries to read.*

HENRIETTA. Steve, you never used to be so disagreeable. You certainly have got some sort of a complex. You're all inhibited. You're no longer open to new ideas. You won't listen to a word about psychoanalysis.

STEVE. A word! I've listened to volumes!

HENRIETTA. You've ceased to be creative in architecture — your work isn't going well. You're not sleeping well —

STEVE. How can I sleep, Henrietta, when you're always waking me up in the night to find out what I'm dreaming?

HENRIETTA. But dreams are so important, Steve. If you'd tell yours to Dr. Russell he'd find out exactly what's wrong with you.

STEVE. There's nothing wrong with me.

HENRIETTA. You don't even talk as well as you used to.

STEVE. Talk? I can't say a thing without you looking at me in that dark fashion you have when you're on the trail of a complex.

HENRIETTA. This very irritability indicates that you're suffering from some suppressed desire.

STEVE. I'm suffering from a suppressed desire for a little peace.

HENRIETTA. Dr. Russell is doing simply wonderful things with nervous cases. Won't you go to him, Steve?

STEVE (*slamming down his newspaper*). No Henrietta, I won't!

HENRIETTA. But, Stephen —!

STEVE. Tst! I hear Mabel coming. Let's not be at each other's throats the first day of her visit.

[*He takes out cigarettes. Enter Mabel from door left, the side opposite Steve, so that he is facing her. She is wearing a rather fussy negligee and breakfast cap in contrast to Henrietta, who wears "radical" clothes. Mabel is what is called plump.*

MABEL. Good morning.

HENRIETTA. Oh, here you are, little sister.

STEVE. Good morning, Mabel. [*Mabel nods to him and turns, her face lighting up, to Henrietta.*

HENRIETTA (*giving Mabel a hug as she leans against her*). It's so good to have you here. I was going to let you sleep, thinking you'd be tired after the long trip. Sit down. There'll be fresh toast in a minute and (*rising from her chair*) will you have —

MABEL. Oh, I ought to have told you, Henrietta. Don't get anything for me. I'm not eating any breakfast.

HENRIETTA (*at first in mere surprise*). Not eating breakfast? [*She sits down, then leans toward Mabel and scrutinizes her.*

STEVE (*half to himself*). The psychoanalytical look!

HENRIETTA. Mabel, why are you not eating breakfast?

MABEL (*a little startled*). Why, no particular reason. I just don't care much for breakfast, and they say it keeps down — that is, it's a good thing to go without it.

HENRIETTA. Don't you sleep well? Did you sleep well last night?

MABEL. Oh, yes, I sleep all right. Yes, I slept fine last night, only (*laughing*) I did have the funniest dream!

STEVE. S — h! S — t!

HENRIETTA (*moving closer*). And what did you dream, Mabel?

STEVE. Look-a-here, Mabel, I feel it's my duty to put you on. Don't tell Henrietta your dreams. If you do she'll find out that you have an underground desire to kill your father and marry your mother —

HENRIETTA. Don't be absurd, Stephen Brewster. (*Sweetly to Mabel*) What was your dream, dear?

MABEL (*laughing*). Well, I dreamed I was a hen.

HENRIETTA. A hen?

MABEL. Yes; and I was pushing along through a crowd as fast as I could, but being a hen I couldn't walk very fast — it was like having a tight skirt, you know; and there was some sort of creature in a blue cap — you know how mixed up dreams are — and it kept shouting after me and saying, "Step, Hen! Step, Hen!" until I got all excited and just couldn't move at all.

HENRIETTA (*resting chin in palm and peering*). You say you became much excited?

MABLE (*laughing*). Oh, yes; I was in a terrible state.

HENRIETTA (*leaning back, murmurs*). This is significant.

STEVE. She dreams she's a hen. She is told to step lively. She becomes violently agitated. What can it mean?

HENRIETTA (*turning impatiently from him*). Mabel, do you know anything about psychoanalysis?

MABEL (*feebly*). Oh — not much. No — I — (*brightening*) It's something about the war, isn't it?

STEVE. Not that kind of war.

MABEL (*abashed*). I thought it might be the name of a new explosive.

STEVE. It *is*.

MABEL (*apologetically to Henrietta, who is frowning*). You see, Henrietta, I — we do not live in touch with intellectual things, as you do. Bob being a dentist — somehow — our friends —

STEVE (*softly*). Oh to be a dentist!
[*Goes to window and stands looking out.*

HENRIETTA. Don't you ever see anything more of that editorial writer — what was his name?

MABEL. Lyman Eggleston?

HENRIETTA. Yes, Eggleston. He was in touch with things. Don't you see him?

MABEL. Yes, I see him once in a while. Bob doesn't like him very well.

HENRIETTA. Your husband does not like Lyman Eggleston? (*Mysteriously*) Mabel, are you perfectly happy with your husband?

STEVE (*sharply*). Oh, come now, Henrietta — that's going a little strong!

HENRIETTA. Are you perfectly happy with him, Mabel?
[*Steve goes to work-table.*

MABEL. Why — yes — I guess so. Why — of course I am!

HENRIETTA. Are you happy? Or do you only think you are? Or do you only think you *ought* to be?

MABEL. Why, Henrietta, I don't know what you mean!

STEVE (*seizes stack of books and magazines and dumps them on the breakfast table*). This is what she means, Mabel. Psychoanalysis. My work-table groans with it. Books by Freud, the new Messiah; books by Jung, the new St.

Paul; the Psycho-analytical Review — back numbers two-fifty per.

MABEL. But what's it all about?

STEVE. All about your sub-un-non-conscious mind and desires you know not of. They may be doing you a great deal of harm. You may go crazy with them. Oh, yes! People are doing it right and left. Your dreaming you're a hen —

[*Shakes his head darkly.*

HENRIETTA. Any fool can ridicule anything.

MABEL (*hastily, to avert a quarrel*). But what do you say it is, Henrietta?

STEVE (*looking at his watch*). Oh, if Henrietta's going to start that!

[*He goes to his work-table, and during Henrietta's next speech settles himself and sharpens a lead pencil.*

HENRIETTA. It's like this, Mabel. You want something. You think you can't have it. You think it's wrong. So you try to think you don't want it. Your mind protects you — avoids pain — by refusing to think the forbidden thing. But it's there just the same. It stays there shut up in your unconscious mind, and it festers.

STEVE. Sort of an ingrowing mental toenail.

HENRIETTA. Precisely. The forbidden impulse is there full of energy which has simply got to do something. It breaks into your consciousness in disguise, masks itself in dreams, makes all sorts of trouble. In extreme cases it drives you insane.

MABEL (*with a gesture of horror*). Oh!

HENRIETTA (*reassuringly*). But psychoanalysis has found out how to save us from that. It brings into consciousness the suppressed desire that was making all the trouble. Psychoanalysis is simply the latest scientific method of preventing and curing insanity.

STEVE (*from his table*). It is also the latest scientific method of separating families.

HENRIETTA (*mildly*). Families that ought to be separated.

STEVE. The Dwights, for instance. You must have met them, Mabel, when you were here before. Helen was living, apparently, in peace and happiness with good old Joe. Well — she went to this psychoanalyzer — she was "psyched", and biff! — bang! — home she comes with an unsuppressed desire to leave her husband.

[*He starts work, drawing lines on a drawing board with a T-square.*

MABEL. How terrible! Yes, I remember Helen Dwight. But — but did she have such a desire?

STEVE. First she'd known of it.

MABEL. And she *left* him?

HENRIETTA (*coolly*). Yes, she did.

MABEL. Wasn't he good to her?

HENRIETTA. Why yes, good enough.

MABEL. Wasn't he kind to her!

HENRIETTA. Oh, yes — kind to her.

MABEL. And she left her good kind husband — !

HENRIETTA. Oh, Mabel! 'Left her good, kind husband!' How naïve — forgive me, dear, but how bourgeoise you are! She came to know herself. And she had the courage!

MABEL. I may be very naïve and — bourgeoise — but I don't see the good of a new science that breaks up homes. [*Steve clap hands, applauding.*

STEVE. In enlightening Mabel, we mustn't neglect to mention the case of Art Holden's private secretary, Mary Snow, who has just been informed of her suppressed desire for her employer.

MABEL. Why, I think it is terrible, Henrietta! It would be better if we didn't know such things about ourselves.

HENRIETTA. No, Mabel, that is the old way.

MABEL. But — but her employer? Is he married?

STEVE (*grunts*). Wife and four children.

MABEL. Well, then, what good does it do the girl to be told she has a desire for him? There's nothing that can be done about it.

HENRIETTA. Old institutions will have to be reshaped so that something can be done in such cases. It happens, Mabel, that this suppressed desire was on the point of landing Mary Snow in the insane asylum. Are you so tight-minded that you'd rather have her in the insane asylum than break the conventions?

MABEL. But — but have people always had these awful suppressed desires?

HENRIETTA. Always.

STEVE. But they've just been discovered.

HENRIETTA. The harm they do has just been discovered. And free, sane people must face the fact that they have to be dealt with.

MABEL (*stoutly*). I don't believe they have them in Chicago.

HENRIETTA (*business of giving Mabel up*). People "have them" wherever the living Libido — the center of the soul's energy — is in conflict with petrified moral codes. That means everywhere in civilization. Psychoanalysis —

STEVE. Good God! I've got the roof in the cellar!

HENRIETTA. The roof in the cellar!

STEVE (*holding plan at arm's length*). That's what psychoanalysis does!

HENRIETTA. That's what psychoanalysis could *un*-do. Is it any wonder I'm concerned about Steve? He dreamed the other night that the walls of his room melted away and he found himself alone in a forest. Don't you see how significant it is for an architect to have *walls* slip away from him? It symbolizes his loss of grip in his work. There's some suppressed desire —

STEVE (*hurling his ruined plan viciously to the floor*). Suppressed hell!

HENRIETTA. You speak more truly than you know. It is through suppressions that hells are formed in us.

MABEL (*looking at Steve, who is tearing his hair*). Don't you think it would be a good thing, Henrietta, if we went somewhere else? (*They rise and begin to pick up the dishes. Mabel drops a plate which breaks. Henrietta draws up short*

and looks at her — the psychoanalytic look) I'm sorry,
Henrietta. One of the Spode plates, too. (*Surprised
and resentful as Henrietta continues to peer at her*) Don't
take it so to heart, Henrietta.

HENRIETTA. I can't help taking it to heart.

MABEL. I'll get you another. (*Pause. More sharply as
Henrietta does not answer*) I said I'll get you another plate,
Henrietta.

HENRIETTA. It's not the plate.

MABEL. For heaven's sake, what is it then?

HENRIETTA. It's the significant little false movement that
made you drop it.

MABEL. Well, I suppose every one makes a false movement
once in a while.

HENRIETTA. Yes, Mabel, but these false movements all mean
something.

MABEL (*about to cry*). I don't think that's very nice! It
was just because I happened to think of that Mabel Snow
you were talking about —

HENRIETTA. *Mabel* Snow!

MABEL. Snow — Snow — well, what was her name, then?

HENRIETTA. Her name is Mary. You substituted *your own*
name for hers.

MABEL. Well, *Mary* Snow, then; *Mary* Snow. I never
heard her name but once. I don't see anything to make
such a fuss about.

HENRIETTA (*gently*). Mabel dear — mistakes like that in
names —

MABEL (*desperately*). They don't mean something, too, do
they?

HENRIETTA (*gently*). I am sorry, dear, but they do.

MABEL. *But I am always doing that!*

HENRIETTA (*after a start of horror*). My poor little sister,
tell me all about it.

MABEL. About what?

HENRIETTA. About your not being happy. About your
longing for another sort of life.

MABEL. But I *don't*.

HENRIETTA. Ah, I understand these things, dear. You feel
Bob is limiting you to a life which you do not feel free —

MABEL. Henrietta! When did I ever say such a thing?

HENRIETTA. You said you are not in touch with things intellectual. You showed your feeling that it is Bob's profession — that has engendered a resentment which has
colored your whole life with him.

MABEL. Why — Henri*e*tta!

HENRIETTA. Don't be afraid of me, little sister. There's
nothing can shock me or turn me from you. I am not
like that. I wanted you to come for this visit because I
had a feeling that you needed more from life than you
were getting. No one of these things I have seen would
excite my suspicion. It's the combination. You don't
eat breakfast; you make false moves; you substitute your
own name for the name of another *whose love is misdirected.*
You're nervous; you look queer; in your eyes there's a
frightened look that is most unlike you. And this dream.
A *hen* — come with me this afternoon to Dr. Russell!
Your whole life may be at stake, Mabel.

MABEL (*gasping*). Henrietta, I — you — you always were
the smartest in the family, and all that, but — this is
terrible! I don't think we *ought* to think such things,
and (*brightening*) Why, I'll tell you why I dreamed I
was a hen. It was because last night, telling about that
time in Chicago, you said I was as mad as a wet hen.

HENRIETTA (*superior*). Did you dream you were a *wet* hen?

MABEL (*forced to admit it*). No.

HENRIETTA. No. You dreamed you were a *dry* hen. And
why, being a hen, were you urged to step?

MABEL. Maybe it's because when I am getting on a street
car it always irritates me to have them call "Step lively."

HENRIETTA. No, Mabel, that is only a child's view of it —
if you will forgive me. You see merely the elements used
in the dream. You do not see into the dream; you do
not see its meaning. This dream of the hen —

STEVE. Hen — hen — wet hen — dry hen — mad hen!
(*Jumps up in a rage*)   Let me out of this!

HENRIETTA (*hastily picking up dishes, speaks soothingly*).
Just a minute, dear, and we'll have things so you can work
in quiet.   Mabel and I are going to sit in my room.   [*She
goes out with both hands full of dishes.*

STEVE (*seizing hat and coat from the costumer*).   I'm going
to be psychoanalyzed.   I'm going now! I'm going
straight to that infallible doctor of hers — that priest of
this new religion.   If he's got honesty enough to tell Henrietta there's nothing the matter with my unconscious
mind, perhaps I can be let alone about it, and then I *will*
be all right.   (*From the door in a low voice*)   Don't tell
Henrietta I'm going.   It might take weeks, and I couldn't
stand all the talk.

[*Exit desperately.   Enter Henrietta.*

HENRIETTA.   Where's Steve? Gone?   (*With hopeless gesture*)   You see how impatient he is — how unlike himself!
I tell you, Mabel, I am nearly distracted about Steve.

MABEL.   I think he's a little distracted, too.

HENRIETTA.   Well, if he's gone — you might as well stay
here.   I have a committee meeting at the book-shop, and
will have to leave you to yourself for an hour or two.   (*As
she puts her hat on, her eye, lighting up almost carnivorously,
falls on an enormous volume on the floor beside the work table.
The book has been half hidden from the audience by the waste-
basket.   She picks it up and carries it around the table
toward Mabel*)   Here, dear, is one of the simplest state-
ments of psychoanalysis.   You just read this and then
we can talk more intelligently.   (*Mabel takes volume and
staggers back under its weight to chair rear center.   Henrietta
goes to outer door, stops and asks abruptly*)   How old is
Lyman Eggleston?

MABLE (*promptly*).   He isn't forty yet.   Why, what made
you ask that, Henrietta?

[*As she turns her head to look at Henrietta her hands move
toward the upper corners of the book balanced on her knees.*

HENRIETTA. Oh, nothing. Au revoir.
(*Exit.*
Mabel stares at the ceiling. The book slides to the floor. She starts; looks at the book, then at the broken plate on the table) The plate! The book! (*She lifts her eyes, leans forward elbow on knee, chin on knuckles and plaintively queries*) Am I unhappy?

CURTAIN

SCENE II

The stage is set as in Scene I, except that the breakfast table has been removed or set back against the wall. During the first few minutes the dusk of a winter afternoon deepens. Out of the darkness spring rows of double street-lights almost meeting in the distance. Henrietta is disclosed at the psychoanalytical end of Steve's work-table. Surrounded by open books and periodicals she is writing. Steve enters briskly.

STEVE. What are you doing, my dear?

HENRIETTA. My paper for the Liberal Club.

STEVE. Your paper on —?

HENRIETTA. On a subject which does not have your sympathy.

STEVE. Oh, I'm not sure I'm wholly out of sympathy with psychoanalysis, Henrietta. You worked it so hard. I couldn't even take a bath without its meaning something.

HENRIETTA (*loftily*). I talked it because I knew you needed it.

STEVE. You haven't said much about it these last two weeks. Uh — your faith in it hasn't weakened any?

HENRIETTA. Weakened? It's grown stronger with each new thing I've come to know. And Mabel. She is with Dr. Russell now. Dr. Russell is wonderful. From what Mabel tells me I believe his analysis is going to prove that I was right. To-day I discovered a remarkable confirmation of my theory in the hen-dream.

STEVE. What is your theory?

HENRIETTA. Well, you know about Lyman Eggleston. I've
wondered about him. I've never seen him, but I know
he's less bourgeois than Mabel's other friends — more
intellectual — and (*significantly*) she doesn't see much of
him because Bob doesn't like him.

STEVE. But what's the confirmation?

HENRIETTA. To-day I noticed the first syllable of his name.

STEVE. Ly?

HENRIETTA. No—egg. (*Patiently*) Mabel dreamed she was
a *hen*. (*Steve laughs*) You wouldn't laugh if you knew how
important names are in interpreting dreams. Freud is full
of just such cases in which a whole hidden complex is
revealed by a single significant syllable — like this egg.

STEVE. Doesn't the traditional relation of hen and egg suggest rather a maternal feeling?

HENRIETTA. There is something maternal in Mabel's love
of course, but that's only one element.

STEVE. Well, suppose Mabel hasn't a suppressed desire to
be this gentleman's mother, but his beloved. What's to
be done about it? What about Bob? Don't you think
it's going to be a little rough on him?

HENRIETTA. That can't be helped. Bob, like every one
else, must face the facts of life. If Dr. Russell should
arrive independently at this same interpretation I shall
not hesitate to advise Mabel to leave her present husband.

STEVE. Um — um! (*The lights go up on Fifth Avenue.
Steve goes to the window and looks out*) How long is it we've
lived here, Henrietta?

HENRIETTA. Why, this is the third year, Steve.

STEVE. I — we — one would miss this view if one went
away, wouldn't one?

HENRIETTA. How strangely you speak! Oh, Stephen, I
wish you'd go to Dr. Russell. Don't think my fears have
abated because I've been able to restrain myself. I had
to on account of Mabel. But now, dear — won't you
go?

STEVE. I — (*He breaks off, turns on the light, then comes and sits beside Henrietta*) How long have we been married, Henrietta?

HENRIETTA. Stephen, I don't understand you! You must go to Dr. Russell.

STEVE. I *have* gone.

HENRIETTA. You — what?

STEVE (*jauntily*). Yes, Henrietta, I've been psyched.

HENRIETTA. You went to Dr. Russell?

STEVE. The same.

HENRIETTA. And what did he say?

STEVE. He said — I — I was a little surprised by what he said, Henrietta.

HENRIETTA (*breathlessly*). Of course — one can so seldom anticipate. But tell me — your dream, Stephen? It means — ?

STEVE. It means — I was considerably surprised by what it means.

HENRIETTA. *Don't* be so exasperating!

STEVE. It means — you really want to know, Henrietta?

HENRIETTA. Stephen, you'll drive me mad!

STEVE. He said — of course he may be wrong in what he said.

HENRIETTA. He *isn't* wrong. *Tell* me!

STEVE. He said my dream of the walls receding and leaving me alone in a forest indicates a suppressed desire —

HENRIETTA. Yes — yes!

STEVE. To be freed from —

HENRIETTA. Yes — freed from —?

STEVE. Marriage.

HENRIETTA (*Crumples. Stares*). Marriage!

STEVE. He — he may be mistaken, you know.

HENRIETTA. *May* be mistaken!

STEVE. I — well, of course, I hadn't taken any stock in it myself. It was only your great confidence —

HENRIETTA. Stephen, are you telling me that Dr. Russell — Dr. A. E. Russell — told you this? (*Steve nods*) Told you you have a suppressed desire to separate from me?

STEVE. That's what he said.

HENRIETTA. Did he know who you were?

STEVE. Yes.

HENRIETTA. That you were married to me?

STEVE. Yes, he knew that.

HENRIETTA. And he told you to leave me?

STEVE. It seems he must be wrong, Henrietta.

HENRIETTA (*rising*). And I've sent him more patients — !
(*Catches herself and resumes coldly*) What reason did he
give for this analysis?

STEVE. He says the confining walls are a symbol of my
feeling about marriage and that their fading away is a
wish-fulfillment.

HENRIETTA (*gulping*). Well, is it? Do you want our marriage to end?

STEVE. Well, it was a great surprise to me that I did, Henrietta. You see I hadn't known what was in my unconscious mind.

HENRIETTA (*flaming*). What did you tell Dr. Russell about
me to make him think you weren't happy?

STEVE. I never told him a thing, Henrietta. He got it all
from his confounded clever inferences. I — I tried to
refute them, but he said that was only part of my self-
protective lying.

HENRIETTA. And that's why you were so — happy — when
you came in just now!

STEVE. Why, Henrietta, how can you say such a thing?
I was *sad*. Didn't I speak sadly of — of the view? Didn't
I ask how long we had been married?

HENRIETTA (*rising*). Stephen Brewster, have you no sense
of the seriousness of this? Dr. Russell doesn't know what
our marriage has been. You do. You should have laughed
him down! Confined — in life with me? Did you tell
him that I believe in freedom?

STEVE. I very emphatically told him that his results were
a great surprise to me.

HENRIETTA. But you accepted them.

STEVE. Oh, not at all. I merely couldn't refute his arguments. I'm not a psychologist. I came home to talk it over with you. You being a disciple of psychoanalysis —

HENRIETTA. If you are going, I wish you would go to-night!

STEVE. Oh, my dear! I — surely I couldn't do that! Think of my feelings. And my laundry hasn't come home.

HENRIETTA. I ask you to go to-night. Some women would falter at this, Steve, but I am not such a woman. I leave you free. I do not repudiate psychoanalysis, I say again that it has done great things. It has also made mistakes, of course. But since you accept this analysis — (*She sits down and pretends to begin work*) I have to finish this paper. I wish you would leave me.

STEVE (*scratches his head, goes to the inner door*). I'm sorry, Henrietta, about my unconscious mind.

[*Exit. Henrietta's face betrays her outraged state of mind — disconcerted, resentful, trying to pull herself together. She attains an air of bravely bearing an outrageous thing. Mabel enters in great excitement.*

MABEL (*breathless*). Henrietta, I'm so glad you're here. And alone? (*Looks toward the inner door*) Are you alone, Henrietta?

HENRIETTA (*with reproving dignity*). Very much so.

MABEL (*rushing to her*). Henrietta, he's found it!

HENRIETTA (*aloof*). Who has found what?

MABEL. Who has found what? Dr. Russell has found my suppressed desire.

HENRIETTA. That is interesting.

MABEL. He finished with me to-day — he got hold of my complex — in the most amazing way! But, oh, Henrietta — it is so terrible!

HENRIETTA. Do calm yourself, Mabel. Surely there's no occasion for all this agitation.

MABEL. But there is! And when you think of the lives that are affected — the readjustments that must be made in order to bring the suppressed hell out of me and save me from the insane asylum — !

HENRIETTA. The insane asylum!

MABEL. You said that's where these complexes brought people?

HENRIETTA. What did the doctor tell you, Mabel?

MABEL. Oh, I don't know how I can tell you — it is so awful — so unbelievable.

HENRIETTA. I rather have my hand in at hearing the unbelievable.

MABEL. Henrietta, who would ever have thought it? How can it be true? But the doctor is perfectly certain that I have a suppressed desire for — [*Looks at Henrietta unable to go on.*

HENRIETTA. Oh, go on, Mabel. I'm not unprepared for what you have to say.

MABEL. Not unprepared? You mean you have suspected it?

HENRIETTA. From the first. It's been my theory all along.

MABEL. But, Henrietta, I didn't know myself that I had this secret desire for Stephen.

HENRIETTA (*jumps up*). Stephen!

MABEL. My brother-in-law! My own sister's husband!

HENRIETTA. *You* have a suppressed desire for *Stephen!*

MABEL. Oh, Henrietta, aren't these unconscious selves terrible? They seem so unlike us!

HENRIETTA. What insane thing are you driving at?

MABEL (*blubbering*). Henrietta, don't you use that word to me. I don't *want* to go to the insane asylum.

HENRIETTA. What did Dr. Russell say?

MABEL. Well, you see — oh, it's the strangest thing! But you know the voice in my dream that called "Step, Hen!" Dr. Russell found out to-day that when I was a little girl I had a story-book in words of one syllable and I read the name Stephen wrong. I used to read it S-t-e-p, step, h-e-n, hen. (*Dramatically*) Step Hen is Stephen. (*Enter Stephen, his head bent over a time-table*) Stephen is Step Hen!

STEVE. I? Step Hen!

MABEL (*triumphantly*). S-t-e-p, step, H-e-n, hen, Stephen!

HENRIETTA (*exploding*). Well, what if Stephen is Step Hen? (*Scornfully*) Step Hen! Step Hen! For that ridiculous coincidence —

MABEL. Coincidence! But it's childish to look at the mere elements of a dream. You have to look into it — you have to see what it means!

HENRIETTA. On account of that trivial, meaningless play on syllables — on that flimsy basis — you are ready — (*wails*) O-h!

STEVE. What on earth's the matter? What has happened? Suppose I *am* Step Hen? What about it? What does it mean?

MABEL (*crying*). It means — that — I — have a suppressed desire for *you!*

STEVE. For me! The deuce you have? (*Feebly*) What — er — makes you think so?

MABEL. Dr. Russell has worked it out scientifically.

HENRIETTA. Yes. Through the amazing discovery that Step Hen equals Stephen!

MABEL (*tearfully*). Oh, that isn't all — that isn't near all. Henrietta won't give me a chance to tell it. She'd rather I'd go to the insane asylum than be unconventional.

HENRIETTA. We'll all go there if you can't control yourself. We are still waiting for some rational report.

MABEL (*drying her eyes*). Oh, there's such a lot about names. (*With some pride*) I don't see how I ever did it. It all works in together. I dreamed I was a hen because that's the first syllable of *Hen*-rietta's name, and when I dreamed I was a hen, I was putting myself in Henrietta's place.

HENRIETTA. With Stephen?

MABEL. With Stephen.

HENRIETTA (*outraged*). Oh! (*Turns in rage upon Stephen, who is fanning himself with the time-table*) What are you doing with that time-table?

STEVE. Why — I thought — you were so keen to have me go to-night — I thought I'd just take a run up to Canada, and join Billy — a little shooting — but —

MABEL. But there's more about the names.

HENRIETTA. Mabel, have you thought of Bob — dear old Bob — your good, kind husband?

MABEL. Oh, Henrietta, "my good, kind husband!"

HENRIETTA. Think of him, Mabel, out there alone in Chicago, working his head off, fixing people's *teeth* for you!

MABEL. Yes, but think of the living Libido — in conflict with petrified moral codes! And think of the perfectly wonderful way the names all prove it. Dr. Russell said he's never seen anything more convicing. Just look at Stephen's last name — Brewster. I dream I'm a hen, and the name Brewster — you have to say its first letter by itself — and then the hen, that's me, she says to him: "Stephen, Be Rooster!"

[*Henrietta and Stephen both collapse on chair and divan.*

MABEL. I think it's perfectly wonderful! Why, if it wasn't for psychoanalysis you'd never find out how wonderful your own mind is!

STEVE (*begins to chuckle*). Be Rooster, Stephen, Be Rooster!

HENRIETTA. You think it's funny, do you?

STEVE. Well, what's to be done about it? Does Mabel have to go away with me?

HENRIETTA. Do you want Mabel to go away with you?

STEVE. Well, but Mabel herself — her complex — her suppressed desire — !

HENRIETTA. Mabel, are you going to insist on going away with Stephen?

MABEL. I'd rather go with Stephen than go to the insane asylum.

HENRIETTA. For Heaven's sake, Mabel, drop that insane asylum! If you *did* have a suppressed desire for Stephen hidden away in you — God knows it isn't hidden *now*. Dr. Russell has brought it into your consciousness — with a vengeance. That's all that's necessary to break up a complex. Psychoanalysis doesn't say you have to *gratify* every suppressed desire.

STEVE (*softly*). Unless it's for Lyman Eggleston.

HENRIETTA (*turning on him*). Well, if it comes to that, Stephen Brewster, I'd like to know why that interpretation of mine isn't as good as this one? Step, Hen!

STEVE. But Be Rooster! (*He pauses, chuckling to himself*) Step-Hen B-rooster. And *H*enrietta. Pshaw, my dear, Doc Russell's got you beat a mile! (*He turns away and chuckles*) Be rooster!

MABEL. What has Lyman Eggleston got to do with it?

STEVE. According to Henrietta, you, the hen, have a suppressed desire for *Egg*leston, the egg.

MABEL. Henrietta, I think that's indecent of you! He is bald as an egg and little and fat — the idea of you thinking such a thing of me!

HENRIETTA. Well, Bob isn't little and bald and fat! Why don't you stick to your own husband? (*Turns on Stephen*) What if Dr. Russell's interpretation has got mine "beat a mile"? (*Resentful look at him*) It would only mean that Mabel doesn't want Eggleston and does want you. Does that mean she has to have you?

MABEL. But you said Mabel Snow —

HENRIETTA. *Mary* Snow! You're not as much like her as you think — substituting your name for hers! The cases are entirely different. Oh, I wouldn't have believed this of you, Mabel. I brought you here for a pleasant visit — thought you needed brightening *up* — wanted to be nice to you — and now you — my husband — you insist — [*Begins to cry. Makes a movement which brushes to the floor some sheets from the psychoanalytical table.*

STEVE (*with solicitude*). Careful, dear. Your paper on psychoanalysis!
[*Gathers up sheets and offers them to her.*

HENRIETTA (*crying*). I don't want my paper on psychoanalysis! I'm sick of psychoanalysis!

STEVE (*eagerly*). Do you mean that, Henrietta?

HENRIETTA. Why shouldn't I mean it? Look at all I've done for psychoanalysis — and — what has psychoanalysis done for me?

STEVE. Do you mean, Henrietta, that you're going to stop *talking* psychoanalysis?

HENRIETTA. Why shouldn't I stop talking it? Haven't I seen what it does to people? Mabel has gone crazy about psychoanalysis!

[*At the word "crazy" Mabel sinks with a moan into the arm-chair and buries her face in her hands.*

STEVE (*solemnly*). Do you swear never to wake me up in the night to find out what I'm dreaming?

HENRIETTA. Dream what you please — I don't care what you're dreaming.

STEVE. Will you clear off my work-table so the Journal of Morbid Psychology doesn't stare me in the face when I'm trying to plan a house?

HENRIETTA (*pushing a stack of periodicals off the table*). I'll *burn* the Journal of Morbid Psychology!

STEVE. My dear Henrietta, if you're going to separate from psychoanalysis, there's no reason why I should separate from *you*.

[*They embrace ardently. Mabel lifts her head and looks at them woefully.*

MABEL (*jumping up and going toward them*). But what about me? What am I to do with my suppressed desire?

STEVE (*with one arm still around Henrietta, gives Mabel a brotherly hug*). Mabel, you just keep right on suppressing it.

CURTAIN

THE LAST STRAW

BOSWORTH CROCKER

THE WASHINGTON SQUARE Players came into existence in a New York bookshop in 1915; now they are internationally famous, and known as "The Theatre Guild." They have always produced artistic plays, and they have been quick to assimilate talent from every quarter, whether here or abroad.

Robert Edmond Jones, a Harvard Workshop man, was their first scenic artist; Lewis Beach, Eugene O'Neill, and Susan Glaspell furnished them with some of their first plays. Although they gave great encouragement to the one-act playwrights at one time, — particularly those with tendencies toward a sophisticated style, — they have since found that full-length plays are more interesting experiments in expert staging; and their directors, at first Edward Goodman, then Theresa Helburn and Philip Moeller, have demonstrated a technical efficiency that is not surpassed anywhere in the American theatre.

Bosworth Crocker (in private life, Mrs. Ludwig Lewisohn) was among the playwrights introduced by the Washington Square Players, and "The Last Straw" has been one of her most widely acted plays because of its intimate portrayal of a typical American scene.

She was born in Surrey, England, but was brought to the United States in childhood. She has written poetry, criticism, and feature articles for magazines and newspapers, over this pen name and others, and was dramatic critic for *Town Topics* in New York City from 1918 to 1925.

She has published "Pawns of War" (a three-act play, with introduction by John Galsworthy); *Humble Folk*, a collection of one-act plays; and "Coquine", based on an episode in the life of Heinrich Heine. These plays, and her "The First Time", "The Cost of a Hat", "The Hour Before", "Stone Walls" (a play in three acts), and "Heritage", (a play in four acts), have been successfully given throughout the United States. "The Baby Carriage" has had production in England and Australia, and many of the plays have been broadcasted.

THE LAST STRAW

By BOSWORTH CROCKER

"The Last Straw" was originally produced by The Washington Square Players at the Comedy Theatre, New York City, February 12, 1917.

Original Cast

FRIEDRICH BAUER, janitor of the Bryn
    Mawr . . . . Arthur E. Hohle
MIENE, his wife . . . . . . Marjorie Vonnegut
                              (Mrs. Don Marquis)
KARL, elder son, aged ten . . . Nick Long
FRITZI, younger son, aged seven . Frank Longacre
JIM LANE, a grocer boy . . . . Glenn Hunter

THE LAST STRAW

TIME. *The present day.*

SCENE. *The basement of a large apartment house in New York City.*

SCENE. *The kitchen of the Bauer flat in the basement of the Bryn Mawr. A window at the side gives on an area and shows the walk above and the houses across the street. Opposite the windows is a door to an inner room. Through the outer door, in the centre of the back wall, a dumb-waiter and whistles to tenants can be seen. A broken milk bottle lies in a puddle of milk on the cement floor in front of the dumb-waiter. To the right of the outer door, a telephone; gas-range on which there are flatirons heating and vegetables cooking. To the left of the outer door is an old sideboard; over it hangs a picture of Schiller. Near the centre of the room, a little to the right, stands a kitchen table with four chairs around it. Ironing board is placed between the kitchen table and the sink, a basket of dampened clothes under it. A large calendar on the wall. An alarm-clock on the window-sill. Time: a little before noon. The telephone rings, Mrs. Bauer leaves her ironing and goes to answer it.*

MRS. BAUER.   No, Mr. Bauer's out yet. (*She listens through the transmitter*) Thank you, Mrs. Mohler. (*Another pause*) I'll tell him just so soon he comes in — yes ma'am.

[*Mrs. Bauer goes back to her ironing. Grocer boy rushes into basement, whistling; he puts down his basket, goes up to Mrs. Bauer's door and looks in.*

LANE.   Say — where's the boss?

MRS. BAUER.   He'll be home soon, I — hope — Jim.   What you want?

[*He stands looking at her with growing sympathy.*

LANE. Nothin'. Got a rag 'round here? Dumb-waiter's all
wet. . . . Lot of groceries for Sawyers.

MRS. BAUER (*without lifting her eyes, mechanically hands him
a mop which hangs beside the door*). Here.

LANE. What's the matter?

MRS. BAUER (*dully*). Huh?

LANE (*significantly*). Oh, I know.

MRS. BAUER. What you know?

LANE. About the boss. (*Mrs. Bauer looks distressed*)
Heard your friends across the street talkin'.

MRS BAUER (*bitterly*). Friends!

LANE. Rotten trick to play on the boss, all right, puttin'
that old maid up to get him pinched.

MRS. BAUER (*absently*). Was she an old maid?

LANE. The cruelty to animals woman over there (*waves
his hand*) — regular old crank. Nies* put her up to it
all right.

MRS. BAUER. I guess it was his old woman. Nies ain't
so bad. She's the one. Because my two boys dress up a
little on Sunday, she don't like it.

LANE. Yes, she's sore because the boys told her the boss
kicks their dog.

MRS. BAUER. He don't do nothin' of the sort — jus' drives
it 'way from the garbage pails — that's all. We coulda
had that dog took up long ago — they ain't got no license.
But Fritz — he's so easy — he jus' takes it out chasin'
the dog and hollerin'.

LANE. That ain't no way. He ought to make the dog holler — good and hard — once; then it'd keep out of here.

MRS. BAUER. Don't you go to talkin' like that 'round my
man. Look at all this trouble we're in on account of a
stray cat.

LANE. I better get busy. They'll be callin' up the store
in a minute. That woman's the limit. . . . Send up the
groceries in that slop, she'd send them down again. High-
toned people like her ought to keep maids.

* Pronounced *niece.*

[He mops out the lower shelf of the dumb-waiter, then looks at the broken bottle and the puddle of milk inquiringly.

MRS. BAUER *(taking the mop away from him).* I'll clean that up. I forgot — in all this trouble.

LANE. Whose milk?

MRS. BAUER. The Mohlers'. — That's how it all happened. Somebody upset their milk on the dumb-waiter and the cat was on the shelf lickin' it up; my man, not noticin' starts the waiter up and the cat tries to jump out; the bottle rolls off and breaks. The cat was hurt awful — caught in the shaft. I don't see how it coulda run after that, but it did — right into the street, right into that woman — Fritz after it. Then it fell over. "You did that?" she says to Fritz. "Yes", he says, "I did that." He didn't say no more, jus' went off and then after a while they came for him and —

[She begins to cry softly.

LANE. Brace up; they ain't goin' to do anything to him. . . . *(Comes into kitchen. Hesitatingly)* Say! . . . He didn't kick the cat — did he?

MRS. BAUER. Who said so?

LANE. Mrs. Nies — says she saw him from her window.

MRS. BAUER *(as though to herself).* I dunno. *(Excitedly)* Of course he didn't kick that cat. *(Again as though to herself)* Fritz is so quick-tempered he mighta kicked it 'fore he knew what he was about. No one'd ever know how good Fritz is unless they lived with him. He never hurt no one and nothing except himself.

LANE. Oh, I'm on to the boss. I never mind his hollerin'.

MRS. BAUER. If you get a chance, bring me some butter for dinner — a pound.

LANE. All right. I'll run over with it in ten or fifteen minutes, soon as I get rid of these orders out here in the wagon.

MRS. BAUER. That'll do.

[She moves about apathetically, lays the cloth on the kitchen

table and begins to set it. Lane goes to the dumb-waiter, whistles up the tube, puts the basket of groceries on the shelf of the dumb-waiter, pulls rope and sends waiter up. Mrs. Bauer continues to set the table. Boys from the street suddenly swoop into the basement and yell.

CHORUS OF BOYS' VOICES. Who killed the cat! Who killed the cat!

LANE (*letting the rope go and making a dive for the boys*). I'll show you, you —

[*They rush out, Mrs. Bauer stands despairingly in the doorway shaking her clasped hands.*

MRS. BAUER. Those are Nies's boys.

LANE. Regular toughs! Call the cop and have 'em pinched if they don't stop it.

MRS. BAUER. If my man hears them — you know — there'll be more trouble.

LANE. The boss ought to make it hot for them.

MRS. BAUER. Such trouble!

LANE (*starts to go*) Well, — luck to the boss.

MRS. BAUER. There ain't no such thing as luck for us.

LANE. Aw, come on. . . .

MRS. BAUER. Everything's against us. First Fritz's mother dies. We named the baby after her — Trude. . . . Then we lost Trude. That finished Fritz After that he began this holler'n' business And now this here trouble — just when things was goin' half ways decent for the first time.

[*She pushes past him and goes to her ironing.*

LANE (*shakes his head sympathetically and takes up his basket*). A pound you said?

MRS. BAUER. Yes.

LANE. All right. (*He starts off and then rushes back*) Here's the boss comin', Mrs. Bauer.

[*Rushes off again.*

LANE'S VOICE (*cheerfully*). Hello, there!

BAUER'S VOICE (*dull and strained*). Hello!

[*Bauer comes in. His naturally bright blue eyes are tired*

and lustreless; his strong frame seems to have lost all vigor and alertness; there is a look of utter despondency on his face.

MRS. BAUER (*closing the door after him*). They let you off?

BAUER (*with a hard little laugh*). Yes, they let me off — they let me off with a fine all right.

MRS. BAUER (*aghast*). They think you did it then.

BAUER (*harshly*). The judge fined me, I tell you.

MRS. BAUER (*unable to express her poignant sympathy*). Fined you!. . . O Fritz!

[*She lays her hand on his shoulder.*

BAUER (*roughly, to keep himself from going to pieces*). That slop out there ain't cleaned up yet.

MRS. BAUER. I've been so worried.

BAUER (*with sudden desperation*). I can't stand it, I tell you.

MRS. BAUER. Well, it's all over now, Fritz.

BAUER. Yes, it's all over . . . it's all up with me.

MRS. BAUER Fritz!

BAUER. That's one sure thing.

MRS. BAUER. You oughtn't to give up like this.

BAUER (*pounding on the table*). I tell you I can't hold up my head again.

MRS. BAUER. Why, Fritz?

BAUER. They've made me out guilty. The judge fined me. Fined me, Miene! How is that? Can a man stand for that? The woman said I told her myself — right out — that I did it.

MRS. BAUER. The woman that had you — (*He winces as she hesitates*) took?

BAUER. Damned —

MRS. BAUER (*putting her hand over his mouth*). Hush, Fritz.

BAUER. Why will I hush, Miene? She said I was proud of the job. (*Passionately raising his voice*) The damned interferin' —

MRS. BAUER. Don't holler, Fritz. It's your hollerin' that's made all this trouble.

BAUER (*penetrated by her words more and more*). My hollerin'! . . . .

[*The telephone rings; she answers it.*

MRS. BAUER. Yes, Mrs. Mohler, he's come in now. — Yes. — Won't after dinner do? — All right. — Thank you, Mrs. Mohler. (*She hangs up the receiver*) Mrs. Mohler wants you to fix her sink right after dinner.

BAUER. I'm not goin' to do any more fixin' around here.

MRS. BAUER. You hold on to yourself, Fritz; that's no way to talk; Mrs. Mohler's a nice woman.

BAUER. I don't want to see no more nice women. (*After a pause*) Hollerin'! — that's what's the matter with me — hollerin', eh? Well, I've took it all out in hollerin'.

MRS. BAUER. They hear you and they think you've got no feelings.

BAUER (*in utter amazement at the irony of the situation*). And I was goin' after the damned cat to take care of it.

MRS. BAUER. Why didn't you tell the judge all about it?

BAUER. They got me rattled among them. The lady was so soft and pleasant — "He must be made to understand, your Honor," she said to the judge, "that dumb animals has feelin's, too, just as well as human beings" — *Me, Meine,* — made to understand that! I couldn't say nothin'. My voice just stuck in my throat.

MRS. BAUER. What's the matter with you! You oughta spoke up and told the judge just how it all happened.

BAUER. I said to myself: I'll go home and put a bullet through my head — that's the best thing for me now.

MRS. BAUER (*with impatient unbelief*). *Ach,* Fritz, Fritz! [*Clatter of feet.*

CHORUS OF VOICES (*at the outer door*). Who killed the cat! Who killed the cat!

[*Bauer jumps up, pale and shaken with strange rage; she pushes him gently back into his chair, opens the door, steps out for a moment, then comes in and leaves the door open behind her.*

BAUER. You see? . . . Even the kids . . . I'm disgraced all over the place.

MRS. BAUER. So long as you didn't hurt the cat —

BAUER. What's the difference? Everybody believes it.

MRS. BAUER. No, they don't, Fritz.

BAUER. You can't fool me, Miene. I see it in their eyes. They looked away from me when I was comin' 'round the corner. Some of them kinder smiled like — (*Passes his hand over his head*) Even the cop says to me on the way over, yesterday: "Don't you put your foot in it any more'n you have to." You see? He thought I did it all right. Everybody believes it.

MRS. BAUER (*putting towels away*). Well, then *let* them believe it. . . . The agent don't believe it.

BAUER. I dunno. He'da paid my fine anyhow.

MRS. BAUER. He gave you a good name.

BAUER (*with indignant derision*). He gave me a good name! . . . Haven't I always kept this place all right since we been here? Afterwards he said to me: "I'm surprised at this business, Bauer, very much surprised." That shows what he thinks. I told him it ain't true, I didn't mean to hurt it. I saw by his eyes he didn't believe me.

MRS. BAUER. Well, don't you worry any more now.

BAUER (*to himself*). Hollerin'!

MRS. BAUER (*shuts the door*). Well now holler a little if it does you good.

BAUER. Nothin's goin' to do me good.

MRS. BAUER. You just put it out of your mind. (*The telephone rings. She answers it*) Yes, but he can't come now, Mrs. McAllister. He'll be up this afternoon. [*She hangs up the receiver.*

BAUER. And I ain't goin' this afternoon — nowhere.

MRS. BAUER. It's Mrs. McAllister. Somethin's wrong with her refrigerator — the water won't run off, she says.

BAUER. They can clean out their own drain pipes.

MRS. BAUER. You go to work and get your mind off this here business.

BAUER (*staring staight ahead of him*). I ain't goin' 'round among the people in this house . . . to have them lookin' at me . . . disgraced like this.

MRS. BAUER. You want to hold up your head and act as if nothin's happened.

BAUER. Nobody spoke to me at the dumb-waiter when I took off the garbage and paper this morning. Mrs. Mohler always says something pleasant.

MRS. BAUER. You just think that because you're all upset. (*The telephone rings; she goes to it and listens*) Yes, ma'am, I'll see. Fritz, have you any fine wire? Mrs. McAllister thinks she might try and fix the drain with it — till you come up.

BAUER. I got no wire.

MRS. BAUER. Mr. Bauer'll fix it — right after dinner, Mrs. McAllister. (*Impatiently*) He can't find the wire this minute — soon's he eats his dinner.

BAUER (*doggedly*). You'll see. . . .

MRS. BAUER (*soothingly*). Come now, Fritz, give me your hat.

[*She takes his hat from him.*

VOICES IN THE STREET (*receding from the front area*). Who killed the cat! Who killed the cat!

[*Bauer rushes toward the window in a fury of excitement.*

BAUER (*shouting at the top of his voice*) *Verdammte* loafers! *Schweine!*

MRS. BAUER (*goes up to him*). Fritz! Fritz!

BAUER (*collapses and drops into chair*). You hear 'em.

MRS. BAUER. Don't pay no attention, then they'll get tired.

BAUER. Miene, we must go away. I can't stand it here no longer.

MRS. BAUER. But there's not such another good place, Fritz — And the movin' . . .

BAUER. I say I can't stand it.

MRS. BAUER (*desperately*). It . . . it would be just the same any other place.

BAUER. Just the same?

MRS. BAUER. Yes, something'd go wrong anyhow.

BAUER. You think I'm a regular Jonah.

[*He shakes his head repeatedly in the affirmative as though wholly embracing her point of view.*

MRS. BAUER. Folks don't get to know you. They hear you hollerin' 'round and they think you beat the children and kick the dogs and cats.

BAUER. Do I ever lick the children when they don't need it?

MRS. BAUER. Not Fritzi.

BAUER. You want to spoil Karl. I just touch him with the strap once, a little — like this (*illustrates with a gesture*) to scare him and he howls like hell.

MRS. BAUER. Yes, and then he don't mind you no more because he knows you don't mean it.

BAUER (*to himself*). That's the way it goes . . . a man's own wife and children . . .

MRS. BAUER (*attending to the dinner. Irritably*). Fritz, if you would clean that up out there — and Mrs. Carroll wants her waste-basket. You musta forgot to send it up again.

BAUER. All right.

[*He goes out and leaves the door open. She stands her flatiron on the ledge of the range to cool and puts her ironing-board away, watching him at the dumb-waiter while he picks up the glass and cleans up the milk on the cement floor. He disappears for a moment, then he comes in again, goes to a drawer and takes out rags and a bottle of polish.*

MRS. BAUER (*pushing the clothes-basket out of the way*). This ain't cleanin' day, Fritz.

BAUER (*dully, putting the polish back into the drawer*). That's so.

MRS. BAUER (*comforting him*). You've got to eat a good dinner and then go upstairs and fix that sink for Mrs. Mohler and the drain for Mrs. McAllister.

BAUER (*in a tense voice*). I tell you I can't stand it. . . . I tell you, Miene. . . .

MRS. BAUER. What now, Fritz?

BAUER. People laugh in my face. (*Nods in the direction of the street*) Frazer's boy standin' on the stoop calls his dog away when it runs up to me like it always does.

MRS. BAUER. Dogs know better'n men who's good to them.

BAUER. He acted like he thought I'd kick it.

MRS. BAUER. You've got all kinds of foolishness in your head now . . . . You sent up Carroll's basket?

BAUER. No.

MRS. BAUER. Well —
[*She checks herself.*

BAUER. All right.
[*He gets up.*

MRS. BAUER. It's settin' right beside the other dumb-waiter. (*He goes out*) O Gott! — O Gott! — O Gott!
[*Enter Karl and Fritzi. Fritzi is crying.*

MRS. BAUER (*running to them*). What's the matter?
[*She hushes them and carefully closes the door.*

KARL. The boys make fun of us; they mock us.

FRITZI. They mock us — "Miau! Miau!" they cry, and then they go like this —
[*Fritzi imitates kicking and breaks out crying afresh.*

MRS. BAUER. Hush, Fritzi, you mustn't let your father hear.

FRITZI. He'd make them shut up.

KARL. I don't want to go to school this afternoon.
[*He doubles his fists.*

MRS. BAUER (*turning on him fiercely*). Why not? (*In an undertone*) You talk that way before your little brother. — Have you no sense?

FRITZI (*beginning to whimper*). I d-d-d-on't want to go to school this afternoon.

MRS. BAUER. You just go 'long to school and mind your own business.

KARL AND FRITZI (*together*). But the boys. . . .

MRS. BAUER. They ain't a goin' to keep it up forever. Don't you answer them. Just go 'long together and pay no attention.

KARL. Then they get fresher and fresher.

FRITZI (*echoing Karl*).   Yes, then they get fresher and fresher.
[*Mrs. Bauer begins to take up the dinner. The sound of
footfalls just outside the door is heard.*

MRS. BAUER.   Go on now, hang up your caps and get ready
for your dinners.

FRITZI.   I'm going to tell my papa.

[*Goes to inner door.*

MRS. BAUER.   For God's sake, Fritzi, shut up.   You mustn't
tell no one.   Papa'd be disgraced all over.

KARL (*coming up to her*)   Disgraced?

MRS. BAUER.   Hush!

KARL.   Why disgraced?

MRS. BAUER.   Because there's liars, low-down snoopin'
liars in the world.

KARL.   Who's lied, Mamma?

MRS. BAUER.   The janitress across the street.

KARL.   Mrs. Nies?

FRITZI (*calling out*).   Henny Nies is a tough.

MRS. BAUER (*looking toward the outer door anxiously and
shaking her head threateningly at Fritzi*).   I give you somethin', if you don't stop hollerin' out like that.

KARL.   Who'd she lie to?

MRS. BAUER.   Never mind.   Go 'long now.   It's time you
begin to eat.

KARL.   What'd she lie about?

MRS. BAUER (*warningly*).   S-s-sh!   Papa'll be comin' in now
in a minute.

KARL.   It was Henny Nies set the gang on to us.   I coulda
licked them all if I hadn't had to take care of Fritzi.

MRS. BAUER.   You'll get a lickin' all right if you don't keep
away from Henny Nies.

KARL.   Well — if they call me names — and say *my* father's
been to the station-house for killing a cat . . . ?

FRITZI.   Miau! Miau! Miau!

MRS. BAUER.   Hold your mouth.

FRITZI (*swaggering*).   My father never was in jail — was he,
Mamma?

KARL. Course not.

MRS. BAUER (*to Fritzi*). Go, wash your hands, Fritzi.

[*She steers him to the door of the inner room, he exits.*

MRS. BAUER (*distressed*). Karl . . .

KARL (*turning to his mother*). Was he, Mamma?

MRS. BAUER. Papa don't act like he used to. Sometimes I wonder what's come over him. Of course it's enough to ruin any man's temper, all the trouble we've had.

CHORUS OF VOICES (*from the area by the window*). Who killed the cat! Who killed the cat!

[*Sound of feet clattering up the area steps. Fritzi rushes in, flourishing a revolver.*

FRITZI. I shoot them, Mamma.

MRS. BAUER (*grabbing the revolver*). Mein Gott! Fritzi! Papa's pistol! (*She examines it carefully*) You ever touch that again and I'll . . . .

[*She menaces him.*

FRITZI (*sulkily*). I'll save up my money and buy me one.

MRS. BAUER (*smiling a little to herself*). I see you buyin' one.

[*Carries revolver into inner room.*

FRITZI (*in a loud voice and as though shooting at Karl*). Bang! Bang! Bang!

[*Karl strikes at Fritzi; Fritzi dodges.*

KARL (*to his mother as she re-enters*). Trouble with Fritzi is he don't mind me any more.

MRS. BAUER. You wash your dirty hands and face this minute — d'you hear me, Fritzi!

FRITZI (*looking at his hands*). That's ink stains. I got the highest mark in spelling today. Capital H-e-n-n-y, capital N-i-e-s — Henny Nies, a bum.

[*Mrs. Bauer makes a rush at him and he runs back into the inner room.*

KARL (*sitting down beside the table*). Do we have to go to school this afternoon?

MRS. BAUER. You have to do what you always do.

KARL. Can't we stay home. . . .

MRS. BAUER (*fiercely*). Why? Why?

KARL (*sheepishly*) I ain't feelin' well.

MRS. BAUER. Karlchen! . . . *sham dich!*

KARL. Till the boys forget. . . .

MRS. BAUER. Papa'd know somethin' was wrong right away. That'd be the end. You mustn't act as if anything was different from always.

KARL (*indignantly*). Sayin' *my* father's been to jail!

MRS. BAUER. Karl. . . .

KARL. Papa'd make them stop.

MRS. BAUER (*panic-stricken*). Karl, don't you tell Papa nothing.

KARL. Not tell Papa?

MRS. BAUER. No.

KARL. Why not tell Papa?

MRS. BAUER. Because —

KARL. Yes, Mamma?

MRS. BAUER. Because he *was* arrested yesterday.

KARL (*shocked*). What for, Mamma? Why was he —

MRS. BAUER. For nothing. . . . It was all a lie.

KARL. Well — what was it, Mamma?

MRS. BAUER. The cat got hurt in the dumb-waiter — Papa didn't mean to — then they saw Papa chasin' it — then it died.

KARL. Why did Papa chase it?

MRS. BAUER. To see how it hurt itself.

KARL. Whose cat?

MRS. BAUER. The stray cat.

KARL. The little black cat? Is Blacky dead?

MRS. BAUER. Yes, he died on the sidewalk.

KARL. Where was we?

MRS. BAUER. You was at school.

KARL. Papa didn't want us to keep Blacky.

MRS. BAUER. So many cats and dogs around. . . .

FRITZI (*wailing at the door*). Blacky was my cat.

MRS. BAUER. S-s-h! What do you know about Blacky?

FRITZI. I was listening. Why did Papa kill Blacky?

MRS. BAUER. Hush!

FRITZI. Why was Papa took to jail?

MRS. BAUER. Fritzi! If Papa was to hear. . . .

[*Mrs. Bauer goes out.*

FRITZI (*sidling up to Karl*). Miau! Miau!

KARL. You shut up that. Didn't Mamma tell you.

FRITZI. When I'm a man I'm going to get arrested. I'll shoot Henny Nies.

KARL (*contemptuously*). Yes, you'll do a lot of shooting.
[*Fritzi punches Karl in back.*

KARL (*striking at Fritzi*). You're as big a tough as Henny Nies.

FRITZI (*proud of this alleged likeness*). I'm going to be a man just like my father; I'll holler and make them stand around.

KARL (*with conviction*). What you need is a good licking.
[*Telephone rings; Karl goes to it.*

KARL. No, Ma'am, we're just going to eat now.

FRITZI (*sits down beside the table*). Blacky was a nice cat; she purred just like a steam engine.

KARL. Mamma told you not to bring her in.

FRITZI. Papa said I could.

[*There is the sound of footfalls. Bauer and his wife come in and close the door behind them.*

MRS. BAUER (*putting the dinner on the table*). Come, children. (*To Bauer*) Sit down, Fritz.

[*She serves the dinner. Karl pulls Fritzi out of his father's chair and pushes him into his own; then he takes his place next to his mother.*

MRS. BAUER (*to Bauer, who sits looking at his food*). Eat somethin', Friedrich.

[*She sits down.*

BAUER. I can't eat nothin'. I'm full up to here.

[*He touches his throat.*

MRS. BAUER. If you haven't done nothin' wrong why do you let it worry you so?

[*Children are absorbed in eating.*

FRITZI (*suddenly*). Gee, didn't Blacky like liver!

[*Mrs. Bauer and Karl look at him warningly.*

MRS. BAUER (*fiercely*). You eat your dinner.

BAUER (*affectionately, laying his hand on Fritzi's arm*). Fritzi.

FRITZI (*points toward the inner room*). I'm going to have a gun, too, when I'm a man.

[*Bauer follows Fritzi's gesture and falls to musing. There is a look of brooding misery on his face. Karl nudges Fritzi warningly and watches his father furtively. Bauer sits motionless, staring straight ahead of him.*

MRS. BAUER (*to Bauer*). Now drink your coffee.

BAUER. Don't you see, Miene, don't you see? . . . Nothing makes it right now; no one believes me — no one believes me — no one.

MRS. BAUER. What do you care, if you didn't do it.

BAUER. I care like hell.

MRS. BAUER (*with a searching look at her husband*). Fritzi, when you go on like this, people won't believe you didn't do it. You ought to act like you don't care . . . (*She fixes him with a beseeching glance*) if you *didn't* do it.

[*Bauer looks at his wife as though a hidden meaning to her words had suddenly bitten into his mind.*

BAUER (*as though to himself*). A man can't stand that. I've gone hungry . . . I've been in the hospital . . . I've worked when I couldn't stand up hardly. . . .

MRS. BAUER (*coaxingly*). Drink your coffee, drink it now, Fritz, while it's hot.

[*He tries to swallow a little coffee and then puts down the cup.*

BAUER. I've never asked favors of no man.

MRS. BAUER. Well, an' if you did . . .

BAUER. I've always kept my good name. . . .

MRS. BAUER. If a man hasn't done nothin' wrong it don't matter. Just go ahead like always — if —

BAUER (*muttering*). If — if —

MRS. BAUER (*to the boys*). Get your caps now, it's time to go to school.

[*Karl gets up, passes behind his father and beckons to Fritzi to follow him.*

FRITZI (*keeping his seat*).   Do we have to go to school?

BAUER (*suddenly alert*).   Why, what's the matter?

FRITZI.   The boys —

MRS. BAUER (*breaking in*).   Fritzi!

(*The boys go into the inner room. Bauer collapses again. Mrs. Bauer, looking at him strangely*) Fritzi — if you didn't —

BAUER.   I can't prove nothing — and no one believes me. (*A pause. She is silent under his gaze*) No one! (*He waits for her to speak. She sits with averted face. He sinks into a dull misery. The expression in his eyes changes from beseeching to despair as her silence continues, and he cries out hoarsely*) No one! Even if you kill a cat — what's a cat against a man's life!

MRS. BAUER (*tensely, her eyes fastened on his*).   But you *didn't* kill it?

[*A pause.*

MRS. BAUER (*in a low appealing voice*).   *Did* you, Fritz? DID you? (*Bauer gets up slowly. He stands very still and stares at his wife. Karl's voice.* "Mamma, Fritzi's fooling with Papa's gun.")

[*Both children rush into the room.*

KARL.   You oughta lock it up.

MRS. BAUER (*to Fritzi*). Bad boy! (*To Karl*) Fritzi wants to kill himself — that's what. Go on to school.

[*Boys run past area.*

VOICES.   Who killed the cat! Who killed the cat!

[*At the sound of the voices the boys start back. Instinctively Mrs. Bauer lays a protecting hand on each. She looks around at her husband with a sudden anxiety which she tries to conceal from the children, who whisper together. Bauer rises heavily to his feet and walks staggeringly toward the inner room.*

MRS. BAUER (*in a worried tone as she pushes the children out*). Go on to school.

[*At the threshold of the inner room, Bauer stops, half turns back with distorted features, and then hurries in. The door slams behind him. Mrs. Bauer closes the outer door, turns, takes a step as though to follow Bauer, hesitates, then crosses to the kitchen table and starts to clear up the dishes. The report of a revolver sounds from the inner room. Terror-stricken, Mrs. Bauer rushes in.*

MRS. BAUER'S VOICE. Fritz! Fritz! Speak to me! Look at me, Fritz! You didn't do it, Fritz! I know you didn't do it!

[*Sound of low sobbing . . . After a few seconds the telephone bell . . . It rings continuously while the* CURTAIN *slowly falls.*

THE WONDER HAT

BEN HECHT AND KENNETH SAWYER GOODMAN

THE CHICAGO WORKSHOP THEATRE opened in 1916 for the purpose of giving plays written by Chicago authors, acted by Chicago amateurs, and staged by Chicago artists. Ben Hecht and Kenneth Sawyer Goodman, together with Alice Gerstenberg, Oscar Wolff, Mary Aldis, and other one-act playwrights, were prominent members of the group. "The Wonder Hat", one of the perennial comedies about Pierrot and his loves, was a popular offering that was first published in this collection.

Ben Hecht, who has been newspaper reporter, playwright, novelist, short story writer, and Little Theatre producer, was born in New York City in 1893. When he was eight, his family moved to Racine, Wisconsin; at seventeen, he graduated from the Racine High School. A month later he arrived in Chicago and secured a job on the *Chicago Journal*, where he worked for four years. Then he joined the *Chicago Daily News*, and was official Berlin correspondent for that paper during the World War. In recent years, he has been writing plays and novels and producing motion pictures.

He has, either as co-author or sole author, contributed the following one-act plays: "The Hero of Santa Maria", "The Idyl of the Shops", "Poem of David", "The Hand of Siva", "The Quitter", and "Dregs." Among the principal long plays associated with his name are "The Egoist", "The Front Page", "The Great Magoo", and "Twentieth Century." In preparation is "To Quito and Back." He has done outstanding independent work in motion-picture writing and production, in "Crime Without Passion" and

"The Scoundrel"; and he has contributed to the achievement of such superior films as "Viva Villa", "Scarface", "Topaze", and "A Design for Living."

KENNETH SAWYER GOODMAN

THE BIOGRAPHY of Kenneth Sawyer Goodman is to be found with the play "Ryland."

THE WONDER HAT

A HARLEQUINADE

By BEN HECHT AND KENNETH SAWYER
GOODMAN

"The Wonder Hat" was originally produced at the Arts and Crafts Theatre, Detroit, Michigan, in 1916.

Original Cast

HARLEQUIN . . . . Sam Hume
PIERROT . . . . Charles E. Hilton
PUNCHINELLO . . . . A. L. Weeks
COLUMBINE . . . . Lento Fulwell
MARGOT . . . . Betty Brooks

THE WONDER HAT

SCENE. *The scene is a park by moonlight. The stage setting is shallow. At the back center is a formal fountain, backed by a short wall about seven feet high and having urns at its two ends. At each side of the fountain are low groups of shrubbery. There is a clear space between the fountain and back drop so that the characters may pass round the shrubbery and the fountain. The back drop represents a night sky with an abnormally large yellow moon. A path crosses the stage parallel to the footlights.*

As the curtain rises, Harlequin and Pierrot saunter in from the left, arm in arm. They both have on long cloaks and are swinging light canes with an air of elegant ennui. They pause in the center of the stage.

HARLEQUIN (*indicating with a wave of his cane*). Dear fellow, this is a circular path. It runs quite around the outer edge of the park, a matter of a half mile or thereabouts. It delights me. I always spend my evenings here. One can walk for hours with the absolute certainty of never getting anywhere.

PIERROT (*removing his eyeglass*). Dear chap, in these days of suburban progress, I had not supposed such a place possible.

HARLEQUIN. There is another point in its favor. As you may have noticed, all the promenaders move continuously in the same direction. It is therefore only necessary to maintain an even pace in order to avoid making acquaintances.

PIERROT. One might retrace one's steps.

HARLEQUIN. It has been tried by certain elderly roués and ladies from the opera, but always with disastrous results. Our best people no longer attempt it.

PIERROT (*with a slight yawn*). How delightfully like life.

HARLEQUIN. In certain ways, yes. Those of a genial disposition may lag and allow others to catch up. The more adventurous may press on and possibly overtake somebody. But unlike life, one is never troubled by one's creditors.

PIERROT. How thoroughly charming. (*Takes pose at fountain*) Tell me, does Columbine ever come here?

HARLEQUIN (*becoming serious; takes pose other side of fountain*). That is the one drawback. She comes here very often.

PIERROT (*snappishly*). Humph! That is really annoying, deucedly, devilishly, foolishly annoying!

HARLEQUIN. You're very emphatic.

PIERROT (*still more snappishly*). I have never liked that woman, in spite of what the poets say about us.

HARLEQUIN. By keeping a sharp lookout, I have thus far managed to avoid her myself and yet keep her often in sight without her laying eyes on me.

PIERROT (*pleased*). I see that we are both confirmed bachelors, without a grain of sentiment in us. We agree perfectly.

HARLEQUIN. On the contrary, we don't agree at all. Because you dislike Columbine, you're too confoundedly polite to others. You make cynical love to all sorts of women and nobody likes you for it. On the other hand, I am immensely partial to the same young lady and detest all the rest of the sex. For that reason I am simply overwhelmed with dinner invitations.

PIERROT. If you're in love with Columbine, why don't you catch up with her some evening and have it out with her?

HARLEQUIN (*preening himself*). Gross materialist! For the sake of a few honeyed kisses would you have me risk the crumbling of an ideal? She would certainly fall in love with me like all the others.

PIERROT (*with equal self-satisfaction*). At least I should be spared the possibility of her falling in love with me.

HARLEQUIN. How selfish of you! (*Moves from the fountain*) But come, if you are quite rested, let us continue our walk.

PIERROT (*moves from fountain*). To be perfectly frank, dear chap, I find your conversation has made me extremely sleepy.

HARLEQUIN (*haughtily*). There is a beautiful stone bench just beyond that clump of lilacs.

PIERROT. Thanks. When we reach it, I shall sit down.

HARLEQUIN. By all means, dear fellow. I can then resume my stroll without the encumbrance of your society.

[*They saunter off, arm in arm. Punchinello enters, dressed in a long, ragged, green coat, carrying a large sack and a little bell. He wears long whiskers and a pair of bone-rimmed spectacles. He advances, tapping before him with a staff and ringing his little bell.*

PUNCHINELLO (*in a whining singsong*). New loves for old! New loves for old! New loves for old! I will buy broken ambitions, wasted lives, cork legs, rejected poems, unfinished plays, bottles, bootjacks, and worn-out religions. (*Drops pack*) Oyez! Oyez! Oyez! New loves for old! New loves for old! (*He wags his head, listening*) Nobody here. Damn it all, I've walked three times round this accursed park with never so much as a squirrel to nibble at my heels. I've seen moon-faced boys asleep on stone benches, stone tritons blowing water into the air, and a rabble of sick looking poets and silly looking girls, all walking in the same direction. But not a bona fide customer. I'll sit down. Yes, yes, I'll sit down, curse them, and ease this infernal crick in my back.

[*He unfolds a little camp stool, which he carries slung by a strap, and sits down. Columbine and Margot enter from the left and advance timidly to the center of the stage without noticing Punchinello.*

COLUMBINE. I'm sure, Margot, that I saw him here only a minute ago talking to that silly clown in the yellow suit.

MARGOT. Well, anyway, whether it was him or an hallucination he's gone now.

COLUMBINE. Oh, dear! I thought he might have stopped to let me catch up with him.

MARGOT. Do you want my honest opinion, Mistress Columbine?

COLUMBINE (*stamping her foot*). How can an opinion be anything but honest? An opinion is naturally and automatically honest.

MARGOT. Mine ain't, m'am. I always formulates my opinions to conform.

COLUMBINE. I don't want them. I'm miserable. I'm wretched.

MARGOT (*severely*). Then I won't give them to you. But if you'd act more like a lady and stop trapesing around in the damp of the night trying to scrape acquaintance with — with this Harlequin who, God knows, may have six or seven wives already —

COLUMBINE. I'm not trapesing after him!

PUNCHINELLO (*in his singsong voice*). New loves for old! New loves for old!

COLUMBINE (*frightened*). Oh, how you startled me!

MARGOT (*her hand on her heart*). Lord love us! I near swallowed my tongue with the jump he gave me.

PUNCHINELLO (*rubbing his hands*). Bargains! Cheap, wonderful bargains! What will the young lady buy? Something for her parlor? Something for her bedroom? Something for herself? Wall paper, eggbeaters, canary birds, salt shakers, oriental rugs, corset covers, diamonds, water bags, chums, potato peelers, hats, shoes, gas fixtures, new, old — bargains, lady, bargains.

COLUMBINE. No, no, no! I don't want to buy anything.

PUNCHINELLO (*kneeling and spreading out his wares*). I have cures to sell, and charms.

MARGOT. Can't you see she doesn't want any of your patent medicines?

COLUMBINE (*fascinated in spite of herself*). What — what charms have you?

PUNCHINELLO. Ho, ho! I have a charm to ward off evil spirits.

MARGOT (*in disgust*). Get along with you!

PUNCHINELLO. Against nightmares, then; against mice, toothaches, bunions, burglars, and broken legs.

COLUMBINE. I don't want them, any of them.

PUNCHINELLO (*wagging his head*). Ho, ho! Ha, ha! Then you're in love. You want a love charm.

COLUMBINE (*stamping her foot*). You're impudent! I tell you I'm not in love.

MARGOT (*beginning to be interested*). What makes you pipe her off as being in love?

PUNCHINELLO. A lady who isn't interested in mice, bunions, or burglars must be in love. There's no two ways about it.

MARGOT. What about the broken legs and toothaches?

PUNCHINELLO (*spreading his hands*). I just put that in for good measure.

COLUMBINE. Enough! I won't listen to you. I'm — not in love.

PUNCHINELLO. I can remedy that with a charm.

COLUMBINE (*almost in tears*). I don't want your charms. I don't want to be in love. I hate him! I hate him! I hate him!

PUNCHINELLO. Yes, yes, pretty lady. I know that sort of talk very well. But I have also a charm to attract love.

COLUMBINE (*brightening immediately*). You have a charm to attract love?

PUNCHINELLO. It will bring all men to you; little men, big men, pretty men, noble men, fat men —

COLUMBINE (*clasping her hands*). I want only one man — only Harlequin.

MARGOT (*interrupting*). If you want my opinion, m'am —

COLUMBINE. But I don't.

MARGOT. I'd leave this fellow's stuff alone, if I was you.

COLUMBINE. But I'm not you and I want the charm.

PUNCHINELLO (*searching through his wares*). It will bring Harlequin to you with the rest.

COLUMBINE (*on tiptoe with eagerness*). Oh, quick! Give it to me.

PUNCHINELLO (*taking an old slipper from his pocket*). Ho, ho! Here it is. An old slipper! Each stitch of it more effective than Sappho's complete works. Each thread more potent than the burning caresses of Dido. They say Cinderella wore a crystal slipper. It's a lie. This — this is what she wore. Ah, ha! Look at it!

COLUMBINE (*taken aback*). Do I have to wear *that*.

MARGOT (*scornfully*). Land's sake, it's all run down at the heel.

PUNCHINELLO. That's because it has been worn so often. Semiramis of Babylon, Lais of Corinth, and Thais of Alexandria all wore this boot.

MARGOT (*with a sniff*). Them names don't sound like respectable ladies to my way of thinking.

COLUMBINE (*dubiously*). It looks very old. Are you sure it has been fumigated?

PUNCHINELLO. It's no older than the light it will kindle in a thousand eyes when you wear it. But in its antiquity lies its chief charm. Cleopatra of Egypt abetted the lures of her person with this same ragged boot. Mary of Scotland and a hundred other beauties of history have inspired the enraptured supplications of their adorers with no more tangible asset then this homely boot. Put it on, pretty lady, and all the men will flock to your feet, especially to the foot that wears the slipper.

[*He hands Columbine the slipper.*

COLUMBINE. Ooh, ooh! How wonderful!

MARGOT (*with a superior air*). Take my word, miss, it'll be a nuisance to you.

COLUMBINE. I don't care. I'm going to teach Harlequin a lesson he won't forget in a hurry.

[*She takes off her own shoe, hopping on one foot and holding Margot's arm. She then puts on the magic slipper.*

MARGOT. Mind, I warned you.

COLUMBINE (*stamping her foot down*). There! It doesn't look so badly once I get it on. It fits perfectly.

PUNCHINELLO (*groveling on his knees*). Oh, most wonderful lady! Oh, most beautiful, most gracious, most divine lady!

MARGOT (*amazed at Punchinello's sudden fervor*). Lord love us! What's got into the old bag of bones?

PUNCHINELLO (*to Columbine*). You have melted the lump of ice in my old breast. I am young again. I can hear the birds singing and sweet waters falling.

MARGOT (*to Punchinello*). Get up this minute, before I burst a lung bawling for help.

COLUMBINE (*dancing up and down with delight*). Oh, oh, oh! Now I know it works. Don't you understand, Margot? It's the slipper, the magic slipper.

PUNCHINELLO. I love you! I love you! I love you!

MARGOT. Stop it, I tell you.

COLUMBINE (*gently*). That's very nice in you, of course, but get up, please, and tell me how much I owe you.

MARGOT. We can't stand here all night.

PUNCHINELLO (*still on his knees*) Oh, oh, oh!

COLUMBINE (*stamping her foot*). Don't you hear me? I say how much do I owe you for the magic slipper?

PUNCHINELLO (*still groveling*). Nothing! Nothing! You owe me nothing at all. I will give you everything in my sack, all my bargains, all my spells, all my charms.

MARGOT. She wouldn't touch them with the tip of a barge pole.

COLUMBINE (*to Margot*). I really think I ought to pay him.

MARGOT If he won't take anything he won't. That's all there is to it.

PUNCHINELLO. Speak to me. My heart is bursting.

MARGOT. Let it burst then. Come, m'am. It's my advice to get away from here before he throws a fit and the police come for him.

COLUMBINE. Yes, yes. Let's run.

[*Columbine takes Margot by the hand and they run off right, laughing.*

PUNCHINELLO (*attempting to rise*). Wait, wait! You must listen to me. I love you. I — I — Oh, this stitch in my side!

[*As the girls' voices die away he struggles to his feet and rubs his head in a dazed sort of way.*

Gone! What have I done? By the seven witches of Beelzebub, by the long fanged mother of the great green spider, I have given my magic slipper away for nothing. (*He shakes his staff*) I've been tricked, cheated. Curses on her golden head. May she have nightmares and toothache! May — Old fool! A blight on my whiskers! I've given my darling slipper away for nothing. (*He sits down again on his camp stool and rocks to and fro, muttering. Harlequin, having completed his circle of the park, enters from the left. He is smoking a cigarette and strolls along, wearing a gloomy and troubled expression. Punchinello sees him and resumes his whining chant*) New loves for old. New loves for old. Bargains in cast-off sweethearts, old coats, umbrellas, glove buttoners, and household pets. Bargains sir. Cheap, wonderful bargains!

(*Harlequin passes and regards Punchinello with absolute indifference*) I have pipes, swords, hosiery, snuff-boxes, underwear, wines, trinkets for beautiful ladies, furniture, spyglasses, motor cars, and bottle openers.

HARLEQUIN (*impatiently*). I want none of your bargains.

PUNCHINELLO. I have magic charms, sir. Spells and charms.

HARLEQUIN. Ah, more like it! You have charms, eh? What kind of charms?

PUNCHINELLO. I have charms against bunions, burglars, broken legs, nightmares, stomach-aches, and hangnails.

HARLEQUIN. Ordinary trash. I don't want them.

PUNCHINELLO (*looking furtively about*). I have a love charm.

HARLEQUIN (*in alarm*) God forbid!

PUNCHINELLO (*rubbing his hands*). Ho, ho! He, he!

HARLEQUIN. Have you, by any chance, a charm against love? Aye, more, have you some efficacious armour against womankind in general?

PUNCHINELLO. Ho, ho! A man after my own heart. A cautious man. A sensible man.

HARLEQUIN (*loftily*). Know you, antiquated pander, that in this day, a young man's lot is not a happy one. Everywhere I go, excepting only this park, women follow me. They stalk me. They covet me. They make my days miserable. They haunt my sleep. They simper about me, wink at me, rub against me like silken cats. (*With vexation*) Ah, I would almost end my life from very irritation with their wiles, their snaring pursuits, from the very annoyance of their cloying affection. And the worst part of it is that I know myself susceptible.

PUNCHINELLO (*slyly*). There is no charm in the world against falling in love, but I can sell you a powder which, tossed into the air, will bring destruction to women alone.

HARLEQUIN (*rubbing his chin doubtfully*). No, that's too brutal. I couldn't kill them all even if I wanted to. And what use to destroy a hundred, a thousand, even a million women, and have one sneak up behind you and get you after all. It would be an effort wasted. Love is inevitable.

PUNCHINELLO. Wait. Ho, ho! I have it, the very thing. If one cannot remove the inevitable, at any rate one can hide from it. What doesn't see you, can't get you. Ha, ha! I can sell you a hat.

HARLEQUIN. I am not in the market for a hat.

PUNCHINELLO (*triumphantly*). But, a magic hat! A Wonder Hat! It will make you invisible.

HARLEQUIN (*incredulously*). Invisible!

PUNCHINELLO (*fishing in his bag*). When you put it on, you will be invisible to the world. You will exist only in your own mind. You will escape the pernicious sentimentality, the never-ending blandishments, the strategic coquetry of women. Ho, ho! Ha, ha!

HARLEQUIN (*eagerly*). Come, you millinery sorcerer. You have convinced me. Invisibility is the one thing I crave to make me sublimely happy. Splendid. They shall never simper at me again, never undulate before my tormented eyes. I will buy it.

PUNCHINELLO (*holding up the hat*). Is it not a creation?

HARLEQUIN (*looking at the hat with distaste*). God, what a thing to wear! I would not wear it, you may be sure, were it not invisible. Being invisible, I assure you, is its chief charm. Indeed, any man would prefer not to be seen in such a hat.

PUNCHINELLO. It may be unlovely in outline, coarse in texture, unrefined in color, but there is only one other such hat in the world. It belongs to the Grand Llamah of Thibet. Ha, ha! This one will cost you gold.

HARLEQUIN (*cautiously*). But, first I must see if it is really a wonder hat.

PUNCHINELLO. I will put it on.

[*He does so.*

HARLEQUIN (*delighted*). A miracle! Where are you?

PUNCHINELLO (*removing the hat with a flourish*). Now!

HARLEQUIN. What wonders I will do with that hat. I will walk the streets in comfort and security. But stay! What if the hat is only charmed for you? What if the charm does not apply to me?

PUNCHINELLO. You shall try it yourself. Put it on.

[*Harlequin takes the hat and puts it on.*

HARLEQUIN. Can you see me?

PUNCHINELLO. By St. Peter of Padua, not a speck of you! [*He gropes with his hands, then strikes out with his staff and strikes Harlequin on the shins.*

HARLEQUIN. Ooh! Ouch!

PUNCHINELLO. You see you are quite invisible.

HARLEQUIN. But not invulnerable.

[*He rubs his shin.*

PUNCHINELLO. How much will you give me for this Wonder Hat?

HARLEQUIN. Are you sure you can't see me?

PUNCHINELLO. You are one with the thin air and the fairies that inhabit it.

[*Rubbing his hands.*

HARLEQUIN. There's no uncanny trick by which Columbine can discover me?

PUNCHINELLO. None! None! I swear it. It's only by
your voice that I know where you are.

[*He swings out with his staff. Harlequin leaps nimbly aside.*

PUNCHINELLO. For years I have treasured this wonder hat.
A blind woman with seven teeth and one eye made it in
a haunted hut. It was cooked over a fire of serpents'
skins. (*As Punchinello speaks, Harlequin tiptoes away to
the right around the central group of shrubbery*) It is colored
with the dye of a magic root. It is older than the oldest
cloud and you can figure out for yourself how old that
would be. Ho, ho! There's no charm like it to be had
from one peak of the world to the other. (*He swings
out again with his staff*) Five bags of gold, sir. Cheap,
a bargain. Hey! (*He swings his staff*) Hey! Hey!
Where are you? Take off my hat so that I can see you.
Give me back my hat. (*He stands still and listens*)
Thief! Thief! He's gone. Oh, what a fool. First
my magic slipper, worth fifty pots of gold. What
a doddering idiot! I have lost my magic hat, my wonder
hat. I've been cheated, robbed. Oh, what a stitch in
my side. Oh, oh! (*He gathers up his pack hurriedly, then
stops and taps the side of his nose with his finger*) Ho, ho!
A thought! What a pair of lovers they will make! She
with her slipper. He with his hat. She said Harlequin.
He said Columbine. Yes, yes! I shall have my reward.
They are the fools, not I. As if love were not enough
magic of itself. Ho, ho, ho! I must follow her. She
went this way.

[*He moves off toward the right, leaving his camp stool. Harlequin appears round the left end of the shrubbery and advances cautiously to center of stage.*

HARLEQUIN (*looking after Punchinello*). I should have paid
him if he hadn't run away like that. I detest the idea of
cheating anybody. But of course, one can't be running
after tradespeople, pressing money upon them. It simply
isn't done. (*He looks in the other direction*) Columbine
should have made the round of the park by this time.

What's keeping her? Here I am waiting for her, as safe and invisible as the angels themselves. (*He sits down on the camp stool and holds his hand before his face*) No, I can't see it. I wonder if I have a hand or a leg, or a stomach, or a heart? If I don't take off my hat and look at myself I shall soon become a total stranger to myself. What a wonder hat! (*There is the sound of women's voices in the distance. He pricks up his ears*) Ah, her voice! Like the tinkling bells in a shrine of ivory. Like the patter of crystal rain in a pool of scarlet lilies. (*He slaps his leg*) Ah, ha! I'm in love. In love! To the tips of where my fingers ought to be. (*He becomes serious*) If I should take off my hat, I'd be lost. She would pounce on me, and, being in love, I should pounce back. My hat must stay on. I will tie it on. I will nail it on. Curse me if I take off my hat. (*He pulls his hat down to the tips of his ears, then clasps his hands*) Ah, to sit by her, safe and unseen! To bask in the splendor of her presence. To love and be loved only as a dream. To be free from all material entanglements and responsibilities. To touch her with invisible fingers and permit the stolen thrills to course up and down my invisible spine! (*He sings*)

Wandering Minstrel Air

A love-sick atom I,
A thing unseen and seeing,
For in my hat am I
A hypothetical being.

(*He suddenly has a new thought*) But what if, being unable to see me, she should fall in love with somebody else? That vapid ass, Pierrot, for instance? Oh, God, what if he should strike fire in her heart? But I will not take off my hat. Kind heaven, give me the strength to keep my hat on.

[*He pulls the hat still further over his ears, just as Columbine and Margot enter from the left.*

COLUMBINE. This is too much! Did you ever see such a rabble?

MARGOT. I shouldn't be so particular, miss, seeing as how you brought it on yourself.

COLUMBINE. They've risen from every bench to follow me. They've come from every corner of the park; burglars, doctors, poets, whiskered Don Juans, rumbling Romeos. Great Heavens, the idiots! If they hadn't fallen to fighting among themselves, we'd have been trampled to death. I — I hope they exterminate each other. I hope I never see them again. I — I —

[*Harlequin, seeing Columbine in such an angry mood, rises cautiously and in so doing upsets the camp stool. He stands trembling and holding on to his hat.*

MARGOT (*starting*). Bless me, what's that?

[*Both look around. Their eyes pass over Harlequin without seeing him.*

COLUMBINE. Nothing. There's nobody here.

[*Evidently much relieved, Harlequin tiptoes to the right end of the fountain.*

MARGOT. If you want my honest opinion, miss —

COLUMBINE (*stamping her foot*). How many times must I tell you —

MARGOT. Be careful with that magic boot, miss.

COLUMBINE. What's the good of it? It's brought me nothing but trouble.

MARGOT. Well, what did you expect?

COLUMBINE (*almost weeping*). It hasn't brought him. It hasn't brought Harlequin.

MARGOT. If you want my opinion, miss, honest or otherwise —

COLUMBINE (*stamping her foot again*). I don't!

MARGOT. Then I won't give it to you.

COLUMBINE. Oh, Margot, be gentle with me. I love him — and I'm dreadfully uncomfortable about it.

MARGOT. Well, there's worse discomfort. There's clergyman's sore throat, for instance, and housemaid's knee.

COLUMBINE (*clinching her hands*). Oh, if I could only see him now, the cold-hearted fish! I'd fix him! I'd melt his icy blood for him!

[*Harlequin holds tight to his hat.*

MARGOT (*soothingly*). Of course you would. Of course you would.

COLUMBINE (*sits on fountain*). But he can't escape. The magic slipper will draw him from the ends of the earth. I'll marry him. I'll have him for my own, locked under key in a house; a beautiful little house, all new and spick and span, with white trimmings and green shutters.

MARGOT. If I may put in a word for myself, miss, I hope you won't have a basement kitchen.

COLUMBINE. But I'll make him suffer first. I'll — I'll (*spitefully*) —

[*Harlequin jams his hat down tighter and disappears behind the fountain.*

MARGOT. If you must get het up and stamp, miss, I'd advise you to confine your stamping to the foot which ain't got the magic boot on.

COLUMBINE. Margot, were you ever in love?

MARGOT. You know very well, miss, I have three babies at home.

COLUMBINE. Tell me, did you love their father?

MARGOT. It's my honest opinion, miss, there were three fathers, and I loved them all very much.

COLUMBINE (*shocked*). Then you're a wicked woman.

MARGOT. There are opinions concerning that question, miss, honest and otherwise.

COLUMBINE. You are, I say.

MARGOT. Which I choose, begging your pardon, to consider as an otherwise opinion. Being a father to three babies puts an awful responsibility on a man, as you may find out for yourself some day. So I was careful to distribute the burden.

[*Pierrot enters dishevelled and breathless. He advances and flings himself on one knee before Columbine.*

PIERROT. At last, exquisite Columbine, ravishing vision, I have overcome my rivals. I have vanquished a legion of your adorers.

[*Harlequin peeps round the left side of the fountain.*

MARGOT. Lord love us, you look as though you'd been run through a threshing machine.

PIERROT. I have. I kicked Scaramouche in the stomach and pushed the Doctor of Bologna into a lily pond. Divine Circe, I have come to claim my reward.

[*He clutches at the edge of Columbine's dress.*

COLUMBINE. You're tearing the trimming off my petticoat.

PIERROT. Columbine, Columbine, I love you!

MARGOT (*taking his arm and pulling him to his feet*). Get up, you big baby.

[*Harlequin tiptoes across the stage and stands behind Margot and Pierrot.*

PIERROT (*clasping his hands*). I love you, Columbine. Listen to me.

COLUMBINE (*haughtily*). This is a very sudden change on your part, Mr. Pierrot. Yesterday you snubbed me quite openly.

PIERROT. Forgive me! I was blind! I was a dolt. I have only just now come to my senses.

MARGOT (*turning her shoulder to him and folding her arms*). You'll come to something worse presently.

PIERROT. I love you. I love you.

[*Harlequin reaches out and deftly extracts a long hat pin from the back of Margot's cap. Margot puts her hands to her head and turns fiercely on Pierrot.*

MARGOT. How dast you grab my hat?

PIERROT (*in astonishment*). I never touched your hat.

MARGOT. You did.

PIERROT (*turning on her*). I — I did nothing of the sort.

MARGOT. There's laws to cover this sort of thing — annoying women in a public park.

PIERROT. You're an impudent hussy.

MARGOT. You're nothing but a common, ordinary home wrecker.

[*Harlequin approaches Columbine and gently touches her hair. Pierrot and Margot glare at each other.*

COLUMBINE (*clasping her hands*). Margot, Margot, it's wonderful! It's divine. I feel as if the air were suddenly full of kisses.

[*Harlequin strikes an attitude of complete satisfaction.*

MARGOT. It's full of dampness and nasty language, that's what it is.

[*She gives Pierrot a venomous look.*

PIERROT (*again falling on his knees*). It's full of unspeakable ecstasy of my adoration.

COLUMBINE (*paying no attention to him*). It's full of marvelously shy caresses. They are like the wings of happy butterflies, brushing the white lilac blooms.

PIERROT. Ah, what did I tell you? The love I offer you is a gift, a treasure.

COLUMBINE (*her hands still clasped*). I can almost hear invisible lips sighing my name — his lips — Harlequin's lips.

PIERROT (*straightening himself up on his knees*). What's that you say about Harlequin?

COLUMBINE (*coming to herself*). It's none of your business.

PIERROT (*spitefully*). Good God! To think of intruding that fellow's name at a time like this. Why, the chap's positively a bounder. He has no taste, no education, no refinement. And his face — ugh! He'd frighten himself to death if he looked in a mirror before his barber got to him in the morning.

[*Harlequin steps behind Pierrot and prods him in the back with the hat pin.*

PIERROT. Ooh! Ouch! (*He springs to his feet and turns on Margot*) You — you did that. You — you know you did.

[*Shaking his finger in her face.*

MARGOT (*taken aback*). Did what?

PIERROT (*in a rage*). You — you stabbed me in the back and don't you deny it.

MARGOT. The man's stark, staring mad!

COLUMBINE (*to Pierrot in an icy tone*). Will you be good
enough to explain what's the matter with you?

PIERROT (*his eyes still on Margot*). I've been attacked,
lacerated.

MARGOT. If you don't behave yourself, I'll give you something to howl about.

PIERROT (*again falling at Columbine's feet*). But it's nothing,
nothing to the torments I suffer from your heartlessness.
Nothing to the —
(*Harlequin stabs again*)
Ouch! Wow! Hell's fire! Animals! I'm being bitten
to death!
[*He clasps his hand to the spot.*

MARGOT. And a good riddance, too!

COLUMBINE. Come, Margot. I won't stay here. I won't
be insulted.

PIERROT (*again grasping the hem of her gown*). No, no, I'll
suffer everything. I'll suffer in silence. Only don't
leave me. Speak to me. I love you. I —

COLUMBINE. Let go my dress or I'll scream for help.

MARGOT. If you really want help, miss, it's my advice take
off the slipper.
[*Harlequin, who has been about to attack Pierrot, hesitates and
looks puzzled.*

COLUMBINE. Yes, yes. Why didn't I think of it.
[*She whips off the magic slipper and holds it in her hand.
The moment the slipper leaves her foot, Pierrot sits back
on his haunches and lets go of the edge of Columbine's
dress.*

PIERROT (*in a feeble voice*). I love you. I — (*He rubs his
head*) By Jove, this is most extraordinary!

MARGOT (*clapping her hands*). Toss it to me, miss.
[*Columbine tosses the slipper to Margot.*

MARGOT (*examining the slipper*). What a rummy slipper!
(*She takes off her shoe*) I wonder what's inside of it. Love?
(*She puts it on her own foot*) Ooh! How it tickles!

[*Pierrot rises from his knees and looks helplessly from Columbine to Margot.*

COLUMBINE. Well, Mr. Pierrot?

PIERROT (*completely puzzled*). I am quite at a loss to explain my feelings.

[*He hesitates, then turns and kneels before Margot. Harlequin appears even more puzzled. He is also drawn toward Margot by the spell of the slipper, but his natural infatuation for Columbine seems to neutralize the charm. He is visibly perplexed.*

PIERROT. Incomparable Margot! Queen among housemaids! Divine custodian of my deepest affections.

MARGOT. You see, miss, the gentleman is now in love with me.

COLUMBINE. Disgusting!

PIERROT. I am drawn by some irresistible power of fascination. I — belong to you utterly.

MARGOT. You belong in jail, that's where you belong. You're nothing but a — a shameless affinity.

PIERROT (*clinging to the hem of Margot's skirt*). I love you. I swear it. See, I kiss the hem of your gown. I throw myself on your mercy.

MARGOT (*weakening*). Oh, la, la! Listen to the man talk!

COLUMBINE. You're a brazen hussy to take advantage of your social superior.

MARGOT (*haughtily*). My superior? Him?

COLUMBINE (*stamping her foot*). You're forgetting your place.

PIERROT. I love you. I love you.

MARGOT (*slyly*). Suppose, miss, I was to say I believe every word he says to me?

COLUMBINE. I'd say you were an artful, designing minx. I'd discharge you without a shred of character.

MARGOT. Well, you won't have to — because I ain't going to say it.

PIERROT (*making another grab at her skirt*). You must listen to me. You must.

[*Harlequin stabs him once more with the hat pin.*

Ouch! Wow! This is terrible. I love you.

MARGOT. Hey! Get up. A woman what works for a living can't afford to have her good nerves shattered for her. [*She tries to shake off Pierrot.*

COLUMBINE. Give me back the slipper, this instant.

MARGOT. You're welcome to it, I'm sure. (*She snatches off the slipper and tosses it away from her. Columbine picks it up, but does not put it on*) Now will you leave go of me? [*To Pierrot. He releases her in a dazed way.*

PIERROT. I love you. I — [*He arises and again looks from one to the other. Columbine holds the slipper in her hand.*

COLUMBINE. Well, sir?

MARGOT. Well?

PIERROT (*adjusting his collar and speaking quite calmly*). I consider myself fortunate in having escaped you both. I see now that there is something deadly about that slipper. To think that a man of my intellectual and artistic attainments should have been affected by such a slippery artifice. In love with a boot! How very trivial!

MARGOT. Well, what are you going to do now?

PIERROT. I don't know exactly. Perhaps I shall drown myself in the fountain. [*He turns his back on Margot and Columbine and assumes a pose of thoughtful indifference. Harlequin again approaches Columbine.*

COLUMBINE. Margot, Margot, what shall I do? I'm faint. I'm intoxicated. He hasn't come and yet I feel as if he were near me, almost touching me. I feel all the exquisite uncertainty of love. Yes, yes, I love him. I love Harlequin and I know that he loves me in return. I know it, and yet, and yet —

MARGOT. Yes, miss, and yet —?

COLUMBINE (*wringing her hands*). And yet I don't know what under heavens to do about it. [*Harlequin clasps his hands in an ecstasy of complete satisfaction. Margot and Columbine are now at one side and*

Margot speaks in a tone which Harlequin and Pierrot are not supposed to hear.

MARGOT. It's my advice, miss, put the slipper on again. What if it don't catch this here Harlequin? There's just as big perch in the puddle as ever came out of it. That's my motto. Besides, there is such a thing as making the right man jealous.

COLUMBINE (*brightening immediately*). I believe you're right. I'll put on the slipper. I'll have a desperate flirtation with Pierrot. I'll take him everywhere with me. I'll dangle him before Harlequin's eyes. It will serve them both right. (*She puts on the slipper and speaks archly*) Mr. Pierrot.

PIERROT (*turning*). Eh? I beg your pardon.

COLUMBINE. I — don't want you to be angry with me.

[*Pierrot looks puzzled for a moment, then succumbs to the spell of the slipper again and rushes toward her.*

PIERROT. I — I don't — (*He throws himself on his knees*) Columbine, Columbine, my angel, my flower, my enchantress!

COLUMBINE (*shaking her finger at him*). You were very rude to me a few moments ago.

[*Harlequin watches with puzzled interest.*

PIERROT. Forgive me! It was a dream. I love you!

COLUMBINE. You accused me of having ensnared your affections by means of a charm.

PIERROT. A charm? I don't know anything about a charm. I am charmed only by your eyes, your lips, the flow of your voice.

COLUMBINE. Do you know I think it's very sweet of you to say that, after all that's happened this evening.

PIERROT. I can say more, a thousand times more.

COLUMBINE. Perhaps I shall give you the chance.

HARLEQUIN (*aloud, completely overcome with jealousy*). Here's a fine kettle of fish!

PIERROT. You — you do love me then, after all?

COLUMBINE. I haven't said so.

HARLEQUIN. I shall put a stop to this. (*He seems to come to a tremendous resolution*) I — I shall take off my hat.

MARGOT. Lord have mercy, what is that?

COLUMBINE. Please give me your arm.

HARLEQUIN. Thousand devils, I can't get it off!

COLUMBINE. You may see me to my door.

HARLEQUIN (*frantically*). Wait! Stop! — If, — if I could only get my hat off!

MARGOT (*alarmed*). I want to get away from here.

COLUMBINE (*listening*). It's Harlequin's voice.

PIERROT. I don't see anybody.

[*They all look about them. Punchinello enters from the left with his pack on his back. They all see him.*

PUNCHINELLO. Ho, ho, ha ha! There you are, eh? There you are. I've been looking for you. Ho, ho! And now I've caught up with you.

[*Columbine hastily snatches off her slipper and hides it behind her. They all face Punchinello. Harlequin tiptoes to one side and watches curiously.*

COLUMBINE. What do you want?

PUNCHINELLO. What do I want, eh? You know very well what I want. I want my magic slipper, my magic slipper that you stole from me.

COLUMBINE. I didn't steal it. You gave it to me.

PUNCHINELLO. Ho, ho! That's a pretty story. I gave it to you, eh? Well, I changed my mind.

COLUMBINE. I — I'm perfectly willing to pay you for it.

MARGOT. Don't you give him a cent, the miserable oyster.

COLUMBINE. How much do you want for it?

PUNCHINELLO. I should think about ten bags of gold.

COLUMBINE. Ridiculous! There isn't so much money in the whole world.

PUNCHINELLO (*pointing to Pierrot*). Perhaps this nice gentleman would like to buy it for you?

PIERROT. I — (*He looks at Columbine*) I have only the most casual acquaintance with this lady.

HARLEQUIN (*in a rage, to Pierrot*). You infernal little cad!
You —
[*He makes a movement toward Pierrot. All start away from
his voice but Punchinello.*

PUNCHINELLO. Ho, ho! So you're here. Two birds with
one stone. (*He rubs his hands*) My magic slipper and
my beloved Wonder Hat. Well, well, well!
(*Harlequin, seeing he has betrayed his presence, stands as if
undecided what to do. Punchinello strikes about him with
his staff*)
Hey, where are you? Take off my hat.

MARGOT. For the love of heaven, what is he raving about
now?

PUNCHINELLO. My hat, my Wonder Hat. I sold it to
Harlequin for five bags of gold — six bags of gold.

COLUMBINE. You sold it to Harlequin?

PUNCHINELLO. Aye, the ruffian, the highwayman. He
clapped it on his head and now he's invisible.

COLUMBINE (*in delighted wonder*). You really mean that
Harlequin is here, near us? Oh, I knew it. I felt it.

PUNCHINELLO. Of course, he's here. Hey, you, take off
my hat. (*He swings his staff and Harlequin dances out of
the way*)
Take off my hat or give me my eight bags of gold. (*He
swings his staff again*) Hey, thief!

HARLEQUIN. I'm not a thief. I'd have paid you for your
hat if you hadn't run away in such a huff. Now, after the
way you've acted, I shall take my own time about it.

COLUMBINE (*stamping her foot*). Harlequin.

HARLEQUIN (*in a dubious voice*). Ye — yes?

COLUMBINE. Take off that silly hat this minute!

HARLEQUIN. I — well, to tell the truth, I —

COLUMBINE. Don't you hear what I'm saying? Give it back
this second.

HARLEQUIN. I would first like some sort of assurance, some
guarantee of good faith, some —

COLUMBINE. I'm not making any promises this evening.

HARLEQUIN (*plaintively*). My dear Columbine, I have learned a good deal about my own feelings in the last half hour. I am perfectly willing to return this man's property and to submit to the ordinary and normal risks of society, but I positively insist that, before I reveal myself, you must also return to him all sundry charms, spells, et cetera, which might, if used either by accident or malice aforethought, affect my own future course of action.

COLUMBINE (*remaining absolutely firm*). I've told you once that I won't make any promises.

HARLEQUIN. Then, I remain invisible.

PUNCHINELLO. I tell you once more, give me back my hat.

HARLEQUIN (*folding his arms*). No.

PUNCHINELLO. Ah, ha! Then I shall have my revenge. Know, miserable butterfly, that you are trifling with magic beyond your own powers of control. There is a terrible clause in the incorporation of this hat. Listen. He who steals this Wonder Hat and places it upon his own head, cannot remove it again except in the presence and with the consent of its rightful owner. When I have left you, you will become for all time one with the interstellar atoms. You will never resume your mortal shape. You will haunt the cafés. You will moon among the boxes at the opera. You will sigh and pine in the wake of beautiful women, as futile and impalpable as a gust of summer wind. (*He picks up his pack*) Now, will you give me back my hat?

HARLEQUIN (*with evident effort at firmness*). No, not unless Columbine first returns the slipper.

PUNCHINELLO. Madam, I make my last appeal to you.

COLUMBINE (*folding her arms*). Not unless Harlequin first returns the hat.

[*Punchinello looks from one to the other.*

PUNCHINELLO. Come, ladies and gentlemen, I have urgent business elsewhere.

PIERROT. Might I suggest that the simplest way out of the dilemma would be for each of the principal parties to return the pilfered articles at the same exact time.

PUNCHINELLO. An excellent idea.

PIERROT. I shall count, and at the word "three" — is that satisfactory to everybody?

HARLEQUIN (*doubtfully*). Ye — yes.

COLUMBINE (*doubtfully*). Ye — yes.

PIERROT. Very well, then. One — (*Harlequin begins to loosen the hat*) Two —

MARGOT (*stepping forward*). Stop, everybody. You, Mistress Columbine, and you, invisible Mr. Harlequin. Because no matter what you do, somebody's bound to regret it. You, wherever you are, keep your lid on and your mouth shut. I want to put it up to the kind ladies and gentlemen that have been studying this performance and I asks them openly, what should be done at this point? Should Columbine give back the slipper or should she hang on to what she's got? Should Harlequin take off his hat? Personally, my honest opinion is that the question can't be answered to suit everybody so it's my advice that we ring down right here and allow every one to go home and fix up an ending to conform to the state of one's own digestion.

PIERROT. But you know, we're being paid to finish this thing.

HARLEQUIN. Paid? We're not working for money. We're working for love.

COLUMBINE. Love!

MARGOT. Aw, hell!

QUICK CURTAIN

TUNING IN

ALICE GERSTENBERG

To Alice Gerstenberg must go the credit for originating a dramatic formula which has been employed widely, with slight modification, in what are known as "expressionistic" plays. It is the duplex method which enables all of the characters to speak their individual thoughts as well as their social ones, or (to put it otherwise) to converse subconsciously as well as consciously. Her one-act play, "Overtones", which was an early success of the Washington Square Players, introduced this method.

"Tuning In", which was first played by The Playwrights' Theatre of Chicago as "Sentience", carries the idea one step further: it develops the unspoken values inherent in "things."

Miss Gerstenberg was born in Chicago and was educated there and at Bryn Mawr College. Her first novel, *Unquenched Fire*, was published in 1912 and republished in England the following year. Her next novel was *The Conscience of Sarah Platt*.

Her published collections of one-act plays are: *Ten One-Act Plays*, *Comedies All*, and *Four Plays for Four Women*. Her one-act plays, in addition, that may be found in compilations are: "Star Dust", "The Trap", "The Patroness", "Tuning In."

Her dramatization of Lewis Carroll's *Alice in Wonderland* was produced at the Booth Theatre, New York, in 1915; of Charles Kingsley's *Water Babies*, at the Repertory Theatre of Boston in 1929. In collaboration with Herma Clark, she wrote and produced a historical play, "When Chicago Was

Young", at the Goodman Theatre in Chicago in 1932; and in collaboration with Maude Fealy wrote a play on spiritualism, which was produced by the Playwrights' Theatre of Chicago in 1936.

Other plays are: "Within the Hour", "Glee Plays the Game" (in three acts), and "The Land of Don't Want To" (dramatization, in collaboration with Lillian Bell).

Alice Gerstenberg is past President of the Society of Midland Authors; past President of the Bryn Mawr Club of Chicago; Co-founder of the Chicago Junior League Theatre for Children (1921); founder, and since 1922 President, of the Playwrights' Theatre of Chicago.

TUNING IN

By ALICE GERSTENBERG

"Tuning In" was originally "Sentience", produced by the Playwrights' Theatre of Chicago at the Arts Club, April 27, 1933, and repeated under sponsorship of the Chicago Drama League, May 11, 1933.

Original Cast

DAHLIA MOORE	Kathleen Harvey
KENNETH HEATON	George Francis Wolff
TOM MICHAELSON	Ernst von Ammon
VIOLIN VIBRATIONS	Ruth Breytspraak
VOICES	Marion Russell / Charlotte Flatley

Stage set by Marie Blanke and Lewis P. Evans.
Directed by Channing Overton.

TUNING IN

SCENE. *A well-furnished apartment. Doors* R. *and* L. *Windows* R.C. *and* L.C. *at back looking out to the street. Large armchair down* R. *Table desk* R.C. *with chair* L. *of it. Console table* C. *at back, on which are vases,* R. *and* L., *statue between them. Couch up* L. *Table down* L. *against wall with vase of flowers. Portrait on wall above this table. Chair* R. *of it. Writing materials and cigarette box on desk table. Other characteristic furniture.*

[*As the Curtain rises one hears Voices off Right, and Dahlia, very smartly gowned and very attractive, enters from Right, followed by Kenneth, who looks handsome, healthy, prosperous, lovable, but of unimaginative type.*

DAHLIA (*gaily as she starts to take off her opera cloak*). You don't think they'll criticize us, do you, Ken, for leaving the party and coming up here? I do so want to see your apartment and how you live in it.

KEN (*taking her cloak and placing it on a small couch up* L.). Wonderful to have you here.

DAHLIA (*walking down to armchair* L. *of table at down* R.C.). After all, we are engaged — except — I'm not so sure I want to marry you.
[*Sits in armchair.*

KEN (*turns from putting the cloak on couch*). What?
[*Comes down to her and sits on arm of the chair.*

DAHLIA (*a bit serious though teasingly*). I think I want to marry you but I'm not quite sure.

KEN. Oh, I say, Dahlia — (*Embraces her*) It was settled.

DAHLIA (*holds him off*). I'm not so sure. Sometimes I feel so strange about it. Just now in Tom Michaelson's apartment, even though the party is very gay and happy, I felt something *queer* about *his* place.

KEN. Queer?

DAHLIA. As if there were a shadow there — (*Her glance wanders to a portrait of a woman at down* L., *hanging above a side table on which stands a beautiful vase with fresh flowers*) — and sometimes I feel about you a vague uneasiness — as if you are hiding something — not quite straightforward with me.

KEN (*laughs teasingly*). I shouldn't have taken you to Laberti's for dinner. The liquor there can't be very good — if you're *seeing* things.

DAHLIA. I can't explain it exactly, but I feel things to a deeper degree than most people do. (*Glances at the portrait*) It's annoying to *me*, but — (*Gaily to him*) — don't let it trouble *you* — I suppose it's my talent, as painting is to others.

KEN (*with authority*). Oh, you just have a lively imagination. Come, kiss me.

[*Embraces her.*

DAHLIA (*playfully, in his arms*). Is Tom Michaelson happy Ken?

KEN. Why, yes. Why shouldn't he be?

DAHLIA. He's never married. Is he in love?

KEN. How should I know?

DAHLIA. You're his best friend.

KEN. He has a lot of parties but doesn't seem to specialize. (*Rises, a bit worried*) Why do you ask? Does he like *you*?

DAHLIA (*flirtatiously*). I hope so, but that's not it. (*Rises*) So this is how you live.

KEN. Don't you think you might give me one more kiss before we go back to Tom's?

DAHLIA (*goes to Ken and puts her arms about his neck*). Yes, I do, darling.

KEN. Why, you're trembling.

DAHLIA. Am I?

KEN. What is the matter with you, my dear?

DAHLIA (*at* R. *of Ken, finds her glance pulled to the portrait*

down L. *and crosses to gaze at it throughout her speech).*
Oh, Ken, that portrait. I can't forget that you have been
married before.

KEN (*has allowed his glance to follow Dahlia's but he withdraws it quickly).* But it's five years since Virginia
died.

DAHLIA. You and Virginia must have spent many happy
evenings here. Did you love her very much?

KEN. Must you mention Virginia?

DAHLIA (*glances at the portrait but tries to say lightly).* Perhaps
her spirit still lingers here.

KEN. You imagine it.

DAHLIA. Can a husband forget so soon?

KEN. Five years is a long time.

DAHLIA (*not over serious but something of the glance of a mystic
in her eyes).* They say what *was, is,* and *ever* shall be.

KEN (*triumphantly and with definite assurance, embraces her).*
Are you jealous? That means, then, that you *do* love me
and *will* marry me.

DAHLIA (*starts).* What's that noise?

KEN (*undisturbed).* I don't hear anything.

DAHLIA. It's sort of a rasping sound, very unpleasant.

KEN. I'll never dine you at Laberti's again. Their liquor
must be —

DAHLIA. All right, I'll behave. Kiss me again.

KEN (*impetuously embracing her).* Oh, Dahlia, Dahlia.

DAHLIA (*pulls away).* There, that noise again.
[*Walks up* R.

KEN. I don't hear a thing.
[*Follows up* L.

DAHLIA (*puzzled and changing the subject).* It doesn't look
like you. I suppose Virginia furnished it.

KEN. Our wedding presents started us off.

DAHLIA (*walks down and leans against the back of the armchair,*
L. *of the table down* R.C.; *the chair faces the audience).* And
this is your chair. You are comfortable here. The chair
tells me so. (*Pats the back of the chair*) The chair loves

you. (*Motions to him to sit down in it*) So this is how you look when you are here alone and reading.

KEN (*settling in his chair and lifting his arms to take her as she stands behind the chair*). But I don't read. Thoughts of you distract me.

DAHLIA (*sits on* L. *arm of his chair and says teasingly as she looks at the table at his* R.). Your desk is rather messy. Why is the ink-stand shoved into a corner? It belongs in the middle.

KEN (*reaches out with his right hand and puts the ink-stand back into place*). So it does. I was working over some reports last night; pushed everything out of the way.

DAHLIA (*flirtatiously and charmingly*). Thanks. The inkwell feels happier about it and so do I. (*Puts her right arm around his neck*) Everything has its proper, harmonic place. Misfits are out of tune, they shriek discords.

KEN. That's amusing, you funny dear.

DAHLIA. The ink-stand was desperately anxious to get back into place.

KEN (*playfully raising the ink-stand and looking at it*). After this I shall respect its wishes. Why, you have me talking to it. You make me feel it is a living thing.

DAHLIA (*cheerfully and laughingly*). All things live. That is, I think they do, in different *degrees* of consciousness. And if you are sentient enough you can fairly hear them shriek or sing —

KEN (*laughs*). You silly dear.

DAHLIA (*rises from the arm of the chair, drops his hand rather impatiently, and walks away to the little couch up* L.) Why are men always so afraid of listening to the inner voice of things?

[*Sits on the couch.*

KEN (*turns in his chair to face her*). Meaning what?

DAHLIA. You are always evaluating things for what they are, instead of for what they *do* to one. You talk of how much you have paid, always a question of cost; and we miss all the enjoyment which costs nothing to enjoy ——

KEN (*teasingly*). Such as ——

DAHLIA. Being aware of that console — (*Waves her hand toward a large console or a mantelpiece back* C. *upon which stand two vases on either side of a statue*) — because its architectural lines keep running in perpetual proportion. Being aware of those curtains not because they are the color they are but because the satin folds so softly. Being aware of you, not for what you are but for what — I am — because of — loving you.

KEN. My dear, you mustn't go into this hocuspocus stuff — it's not healthy.

DAHLIA. I do it for fun, of course. (*Rises and walks down to him*) Don't *you* get serious about it.

KEN. Come, sit down.

DAHLIA. First, give me a cigarette — (*Puts out her hand to suggest he offer her a cigarette box she seems to see on the nearest corner of the table. There is no box there and she retreats. Dahlia, startled*) Oh.

KEN (*surprised*). What is it?

DAHLIA (*tossing her answer off with a laugh*). I thought I saw a brass cigarette box there.

KEN (*stretches his right hand to bring from the back of the table such a box into view, and offers it open to her*). I pushed it way back here yesterday, but it does belong where you thought you saw it.

DAHLIA. My mistake.

[*Airily takes a cigarette out of the box.*

KEN (*puts box down where it ought to be and offers her a lighted match*). That *was* weird.

DAHLIA (*smokes and tries to conceal her amusement as she stands at his* L.). Darling, I'm teasing you again. When I was standing — I saw it over there and it — shrieked out at me to be put back into place.

KEN (*nods to an armchair way down* R. *which exactly faces the portrait. His voice is politely nonchalant*). Take that chair. It's comfortable.

DAHLIA (*carelessly*). Is it?

[*Crosses to take it, but retreats in dismay as her approach is repelled by the fact that the chair shrieks at her.*

VOICE FROM CHAIR (*is masculine and annoyed*). Don't sit in me. I — am — Virginia's — chair.

DAHLIA (*retreats to* C., *her hands to her ears*). Oh, oh.

KEN (*rises in alarm*). Dahlia, what is it?

DAHLIA (*laughs*). You didn't hear anything?

KEN. No, are you crazy?

DAHLIA (*laughing*). No, you're crazy *not* to hear it. You see we're never going to get along together happily unless we *both* understand. (*Glances at portrait quickly and away again*) Suppose I say I don't like the color of that chair. It clashes in the room. If *I* came to live here, *it* would have to go out.

KEN (*embarrassed*). B — b — but I inherited it from my — my — gr — grandmother.

DAHLIA. Or do you mean it was Virginia's? Kenneth, listen to me. The whole room would have to be refurnished. (*Walks up stage and about*) You know some colors don't agree. (*Glances around and seizes some vivid covered books from table at* L.) If I put these two colors together, don't you feel the harmony? Don't you almost hear music — in harmony? (*Violin plays "Elegy", Massanet, first five measures ending with double stop E and G*) Now if I put these together — discord — discord — (*Violin plays discords*) It actually hurts me. It is true pain to me. You are so callous to these things. *Can* we make a harmony of our marriage?

KEN (*going to her*). Darling, you can have it all your own way.

DAHLIA (L. *of Ken*). I would never have told you if this place had pleased me — (*Her wandering glance rests upon the portrait and remains there as she says with intensifying passion*) — but there's something about it that *is driving me wild*.

KEN (*in alarm*). It's all the fault of Laberti's. I'll make some black coffee for you. Come into the kitchen.

DAHLIA (*masking her reason for not wanting to go*). No, I'll stay here — and rest. (*Waits until he has gone out at L., then hurries to armchair way down R., and putting her hands on the arms of the chair, begins a confidential conversation with it*) Now tell me quickly, Virginia, you don't want me to marry him, do you? Do you come back in spirit to sit here? No, you are not here. I am not conscious of you. You are not here. I am glad. But this was where you sat. You made the chair part of you —

CHAIR. I belong to Virginia.

DAHLIA (*pats the chair and is amused*). That's very loyal of you. Don't be worried. I'm not going to sit in you.

CHAIR. I'm lonely without Virginia.

DAHLIA. Why doesn't she come back then in spirit, and sit in you?

CHAIR. I don't know.

DAHLIA. She doesn't come back?

CHAIR. No.

DAHLIA. But she loved him. (*Chair does not answer*) Why doesn't she come back to sit opposite him when he is here reading alone at night? (*Chair does not answer*) Do you know why?

CHAIR. I don't want anyone else to sit in me. I want Virginia.

DAHLIA. Well, why doesn't Virginia come back?

CHAIR. I want Virginia.

DAHLIA. Stupid chair, aware of so much and no more! I must find out —

CHAIR. I want Virginia.

DAHLIA. Oh, shut up. Do you think I can marry him and move in here with everything shrieking "Virginia" at me? (*Crosses to L. to look at portrait*) And her portrait — with a vase of fresh flowers under it.

VOICE OF VASE (*is feminine, high-pitched and brittle*). Fresh flowers in me every day.

DAHLIA (*startled*). Oh, oh — who said that, you?

VASE. I, the vase.

DAHLIA. Glad to meet you, Vase. You're really very handsome.

VASE. A wedding present from Virginia's brother.

DAHLIA. Is that so?

VASE. Yes, there are three.

DAHLIA. Three brothers?

VASE. No, three vases.

DAHLIA. Three vases?

VASE. Over there on the console, two side vases.

DAHLIA. Ah, yes, they do match you.

VASE. I belong in the middle. Can you put me over there?

DAHLIA. Why, yes, glad to oblige.

VASE. I've been waiting five years for some one to rescue me.

DAHLIA. Well, my dear. I'll put you right back where you belong.

VASE. The others will be glad to have me back with them again. We'll sing a song of happiness for you.

DAHLIA. Why, of course.

[*Carries vase to console and puts it in the place of the statue. Takes statue in her arms.*

VOICES OF THE TWO VASES ON CONSOLE (*brittle, cheerfully exultant*). Hello, hello, hello!

[*Violin plays first four measures "From the Canebrake" — Samuel Gardner. Dahlia laughs and stands listening.*

VOICES OF THREE VASES. Thank you, thank you, thank you!

DAHLIA. You are really magnificent, the three of you there. It was a pity to separate you. Now, Statue, where shall I place you? Where the vase was, I suppose. (*Places statue on table under portrait*) How's that? Satisfied?

[*Violin continues next four measures.*

VOICE OF STATUE (*is masculine and rather heavy*). Thanks. This is where I stood five years ago.

DAHLIA. Five years? So *Kenneth* moved you. *Why?*

STATUE. He's *so* sentimental.

DAHLIA. Kenneth — sentimental?

STATUE. Don't you understand? *I* have no place to hold *flowers*.

KEN (*enters from* L. *with tray, coffee pot, small cups, and spoons*). Here's fresh, hot coffee. This will settle your head. [*Places tray on table under portrait and passes cup to Dahlia.*

DAHLIA (*at his entrance has quickly retreated from the portrait and has taken his chair at the* L. *of table* R.C.). Thanks, my darling. Have some with me.

KEN. I'm going to. [*Takes cup of coffee and sits near table* L. *on which the statue is now standing.*

DAHLIA (*after a sip of coffee*). You know, Ken, I've been taking that diet to get thin, and it's been making me a little light-headed. (*Laughs as if amused at herself, but really trying to allay his alarm about her condition*) I really want to move out of town into the country where I can get back to earth — you know — into the garden to dig around in flower beds and vegetables. You couldn't be persuaded to sell this apartment, could you?

KEN. Be a suburbanite? Drag my town customers into the country? Why, most of my bond sales are made in this room at midnight supper parties.

DAHLIA. But I would have to stay here alone all day —

KEN (*is about to put his coffee cup to his lips when he suddenly becomes aware of the statue on the table before him, and he sets the cup down in amazement*). Of all — (*Looks around to console*) How did that vase get there?

DAHLIA (*pretending indifference*). What vase?

KEN (*rising*). Why, the one with the flowers. They must have sent a new housemaid in to clean to-day. Funny I didn't notice it before. (*Approaches Dahlia with gallantry*) But then I was looking at *you*. [*Turns to go to console.*

DAHLIA (*rises pleadingly*). Oh, Ken, don't take the vase away; don't separate them, they all belong together. [*Ken picks up vase with flowers.*
Instruments off stage play discords and vases shriek shrilly.

DAHLIA (*puts her hands to her ears*). Please, for my sake! Oh, you're spoiling the appearance of the room! Oh, you have no idea of the fitness of things! I implore you do not take the vase away from its family!

KEN. Family? That's a good one.

DAHLIA (*following him as he places vase under portrait*). Well, aren't things related? Aren't knives and forks wedded? Cups and saucers, aren't they mates? Oh, my nerves! The statue doesn't like to be between the two little vases any more than they want to have it there. They hate one another or rather they're not in harmony — Oh, please, Ken —

KEN. Silly dear.

[*Places statue back on console.*

DAHLIA (*with a gesture of apology to the little vases*). I'm so sorry, there's nothing I can do.

KEN (*blandly unconscious of the unseen drama of vibration*). There now — that's better. I *must* tell the new maid not to disturb things again.

DAHLIA. Ken, *I* changed them.

KEN. What?

DAHLIA. I could almost hear them scream with anger because they were apart. How could you live five years with those vases separated! Even though you do want to keep flowers in front of her portrait every day!

KEN. How do you know the flowers are there every day?

DAHLIA. I guessed it, maybe.

KEN. I have a standing order at the florist's. Is that so criminal? Must you be jealous over that?

DAHLIA. I'm not jealous.

KEN. You are absurdly jealous and I won't give in to it.

DAHLIA. I'll never move in here, never — if you don't put the vases where they belong.

VASE. Put me back.

STATUE. Put me back.

DAHLIA. If you don't move them, I'll go —

KEN. No, no, the vase must stay under the portrait. I won't put up with your silly whim.

DAHLIA. You have no right to torture them, me — like this.

KEN (*sternly*). Dahlia, you are losing your mind.

DAHLIA (*with a little stamp of her foot*). Will you or will you not exchange the vase and statue!

KEN (*rather angrily*). I can't do it!

DAHLIA (*angrily, starting to go for her cloak*). Then I'm going back to Tom's party — and — home —

KEN (*barring her path*). It's getting you, your jealousy of Virginia. Why should it? You don't mean this. I can't let you go. I can't.

VASE. Don't leave us.

STATUE. Don't leave me.

DAHLIA. Will you or will you not change the vase?

KEN. Are you mad to make an issue of so small a thing?

DAHLIA. Mad, yes, and leaving — forever.

[*Crossing to door* R.

KEN (*barring her path*). No. Dahlia, I can't give you up.

DAHLIA (*retreats*). There's your doorbell.

KEN. I didn't hear a ring.

DAHLIA. Didn't you? My mistake!

[*The doorbell rings.*

KEN. Who's that?

DAHLIA (*walks down* L.). It might be Tom Michaelson.

KEN (*goes out* R. *and reënters immediately*). Tom — oh, it's you. Come in.

TOM (*enters from* R. *in advance of Ken and comes down* C. *He is very attractive and more imaginative than Ken*). Hello, aren't you coming down again? They're all asking for you. We want to start some contract. I said I could get you down. What's the matter?

DAHLIA (*face averted, pouting*). Matter?

TOM (*to Ken at his* R.). What's the matter with you, Ken? What's in the air?

KEN. What do you mean, what's in the air?

TOM. Something's wrong. I sense that something's wrong.

KEN. What makes you think that?

TOM (*to Ken*). A hunch. Don't you have hunches? I listen to 'em in business. (*To Dahlia*) If I start out to sell and feel that the prospect isn't in a buying mood, I just wait until another day. (*Glancing at Both of them*) I can feel the air here just sizzling with something.

KEN. Are you crazy too?

TOM. What do you mean, crazy?

DAHLIA. Yes, Mr. Michaelson, we've been quarreling.

KEN (*with irritation*). It is all because she is jealous of Virginia.

DAHLIA. It's the *furniture* that bothers me.

TOM. I'm glad *you* feel that way about it. I need some changes myself downstairs and perhaps you'll help me with them. I've always had my eye on some of Ken's things. What about selling me — (*Glances about room and goes to touch table under the portrait*) — this table and — [*Hesitatingly crosses to* R.

DAHLIA (*follows him and touches table under portrait, a look of the mystic in her eyes as her fingers linger on the table*). This table wants to go.

KEN. *Wants* to go?

DAHLIA (*nonchalantly*). Ought to go.

[*Crosses to* C. *Ken comes down* L.

TOM. And I'll take this chair. (*Sits in Virginia's chair way down* R. *as if he were very comfortable in it*) I've always liked it.

VOICE OF CHAIR. *I should say he — did —*

DAHLIA. What did you say?

TOM (*surprised at her question*). I didn't say anything.

DAHLIA (*goes a little nearer*). Oh — oh — *you* are comfortable in it.

TOM. I certainly am.

VOICE OF CHAIR (*with amusement*). Of course *he* is!

DAHLIA (*with the look of a mystic*). I see.

TOM (*startled*). *What* do you see?

DAHLIA (*surprised*). Did I say "*see*"?

KEN. You said you see. What *do* you see?

DAHLIA (*realization of the truth gives her a roguish enjoyment of the situation as she turns to Ken*). A figure of speech, that's all. (*Turns to Tom and measures him amusedly*) Yes — *sell* him — that — *chair* —

KEN. B-but it was —

DAHLIA. Your grandmother's, you said.

KEN (*worried*). It is the one thing I cannot sell.

DAHLIA. That he won't sell. (*Petulantly*) I must be leaving. (*Goes to Tom*) What time is it, Mr. Michaelson?

TOM (*rises and takes out his watch*). Ten o'clock.

DAHLIA. What a beautiful watch! May I see it?

TOM. Why, certainly.

DAHLIA (*takes the watch, turns away quickly, opens the back of it, discovers a photograph as she had suspected, appraises it with a swift glance at the portrait of Virginia and returns it open to Tom with a knowing smile*). I thought so, Mr. Michaelson.

KEN (*who has been sullenly inattentive*). What did you think?

DAHLIA (*turning and going up stage to get her cloak*). That it's ten o'clock.

TOM (*hastily as if to make sure she will keep the secret of his romance*). May I escort you home?

KEN (*annoyed*). No, thanks, *I'll* do that.

TOM (*apologetically*). I thought you had quarreled.

DAHLIA (*gaily and happily, and coming down again as if she had changed her mind*). Oh, we've forgotten all about that now. I've just been teasing Ken — pretending I was jealous of Virginia — thinking how *much* they had *loved* each other — but I'm not really — Of course Ken *had* to love his wife — I was foolish — I see it — all.

TOM (*looking straight into Dahlia's eyes*). All?

DAHLIA (*returning a straight gaze*). All.

TOM. How can you know —

KEN. What's all this?

DAHLIA. Oh, just that Tom and I understand each other about the furniture : a language you don't know and don't

have to. You want us all to be friends, don't you, Ken? Tom and — (*Nods toward portrait*) — Virginia, and you and I. Well, we are a little *foursome* — with the memory of Virginia with us. Now, I know, too, what's wrong with your rooms downstairs, Tom. You do need more chairs. Now, Ken, if you'll just let me move this vase back to where it belongs —
[*Takes vase from table under portrait and starts upstage toward console.*

KEN (*bewildered*). But you're starting it all over again. Dahlia insists she can't live here unless I move the vase.

DAHLIA. It belongs up here with its complements.

TOM (*crosses to* C., *takes vase from Dahlia, and places it on the console between the two side vases. Takes statue in his arms*). Certainly it does. (*Violin plays "Caprice Viennois" — Kreisler. Andante con moto. Music is harmonious when the three vases are together again*) And the statue should be down here.
[*Music. Double stop 1–10th measure. Goes to place it on the table under the portrait. Music rises into beautiful harmony — 19th — 23d measure. For the moment All admire the statue while Music plays.*

KEN. Yes, Tom gave it to us as a wedding present.
[*Walks toward statue on table under portrait.*

DAHLIA (*talking fast as she comes down stage between Ken at* L. *and Tom at* R.). The statue really does belong below the portrait. Although I really can't look at that portrait every day, Ken, couldn't you loan it to Tom?

KEN (*stutters*). Why — why —

DAHLIA (*continuing very fast, scarcely allowing the Men to make their exclamations, as she maneuvers, with charm and a sense of comedy, to get the portrait and the chair out of the house so she can move into it contentedly herself*). You wouldn't mind our loaning you the portrait, would you, Tom, would you?

TOM. Why, no, why, yes — why —

DAHLIA (*hastily and with a tantalizing smile at Tom*). And

then *you* could keep fresh flowers in a vase under it every day.

TOM (*very eager and happy at the realization he is going to get the portrait*). So I could.

DAHLIA (*turning hastily to Ken and with mock-seriousness*). And Ken can come in to see you when he wants to devote his thoughts to Virginia. Wouldn't it be more polite toward me for him not to fling my predecessor at me every day?

KEN. I suppose it would —

DAHLIA. And Tom's your best friend, Ken. He will take awfully good care of the portrait —

KEN. Yes —

DAHLIA. And then when you go to pay your respects to Virginia, I won't have to see you do it. And we can loan you his grandmother's chair —

TOM. *Grandmother's?*

DAHLIA. Because it does remind *me* of Virginia and I'm sure Virginia needs the chair in your apartment.

KEN. What?

DAHLIA (*hastily*). I mean — the portrait's been so used to gazing across at the chair and the chair at the portrait that they belong together just as the vases do — (*Turns to walk up to look at the vases as well as to hide her amusement at her cleverness of achieving what she wants*) — and *ought not to be separated.*

KEN. Tom, I love Dahlia but is she going mad?
[*Dahlia, amused, takes a flower out of the vase and sits on the couch up L. Twirls flower.*

TOM (*amused and very kind and reassuring*). Why, no, Ken, she just has a marvelous intuition. Besides, you couldn't expect her to be daily reminded of your past.

KEN (*in desperate confession looking at Tom, and in the slowness and difficulty of saying it, reveals the unhappiness of years*). Of course, I'd almost rather die than say it. (*Dahlia, on the couch in the background, takes an attitude of still attention*) You see she's so jealous of Virginia and the truth is —

I — never — really — loved — Virginia.
[*Warn curtain.*

TOM (*gazes for a moment straight into Ken's eyes and in that moment one feels the years of unhappiness he has lived through*). My God, man — you never — loved — Virginia? Then — (*Sinks into Virginia's chair*) — why didn't you say so before?

KEN (*waits a moment. Turns away*). I did everything I could to *pretend* I did, and to cover my conscience about it because I never wanted her even to guess it!

DAHLIA (*contemplates them Both a moment, then comes down to Ken's chair* L. *of table and smiles, amused at Tom*). You don't know so much about hunches after all, do you, Tom? (*Looks at Ken standing at* L.) And I'm so glad you don't have them, Ken. Oh, Ken, how wonderful you are! (*Ken glances at her in surprise and crosses quickly to take her in his arms. Dahlia, triumphantly with her arms around him*) And now it's all settled, isn't it, when I come in, the *portrait* and the *chair* go *out!*

KEN (*with a happy glance at Dahlia, at Tom, and back to Dahlia*). I guess — I guess the ayes have it.

DAHLIA (*looking over her shoulder with a roguish glance at the chair in which Tom is still seated*). And what does the chair say?

VOICE OF CHAIR (*chuckles and shouts*). The *ayes* have it!
[*Tom starts, surprised, as if he had heard something. His eyes turn to Dahlia. Violin plays "2d Mazurka" — Wienianski — Tempo di Maznika — eight measures. Dahlia accepts Tom's startled look with amusement and turns with final triumph to Ken.*

CURTAIN

SINTRAM OF SKAGERRAK

SADA COWAN

THE RECORD of writers of one-act plays whose names are by-words in Little Theatres the country over is an honorable one: such names as Booth Tarkington, Christopher Morley, Alice Brown, Thornton Wilder, Beulah Marie Dix, Edna St. Vincent Millay, Glenn and Babette Hughes, the Nicholsons, Hall and Middlemass, Rachel L. Field, Constance D'Arcy Mackay, the Colin Clementses, Alice C. D. Riley . . . one could go on and on, — beginning with the popular parlor sketches which William Dean Howells created long before Americans were ready for them, — and still not be able to complete the record of popular one-act play production. These writers, like Sada Cowan, have written plays that have been produced from coast to coast, that have won tournament prizes, that have been reprinted in anthologies; yet space permits the barest mention of them here, with the statement that they have each and all contributed to Little Theatre progress.

Sada Cowan's impressionistic episode, "Sintram of Skagerrak", first appeared in this anthology.

She was educated at a private boarding school near Boston, but at the age of fifteen she went to Germany to study music, and later traveled extensively.

Her published one-act plays are: *Pomp and Other Plays* (a collection); "The Moonlit Way" (also called "The Cat"); "A Woman's Touch"; "Auf Wiedersehen." One-act plays which have been produced are "Other Men's Shoes", "The Wonder of the Age" (also called "The Dream Woman"), "Abdul the Azra", "The Honor of America", "I Wish I

Knew", and "Investigation." Her full-length plays which have been produced are: "Playing the Game", "Defiance", "Napoleon Had It Too", "Vultures", "Bamboo", "Rusty Keys."

Although the paths of many of our Little Theatre dramatists have led recently from playwriting to scenario writing, Sada Cowan has been a scenario writer for more than fifteen years. Her outstanding original screen plays have been: "Peter the Great" (UFA, Berlin), "Smouldering Fires" (Universal), and "Trouble with Wives" (Paramount). In addition, she has written adaptations or continuities for more than fifty feature films, and has contributed occasional articles to magazines and newspapers.

SINTRAM OF SKAGERRAK

By SADA COWAN

"Sintram of Skagerrak" was originally produced by the Brooklyn Repertory Theatre, April 27, 1917.

Original Cast

SINTRAM . . . . Harmon Cheshire
GUNHILDE . . . . Ethel Rosemon

SINTRAM OF SKAGERRAK

SCENE. *A high, bare cliff, situated on the edge of the shore, in a bleak, barren country. Against this cliff the breakers dash unceasingly, splitting with a roar and thud; tossing their spray high into the air.*

It is a moonlight night in summer.

*On the peak of the cliff, and looking out upon the ocean, stands Sintram, an emaciated, frail, sickly lad of about twenty. As the curtains part, he stretches his arms out impetuously towards the sea, uttering a prolonged "*Ah . . . h . . . h!*" then lets them fall languidly to his side and hangs his head, as though weary of his whole existence. He continues to stand, apathetic and listless, for several moments, gazing spellbound upon the ocean. Unobserved by him across the rocks, Gunhilde enters: a vivacious girl of eighteen, plainly dressed as befits her lowly station. She looks about and behind her as if afraid of being followed, then, a rock hiding Sintram from her view, calls softly.*

GUNHILDE. Sintram . . .! Sintram . . .! (*Sintram, lost in his morose brooding, does not hear her, but continues to stand staring at the ocean*) Sintram . . .! Sintram . . .! Ah, there you are. I hoped that I should find you.

[*Sintram turns slowly and descends the cliff with tired, dragging step; she runs eagerly towards him.*

SINTRAM (*angrily*). What are you doing here, Gunhilde, at this hour?

GUNHILDE. Sh . . . h . . . h . . .! Not so loud! Some one will hear you.

SINTRAM. What are you doing here! Have I not forbidden your creeping out of your house, like a thief in the night, to look for me!

GUNHILDE. Be kind . . . be gentle, Sintram.

SINTRAM (*sternly*). Your Father thinks you at home. Why
do you deceive him? Go home! (*She does not move.
Kindly*) Go, little friend, little playmate! You know it
is for your good I would have you go . . . go home!

GUNHILDE. No.

SINTRAM. We have said all that we had to say to each other.
Why have you come back again?

GUNHILDE. I had to see you once more Sintram before . . .
(*her voice breaks*) . . . before they take you away. I shall
be at work in the morning when they come for you.
[*She covers her face with her hands and begins to sob.*

SINTRAM (*furiously*). Stop that senseless crying! Leave me
alone. Do you think that my soul is not racked enough?
(*Sadly*) All night I have sat on the edge of the cliff saying
"Good-by" to the sea. We understand each other, the
mad, wild, restless ocean and I. And all night she has
wept for me . . . wept in her anguish. (*Pushing Gunhilde
aside*) I have no need of woman's tears.

GUNHILDE (*awed*). Often it seems to me, Sintram, as though
there were something uncanny about you. As though you
lived on this earth among us, without really being one of
us. When you have taken me in your arms and have
kissed me tenderly . . . (*bitterly*) just as if I were a little
child, I have felt that worlds and worlds lay between us.
What is it, Sintram? Have you a secret which you have
kept from me? (*He gives no answer, but dumbly nods his
head in assent*) I thought so. Will you not tell it to me
before you go?

SINTRAM (*hastily*). No . . . no . . . you could not understand.

GUNHILDE. Let me try . . . come . . . tell me! (*She
leads him to a rock where they sit beside each other, she still
holding his hand. He shivers nervously and coughs*) You
ought not to be here in the night air.

SINTRAM. I am not cold (*shivers again*) but . . . . I feel —
afraid. Gunhilde, come closer . . .

GUNHILDE (*moves nearer to him*). Why, you are shivering! Here, let me fasten your coat, you poor boy.

SINTRAM (*shaking her off and turning on her with sudden, unexpected fury*). Bah! Do you begin too? Can I not have just this one night in peace? Is it not time enough for me to begin my life as a puppet . . . to-morrow?

GUNHILDE (*hurt*). Why, Sintram!

SINTRAM. I mean what I say, every word of it and I know what I'm saying. (*She attempts to touch him*) Leave me alone! Do you hear? Do not touch me. To-night is mine . . . MINE! And if the night air kills me . . . let it kill. But just this once I am going to forget that I am nothing but the shadow of a man, sick and miserable, cheated by nature of all that a man should have; blindfolded and handicapped in Life's race . . . even before I entered it. Beaten before the first step was taken! But to-night I am a man! To-morrow I will be the half-dead invalid dragged, against my will, to warmer climes, where my soul will sicken . . . (*harshly*) that my body may live.

GUNHILDE (*gently*). How bitterly you speak. It is not for long that you are going.

SINTRAM. You know that it is forever. (*Takes a deep breath, then coughs*) That this air . . . cool and sharp . . . this air I love is as so much poison to me. And you know just as well as I do that I will never come back.

GUNHILDE (*hiding her tears and trying to cheer him*). But it must be wonderful in the warm sunshine, among eternal flowers. Oh, I should love it — I wish that I too might go. This land is hateful to me. 'Tis so cold and bleak, and nothing green ever grows. Nothing but seaweed and nasty slimy things from the sea. I asked your guardian to-day to tell me about the place to which he was taking you and he said that it was like fairyland . . . like Paradise; full of roses and palms and . . . Why, it must be glorious, Sintram!

SINTRAM. Things to please a soft woman . . . not for a man. (*A moment's pause, them to himself*) And I must go away and leave her. (*Covers his eyes with his hands and rocks to and fro with emotion*) Oh, God, that is beyond my strength!

GUNHILDE. Her? Whom do you mean . . . me?

SINTRAM. That is my secret, Gunhilde.

GUNHILDE (*passionately*). Tell me . . . you must tell me.

SINTRAM. No . . . no . . . you would not understand. I am afraid that you would think me mad.

GUNHILDE. Tell me.

SINTRAM. I have kept it to myself these three years. I will keep it to the end.

GUNHILDE. But you can have no secrets from me. You should have none. 'Tis breaking your oath.

SINTRAM (*perplexed*). My oath? My oath?

GUNHILDE. Why, do you not recall the day we stood here on the cliff and drank the red wine together from your little silver cup?

SINTRAM. Yes.

GUNHILDE. And you said, as you held the cup up . . . so (*she raises one arm above her head, laughing, and looks towards the sea*) "I swear to you, little comrade, that as long as I live I shall never withhold one thought, keep back one single feeling, or shut out my soul for one single instant from . . . her whom I love! And then you threw the cup far out into the sea. Do you not remember, Sintram?

SINTRAM. Yes . . . yes . . . I remember.

GUNHILDE. So you must trust me and if you have kept anything hidden from me you must tell it to me now.

SINTRAM. I will tell it to you Gunhilde . . . I will. (*He looks at her a moment sympathetically as though he would like to spare her the pain of that which he is about to say*) You love me . . . do you not?

GUNHILDE. I adore you.

SINTRAM. You have been a dear little friend, a loyal comrade these two years; I shall miss you.

GUNHILDE. Oh, Sintram . . . ! (*With a voice too old for her years*) I wish that I could have been more to you than I have been.

SINTRAM. What do you mean?

GUNHILDE. Nothing . . . nothing! (*Hastily trying to hide her emotion*) I have no wish to burden you with my secret. Let me hear yours.

SINTRAM. Presently. First I want you to tell me something. You are sorry that I have to leave you . . . are you not?

GUNHILDE. How can you ask? You know it.

SINTRAM. But you hope some day to see me again, or to hear from me at least, do you not?

GUNHILDE. Yes, soon.

SINTRAM. Then listen and see if you can possibly feel as I feel, for even as you love me, and more . . . much more, I too love. (*Gunhilde tightens her hold upon his hand and smiles happily, thinking that he is alluding to her. Sadly and slowly*) No . . . not you, little playmate, little friend; but a wild, beautiful woman who sometimes mocks me and torments me, and sometimes caresses and quiets me. Her moods are my moods. Her feelings are mine. When she is angry, my soul responds and is filled with a vague restlessness; when she is calm, her peace rests on me; when she is powerful, my poor, sickly body feels her strength; and when she is vindictive, I too cry for human life . . . and blood! [*During his entire speech Gunhilde has sat dumbfounded, now she breaks forth passionately.*

GUNHILDE. You love some one else! You have deceived me, telling me that you had no mistress; you love a cruel, bad woman . . . Who is she?

SINTRAM. Be quiet, Gunhilde, and I will tell you everything. Only be quiet . . . you will not be jealous when you have heard all.

GUNHILDE (*dreamily*). And I thought that you cared because you were leaving me.

SINTRAM. I do care . . . but listen. I want you to understand. (*Calmly*) I have always lived here, as you know, little comrade. In that old house, just the other side of the cliff, I was born; weighed down with riches and an untarnished name. My people had intermarried closely: (*bitterly*) no strong, vital peasants' blood ran in my veins. (*Quietly*) My Mother's bed-room faced the ocean, so the first sound which reached my ears when I came to the world was . . . the moan of the sea. My Mother died when I was born, so the sea became my Mother and sang her lullabys to me until I fell asleep, stilled by her soft crooning. (*Scornfully*) Then I grew up . . . weak . . . delicate . . . sick . . . ! The boys used to ridicule me because I was not able to spring from one rock to another, laughing and shouting as they did. They made fun of me and then went away, leaving me sitting (*points*) just there. Hour after hour I would stay there with tears in my eyes gazing out at the sea. And then, ah . . . how grateful I was . . . she would dance and prance and splash and roar . . . all to please and amuse me; calling softly to me not to be sad! And she would weave her most beautiful fairy tales for me in the loom of the waves. In the ever-changing whitecaps I saw all the heroes of my boyhood fancy pass before me. So, as the sea had once taken the place of my Mother, she became, in turn, my playmate. Are you tired listening, Gunhilde?

GUNHILDE. No, dear, no. Go on . . . !

SINTRAM. Then my boyhood vanished and I grew to be a man: a weak, puny man, able to dream dreams in the moonlight, to write sad verse, to kiss your soft lips — and there my strength ended. Often when you had left me in the evening, my soul afire from the moonbeams and the light on the waves; when my body . . . (*Breaks off suddenly, remembering that she is little more than a child*) What am I saying to you? I forgot, little girl, forgive me. I am so used to talking to myself, forgive me . . . Gunhilde.

GUNHILDE.   What happened to you, Sintram, when you
stayed alone in the moonlight after I had gone? Tell me.
I will understand.   I am not such a child as you think.

SINTRAM (*reflects, then almost spontaneously*).   I used to sit
on the edge of the peak, just where you found me to-night,
and listen to the same soft voice calling to me not to be
sad.   Then I would close my eyes and lie on the very
edge of the rock so that the spray might dash into my face.
(*Rapturously*) It felt like woman's tears upon my eyes
and lips, and I used to wonder why the ocean wept.   But
now I know.   To all my longings, thoughts, and desires
the ocean responded; so, in turn, she became . . . my
mistress . . . and I love her!   There you have my secret
(*Laughs loudly and harshly*) "Sintram the Scatter-
brained" in love with the sea!

GUNHILDE.   There is nothing so strange about that, Sintram;
you have lived here always and the ocean has become a
part of your life.   If you had been strong and poor you
could have been a sailor.   Why, look at all the boys who
have run away from home to become sailors.   Many men
love the sea . . . that is not strange.

SINTRAM (*interrupting passionately*).   They never loved her
as I love her.   (*Takes her hand violently and speaks rapidly*) To me she is not a thing of water and foam, as she is
to you, Gunhilde, but she is a woman!   A moody, beautiful
woman, with a wonderful body and golden hair, and her
soul . . . . Ah! how shall I tell you of her soul or of her
soft voice when she loves me and takes me in her arms?
But she is capricious . . . as capricious as she is beautiful.

GUNHILDE.   What do you mean?   Is this some poem that
you have written?

SINTRAM (*oblivious to her, and talking to himself, staring all
the while before him*).   How many nights have I lain awake
in my bed and have listened to her murmur and sing and
call me.   Then, in an uncontrollable frenzy, when I have
rushed bare-footed to answer her bidding, she has mocked
me and scoffed me; she has risen up in stormy anger, cut-

ting my face with her lashes of spray and has laughed and laughed at me, until I have covered my face with my hands and gone sobbing back to my bed.

GUNHILDE. I cannot understand you, Sintram.

SINTRAM. No, dear, no . . . I did not think you would. I hardly understand myself; only this I know, Gunhilde, that to go away from here and never to look upon her again is like tearing my heart out of my body. (*A pause in which he listens to the crash of the breakers on the rocks below*) Here . . . ! Listen how angry she is, and how she hates me to-night.

GUNHILDE. What foolishness! It is going to storm, that is all.

SINTRAM. Oh, you have not learned her language as I have. Listen! see if her voice carries no meaning to you. (*They both listen silently for several moments, in which a dull roar and thud is heard; then Sintram begins to chant, strongly accenting every other syllable*) Sintram . . . ! Sintram . . . going . . . away . . . ! Away . . . ! To new loves . . . ! He is false . . . ! False . . . ! Ugh . . . ! Did you hear her shriek then . . . ?

GUNHILDE. No, I heard nothing; not even the wind.

SINTRAM. She hates me, Gunhilde . . . my Beloved hates me! [*He shudders.*

GUNHILDE (*tenderly and sadly*). Would that your voice were so when you talk of me; your eyes never looked for me as they look when you speak of her. I love you, Sintram.

SINTRAM (*indifferently*). Yes . . . yes . . . I know.

GUNHILDE. No . . . you do not know; not as you think. You have treated me always as a child . . . a little child.

SINTRAM. But you are a child!

GUNHILDE. I am a woman . . . a woman . . . and I love you. (*He looks at her surprised, almost startled. She lays her hand on his*) Forget your foolish fancy, for it is only a fancy, and let me be your love; take me away with you to-morrow and I will love you forever. Take me . . . do! You

little know how I have suffered since I have cared for you,
how my passion for you has nearly killed me.   All that gave
me strength and courage was to feel that you loved no one
else, and now . . . !   But soon you will be well and strong
again, and then you will look back upon all this as on some
wild, strange dream.   [*While speaking, she has been drawing closer to him and has been caressing him.   Now she sits
with one arm about his neck, her cheek pressed to his.*

SINTRAM.   Oh . . . how warm you are . . . how warm!   [*He
shivers.*

GUNHILDE.   Kiss me . . . Sintram!

SINTRAM (*opening his eyes, looking into space and talking to
himself*).   If I take her with me perhaps I would grow
well and strong; perhaps I would no longer be lonely . . .
and I might forget. . . .

GUNHILDE (*whispering*).   Kiss me, Sintram . . . I love you!
[*He looks at her a moment, then takes hold of her, and crushing
her with all his strength to him, he gives her a long kiss.   Suddenly he jumps up, startling her, and looks about excitedly.*

SINTRAM.   What was that?

GUNHILDE (*dazed from the suddenness of the interruption*).
What, Sintram . . . ?   What is it . . . ?

SINTRAM.   I heard a dull thud . . . and a moan from the sea.

GUNHILDE (*drawing him back to the rock*).   You are fanciful
and nervous to-night.   There was no noise.   (*Sintram
sits for a moment beside her, but he is restless and a strained
tension is visible in his every motion.   Finally he springs up
and runs to and fro on the cliff, peering on every side; seeing
nothing, he comes back to Gunhilde.   Rising*)   How strange
you are!   I never saw you so before.   Is it because you
are going away to-morrow?   Look at me. . . .   AT me
. . . not into space!   (*Awed*)   There is a distant, far-away
. . . something . . . in your eyes which I have never seen
in the eyes of any man. . . .   It frightens me!   [*She
draws away from him.*

SINTRAM (*stands as though listening to a far-away voice, then
breaks out suddenly*).   There . . . !   Did you not hear it

then? (*This time he dashes to the top of the cliff, where he had originally been standing; she follows him. He stares silently out at the ocean, moving nervously and excitedly the while; finally he takes Gunhilde's hand*) Look . . . Gunhilde . . . look!

GUNHILDE (*looking in the direction in which he is pointing*). Where? What?

SINTRAM (*straining his eyes*). Far out beyond those jagged rocks, far . . . far out!

GUNHILDE. I see nothing! (*Horrified*) At what are you staring so, Sintram?

SINTRAM. There is something white floating on the waves . . . it is coming nearer and nearer. (*Pause*) I think it is . . . a corpse!

GUNHILDE (*utters a long drawn out*) "Oh . . . h . . . h . . . h . . . !" (*She lies down and leans way over the cliff. Then she rises*) But I see . . . nothing!

SINTRAM (*pointing*). Not below us! There . . . there! Can you not see? It is a woman with open, glassy eyes and golden hair, entwined like a fisherman's net about her white body.

GUNHILDE. All I see is a shimmer of gold from the moon.

SINTRAM. She is floating nearer . . . nearer . . . ! Look, she is not dead! She moves! She breathes . . . ! Her breast heaves slowly!

GUNHILDE (*puzzled*). I see nothing but the waves rising and falling in the moonbeams.

SINTRAM (*leaning over the cliff*). Now she lies at the very foot of the cliff . . . see . . . see . . . (*Pause*) She is rising . . . she is standing upon the water. (*Surprised*) Gunhilde . . . ! She is looking at us! She is calling me! Can you not hear her?

GUNHILDE (*laying her hand on his arm restrainingly*). Are you mad . . . Sintram . . . !

SINTRAM (*happily*). She is jealous of you, Gunhilde . . . my ocean love is jealous. (*He laughs loudly. Then he is suddenly very still and peers tensely below him, in happy as-*

tonishment) She is beckoning to me . . . she holds out her arms to me! (*In ecstasy*) Oh, Beloved . . . At last . . . ! [*He extends his arms to the imaginary woman and plunges headlong over the cliff.*

GUNHILDE (*shrieks*). Sintram . . . ! Sintram . . . !

(*As the curtains close*).

THE ROBBERY

CLARE KUMMER

COINCIDENTALLY with the rise of the Little Theatres, several brave professional producers, principally in New York and Chicago, tried out short plays as experiments at special matinées. Clare Kummer (now Mrs. Arthur Henry) was one of those whose one-act plays were introduced in this way.

She was born in Brooklyn, N. Y., the great-niece of Henry Ward Beecher and Harriet Beecher Stowe. As she was a fragile child, her schooling was light, and she was allowed to wander into the bypaths of music, books, and other things she loved. Her mother was an accomplished amateur actress, and Clare almost learned to read by means of the yellow-covered books of plays with which the shelves of her mother's desk were stacked.

Although her first one-act play, "The Choir Rehearsal", was originally produced in vaudeville, "The Robbery" and "Chinese Love" were introduced as matinée performances during the run of her full-length play "Rollo's Wild Oat." Her other one-act plays, all of which have been published, are "Bridges", "So's Your Old Antique", "Papers." Her other published full-length plays are: "Be Calm, Camilla", "Good Gracious, Annabelle!", "Pomeroy's Past", "The Rescuing Angel", "A Successful Calamity."

THE ROBBERY

By CLARE KUMMER

"The Robbery" was originally produced at The Punch and Judy Theatre, New York, Monday, February 13–28, 1921.

Original Cast

John Upton, a father	J. M. Kerrigan
Margaret Upton, a mother	Mrs. Alice Chapin
Edie Upton, a daughter	Ruth Gillmore
Robert Hamilton, a son	Sidney Blackmer
Fielding, a butler	George Bliven

THE ROBBERY

SCENE. *The sitting-room of the Uptons' house on Seventy-second Street. A door* L.U.E. *leading into hall and sleeping rooms, and window and window-seat below. Another door* R.U.E. *leading into hall and downstairs. It is an English basement house and the sitting-room is on the second floor.*

It is summer and the furniture is covered with linen.

[On rise, the clock is striking twelve. Fielding enters stealthily L.U.E. *with case containing silver. He extinguishes the light which is burning dimly. As he goes to pick up the suit-case, his foot upsets it, making a light crash. He picks it up and hurriedly exits.*

Enter Edie almost immediately. She wears a negligee and slippers. She peers into the room, runs to door R.U.E., *looks out, comes back, rings bell, and runs to the window, opens it and calls out.*

EDIE. Help! Help! (*Looking in, greatly frightened*) Oh, dear — what shall I do, if someone comes! (*Bell rings. Edie again looks out*) Who is it? Are you a policeman? Yes, I'm afraid something is the matter — but I can't let you in unless you're a policeman — I'm all alone in the house, and I think there's a burglar! Wait!

[She switches on the lights. By this time Hamilton is coming through the window. He is a little dishevelled, but very serious and polite. He wears a dinner coat and carries a soft hat. This he lays on chair almost immediately.

BOB. I thought I'd better come right in — you see, I don't know any policemen around here — yet.

EDIE. Oh, mercy!

BOB. Don't be frightened. I live just across the street.

EDIE. Are you sure?

BOB. Yes — really. My mother's in the country, but my father's there — he's bought the house and gone to bed — and I was just sitting on the front steps asleep when I heard you call "Help!"

EDIE. Sitting on the front steps asleep!

BOB. Yes. My father has my key. He doesn't like my being out nights. So I either have to go to a Turkish bath or sit on the steps all night.

EDIE. But it's only twelve o'clock.

BOB. Splendid of you to say so. My father likes to have the lights out at ten. You see, I'm going to be his partner some day, so he wants me to be down bright and early to sweep out the office —— What was it that frightened you?

EDIE. I heard things!

BOB. *Really?* What sort of things?

EDIE. I don't know. Then there was a crash — and I ran out and saw a man disappearing down the stairs.

BOB. Oh — you did!

EDIE. Then I rang for Fielding, and there was no answer — and then I opened the window and called for help.

BOB. Fielding?

EDIE. The butler.

BOB. There's no one else in the house?

EDIE. Well, mother's maid is supposed to be here, but she isn't.

BOB. I see.

EDIE. I let her go to her sister's down on Long Island, because poor Maggie's husband has broken his leg, and Maggie wanted to come to town and see him — she has so little pleasure — so I let Ellen go to look after Maggie's children.

BOB. I see.

EDIE. Do you suppose Fielding is dead?

BOB. Probably a sound sleeper.

EDIE. Father has the bell in the servants' room specially hung — he could never sleep through it.

BOB. Well, it wasn't long ago. Maybe he's dressing. If butlers ever take off their clothes — I don't know whether they do or not. Shall I go and look for him?

EDIE. No — I'll ring again. But I'm sure there's no one alive in the house. Don't you have that feeling?

[*She rings again.*

BOB. Well, no, I must say it's awfully cheerful and pleasant after the front steps.

EDIE (*hesitating prettily*). Won't you sit down — while we're waiting?

[*She sits at one end of couch.*

BOB. Thanks. Excuse my collar, won't you? I'd have taken more care of it at the banquet if I'd known I was coming.

EDIE. Oh — you've been to a banquet?

BOB (*sits* L. *end of couch*). Yes. It was jolly, but it lasted a little too long. Our class is going to the boat race to-morrow and one of the fellows unfortunately had a birthday.

EDIE. I see. Well, do you think we ought to telephone for the police?

BOB. Why, not on my account. Are you afraid now?

EDIE. No, not now. But —

BOB. I'll stay till the butler gets dressed. I'm sure he's not dead. They always live to be awfully old.

EDIE. I wonder what it could have been that made that dreadful crash. It sounded as if all the chandeliers in the house were falling.

BOB. They don't usually take those.

EDIE (*darting forward, picking up salt spoon*). Oh, look —

BOB. What is it?

EDIE. It's one of the little silver salt spoons!

BOB. Oh — he was after the silver!

EDIE. Yes — but you don't understand — this is one of Aunt Abingdon's salt spoons.

BOB. Does that make it better or worse?

EDIE. Oh, it makes it dreadful — for he must have taken it all! The whole case!

BOB (*taking the spoon*). Well — we've got this much left of it — anyway.

EDIE. It was in father's room — wait — I shall look and see if it's gone. But I'm sure it is — aren't you?

BOB. Oh, absolutely. Let me go first. . . .

EDIE. It's the room across the hall. Wait! You'd better take the poker — but I don't believe there's anyone in there — now. (*They go up to door* L. *Edie holds the door open. Bob looks in door across hall. Edie closes her eyes*) Do you see anybody?

BOB. No.

EDIE. Is there a suit-case lying on the couch at the foot of the bed?

BOB. No.

EDIE. Then it's gone. (*They come back*) He did take it! How terrible!

BOB. Is it? Can't you get some more?

EDIE. Not like this. . . . It's been in the family for years (*Replaces poker*) Sit down and let me tell you — (*They sit on the couch, a space between them*) Father and mother were taking it to Rochester to-night to Aunt Abingdon's wedding. No one ever thought she would marry, you see — and *she* didn't think so — so she let father keep the silver for me in his safe deposit vault —

BOB (*rousing himself*). I see!

EDIE. Then she suddenly decided to marry — and sent for it, and father and mother started with it — they took the midnight train. But there were so many suit-cases that father evidently left the wrong one — and I saw it lying on the couch at the foot of the bed in his room after they'd gone — (*During this recital Bob falls asleep*) Why, he's asleep.

[*Takes Bob's hand.*

BOB (*singing cheerfully*). Cheer, cheer, the gang's all here! (*Opening his eyes*) I beg your pardon —

EDIE. I'm awfully sorry to wake you up — but I was telling you about the silver.

BOB. I know it — I remember perfectly — it's gone. Do you feel very badly about it?

EDIE. Well, it would have been terribly nice to have it. The tea-pot was so cunning.

BOB. Well, I'll tell you. You can have mine. I have a lot of silver coming to me and I don't care anything about it, at all. There ought to have been a girl to have it, but there wasn't. It's marked with an E. What's your name?

EDIE. My name is Edie — isn't that wonderful? But of course I couldn't take it —

BOB. Oh — you couldn't?

EDIE. No — because those things descend in families, you know. There's a regular form that has to be gone through.

BOB. I see. Well, can't we go through it? Anyhow, there's nothing very regular about the way yours has descended. It may not even have the right initials for the burglar's family.

EDIE. I know — and doesn't it seem dreadful for all the little burglars to be eating with Aunt Abingdon's spoons?

BOB. Sorry I made you think of that.

EDIE. You know I ought not to keep you here — but there's no one I could telephone to come and stay with me — everyone is out of town. We're out of town, too, if it hadn't been for the wedding.

BOB. Lucky for me that Aunt Abbie decided to get married. I'd go, but I really don't think I ought to leave you — do you? If you send me away there's nothing but the cold steps across the street.

EDIE. Wouldn't they really let you in?

BOB. Here I am.

EDIE. I'm surprised you didn't go to a hotel!

BOB. Well, it takes quite a lot of time and courage to get home. And somehow, after you get home you haven't the heart to go anywhere else. It seems as though the least they could do is to let you in.

EDIE. I should think so. You're sleepy — if only you could stay until it gets just the least little bit light.

BOB (*rises*). Certainly I will. I'll stay — and I'll try to stay awake. And you go and get some sleep — there's nothing for you to worry about any more. There's a man in the house.

EDIE (*rising*). I wish I could make you more comfortable.

BOB. Oh, I'm all right.

EDIE. No, you're not. I think it's your collar.

BOB. I know it is.

EDIE. I know — you shall put on father's dressing-gown — then you can lie down — if you find you can't sit up. (*She hurries to door* R.U.E.) Of course if you could keep awake until it's just a little bit light, it would be better. [*Exit.*

BOB. I'll keep awake — here's how I'll do it!

[*Starts Victrola, which is already wound. It plays "The Brook." Bob goes to couch and sits on the arm for a moment. Blinks his eyes, goes back to Victrola. Closes it. Places one arm on top, his head in his hand. Enter Edie. She has the dressing-gown.*

EDIE (*laying the dressing-gown on the table*). Oh, what a splendid idea!

BOB. Isn't it? But I think a waltz or a fox-trot would be more effective.

EDIE. Oh, but haven't you ever waltzed to this? I have. It's heavenly!

BOB. Is it? (*They dance. After a few steps*) Why, it *is* heavenly!

EDIE. It's "The Brook", you know.

BOB (*as they dance*). "The Brook"? Does it go on forever? I hope it does. It's wonderful — so dreamy . . .

EDIE. Dreamy — yes — perhaps we'd better stop.

BOB (*stopping the Victrola. Edie sits on arm of couch*). Every time I go to sleep I'll just wake up and start the music. I guess Fielding is dead — or he 'd be here by this time. By Jove — I 've an idea! Have you had him long?

EDIE. No — not very.

BOB. Maybe he took the silver!

EDIE. Oh — do you think he did?

BOB. If it makes you feel any better, I 'm sure he did.

EDIE. Well, if he did I 'm sure he won't come back. At least I shouldn't think he would. So I shouldn't be in danger any more and perhaps I ought to let you go.

BOB. Please don't. Anyway — you can't be sure with a man like that. Even if he 's taken the silver — he might decide to bring it back.

EDIE. It 's the idea of being alone in the house, that 's sort of terrifying —

BOB. Of course. I shouldn't think of allowing it. I 've taken charge of things now — and I order you to talk to me for just a few minutes more, then go to bed.

[*He puts on the dressing-gown; it is a soft silk one and slips on easily over his coat. Edie sits on the couch.*

EDIE. What sort of things are you interested in? Do you like going to college?

BOB. Oh, I 'm all through college — yes — didn't I tell you I 'm going into business? I 'm interested in electricity and motor boats and girls.

EDIE. Don't you care for anything else?

BOB (*sitting beside her. A little nearer this time*). Oh, yes. I 'm awfully fond of my mother.

EDIE. Do you know what I want to do? I want to raise violets. I simply adore them — sweet ones, I mean.

BOB. So do I. Let 's raise them.

EDIE. You never can buy them any more, you know — they 're not the least bit sweet. And it 's a pity to let such an exquisite fragrance die out of the world.

BOB. Why, it 's terrible. Is it dying really? No one ever told me.

EDIE. Girls can't, you know. They can't say, "The violets you sent me were perfectly horrid." But they always are.

Because they're not raised right. They're hurried, and chilled and dead. Just dead violets with a ribbon 'round them.

BOB. Where's my handkerchief! — Can we do anything about it to-night?

EDIE. No — but I'm going to have violet frames under my window in the country. Father says I may. Won't that be heavenly? Then if I make a success of them I'll send them in to shops. Just so that people can buy them and not be disappointed.

BOB. You must let me buy the first bunch — and send it to you.

EDIE (*wishing to inject a little formality into the conversation*). What have you been reading lately?

BOB. Why — the last thing I read was the newspaper. Don't feel that you have to talk to me, Edie.

EDIE. Oh, I love it.

BOB. But aren't you sleepy?

EDIE. Oh, no, it's only that I got up awfully early to come to town, so I could go to the wedding. And then mother decided it was too much for me. To be on the train all night.

BOB. I'm so glad. Tell me — would you like to have a dog?

EDIE. I have two, but I'd *love* to have another.

BOB. I've got a lovely dog — he's just a pup.

EDIE. But don't you want him?

BOB. Yes, but I'm going into business. And he's a bird dog and he's awfully unhappy in the back yard.

EDIE. I'll take him up to the country — to-morrow.

BOB. All right. He's a thorough-bred — very good — but he's just the age where he needs a lot of care. His ears don't stand up quite right.

EDIE. And what do you do about them?

BOB. Well, when I'm reading I sit and hold them forward and up a little — he likes it.

EDIE. The darling. I'll remember to do it.

BOB. He doesn't know much, but he'll be a fine watch dog for the violets. You know, that idea about the violets is immense. I can't wait for the great day when the first fragrant violet in years hits New York. Why not call it "violet day", and have a holiday?

EDIE (*laughing a little*). Wouldn't that be lovely? (*The tiniest yawn. She glances hastily to see if it was observed. It was not*) You know, I can't understand mother's letting father forget the silver.

BOB. Maybe father let mother forget.

EDIE. Oh, no — mother never forgets.

BOB. Mothers are wonderful.

EDIE. Aren't they? Fathers are nice, too.

BOB. Yes, sometimes. But they can't keep it up like mothers.

EDIE. Oh, no, of course not. You couldn't expect that. [*A tiny yawn. She puts her finger on her mouth and looks very serious.*

BOB. No, anyone that expects to be like a mother has got to *be* one, that's all. . . . I'm going to tell you something — when I sat there on those steps a little while ago — What I thought about life — well, it wouldn't do at all for a little girl like you to hear. But I was wrong, I don't care what anyone says, it's all right. And we ought to realize when we're unhappy, that any time, a little thing like a robbery can make it beautiful.

EDIE (*sleepily*). I think life is beautiful.

BOB. I know it is.

EDIE. I don't understand people who are unhappy — Aunt Abbie was always unhappy.

BOB. Because she wasn't married, I suppose.

EDIE. I suppose so. And now she'll be unhappy because she is.

BOB (*a little sleepy*). When would you like to get married? I mean do you believe in early marriage or do you think it's better to wait?

EDIE. Well, I think it depends.

BOB. So do I. But why wait? I mean if a thing's worth doing it's worth doing well — I mean — quick. After all, love is just love, isn't it? If it's going to last it is — if it doesn't, it isn't. I mean if it isn't, it doesn't. So it's not going to make things any better as far as I can see, to wait.

EDIE. No. Not in the least.

[*Edie goes to sleep.*

BOB. Dear little thing, she's gone to sleep. Thank goodness, she won't have to worry any more about my keeping awake. Edie, are you asleep? (*Very softly*) She is. Now how am I going to tell when it gets the least little bit light? [*Edie's head droops against his shoulder. A little disturbed he uncrosses his knees carefully, then deciding not to wake her, re-crosses them. He goes to sleep. He gently, in his sleep, puts his arm around her. His head rests against hers. After a few moments, Voices off.*

MARGARET. Well, I know her better than you do, dear. You'd have had a very cold reception without the silver, I can tell you.

JOHN. All right, all right. You know best, about your own relatives — but I must say if it weren't for Edie's future I wouldn't go a step — not a step.

MARGARET. Don't wake Edie talking so loud. Just slip in and get it, and come right out again.

[*John enters, followed by Margaret. John's eyes rest on the sleeping pair.*

JOHN (*horrified*). Margaret! — Margaret!

MARGARET. John?

JOHN (*hardly able to speak*). Will you — will you look on the couch? Edie! And a strange young man — (*Peering at them*) Yes — in my dressing-gown!

MARGARET (*greatly interested*). Why, John! Who do you suppose it is! I never saw him before in my life!

JOHN. Margaret, I have told you all along that your ideas about bringing Edie up would result in disaster. Now you see for yourself.

MARGARET. See? See what? I don't see any particular disaster about it yet. Of course I don't understand it, but the boy is a very nice-looking, in fact quite a distinguished-looking boy. . . .

JOHN. And he's here in my house asleep in my dressing-gown, with my daughter in his arms! That's all right, I suppose. Quite all right if one is modern enough to think so.

MARGARET. John, do lower your voice and don't talk about *your* house and *your* dressing-gown and *your* daughter. The house is ours and the dressing-gown I gave you for Xmas and Edie is certainly mine. . . .

JOHN (*gloomily*). I fear the worst.

MARGARET. I don't. I have perfect confidence in my child. I don't know anything about your ancestors, John, but mine alone would prevent any scandal occurring in the family.

JOHN. She said going to Rochester would be too much for her — but she's killed her father — that's what she's done!

MARGARET. John, don't be ridiculous — why don't you wake him up and ask him what he's doing here?

JOHN. I don't need to ask him. But I will. . . .

[*He leaps upon Bob. They fight.*

BOB. It's Fielding! So you're back, are you, after that salt spoon? — you avaricious old thief!

EDIE. Stop! Mercy!

BOB. Don't be worried — I can handle him.

EDIE. Don't! That's my father!

MARGARET. Stop him, Edie!

BOB. Oh, I beg your pardon — I thought you were the Butler!

JOHN. And who are you, if I may ask?

EDIE. Father, don't — don't tremble so!

JOHN. I'm not trembling — or if I am it's not with fear.

EDIE. Of course not, dear. I didn't mean that.

JOHN.   To come into my house at this hour and find a perfect stranger and in my dressing-gown —

BOB.   I 'll take it off —

[*Does so.*

MARGARET.   Edie, who is he?

EDIE.   His name is — I forget — but he lives across the street.

JOHN.   Then what is he doing here — if he lives across the street?

EDIE.   Father, you don't understand. . . .

JOHN.   No — I don't.   Why isn 't he across the street where he belongs?

BOB.   I was.   But I heard a call for help and I came in and found your daughter alone in the house —

JOHN.   I should hope so —

BOB.   I couldn't leave her alone in the house —

JOHN.   Why couldn't you?

EDIE.   Father, listen to me — don't you realize that the house has been robbed?   All Aunt Abingdon's silver and I don't know what besides — you know you left it.

MARGARET.   Where did you leave it, John?

JOHN.   I didn't leave it at all — you left it.

MARGARET.   Why, I didn't — you said in the cab, it was somewhere.

EDIE.   Well, it isn't anywhere now — and we think Fielding has taken it — for he doesn't answer the bell — either that or Fielding is dead — but we don't think he is — for we turned the Victrola on and still he didn't come.

[*John goes to bell.   Rings, exits.*

MARGARET.   Isn't even Ellen here?

EDIE.   No, darling — she 's gone down to Maggie's house. But it 's all right, mother.   This is Robert Hamilton — I remember now.   He was sitting on the steps of his house when I called for help.

BOB.   I suppose you think that 's very strange, Mrs. Upton?

MARGARET.   Why, not any stranger than anything else.

BOB. I was locked out, you see. My father is — well —
he's a little like Mr. Upton.

[*Mr. Upton returns.*

JOHN. The silver is gone — and Fielding is not in his room.
Well, I never liked his face. I said he had a shifty eye.

MARGARET. But only one — the other was very nice — and
he told me the shifty one was hit by a boy with a bean-
shooter.

JOHN. You will engage the servants, in spite of any protests
from me. Well, we won't go to Rochester without that
silver. At least I won't. (*Telephone*) Now who's that?

MARGARET. Maybe it's Fielding! — To say he's sorry!

JOHN (*at the phone*). Yes — that's very likely. (*Into
phone*) Who is it? Fielding? Yes, yes! Where are
you? At the station? With the silver? Well, my good
man — you have made us all a great deal of trouble. . . .
Of course we won't go to-night. No, Mrs. Upton is too
upset. Bring the silver back, here to the house.

MARGARET (*to Edie*). Isn't it wonderful how your father is
always wrong about everything?

BOB. I suppose I'd better go.

JOHN. Indeed you'll not go. I want an explanation of how
you come to be here and who you are.

BOB. My name is Hamilton. Robert Hamilton. My
father has just bought the house across the street.

JOHN. Edie, have you ever met this young man before?

EDIE. No, father.

JOHN. And — and — I find you asleep in his arms?

EDIE. Father, was I? How dreadful!

[*Turning to her mother.*

MARGARET (*putting her arms around Edie*). John, you
shouldn't have told her.

BOB. It wasn't dreadful. She went to sleep and I didn't
like to wake her up. She's nothing but a tired child — if
you scold her I — I have my opinion of you.

JOHN. Indeed! And your name is Hamilton. Where do
you live?

BOB. Just where I did before, across the street.

JOHN. That's easily verified. (*Going to phone*) Hamilton.

BOB. The phone is 4664 River, but I wouldn't advise you to call him.

JOHN. Indeed . . . (*At phone*) 4664 River.

BOB. He's a brave man.

EDIE. I'm so sorry!

JOHN (*in phone*). Is this Mr. Hamilton? Well, I'm sure — Wait — But I — why, you — This is Mr. Upton speaking. Your son — your son — your son!

[*His voice increasing in volume. Retreats from phone, defeated.*

BOB (*going to the rescue*). Allow me — (*At phone*) Hello, Dad — I had to save a girl's life across the street. A robbery. . . . Yes, sir, case of silver. But it's been returned now and I can come home. That's what made me late. I'm there now — I mean here. I knew you wouldn't let me in. All right, sir — all right.

[*Picks up his hat.*

EDIE. Are you going?

JOHN. My boy, you put my dressing-gown right on again and stay. I wouldn't go home at all — if I were you.

BOB. Oh, it's all right — he says he'll open the door. Good night. . . .

[*Bob goes. John goes with him.*

EDIE. Oh — he'll never come again — father acted so dreadfully.

MARGARET. Well, he won't come to see your father certainly.

[*Sits on couch. Edie sits beside her.*

EDIE. He was so nice. He'd been to a banquet, mother, and he was terribly tired — and still, he was nice.

MARGARET. I really think he was, and I loved the way he fought with your father. And I thought your father fought very well.

EDIE. I should say so — especially after they stopped. Oh, dear! I liked him so much and he was going to give me a dog, and now it's all over!

[*Bob offstage whistles a bar of " The Brook." Edie runs to the*

*window, she turns and smiles at her mother.   Margaret goes
a few steps toward her.*

EDIE (*looking out*).   Father 's going across the street with him.
Father 's gone in — (*Runs to her mother, taking her hands*)
Oh, mother — now we know the Hamiltons!
[*Embracing her mother.*

CURTAIN

POOR AUBREY

GEORGE KELLY

Not many of the playwrights who have become popular with Little Theatre audiences received their early training in the vaudeville circuits, but George Kelly's one-act plays were all produced successfully in the principal Keith and Orpheum theatres of the United States and Canada. It is seldom, also, that a one-act play is expanded into a full-length drama, but after two years of continuous production in the short form, George Kelly used the character of Aubrey Piper for his three-act play, "The Show-Off." In both its short and in its long forms, the comedy of "Poor Aubrey" has been a Little Theatre favorite for many years, and has been produced in many parts of the world.

Mr. Kelly was born in 1887 in a suburb of Philadelphia. At the age of twenty-one he came to New York and entered the dramatic profession as an actor.

He has published his one-act plays in a collection, *The Flattering Word and Other One-Act Plays*. His full-length plays are "The Torch-Bearers", "The Show-Off", "Craig's Wife" (which was awarded the Pulitzer prize of 1926), "Daisy Mayme", "Philip Goes Forth", "Reflected Glory", and "Behold the Bridegroom."

POOR AUBREY

By GEORGE KELLY

"Poor Aubrey" was originally presented at the Palace Theater, New York City.

Original Cast

AUBREY PIPER	Frederick Sumner
AMY, his wife	Margaret O'Neill
MRS. FISHER, Amy's mother	Bertine Robinson
MRS. COLE, Marion Brill, a friend of Amy's	Corinne Cantwell

Reprinted from *The Flattering Word and Other One-Act Plays* by permission of and special arrangement with George Kelly and Little, Brown and Company, Boston, Massachusetts.

This play, in its printed form, is designed for the reading public only. All dramatic, motion-picture, and other rights are fully protected by copyright, *and no performance — professional or amateur — may be given without the written permission of the author, and the payment of royalty.* Communications may be addressed to the author, George Kelly, 3665 Midvale Avenue, Philadelphia, Pennsylvania.

POOR AUBREY

SCENE. *The sitting room in Fisher's house, about four o'clock of a Saturday afternoon in February.*

[Amy enters briskly through the portières at the right, carrying a fancy cushion, which she sets in the armchair at the back of the room; then continues on over to an arched doorway at the left and draws the curtains together. She is a dark-haired, trim-looking woman, in her late twenties, dressed in black — a very pretty dress, of black crêpe, with a graceful side sash of the goods, piped with buff-colored silk. She has on black slippers and stockings, and wears a string of buff-colored beads — quite large. Her general manner suggests a quality of intelligent definiteness; something of which is even evident in the arrangement of her hair. While she is engaged at the curtains, the portières over at the right are brushed aside, and her husband swings into the room, and stands preening himself near the table. He is fearfully and wonderfully gotten up! — a perfect flash of cross-barred gray and brilliantine. Poor Aubrey! He is painfully arrayed, even to the toupee; a feature that, as Dickens remarked of Sairey Gamp's transformation, could scarcely be called false, it is so very innocent of anything approaching to deception. And the quantities of brilliantine that have obviously been employed upon it only serve to heighten its artificiality. He is wearing a glistening white vest and a shiny gold watch-chain, a necktie of living green, with a rather large horseshoe tie-pin of imitation diamonds, and a very high collar. He has a flashily bordered silk handkerchief set forth in the breast pocket of his coat, and there is a pair of heavy-rimmed nose-glasses depending from his neck on a black tape.

AUBREY (*touching his toupee gingerly*). Does this thing look all right?

AMY. What?

AUBREY. This toupee. (*She glances over her right shoulder indifferently*) I put some of that brilliantine on it.

AMY (*resuming her arrangement of the curtains*). It's all right.

AUBREY (*turning to the little wall mirror just below the portières at the right*). You don't seem very enthusiastic about it.

AMY (*turning from the curtains and crossing quickly to the table — an oblong table, in the middle of the room, and towards the back*). Because I don't think you need it.

[*She picks up a small folded cover from the table, shakes it out, and tosses it across her left shoulder; then commences to gather up the scattered books and put them into the little table-rack.*

AUBREY (*settling the toupee at the mirror*). What do you want your friend to think, that you married an old man?

AMY. Why, a man doesn't look old simply because he hasn't a big head of hair.

AUBREY. Well, mine's pretty thin here on top.

AMY. Well, that's nothing; lots of young men haven't much.

AUBREY (*turning to her*). Why, it was you that suggested my getting a toupee in the first place!

AMY (*stopping, and resting her hands on the table; and speaking directly to him*). I know very well it was; because I knew I'd never have a minute's peace till you'd get one. All I heard morning, noon, and night was something about your hair coming out. You might think nobody ever heard of anybody being baldheaded.

AUBREY (*turning back to the mirror*). Well, a man's got to make the most of himself.

AMY. Well, if you think that thing's adding anything to *your* appearance, you've got another think. (*She starts towards the tabourette in front of the bay-window over at the left*) Lift up this plant here for me, I want to put this cover on. (*She picks up a dead leaf or two from the floor and tosses them out the window. He remains standing at the mirror, looking at the toupee very critically from various angles*) Aubrey!

AUBREY (*without moving, and with a touch of irritation*). All right, all right!

AMY. Well, hurry up! — I want to change these covers. (*He withdraws lingeringly from the mirror*) You'll keep fooling with that wig till there isn't a hair left on it.

AUBREY (*crossing to her*). It isn't a wig, now, Amy! I've told you that half a dozen times!

AMY (*raising her hand quietly, to silence him*). Well, a toupee then, dearie, — don't get excited.

AUBREY. I'm not getting excited at all!

AMY (*indicating the plant with an authoritative gesture*). Lift up this plant and shut up. (*He lifts up the plant and holds it, till she has changed the covers*) There.

[*He sets the plant down again, and she settles it more precisely.*

AUBREY (*starting back across the room, in front of the sofa*). You just call it a wig because you know it makes me mad!

AMY (*straightening up and looking after him, with one hand on her hip*). I don't know why it should make you so mad, to have it called a wig.

AUBREY (*turning to her sharply*). Because it *isn't* a wig! It's a toupee!

AMY (*turning to the plant again and giving it a final touch*). Well, it's pretty, whatever it is.

AUBREY. It isn't even a toupee; it's just a patch!

AMY (*starting across to the back of the center table, carrying the soiled cover*). It's a young *wig*, that's what it is. (*He turns and glares at her. She settles the scarf on the center table*) And if it were only half as big as it is, anybody that'd look at it a mile away'd know that it never grew on you.

[*She goes quickly out through the portières at the right, and he returns to the mirror and preens himself generally. Immediately she comes back into the room again, carrying a big, dark dust-cloth, with which she commences to dust the center table; while he struts across the room in front of the table, settling his cuffs and whistling the opening bars of the chorus of "I'm Forever Blowing Bubbles."*

AUBREY (*as he approaches the bay-window*). What do you say about putting a couple of these plants out on the front porch?

AMY. What for?

AUBREY. I think it adds a lot to the appearance of the house as you come up the street.

AMY. Oh, don't be silly, Aubrey!

AUBREY (*wheeling around and looking at her in astonishment*). What do you mean, don't be silly?

AMY (*pausing in her dusting*). Why, who ever heard of anybody putting plants on a front porch in February!

AUBREY. I don't mean to leave them out there! We could bring them in again as soon as she goes.

AMY (*starting for the little corner table down at the right*). Yes, and she'd go away thinking we were both crazy.

[*She arranges the few magazines on the table, and then commences to dust it.*

AUBREY (*sauntering back to the center table, where he proceeds to take the books which she has just arranged out of the little rack, and stand them on their ends*). Oh, everybody's thinking you're crazy, with you!

AMY (*turning to him and speaking emphatically*). Well, I know that's exactly what *I'd* think, if I were to come along and see plants on an open porch in the middle of winter.

AUBREY (*occupied with the book arrangement, and without looking up*). Well, I've seen *lots* of plants on front porches in the winter.

AMY (*returning to her work of dusting the table*). Well, if you did, they were *enclosed* porches. (*She finishes the dusting, and starts back towards the center table; but comes to a dead stop upon seeing the arrangement of the books, and her husband's intense absorption in it. There is a slight pause*) What are you doing with those books?

AUBREY (*still busy*). I'm just standing them up this way, so you can see what they are.

AMY. Can't you see what they are in the rack?

AUBREY. Certainly you can; but I think they show up better this way.

AMY (*stepping towards him and pushing him out of the way*). Go away! and let them alone!

[*She hurriedly commences to gather them up and restore them to the rack.*

AUBREY (*wandering towards the arched doorway at the left*). That's the way they have them in all the store windows.

[*He proceeds to push the curtains back at the arched doorway.*

AMY. Well, this isn't a store window. (*She glances at what he's doing, and starts towards him*) And don't push those curtains back that way, Aubrey! I just fixed them.

[*She pushes him towards the back of the room. He wanders around her and comes forward at the left.*

AUBREY. They cover up the Victrola, that way.

AMY (*settling the curtains*). That doesn't matter. These doors look too bare with the curtains pushed back. (*She starts back towards the center table to complete her rearrangement of the books*) Now, let things alone, for heaven's sake! She can see the Victrola when she goes in there.

AUBREY (*sauntering a little towards the right, in front of the center table*). She may not go in there.

AMY (*addressing him, as she crosses to the portières at the right, taking the dust cloth with her*). Well, I guess she's seen Victrolas before, even if she *doesn't* go in there. (*She goes out through the portières. He stands for a second fixing himself, then breaks into "I'm Forever Blowing Bubbles" again. The detection of a speck of dust on his left shoe brings his whistling to a close; and, whipping out the eloquent handkerchief from his breast pocket, he leans over to flick it off. The effort dislodges the toupee, which drops to the floor in front of him. He snatches it up frantically, and claps it back upon his head; thrusts his handkerchief back into his pocket, and, with a panic-stricken glance over his right shoulder, in the direction of the portières, bolts to the bay-window, at the left, holding the toupee in place with his left hand. Amy hurries in from the right carrying a small vase, which she takes to the little stand down at the right)* Any sign of her?

AUBREY (*adjusting the toupee, and pretending to look out the window*). I don't see any sign of her yet.

AMY (*turning from the little stand and moving towards the front of the center table*). Maybe her train's late.

[*She glances about the room, to see that everything is all right.*

AUBREY. I don't know why it *should* be; there wasn't any hold-up along the line to-day that *I* heard of.

AMY (*settling her sash*). She said in her telegram that she'd get into Broad Street at three o'clock sharp, and that she'd come right out here — Because she had to leave again on the Bridge train at four-fourteen.

AUBREY (*turning from the window and coming towards her*). Too bad she didn't know, she could have gotten right off here at North Philadelphia — And then she could have gotten that Bridge train right there again at — a — four-twenty-seven.

[*He finishes his remarks with an explanatory gesture, and stands looking at his wife. She is still settling her sash. There is a fractional pause. Then she finishes and looks up at him. Then there is another pause, during which her eyes shift to his toupee, which is on askew, — a bit over the left eye.*

AMY (*with a kind of wearied impatience*). Fix your toupee.

AUBREY (*putting his hand to it, and with a note of challenge in his voice*). What's the matter with it?

AMY. Why, it's all over the place.

AUBREY. Is that so!

AMY. Well, look at it!

AUBREY. Well, I fixed it that way!

[*He emphasizes the remark with a little bob of his head, and starts up around the center table towards the mirror.*

AMY. Well, it's pretty.

AUBREY. To let the air get to my scalp.

AMY. Well, for Heaven's sake, don't have it fixed that way when Marion comes! (*Fixing the lace at her left cuff*) You look as though your head were lopsided.
[*He turns from the mirror, and gives her a withering look. But she is occupied with her cuff.*

AUBREY (*turning back to the mirror*). How is it you didn't put on your other dress?

AMY. What other dress?

AUBREY. The one with all the beads.

AMY (*looking at him*). Why, this is my good dress.

AUBREY. I think that other one's more of a flash.

AMY (*turning away again and settling the front of her dress*). Oh, don't be such a show-off, Aubrey!

AUBREY (*turning sharply and looking at her*). Show-off!

AMY. That's what I said.

AUBREY. I don't know how you figure that's showing off! — Because I want you to *look* good.

AMY (*looking at him stonily, and speaking in a level key*). You want me to look good because I'm *your* wife. And you want this friend of mine to *see* me looking good; just as you want her to see that Victrola in there — (*She indicates the arched door on the left with a slight nod*) that isn't half paid for.
[*She looks out.*

AUBREY (*coming towards her a step or two*). I suppose *you'd* rather have her think you married some poor thing!

AMY. Listen, Aubrey — It won't make the least bit of difference *what* we want her to think — She's a very smart girl; and all she'll have to do is glance around this room, and she'll know *exactly* what I married.
[*She looks straight out again.*

AUBREY (*mimicking her tone*). Is that so! (*She simply emphasizes her remarks with a slow and very positive nod*) Well, now, you listen to me for a minute, Amy! You know I can beat it right over to the barber shop (*She breaks into a rather tired little laugh*) and stay there, till this friend of yours has gone, (*He moves over towards the little stand at the right*) if you 're so awfully afraid that I 'm going to show up so badly in front of her!

AMY (*looking after him with a very knowing expression*).   No fear of your beating it over to the barber shop.

AUBREY.   No?

AMY.   You 'll be strutting around here in front of her if she stays till midnight.

AUBREY (*very nettled, and securing his tie and tie-pin*).   All right.

AMY (*taking a step or two towards him*).   And, by the way, Aubrey — When Marion comes — I want you to do me a little favor; and don't be giving her a lot of big talk, — the way you were doing to that insurance man the other night; (*He turns and looks at her in astonished indignation*) for I don't want her to think you 're silly.

AUBREY.   When was I doing any big talk to any insurance man?

AMY.   The other night when you were talking to that man about the price of a fifty-thousand dollar policy.

AUBREY.   Well, what about it?

AMY.   Nothing; only that he was just laughing up his sleeve at you.

AUBREY.   Is that so!

AMY.   Well now, what else *could* he do, Aubrey?   He knew you hadn't the slightest intention of taking any such policy.

AUBREY.   How do you know he did?

AMY.   Because he knows you 're only a clerk.   And that you don't get enough salary in six months to pay one year's premium on a policy like that.   So when Marion comes, please don't be trying to impress her; (*She turns away from him rather slowly and moves up at the right of the center table*) for she 's a very sensible woman.

AUBREY (*turning and going up to the mirror*).   I won't have anything to say to the woman at all.

AMY (*standing above the center table glancing through a magazine*).   Oh, yes, you will, dearie.

AUBREY. She's not coming to see me.

AMY. That doesn't make any difference to you.

AUBREY. No reason why I should stand around *gabbing* to her.

AMY. Well, you'll stand around gabbing, if you can get anybody to listen to you.

AUBREY. Well, now, you watch me.

AMY. I've been watching you; and listening to you too; for nearly four years.

AUBREY (*turning to her from the mirror, very peevishly, and holding up his right hand*). All right, I'll raise my hand, — if I want to say anything.

[*He moves forward at the right.*

AMY. I know what you'll do, if you get the chance; I've heard you before.

[*There is a slight pause, during which he frets a bit, down at the right. Then his mood shifts and he breaks into whistling his familiar "I'm Forever Blowing Bubbles." But this dies gradually as he becomes conscious of the little vase which Amy brought in for the stand at his right. He tilts his head a bit to one side and looks at it with critical disapproval.*

AUBREY. You know, it's too bad we haven't got something flashier for this stand here.

AMY (*just lifting her eyes over the top of the magazine*). There's that vase up in Mother's room.

AUBREY. Is she up there now?

AMY. She was when I came down.

AUBREY (*with a gesture of finality, and starting across in front of the center table*). Well, *that's* out.

AMY. Why, she wouldn't mind my taking it.

AUBREY (*turning to his left and speaking emphatically*). It isn't that! But if she sees you taking anything out of her room, she'll get an idea there's something going on down here, and she'll be right down for the rest of the night and you won't be able to chase her!

[*He turns to his right and looks out the bay-window.*

AMY. Why, she knows that Marion Brill is coming here this afternoon.

AUBREY (*turning to her sharply, with a distressed expression*). Did you tell her?

AMY. Certainly I told her.

AUBREY (*despairingly, and crossing over again in front of the center table*). Good night!

AMY. Why, I want her to *meet* Marion! She's never *met* her!

AUBREY. Well, if your mother ever gets *talking*, this friend of yours'll know everything from *your* age to *my* salary! (*He turns away to his right*) Now, I'm telling you!

AMY (*with a glance towards the portières at the right, and speaking in an emphatic but subdued manner*). I don't care whether she does or not.

AUBREY. Well, I *do.*

[*Amy glances quickly towards the bay-window at the left; then, dropping the magazine, she steps eagerly towards it.*

AMY. There's a taxi, now.

[*She draws the curtain aside and looks keenly out.*

AUBREY (*whirling round and striding towards the bay-window, — holding on to his toupee with his left hand*). Is it stopping?

AMY (*suddenly, and in a tone of suppressed excitement*). *There* she is! (*She runs to the door at the back of the room and vanishes into the hallway*) She's looking for the number!

[*Aubrey peers eagerly through the bay-window, then steps quickly up to the door at the back.*

AUBREY. Don't stand out there talking, now, Amy, without something around you!

[*He rushes across at the back, still holding on to the toupee and, after a fleeting glance through the portières at the right, reaches the mirror, where he gives himself a hasty and critical survey. Then the laughter and greetings of his wife and Mrs. Cole reach him from the front door; so, with a glance in*

*that direction, he struts forward at the right and strikes a pose,
swinging his nose-glasses carelessly back and forth, and
looking away off.*

AMY (*out at the left*).   I knew you through the window of the
taxi!

MRS. COLE.   Well, you know, I was thinking all the way out,
"Now, I wonder if Amy got my wire."

AMY.   I got it yesterday morning.

MRS. COLE and AMY (*together*).

{ (*Mrs. Cole*)   Because, you know, I couldn't wait to
hear from you.

{ (*Amy*)   But I said to Aubrey, "There's no use in my
sending any word now, for she's already left Chicago by
this time."

[*The front door closes.*

MRS. COLE.   Well, you see, dear, I didn't know *definitely* —

MRS. COLE and AMY (*together*).

{ (*Mrs. Cole*)   Up until Thursday night that I was coming.

{ (*Amy, appearing in the hall door*)   Oh, well, it doesn't
matter!   (*Coming into the room*)   Just so long as I get to
see you.

[*She glances at her husband, then turns and faces the hall
door.   There is a second's pause;   then Mrs. Cole enters
the room;   and, glancing about, stops just inside the door.
She is a bit older than Amy, — probably three or four years,
and considerably lighter in coloring.   And very smart.
Amy said she was, and she is — extremely so.   It's in the
clearness of her eye, and the peculiarly deft coördination of
her general movement.   Her clothes are smart too;   and by
the looks of them, she must have married rather well;   they are
quite gorgeous.   A fine seal coat, full length, with a cape
effect, and an enormous muff made of black fox;   rather large
hat of black lace over black satin, faced with pale coral, and
black slippers and stockings.   She doesn't remove her coat,
but when she opens it, there is a glimpse of a light coral-
colored dress, heavily trimmed with steel beads, a long neck-
scarf in steel silk, and a lovely-looking necklace of pale jade.*

*She is wearing white kid gloves and carries a fancy bag made
of jade and coral beads on her left wrist.*

MRS. COLE.   What an attractive house you have, Amy.

AMY (*smiling, and indicating her husband*).   There's the
principal attraction, over there.

[*Aubrey acknowledges the compliment by melting slightly.*

MRS. COLE (*smiling graciously and passing down at the left of
the center table, towards Aubrey*).   Is this *him?*

[*He advances.*

AMY (*coming forward at the left of the center table*).   That's
him.

MRS. COLE.   I'm *so* glad to meet you, Mr. Piper.

AUBREY (*with a touch of condescension*).   How do you
do.

[*They shake hands.*

MRS. COLE.   You know, I've always been enormously *curious*
to see Amy's husband.

AUBREY.   That so?

AMY (*looking straight out, and securing a hairpin in the right
side of her head*).   There he is.

MRS. COLE (*tilting her head a bit to the left side and looking at
Aubrey with a smile*).   He's terribly good-looking.

AMY (*turning away*).   Oh!

[*Mrs. Cole turns her head sharply and looks at her, still
smiling.*

AUBREY (*addressing his wife*).   You hear *that?*

[*Mrs. Cole turns again to Aubrey.*

AMY.   Please don't tell him that, Marion! he's bad enough
as it is.

MRS. COLE.   I don't know how you managed it, Amy.   I
could never do it.   You should see *my* husband, Mr.
Piper.   I don't suppose he's any *older* than Mr. Piper,
but, my dear, he *looks* old enough to be your father.   (*Amy
gives a little laugh of incredulity, and Mrs. Cole turns suddenly to her*)   Really!   (*Then she turns suddenly again to
Aubrey*)   He's almost bald!

[*Aubrey's smile freezes.*

AMY. Let me take your coat, Marion.

[*Aubrey turns quietly around to the right, touching his toupee with his right hand, and moves up to the mirror, where he takes a reassuring peep at it, unobserved.*

MRS. COLE. I don't think I'll bother, dear, really; that taxicab's waiting out there for me. You see, I've got to get that Bridge train out of Broad Street at four-fourteen.

AUBREY (*coming forward at the right*). I was just saying to Amy, it's too bad you didn't know, you could have gotten right off here at North Philadelphia, and wouldn't have had to go downtown at all.

AMY. You know, that Bridge train makes a stop here, Marion, at North Philadelphia, on the way to Atlantic City.

MRS. COLE. Oh, does it!

AMY. Gets there at four-twenty-seven.

MRS. COLE. Isn't it too bad I didn't know that.

AUBREY. Well, you won't have to go back downtown now, as it is, will you, Mrs. Cole?

MRS. COLE. Yes, I've checked my grip at Broad Street.

AMY. Oh, isn't that too bad!

MRS. COLE. Well, it doesn't matter! Just so long as I got to see you.

AMY. That's about all you'll be able to do.

MRS. COLE. Well, sometime I'm going to invite myself to spend a few days with you, and then we'll have lots of time to talk.

AMY. I wish you could spend them now.

MRS. COLE. So do I, dear child; but what can a poor woman do with a sick husband on her hands.

AMY. How is he, Marion?

MRS. COLE. Why, he's pretty good, now.

AMY. Sit down.

[*She picks up the cushion from the right end of the sofa to make a place for Mrs. Cole.*

MRS. COLE (*stepping over to the sofa and unfastening her coat*). I must unfasten this coat. (*Amy sits at the left end of the*

sofa; then Mrs. Cole sits down) You know he had quite
an attack of the flu last winter; and, I don't know, he
never seemed to really get over it.

[*Aubrey has assumed a position over at the right of the center
table, and is listening with a general expression of heavy
consequence.*

AMY. So many people didn't.

AUBREY. One of the bookkeepers down at my office was
telling me the other day that the flu has left him with a
weak heart.

MRS. COLE. Yes, I've heard of that, too. But with my
husband, it all seems to be in his nerves. That's the reason
he's at Atlantic City now.

AMY. How long has he been there, Marion?

MRS. COLE. Since the week after New Year's.

AUBREY. They say Atlantic City's a great place for the
nerves.

MRS. COLE. Well, Ralph says he feels ever so much better.
I had a letter from him on Tuesday, and he said he was
only going to stay another week. So I thought I'd better
just run down there myself and see how he is before he
starts that long trip back to Chicago.

AMY. That flu was a dreadful thing, wasn't it?

MRS. COLE. Dreadful! My dear, you've never seen anything change a person the way it has changed my husband.
(*She turns suddenly to Aubrey*) He's even lost his hair.

[*She coughs a little, and uses her handkerchief; while
Aubrey glides to the mirror again, touching his toupee dis-
creetly.*

AMY (*picking up the muff from Mrs. Cole's lap*). I love this
muff, Marion.

MRS. COLE. Do you know how long I've had that?

AMY. How long?

MRS. COLE. Three years last Christmas.

AMY. Really!

MRS. COLE. Ralph gave it to me the first Christmas we were
married.

AMY (*holding it out on her left arm*). It's beautiful!

[*Aubrey comes forward again.*

AUBREY. What kind of fur *is* that, Mrs. Cole?

MRS. COLE. Fox.

AUBREY. Makes a nice looking fur.

MRS. COLE (*turning and looking at it*). It was pretty when I first got it. (*Turning again to Aubrey*) But it's getting old now; (*Looking back to the muff*) the hair's commencing to fall out. (*He turns and drifts to the back of the room*) I was so sorry to hear about your father, Amy.

AMY. Yes, it was so sudden.

MRS. COLE. How is your mother, Amy?

[*Aubrey turns and looks towards his wife.*

AMY. She keeps pretty well.

MRS. COLE. That's good.

AMY. She's here with us, you know.

[*Aubrey makes a despairing gesture.*

MRS. COLE. Oh, is she?

AMY. Yes.

MRS. COLE. Living with you, you mean?

AMY (*getting up, and going round back of the sofa*). Hum-hum. I must tell her you're here.

MRS. COLE. Well, now, don't bother her, Amy, if she's doing anything.

AMY (*crossing to the portières at the right*). Not a thing — She's crazy to see you.

MRS. COLE and AMY (*together*).

{ (*Mrs. Cole*) I don't want to bother her.
{ (*Amy*) I told her I'd call her as soon as you came. (*Going out through the portières*) I'll be down in a second. [*Aubrey, standing up at the back of the room, glances after his wife, then turns and looks at Mrs. Cole. She is settling her muff beside her on the sofa. He glances at himself in the mirror, and then comes forward at the right, rather grandly, flipping the nose-glasses back and forth.*

MRS. COLE. Isn't it nice that Amy can have her mother here with her?

AUBREY. Yes; I've had her here ever since Mr. Fisher died.

MRS. COLE. She must be so much company for you.

AUBREY. Yes; a person'd never be lonesome.

MRS. COLE. I often say to *my* husband, I wish there were some one like that with us; I get so lonesome sometimes in the house during the day.

AUBREY. Well, when my father-in-law died, I thought Amy's mother might just as well come here with us. She was alone; and we had plenty of room; so I said, "Come ahead! (*He makes a rather magnificent gesture with his right hand*) The more the merrier!"

MRS. COLE. This *is* rather a large house, isn't it?

AUBREY. Yes, it is. Quite a wonderfully made house, too. They were put up by the McNeil people out here at Jenkintown. They're considered to build the best dwelling-house of anybody in the country. They just put up the twenty of them, as kind of sample houses — ten on that side, and ten on this. Of course, these on this side have the southern exposure; so a person's got to have quite a little pull to get hold of one of these. (*He catches his thumbs in the armholes of his vest, and, tilting his head a bit to the left side, looks away out and off, tapping his fingers on his chest*) But I have a friend — that's one of the biggest real estate men here in town, and he was able to fix it for me.

MRS. COLE. You were very lucky, weren't you?

AUBREY. Yes, I *was* pretty lucky in a way. Although I'd like to have gotten hold of one of the corner ones.

MRS. COLE. Are they a much larger house than these?

AUBREY. They're a fifteen-thousand-dollar house; these are only ten.

[*He moves across in front of her, with ever so slight a suggestion of strut.*

MRS. COLE. I see.

AUBREY (*with a casual glance out of the bay-window*). I'm very anxious to get hold of one of them. I told this friend of mine to keep his eye open, and if there's a chance, I'll go as high as twenty thousand. Then, of course, I could always rent this.

MRS. COLE. It's an awfully nice street.

AUBREY. Nice in summer.

MRS. COLE. I was so surprised when I saw it, because the taxicab driver didn't know where it was when I asked him. [*Aubrey looks at her, with a quick movement of his head.*

AUBREY. Didn't know where Cresson Street was?

MRS. COLE. He said not.

AUBREY (*shaking his head from side to side and smiling with heavy amusement*). He must be an awful rube.

MRS. COLE. He had to ask the traffic officer down on Broad Street.

AUBREY. Well, I'll tell you — I don't suppose they *have* many calls for taxis out this way. You see, most everybody in through here has his own car.

MRS. COLE. Oh, I see.

AUBREY. Some of them have a half a dozen, for that matter. (*He laughs consequentially, and she reflects his amusement faintly*) I was saying to Amy, when we got your wire yesterday, it was too bad *my* car was laid up, I could have picked you up at the station to-day.

MRS. COLE. Oh, that didn't matter.

AUBREY. But I've been working it pretty hard lately, and I had to turn it in Thursday to have the valves ground.

MRS. COLE. There's always something to be done to them, isn't there?

AUBREY. I should say so. Funny thing, too, — people have an idea if they get hold of a high-priced car their trouble's over. (*She smiles and shakes her head from side to side in appreciation of that illusion*) I swear, I've had just as much trouble with my *Pierce Arrow* as I ever had with my Buick.

[*They both laugh, and Aubrey looks out the window.*

AMY (*coming in through the portières at the right*). Mother says she was just coming down to inquire how it was you hadn't come. (*Aubrey turns and looks at his wife, then turns around to his right and moves towards the back of the room. Mrs. Fisher comes in through the portières, and Mrs. Cole rises) This* is Mrs. Cole, Mother — Marion Brill that you've heard so much about.

MRS. FISHER (*coming forward at the right of the center table*). Well, indeed I have.

MRS. COLE (*advancing*). I'm *so* glad to meet you, Mrs. Fisher.

MRS. FISHER (*shaking hands with her*). How do you do. I'm certainly pleased to meet you, too.

MRS. COLE. Thank you.

MRS. FISHER. For I think I've heard your name more than any other girl's name I ever heard in this house.

MRS. COLE. Well, Amy and I worked beside each other so long.

MRS. FISHER. All I used to hear morning, noon, and night was, "Marion Brill said so and so" (*Mrs. Cole and Amy laugh*) or, "Marion Brill is going to do so and so."
[*Mrs. Fisher laughs.*

AMY (*standing at her mother's right*). I'm afraid that's about all we did was talk, wasn't it, Marion?
[*She laughs again.*

MRS. COLE. It's about all *I* used to do.
[*She laughs.*

MRS. FISHER (*indicating the sofa*). Won't you sit down, Mrs. Cole?

MRS. COLE (*turning to her right, towards the sofa*). Thanks.

AMY (*indicating the armchair at the right of the center table*). Sit here, Mother.

MRS. FISHER (*passing to the armchair, in front of Amy*). Amy, why didn't you ask Mrs. Cole to take off her coat?

MRS. COLE (*sitting on the sofa*). She did, Mrs. Fisher.
[*Mrs. Fisher sits down.*

AMY (*sitting on the edge of the center table*). Marion can't stay, Mother.

MRS. COLE. I've got to go almost immediately, Mrs. Fisher.

MRS. FISHER. It's too bad you can't stay for a cup of tea, anyway.

MRS. COLE. I'd love it, Mrs. Fisher, but I really haven't time.

MRS. FISHER. You're going to Atlantic City, aren't you?

MRS. COLE. Yes.

MRS. FISHER (*as though admitting a weakness in herself*). I wish I was going with you.

[*She laughs shyly. And when she laughs she's pretty. She must have been a rather pretty girl; for there are traces of it yet; even after nearly thirty years as the wife of a poor man. Her husband was a wage-earner, always; and it was only by dint of vigilance and excessive scrimping that they were able to purchase and pay for the house in which she now lives. But the economic strain has told upon her, in many ways; perhaps, most obviously, in the developing of a certain plainness of personal quality, — a simplicity that is at once pathetic and, in a way, quaint. And her manner of dressing and the arrangement of her hair rather heighten this impression. She looks old-fashioned. But her hair is quite lovely; it's thick and silvery, with the loveliest wave in it; and she has it simply parted in the middle and drawn back over her ears. She must have been a decided blonde. Her dress, which looks as though she might have made it herself, a long time ago, has no particular pattern; simply a plain, brown poplin dress, without a bit of trimming except a little ruffle of the goods, about two inches deep, around the hem of the skirt. This skirt is one of the old-fashioned, full kind, — touching all the way round. She is wearing a deep lace collar, probably to relieve the almost basque-like tightness of the body, and an enormous breastpin, featuring a very vague likeness of a delicate-looking gentleman in a straw hat; presumably, Mr. Fisher.*

MRS. COLE. Do you like Atlantic City, Mrs. Fisher?

[*She nods, still smiling.*

AMY. Yes, Mother's always been crazy about Atlantic City.

MRS. FISHER. I like the bathing.

MRS. COLE. Yes, wonderful, isn't it?

MRS. FISHER. I used to go in sometimes twice a day.
[*She laughs a little again.*

MRS. COLE. You must have liked it.

MRS. FISHER (*with an instant change to seriousness of expression and voice*). Of course, that was before my
operation.

[*Aubrey, who has been standing at the back of the room
watching her with an expression of contemptuous pity, makes
an impatient gesture and turns to the bay-window. Amy
feels the movement, and, under the pretext of touching her
hair, glances towards him.*

MRS. COLE. It certainly is a wonderful place.

MRS. FISHER. I haven't been there now since my husband
died.

MRS. COLE. Is that so?

MRS. FISHER. Yes; it'll be four years the seventeenth of
next October. He died the day Amy was twenty-five.
(*Aubrey turns from the bay-window and looks daggers at her*)
Died on her birthday. Didn't he, Amy?

AMY. Yes.

[*She glances towards Aubrey again, and he says voicelessly
to her, but with very eloquent gestures, "Didn't I tell you!"
and goes towards the back of the room again.*

MRS. COLE. And you haven't been to Atlantic City *since*
then?

MRS. FISHER. No, not since then. But before that, we used
to spend two days there every single summer. (*Aubrey
turns at the back of the room and looks at her stonily*) Go
down on Saturday morning, and come up Sunday night.
Of course, it didn't cost us anything, you know, 'cept our
fares; because we used to carry our lunch with us. (*Aubrey
begins to boil*) And in those days, they used to allow
the excursionists to sleep under the board walk, if you remember.

[*Aubrey raises his hand in the hope of attracting her attention and silencing her; but she is oblivious of him. He's*

away up in the left-hand corner of the room, out of the range
of Mrs. Cole's eye.

MRS. COLE. Yes, I remember.

MRS. FISHER. Dear me, I used to look forward to those two
days the whole year round. (*She laughs a little*) I was just
saying to Amy the other day, that if I could see my way
clear to do it, I believe I'd enjoy a day down there now,
just as much as ever I did.

MRS. COLE. Well, I don't see why you shouldn't, Mrs. Fisher.

MRS. FISHER (*with another instantaneous shift to seriousness*).
Well, of course, since my operation,
[*Aubrey makes a movement of excessive irritation, and Amy*
gets it; and thinks it wise to interrupt her mother.

MRS. FISHER and AMY (*together*).

⎧ (*Mrs. Fisher*) I've got to be more careful. I can't
⎨ do the things — that — I —
⎩ (*Amy, turning suddenly to Mrs. Cole*) You haven't
been in Atlantic City since you were married, have you,
Marion?

MRS. COLE. No, it's five years since I've been there.

MRS. FISHER. Are you going to stay there for any length of
time, Mrs. Cole?

MRS. COLE. No, I'm not, Mrs. Fisher; I just want to see
how my husband is.

MRS. FISHER. Has he consumption?
[*Aubrey snaps with irritation.*

MRS. COLE. No-o, he had the flu last winter; (*Mrs. Fisher*
folds her lips in, shakes her head slowly from side to side, and
looks at the floor in front of her) and he's never been exactly
himself since.

MRS. FISHER. They never do much good after that flu.
[*Amy rises and crosses towards the left, above the sofa.*

AMY. I suppose it depends upon how bad a person's had it,
Mother.
[*As soon as she passes out of the range of Mrs. Cole's vision,*
Aubrey appeals to her to know if there isn't something she
can do to shut her mother up. She simply dismisses him with

*a deft gesture; and, with a sharp nod of her head, indicates
the immediate presence of Mrs. Cole.*

MRS. FISHER (*unaware of the situation*). Well, now, this doctor that tended me during my operation (*Aubrey whirls
round and goes to the hall door, at the back, and Amy comes
around and sits down on the sofa, to Mrs. Cole's left*) Doctor
Stainthorpe — she's a lady doctor — she was telling me
that the flu is like scarlet fever; if it don't leave you with
one thing, it'll leave you with something else.

MRS. COLE. Well, Mr. Cole seems pretty good, most of the
time, but occasionally he has a spell of sort of — nervous
exhaustion.

[*Aubrey wanders over and stands resting his right hand on
the left end of the center table, listening to Mrs. Cole.*

MRS. FISHER. Maybe he works too hard.

MRS. COLE. No, I don't think it's that; (*Speaking directly to
Aubrey*) his work is easy enough. (*Shifting her eyes again
to Mrs. Fisher*) He's just a wig-maker. (*Aubrey drifts
towards the mirror*) Makes all kinds of hair goods, you
know.

MRS. FISHER. Oh, yes.

AMY. I don't think I ever knew your husband's business,
Marion.

MRS. COLE. Didn't I ever tell you?

AMY. You *may* have, but I've forgotten.

[*With a glance at his toupee in the mirror, Aubrey glides
down at the right of Mrs. Fisher.*

MRS. COLE. That's what he does — Makes all these toupees
that you see — (*Aubrey turns quietly away to the right and
glides up again towards the back of the room*) and switches
and — patches — All that kind of thing.

MRS. FISHER. Did you have any trouble finding the house,
Mrs. Cole?

MRS. COLE. No, not very much.

AMY. Marion came out in a taxi.

MRS. FISHER (*as though coming out in a taxi were quite an
experience*). Oh, *did* you!

MRS. COLE (*dropping her handkerchief at her left foot*). Yes,
I came right out Broad Street.

AMY (*handing her the handkerchief*). Here's your handkerchief, Marion.

MRS. COLE and MRS. FISHER (*together*).

{ (*Mrs. Cole*) Oh, thanks. Did I drop that?
{ (*Mrs. Fisher*) Have you any children, Mrs. Cole?

MRS. COLE. What did you say, Mrs. Fisher?

MRS. FISHER. I say, have you any children?

MRS. COLE. No, I haven't, Mrs. Fisher.

MRS. FISHER. Didn't you ever have any?

[*Aubrey looks helplessly at his wife, then back to his mother-
in-law.*

MRS. COLE. No.

MRS. FISHER. Well, maybe you're just as well off.

MRS. COLE. Yes, I suppose I am, in a way.

MRS. FISHER (*looking at the floor in front of her, and shaking
her head philosophically*). If they never make you laugh,
they'll never make you cry.

MRS. COLE. That's true.

MRS. FISHER. I buried a boy, when he was eight years old;
and, dear me, it seemed as though I never in this *world*
would get over it. But when I read in the newspapers now
about all these bandits, and moving-picture people, — I'm
kind of glad he went when he did. He might have gotten
in with bad company and turned out just as bad as any of
the others.

MRS. COLE. It's hard to tell how they'll turn out.

MRS. FISHER. Well, you see, this is such a terrible neighborhood in through here, to bring a boy *up* in. (*Aubrey makes
a movement of controlled desperation towards the left. Amy
glances at him, and he gives her a speaking look*) So many
foreigners.

MRS. COLE. Is that so?

MRS. FISHER. Oh, it's just dreadful. (*Aubrey tries to signal
her from the upper left-hand corner of the room, with divers
shakes and waves of his hands. But it is utterly lost upon*

*Mrs. Fisher.   She is all set for a good chat; and it will
require more than the gesticulations of Mr. Piper to distract
her.   So she goes serenely on; never even casting a glance in
his direction)* A body'd be afraid to put their nose outside
the door, after dark.   Why, right across the street here
(*She extends her arm and hand towards the right*) in two-
twenty-eight, there's a big *Polish* family; and I don't
believe there's a soul in that house speaks a word of
English.   And there's a *colored* organization of some kind
has just bought two-forty-nine — (*Aubrey has passed into
a state of desperate unconsciousness, and stands glaring at
his mother-in-law*) that's the corner property on this side.
(*She points to the right*) Paid three thousand dollars cash
for it, too.   So you can see what the neighborhood's
coming to.

AMY (*tactfully*).   Aubrey, — I wish you'd go down and close
the heater; the house is getting cold again, I think.

[*He starts for the portières immediately, and Mrs. Cole turns
and says something to Amy.   As Aubrey crosses the back of
the room, he fixes Mrs. Fisher with an icy glare, which he
holds until he passes through the portières.   Not knowing
wherein she has offended, she turns and looks over her right
shoulder after him with an expression of puzzled resentment.
Then she turns to Amy.*

MRS. FISHER.   Amy, you'd better go down, too; he'll be
locking those grates again, the way he did last week.

AMY (*rising and going around back of the sofa and over towards
the portières*).   He doesn't need to touch those grates;
that fire's all right.

[*Goes out.*

MRS. FISHER.   We have one of those old-fashioned heaters;
and when you're raking it, unless you turn it just a certain
way, the grates'll lock.   It's a perfect nuisance.   I often
say, I don't wonder people want to live in apartments;
where they won't have to be bothered with all this heater
business.

MRS. COLE.   It is a bother.

MRS. FISHER. Oh, it's a pest.

MRS. COLE. Although I had the hardest time getting used to an apartment when I was first married.

MRS. FISHER. Oh, do you live in an apartment in Chicago, Mrs. Cole?

MRS. COLE. Yes, I've lived in one ever since I've been out there.

MRS. FISHER. Well, you ought to be glad of it.

MRS. COLE. Well, really, it was the only place we could get — there have been so few houses go up in Chicago in the last few years.

MRS. FISHER. That's just the way it's been here. Why, when Amy was married four years ago, she couldn't get a house for love or money. That is, I mean, one that she could afford the rent, you know.

MRS. COLE. Yes, I know.

MRS. FISHER. Of course, she could have gotten plenty at fancy rents; but as I said to her, "How are you going to pay it on his wages?" (*She turns carefully in her chair and glances over her right shoulder towards the portières, for fear Aubrey might be within hearing distance. Then she turns back to Mrs. Cole, and leaning towards her a bit, speaks in a rather subdued tone*) He's only a clerk, you know — down here in the Pennsylvania Freight Office. But she couldn't get a thing. Of course, I'd have liked to have her stay here; because there was only Mr. Fisher and myself; but — a — (*She turns again and glances over her right shoulder, then back again to Mrs. Cole; this time with even more confidence*) my husband never liked *him*. (*She indicates Aubrey with a nod towards the portières. Then to emphasize the fact, she looks straight at Mrs. Cole and gives her head a little shake from side to side. But evidently she feels that she hasn't stated the circumstance sufficiently; or that, having mentioned it at all, it implies some measure of elucidation; for she rises gingerly, and, tiptoeing over to the center table, rests her left hand upon it and leans towards Mrs. Cole in an attitude of extreme caution and confidence*)

Said he was kind of a blatherskite, you know — (*She tiptoes towards the portières, but stops halfway and turns again*) Very big ideas and very little brains. (*She continues on to the portières and glances out; then returns to the table*) So — a — finally, they had to take two little rooms over here on Lehigh Avenue. Nine dollars a month, so you can imagine what they were like. But you couldn't *tell* them anything. As I said to them, the night they first told me they were going to be married — I said, "How do you two ever expect to make ends meet on thirty-two dollars a week?" "Oh," he says, "that's only temporary," he says, — "I'll *own* the Pennsylvania Railroad within the next five years." This is the way he's owning it. (*She looks towards the portières; then turns back and says emphatically*) He's never even gotten a raise. He's been getting thirty-two dollars a week for the last four years. (*She moves stealthily towards the portières again; far enough over to enable her to glance through them; then comes back to the table*) But — a — as soon as Mr. *Fisher* died, I told Amy she could come here, and I'd take my rent out in board. And then she makes me different things to wear; she's very handy, you know.

MRS. COLE. Yes, she's a wonderful *girl*.

MRS. FISHER. But, you know, you'd think *he* was doing me a favor to *live* here. (*Mrs. Cole doesn't know exactly what to say, so she simply shakes her head from side to side and smiles*) He doesn't like me, you know. Hardly ever speaks to me. I suppose you noticed it, didn't you?

MRS. COLE. No, I didn't, Mrs. Fisher.

MRS. FISHER. He's been *furious* ever since last spring. (*She turns away again and glances towards the portières; then turns hurriedly back, as though she had a particularly incredible item of information to communicate*) Wanted *me* to put a *mortgage* on this house to get him an automobile. Can you imagine that! He's *crazy* about automobiles. And, Mrs. Cole, I know just as well as I'm standing here,

that if he *got* one, he'd only kill himself — for he has no
more brains than a rabbit. So I told him. I sez —

[*Amy's voice, out at the right, interrupts her.*

AMY.   Be sure and close this cellar door, Aubrey; there's a
draught here if you don't.

MRS. FISHER (*tiptoeing back to her chair, with a significant
gesture to Mrs. Cole*).   Well, I hope you find your husband
all right, Mrs. Cole.

[*She sits down.*

MRS. COLE.   I hope so, thanks, Mrs. Fisher.   He *seems* pretty
good, from his letters.

AMY (*coming through the portières*).   I'm sorry, Marion, but
I seem to be the only one around here that knows how to
tend to that heater.

MRS. COLE (*rising*).   Well, you know, you were always able to
do everything, Amy.

[*She moves a little towards the front of the center table, fasten-
ing her glove.*

AMY.   You don't have to go already, do you, Marion?

MRS. COLE.   I'm afraid so, dear; (*Mrs. Fisher rises*) it's
getting on to four o'clock.

[*Aubrey sways in through the portières, flicking imaginary
ashes from himself with the fancy handkerchief.*

MRS. FISHER.   Couldn't you take a later train, Mrs.
Cole?

[*Aubrey comes forward at the right.*

MRS. COLE.   Why, I suppose I could, Mrs. Fisher; but I've
wired Mr. Cole that I'll be on *that* one.

MRS. FISHER.   Oh, I see.

MRS. COLE.   And he's so nervous and worrisome since he's
been sick, that I'm afraid if I'm *not* on it, he'll be tearing
his hair out.

[*She turns, laughing a little, which Amy and her mother reflect,
and goes back to the sofa for her muff.   Aubrey is feigning
a profound absorption in an examination of his finger nails.
Amy crosses over after Mrs. Cole and goes up back of the sofa
towards the bay-window.*

MRS. FISHER.   Are you going back to the station on the trolley, Mrs. Cole?

MRS. COLE.   No, I told the taxi to wait, Mrs. Fisher.   I hope he's still out there.   Is he, Amy?

AMY (*at the window*).   Yes, he's still there.

MRS. FISHER (*hurrying across in front of Mrs. Cole*).   Oh, I must see it!   Pardon me.

MRS. COLE.   Certainly.   (*Turning around to her right and going up towards the hall door*)   Now, Amy, I *do* hope you're going to write to me occasionally.

AMY (*coming away from the window, towards her*).   You're the one who never writes.

MRS. COLE (*laughing guiltily*).   I know, darling; but I'm going to reform, really.

AMY.   Well, now, I'm going to wait and see.

MRS. COLE.   But, really, I've been so terribly busy since Mr. Cole's been ill, that I don't seem to be able to —
   [*She becomes confidential.*

MRS. FISHER (*turning, at the window, and addressing Aubrey, who is standing directly opposite her at the right, and who happens to be the first one her eye lights upon*).   Seems so funny to see an automobile in this street.   (*Aubrey is paralyzed; and before he can recover the use of his arm sufficiently to try to silence her, she has turned again to the window; and he stands watching her, frozen with the fear that she may turn again, and sustained only by the hope that Mrs. Cole did not hear her.   His agony is very brief, however, for almost immediately, Mrs. Fisher turns again and addresses him*)   I don't think I've ever *seen* one in this street before.   (*Aubrey makes a frantic gesture to her, and, turning around to his left, strides up to the back of the room, pointing vigorously at Mrs. Cole.   Mrs. Fisher is bewildered — She simply stares blankly at the goings-on of her son-in-law; and it is not until he strides forward again at the right, glowering at her savagely, that it occurs to her to speak*)   Why, what's the matter with you!

[*Aubrey suddenly raises his left arm and hand as though he'd*

*like to sweep her from the earth, but the opportune turning of
Mrs. Cole to say good-by to Mrs. Fisher, restores order.*

MRS. COLE. Good-by, Mrs. Fisher.

MRS. FISHER (*shaking hands with her*). Good-by, Mrs. Cole.

MRS. COLE. I'm sorry to have to run away like this.

[*Amy moves around to Mrs. Cole's right.*

MRS. FISHER. Well, I know how you feel.

MRS. COLE (*turning and chucking Amy under the chin*). But I
did want to see my child here. And her husband — probably the *best*-looking man I've seen in Philadelphia so far.
[*Amy, with an exclamation of deprecation, turns to her left
and goes laughing out into the hallway. Mrs. Fisher laughs
a little, out of courtesy.*

AUBREY (*swaggering up at the right of the center table, exces-
sively self-satisfied, and pointing after his wife*). Tell *her*
that!

MRS. FISHER. I hope the next time you come this way you'll
be able to stay a little longer, Mrs. Cole.

MRS. COLE. Thanks; I hope so, too, Mrs. Fisher. (*She
turns to the right to greet Aubrey, who has come across above
the center table*) Good-by, Mr. Piper.

AUBREY. Good-by, Mrs. Cole.

[*They shake hands.*

MRS. COLE (*dropping her glove at her right foot*). I'm *so* glad
to have met you. — Oh!

AUBREY (*stooping*). I'll get it.

[*The toupee glides off and falls on to the black fur rug on
which they're standing; but he doesn't observe the circumstance, and restores the glove with a touch of flourish.*

MRS. COLE. Thanks.

[*She simply takes the glove, without the slightest evidence of
an appreciation of the situation. But old Mrs. Fisher is in a
state of siege; and, taking advantage of her position behind
Mrs. Cole, endeavors to communicate to her son-in-law, by
means of funny little pointings and movements with her head,
some knowledge of his condition. But Aubrey is mercifully
oblivious of everything, save that he is in the presence of a very*

*attractive woman, who has admitted that she considers him
probably the best-looking man she has seen in Philadelphia.*

AUBREY. Sorry you have to go so soon.

MRS. COLE. I'm sorry, too, Mr. Piper. But if I'm not on
that train (*She turns to Mrs. Fisher*) I'm afraid I'll
get scalped.

[*She goes out into the hallway.*

MRS. FISHER (*stepping to the hall door*). Don't let her stand
out there in the cold with nothing around her, Mrs. Cole.

MRS. COLE. No, I'll send her right in, Mrs. Fisher.

MRS. FISHER. Good-by.

MRS. COLE. Good-by.

AUBREY (*standing immediately behind Mrs. Fisher, looking
out into the hallway*). Good-by.

MRS. COLE. Amy, your mother says you mustn't stand out
here in the cold with nothing around you.

[*Mrs. Fisher turns, and with a glance at Aubrey, steps to
the bay-window, to watch Mrs. Cole get into the taxi. Aubrey
follows her and takes up his position just back of her, looking
out.*

MRS. FISHER (*after a slight pause*). Good-by. (*She waves to
Mrs. Cole; and so does Aubrey, — perhaps with a trifle more
dignity than the occasion implies. Then the taxi moves
away, and they watch it, smiling, down the street. Suddenly
Mrs. Fisher looks sharply in the opposite direction*) There's
the boy with the paper. (*Turning from the window, folding
her arms tightly together*) I've got to get my little woolen
shawl (*She crosses to the right, above the center table*); this
room's too chilly for me.

[*She goes out through the portières at the right. The front
door, out at the left, closes; and Aubrey turns from the
window to the hall door.*

AMY (*entering briskly through the hall door, carrying the evening
paper*). Here's the *Ledger.*

AUBREY. You ought to have something around you.

AMY (*stepping to the bay-window*). I'm not cold. Where's
Mother?

AUBREY (*opening the paper, as he strolls across above the center table*). She's gone up for her shawl.

[*He sits in the armchair, down at the right, and Amy peers through the bay-window, as though trying to catch a last glimpse of the departing taxi.*

AMY (*suddenly turning from the window and coming across to the right, above the center table*). Isn't Marion nice?

AUBREY. Yes, she's very pleasant.

AMY (*looking at herself in the mirror*). She's an awfully smart girl, too. She had charge of our entire department when I worked at the Bank.

[*There is a slight pause.*

AUBREY (*half-turning, and very significantly*). Say, Amy.

AMY. What?

AUBREY. Listen.

[*She turns her head sharply and looks at him. He beckons her to him with a rather mysterious nod, and she comes around to his left.*

AMY. What?

AUBREY (*in a subdued, level tone*). Did you get your mother telling her your age?

AMY. That's nothing; Marion knows my age.

AUBREY. I *told* you what she'd do.

AMY (*starting towards the portières*). Well, now, it doesn't make the least bit of difference; so don't start anything. [*She glances through the portières.*

AUBREY. It's a good thing she didn't have any longer to stay.

MRS. FISHER (*out at the right*). You know, Amy, —

AMY (*turning suddenly to him with a deft gesture*). Sh — sh — [*She steps to the mirror and pretends to be fixing her hair.*

AUBREY. Or she'd have told her a whole lot more.

MRS. FISHER (*coming through the portières wearing a rather skimpy-looking white shoulder-shawl and carrying some pale-pink knitting*). I always pictured that girl as a much bigger woman than she is, when you used to talk about her. [*She walks down between Aubrey and the center table and crosses over to the sofa. She appears to be having difficulty in disentangling her yarn.*

AMY. Don't you think she's a big girl?

MRS. FISHER. Well, *stouter*, I mean.

AMY. No, she never was stout.

MRS. FISHER (*sitting on the sofa, and settling herself*). I'd never know her in the world from that picture you have of her upstairs.

AMY (*turning from the mirror*). Don't you think she's nice?

MRS. FISHER. Very nice.

AMY (*standing at her husband's right*). Give me a piece of that paper.

MRS. FISHER. And very stylish, too.

AMY. Any part 'll do.

[*He detaches a section of the paper and gives it to her. She moves a step or two to the right and forward and commences to read. Aubrey resumes his reading; and Mrs. Fisher knits.*

MRS. FISHER (*after a pause*). I'll bet there was five hundred dollars right on her back there to-day if there was a penny. And that's not counting her hat nor her shoes, either. (*There is another little pause*) That wig business must be a very good business. (*Aubrey looks over at her stonily; but she's occupied with her knitting*) I saw a piece in the *North American* the other morning, that a lot of people were wearing wigs now that don't need them at all. (*She looks over at Amy, to find Aubrey glaring at her*) That's what it said. (*He snaps his head round and continues reading*) She was telling me, Amy, that she lives in an apartment there in Chicago. Sez they couldn't *get* a house when they first went there. Sez there hasn't been a house go up in Chicago since before the war. (*She laughs faintly to herself*) I was telling her about the time you and Aubrey had, when you were first married — (*He looks over at her, with a dangerous squint*) trying to get even a couple of rooms somewhere. And the kind they were when you *did* get them. (*She laughs a little more, at the recollection of them*) But they had the nerve to charge you nine dollars a month for them, just the same.

[*She smiles and looks at Aubrey.*

AUBREY (*explosively*). I suppose you told her *that*, too, didn't you!

[*Amy is startled out of her interest in the newspaper.*

MRS. FISHER (*after a second's amazement*). Told her what?

AUBREY. When were you handing out all this information?

AMY. Now, Aubrey, don't start, please!

AUBREY (*jumping to his feet*). It's enough to *make* (*He slams the piece of newspaper down on to the chair violently*) a fellow start! (*He thrusts his hands into his trousers' pockets and strides towards the back of the room*) Trying to make me look like a poor *sap!*

[*He crosses to the hall door and right back again.*

MRS. FISHER (*looking in bewilderment at Amy*). Why, what's the matter with *him!*

AMY and AUBREY (*together*).

{ (*Amy*) Nothing at all, Mother.
{ (*Aubrey, at the upper right-hand corner of the center table*). You know very *well* what's the matter with me!

MRS. FISHER. What?

AUBREY. Handing out a line of *gab* about my *business!* every time you can get anybody to *listen* to you.

MRS. FISHER. Who was handing out any line of gab about your business?

AUBREY. *You* were! — and you're always doing it!

MRS. FISHER. Why, you haven't got any line of business for anybody to hand out any line of gab about — that I ever heard of.

[*She turns away.*

AUBREY. It doesn't matter whether I have any line of business or not! It isn't necessary for you to be gabbing to perfect strangers about it.

MRS. FISHER. What did you want me to do, sit there lookin' at the woman, like a cow?

AMY. Mother, please.

AUBREY. You don't have to talk about my affairs!

MRS. FISHER (*with vast amusement*). Your affairs —

AUBREY. That's what I said, my affairs! (*Mrs. Fisher laughs derisively, and Aubrey turns to his wife, desperately*) You hear her!

MRS. FISHER. That's funny.

AMY. She wasn't talking about you, Aubrey.

AUBREY. She *was* talking about me! That's all she ever *does*, is talk about me!

[*Mrs. Fisher whirls around.*

MRS. FISHER. I was talkin' about houses! — that ain't you, is it?

AUBREY. I know what you were talking about, you needn't tell me.

MRS. FISHER. I had to talk about something, didn't I?

AMY. Keep quiet, Aubrey!

AUBREY and MRS. FISHER (*together*).

⎰ (*Aubrey, whirling around and going towards the hall door*)
⎱ No, I won't keep quiet!
⎩ (*Mrs. Fisher*) You two were down in the cellar fixing the fire! And you can't sit there with your two hands as long as each other when a person's visiting in your house!

AUBREY (*stopping abruptly above the center table, on his way back towards the portières*). I suppose you mentioned *that*, too, didn't you!

MRS. FISHER (*half-turning and listening narrowly*). Mentioned what?

AUBREY. That it was *your* house!

[*Mrs. Fisher turns her whole body round to him in a literal bounce.*

MRS. FISHER (*shrilly*). Well, whose house *would* I mention that it was!

AUBREY (*turning to Amy with a broad gesture of his right hand*). You see! Didn't I tell you!

AMY and AUBREY (*together*).

> (*Amy*) Well, what of it, Aubrey! What of it!
> (*Aubrey*) Every opportunity she gets she's trying to make me look like a poor thing!

[*He brings his right hand down thunderously upon the center table. Then, thrusting his hands into his trousers' pockets again, strides over to the arched door and back again to the portières.*

MRS. FISHER (*after a strained pause*). Why, what's the matter with the crazy Jack!

AMY. Pay no attention to him, Mother.

MRS. FISHER. I suppose I won't be able to say this house *is* my own after a while.

AUBREY (*stopping above the center table and rapping his fist upon it*). It isn't necessary for you to be gabbing to perfect strangers about *whose* house it is!

MRS. FISHER (*keenly*). I guess it'd have been all right if I'd told her it was yours, wouldn't it?

AUBREY (*repudiating her remark with a sharp gesture of his left hand*). You don't have to tell anybody *anything!*

[*Mrs. Fisher springs to her feet.*

MRS. FISHER. I suppose that's what's the matter with you, isn't it?

AUBREY and MRS. FISHER (*together*).

> (*Aubrey*) There's nothing at all the matter with me!
> [*He touches his handkerchief to his forehead.*
> (*Mrs. Fisher, taking a few steps towards Amy*) He's very

likely been telling this friend of yours, Amy, that this is *his* house! And I guess with a lot of big talk about taking *me* in, and giving *me* a home! Trying to make *me* look like a poor thing!

AMY (*trying to pacify her mother*). Now, he didn't tell her anything of the kind, Mother!

MRS. FISHER (*shaking with wrath*). He did if he got the chance! I know him.

AMY. Well, he didn't *get* the chance; I was only out of the room two minutes.

MRS. FISHER (*returning to the sofa*). Well, that's long enough for him! I've heard *him* before. (*She gathers up her knitting, preparatory to sitting down*) Blowing his bubbles! (*She sits down, fuming*) The big blatherskite! (*There is a pause. Amy and Aubrey look at each other, then at Mrs. Fisher, who knits violently*) I'm very glad now I *did* tell her this was my house! — (*She knits a little more*) I'm glad I had sense enough! (*More knitting*) For I know he'd very soon tell her it was *his*, if he got my back turned long enough! (*She draws some yarn from the ball*) And it wouldn't be mine long, either, if I listened to all his silly blather about stocks, and bonds, and automobiles, and every other thing! — On his thirty-two dollars a week. (*Aubrey looks stonily at her for a second; then she turns sharply and leans on the arm of the sofa towards him*) I told her *that*, too!

AUBREY (*turning to Amy, who is standing back of the armchair*). You see! Didn't I tell you!

[*He passes forward at the right of his wife.*

MRS. FISHER (*resuming her knitting*). So she'd know how much brains you had!

AMY. It wasn't at all necessary, Mother, for you to tell Marion that.

MRS. FISHER (*without looking up from her work*). Well, I told her; whether it was necessary or not. (*She looks at Amy and speaks emphatically*) It was the truth, anyway. And I guess that's more than can be said for a whole lot that *he* told her.

[*She indicates Aubrey with a nod; then resumes her work. There is a pause. Aubrey is standing fuming down at the right. Amy picks up the piece of the paper that he threw on the chair, then extends the piece that she has been reading towards him.*

AMY. Do you want this?

AUBREY (*half-turning, and with a shade of hauteur*). What is it?

AMY. Why, it's the newspaper of course! what do you think it is?

[*He deigns to take it. She gives him a long look, then opens the other half of the paper and reads.*

AUBREY (*opening his part of the paper*). A man'd certainly have a swell chance trying to make anything of himself around this *hut!*

MRS. FISHER. I don't see that anybody's trying to *stop* you from making something of yourself.

AUBREY. No, and I don't see that anybody's trying to *help* me any, either. Only trying to make me look like a *pin-head* every chance they get.

MRS. FISHER. Nobody'll have to try very hard to make *you* look like a pin-head. Your own silly talk'll do *that* for you, any time at all.

AUBREY (*turning to her sharply*). I suppose it's silly talk to try to make a good impression.

MRS. FISHER (*looking over at him, and inclining her head conclusively*). Yes — It's silly to try to make an impression of *any* kind; for the only one that'll be made'll be the *right* one; and that'll make itself.

[*She reverts to her work.*

AUBREY. Well, if you were out in the world as much as I am, you'd very soon see how much easier it is for a fellow to get along if people think he's *got* something.

MRS. FISHER. Well, anybody'd listen to you very long'd know you *couldn't* have very much.

AUBREY. Is that so.

MRS. FISHER (*quietly*). You heard me. (*Aubrey steps over to the armchair at his left and sits down, looking bitterly at his mother-in-law*) People that are smart enough to be able to make it easier for anybody, are not interested in what you've *got*. (*Looking over at him*) It's what you've got in your *brains* that they're interested in. And nobody has to tell them that, either. They'll know all about it, if you never opened your mouth.

AMY. Oh, stop talking, Mother.

[*She turns, with a movement of wearied impatience, from the right end of the center table, and crosses over back of the*

armchair to the right, where she continues to read. There is a
quiet pause; Amy and Aubrey reading, and Mrs. Fisher
knitting. Then Aubrey looks up from his paper, thinks for a
second, and half turns to his wife.

AUBREY. Did you get that remark your friend made, as she
was going out?

AMY. What remark?

[*Mrs. Fisher looks over.*

AUBREY (*with a self-satisfied smile*). About the best-looking
man in Philadelphia?

MRS. FISHER (*rearranging her knitting*). Oh, dear!

[*Aubrey gives her a narrow look; then turns back to his wife.*

AUBREY. She made it twice, too.

AMY. I suppose I'll never hear the end of that now.

AUBREY. No, but it made an awful hit with me, after all the
talk you made about putting on the toupee.

AMY. Oh, it wasn't the toupee that made her say it; don't
flatter yourself.

AUBREY. I don't think it hurt any.

AMY. No, and I don't think you're so crazy about the toupee
yourself.

AUBREY. It's better than being baldheaded.

AMY. I noticed you got rid of it very quickly, as soon as she
went.

[*Mrs. Fisher listens.*

AUBREY. What?

AMY (*without looking up from the paper*). You heard me.
(*Mrs. Fisher can't resist a glance at Aubrey; but realizing that
her expression might precipitate another row, she turns away
quietly and continues with her knitting. Aubrey hasn't
grasped the significance of his wife's remark. He turns and
looks at her with a puzzled expression; but she is reading; so
he turns back again and looks straight out, baffled. Then a
thought occurs to him. He reaches up and touches his head.
The toupee is off. His brows lift and his mouth falls open,
and he sits staring straight ahead for a second. Then he
glances furtively at his mother-in-law, but she is studiously*

avoiding the situation. He gets up, very quietly; and, with a little glance over his right shoulder at his wife, turns and gives a quick look on the armchair and under it. No sign of the toupee. He feels all over his head and around the back of his neck; puts his hand up under his coat, and looks on the floor back of the armchair. All very quietly, and with a pathetic attempt at nonchalance. But the toupee is not to be seen. He saunters up towards the back of the room, steps over and glances at himself in the mirror, then stands looking about the floor in a quandary. His wife observes him out of the corner of her eye, and turns to him) What are you looking for?

[He glances at Mrs. Fisher, then goes very close to his wife and speaks in a confidential tone.

AUBREY. My toupee. Did you see anything of it?

AMY. Where 'd you put it?

AUBREY *(with a shade of impatience)*. I didn't put it anywhere.

AMY. Well, where did you have it?

AUBREY *(becoming more impatient)*. I had it on my head, of course! where 'd you think I had it!

AMY. I thought you took it off, when Marion went.

AUBREY. No, I didn't take it off!

AMY. Well, where is it?

AUBREY *(throwing discretion to the winds)*. I don't know *where* it is! That 's why I 'm asking *you!* *(Mrs. Fisher can no longer contain herself, and bursts into unrestrained laughter. They both turn sharply and look at her, Aubrey glaring)* Funny! isn't it!

[Amy crosses quickly to the center table, in front of her husband.

AMY. Did you see anything of it, Mother?

MRS. FISHER *(bursting out afresh)*. I saw it *fall off,* that 's all *I* know about it.

[They stand looking at her.

AUBREY. You see that! She 'd let me walk around here all day with it off, and never tip me off that it was off!

MRS. FISHER.   What good was it to tip you off that it was off after it was off! (*Turning back to her knitting*) The cat was out of the bag, then.

AMY.   Where'd it fall off, Mother?

MRS. FISHER.   When he was picking that woman's glove up, up there at the hallway. (*Amy turns quickly towards the hall door, glancing about the floor; and Mrs. Fisher turns to Aubrey*) It isn't *my* fault if his old *wig* doesn't fit him.

[*He is looking at her with murder in his eye; but she doesn't flinch. If anything, there is a glint of challenge in her look. And it's quite as steady as his own. Amy finds the toupee where it fell, and holds it up towards Aubrey by one hair.*

AMY.   Is this it?

[*But the duel of eyes is still on between Aubrey and his mother-in-law; and he is oblivious of both his wife and her question. So the toupee, looking very much like a dead cat, depends from Amy's uplifted fingers. Then, suddenly, Aubrey snatches it, with a whirling movement to the left, and goes towards the mirror to adjust it.*

MRS. FISHER (*following him with her eyes*).   It just serves him right! That's what he gets for showing off!

AUBREY (*whirling at the mirror, and literally shouting at her*). Shut up, will you!

[*The violence of his turning sends the toupee flying off his head on to the floor, and causes Mrs. Fisher to start so that her ball of yarn flies four feet into the air.*

AMY (*taking a step towards her husband and lifting her hand to enjoin silence*).   Sh — sh — sh —

AUBREY (*looking at her with an eye of fire*).   I won't stand much more of this Amy! now, I'm telling you!

AMY.   Keep quiet, Aubrey! Marion probably never noticed it at all.

MRS. FISHER.   I don't know how she could *help* noticing it. *I* noticed it; and I don't think my eyesight's as good as hers.

AUBREY. Then, why didn't you say something!

MRS. FISHER. Because I knew if I did I'd very likely get snatched baldheaded!

[*Aubrey starts violently, and Mrs. Fisher snaps back to her knitting.*

AUBREY (*appealing to his wife*). You hear that! Is it any wonder my nerves are the way they are!

AMY. Oh, keep quiet, Aubrey! for Heaven's sake! (*Pointing to the toupee on the floor, as she steps forward at the right of the center table*) And pick up your wig.

[*This is too much for Aubrey. He literally sways against the portières above the mirror.*

AUBREY (*recovering himself*). It isn't a wig, now, Amy! I've told you that a half a dozen times!

AMY (*looking up from the paper which she has commenced to read, and in an exhausted tone*). Well, then, pick up your toupee!

[*He picks it up and simply slaps it back on to his head. The effect is weird; for it is quite disheveled from its recent experiences, and, in his temper, he has put it on backwards. He swings forward at the right and sits in the armchair, very sulkily. Amy crosses over back of the armchair and stands down near the little table at the right, where she continues to read the evening paper. Mrs. Fisher knits, and Aubrey sits sulking, looking straight ahead. There is a pause. Then, possibly at the recollection of certain of the remarks that his mother-in-law made earlier in the battle, Aubrey darts a sudden glare in her direction; only to find that she has been the victim of similar memories. So they sit and scowl at each other; then turn away. Then turn back again, and away again. Then Aubrey becomes conscious of his wife; and of the fact that she is reading the evening newspaper; and, by the association of ideas, his thought is diverted into more becoming channels. He half-turns to Amy, with something of the self-importance that characterized his earlier manner, and, after a slight pause, addresses her.*

AUBREY.   Have you got the — a — financial page there?
[*Amy hands it to him; and the curtain commences to descend very slowly.*

MRS. FISHER.   Hum!
[*He glares over at her, but she's knitting; so, withdrawing his eyes, he reaches into his vest pocket and brings forth the rimmed nose-glasses, which he settles rather authentically upon his nose.   Then he takes a silver pencil from the other vest pocket, and, turning to his wife, accepts the newspaper. Then he crosses his knees, and, spreading the newspaper upon them, proceeds to figure profits in the margin.   Amy stands looking at him, and Mrs. Fisher knits.*

· THE CURTAIN IS DOWN

GOOD VINTAGE

DAN TOTHEROH

DAN TOTHEROH is also one of a few whose early play-writing was done for the vaudeville stage. Born in Oakland, California, in 1894, and educated in San Rafael, he became an actor in both stock and vaudeville immediately after leaving high school. He is now in Hollywood, writing for the screen.

Eleven of his one-act plays have been published in a collection entitled *One-Act Plays for Everyone;* and "The Kelly Kid" (in collaboration with Kathleen Norris) has been published separately. His full-length plays are: "Wild Birds", a California prize play; "The Princess Salome"; "Daughters of Music" (first produced by Stuart Walker); "Mother Lode" (written in collaboration with George O'Neil); and "Searching for the Sun."

GOOD VINTAGE

By DAN TOTHEROH

Although "Good Vintage" has been produced widely throughout the United States, the record of the original cast has been lost.

Characters

JULIA GARCIA	AUNT ROSE
MAMMA GARCIA	LEONORA
JOE GARCIA	MARIE
AUNT ANNIE	HARRY BARTO

GOOD VINTAGE

SCENE. *Julia Garcia's bedroom in her father's ranch house, Sonoma County, California, not very far from the Valley of the Moon. It is the typical room of a young Italian girl whose father is now wealthy and can afford to give her a room to herself. Before Prohibition, when Joe Garcia was a struggling vine-grower, Julia slept in the same room with four brothers and sisters. The room is box-like and unimaginative, with white-washed walls. The white-wash is fresh and clean, however, and gives the room a singularly virginal appearance. Julia's highly polished brass bed is at the center, with a sky-blue counterpane, now flung back, for it is early morning and the bed is not made up. The rest of the furniture is a shiny mission set, bought in Napa at the Star furniture store, the leading one in the county. It is golden oak, highly polished, outdoing the glittering brass of the bed. On the dresser are many little girlish trinkets such as souvenir pin trays, a pin cushion shaped like a silver slipper, a burnt-wood box for handkerchiefs, some fancy bottles of cologne, a white ivory toilette set painted with small pink roses and a red porcelain vase for flowers. There is also a little chalk statue of the Virgin in a bright blue robe edged in gold. Over the bed is a wooden crucifix from which dangles a string of rosary beads, and there are numerous holy pictures on the walls. The Virgin holding up her red and gleaming heart, Christ holding out his pierced hands, The Visit of the Wise Men, etc. — all highly colored lithographs. Julia's communion veil and wilted wreath are also hung up on a peg near the dresser. The carpet on the floor is gay and garish with bright pink and red roses on a field of dove-gray. The early fall day is already warm, the sun streaming through the flowered curtains of Julia's room, bringing*

*a promise of baking heat at noon.   Indeed, the morning could
not be more propitious for a Grape Festival.   This is real grape-
weather — the sun kissing the grape into sweetness on the vine
— and even though the day will be a scorcher, the nights in the
valley are always cool and there will be a moon for dancing on
the open-air platform in the square.*

[*Julia Garcia is discovered standing in the center of a fluttering
group of relatives, being dressed in the robes of the Queen of
the Vineyards.   She is lithe and Latin — dusky as a purple
grape herself — her hair thick and blue-black, and her eyes
liquid brown, swimming with dreams.   She has been up since
dawn and so has the Garcia household.   Joe Garcia has out-
done himself, sparing no expense in costuming his daughter.
The voluminous gown is of varied-colored silks, and there is
a heavy satin cloak terminating in a long train.   The colors
of the gown are the colors of the grape, the leaves of the vine
and the wine of the vintage.   There are touches of young
green also — the whole dress symbolic of the grape from the
time it is green on the branch to the time it ripens.   Mamma
Garcia, fat and swarthy of skin, with gray streaks in her
once satin-black hair, is just putting the dress over Julia's
head.   Julia's Aunt Annie, thin and wiry, with a beak-like
nose and brown, leathery skin, is helping her.   Then there is
Aunt Rose who is small and all shriveled up like a dried
apricot.   She is in a lachrymose state for she has recently
lost her husband and cannot forget it.   Her hair is white with
a tinge of yellow like an old bone, and she is dressed in shoddy
black.   Around her neck is a black chain, dangling a crucifix
of yellowed ivory.*

*Julia's cousin, Leonora, a girl of fourteen, overgrown and
thin, her skirts too short for her spindly legs, sits on the edge
of the unmade bed, watching Julia with an envy which she
attempts to conceal under a childish cloak of nonchalance.*

AUNT ANNIE (*clasping her hands in ecstasy as the folds of the
    dress drop to the floor*). Beautiful! Beautiful! *Dio Mio,*
    how beautiful!

AUNT ROSE (*tearfully*).   Ah, pretty Julia *mia* — She is like a saint . . . (*She blows her sharp nose which is always red from blowing*) . . . The little Saint of the Flowers.

MAMMA GARCIA (*who is always practical*). No, no, not of the *flowers*, Rosie — of the grapevines!

AUNT ANNIE (*who always agrees with her wealthy sister*). Yes, that is right — little Saint of the Grapevines. (*To her daughter, sitting on the bed*) Ain't she beautiful, Leonora?

LEONORA. Swell.

AUNT ANNIE (*laughing and winking at Aunt Rose*). Swell, she says! That's all she learns in high school.

MAMMA GARCIA (*straightening out the folds of the dress*). How does that feel, Julie?

JULIA. Fine — but warm, Mamma.

MAMMA GARCIA. Warm, of course! What do you think? An' you will be warmer than this when you ride on the float. It's what you must expect.

JULIA. Yes, Mamma.

MAMMA GARCIA. Didn't you almost faint last year, when you was maid-of-honor? (*Julia nods*) But then you had to ride down hot Main Street all that time with no cover over your head. It's dif'rent bein' queen, Julie. You get to ride on the throne with grapevines to keep the sun off.

JULIA. Yes, Mamma.

AUNT ROSE. It was hotter last year.

AUNT ANNIE. What are you talkin' about, Rosie? You can't tell so early in the mornin'.

AUNT ROSE. But I remember last year — Tony, he says to me, right after breakfast — (*Crossing herself*) You know, Tony was alive this time last year —
[*She blows her nose.*

MAMMA GARCIA. Now, Rosie, you promised not to talk about Tony till next Sunday mass, didn't you?

AUNT ROSE. Yes, but I remember he said, "Rosie *mia*, this is the hottest mornin' in August since I come to Sonoma an' that was fifteen years ago."

MAMMA GARCIA. All right, but that is over now. Now, walk

up and down, Julie. Let Mamma see how the train goes.
[*Julia, with the dignity and pride of a little queen, walks up
and down the room.*

AUNT ANNIE. Beautiful! Wonderful! *Dio Mio! Dio Mio!*

AUNT ROSE. The little Saint! Like in a church window
she is!

MAMMA GARCIA. That is fine, Julie. Never was there such
a beautiful queen in Sonoma county!

AUNT ANNIE. Or in all California!

AUNT ROSE. Cara Arbini was so ugly last year. So fat!
When the float bumped she jiggled like jelly.

LEONORA (*giggling*). An' she has a mustache!
[*They all laugh, in spite of the fact that Mamma Garcia has a
mustache of her own.*

MAMMA GARCIA. Cara Arbini is a fool.

AUNT ANNIE. *All* the Arbinis are fools.

AUNT ROSE. They are dangerous people.

AUNT ANNIE. Poof! Don't talk crazy, Rosie.

MAMMA GARCIA (*to Julia who is still walking up and down,
pausing to preen in front of the dresser mirror*). Now turn
around slow, Julie, an' make your bow like when they
crown you queen.
[*Julia stops, turns, and makes a low bow, bending her head.*

THE TWO AUNTS. Beautiful! Wonderful! Don't she do it
beautiful! Just like a dancer!

AUNT ANNIE. See. She stays like that till they put the
crown on her and read the speech.

MAMMA GARCIA (*as Julia rises again, flushed and with sparkling
eyes*). That was good, Julie.

AUNT ANNIE. Just like a movie queen.

MAMMA GARCIA. Shall I call Papa?

AUNT ROSE (*blowing her nose again*). If Tony could only see
her. Tony always loved Julie.

AUNT ANNIE. Yes, call Joe, Amelia. He will be so proud
of her.

MAMMA GARCIA (*going to the door and calling down the stairs*).
Papa! Oh, Papa! Come up an' see Julie all dressed.

JOE GARCIA. Just a minute, Amelia.

AUNT ROSE. All the girls will be so jealous of her.

JULIA. I don't *want* them to be jealous, Auntie.

MAMMA GARCIA. Of course not! Julie is a sweet girl.

A YOUNG GIRL'S VOICE (*from downstairs*). Oh, Julie, can I come up?

JULIA (*eyes dancing*). It's Marie! Tell her to come up, Mamma!

MAMMA GARCIA. Come up, Marie! We are in Julie's room.

[*Julia walks up and down again, her little chin tilted. In a moment, Marie rushes in, a girl of Julia's age, dressed as a maid-of-honor. She is a plain-looking girl with chestnut brown hair and many freckles scattered across her snubby nose. She pauses a moment in the doorway, eyes round with admiration; then she squeals and rushes to Julia with outstretched arms.*

MARIE. Oh, Julie — Julie — you look simply wonderful!

[*The girls kiss each other, squealing, giggling, half crying.*

MAMMA GARCIA (*studying Marie with keen, analytical eyes*). *You* look nice, too, Marie.

MARIE (*stepping away from Julia to get a better view*). Yes — but I'm only a maid-of-honor. *Julie's* the *queen!* I *never* saw anybody look so *wonderful!*

JULIA. I'm glad you like it, Marie.

MARIE. I just been down to see the float. It looks *simply* beautiful — just like a big wedding cake!

AUNT ANNIE. Wedding cake! That's funny.

MARIE. Yes, it does. A beautiful, big wedding cake.

AUNT ROSE. A wedding cake with grapes on it. That's a good one.

MARIE. The throne's awful high. Everybody'll see Julie easy — above everybody else. Some of the maids-of-honor were there already, picking out the best seats. Helen Raymond was acting like a pig.

LEONORA. She only got twenty-five votes. I saw the list in the drug store.

MARIE (*giggling*). Who would buy votes for Helen Raymond!

AUNT ANNIE. Her papa is stingy. He makes a lot of money
with plumbing.

MARIE. The Native Sons' float looked pretty.

LEONORA. They decorated the new fire wagon.

MARIE. My brother Johnny's going to drive the horn of
plenty.

JULIA. What time is it, anyway?

MARIE. Almost ten.

JULIA. I didn't know it was *that* late. The parade's
supposed to start at eleven.

AUNT ANNIE. They *never* start on time.

LEONORA. I haven't heard the firemen's band yet.

MAMMA GARCIA. They can't start without the queen.

AUNT ROSE. That would be bad luck, an' the grapes would
be bad next year.

AUNT ANNIE. Such crazy talk, Rosie. You talk like the old
country.

MAMMA GARCIA. This is California, Rosie.

AUNT ROSE (*shaking her head*). Grapes are the same here
as in Italy.

AUNT ANNIE. You talk old-fashion, Rosie.

AUNT ROSE. What do we have the festival for? It is to
make thanks for a good vintage, is it not? What is Julie
a queen for?

MAMMA GARCIA. It is all for fun! (*As Joe Garcia comes in*)
Oh, here's Papa. Look at her, Papa! Look at your Julie!
[*Joe Garcia is a thick-set, middle-aged Italian with a round
stomach and a red-brown face. His eyes are small and good-
natured, and his coarse black hair, a little greasy, is streaked
with gray. He is dressed for the occasion in a flashy,
chocolate-brown suit and wears a red vest which fits over his
stomach as snugly as red feathers fit a robin's breast. His
cream-colored satin tie has a ruby stick-pin in it and there
is a ruby ring on his little finger. He is inordinately proud
of his daughter and now becomes almost hysterical over her
appearance.*

JOE GARCIA. Oh, Julia *mia*, you are wonderful! Wonderful!

You are like — like all the leaves in my vineyard!
[*His eyes fill with tears.*

MAMMA GARCIA. Walk up an' down for Papa, Julie — up an' down.
[*Julia walks up and down.*

JOE GARCIA (*wringing his hands in ecstasy*). Beautiful! Wonderful! Everybody will be so jealous of her! My beautiful Julie! She is the most beautiful queen in the world! If only Mussolini could see her. *He* would say she was beautiful! Oh, Julie — Julie — you make your old Papa cry.
[*He sniffs and clasps and unclasps his pudgy, red hands. Aunt Rose weeps a little in her handkerchief.*

MAMMA GARCIA. Now bow for him, Julie — just like you did for us. Look, Papa — this is how she'll bow when they put the crown on her.
[*Julia turns and bows, sinking gracefully to one knee.*

JOE GARCIA (*clapping his hands like an excited small boy*). *Dio Mio*, you are an angel. Everybody will cry when you do that — *everybody* — even people who are jealous of me — even my enemies. They will all cry!

MAMMA GARCIA. See? She stays like that till the mayor puts the crown on her.

MARIE. And we'll all bow behind her, like this.
[*Marie bows awkwardly.*

AUNT ANNIE. Good!

MAMMA GARCIA. Get up now, Julie.

JULIA (*rising*). It's about time for us to go, Mamma.

JOE GARCIA. I am going to take you down in the new car, Julie. (*He rubs his hands together*) You'll look beautiful in the new car.

MAMMA GARCIA. Ain't that fine, Julie? You'll be the first to ride in Papa's new Pierce Arrow.

MARIE (*squealing, quite beside herself*). Oh, Julie — Julie —
[*She crushes Julia in her arms.*

MAMMA GARCIA. Look out, don't mess her, Marie.
[*A bell rings downstairs.*

JOE GARCIA. Ain't that somebody at the door?

MAMMA GARCIA. Mary 'll answer it.

AUNT ANNIE. We 're forgettin' all about dressin'. Come on, Leonora, get yourself washed.

AUNT ROSE. I must get my corset on.

MARY (*the servant, calling at the foot of the stairs*). It 's Mister Barto, Mr. Garcia.

JOE GARCIA (*still excited*). Harry! Harry must see my Julie!

MAMMA GARCIA. He can see in the parade, Papa.

JOE GARCIA. No, I want him to see her here. Have him come up, Mary.

MARY. All right, Mr. Garcia.

MAMMA GARCIA. Well, don't be long, Papa. We got to go.

AUNT ANNIE (*to Leonora who is looking out of the window*). Come along, Leonora. You got to get your new pink dress on.

LEONORA. There was a man lookin' up at this window from the grape arbor.

JOE GARCIA. Huh? — Somebody lookin' up here? (*He trots to the window and peeks out, rather cautiously*) Who was lookin' up at my Julie's bedroom?

LEONORA. He ain't there now. (*Pointing out the window*) But he was right over near that wine barrel.

JOE GARCIA. What did he look like?

LEONORA. I couldn't see very well. The leaves was in front of his face.

JOE GARCIA. A tall man?

LEONORA. I don't know. Maybe. I just saw him and then he went away.

AUNT ANNIE. Funny the dogs didn't bark.

MAMMA GARCIA. Just one of the new pickers, Papa.

JOE GARCIA (*rubbing his chin, thoughtfully*). Maybe, an' maybe not. Maybe one of my enemies. I got lots of enemies since I got rich.

AUNT ROSE. That is always the way. When you was poor, everybody liked you.

JOE GARCIA (*rubbing his hands*). They are all jealous of me.

They laughed at me when Prohibition came in. They made believe to be sorry for me. "Poor old Joe Garcia," they said — "All them grapes planted an' now no place to sell his wine." They made believe to be sorry, but they was all glad. (*Chuckling*) But — but I fooled 'em — They laughed too quick. Yes, I got lots of enemies.

MAMMA GARCIA. Don't talk like a fool, Joe — an' don't go talkin' so loud. The windows are open.

[*Enter Harry Barto, a short, very dark Italian, younger than Joe. He wears a heavy, black mustache and his eyes are beady-black and snapping. Usually a placid little man, he is now excited. He too is dressed for the festival, but his attire is less conspicuous than Garcia's, although he wears a very bright red necktie and his suit is a light gray with a thin stripe.*

HARRY. Hello.

MAMMA GARCIA. Hello, Harry.

JOE GARCIA. Harry — Harry — you are just in time — (*Trotting over to him, shaking his hand and dragging him into the room toward Julia, who stands before the mirror*) Look at my little Julie — my little queen — Is she not beautiful, huh? (*Turning Julia around as though she were a wax model*) All real silk, Harry — real silk. How much did it cost in Napa, Mamma?

MAMMA GARCIA. Thirty dollars, Joe.

JOE GARCIA. Do you hear that? Thirty dollars just for a costume, Harry — but it's worth it, eh?

HARRY. Sure.

AUNT ANNIE. An' the cloak, Joe — real *satin*.

JOE GARCIA. Yes, real satin. How much was that, Mamma?

MAMMA GARCIA. Twenty-five dollars, Joe.

JOE GARCIA. Twenty-five dollars, just for the cloak. (*Chuckling*) An' that's only part of it. One hundred dollars for votes. One hundred dollars to make Julie queen. But what do *I* care? I showed all my enemies. Last year Arbini bought all the votes. He thought he was so smart. Julie could only be maid-of-honor. They laughed at me, but I showed 'em. Julie will look so beautiful on the float — (*Pinching Julia's cheek*) Won't you, Julie — huh? You will hold your head up way, way high, huh, Julie? He-he-he, look at her blushing. She is so happy — Now, make one of them pretty bows for Harry, Julie, like you did for me. A bow for Papa's best friend. (*Pulling Harry back a little*) Now, now look, Harry — Watch. She will bow like this when Spengenni puts the crown on her. Go ahead, Julie.

[*Julia bows as before.*

JOE GARCIA. Ha, ha, ha — beautiful, eh? — beautiful! My God, Julie, you are beautiful! (*Slapping Harry on the back*) What say, Harry?

HARRY. Fine, Joe — just fine.

[*He shuffles his feet impatiently.*

MAMMA GARCIA. Get up, Julie — don't you get tired now. (*Putting her arm around her as Julia rises*) Come in my room a minute. I want to give you something. A present Mamma has for you.

JULIA. A *present*, Mamma?

MAMMA GARCIA. Yes, a little surprise, Julie.

[*They go toward the door.*

AUNT ANNIE. Let us see too, Amelia.

MAMMA GARCIA. Yes, you can all come.

JULIA. Come on, Marie.

AUNT ANNIE. Come on, Leonora. Then you must get dressed an' look pretty.

JOE GARCIA. Don't be long, Amelia. I got the new car waitin'.

AUNT ROSE (*pointing to a wreath of grape leaves and artificial grapes lying on the bed*) You forgot the wreath, Amelia.

MAMMA GARCIA. We'll get that in a minute. Come on.

[*All the women crowd out, following Mamma Garcia.*

AUNT ROSE (*shaking her head and blowing her nose*). This is a sad day for me. No Tony — Tony he used to like the festivals. In Italy we would dance all day an' night when

it was a good vintage. Everybody would get drunk but
nobody would hurt each other —

[*She goes out, mumbling.*

JOE GARCIA. What's the matter, Harry? You don't act
right.

HARRY (*looking around him and speaking in a low, cautious
voice*). They're all in town, Joe.

JOE GARCIA. The Arbinis?

HARRY. Yep. They came over from Santa Rosa in a truck,
early this mornin'. It don't look good.

JOE GARCIA (*purple in the face*). Let him try anything!

HARRY. There's a lot of 'em. Ten, I think. They all got
guns.

JOE GARCIA. Guns!

HARRY. Yep. Eddie thinks they mean business.

JOE GARCIA. Goddam — just let 'em try things. I ain't
scared of them.

HARRY. They think you'll be off guard, tendin' to the
festival. Eddie says two or three of 'em was talkin' in the
barber shop an' not carin' who heard 'em. They came
right out about hi-jackin'.

JOE GARCIA. They better keep out of my territory!

HARRY. We went into theirs, didn't we?

JOE GARCIA. That was dif'rent. Jesus, I don't carry no
guns to go around killin' people.

HARRY. No, but *I* do. An' *you* better carry one
to-day, Joe. In them crowds there's no tellin' *what*
they'll do.

JOE GARCIA. Is that Goddam Arbini here, too?

HARRY. Not yet — just his gang. But he'll come over
later, I'll bet, when things get goin'.

JOE GARCIA. That Goddam wop! Let him start tryin'
things. I wouldn't mind killin' *him*. Ever since he come
up from 'Frisco he's been dirty with me.

[*He trots up and down.*

HARRY. We don't want no scraps at the festival, if we can
help it.

JOE GARCIA. Of course we don't. We all ought to be happy. *Everybody* in Sonoma ought to be happy. We ought to give thanks to God, Harry. He gave us a good vintage this year — *never* such a good vintage. We ought to thank God an' make merry.

HARRY. Arbini's crop wasn't so good. That early frost got him, you remember?

JOE GARCIA. It got *him* an' left *me* alone.

HARRY. Yes. Well, maybe that's what makes him so sore.

JOE GARCIA. Serves that wop right! Goin' around with guns — hatin' people. Serves him right!

HARRY. Well — we got to be careful to-day, anyhow. You better not go ridin' around in that new big car. You'll be a regular target in that.

JOE GARCIA. Like Hell! I'll go around in that car, all right. (*Mopping his perspiring forehead with a flashy handkerchief*) Hot, ain't it? We better tell the sheriff to keep on the job, Harry.

HARRY. Sheriff knows we hi-jacked over in Santa Rosa, last week.

JOE GARCIA. Sure, but he won't say nothin'. I got him fixed, all right. I'll phone George downstairs. He's a good feller.

HARRY. I don't trust him a inch. If Arbini gave him more money, he'd —

JOE GARCIA. Arbini *won't!* That Goddam wop, he pinches every nickel. He won't even give to the church! But look at *me*. I give a fat sum every month, an' two weeks ago I gave Father Roni one hundred dollars to put a new wall on the mission.

HARRY. Sure, *I* know. You're a good man, Joe. But all them things make Arbini more mad, all the time. He don't like to see you act so rich — so, so we better watch out to-day. See?

JOE GARCIA. Sure, I see. (*Patting Harry on the back, affectionately*) You're a good friend to me, Harry — a damn good friend. You help me lots. I don't forget, see? Come on, I'll phone George an' then you an' me'll have a big drink of vino. Then we go downtown, huh?

HARRY. Sure.

JOE GARCIA. Don't let the women know about Arbini, Harry. We can't get them scared. I want them to have a good time to-day.

HARRY. Sure.

[*They start for the door, when the women return.*

JULIA (*bursting in, flushed excitedly. Marie follows; then Leonora and the three sisters, Mamma Garcia beaming broadly*). Look, Papa — Look at the present Mamma gave me! (*She runs over to her father and shows him a chain of bright blue beads around her neck which terminates in a little blue-lacquered crucifix*) Isn't it pretty, Papa?

JOE GARCIA. Ah — it is very pretty, Julie. It goes pretty with your costume. You'll wear it to-day, huh? (*Joe, somewhat sobered, kisses the little crucifix*) It will protect you from harm.

JULIA. Yes. Mamma had Father Roni bless it for me.

JOE GARCIA. That was good, Amelia. That was very good. (*Letting the cross drop back against Julia's little breast*) You did right. It will protect my little Julie from all harm.

MAMMA GARCIA. You talk like there is some sort of danger, Joe.

JOE GARCIA (*shrugging and glancing at Harry*). You never can tell.

AUNT ROSE (*blowing her nose*). No, you can't. Look what happened to Tony. This time last year he was stronger than anybody — drivin' a big truck, good as anybody — then, all of a sudden —

AUNT ANNIE. Rosie! To-day we are all goin' to be merry!

MAMMA GARCIA. What a lot of crazy jabber. This is a festival, not a funeral! (*Picking up the wreath of vine leaves from the bed*) Here, put on the wreath, Julie. Then we must go.

[*The wreath is placed around Julia's blue-black hair. It is very lovely with her dark skin and eyes.*

AUNT ANNIE. How beautiful!

MAMMA GARCIA. She'll wear that until they put the crown on her.

MARIE. The crown is *simply* beautiful. It looks like real gold an' has rubies an' emeralds in it.

LEONORA. They ain't real!

[*She turns to the window and looks out.*

JOE GARCIA. They wanted to give her the old one they used last year, but I bought a new one for her, out of my own pocket. It was the best I could get in 'Frisco.

AUNT ANNIE. Imagine usin' the one Cara Arbini wore!

JOE GARCIA. This one will be mine after the festival is over. Julie can hang it up in her room. Would you like that, Julie?

JULIA. Oh, yes, Papa.

HARRY. Come on, Joe — we got to 'phone.

JOE GARCIA. All right — (*Turning to look once more at Julia*) *Dio Mio*, I can't get enough of her. She is beautiful. Walk up and down just once more for your Papa, Julie — just once more, a little bit.

MAMMA GARCIA. Listen to him! You are so crazy, Papa.

JOE GARCIA (*winking at Mamma Garcia*). Like I was about *you*, Amelia. (*He puts his hand on his heart and sighs loudly*) Ha, ha, ha, just like that!

AUNT ANNIE. Don't *I* remember them days, Joe. She thought you'd *never* ask her. Ha, ha, ha.

MAMMA GARCIA. What a lot of foolishness!

JOE GARCIA. Go on, Julie. Walk up an' down for Papa, once more!

AUNT ANNIE. You'll get her all tired out, Joe.

JOE GARCIA. Shut up, Annie. Go on, Julie.

[*Julia walks up and down, tilting her chin.*

LEONORA (*at the window, drawing back a little as Julia is walking*) Look! There's that man again, Uncle Joe!

JOE GARCIA. Where?

[*He cautiously tiptoes toward the window. Julia, in her glory and pride, is still walking, looking back to see herself in the dresser mirror.*

LEONORA (*suddenly crouching*). Look out, Uncle Joe! He has a gun. He's pointin' it right at you!

HARRY (*nearer to the window*). For Christ's sake, duck, Joe — Duck!

[*Joe Garcia drops down to his knees. There is a shot outside. Julia screams. She stands still as though transfixed; then crumples up and falls in her glory of robes to the floor.*

MAMMA GARCIA. Julie! Baby — Julie.

[*She drops to her knees beside Julia.*

HARRY. It's one of Arbini's gang!

[*He pulls out his gun and runs swiftly down the stairs.*

LEONORA (*peeking out*). There he goes! He jumped the fence. He's runnin' down the road!

JOE GARCIA (*dazed and stumbling to Julia*). Julie — my little Julie — That was meant for your papa — not for you — not for you — not for my baby — for her bad papa — (*He, too, is on his knees, lifting Julia in his arms*) Julie — my little girl —

MAMMA GARCIA. Run, Annie — quick — quick — telephone the doctor.

AUNT ANNIE. Yes, yes — the doctor —

[*She is running out.*

AUNT ROSE. Get Father Roni, quick!

AUNT ANNIE. Yes, Father Roni —

[*She stumbles down the stairs and out of sight.*

JOE GARCIA (*stroking back Julia's hair*). Julie — speak to Papa — speak to Papa — Julie, open your eyes — Look at Papa.

JULIA (*in a whisper*). Papa —

MARIE (*sobbing wildly*). Julie — Julie — don't die —

MAMMA GARCIA. Put her on her bed, Papa.

[*Joe Garcia lifts up Julia and carries her to the shiny brass bed and puts her down gently, her head on the pillow.*

JOE GARCIA. There, Julie — that's all right — you'll be all right — There, Julie —

JULIA (*whispering*). Papa — Mamma —

MAMMA GARCIA. Yes, Baby — here I am, Baby.

[*Julia's hands flutter a moment; then she dies without another sound.*

JOE GARCIA (*patting her hands*). You're all right — you're all right, Julie — You're a queen, Julie — the queen — You got to ride on the float, Baby — don't forget that — Papa is so proud of you —

MAMMA GARCIA. Oh, blessed Virgin — Oh, blessed Jesus — (*Stroking her brow*) She's gone, Papa — She's gone —

JOE GARCIA (*fiercely*). What are you talkin' about, Amelia! What are you talkin' about! Julie's here — Julie's here —

[*Suddenly, far off, the town band is heard, playing, rather discordantly, one of Sousa's marches.*

MARIE (*between sobs*). There — there comes the band — They're — they're getting ready for the parade —

MAMMA GARCIA. Make 'em stop — Make 'em stop — They don't know what they're doin' —

AUNT ROSE (*sinking to her knees beside the bed and slowly crossing herself*). Thy will be done — (*She pats Julia's hand*) Tony will take care of you now.

[*The town band draws nearer, up the dusty road, the brasses blaring. It drowns out the sound of weeping around the bed.*

CURTAIN

UNTO SUCH GLORY

PAUL GREEN

THE FOLK-PLAY and pageant movement — which Percy MacKaye's work first suggested, the Wisconsin Players first attempted, and Professor Frederick H. Koch first created at the University of North Dakota — matured in the Professor's work with the Carolina Playmakers at Chapel Hill. Among the students who have been encouraged to create a drama of North Carolina folklore and tradition, the outstanding artist is Paul Green, winner of the Pulitzer award in 1927 for his full-length version of "In Abraham's Bosom."

Mr. Green was born on a farm near Lillington, North Carolina, on March 17, 1894, and lived there for twenty-two years. He farmed in the spring and summer and went to country school for a few months every winter. His secondary school education was received at Buies Creek Academy, from which he graduated in 1914. His study at the University of North Carolina was interrupted by enlistment in the army, four months of which were in service on the Western front. He returned to the University, and graduated from there in 1921. After a year's graduate work there and at Cornell University, he returned to the University of North Carolina as assistant professor in the Department of Philosophy. In 1928–1929 he was on leave of absence traveling abroad, on a Guggenheim fellowship.

Paul Green's published collections of one-act plays are: *The Lord's Will and Other Carolina Plays; Lonesome Road (Six Plays for the Negro Theatre)*; *In the Valley and Other Carolina Plays*. His one-act plays that have been published otherwise are: "Old Christmas", "Bread and Butter

Come to Supper", "Fixin's", "Blue Thunder", "Hymn to the Rising Sun."

His long published plays are: "The Field God", "In Abraham's Bosom", "The House of Connelly", "Potter's Field" (rewritten as "Roll Sweet Chariot"), "Tread the Green Grass", "Shroud My Body Down", "Johnny Johnson."

Recent plays are the one-act "Texas Calls", and the full-length plays "The Southern Cross", "The Enchanted Maze", "The Lost Colony."

UNTO SUCH GLORY

By PAUL GREEN

The record of the original production of "Unto Such Glory" has been lost.

Characters

BROTHER SIMPKINS, an itinerant revivalist preacher
WALT ENNIS, a young farmer
LANIE ENNIS, his wife
JODIE MAYNARD, her brother
SUT MAYNARD, her father

UNTO SUCH GLORY

Time. *The latter part of the nineteenth century.*
Place. *The southern part of the United States.*

In the rural sections of the South the people begin to think about the Lord when late July and August come. Crops are laid by — corn hilled and cotton ploughed for the last time, even tobacco-curing held in abeyance — and every little church from Bethel to Shiloh is rocked for a week by the fighting paradox of God and the Devil. Then it is that the way of the transgressor grows hard. Little children are herded terrified into the fold, the drunkard denies his dram, the profane man softens his speech, and shy, tough-knotted old fellows with land lawsuits greet each other gently as "Brother." Then too the way of the chicken grows hard. He is slaughtered by the thousands and his plucked feathers blow heavenward by the impersonal winds. The smoke-house suffers its onslaughts, the bin is visited and revisited, the pig is snatched and barbecued, the watermelon and "mushmelon" patches are devastated. The tired housewife sings "Blessed be the name", sweats and grows sick before a red-hot stove, and the farmer's last dollar is pleaded forth from its hiding place. For now it is that the preachers are abroad in the land. And now too the city cousins and their kin come down like Assyrian kings to eat and talk of the pleasures of farming and the open air — and to attend "big-meeting." Through it all the providing farmer moves quiet and subdued, comforted by the presence of the men of God and vaguely hoping to profit somehow thereby. He listens to the blarney of the city-bred, his impassive face concealing the superiority he knows is his. To the preachers he is all respect and gentleness. And bless God, even when he suspects their thievery and quackery, he comforts himself that the True Message can never be contaminated by scurvy containers — a metaphysic St. Thomas

*himself could not surpass. And accordingly under all pomp
and circumstance his faith remains. There are exceptions, of
course — for instance one of the farmers depicted in this piece.
But all glory to the general type, for I doubt that even in the time
of Piers the Plowman when the land was likewise overrun by
heavenly grafters was the burden borne more dutifully and stoi-
cally. But wonderful cures were wrought then and wonderful
cures are wrought now, and the response now as then remains a
general and irrational "hallelujah." And these gentlemen go
their rounds and will go. Let them. They saved me and they
may save others. — Preachers thin and wan and holy; preachers
fat, oily, and unctuous; preachers dashing and handsome crying out with pleasurable anguish the story of their red-light days
— God wot; — preachers Hebraic, awful and thundering. They
will go their way in the service of imagination and the Lord.
Thanks be. . . . Where is he who used to leave his photograph
to delight the daughters? — it meets me now from many a country mantelpiece. — He is still doing the Lord's work and passing
the plate to pay the photographers. And he who was wont in
the old days to leave more real and distressing images of himself
behind? He too pursues his labors to the glory and profit of
God. All honor to them and their " brethering." Let us continue
to feed and clothe them and leave the subtlety of an ethic to furnish
them forth to action. For fairies and fierce convictions are salty
savor to a land. ·*

*So it is as the curtain rises on Lanie Ennis sweating up
supper on a hot August evening for a carnivorous man of God.
She is a rather pretty young country woman, neatly and plainly
dressed, with large babyish blue eyes and a quick bird-like step.
From behind a door on the left come desultory sounds of a booming voice lifted in exclamations, snatches of song, and hallelu-
jahing. Lanie stands listening a moment with a steaming dish
of food in her hands. She places the food on the table and waits,
abstractedly fingering the chain of a locket around her throat.*

VOICE (*within*). Hallelujah, hallelujah.

LANIE (*softly*). Hallelujah! (*The sound of her own voice
seems to wake her from her abstraction and she moves swiftly*

through an open door at the right onto the porch and calls out through the darkness) Come on to supper, Walt!

A VOICE (*near at hand, outside*). I'm coming.

[*Lanie turns back into the room and goes into the kitchen at the rear. Walt enters at the right, carrying a bucket. He is a hot sunburned young farmer below medium height, slender and wiry and with a steel-like hardness about him.*

WALT. Got any slops for the pigs, Lanie?

LANIE. There's some pot liquor there by the stove. (*He disappears into the kitchen. The voice at the left is quiet and Lanie goes to the door and calls*) Supper's about ready, Brother Simpkins.

VOICE. Thankee, sister, thankee. . . .

WALT (*reappearing with his bucket*). How long till you're ready to eat?

LANIE. Soon as the coffee boils.

WALT. I'll be back in a minute then. (*He starts out at the right and then stops*) Won't your Brother Simpkins be too late for service?

LANIE (*working rapidly about the table*). Brother Jackson preaches first to-night.

WALT. Ah!

[*He goes out, but immediately returns and sits down in a chair near the door.*

LANIE. Ain't you going to feed the pigs?

WALT. Are you going to the church tonight?

LANIE (*defensively*). I can't miss the last meeting, Walt.

BROTHER SIMPKINS (*within*). Hallelujah, hallelujah, glory!

[*He is heard singing and clapping his hands.*

WALT. Makes more racket than usual.

LANIE (*quickly*). He's thinking of certain sinners that'll not be saved when the meeting ends. (*With a catch in her voice*) Might be singing with you in his mind, Walt.

WALT. Better change his tune then.

LANIE. Oh, Walt!

WALT. Yeh and he had.

LANIE. All of them preachers and prayers ain't made any impression on you.

WALT. Made an impression on my smokehouse all right. Been feeding Brother Simpkins for the last week. That's an eating white man, I'm here to tell you.

LANIE. We'd ought to count it a privilege to feed him, a chosen disciple of God. (*Walt sits looking at the floor, pondering*) Ain't you going to-night?

WALT. No.

[*Brother Simpkins is heard washing himself in a basin, splashing and blowing through his hands.*

LANIE. All the evening I been thinking about that song — "Why not to-night?" (*Chanting in a childlike voice*)
"To-morrow's sun may never rise,
To bless thy long deluded sight."

WALT. Don't worry about me.

LANIE. I can't help it.

WALT. And I'm worried about a heap of other folks myself.

[*He gives Lanie a sharp look.*

LANIE. You're about the only sinner in the neighborhood not saved.

WALT. No, your daddy'll keep me company.

LANIE. He got saved this evening, and went home shouting.

WALT. Good gracious!

LANIE. He did, Walt. And he stood up in the church and testified to every single mean thing he'd ever done.

WALT. He couldn't a-done that.

LANIE. Oh, Walt, to-night's the last night and won't you go?

WALT (*a bit sharply*). You've been going enough lately for both of us.

LANIE. And two weeks ago I was lost to God and the world and now —

[*She raises her face to heaven.*

WALT. Ah!

[*He sits looking at her mournfully and then picks up his bucket and goes quickly out and down the steps. Brother Simpkins*

*comes through the door at the left carrying a Bible in his hand.
He is a dark bearded man of middle age, heavy-set, with a
bloated ignorant face, but somewhat kindly withal. He is
dressed in a thin black seersucker suit and a celluloid collar
with an enormous white tie.*

BROTHER SIMPKINS (*in a deep throaty voice, hoarse from thundering in the pulpit*). Ah, sister, he's unworthy. Yes,
I fear he is.

LANIE. I don't know — I —

BROTHER SIMPKINS (*coming close to her*). I've told you —
(*Suddenly opening the Bible and pointing to a verse*) Read
there — it's the message again, coming another way —
plain — plain. (*Reading in a low vehement voice*) "For
both he that sanctifieth and they who are sanctified are
of one."

[*His eyes bore into hers and he lays his hand on her shoulder.*

LANIE. Yes, yes.

BROTHER SIMPKINS. Ah, you are sanctified — the seal is
on your forehead — pure and holy.

[*He bends quickly and kisses her.*

LANIE. Oh — I —

BROTHER SIMPKINS. It is written in Corinthians, one, one
and two, "They that are sanctified are called the saints."
And the saints are those saved forever, sealed for the
rapture, and they can do no harm.

LANIE. I know it, I feel it —

BROTHER SIMPKINS. Amen!

[*Walt comes abruptly in again with his bucket.*

WALT. I forgot to put any meal in these slops.

[*He brings a dipper of meal from the kitchen, pours it into
the bucket, and stirs it.*

BROTHER SIMPKINS. How ye to-night, Brother Ennis?

WALT. Tired — How're you?

BROTHER SIMPKINS. Bless God I'm carrying on happy
towards the Glory Land.

[*Lanie moves around the table arranging supper, now and
then looking at Walt with a puzzled expression.*

WALT (*with sudden admiration in his voice*). You *are* a big strong man, ain't you?

BROTHER SIMPKINS. Nothing but sinful clay. (*Lanie looks at him with undisguised admiration. Walt's eyes narrow a bit*) God gave me a big voice and a big body to use in his vineyard and I've brung him big harvest for twenty year.

WALT. He's proud of you, I bet.

BROTHER SIMPKINS (*softly*). Hanh — And the biggest harvest of all has been gathered here in this neighborhood these two weeks. . . .

WALT. Can you shoulder a sack of guano?

BROTHER SIMPKINS. Well, I don't know — I've never —

WALT. They don't have guano 'way off yonder where you come from, do they?

BROTHER SIMPKINS. I don't know — My work has been in the church.

WALT. You were talking about a vineyard.

BROTHER SIMPKINS (*perplexed*). The Lord's Vineyard.

WALT. Brother Simpkins, let me tell you something.

BROTHER SIMPKINS. Yes.

WALT. I can shoulder a sack of guano.

LANIE. Yes, he can.

BROTHER SIMPKINS. Yes.

WALT. Two hundred pounds.

BROTHER SIMPKINS. That's a right smart weight.

WALT. Yeh, it is, and that ain't all. I can shoulder it standing in a half bushel peck-measure.

BROTHER SIMPKINS (*looking around him uncertainly*). Yes, yes.

WALT (*pleasantly*). I weigh a hundred and fifteen pounds. How much do you weigh, Brother Simpkins?

BROTHER SIMPKINS. Two hundred and twenty.

WALT. A right smart weight. Hum — well, Lanie, you and Brother Simpkins better go ahead with your supper. I hear the folks starting their music over at the church. [*He gets up and goes out again with his bucket.*

BROTHER SIMPKINS. Seemed like your husband was making fun.

LANIE. No, he wan't thinking of that.

BROTHER SIMPKINS. I fear he'll never turn from his ways. Ah, I mis-doubt it.

LANIE. We must do all we can this last night.

BROTHER SIMPKINS (*after a moment, sternly*). No. He's refused again and again, and there's nothing to be done.

LANIE (*nervously*). I don't know — I've tried to get him to the meeting to-night.

BROTHER SIMPKINS. It's better for him not to be there.

LANIE. Yes —

BROTHER SIMPKINS. We'll go straight on from the church.

LANIE (*sitting down in her chair by the table*). Oh, I don't see how I can do it.

BROTHER SIMPKINS. It's the hand of God behind it. He's sending us forth to labor together for bringing souls to the anxious seat, and set them forth in the morning light.

LANIE (*standing up, as he puts his arm around her*). Yes, yes. . . .

BROTHER SIMPKINS. Like a lily of the valley, a sister of mercy. . . . (*He kisses her and strokes her hair*) Unto such glory thou wilt go.

LANIE (*her face shining*). Wonderful, wonderful! It is fine there where we're going?

BROTHER SIMPKINS. Fine, fine, but sinful. The wastefulness of the rich, the pride of the haughty, the sweating and groaning of the poor and oppressed, injustice and crime, sin — sin — sin. The houses lift themselves up high to heaven, their chimneys spit dust and ashes in God's face, silk and finery, lights and crowds and moving, moving, moving down the devil's sinful road. I've stood on the streets there and cried: "Repent, repent, remember Sodom and Gomorrah!" Like them sunken cities they pay no heed — but you and me'll go back there, go back there and keep crying: "Repent!"

LANIE. Keep crying repent, and they will repent. (*Slip-*

ping out of his arms) Oh, but people will think hard of me, I'm afraid.

BROTHER SIMPKINS. They hadn't ought to.

LANIE. No, they can't, they won't, and me going with you, will they? (*Looking up at him suddenly*) But I ain't told him yet — Walt, I mean.

BROTHER SIMPKINS. You mustn't tell him . . . maybe.

LANIE. But you've preached about deceiving.

BROTHER SIMPKINS. I don't know. I been thinking . . . while ago he talked funny, like he already knew something.

LANIE. You will explain everything, I know you will. There they go singing at the church.

[*Far off across the fields comes the pulsating rhythm of the meeting's song. Brother Simpkins raises his face in a ragged smile.*

BROTHER SIMPKINS. Hear Brother Jackson's voice — hallelujah, amen!

LANIE (*softly*). Amen.

BROTHER SIMPKINS (*moving up and down the room*). That great old song, how they sing it! (*Listening*) There's Sister Eason's alto, and Sister Jernigan's soprano rising to heaven in the night. Amen, amen, give 'em power, hold up Brother Jackson's arms, touch his tongue with fire, amen, amen. Let him prepare the way, for to-night I come with the power.

LANIE (*watching him in loving terror*). Hallelujah!

BROTHER SIMPKINS (*joining in the far-away song with a roar*).
"As I journey thro' the land, singing as I go,
  Pointing souls to Calvary — to the crimson flow,
  Many arrows pierce my soul — from without, within —"
(*He suddenly flings out his arms, turning upon Lanie*)
Yes, tell your husband everything. He can't stand out against me, nothing can, I'll sweep on, move everything before me with you at my side.

LANIE (*her gestures hypnotically beginning to resemble his*).
Yes, yes.

BROTHER SIMPKINS (*singing*).

"On the streets of Glory let me lift my voice,
Cares all past,
Home at last,
Ever to rejoice."

LANIE (*joining in with a high piping voice*). "When in valleys low I look towards the mountain height."

BROTHER SIMPKINS. Yea, yea, sealed for the rapture! (*Brokenly*) Lanie, Lanie! (*Speaking into the air*) Hurt not the earth, neither the sea nor the trees, till we have sealed the servants of God in their foreheads.

LANIE (*chanting and staring at him wide-eyed*). Sealed and set unto the day of redemption.

BROTHER SIMPKINS. Glory!

LANIE (*with a sharp hysterical giggle*). Hallelujah.

BROTHER SIMPKINS (*shouting*). The power, the blessing coming down!

LANIE (*moaning*). I can't stand it no more. I can't stand it —

BROTHER SIMPKINS. Pour out, pour it out on us, God. Let it come down like buckets of water, let it come down, let it come down drenching us, flooding us.

LANIE (*springing up and down in the room, her face set in a sort of mask*). Let it come down, let it come down — give it to me, give it to me — give — give — give —

BROTHER SIMPKINS (*prancing back and forth as he throws his hands above his head*). Glory — glory — glory — glory. Give it to us — gloryglorygloryglory-rrry. (*His words pass into a frenzy of senseless sounds*) Meeny-meeny-meeny-eeny-eeny — yari-yari-yari-hi-hi-hi-ee-ee-ee-ee — (*He shudders, closes his eyes, swings his head from side to side, his lips fluttering in a flood of sound*) Hic-y-hic-y-hic-hree-hree — whizzem-whizzem — loki-loki —

LANIE (*fluttering towards him and stretching out her arms before her*). Manny-yan-manny-yan — kari-kari — manny-yan-yan-manny-yan-yan.

[*She dances into his arms, and wrapped in each other's embrace they dance up and down, skip back and forth, all the while with their faces lifted towards the sky as if peering directly at a blinding light.*

BROTHER SIMPKINS. Hah-hah-hah.

LANIE (*laughing in oblivion*). Hee-hee-hee.

[*Brother Simpkins closes his eyes, a smile spreads over his face, and he falls to whistling a thumping barbaric tune to which their heels click rhythmically against the floor. Lanie closes her eyes and abandons herself to him. They whirl up and down the floor faster and faster. Now and then the whistled tune is punctuated by a shout or scream.*

BROTHER SIMPKINS (*with a blood-curdling yell*). Yee-ee-ee-h!

LANIE. Glory — glory — glorrrryyyrryyrryy!

[*Presently Walt rushes in at the right and stops thunder-struck.*

WALT (*shouting*). Heigh, you! Lord have mercy! Stop that!

BROTHER SIMPKINS. Give it — give it — give it —

WALT. Great God A'mighty!

BROTHER SIMPKINS. The blessing — the blessing — it's come — it's here — here —

LANIE. Hallelujah — hallelujah!

BROTHER SIMPKINS. Hallelujah — glory — hoofey-beigh — hoofey-beigh — loki-loki —

WALT (*running up and snatching Lanie from him*). Stop it, stop it!

[*He spins Lanie around and shakes her like a rag.*

BROTHER SIMPKINS (*slapping himself as if trying to beat off a spell*). Brother Ennis, Brother Ennis!

WALT. Don't "Brother Ennis" me. (*He flings Lanie down in a chair by the table*) I thought you'd done enough of that unknown tongue business at the church without doing it here.

LANIE. Everything looks so purty. Walt, Walt, I love everybody. Your face is so purty. (*She springs up and throws her arms around his neck. He fights her away from him*) Oh, I wisht you could see how purty this room is!

WALT. Have you gone plumb crazy?

[*Lanie drops into her chair and begins to cry softly, her body quivering and jerking.*

BROTHER SIMPKINS (*twisting and looking around him*).   I must get on to the church — we must get on.

WALT.   Yeh, and I reckon so.   From the sound of it there's a big outpouring over there and you'd do better to spill yours in the pulpit.

[*Brother Simpkins rushes into the room at the left and re-appears with a worn derby hat.   He crams it on his head and stands looking down at Lanie.*

BROTHER SIMPKINS.   Sister, let's be going on.

WALT.   She ain't fitten to go nowheres till she's had some supper.

LANIE (*quavering*).   Le's all sit down and eat.

[*Walt furtively sits down, the preacher hesitates a moment and then sits to the table without removing his derby.*

BROTHER SIMPKINS (*regretfully*).   And this is my last supper here.

WALT.   Ah!

LANIE.   I'll get the coffee.

[*She rises to her feet and then falls weakly back in her chair.*

WALT.   I will for you.

[*He goes into the kitchen.*

LANIE.   I'm so h-happy-happy.

[*Her hands writhe and twist uncontrollably in her lap. Brother Simpkins bends over and strokes her head, and she suddenly grasps his hand and covers it with crazy, hysterical kisses.*

BROTHER SIMPKINS.   Let your tears be joyful at your deliverance.

LANIE (*shivering*).   Yes, yes.

BROTHER SIMPKINS.   Now you can tell him — (*Turning from the table*)   Listen, listen, a second day of Pentecost — but wait — wait, when I get there — (*Lifting up his eyes*)   And when the day of Pentecost was fully come, they were all with one accord in one place.   And suddenly there came a sound from heaven as of a rushing mighty

wind, and it filled all the house where they were sitting.
And there appeared unto them cloven tongues like as of
fire and it sat upon each of them. (*Raising his voice*) Yea,
yea, hear my prayer! (*Walt comes in with the coffee*)
Let me bring the wind to them and fetch tongues of fire
for them when I do come. Go on, go on, Brother Jackson
— make ready — make ready! (*Looking through the door
at the right*) I can almost see the fire now.

WALT (*looking out*). What's that — where?

BROTHER SIMPKINS. The fire from heaven!

WALT (*pouring out the coffee*). Let's eat something.

BROTHER SIMPKINS (*bowing his head*). Now may —
[*He remembers his hat and snatches it off.*

WALT (*his face suddenly hard*). Lemme ask the blessing.

BROTHER SIMPKINS. You! . . . Hallelujah . . . amen!
He's beginning to yield, Sister Lanie, he's —

WALT. Bow your heads.

BROTHER SIMPKINS. Him, Sister Lanie! It's him bowing
his head.

WALT (*with sudden roughness*).
          Bless the bread and damn the meat,
          Great God, let's eat!
[*He falls to eating.*

BROTHER SIMPKINS (*starting back*). Blasphemy!
[*Walt goes on eating, watching the two of them now with a hard
face.*

WALT. Have some bread, Brother Simpkins.

BROTHER SIMPKINS. Ah!
[*He bows his head in inaudible prayer a moment and then
begins to eat.*

WALT. Help yourself, Lanie.

LANIE. I can't eat a thing.
[*She drops her head weeping on the table.*

BROTHER SIMPKINS. A man blessed with such a wife as yours,
and such blasphemy!

WALT. Yeh, two weeks ago there wan't no better wife
nowhere.

BROTHER SIMPKINS. Two weeks ago!

LANIE. No, I was lost then, Walt.

BROTHER SIMPKINS. Yes, lost. Now look into her face and see the hand of God. To-day she was consecrated and sanctified.

WALT. Was! Didn't look like it while ago. You two cutting up.

LANIE. Oh, Walt, everything is specially peaceful and happy now. Used to I'd sit here and be so lonesome, the house all so quiet and you off in the field. There was a great emptiness in here around my heart. Now I'm full, full. I feel like crying all the time, I'm so happy.

BROTHER SIMPKINS. Bless God! You hear her, Brother.

LANIE. I feel like I'll never be lonesome any more, never any more.

[*Walt bends his head over his plate eating heavily and saying nothing. There is a step on the porch at the right and Jodie, a country boy about sixteen years old, comes in carrying a rope in his hand.*

JODIE. You all seen Pa?

WALT. No. Ain't he at the church?

JODIE. He ain't.

BROTHER SIMPKINS. Is that Brother Sut Maynard's boy?

JODIE. Yessir.

[*He eyes the preacher rather boldly.*

BROTHER SIMPKINS. In all my twenty years of toiling in the vineyard I ain't seen a happier man than your Pa was to-day when the power come on him.

JODIE. Wish you'd tell me where he is now. Muh's just about crazy.

BROTHER SIMPKINS. No doubt he's in some quiet place offering up prayers on bended knee.

JODIE. Reckon his knees are bended, but I'm misdoubtful about the prayers.

WALT. When'd you see him last?

JODIE. About sunset. (*Bursting out*) He's been like a wild man ever since he got home this evening from the church.

I started off to get the cow in the pasture a while ago, and Muh run out and said Pa was gone. We couldn't find him nowhere. I been all down in the swamp but I can't find him.

WALT. I spect he's at the church then. And who would a-thought it?

JODIE. He come home from church talking them old unknown tongues, and then he took off near-about all his clothes and got down on his all-fours and run about the house like a dog.

BROTHER SIMPKINS. He's humbling himself. To-morrow he'll come out clothed in his right mind and praising God.

JODIE (*almost whimpering*). He's run mad or something.

WALT. You know how your Pa is, Jodie. When he gets a thing he gets it good.

LANIE (*sharply*). It's what'll keep Pa's soul out of the clutches of the old Bad Boy.

BROTHER SIMPKINS (*with a fond look*). Ah, Sister. (*To Jodie*) Go home — no, go to the church and pray for your father.

JODIE. Something bad has happened to him?

BROTHER SIMPKINS. Can't nothing happen to him. He's one of the consecrated now. I told him what to do to test his faith. Romans eight, twenty-eight.

JODIE. Pa's been talking about that man in the Bible that went around on his all-fours.

BROTHER SIMPKINS (*his mouth full of food*). Nebuchadnezzar. But afterwards he returned to the fold a wiser and a better man. Likewise your father.

JODIE. Ma says she bets he's off eating grass like a cow somewhere, and he out in the damp without his shoes.

BROTHER SIMPKINS. He needs no shoes to protect him.

JODIE (*pleadingly*). Walt, come help me ketch him.

WALT (*jumping up from the table*). Yeh, I'll go.

[*He starts out through the door, looks back at Lanie and the preacher and hesitates.*]

JODIE. Come on, he'll mind you if we find him.

WALT (*coming back to the table*). No, I can't go now, Jodie.
I'm needed here.

JODIE. Can't you come, Walt?

WALT. Not to-night. If you ain't found him in the morning,
I'll help you. I just can't leave here to-night.

JODIE. If you folks was in such a fix I'd help you.
[*Jodie suddenly goes off in a huff.*

LANIE. I'm glad you didn't go, Walt.

WALT. Yah.

LANIE. Now tell him, Brother Simpkins, please do.

BROTHER SIMPKINS. No, you'd better tell it like the message
come to you.
[*Lanie looks down and says nothing.*

WALT. Well, go ahead. (*He waits and they are silent*) But
I already know what you're gonna tell.

LANIE. Then I won't have to tell it?

WALT. Brother Simpkins spoke about it while ago. And
I reckon I got eyes to see what I saw when I come in.

BROTHER SIMPKINS (*hurriedly*). I don't remember it.

LANIE. Are you willing to it, Walt?

WALT. I ain't willing, but I don't see what I can do about it.

BROTHER SIMPKINS. No, no, there's nothing you can do
about it. We can't go against the will of the almighty.

LANIE. It'll be hard, I know, but it's all come so clear to me.
And Brother Simpkins has had a vision from above.

WALT. I know it. No, I ain't willing, but the whole country's turned upside down from Rocky Mount to Fayette-
ville, and I can't blame you entirely. (*Nodding his head
at Brother Simpkins*) He's the one to be blamed most.

LANIE. Both of us have received the command.

WALT. I thought you had more sense, Lanie, than to get all
wropped up in such stuff.

LANIE. I don't know how you'll get along at first, I suppose
after while you'll get used to it.

WALT. I betcha Sut Maynard'll be back cussing and chewing
tobacco as bad as ever in a month. And you'll soon forget
it all too, Lanie.

LANIE. No, I won't, no I won't. I'd rather die.

BROTHER SIMPKINS. Never. She's stamped and sealed, and the mark will never pass away.

LANIE. Reckon you'll mind after a month or two, Walt?

WALT. It'll all be passed out of my mind.

[*Brother Simpkins smiles broadly and looks at Lanie happily.*

BROTHER SIMPKINS. Hallelujah.

LANIE. Brother Simpkins said at first you might try to get the law on him.

WALT (*staring at her*). Law on him — not me. I got more sense than that.

BROTHER SIMPKINS. Amen!

LANIE (*piteously*). I got everything fixed where you can find it.

WALT. Hanh?

LANIE. And be sure to feed the chickens regular. And don't you let the flowers dry up. (*Suddenly wringing her hands*) Oh, I don't see how you can get along without me.

WALT. Get along without you?

LANIE. I know it'll be lonesome for you.

WALT. I ain't going to be here by myself.

LANIE. Would you get somebody else to come and stay with you? No, no, I couldn't let you do that.

WALT (*bounding out of his chair*). You mean you're thinking of going away?

LANIE. Yes, yes, I got to go off and leave you.

WALT. Lanie!

LANIE (*wretchedly*). I can't help it. It's got to be done.

WALT (*sitting down with a gasp*). Where you going?

LANIE (*beginning to sob*). Oh, 'way off somewheres.

WALT (*to Brother Simpkins*). Are you mixed up in her wild ideas about leaving?

BROTHER SIMPKINS. It's a power beyond either of us.

WALT. What power?

BROTHER SIMPKINS (*gesturing*). Up there.

WALT. And what does the power up there say?

BROTHER SIMPKINS. That she shall go out and labor in the vineyard with me.

WALT (*springing out of his chair again*). Great God! I thought she was talking about all that getting sanctified and filled with tongues. (*He moves towards the preacher who pushes himself behind his chair*) You old goat, I'll —

BROTHER SIMPKINS. Ask her, ask her about it.

WALT. Lanie, what 'n the world you mean by all this?

LANIE. I can't help it, I can't help it. Don't blame me.

WALT. I ain't blaming you completely.

LANIE. I been feeling the call all the week to do something, to go out and work and help spread the message. It's got stronger all the time. Oh, I've just got to go.

WALT. Has he been talking to you about it?

LANIE. He's sympathized with me all the time.

WALT (*gripping his chair*). 'Y God, I reckon so.

LANIE. Don't think he's the fault, I am. I've been having dreams about it, and several times a voice has come to me telling me I had to give up home and everything — Yes, it said I'd have to give up you — and go forth.

WALT. Did that voice say for you to go with him?

LANIE (*weeping*). Yes, It said, "Lanie Ennis, go with Brother Simpkins."

WALT (*looking helplessly around him a moment and then sitting down in his chair*). What else did it say?

LANIE. That's about all it said to me. But I might have still stayed with you if it hadn't a-been for the vision.

WALT. What did the vision say?

LANIE. He's the one had it; he'll tell you. It was so beautiful. He'll tell you.

WALT. I ain't interested in what he had, nor how beautiful. If you didn't have no vision, why you want to put dependence in his?

BROTHER SIMPKINS. What you do is done at the call of your own sinful self, the movement of man. What I do is in obedience to a higher power. Without him I am nothing; with him I am everything.

WALT. Then why you want her if he's everything to you?

BROTHER SIMPKINS. He will work with me through her.

WALT. Will he?

BROTHER SIMPKINS. He will — glory!

WALT (*suddenly turning upon Lanie*). What's that you got around your neck?

LANIE (*covering her throat with her hands*). A little chain.

WALT. I been watching that. Who give it to you?

LANIE. He did.

WALT. Did God tell you to give that locket to her, Brother?

LANIE. It was so purty I thought I'd wear it.

BROTHER SIMPKINS. I asked you not to.

WALT (*sharply*). Thought you'd wait till you toled her off with it, did you?

BROTHER SIMPKINS (*with childish sullenness*). You never give her nothing.

LANIE (*plaintively*). He don't make a lot of money the way you do, Brother Simpkins.

WALT. No, 'y God, I don't. I don't go around preaching and begging the folks and taking up collections in dishpans. By God, I ain't got that low yet. I work for my living.

BROTHER SIMPKINS (*breaking out*). I had the vision and I'll heed the vision. If she's willing we will go.

WALT. Are you willing, Lanie?

LANIE. There's nothing else to do.

[*She buries her face in her arms weeping.*

BROTHER SIMPKINS. Come, come, and we'll go forth to new fields, to new labors.

WALT (*imploringly*). Lanie, you can't go off thataway. (*Helplessly*) You ain't got your clothes fixed.

LANIE. They're all packed in the suitcase. Brother Simpkins will take 'em up the road. We're gonna leave from the church. Oh, I can't go off and leave all this. (*She begins smoothing a pattern in the tablecloth affectionately*) Aunt Rachel gave me that tablecloth.

[*She bursts into sobs again. Walt looks at her in consternation, beating his hands together. Presently he stands up.*

WALT (*threateningly*). Brother Simpkins, you'd better go on by yourself, and you better go mighty quick.

BROTHER SIMPKINS (*staring ahead of him and booming*). It come to me in the night clear as the broad daytime, an angel, the angel Gabriel. He brung a message to me like the message of old to the prophets. I was in that room there, he come in through that door — (*Gesturing to the left and the right*) — and stood with a flood of glory around him. He spoke to me in a loud voice and said he'd choosed one of the fairest daughters of men to be an aid to me on my way. (*Lanie looks at him with shining face*) And no sooner had he said she was fair than I knowed it was Sister Lanie, for they's none fairer than her, like a pearl, like a dewdrop on the mountain, like a diamond lost among swine. He said stoop down and lift her up, and she will hold up your arms in times of trouble. Your powers will be multiplied, your labors will be fruitful under the sun. Then to make sure I bowed my head and asked who the chosen one was, and he said it was her, Sister Lanie. It was a message. And then I slept and behold she appeared to me in a dream and said that whither thou goest I will go and whither thou lodgest I will lodge. Then I awoke and praised God, hallelujah! Next morning she told me she'd had a dream telling her to go with me. (*Glaring at Walt who sits hunched in his chair, taken aback*) Before the angel Gabriel left, he told me to let no man put his message astray. And no man can.

[*Lanie moves towards him now and takes his outstretched hand.*

WALT. Lanie!

LANIE. I wish it could be different, but it can't. I could never stay here any more. The lonesomeness would eat my heart out. There's something calling me off — calling me on towards it. I don't know what it is, but I know it's wonderful and great.

WALT (*in a low voice*). Suppose the vision hadn't come, Brother Simpkins, would you a' wanted her anyhow?

BROTHER SIMPKINS. But it did come, and that settles it for
me.

WALT (*softly*). Does it?

BROTHER SIMPKINS. I am nothing but a weak and empty
vessel. As I am filled I am powerful and give forth the
waters of salvation in his name — hallelujah!

LANIE (*weeping*). Hallelujah!

BROTHER SIMPKINS (*looking down at Lanie*). The gift of
tongues will come upon the multitude, the sick will be
healed, and such an outpouring of the blessing this night
as these old fields and woods have never seen. (*He leads
her towards the door at the right*) Listen there, listen there
at the children of the Lord.

[*The singing and shouting from the church rise clear and
strong, punctuated by high screams.*

LANIE. Good-by, Walt, good-by.

[*She runs up to him and throws her arms around him, weeping
over him.*

WALT (*suddenly convulsed as if with an electric shock*). What's
that, what's that, what's got hold of me? (*Springing
from his chair and whirling around the room, his eyes set like
one seized with a fit*) Turn me loose, turn me loose!

LANIE (*aghast*). There's something happened to him.

WALT (*staring before him and beginning to talk as if to some per-
son immediately before him*). Who's that? Is that you?
Who? (*He answers himself in a strange far-away voice*)
It's me, the angel Michael.

BROTHER SIMPKINS. The power's coming on him —
hallelujah.

LANIE. Glory, glory!

WALT (*beginning to jabber*). Yimmy-yam-yimmy-yam.
(*He skips up and down the floor*) Yee-yee-yee. Yamm-
yamm-yamm. (*His voice lowers itself into a growl, like an
animal mouthing something*) Hanh — hanh-hanh-we-we-
we-we — whee-ee-h!

BROTHER SIMPKINS. It's come on him like a flood. Glory,
glory to God!

LANIE (*clapping her hands*).   Glory-glory-glory !

WALT (*stopping and speaking as if to an unseen person*).   Yes, yes, yes, I hear you. (*His voice coming out faint and funereally*)   Go towards him, come to him.
[*He moves like a blind man towards the preacher.*

BROTHER SIMPKINS.   He 's seeing a vision.

WALT.   I see an angel with a rod and staff in his hand.

BROTHER SIMPKINS.   Glory !

LANIE.   He 's saved.

WALT (*speaking in the voice of the angel*).   He 's a liar, he 's a dirty low-down suck-egg dog.   (*In his own voice*)   No, he 's a servant of God. I 'm willing for her to go with him. Let her go. (*With the angel's voice*) Step up to him, choke his liver out, crucify him. (*He draws nearer the preacher*)   Oh, I see the angel Michael killing a man with a stick !

BROTHER SIMPKINS.   What is it, Brother, what is it ?

WALT (*in the angel's voice*).   He 's a dirty scoundrel trying to ruin your wife. Scratch his eyes out. (*Shuddering and speaking in his own voice*)   No, no, I can't hurt him, don't make me hurt him. (*In the voice of the angel*)   He 's led women off before, don't let him do it again.
[*With the fury of a wildcat he suddenly flies on the preacher, clawing and biting him.*

BROTHER SIMPKINS (*screaming*).   Help ! Help ! Keep him off'n me, sister !

LANIE.   Walt, Walt, don't you know what you 're doing ?
[*She throws up her hands and drops in a chair. The preacher is helpless before the attack of Walt who is all over him, around him, and under him.*

WALT (*on top of Brother Simpkins and tearing him in the face*). I hate to do it ! I hate to do it !

BROTHER SIMPKINS (*roaring*).   Mercy ! Mercy !

WALT (*astride of the preacher as he crawls about the room squealing in pain*).   Tear him all to pieces !
[*He rips the preacher's coat and shirt from him leaving him almost bare above the waist.*

BROTHER SIMPKINS (*falling exhausted on the floor*). So was the prophets persecuted before me.

[*He lays himself out on the floor whimpering.*

WALT (*standing up presently and shaking himself as if coming out of a dream*). Lord 'a' mercy, what I been doing! [*He stares at the prone figure amazed.*

LANIE. You done beat him near-about to death.

WALT. Is that you, Brother Simpkins? Is that you on the floor there?

BROTHER SIMPKINS (*gasping*). Help, mercy!

WALT. Bring a towel and some water quick, Lanie, there's something happened.

[*Lanie runs into the kitchen and returns with a basin of water and a towel.*

LANIE. Oh, me, look how his face is bleeding!

WALT. It's his nose, ain't it? Worse'n a butchered yearling. (*Bending over him and bathing his face*) Who in the world done it, Brother?

BROTHER SIMPKINS. Lemme leave this place; lemme git away.

WALT (*pushing him down and pouring water over him*). Did I do it? I couldn't 'a' done it.

LANIE. Yes, you did, you sailed on him like a run-mad man, a-biting and a-scratching.

WALT (*contritely*). Good gracious me! A sort of spell come over me — I seen a vision. It wan't my fault, don't blame me. I can't help it. It was a power from above. The angel Michael stood out all of a suddent with a pile o' glory around him and he told me what to do. He give my arm power. He come in through that door there.

BROTHER SIMPKINS (*sitting up*). Git me some clothes. I'm going from here.

LANIE (*coming up to him*). I'll help you.

BROTHER SIMPKINS (*snarling*). You ain't gonna help me nothing. Get back from here, you sinful creature.

LANIE. Oh, Lord have mercy!

[*She begins to sob again.*

BROTHER SIMPKINS. May a curse come on this household for so persecuting a servant of the Lord !

[*Walt runs into the kitchen and returns with a bottle.*

WALT. Here's something that'll take the burn out'n them raw places. Put some on your face.

[*He shoots the bottle to him.*

BROTHER SIMPKINS (*knocking it from him with a shout*). That's liniment ! You're trying to kill me !

WALT. Lord, I didn't mean any harm.

[*There is a stir on the porch at the right, and old man Sut Maynard creeps in on his all-fours, dressed in an old shirt and a torn pair of drawers. A mop of gray hair hangs down over his eyes. His face is swollen, and one eye is closed. He has a rope around his neck by which Jodie tries to pull him back.*

JODIE. Pa, ain't you got no shame about ye? Gracious, what you all been doing to the preacher?

WALT. We all had a spell of unknown tongues a while back. Where'd you find Sut?

JODIE. Down there in the edge of the briar patch. The yellow jackets got after him down there and I heard him hollering. Make him come on home with me, Walt.

LANIE. Pa, what ails you?

WALT. Go on home, Sut. You and the preacher ain't fitten to be seen in public.

[*Brother Simpkins sits up nursing his head in his arms.*

SUT (*going up to Brother Simpkins and whining*). Brother Simpkins, ain't I been humble enough?

BROTHER SIMPKINS (*growling*). I dunno —

SUT. You told me to go a day and night. I can't do it —

BROTHER SIMPKINS. Go on and do what you want to.

SUT. I'm a' old man and I can't stand much of the night air.

[*He waits and the preacher makes no reply.*

JODIE. No, he can't.

SUT. I done suffered my share. About a hundred of them yellow jackets stung me.

SPARKIN'

ELLSWORTH PROUTY CONKLE

The one-act plays of Ellsworth Prouty Conkle depict the folk of typical small towns in the Middle Western states. He was born in Nebraska in 1899, attended Peru State Normal School, and graduated from the University with a Master's degree in 1923.

The influence of the colleges in the creation of the dramas of the farms is again evident in his work, for in 1926 and 1927 he studied under Professor Baker at Yale, and his graduate studies included work as a Rockefeller Fellow at the University of Iowa, and as a Guggenheim Fellow abroad. After teaching for three years at the University of North Dakota, he became Assistant Professor in the University of Delaware, and then went to the University of Iowa. There he has been Research Associate and Lecturer for four years, has received his Doctor's degree, and is now Assistant Professor of Speech.

His collections of published one-act plays are: *Crick Bottom Plays*, and *Loolie and Other Short Plays*. Other one-act plays which have been published are: "Th' 'Nitiated", "Th' Feller from Omaha", "Chief Sittum Bull", "The Juber Bird", " Chick-a-Dee."

His full-length published plays are: "In the Shadow of a Rock", "Prologue to Glory", "Two Hundred Were Chosen" (produced 1936, New York).

Other plays, most of which have had experimental production in community playhouses, are: "Julia Mallory", "Leaven", "In Tamman's Hollow", "Dobey and Sons", "The Mayor of Sherm Center", "Fräulein Klauber", "49 Dogs in the Meathouse", "Oxygenerator", "Death in Her Face", "The Lovings", "Paul and the Blue Ox."

SPARKIN'

By ELLSWORTH PROUTY CONKLE

"Sparkin'" was originally presented by the Department of Drama at Yale University as a class-room exercise. There was no program, either printed or mimeographed.

Characters

SUSAN HANNA
LESSIE HANNA
GRANNY PAINSBERRY
ORRY SPARKS

SPARKIN'

SCENE. *Evening at Tude Hanna's farm home. The room is the kitchen. On the right wall is the kitchen range, with a tea-kettle stewing and simmering. In front of the stove, with her stocking feet stuck into the oven, sits Granny Painsberry. She has a shawl over her shoulders and sits all scrootched up. She shivers at times, and sticks her hands out to warm them.*

In the center of the room is a dining table, covered with a white oil-cloth. There are victuals in dishes and uncovered. In the middle is a lamp. Lessie Hanna, a shy and pretty little girl, is ironing some things. One end of her ironing board rests on the table; the other end lies on the back of a chair. Throughout the play she runs to the stove and changes her irons, the hot for the cold. She irons away busily and adroitly, looking up now and then suspiciously toward the upper door left.

In the rear of the room, Susan Hanna, Tude's wife, is working at a kitchen-cabinet mixing bread.

There is a door in the rear wall right; and there are two in the left wall, both identical, and very close together.

There is a straight-back chair between the two doors.

At the rise of the curtain the women are working.

Granny chews and spits into the wood-box. After a spell of silence, Granny speaks.

GRANNY. Is Tude gone to bed, Susy?

SUSAN. Why, yes, ma. Didn't you hear him say he was a goin' to bed?

GRANNY. Ef I'd a heerd him I wudn't a asted you. (*Pause*) Whut'd Tude go to bed fer s' soon a'ready?

SUSAN. He said he war kind-a tired, ma. He's been a shuckin' corn on that north forty an' et's perty rough in them hills. Et wears a person clean out.

[*Silence.*

GRANNY. What time is et?

SUSAN. Whut time is et, Lessie? I cain't see withouten my spec's.

LESSIE. It's a quarter to eight, mom.

GRANNY. What'd she say?

SUSAN. She said et war a quarter to eight.

GRANNY. Well, why don't she speak plainer-like. No wonder Lessie ain't got no fellers. A pusson cain't hear nothin' she says. Not nothin'!

LESSIE. I don't want no fellers.

SUSAN. Lessie ain't a thinkin' about the fellers, air you, Lessie?

LESSIE. No.

[*She looks toward the door again. Then she lowers her head.*

GRANNY. What say?

SUSAN. Lessie hain't thinkin' 'bout no fellers.

GRANNY. Listen to th' wind blowin'! Hain't thinkin' 'bout no fellers, ain't she? Well . . . ef she hain't, you betterd taik her inter Doc Spellzer an' have her 'zamined. Thur must be somethin' wrong somewhurs about her.

SUSAN. Ma! What air you a talkin' about annyways?

GRANNY. You heerd me th' fust time, Susy. You know well 'nough whut I'm a talkin' about. Uhhhhhh . . .

[*Pause.*

GRANNY. You a arnin' that white calicy dress-a mine, Lessie?

LESSIE. I guess I am, Granny.

GRANNY. What say?

LESSIE. I guess so, Granny.

GRANNY. You guess so? Don't you know so? Don't you ever know nothin', Lessie? A person'd think you was plumb dumb. Maybe you air. I don't know. A pusson never cain hear nothin' you say. You're jest like'n your dead gran'pap Lute Painsberry. He never did know nothin', neither. Leastwise, not more'n th' law wud allow.

LESSIE. I'm a arnin' your dress, Granny. Lands-a-goodness!

GRANNY. That's right! Begin a swearin' at me! Well, see you don't scorch no hole inter et!

SUSAN. A person'd think you war old enough to know better'n to go to dances, ma. You're too old t' be doin' such things.

GRANNY. I hain't too old to do nothin'. Nobody hain't who don't think so! I'm a goin' to Hank Wagnerses barn-dance tomorry night ef I have t' put on a pair-a gum-boots an' wade. Nobody cain't talk me outen et. So shet up. Hang that dress in th' closet thur b'hint ye.

LESSIE. That's what I was a aimin' t' do, Granny.

[*She holds the dress up before her grandmother.*

LESSIE. See. Ain't it perty, Granny?

GRANNY. It'll do . . . cainsiderin' who arned et.

LESSIE. Let's see how you're a goin' to look . . .

GRANNY. Git away with yer lollygaggin' 'round me, will you. You act like you'd never'd a seen me dressed up!

LESSIE. You look like a perty old rosebud, Granny!

[*She lays the dress on the old lady's huddled form.*

GRANNY. I *am* perty old. But I hain't no rosebud. I know I hain't no rosebud. An' you know I hain't no rosebud. You jest want to git my money when I'm gone. You're jest like all th' rest-a them all!

LESSIE. Aw, Granny . . . I don't want your money.

[*She stoops and kisses the old lady. The latter spits and sputters.*

GRANNY. Git away with yer lollygaggin' 'round me, will you? I never cud tolerate no lollygaggin' 'round! Lute usta be all th' time a lollygaggin' round. He didn't care who he lollygagged with, neither.

SUSAN. Ma! You're talkin' about poor pa that-a-way?

GRANNY. He allus sayed as how he wanted t' go to hell, 'cause thur's where a person'll find all th' wayward women-folks.

SUSAN. Ma! You're talkin' that-away before Lessie?

LESSIE. Don't pay no attention to me. She can't hurt me none.

SUSAN. Lessie!

[*Lessie goes to hang the dress in the closet.*

GRANNY. I reckon Lessie 'll be a settin' her cap fer that new hired-hand Cornie Youngseses got.

LESSIE. Granny!

GRANNY. He don't look t' me like he 'mounted to powder an' lead t' blow him up with. One-a them slow-pokey fellers. They don't never get nowheres in this-a world. You got to be up-an'-comin' to amount to much around here. I'll give it to your gran'pap. He war shore up-an'-comin'. 'Specially whenever he seed a woman. I had no complaint t' make 'bout him a bein' a live one.

LESSIE. That feller over to Youngs' is a nice feller.

GRANNY. Oh. You been inspectin' him, have you? Oh.

LESSIE. Well . . . he is!

GRANNY. Susy.

SUSAN. What, ma?

GRANNY. Put another stick-a cord-wood inter th' fyar. My feet is a freezin' off of me. That there slippery-ellum is too wet. Et don't burn good when et 's wet. Tell Tude t' scair up some-a that jack-oak that 's on th' bottom-a th' pile.

SUSAN (*fixing the fire*). It don't seem none too cold in here for me. Does it to you, Lessie?

LESSIE. I'm about burnin' up.

GRANNY. Well, et hain't no heat out-a this-here stove 's a burnin' you up. Ef you 're a burnin' up, et must be with curiosity er somethin'.

SUSAN. We 're a workin', ma.

GRANNY. What you a workin' at?

SUSAN. I'm a mixin' out my bread. Th' starter hain't been right th' last two times.

GRANNY. You don't put enough taters inter your taterwater.

SUSAN. Et hain't that, ma.

GRANNY. Don't you go a tellin' me what ain't, an' what is.

Ef you want to know what — (*There is a heavy step on the porch. All the women turn abruptly towards the upper left door*) Who's that a prowlin' around here this time-a th' night? (*There is a stamping and scraping of feet*) Comin' around time a person's gittin' ready fer their bed.

[*There is a heavy knock on the door like the banging of a mailed fist.*

LESSIE.   Oh!

[*The women turn to her.*

SUSAN.   Who is et, Lessie?

LESSIE.   It's . . . him!

GRANNY.   Who's *him?*

LESSIE.   Him!

SUSAN.   Lessie, who is et?

LESSIE.   It's Orry Sparks.

SUSAN.   Lessie . . . what's Orry Sparks doin' comin' over here?

LESSIE.   T' see about somethin', I reckon.

GRANNY.   Who'd she say et war?

SUSAN.   She said et war that new feller over to Youngses.

GRANNY.   Oh. I was a wonderin' what she was a wearin' them new slippers an' sox t'night fer. So she's a shinin' around fer a man, is she? I ain't got no use for that young feller over . . .

[*The knock comes again.*

LESSIE.   Mom!

SUSAN.   What?

LESSIE.   He's . . . out there, mom!

SUSAN.   Well?

GRANNY.   Don't be so green. Go an' let him in. He won't never amount to nothin'. He . . .

LESSIE.   Mom . . . I don't know what to *do!*

[*Susan goes to the door and opens it.*

GRANNY.   Mil*dew!*

[*Lessie stands back of the ironing board nervous and blushing. Granny scrootches up in her shawl. Orry Sparks slides in.*

He is a big, husky fellow. He is bashful and stands with his cap in his hand. His eyes are on Lessie. Otherwise he doesn't know what to do or say.

SUSAN. Howdy do, Mister Sparks. Nice evenin' out, ain't et?

ORRY. Howdy do, Missus Hanna. Why, yeh, kinda.

SUSAN. Lessie, here's Mister Sparks.

LESSIE (*turning and stammering*). Oh. I didn't know you was here. Howdy do. Let me have your cap.

ORRY. Howdy, Lessie. You arnin' some clo'es?

LESSIE. I'm tryin' to.

GRANNY. What does he want, Susy? Is somebody sick over to th' Youngseses? I reckon that little Betty-Sall has throwed another-a her cat fits, an' . . .

ORRY. Th' Youngses is all right, fer as I know. I jest . . . (*He casts his eyes Lessie-ward*) . . . kinda thought I'd drop in a spell to see you folks. I never been over to see you yet.

SUSAN. I'm right glad you come over, Mister Sparks. Have you ever met up with Granny, here? She's my ma.

ORRY. Oh. She's th' nice old lady comes over visitin' Missus Young, ain't she?

GRANNY. What's he a sayin'?

SUSAN. He said as how you was a nice old lady, ma.

GRANNY. Who sayed that?

SUSAN. Him.

[*Granny turns and looks squarely at Orry.*

GRANNY. Oh. (*She turns back. Pause*) Well . . . (*Pause*) Maybe I hain't so nice as I look, young feller. (*She feels in her pocket*) Have a chaw-a t'baccer?

[*Orry is wide-eyed.*

LESSIE. Granny . . . maybe he don't . . .

GRANNY. In my day all th' real fellers chawed t'baccer an' drunk strong licker.

ORRY. Well. I don't us'ally chew t'baccer. But sometimes I do. I'm a real feller, I am. I'll . . . I'll try a chaw . . . (*He grabs off the plug. He looks to Lessie to see if she is watching. He bites off the chunk and returns the*

plug. Granny looks over her shoulder birdlike) . . . ef
et kills me!

SUSAN. Jest set down annywheres you cain find a chair,
Mister Sparks. Looks like Lessie's got 'em all filled up
with clo'es.

ORRY. Don't mind about me. I cain set on th' floor.
Here's a chair over here.

[*He sits on the chair between the two doors. There are
clothes on the back of it.*

LESSIE (*going about her ironing*). I'm sorry I cain't ast you
into th' front-room, but we ain't got our heatin' stove up
in there yet.

ORRY. Aw, that's all right. I ain't usta no parlor-rooms,
noway. I don't feel at home sittin' on a sofy. Do
you?

LESSIE. It's 'cordin' who I'm sittin' with.

ORRY. Aw.

GRANNY. What you ca'culate t' do around here t'night,
young feller?

SUSAN. Ma . . . it's time you was in bed, ain't et?

GRANNY. What say?

SUSAN. I sayed it was time you was in bed. Your bed's
ready.

GRANNY. What ef et is? Cain't I set up ef I want to?
There's one night ever' year I set up to nigh onto nine
o'clock. I think this year, this is et. Poke up th' fyar,
Susy.

SUSAN. Ma, you'll ketch your death a cold settin' up
here.

GRANNY. Whose death is et, annyway? Why should you
keer? You all got your eye on my money when I do die.
They ain't nobody 'round here cain make me go t' bed
ef I don't want to. Ef they is, I'd like t' see th' color-a her
or his petticoats.

[*Granny scrootches up.*

SUSAN. Don't pay no 'tention to ma, Mister Sparks.
She's gettin' old.

ORRY. 'Tain't th' old ladies worries me much, Missus Hanna. Et's . . . (*He blushes. He looks toward Lessie*) . . . th' young ones.

[*Lessie blushes.*

LESSIE. Don't let them worry you none, Mister Sparks. They ain't worth worryin' none over.

ORRY. I reckon . . . you're a talkin' through your hat, Lessie.

[*Lessie smiles and lowers her head. She irons.*

GRANNY. Ef you air a aimin' t' git inter th' good graces-a this fambly, you want t' treat me nice, young feller. I got all th' say around this fambly. What I says, goes. What I don't say, ain't wuth sayin'.

ORRY. I . . . I brung you over a sack of candy . . . Lessie. Got et into Martinses store this afternoon. Et hain't much, but et's somethin' to chaw on. Save you chawin' th' rag.

[*Orry hands Lessie the candy. She opens the sack and looks into it.*

LESSIE. Oh. It's chocolate drops, isn't it?

ORRY. He'p yourse'f, and give some to th' folks.

[*He arises to spit. He looks at both the doors. He decides on the down-stage one, opens it, and spits out. He closes it and sits. Lessie has taken a piece of candy out to eat.*

LESSIE. Here, mom. Mister Sparks brung us some . . .

ORRY. I brung 'em fer you, Lessie, private.

LESSIE. Oh.

ORRY. But your folks cain eat on 'em if you say so. They're kinda hard an' don't amount to nothin'. I reckon they been in th' store since Norah's Ark.

[*Susan takes one. Lessie goes to the old lady.*

LESSIE. Here, Granny.

[*She holds the sack open for Granny to take one.*

GRANNY. What is et?

LESSIE. Chocolate drops.

GRANNY. What?

LESSIE. Chocolate drops.

GRANNY. Choclit draps?

LESSIE. Yes.

GRANNY. Oh. (*She takes the whole bag. Lessie stands speechless*) Thank ye.

[*Lessie is about to protest.*

ORRY. Shshshsh. Let her have 'em. Don't rile her up none.

GRANNY. Whur'd you git choclit draps at?

LESSIE. Mister Sparks brung 'em.

GRANNY. Oh. (*She turns and casts a suspicious eye towards Orry*) They hain't so bad. (*She samples another one*) I tasted better. (*She chews it*) Yit . . . they ain't so bad. (*She takes another*) How'd you know I like choclit draps, young feller?

ORRY. I . . . didn't.

[*Granny scrootches up over her bag of candy and munches one after another. Susan goes about her business at the cabinet.*

ORRY. I didn't ca'culate t' stay very long. Guess maybe I orta be goin' on back home. Me and Cornie's goin' to cut fodder t'morrow on th' crick bottom. Liable to frost anny night now.

LESSIE. You don't need t' be a runnin' off home yet, Mister Sparks. You ain't only just come over.

ORRY. I know I ain't been here very long. But I just thought I'd just drop in a bit to . . . to see you. An' say . . . you wouldn't mind a-callin' me jest Orry, would you? Nobody never called me Mister Sparks much, an' ha'f th' time when a person calls me that, I don't know who they're talkin' to. Orry ain't much of a name, but I reckon *I* hain't so much, neither.

LESSIE. I got an uncle by the name of Orry, too. He's kind-of-silly-like.

ORRY. Ah . . . yeh. (*He drops his head. Lessie irons. Susan putters around. Granny nibbles. Orry lifts his head*) What you doin'? Arnin'?

LESSIE. I'm arnin' out some things fer Sunday.

ORRY. Oh. (*He gets up and spits out the door again. Lessie looks at Susan. Susan looks at Lessie*) Shore dark out t' night. Must-a clouded up since I come in.

GRANNY. Hain't a cloud in th' sky as I cain see. (*They all look toward Granny. She munches. Orry closes the door and sits down*) You arnin' that new calicy dress-a mine, Lessie?

LESSIE. It 's all arned and hung up, Granny.

GRANNY. What?

LESSIE. Yes.

GRANNY. Well, don't git sassy. I heerd you th' fust time. (*Pause*) Susy.

SUSAN. Yes, ma.

[*Going to Granny.*

GRANNY. These choclit draps shore hits th' spot. You folks don't never git me no choclit draps. That young feller ain't so bad. What 's he a doin' now?

SUSAN. Shshsh. He 's a talkin' to Lessie.

GRANNY. What 's he a talkin' 'bout?

SUSAN. About cuttin' fodder, last I heard.

GRANNY. Fodder? Oh, shucks!

[*She scrootches and nibbles. Susan casts a glance at Orry and Lessie, smiles, and leaves by the rear door.*

ORRY. I usta he'p my ma arn. When I had a ma.

LESSIE. Ain't you got no ma no more?

ORRY. Nope. She went an' died. I ain't got no one t' look after me no more. That 's why I 'm like I am. I ain't got no one to look after me.

LESSIE. Aw.

ORRY. I been kinda on th' look-out fer someone t' look after me. You . . . know.

LESSIE. Who you ca'culate you 'll git, Orry?

ORRY. Gosh durn . . . I don't know. But . . . (*Lowering his head and peeking at her from the corners of his eyes*) . . . I got my eye on someone.

[*She looks up from her work. She catches his glance. She lowers her head and blushes.*

LESSIE. Oh.

[*There is an awkward pause. Then Orry breaks it.*

ORRY. Lessie . . . cud I he'p you arn a bit?

[*He gets up.*

LESSIE. I reckon you cud ef you was a mind to, Orry. But Granny wudn't like et.

ORRY. Why not?

LESSIE. Cause she don't like t' see men-folks doin' th' women-folks' work.

ORRY (*sitting down*). Oh. Well. I guess I better not do it then. She's got a lot-a power around this house, ain't she? [*He pulls out his handkerchief and blows his nose very, very audibly.*

LESSIE. She ain't got so much as she thinks she has. Us folks all 'umors her.

ORRY. I bet her husban' had to mind his P's and Q's, didn't he? [*Orry puts his handkerchief into his pocket. Not noticing, he gets it mixed up with an ironed piece on the chair. The next few minutes he spends stuffing a garment — it is a lady's garment — into his pocket. He is talking and doesn't notice it.*

LESSIE. Gran'pa Painsberry never went to school. He never knowed no more 'n th' law 'll allow.

ORRY. You 're perty smart, though, ain't you, Lessie?

LESSIE. Oh, not very. But I cain read quite a bit.

ORRY. Gosh darn, I wisht I cud read more. I don't have much time to read or nothin'. I never had many books. I . . . (*Lessie has caught sight of Orry stuffing the garment into his hip pocket. She doesn't know what to say. She smiles*) . . . I never been to school, much. But when I git a little money ahead . . . Whut you . . . grinnin' at, Lessie? [*He stops.*

LESSIE. Oh. I was jest a grinnin' at myse'f.

ORRY. I was only a puttin' my handkerchief away, Lessie.

LESSIE. I didn't mean no harm, Orry.

ORRY (*looking toward Granny*). Don't your folks never go to bed?

LESSIE. She's jest stayin' up 'cause you're here.

ORRY. I hain't much t' set up for.

LESSIE. No one ever comes in, much. Specially in the evenings. It gets kinda lonesome . . . for me . . . around here.

ORRY. I git kinda lonesome over to Youngses, too. They're all right. But I ain't nothin' but a hired man. They ain't no one there fer me t' talk to.

LESSIE. Us folks 'ud like t' have you come over ever' now an' then.

ORRY (*shyly*). That's whut I ca'culated on doin'.

[*He grins.*

LESSIE. Aw.

ORRY. It'd be kinda cold out t' taik a walk, wouldn't et?

LESSIE. It's perty cold out.

ORRY. Yeh. Still . . . et hain't *very* cold out. Do you ca'culate you cud go a buggy-ridin' with me some time next summer, Lessie?

LESSIE. I reckon I cud ef th' weather wa'n't too bad. Of course . . . bein's you was to ast me to.

ORRY. I'm a astin' you to now, Lessie.

LESSIE. Oh. Why . . . (*Pause*) I'd . . . kind-a like to, Orry. I never been buggy-ridin' with no boy . . . yet.

ORRY. I never neither.

LESSIE. I heard tell et's awful nice, though.

ORRY. I heard tell th' same thing. I'd like t' see fer myse'f, though. A person cain't tell nothin' from hearsay. (*He gets up and opens the door to spit out*) Shore is dark out. Don't see a solitary star. (*Lessie laughs to herself, but says nothing. He closes the door and sits down again*) Well . . . (*Gets out his watch and winds it*) . . . I reckon I orta be a moseyin' on home.

LESSIE. Don't be in no hurry.

ORRY. Don't think I have been, Lessie. When I come,

I didn't ca'culate t' stay this long. I thought maybe you'd run me offn th' place.

LESSIE. Aw. You know I wouldn't run you offn th' place, Orry. You jest come on over when you git lonesome an' want to.

ORRY. Thanks, Lessie. I'll r'member that. I like t' stick around here. You folks is all so homely.

LESSIE. Homely?

ORRY. I mean . . . so kinda home-like.

LESSIE (*low*). Oh. I . . . guess . . . that's 'cause we like you, Orry.

ORRY (*blushing*). Aw, Lessie! Gosh durn!

GRANNY (*turning her head*). You hain't very fast t' do business, air you, young feller?

ORRY (*perking up his head*). Ah . . .

GRANNY. I heard ever' word you been a sayin'. I cain see you're perty sweet on Lessie. Them choclit draps you brung me is first-rate. Th' folks 'round here don't give me nothin' to chew on but t'baccer. I guess you hain't so bad. You ain't got much spunk, though. A feller's got to have spunk t' git on in this world.

ORRY. Ag'in I gits all riled up, a person'd never know how much spunk I got in me! Nobody knows how much spunk I got!

GRANNY. I'm a goin' to poke off t' bed. Oh, Susy. Susy!

LESSIE. Mom's gone to bed already, Granny.

GRANNY. Well . . . why didn't she tell me she was a goin' t' bed?

[*Granny gets up from her chair. She holds the sack of candy close to her.*

GRANNY. Come yur, young feller.

ORRY. What you want?

GRANNY (*eyeing him closely*). Lessie's a right nice little girl. But you got a good voice. You got good eyes. I reckon you ain't so bad.

ORRY. I'm perty good. Leastwise . . . I always try to be.

GRANNY. Them choclits shore filled me up right. Jest drap

in anny night t' see Lessie. I likes peppamint-draps, too.
Peppamint-draps is good fer th' stomick t' settle et.
They 're a kind of a physic, too, they say.

LESSIE. Granny!

GRANNY (*scornfully*). What's wrong with you?

[*She passes Lessie and starts for the lower door left.*

LESSIE. What you goin' to do, Granny?

GRANNY. I 'm a goin' to show this-yur young feller my bran'
new white calicy dress.

ORRY. But . . . but . . .

[*He doesn't understand why she goes to the door downstage.
To Lessie.*

ORRY. But . . . her dress ain't out-doors, is et?

LESSIE. It 's in the closet.

[*Granny opens the door and goes in. Orry stands dumbfounded. Lessie breaks out laughing.*

ORRY. But . . . Lessie! What 've I been a doin'?

LESSIE. You been a spittin' into th' closet, Orry!

ORRY. Aw.

[*His jaw drops ten degrees. Lessie has great fun. Granny
comes out with the dress. She holds it before her spread out.
It is spattered with tobacco juice. She hasn't seen that yet.
Orry is paralyzed when he discovers it. Lessie stares.*

GRANNY. They all aroun' here think I 'm dead an' gone
a'ready. I 'm a goin' t' fool 'em a trip or two. They 's a
barn-dance over to Hank Wagnerses t'morry an' I 'm a
goin' over t' show 'em all how t' cut th' pigeon's wing.
This ol' chicken . . .

[*She sees the two standing speechless. She views them over
her spectacles. Then she looks down at the dress. Immediately she becomes alive.*

GRANNY. Lessie . . . is them fly-specks on my bran' new
white calicy dress?

[*She hurries to the table and lays the dress on it to examine it.*

ORRY. I . . . I guess I . . . better 'd be goin' . . . home,
Lessie.

GRANNY. T'baccer spit! (*She smells and examines*) T'bac-

cer spit! (*She frets and stews*) T'baccer spit on my bran'
new calicy dress! (*She turns furiously*) Lessie! You
. . . you . . .

[*She spies Orry's looks. He is about ready to break out
crying.*

ORRY. I . . . I . . . I . . . I . . . I . . .

GRANNY. You been a spittin' all over my dress, ain't you?
You're a fine one, hain't you? Th' best thing you cain do
is t' hit fer home as fast as you cain, an' never step foot
onto this forty ag'in as long's I live! Th' idea-a you a
comin' into a person's house an' spittin' all over his bran
new calicy dress! You're a nice one, ain't you? Et
won't come out, neither. Nothing'll take t'baccer spit
out! I've tried many's-th'-time t' warsh t'baccer spit
out-a Lute's underpants. An' et won't warsh out no way!
Hain't you a nice feller to come a sparkin' a gal an' hain't
got no more manners about you as to spit all over th' house
this-a-way! Look at th' floor in there! Pity me!

[*She stoops to examine.*

ORRY. I . . . I . . . I guess I better'd go on . . . home,
Lessie. I done enough mischief fer one night. An' I
wanted to be so nice!

GRANNY. Yes. I guess you'd better'd! I'm a goin' to tell
Missus Young all about this! She orta know th' kind-a
feller you air. Most likely you been a spittin' in th' butter,
an' spittin' down into th' cistern, an' . . . spittin' . . .

ORRY (*to Lessie*). I guess I . . . shore made a . . . mess-a
things tonight . . . didn't I, Lessie?

LESSIE. Don't feel bad, Orry. 'Twa'nt your fault.

ORRY. My pa always sayed I was a blockhead. Now I
know I am.

LESSIE. No you ain't, Orry. You ain't neither!

GRANNY (*raising her head from the dress which she frets over*).
Well . . . what you stickin' around fer? You done your
do. You shore done a plenty, too. (*She holds out the
dress*) Hain't that a nice lookin' spectacle after you gone
an' messed all over et?

ORRY. I'll . . . buy you another'n.

GRANNY. I'd like t' know how you'll buy me another'n? You ain't got a second paar-a pants to your name, let alone buyin' me a new calicy dress!

ORRY. I . . . I know . . . et.

GRANNY. Well.

[*She wads the dress up and puts it under her arm.*

ORRY (*to Lessie*). I'm awful sorry I . . . went an' done that. I guess I hadn't . . . orta come over . . . but I . . . you know . . .

LESSIE. You don't need to be sorry, Orry.

ORRY. I . . . I guess I . . . ah . . . (*He turns abruptly and takes a few steps*) . . . good-bye, Lessie.

LESSIE. Orry . . . what you a goin' t' do?

ORRY. I'm a goin' home . . . maybe. An' . . . maybe I ain't.

[*He starts out the wrong door; becomes confused; goes to the other one.*

GRANNY (*mumbling*). A perty sight, ain't et? A perty sight t' b'hold! I'd like t' know how a person cain ever . . .

[*She grumbles and starts for the rear door.*

ORRY (*turning at the door*). Good . . . good . . .

LESSIE. Orry . . . please don't go. Perty please!

ORRY. I'm goin'. An' you mayn't never see me ag'in, Lessie!

[*He lunges out and slams the door after him.*

LESSIE. Granny . . . Granny . . . looky what you've gone an' done!

GRANNY. Looky what he went an' done!

LESSIE. He's goin' out to kill hisse'f!

GRANNY. Don't be no fool, Lessie.

LESSIE. But . . . Granny? . . . (*Lessie runs to the outside door. She throws it open, steps onto the porch, and calls*) Orry! Orry! Orry!

[*There is no reply. She comes back in and closes the door. Granny goes into the other room muttering to herself. Lessie goes to a chair, drops into it, and cries.*

Soon the outside door opens, and Orry comes in, silently.
He goes to Lessie's chair and drops on his knees at her feet.
He touches her hand with the tips of his big fingers.

LESSIE. Orry!

ORRY. Lessie . . . I heard you a-callin' me. I couldn't go
nowheres 'thouten astin' you . . . cud you forgive me th'
way I sinned, Lessie? I guess I was . . . born silly . . .
Lessie.

LESSIE. 'Course I'll forgive you, Orry. B'sides . . . you
ain't silly.

ORRY. Don't cry, Lessie. Here. (*He reaches into his hip*
pocket for his handkerchief. He pulls out the woman's gar-
ment and dries her eyes with it) Don't cry, Lessie. Me and
. . . you . . . we could . . . we . . . could . . .
[*They both discover the "handkerchief." Lessie breaks out*
laughing.

LESSIE. Oh, Orry! What you got in your hand?

ORRY (*arising, horrified, bashful, delighted*). Lessie . . .
gosh durn et . . . how . . . (*A gasp for breath*) . . .
how did that thing-a-ma-jigger get about me, annyways?
[*Lessie laughs. Orry breaks out laughing. He puts the gar-*
ment onto the table; but not before touching his face surrepti-
tiously with it.

LESSIE. I . . . I guess you ain't yourse'f t'night, are you,
Orry?

ORRY. Dog-gone, I don't know what's th' matter with me
t'night. I guess . . . (*He goes to the stove to get Granny's*
chair to draw up to Lessie's) . . . I guess . . . (*Looking*
shyly over his shoulder toward her) . . . et must be . . .
you, Lessie.

LESSIE. I . . . guess *you're* a talkin' through *your* hat now,
ain't you, Orry?
[*He starts toward her with the chair. Granny pokes her head*
in. She has on a nightcap. Orry stops short.

GRANNY. You cain't fool me. I knowed you was there all
th' time! You ain't such a big dunce arter all. I knowed
you'd come back. You don't need t' be 'fraid-a me none

no more, young feller.   I figured out I'll color that-thur
dress coal black an' wear et t' old granny Dill's funeral
when she dies.   An' ef I die fust . . . I'll wear et t' my
own.
[*She grins.   Orry grins.   Lessie grins.*

CURTAIN

RECKLESS

LYNN RIGGS

THE PLAYS of Lynn Riggs are the "Westerns" of folk drama, if one may use the term in a nostalgic sense that suggests poetic interpretation of the lives of the pioneers and the Indians who met in the great Southwest.

Mr. Riggs was born at Claremore, now Oklahoma, but in 1899 Indian Territory; and like most boys of the day his first reading included the works of Horatio Alger and the stories about Diamond Dick. The jobs he held while acquiring an education were many: driving a grocery store delivery-wagon, working in a glass factory or an express office, singing in a movie house, acting in the movies, selling books in Macy's, and reading proof for the *Wall Street Journal*. Before graduating from the University of Oklahoma, he had been to the Western coast and to New York, and he had taught Freshman English.

Then he toured the Middle West as a singer with a Chautauqua circuit; worked on a ranch in Santa Fe, worked in Chicago and in New York. Recently he has been in Hollywood, writing for Schulberg Pictures.

His two one-act published plays are "Knives from Syria" and "Reckless." His longer plays that have been published are: "Big Lake", "Sump'n Like Wings", "A Lantern to See By", "Green Grow the Lilacs", "Roadside" (also called "Borned in Texas"), "Russet Mantle" and "Cherokee Night." In addition, his "Rancor" has been much produced since Jasper Deeter first gave it at the Hedgerow Theatre near Philadelphia.

Lynn Riggs has also contributed poetry to various magazines and periodicals.

RECKLESS

BY LYNN RIGGS

"Reckless" was originally produced by the Little Theatre of Davis, at Norman, Oklahoma, on April 2, 1930.

Original Cast

PAP RADER . . . . Hardin McAdoo
BUZZEY HALE . . . . Gordon Slover
HANNIE . . . . Pauline Edwards
RED IKE BRAZIER . . . . Jack Garrison
BLACK IKE BRAZIER . . . . Lynn Norman
RECKLESS . . . . Page Willis

Directed by Grace Garrison

RECKLESS

Scene. *By the side of a road through the woods, in Indian Territory, many years ago. The back end of a covered wagon, with a box for stepping down out of it, can be seen at left. The road, coming in at the back from deep in the woods, has been widened here by hundreds of campers. Trash and tin cans litter the roadside. A large black pot with a fire under it stands at the right. Some old camp chairs, a battered stool or two, dishes, tin pans, etc. It is near sundown of a day in June, and the air is summery and sweet.*

[*Buzzey Hale, a little, bluish, dried-up man, is sitting disconsolately by the fire. Pap Rader, a tall, wiry, good-natured old man, with dirty, falling-apart clothes, comes from around the wagon.*

PAP RADER (*snorting*). Set there a-pinin'. Damned if you doan look like a ole turkey buzzard! No wonder Hannie called you Buzzey.

BUZZEY (*shortly*). That ain't it. Buzzey is short — fer beautiful.

PAP. Beautiful! Huh! If you're beautiful, I'm a bob-tailed witch. Looky here, I doan see whut you make outa follerin' us around anyway, Mister Turkey Buzzard. They ain't nuthin' dead around here fer you to chaw on. Clappin' yer wings! An' damned if that sorry face o' yourn ain't blue, too, same as a buzzard! After you've et, things must be a sight. I doan wanna be around.

BUZZEY. I ain't wantin' you around.

PAP. I'm gonna *be* around, though. Smoke that.

BUZZEY (*with anxiety*). Yeow, you'll be. If it hadn't a-been fer you, Hannie wouldn't a-left me in the first place. You done it with yer damned ole covered wagon. Tellin' her about the roads again. Remindin' her of when she uz a girl ridin' hell-bent from Arkansaw to Panhandle alongside you an' yer ole womern. You brung her up. I'll say you brung her up, with her ways! Wonder I ever married her a-tall an' her with a ole man like you couldn't read a sign on a hitch-post. Whut'd you think about? Ridin' on the road, that's all you think about. From here t' Texas, and back to Wyoming and all over the cattle roads, and little shike-pole towns from here to Missouri. Stealin' chickens an' roast'n'-ears an' sich, t' keep you alive. (*In disgust*) The road! That's all you think about!

PAP. Whut you think about is plowin'.

BUZZEY. Yeow, an' makin' hay an' plantin' corn an' oats an' feedin' cattle an' shoats — livin' outa the ground, is whut I think about. I'd like to know whut's better?

PAP. This *here's* better. An' I'm tellin' you Hannie'd *orter* divorced you like she did. You ain't no kind of a man, an' yore life ain't no kind of a life fer Hannie t' be havin'. She's a strappin' girl that wants to roam, like me, an' see life 'stid of a milk churn.

BUZZEY. I'll git her back, you'll see. If I have to foller you up Salt Crick.

PAP (*chuckling*). If you foller us too long, yer crops'll all be ruint. Here it is June an' I'll bet yer hay ain't even first cut.

BUZZEY. It's cut, Pap Rader. I got money t' h'ar me h'ard hands.

PAP. An' while you ain't there how hard you reckon they work? (*Chortling*) I used t' be a h'ard hand myself. When ole man Hardgraves uz away we'd se' down an' not git up till his buggy wheels rattled the pike comin' home from Joplin.

BUZZEY. When *I* h'ar men, I ha'r *men*. Red Ike and Black Ike Brazier — that's the kinda men *I* h'ar. I've knowed em from boys up. Ever since Hannie married me, Red Ike an' Black Ike has worked on my farm same as if uz theirn, an' ud git the last drap of growin' out of it.

PAP. Well, I hope yer right. 'Cause if you ain't, you'll git
sick an' turn bluer 'n you be a'ready.

BUZZEY. I'm right, Pap Rader.

PAP. Ain't nobody right fer too long at a time, I noticed.

HANNIE'S VOICE (*from inside the wagon*). Pap!

PAP. Whut is it?

HANNIE (*excitedly*). Pap, come 'ere!

PAP. Come 'ere, yerself. I'm busy. (*To Buzzey*) If you
doan git sense enough to stop follerin' us from county to
county the way you been doin' fer a week, you'll sleep here
on the cold ground till you die of the shakin' aygers.

HANNIE (*from the wagon*). Pap! You heard me, you tarna-
tion ole fool! Come a-runnin'! Cain't you hear nuthin'?

PAP. Well, whut is it? Come out here an' tell it.

HANNIE (*sticking her head out*). I ain't got s' many clothes
on. An' I doan 'spect t' come out an' give that ole buzzard no free show. He's crazy enough fer a womern 'thout
seein' one naked. Case you'd like t' know it, that hound
of yourn is eatin' up yer hog shoulder.

PAP (*flying around the wagon and out of sight*). Well, why in
blazes didden you say so!

HANNIE. I said so.

[*She withdraws her head. A hound lets out a dismal wail
and a series of short yelps.*

BUZZEY (*going up to the wagon*). Whur'd yer Pap git a hog
shoulder, Hannie? Guess he bought it —

HANNIE (*putting her head out again*). Bought it, huh? Stole
it offen the slaughter house at Claremore.

BUZZEY. I knowed it.

HANNIE. You're s' smart.

[*She withdraws.*

PAP (*coming around the wagon*). I saved that dog from
drownin' an' this is the way he does me. A good hog shoulder plum ruint. (*He holds up a mutilated hog shoulder*)
Here, might as well have it all now you've ruint it, you
yeller cur. (*He throws the shoulder back to the dog*) I'm
goin' down along the crick bank an' see whut I c'n see.

BUZZEY (*nastily*). Watermelons ain't ripe yit, Pap.

PAP. Who said watermelons?

BUZZEY. Roast 'n' ears 'll be ripe in July, though.

PAP. I 'm gonna git a mite of hay fer the horses. Stir that stew if you 're gonna stick round here. You 'll be wantin' some in yer measly gullet afore long. (*He starts out*) I 'm gonna jist look t' see if they 's any fish while I 'm about it. (*Turning back*) Looky here, you let Hannie alone. She ain't gonna marry you *again*. An' she ain't gonna have no *truck* with you 's long 's I 'm around, you hear me?

BUZZEY. I hear you.

PAP. You better heed me.

[*He goes out.*

Buzzey stirs the stew, tastes it, and is about to pour some in a bowl when he hears singing down the road. He puts the bowl down hastily, wrinkles his forehead, trying to make out something. Hannie comes out of the wagon and down the steps. She is a buxom, well-made girl about twenty, with black snapping eyes and a rich, vulgar, earthy humor. She crosses over past the fire.

BUZZEY. Hannie. (*She stops*) Hannie, you ain't runnin' away from me, air you?

HANNIE. I doan know you from Adam.

BUZZEY. Don't you do me this a-way, Hannie.

HANNIE. What a-way?

BUZZEY. Not havin' no words with me, even.

HANNIE. Why 're you follerin' us all the way from Vinita, me and Pap?

BUZZEY. I cain't he'p it. Cain't you come back to me?

HANNIE. Not to you ner no one like you. I want me a man, not a broomstick. Besides, I had enough of bein' a farmer's wife.

BUZZEY. It uz cause you 'd been s' sharp to me, I done whut I done. You wouldn't a-got no divorce from me if some-one hadden fixed it up fer you t' find me the way you did.

HANNIE. Oh, woulden I? Sich a womern I found you with too! You must been in a bad way. Who fixed it then?

BUZZEY. I ain't sayin'.

HANNIE. Well, whoever fixed it, you fixed yerself with me.

BUZZEY. Hannie, come on back! The — the ca'ves even doan know me. Old Roan kicks at me ever time I go in the barn. They won't have nuthin' t' do with *me*. They're missin' you, I reckon.

HANNIE. Well, I been missed by ca'ves and horses afore. I'm that kind of a womern. But I never heared of no dumb animals dyin' of a broke heart. Quit a-botherin' me now.

BUZZEY. Aw, Hannie, lemme go with you. Air you goin' to pick up sticks?

HANNIE. No, I ain't.

BUZZEY. Er find wild ingerns? I'll help you do whutever you're a-goin' fer. Guess I'll foller you.

HANNIE. Guess you won't, Mister Buzzey Hale. (*Roguishly*) I ain't gonna do nuthin' you c'n he'p me do.

[*She goes out.*

The song down the road comes nearer. Buzzey listens, uncertain and worried. Then he straightens up decisively and is a rod of cold anger, when Red Ike and Black Ike Brazier burst into sight through the trees along the road. They have on straw hats, overalls, dirty blue shirts, heavy brogans, and are leaning on each other's shoulders, singing loudly. Black Ike's hair is coal black, Red's a flaming red. They are stupid and elfin at the same time. Seeing Buzzey, they stop short, and make a sudden instinctive move to run away, which they quickly suppress.

BUZZEY. Well, by God! It's you, is it?

RED IKE (*swallowing hard*). Yeow, it's us.

BLACK IKE. Red Ike and Black Ike — *both* of us.

BUZZEY (*furiously*). Red Ike and Black Ike, hell! Of all the sorry, mangy — dirty — Whut in hell're you doin' here anyhow? Whut'd you mean flyin' off leavin' my farm t' run itself? How long you been gone? You're two days away now! I'll bet the hogs've died fer slop! I'll bet

the hay's burnt up in the field! I'll bet the corn's just
bakin' in the row —

RED IKE. Is this yore campin' outfit?

BUZZEY (*outraged*). Campin'!

BLACK IKE. You a campin' man now, Mister Hale? We
didden know whur you'd went at.

RED IKE. You got some soup?

BUZZEY. Soup!

BLACK IKE. We're powerful hongry. Ain't et in a
day.

RED IKE. Been a-singin' t' keep up our sperrits.

BUZZEY. Singin'!

BLACK IKE. Et some strawberries, though.

BUZZEY (*violently*). I don't keer if you starve! Whut'd
you leave my farm fur! Thought I could trust it to
you.

BLACK IKE. Mister Hale, we never thunk to a-run onto you,
I swear t' my time. We didden know whur you wuz, not
showin' up. Thought mebbe you drowned in the bottom
some'ers.

RED IKE. We uz a-lookin' fer someone else.

BLACK IKE. Is this the —? (*He is looking over past the
wagon*) By gum it is!

RED IKE. It's the horses.

BUZZEY. You git back quick's you c'n hotfoot it, both of
you. I'd orter thrash you 'thin a inch of yer lives! *Git*,
I tell you!

RED IKE. We're gonna stay.

[*He sits down, cross-legged.*

BLACK IKE (*following suit*). We're gonna set here and stay,
ain't we, Red?

BUZZEY. You're f'ard, both of you!

RED IKE. Suits me. Cain't make *me* mad.

BUZZEY. I'd orter f'ar you.

BLACK IKE. We're a'ready done f'ard.

BUZZEY. No, you ain't! You 'greed t' he'p me git the hay in
an' stay th'ough the thrashin'.

RED IKE. We 'll he'p you.

BUZZEY (*helplessly*). Well, don't set there. Git back like I told you.

RED IKE. We just come.

BUZZEY. Look here. I 'd orten't t' do this — you 're both so onery — but I 'll give you five dollars.

RED IKE. Le 's see it.

[*Buzzey hands him a bill.*

BLACK IKE. Le 's see another 'n.

[*Buzzey hands over another.*

Red Ike and Black Ike look at each other, then hand the bills back.

RED IKE. Don't hurry us.

BUZZEY. You better take it. Why, you 're damn fools! It 'll buy you near ten plugs of Horseshoe.

BLACK IKE (*spitting*). 'Druther chew Star Navy.

BUZZEY. Well, Star Navy.

BLACK IKE (*irrelevantly*). Chew Star Navy an' spit ham gravy.

BUZZEY. Look here, if I give you ten dollars apiece — no, I won't give you ten dollars.

RED IKE. Woulden take it.

BUZZEY (*suspiciously*). How much you tryin' t' bleed outa me?

RED IKE. Not any.

BUZZEY. Whut 'd you come fur anyway?

RED IKE (*evasively*). Oh — jist seen the purty road an' started off a-follerin' it.

BLACK IKE. You caint keep no colt in the pasture when it 's summer. We uz puttin' up the mules an' I says t' Red, "Red," I says, "How about it?" An' Red says, "How about it yerself?" So up we got an' away we went till we come t' Verdigree Switch. There they uz a great to-do of a man shootin' his way into jail, so we hurry up and here we be.

BUZZEY. You got sump'n up yer sleeve.

RED IKE. Why, Mister Hale, no. No, we ain't. Mebbe

you're right though. Mebbe we have got sump'n up our
sleeves. (*Breaking off, excitedly*) Oh!
[*He scrambles to his feet.*

BLACK IKE (*doing likewise*). It's her.

RED IKE. She's a-comin'!

BLACK IKE. She's here!

HANNIE (*coming in, ecstatically*). Hello! Howdy! Red Ike
and Black Ike! *Thought* I heared yer voices!

RED IKE. *Thought* we'd find you! —

BLACK IKE. *Knowed* we'd find you! —

RED IKE. — 'f we looked long enough —

BLACK IKE. — 'n in the right place —

RED IKE. — 'n on the right road.

HANNIE. If I ain't missed you! —

RED IKE. We missed *you*.

BLACK IKE. Come on back, what you say?

RED IKE. 'Spect us to work 'thout you around?

BLACK IKE. Marry the ole buzzard again.

RED IKE. Put up with him.

HANNIE. Quit it! I'm s' glad to see you, I'll be promisin' to,
in a minute!

BUZZEY. Hannie! Go on, promise! I'll be good to you if
you come back. Git you a carpet sweeper.

BLACK IKE. Go on, promise! Think of me an' Red. Not
hardly able to do no work 'thout you around.

RED IKE. Think of me an' Black. In the field honin' fer you.

BUZZEY. Think of *me*, why don't you, Hannie?

HANNIE. Now, now! Quit it! I'm gonna think of my*self*
a while. Here, set down and eat some soup.

BUZZEY (*hopefully*). You ain't said you *wouldn't* come back.

HANNIE. An' I ain't said I *would*.
[*She gives them all soup. They sit down and eat.*

BLACK IKE. We're hungry.

RED IKE. Ain't et in a day.

HANNIE. 'S just like ole times. Me an' Buzzey an' you Ikes
settin' around. If I ain't missed you! Ever once in a while
I git so homesick I'd purt' near kick paw in the pants, an'

hotfoot it back. I wanta set quiet once in a while, an' drink milk out of a cold well.

BUZZEY. We got milk, Hannie. Ever since ole Reddy come in with her calf —

HANNIE. But paw 's sich a goer. Has to cross that next crick, or make the next aidge of town 'fore sundown. Lissen to me, I 'm gonna tell you sump'n. Men is s' crazy. Some wants to set on a farm till they dry up an' blow away — like Buzzey here. Or some wants to go streakin' across the country, hell-bent, like a dose of salts th'ough a widder womern — like paw. If they uz just a half-way crazy man who liked to streak, an' liked to set — *both*. A nonsensical strappin' man who had a good time settin' *or* streakin' — but who had a *good time* — (*She breaks off*) Now tell me things.

BLACK IKE. Whut about?

HANNIE. Oh, anything. The way you used to.

BLACK IKE (*to Red*). 'Bout the ghostes?

RED IKE. On Mabel Gardner's bed post?

HANNIE. I heared that.

BLACK IKE. I know! The man in the sack.

RED IKE. Chinaman!

BLACK IKE. Sewed in a gunny sack.

RED IKE. Mad as a steer!

BLACK IKE. Hung up to the ceiling!

HANNIE. I heared that, too.

BLACK IKE. Oh! She 's heared that. Oh, I know! We 'll tell her about Reckless! Wanta hear about Reckless?

HANNIE. Who 's Reckless?

BLACK IKE. Well, we seen sich a sight. Didden we, Red?

RED IKE. Down at the Switch as we come th'ough.

BLACK IKE. A man th'owed in the jail fer gettin' drunk.

RED IKE. He got drunk an' crazy an' wild. An' he yelled. My, how he yelled!

BLACK IKE. Whut wuz it he yelled? "Borned in Texas —" How 'd it go?

RED IKE (*loudly*).

> Wild an' reckless,
> Borned in Texas,
> Suckled by a bear,
> Steel backbone,
> Tail screwed on,
> Twelve feet long,
> Dare any son of a gun to step on it!

HANNIE. Purty!

BUZZEY (*disgusted*). Purty!

RED IKE. 'Nen the law got a-holt of him, an' the jedge said, "Twelve days in jail, one fer ever foot of yer long tail." So they went to th'ow him in jail an' he kicked the jedge offen the bench an' made just plum hash outa the court room first 'fore they got him in the calaboose.

HANNIE. Good!

BUZZEY (*disgusted*). Good!

RED IKE. My, a big, hulky, curly-headed, han'some ring-tail-tooter, wuzn't he, Black?

HANNIE. An' whur is he?

RED IKE. Sh! Down the road a piece.

HANNIE. Outa jail?

BLACK IKE. Shore. Lissen. Me 'n Red seen him, 's we come along. Like to scairt us to death, too. Come up on us, and said, "I broke outa jail, an' if you tell on me, I'll break yer head." My, we woulden tell on him, would we, Red?

HANNIE (*thoughtfully*). Down the road there?

BLACK IKE (*pointing back*). That road right there.

BUZZEY. You ain't interested in a man like that, air you, Hannie? A man 'at breaks laws, an' don't have no home, an' goes shootin' around —

HANNIE (*cryptically*). Shet up about it. I hate a man like that.

BUZZEY. That's whut I thought. Here comes yer pap.

[*Pap Rader comes in with an armful of hay for the horses. He drops it in astonishment.*

PAP RADER. Red Ike and Black Ike! (*Gleefully*) I knowed it, I knowed it! (*To Buzzey*) Whut'd I tell you about h'ard hands! — Hee! Hee! Knowed they wouldn't work 'thout you around!

[*There is a pistol shot at back, quite near.*

HANNIE (*rushing over to Pap*). Hey, Pap, they's a man comin' along the road! (*In an excited rush, thumping Pap on the chest at every sentence*) Wild an' reckless, borned in Texas! A tail twelve feet long! He shot his way into jail and outa jail, an' he's comin' along that road there, an' heavens an' earth, whut 're you gonna do!

RECKLESS' VOICE (*off back*).
Wild an' reckless,
Borned in Texas!

HANNIE. Hear that! It's him! I'm gonna run in the wagon, quick!

PAP RADER. Why, Hannie! Nuthin' won't hurt you. We got guns.

BUZZEY (*coming over*). Don't you be afeard, little womern. I'll pertect you. An' in the mornin' we'll go back home.

HANNIE (*turns on him*). Why, you little dried-up, stinkin', blue-nosed ole buzzard smellin' of a dead cow in the summer time! Go home with you? (*She laughs uproariously*) Go home with a dead stick! I got better idys 'n that. I'm gonna go in the wagon.

BUZZEY. Whut fer, Hannie?

HANNIE. I'm gonna put flour on my face, an' purty myself up — that's whut fer!

[*She goes up into the wagon.*

BUZZEY (*puzzled*). Now whut on earth's come over her?

PAP RADER. Damned if I know. Whut's this about a man?

BUZZEY. Why, Red an' Black says this is a wild crazy han'-some man, who don't respect no law, ner live nowhur, an' says he uz borned in Texas, an' he's comin' along the road an' —

PAP RADER (*thoughtfully*). Hmm. Oh! Texas.

BUZZEY. Whut'd you mean — *Texas?*

PAP RADER (*with an amused chuckle*). Hannie. That's whur *she* uz borned at.

RECKLESS' VOICE (*coming nearer*).
Steel backbone,
Tail screwed on,
Twelve feet long,
Dare any son of a gun to step on it!

CURTAIN

THE TERRIBLE MEEK

CHARLES RANN KENNEDY

ONE of Charles Rann Kennedy's plays begins thus:
"The Time might be any. It is Always: Even To-day."
In those words also, the place of Kennedy's writings in an
anthology of one-act plays may be suggested. For he was a
pioneer with the earliest in the work of writing short plays;
and The Bennett School of Liberal and Applied Arts, at
Millbrook, New York, of which he and his wife, Edith Wynne
Matthison, are trustees, has conducted a Drama Department
which is a pioneer in the Junior College field. Like the others
who broke away from the commercial theatre, his Repertory
Company of three players has introduced artistic productions
to communities throughout the United States, Canada, and
England. And before American dramatists in general were
aware of the political scene and its social implications, he was
writing about it, and producing his plays in the most modern-
istic, informal ways. In fact, the scope of his activity extends
over the last quarter of a century.

Charles Rann Kennedy is the eldest of the authors included
in this volume. Although born in Derby, England, in 1871,
of a famous English family of scholars and educators, nearly
all of his playwriting has been done in the United States for
production here. He was largely self-educated, and, owing
to an early reversal of the family's fortunes, began to earn
his own living at the age of thirteen. But even by that time
he had picked up the beginnings of a classical education at
home, and had a fair equipment in Latin, Greek, Shakespeare,
Milton, and the Bible.

He has been office boy, lawyer's clerk, telegraph clerk,
socialist lecturer (he fought for the dockers in the Hull Dock

strike when he was about twenty), writer of short stories and poems, and actor with the late Beerbohm Tree.

In recent years his Company of Three Players (Miss Matthison, Miss Gage, and the author himself) have acted chiefly in his own plays.

His two shortest plays are "The Terrible Meek" and "The Necessary Evil." "The Terrible Meek" was written three years and a half before the beginning of the World War, in Passion Week of 1911, and produced in New York the following year. Although it was banned in London, Berlin, and St. Petersburg, it was produced one way or another, and as far as China, some thousands of times before the conflict. During the succeeding years, it has been a regular Lenten and Advent offering in churches of all denominations, and it is broadcasted from a number of stations in many parts of the world every Good Friday.

Kennedy's longer plays are: "The Chastening", "The Admiral", "The Salutation", "Old Nobody", "Crumbs", "Flaming Ministers", "Face of God", "Beggar's Gift" (all collected in *Plays for Three Players*); and "The Servant in the House", "The Winterfeast", "The Idol-Breaker", "The Rib of the Man", "The Army with Banners", "The Fool from the Hills", published with the short plays in *Plays for Seven Players*.

THE TERRIBLE MEEK

By CHARLES RANN KENNEDY

"The Terrible Meek" was originally produced in Lent, 1912, at the Little Theatre, New York, under the management of Winthrop Ames.

Original Cast

A PEASANT WOMAN	Edith Wynne Matthison
AN ARMY CAPTAIN	Sydney Valentine
A SOLDIER	Reginald Barlow

THE TERRIBLE MEEK

Before the curtain rises, a bell from some distant place of worship tolls the hour. Nine brazen notes, far off, out of tune. Then a heavy peal of thunder, and the sharp, cracking strike of a bolt; yet, above all, one other sound, more piercing — a strange, unearthly Cry. There follows a mighty howling of wind, blended with a confused clamour of voices and the hurrying of many feet. The noises have almost all died away, when the Curtain rises upon inky darkness.

[*A sudden hush. The silence deepens. There is a sense of moorlands and desolate places.*

Far off, a cow lows in her stall. Some lost sheep down in the valley bleats dismally. Silence again.

It is broken by the Voice of a Woman, weeping bitterly; a peasant woman.

WOMAN. Oh! . . .

[*Another Voice: the gentlemanly, well-bred voice of an army man, now under some stress of emotion; a Captain.*

CAPTAIN. My God, this is awful. I can't stand it.

WOMAN. Oh! . . .

CAPTAIN. Come, my good woman, it's all over now. There's no earthly help for it. You can't remain here, you know.

WOMAN. Leave me be. Leave me be.

CAPTAIN. All the others left long ago. They hurried off home the moment — the moment the storm came. . . . Come, it's bleak and quite too dreadful for you up on this hill. Let me send you back to the town with one of the soldiers.

WOMAN. One of the — soldiers! . . .

CAPTAIN. Yes: come, come now . . .

WOMAN. Leave me be. Don't touch me. There's the smell of death on you.

CAPTAIN. Well, since you . . . And, after all . . . (*The clank and rattle of his sword and uniform mark his moving away. He sits*) The smell of death. My God, it's true. [*A bitter wind comes soughing up from the valley. The sheep bleats once, piteously. Then all is quiet again.*

Someone else is coming. He is heard stumbling blindly up over the hill, the steel butt of his weapon ringing among the stones; a Soldier.

Groping in darkness, he collides suddenly with the Captain. His Voice is that of a common man, city-bred.

SOLDIER. Gawd blimey, wot the 'ell . . . Oh, beg pawdon, sir. Didn't know it was you, Captain.

CAPTAIN. That's all right, sentry.

SOLDIER. 'Pon my word, sir, you give me a start, fust go orf. Wot with the storm an' the darkness, an' this 'ere little job we been doin', I tek my oath I thought for a moment as you was . . . well, summat else. Wasn't quite a nice thing wot 'appened up 'ere just nah, sir, was it?

CAPTAIN. It wasn't.

SOLDIER. I'm on guard myself, sir; or I don't know as I'd 'a' come up, not for choice. You bin 'ere all the time, Captain?

CAPTAIN. Have I? Yes, I suppose I have. I've been here . . . ever since.

SOLDIER. It's not exactly the place ter spend a pleasant arternoon, is it, sir?

CAPTAIN. No, I suppose not.

SOLDIER. O' course, there's company, as you might say; but not quite congenial company, eh wot?

CAPTAIN. That depends entirely upon the point of view.

SOLDIER. Dam' creepy, I call it! . . . Well, we done for '*im* good an' proper, any'ah.

CAPTAIN. My God, yes. We builders of empire know how to do our business.

SOLDIER. Pretty bloody business, too, ain't it, sir?

CAPTAIN. Yes, that's the word.

[They consider it for a moment. Presently the Soldier laughs at some amusing recollection.

SOLDIER. It's an ill wind wot blows nobody any good. *I* got summat aht o' this, orl said an' done.

CAPTAIN. What's that?

SOLDIER. I got some of 'is togs.

CAPTAIN. His togs. How do you mean?

SOLDIER. Why, I'll tell yer. *'E* didn't want no more togs, not the way 'e was goin'; nah did 'e? So me an' the boys, we got our 'eds together, and arter we'd undressed 'im an' put 'im to bed, so to speak, we pitched an' tossed for the 'ole bag lot, one by one, till they was orl bloomin' well divided aht. I got 'is boots.

CAPTAIN. You got his boots, did you?

SOLDIER. Yes, pore devil. *'E* don't want them no more. Not quite my fit; but they'll do to tek 'ome for a keep-sake — that is, if we ever do get 'ome aht of this 'ere stinkin' 'ole. My little missis 'll think a lot of them boots.

CAPTAIN. They will be a pleasant memento.

SOLDIER. Just wot *I* say, sir. Oh, my missis, she got an 'oly nose for 'orrors : she reely 'ave. Tellin' abaht them boots 'll last 'er a lifetime.

CAPTAIN. She must be an attractive young woman, your — missis.

SOLDIER. Oh, no, sir, just ordinary, just ordinary. Suits *me*, orl right. . . . (*Some memory holds him for a moment*) Funny thing, Captain, 'ow this 'ere foreign service keeps you — well, sort of thinkin', don't it? S'pose it's the lonely nights an' the long sentry duties an' such like. . . .

CAPTAIN. You've felt that too, then, have you?

SOLDIER. Yessir; meks me think abaht my missis. 'Er was in the family way when I left 'ome, sir — expectin' just a couple of month arter I sailed. . . . The little beggar 'll be gettin' on by nah — that is, if 'e come orl right.

CAPTAIN. You've made up your mind for a boy then, eh?

SOLDIER. She allus 'oped for a boy, sir. Women's like that. S'pose it's orl right; it's men wot's wanted these days,

wot with the Army an' the Spread of Empire an' orl
that.

CAPTAIN.   Yes, they make better killing.

[*The Soldier is rather stupid, or he would have laughed.   He
goes on.*

SOLDIER.   Yessir, 'er's bin 'ankerin' arter a kid ever since
we was married six year ago; but some'ow or other it
never seemed to come orf. 'Ealthy woman, too, sir.
You unnerstand 'ow these things is, Captain: there's no
tellin'. Little beggars come by guess an' by Gawd, it
seems to me. . . . I wonder if it's a boy. There's no
gettin' no news aht in this blarsted . . . Good Gawd,
wot's that? . . .

CAPTAIN.   What?

SOLDIER.   Be'ind us.   Summat sort of . . .   There, 'ark!

[*The Woman's Voice rises, sighing like wind.*

WOMAN.   Oh! . . .

SOLDIER.   My Gawd, wot is it?

CAPTAIN.   It's a woman.

SOLDIER.   A woman!   Up *'ere?*

CAPTAIN.   She has every right to be here.   This is her
place.

SOLDIER.   But does she know?   Does she know wot's . . .
danglin' up yonder, over 'er 'ed?

CAPTAIN.   She knows more than we do.   She belongs to him.
She is his mother.

SOLDIER.   'Is mother! . . .

CAPTAIN.   Yes, he was her baby once.

[*The Soldier is affected by this.   He speaks with real com-
passion.*

SOLDIER.   Pore devil!   (*Their minds go wandering through
many troubled by-paths of thought.   Presently the Soldier
speaks again*)   Wot was it 'e done, Captain?

CAPTAIN.   Don't you know?

SOLDIER.   Not exackly.   I got enough to look arter with my
drills an' vittles withaht messin' abaht with politics an'
these 'ere funny foreign religions.

CAPTAIN. And yet you, if I mistake not, were one of the four men told off to do the job.

SOLDIER. Well, I 'ope I know my duty, sir. I on'y obeyed orders. Come to that, sir, arskin' your pawdon, it was you as give them orders. I s'pose *you* knew orl right wot it was 'e done?

CAPTAIN. No, I don't know exactly, either. I am only just beginning to find out. We both did our duty, as you call it, in blindness.

SOLDIER. That 's strange langwidge to be comin' from *your* lips, Captain.

CAPTAIN. Strange thoughts have been coming to me during the last six hours.

SOLDIER. It 's difficult to know wot 's wot in these outlandish places. It 's not like at 'ome, sir, where there 's Law an' Order an' Patriotism an' Gawd's Own True Religion. These blarsted 'eathens got no gratitude. 'Ere 's the Empire sweatin' 'er guts aht, tryin' ter knock some sense inter their dam' silly 'eds ; an' wot do you get aht of it, orl said an' done? Nuthin' ! Nuthin' but a lot of ingratitude, 'ard words, insurrections, an' every nah an' then a bloody example like this 'ere to-day ! Oh, these foreigners mek me sick, they do reely !

CAPTAIN. Yes, perhaps that has been the real mistake all along.

SOLDIER. Wot 'as, Captain?

CAPTAIN. Taking these people — men like this one, for instance — for foreigners.

SOLDIER. Well, you 'll excuse me, sir, but wot the 'ell else are they?

CAPTAIN. I 'm not quite sure ; but supposing they were more nearly related? Supposing, after all, they happened to be made of the same flesh and blood as you and me? Supposing they were men? Supposing, even, they were — brothers?

SOLDIER. Brothers ! Why, that 's exactly wot 'e used ter say — 'im up there. . . . Did you ever 'ear 'im, sir?

CAPTAIN. Once. Did you?

SOLDIER. Once. (*They remain silent for a little*) It was politics when I 'eard 'im. On'y it sahnded more like some rummy religion.

CAPTAIN. When I heard him it was religion — sounding curiously like politics.

SOLDIER. Them two things don't 'ardly seem to go together, do they, sir?

CAPTAIN. They don't. Perhaps they ought to.

SOLDIER. I don't know. Seems to 'ave led *'im* into a pretty mess. . . . It's a queer world! . . . I wonder wot it was 'e reely done.

CAPTAIN. It's rather late in the day for us to be considering that, seeing what *we* have done, isn't it?

SOLDIER. Well, I don't know. P'r'aps it's funny of me, but I never done a job like this yet withaht thinkin' abaht it arterwards. . . . An' I done a few of 'em, too. If you arsk me, sir, it was them — well, them longfaced old jossers dahn there as begun the 'ole beastly business. You know 'oo I mean.

CAPTAIN. Yes, I know whom you mean. But haven't they a name?

SOLDIER. Well, I 'ardly know *wot* ter call them, sir. They're like a lot of old washerwomen. Allus jawin'. We got nuthin' exackly like that sort at 'ome, sir.

CAPTAIN. Oh, I don't know that there's all that difference.

SOLDIER. They was allus naggin' the pore fellow, one way an' another. Couldn't leave 'im alone. They started the 'ole business.

CAPTAIN. Why, what fault did they find with him? What was it they said he did?

SOLDIER. It wasn't nuthin' 'e done, far as I could mek aht. It was summat as 'e said, wot riled them.

CAPTAIN. Something he said?

SOLDIER. Yes, summat 'orrible; that's wot they said. Summat too bad ter be spoken, summat they wasn't a-goin' ter stand from anybody. Least, that's wot I 'eard. . . . Wasn't so very 'orrible, neither. Not ter me. Sahnded a bit mad, that's orl.

CAPTAIN. Oh, then you know what it was?

SOLDIER. Yessir. They 'ad a name for it, too: on'y I can't quite remember. One of them big jaw-crackers, you unnerstand. Seems a bit orf for a bloke ter come ter this, just for usin' a few words.

CAPTAIN. There is great power in words. All the things that ever get done in the world, good or bad, are done by words.

SOLDIER. Well, there's summat in that, too. On'y this thing 'e said — blimey, it was nuthin'! There ain't a loony alive wot doesn't say the same thing 'e said, an' more, a thahsand times a day, when 'e's reel bad in 'is 'ead. At the most, it sahnded like a bit of langwidge, that's orl.

CAPTAIN. And *you* don't mind that, do you?

SOLDIER. Me? 'E could 'a' done it till 'e was blue in the face an' welcome, far as I'd care.

CAPTAIN. You yourself, of course, had nothing at all against him? Nothing personal, nothing political, I mean. No more than I had.

SOLDIER. Lor' bless you, no, sir. Rawther liked 'im, the bit I saw of 'im.

CAPTAIN. Only they — the long-faced gentlemen — found him guilty. So, of course, they had to hand him over to the magistrate.

SOLDIER. Yes, blarst them. What did they want ter go an' do that for?

CAPTAIN. It was perhaps their — duty, don't you see?

SOLDIER (*taken aback on the sacred word*). Oh, was it? Well, since you put it in that way, o' course. . . .

CAPTAIN. Then, again, came the magistrate's duty. I suppose he found he had some duty in the matter? Did *he* very much object to this horrible thing that had been said?

SOLDIER. Not much! 'E ain't that sort, not this fellow! . . . That's the funny thing abaht it. Far as I could 'ear, there weren't no mention of that, by the time the case

come into 'is 'ands. No, it was riotin' an' stirrin' people
up agen the government, as 'e on'y 'ad ter deal with.

CAPTAIN. Was that charge proved against the prisoner?

SOLDIER. They 'ad witnesses, I suppose. On'y you know
wot witnesses are, in a case like this, sir. Got their orders,
you unnerstand.

CAPTAIN. And, of course, they all did their duty. That
sacred obligation was attended to. They obeyed.

SOLDIER. I don't know. Don't arsk me. I know nuthin'
abaht it.

[He is a little nettled at the turn the conversation is taking.

CAPTAIN. Was there no one, from among all those crowds
that followed him, to stand up and say a word for him?

SOLDIER. Well, wot do *you* think? Them greasy blighters!
You saw 'ow they be'aved just nah, when we done the
job.

CAPTAIN. *Their* duty, as voicers of public opinion, I suppose.

SOLDIER (*sullenly*). I don't know.

CAPTAIN. Had they any very strong feelings against this
monstrous thing he said? Were they so stirred with affection for the government? Or didn't their duty cover those
unessential points?

SOLDIER. I don't know.

CAPTAIN. Well, then, this magistrate? Having examined
this poor wretch in the presence of all that exemplary,
patriotic, obedient mob of people, he soon found out where
his duty lay? It was his duty to hand him over to us —
to you and me.

SOLDIER (*shortly*). Yessir.

CAPTAIN (*insisting*). To you and me.

SOLDIER. I said, Yessir.

CAPTAIN. Whereupon, though we were practically ignorant
as to the charge upon which this man was convicted:
though we had grave doubts as to whether he were guilty
at all; and while it is perfectly certain that we had nothing
against him personally, that we even liked him, sympathized with him, pitied him: it became *our* duty, our

sworn, our sacred duty, to do to him — the terrible thing we did just now.

SOLDIER. I can't see wot you're drivin' at, sir. You wouldn't 'ave a man go agen 'is duty, would you?

CAPTAIN. I'm trying to make up my mind. I don't know. I'm blind. I don't think I know what duty is.

SOLDIER. It's perfectly plain, sir. Arter all, duty *is* duty, ain't it?

CAPTAIN. Yes, it doesn't seem to be very much else.

SOLDIER. 'Ow do you mean, sir?

CAPTAIN. Well, for instance, it doesn't seem to be love or neighbourliness or pity or understanding or anything that comes out hot and fierce from the heart of a man. Duty! Duty! We talk of duty! What sort of devil's duties are there in the world, do you think, when they lead blindly, wantonly, wickedly, to the murder of such a man as this!

SOLDIER. Well, far as I'm concerned, I on'y obeyed my orders.

CAPTAIN. Orders! Obeyed orders!

SOLDIER. Well, sir, it was you as give them to me.

CAPTAIN. Good God, man, why didn't you strike me in the blasphemous teeth, the hour I gave them?

SOLDIER. Me, sir? Strike my superior orficer!

CAPTAIN. You struck this defenceless man. You had no scruples about his superiority. You struck him to the death.

SOLDIER (*hotly*). I on'y did my duty!

CAPTAIN. We have murdered our brother. We have destroyed a woman's child.

SOLDIER. I on'y obeyed my orders. When my superior orficer says, *Kill a man*, why, I just kill 'im, that's orl. O' course I kill 'im. Wot's a soldier for? That's duty! (*With sudden lust*) Blood an' 'ell! I'd kill 'im soon as look at 'im, yes, I would, if 'e was Gawd aht of 'Eaven, 'Imself! . . . Not as I 'ave anythin' personal agen this pore devil. On'y I *do* know my duty. (*They are silent for a little while. Then the Soldier, feeling that he has gone*

too far, begins assuaging the situation) There's one thing
certain : it's no use cryin' over spilt milk. 'E's dead an'
done for nah, wotever comes. Dead as a door-nail, pore
cuss. (*The Captain, who has risen during his excitement,
now sits down again. His sword clatters against a boulder.
A pause*) 'E ain't the fust man I done for, neither; an' I
bet 'e won't be the last. Not by a long way.
[*He speaks in an aggrieved tone. It is the way in which
shame comes to a soldier.
A pause.*

CAPTAIN (*deeply*). So you think he is dead, do you?

SOLDIER. Well, wot do *you* think? A man don't live
forever, 'ung up as 'igh as we got 'im yonder. Besides,
we did a bit of business with 'is vital parts, arter we'd got
'im up there.

CAPTAIN. And all that, you think, means — death.

SOLDIER. Well, don't it?

CAPTAIN. That's what I'm wondering.

SOLDIER. Six hours, mind you. It's a long time.

CAPTAIN. There is something mightier than time.

SOLDIER. Well, they don't supply little boys' playthings,
not from our War Office. One of these 'ere beauties . . .
(*He rattles his weapon in the darkness and continues*) . . .
when they *do* start business, generally touch the spot.

CAPTAIN. It would have to reach very far, to touch — this
man's life.

SOLDIER. Nah, wotever do you mean, Captain?

CAPTAIN. I mean that life is a terrible, a wonderful thing.
You can't kill it. All the soldiers in the world, with all
their hate, can't kill it. It comes back, it can't die, it
rises again.

SOLDIER. Good Gawd, Captain, don't you talk like
that!

CAPTAIN. Why, what are you afraid of? We have shown
great courage to-day, you and I. Soldiers should be
brave, you know.

SOLDIER. That's orl very well, when it's a matter of plain

flesh an' blood; but Lor'! Ghosts! . . . Do you believe in them, sir?

CAPTAIN. What?

SOLDIER. Ghosts.

CAPTAIN. Yes. It came to me to-day.

SOLDIER (*slowly*). If I believed there was . . . reely ghosts abaht . . .

CAPTAIN. They are the only realities. Two of them ought to be especially important to you and me just now.

SOLDIER. Two? Blimey! 'Oose?

CAPTAIN. Why, yours, man, and mine. Our ghosts. Our immortal ghosts. This deed of ours to-day should make us think of them forever.

SOLDIER. Yours an' mine? I didn't know we 'ad ghosts, you an' me.

CAPTAIN. It makes a difference, doesn't it? There have been millions of our sort in the long history of the world. I wonder how many more millions there will be in the years to come. Blind, dutiful, bloody-handed: murderers, all of us. A soldier's ghost must be a pitiable thing to see. (*The cloudy darkness slightly lifts from the ground. Their forms can be dimly discerned — vague shadows upon a deeper gloom. Up above there still dwells impenetrable night*) Tell me, brother murderer, have you ever prayed?

SOLDIER. Me, sir? . . . (*Ashamed*) Well, sir, nah you arsk me, yes I 'ave — once.

CAPTAIN. When was that?

SOLDIER. Why, sir, abaht a couple of month arter I set sail for this blarsted little 'ole.

CAPTAIN. I understand. You prayed then for the birth of an innocent child?

SOLDIER. Yessir.

CAPTAIN. You will have need to pray again to-night. Both of us will have need. This time for the death of an innocent man.

[*The Soldier is embarrassed. He does not know what to say. Something about "duty" comes into his head; but somehow*

*it seems inappropriate. A brighter thought occurs to
him.*

SOLDIER. Well, it's time I was dahn yonder, lookin' arter
the boys. Any orders, sir?

CAPTAIN. Orders? No, no more — orders.

SOLDIER. Orl right, sir.

*[There is heard the rattle of his salute, and the dying away of
his footsteps, as he stumbles blindly up and over the hill.*

The Captain does not speak until all is still again.

CAPTAIN. My God! My God! Oh, my God!

[He buries his face in the dirt and stones.

*The faintest moaning of wind. The sheep bleats. A dog,
disturbed by the sound, barks, far off. Then there is a deep
silence, lasting one minute.*

*The Voice of the Peasant Woman is heard, speaking at first
in dull, dead tones, very slowly.*

WOMAN. Thirty-three year ago he was my baby. I bore
him. I warmed him: washed, dressed him: fended for
him. I fed his little mouth with milk. Thirty-three
year ago. And now he's dead. Dead, that's what he is.
Dead. Hung up in the air like a thief: broken and bleeding like a slaughtered beast. All the life gone out of him.
And I'm his mother.

*[A gray, misty light creeps over her face and hands. Moment
by moment, her features limn out faintly through the darkness,
one pale agony.*

Her garments still blend with the general gloom.

That's what they done to my son. Killed him like a beast.
Respectable people, they was. Priests, judges, soldiers,
gentlemen: even common folk like me. *They* done it.
And now he's dead. He didn't hold with their kind, my
son. He was always telling them about it. He would
stand up open in the market-place, at the street corners,
even in the House of God itself, and tell them about it.
That's why they killed him. He had a strange way with
him, my son: always had, from the day he first come.
His eyes . . . They was wonderful. They held folk.

That and his tongue and his tender, pitiful heart. They
didn't understand it down here. None of us understood
it. We was blind — even me. Many a time I got in his
way and tried to hinder him: I was afraid for him,
ashamed. And then he'd look at me. . . . They was
always wonderful, his eyes. He wasn't particular, my
son. He would go with anybody. He loved them so.
There wasn't a drunken bibber in the place, not a lozel,
not a thief, not a loose woman on the streets, but called
him brother. He would eat with them, drink with them,
go to their parties. He would go with grand folk, too:
gentlemen. He wasn't particular: he would go with
anybody. And I tried to hinder him: I got in his way,
because I was ashamed. I kept pushing in. I was afraid
of what the people might think. Like I was blind. Like
I didn't understand. I never told him as I understood.
And now it's too late. He's dead.

[*A gust of anguish takes her, overwhelming her.*

Oh, my son, my own son, child of my sorrow, my lad,
come back to me! It's me, it's your mother, calling to
you. Cannot you hear me out of the lone waste and the
darkness yonder? My lad, come back, come back to
me! . . . He's gone. I shall never know the touch and
the healing gladness of him again, my son, my little lad.
. . . Hark! . . .

[*The wind rises and falls away like a whisper.*

On'y the wind blowing up over the moors. God's breath,
men call it. Ah! It strikes chill to the bones. . . . Is it
cold you are, my lad? I cannot reach you yonder —
on'y your feet, your poor broken feet and the ankles hanging limp toward me. My bosom warms and waits for you,
hungering, yearning like the day I bare you; but I cannot
get up to you: I am cramped and cold and beaten: I
cannot reach you yonder. . . .

[*There is heard a low fluttering as of wings.*

The night-birds and the bats may come anigh you, they
with their black wings; but not your mother, the mother

that gave you life, the mother that held you warm, my son, my son, my little cold lad.

[Her speech breaks away into sobs for a little while. As she recovers, she goes into a dazed dream of memories.

That was a cold night, too — the night you was born, way out in the country yonder, in the barn with them beasties. My man, he was sore about it. He covered us over with his great wool coat, and went and sat out in the yard — under the stars — till them three gentlemen come. Them three gentlemen. . . . They talked wonderful. I have it all here in my heart. Ay, it was rare and cold that night. Like now. Like it is now. . . . Wonderful. They was not common folk. They was like lords, they spoke so fine. About my little lad. About you. And then, that other night, before you come. It was a kind of light : it was a kind of glory. Like sunshine. I remember every word he said. About you. About my little lad.

[The agony begins to prick through again, stab by stab, as she continues.

It was all promise in them days, all promise and hope. Like you was to be somebody. Like you was to be a great man. I kept it inside of me : I fed on it : day by day as you sprung up, I learned you about it. You was to be no common man, you wasn't. You was to lord it over everybody. You was to be a master of men, you was. And now you 'm dead. Oh ! . . . Oh ! . . . Oh me ! . . . That day of the fairing, when we went up to the big city, your father and me and yourself. The wide asking eyes of you, your little hand, how it would go out so and so, your little tongue all a-clatter, the ways, the wonderings of you, and the heartbreak, the heartbreak when we had you lost. Talking to the good priests, you said. Good priests ! My God ! . . . It began that day, that bitter day of the fairing when we went up to the big city. I lost you then. I have lost you ever since. Oh, the big city, the cruel city, the city of men's sin ! Calling, calling the sweet life of a man and swallowing him up in death. There was no doing

with you from that day. No home for you in the little
village from that day. Your father's trade, your tasks,
your companions, all fell off from you that day. The city,
the big city called you, and the country thereabouts. It
was your kingdom, you said. You must find out and build
your kingdom. And the people thronged about you and
followed you wherever you went in them days. They hung
upon your words: they worshipped you. In them days.
It was the way you had — your strange way. A power
went out from you. You was always like nobody else.
A king! A king! It was me as put it first into your head.
You looked like a king. You spoke like a king. You
ruled like a king. You, the little peasant lad I bore. I
never told you: I never lifted up my hand to help you: I
hindered you; but I was proud of you, my lad, proud and
ashamed, and afraid, too! And now it's too late. You'm
dead. All come to nothing. You'm dead. . . . Dead.
Killed by the soldiers and the judges of the great city. I'll
tell them about it. I'll go through all the earth telling
about it. Killed by the men you called your brothers.
Killed by the children of your kingdom. Killed, and the
golden crown of your glory torn off, battered, and cast to
the ground. Beaten, mocked, murdered by the mighty
masters of the world. Hung up, high up in the air like a
thief. Broken and bleeding like a slaughtered beast.
[*She has come to the bottom of her grief. Her voice dies away
through strangled sobs into silence.*
A pause.
*The Captain rises. He halts irresolute for a moment.
Then he can be heard moving over to where she lies prone on
the ground.*
CAPTAIN. Woman, will you let me speak to you?
WOMAN. Who are you?
CAPTAIN. I am the captain who spoke to you just now. I
am in charge here. I am the man who gave the order that
killed your son.
WOMAN. Ah! . . .

CAPTAIN. Won't you hear me? I must speak to you.

WOMAN. What do you want to say? What is there for you to say?

CAPTAIN. It is about myself. . . . I . . .

WOMAN. Go on. I'm listening.

CAPTAIN. I am a murderer. I want you to forgive me. (*She does not answer*) I did it. I did it with a word. It was like magic. One word, one little word, and I was a murderer. There is nothing more terrible in the world than to be a murderer. . . . And now I want you to forgive me. (*She does not answer*) I suppose it's impossible. Forgiveness is impossible for a wretch like me. Because I killed him. For God's sake, speak to me!

WOMAN (*in a stupor*). I want to. I'm trying to. But you say you killed my son.

CAPTAIN. Oh! . . .

WOMAN. Why did you do it?

CAPTAIN. I did not know. Killing's my trade. It was the only thing they brought me up to do. (*She does not answer*) I have been mixed up with it ever since I can remember. My father did it before me. All my people did it. It is considered the thing — the sort of thing a gentleman ought to do. They call it glory: they call it honor; courage; patriotism. Great kings hold their thrones by it. Great merchants get their beastly riches by it. Great empires are built that way.

WOMAN. By murder?

CAPTAIN. By murder. By the blood of just men. Women and little children too.

WOMAN. What makes them do it?

CAPTAIN. They want money. They want power. They want kingdom. They want to possess the earth.

WOMAN. And they have won. They have it.

CAPTAIN. Have they? Not while your son hangs there.

[*She is bewildered.*

WOMAN. What do you mean? My son. . . . My son is dead.

CAPTAIN. Is he? Not while God is in Heaven.

WOMAN. I don't understand you. What were you saying yourself, just now? On'y a little while ago I heard his blood dripping down here in the darkness. The stones are dank with it. Not an hour ago. He's dead.

CAPTAIN. He's alive.

WOMAN. Why do you mock me? You'm mad. Are you God, as you can kill and make alive, all in one breath?

CAPTAIN. He's alive. I can't kill him. All the empires can't kill him. How shall hate destroy the power that possesses and rules the earth?

WOMAN. The power that . . . Who?

CAPTAIN. This broken thing up here. Your son.

WOMAN. My son, the power that . . .

CAPTAIN. Listen. I will tell you . . . I am a soldier. I have been helping to build kingdoms for over twenty years. I have never known any other trade. Soldiery, bloodshed, murder: that's my business. My hands are crimson with it. That's what empire means. In the city I come from, it is the chief concern of the people. Building kingdoms, rule, empire. They're proud of it. The little children in the schools are drilled in obedience to it: they are taught hymns in praise of it: they are brought up to reverence its symbols. When they wave its standard above them, they shout, they leap, they make wild and joyful noises; like animals, like wolves, like little brute beasts. Children! Young children! Their parents encourage them in it: it never occurs to them to feel ashamed: they would be treated like lepers if they felt ashamed. That's what empire does to human beings in the city I come from. It springs from fear — a peculiar kind of fear they call courage.

And so we go on building our kingdoms — the kingdoms of this world. We stretch out our hands, greedy, grasping, tyrannical, to possess the earth. Domination, power, glory, money, merchandise, luxury, these are the things we aim at; but what we really gain is pest and famine, grudged labour, the enslaved hate of men and women, ghosts, dead and death-breathing ghosts that haunt our lives forever. It can't last : it never has lasted, this building in blood and fear. Already our kingdoms begin to totter. Possess the earth! We have lost it. We never did possess it. We have lost both earth and ourselves in trying to possess it; for the soul of the earth is man and the love of him, and we have made of both, a desolation.

I tell you, woman, this dead son of yours, disfigured, shamed, spat upon, has built a kingdom this day that can never die. The living glory of him rules it. The earth is *his* and he made it. He and his brothers have been moulding and making it through the long ages : they are the only ones who ever really did possess it : not the proud : not the idle, not the wealthy, not the vaunting empires of the world. Something has happened up here on this hill to-day to shake all our kingdoms of blood and fear to the dust. The earth is his, the earth is theirs, and they made it. The meek, the terrible meek, the fierce agonizing meek, are about to enter into their inheritance. [*There is a deep, solemn silence for a moment or two, broken only by the tinkle of sheep-bells, which are gradually approaching.*

WOMAN. Then it was not all wasted. It was the truth, that night. I have borne a Man.

CAPTAIN. A man and more than a man. A King.

WOMAN. My peasant lad, a king : Yes. And more yet. He was what he said he was. He was God's Son.

CAPTAIN. It will take a new kind of soldier to serve in his kingdom. A new kind of duty.

WOMAN. A newer courage. More like woman's. Dealing with life, not death.

CAPTAIN. It changes everything.

WOMAN. It puts them back again. What he done, puts all things back again, where they belong.

CAPTAIN. I can see the end of war in this : some day.

WOMAN. I can see the joy of women and little children: some day.

CAPTAIN. I can see cities and great spaces of land full of happiness.

WOMAN. I can see love shining in every face.

CAPTAIN. There shall be no more sin, no pain. . . .

WOMAN. No loss, no death. . . .

CAPTAIN. Only life, only God. . . .

WOMAN. And the kingdom of my Son. . . .

CAPTAIN. Some day.

WOMAN. When the world shall have learned.

CAPTAIN. Mother! . . . I am a murderer! . . .

WOMAN. I have been with Child. I forgive you.

[*It grows a little lighter.*

Some one is heard stumbling blindly over the hill. It is the Soldier. His form emerges gray out of the gloom.

SOLDIER. 'Ello! Are you there, Captain?

CAPTAIN. Yes. I'm here.

SOLDIER. The fog's liftin' dahn below there — liftin' fast. It'll soon be up orf this 'ill, thank Gawd! The General wants ter see you, sir.

CAPTAIN. What does he want with me? Do you know?

SOLDIER. Another of these 'ere bleedin' jobs, I think, sir. Been a bit of a disturbance dahn in the tahn. The boys 'ave their orders, sir. General wants you ter take command.

CAPTAIN. Tell him I refuse to come.

SOLDIER. Beg pawdon, sir. . . .

CAPTAIN. I refuse to come. I disobey.

SOLDIER. I don't think I quite 'eard, sir.

CAPTAIN. I disobey. I have sworn duty to another General. I serve the Empire no longer.

SOLDIER. Beg pawdon, sir, it's not for the likes of me; but . . . Well, you know wot that means.

CAPTAIN. Perfectly. It means what you call death. Tell the General.

SOLDIER. Tell 'im as you refuse to obey orders, sir?

CAPTAIN. His : yes. (*Half to himself*) How simple it all is, after all.

SOLDIER (*after a moment*). I 'm sorry, Captain.

CAPTAIN. Thank you, brother.

[*The Soldier has no word to say.*

The darkness is rapidly melting away. All three figures are now beginning to be seen quite clearly.

SOLDIER. Look sir, wot did I tell yer? It 's comin' light again.

CAPTAIN. Eternally.

[*An unearthly splendour fills the place. It is seen to be the top of a bleak stony hill with little grass to it.*

The Woman is dressed in Eastern garments; the Captain is a Roman centurion; the Soldier, a Roman legionary. Above them rise three gaunt crosses bearing three dead men gibbeted like thieves.

At the foot of the crosses a flock of sheep nibble peacefully at the grass. The air is filled with the sound of their little bells.

CURTAIN

THE LAST MILE

JOHN WEXLEY

THIS version of "The Last Mile" demonstrates that plays of ideas, like impressionistic plays and others where the progressive development of character is not required, can be as effective in one act as in several, and that often a full-length play is simply a concession to Broadway practice. "The Last Mile" was produced professionally for a year's run in New York, and subsequently was given in Spain, Italy, England, and the Soviet Union. The one-act version succeeded the longer form.

Mr. Wexley was born on the island of Manhattan in 1907, and was educated at New York University. He traveled the highroads and byways of the forty-eight states for two years in a variety of jobs, as oil-worker, farm hand, salesman, steel-worker; and acted with the Neighborhood Playhouse in New York, with Eva Le Gallienne's and Leo Bulgakov's companies. He has also had experience as stage manager and director of plays, and as scenario writer for the Hollywood studios.

In addition to "The Last Mile", his plays are: "Steel" (the first labor play to be produced on Broadway, 1931), "They Shall Not Die", and "Running Dogs."

THE LAST MILE

By JOHN WEXLEY

["The Last Mile" was suggested by a short published sketch by Robert Blake, to whom the author acknowledges indebtedness.]

"The Last Mile" was first produced by Herman Shumlin on February 13, 1930, at the Sam H. Harris Theatre in New York City. The play was directed by Chester Erskin; the settings were designed by Henry Dreyfuss.

Original Cast

FRED MAYOR (Cell 3)	Howard Phillips
RICHARD WALTERS (Cell 7) . . .	James Bell
"RED" KIRBY (Cell 9)	Hale Norcross
VINCENT JACKSON (Cell 13) . . .	Ernest Whitman
EDDIE WERNER (Cell 11)	George Leach
DRAKE (Guard)	Don Costello
JOHN MEARS (Cell 5)	Spencer Tracy
O'FLAHERTY (Guard)	Herbert Heywood
PEDDIE (Guard)	Orville Harris
PRINCIPAL KEEPER CALLAHAN . .	Ralph Theadore
HARRIS (Guard)	Richard Abbott
TOM D'AMORO (Cell 1)	Joseph Spurin-Calleia
FATHER O'CONNORS	Henry O'Neill
EVANGELIST	Clarence Chase
FROST ⎫ (Reporters)	Allen Jenkins
BROOKS ⎭	Albert West

THE LAST MILE

SCENE. *The death-house of a state penitentiary. A tier of cells numbering from stage-left — to right: 1, 3, 5, 7, 9, 11, 13. The audience is really supposed to be witnessing the action from the even numbered cells opposite. Therefore between the audience and the odd numbered cells is a corridor. At one end of this, stage-right, is a steel door leading to the offices and to the outside. Stage-left is another door of steel, painted green, opening into the electrocution chamber. The death-house is a one-story structure and through the cell windows that can be seen through the bars of the cell doors, the audience sees some distance away, the sky.*

TIME. *The time is about nine o'clock, two hours before the hour set for Richard Walters' execution. The month is early May. The air is charged with a tenseness, the condemned convicts speak very strangely, very nervously. One of them is to be electrocuted in only two hours.*

At the door Right is the Guard, Drake, seated. Cell 1 is vacant. After the rise of the curtain there is a slight pause.

[*The Curtain rises slowly.*

MAYOR. Nine o'clock, Walters.

WALTERS. How do you know?

MAYOR. Just heard the whistle blow.

WALTERS (*musing*). Funny. I didn't hear it. You got good ears, Three.

MAYOR (*bitterly*). Sure I got good ears. Nothin' to do but listen, is there?

WALTERS (*repeats dully*). Nothin' to do but listen. (*Slight pause*) Well, fellers, this is my last coupla hours.

KIRBY (*encouragingly*). You'll get that stay yet, Seven.

WALTERS (*quietly*). Too late now . . . Red.

KIRBY. The Governor gave a couple last week. No reason why you shouldn't get one.

JACKSON. You'll get it, white boy. You'll get it, jest yuh keep right on prayin' —

WALTERS. I'm prayin' for it, but it's no use. It looks like I ain't been heard at all, Thirteen.

JACKSON (*plaintively*). Don't be callin' me Thirteen. How many times have ah asked yuh not to call me Thirteen. Ain't it bad enough bein' Thirteen without havin' to be called it?

KIRBY. Sure, it's bad enough.

WERNER (*in a loud wailing voice, idiotically*). Hol —— mes!

WALTERS. Well I don't expect that stay, or I'd have gotten it when the Governor gave it to Nine.

KIRBY. It'll come at the last minute, Seven. Just wait. He's refused to commute your sentence, but if you had the priest wire him he might stop the execution to-night and have you examined by the Lunacy Commission.

WALTERS. I did that, Red.

KIRBY. Well . . .?

WALTERS. Well . . . (*Slight pause*) When does the priest come?

MAYOR. He comes whenever you write him or send him a telegram.

WALTERS (*smiling dismally*). Maybe I ought to start yellin' Holmes.

HARRIS. Supper for Number Seven.

DRAKE. O.K.

MAYOR. Too late now. You shoulda done that long ago. (*A noise off-stage left*) Here comes supper.

WALTERS. It better be a good one. It's my last, I guess.

KIRBY. Oh, I dunno. You'll get that stay. It's early yet.

JACKSON. What did youah ohder, Seven?

[*A guard opens the door, delivers the tray to Drake and exits.*

WALTERS. I ordered a tenderloin steak, baked potatoes, fruit cock-tail, jam, bread and lots of butter, coffee, and mushroom soup.

[*Guard gives him food through aperture.*

JACKSON (*meditating*). That oughta be plenty.

WALTERS. Yea, I guess I'll be gettin' good and hungry on my way down.

JACKSON. Ah can't figgah how yo' came to think of that theah mushroom soup. (*Scratches his head*) But ah doan't think ah could eat if ah was you.

WALTERS (*testily*). Aw, shut up. I got the chance to eat to-night, what I want and all I can, and I'm goin' to. I'm sorry I didn't order fried turkey and a lot of side-dishes.

KIRBY. They'll give you anything you ask for.

MAYOR (*sarcastically*). Yeah. Any reasonable request you make now will not be refused you.

JACKSON (*persisting*). Where do you think they got that theah mushroom soup from? Is it canned soup?

WALTERS (*eating*). I dunno. It tastes too good to tell.

JACKSON. Ah wish ah had some.

WALTERS. You'll have it, Thirteen. You'll have all you want.

JACKSON. Please woan't yuh stop callin' me Thirteen? How many times . . . ?

WALTERS. I'll stop. (*Ceases to eat suddenly*) I'm feeling sick. I don't think I can finish this all.

[*A voice off-stage left.*

VOICE. Give these cigars to Number Seven.

DRAKE (*takes them, shuts the door and crosses to Seven*). Some cigars for you, Seven.

WALTERS. Thanks. Who sent 'em?

[*While smelling them.*

DRAKE (*grouchily*). I dunno. Somebody they wouldn't let in to see ya.

WALTERS (*very curious*). But what's the name? Didn't ya get the name?

DRAKE. No, I didn't. I didn't ask.

WALTERS (*angry*). Well, why didn't ya? Didn't ya think a guy might wanna know?

DRAKE. Cause I didn't wanna. That's why. (*Meanly*) Whatsamatter? Don't ya want the seegars?

WALTERS (*suddenly letting down*). Sure I do. But I wanted to know who sent 'em. Give me a light . . . will ya? (*Drake lights one for him. Condemned convicts are not permitted to carry matches, although they may smoke*) Say, I'll never be able to smoke all these.

MAYOR. I'll smoke 'em for ya, Dick. Send 'em down.

WALTERS. Ya want 'em all, ya hog. Take some, Mears. (*Passes some to Mears who takes a few and passes the rest to Mayor*) Say! Fred Mayor! I'm gonna ask them to let me hold your hand to-night.

[*Laughs.*

MAYOR (*laughing*). The hell they will.

WALTERS (*still laughing at what appears to him a great joke*). Sure, they will, and you'll get the juice through you and we'll go to hell together.

[*Everybody lets out a great laugh.*

MAYOR (*laughs a little, then*). Aw, Seven, cut it out. Hey, Screw, give us a light. I'm goin' in a couple of weeks. Ain't that bad enough? (*Drake does so, sullenly*) Some seegar. How do you like the service here, boys? (*Drake glares at him angrily, the match still burning in his hand*) All right, James, that'll do. (*Blows match*) Now bring the Cadillac roadster.

[*The men laugh with abandon. Great joke, even though they've heard it again and again.*

WERNER (*recites suddenly in a ghastly tone*).

The death-house's where they come and go,
They linger just a little time
Before they give you the electric chair,
Sentenced for some awful crime.

WALTERS. Oh, he's begun again. Stop it, Eddie.

MEARS (*shooting his words like rifle shots*). Shut up, you crazy bastard!

WERNER (*going on, unminding*).

I have seen them come, I have seen them go,

I have heard the death-warrants read,
And when I see the bright lights go dim,
In the 'lectric chair, another guy is dead.

WALTERS (*holding his hands to his ears*). Fer Christ's sakes,
Eddie. Have a heart.

WERNER (*undaunted, scarcely pausing*).

When I hear the lonesome hum of the motor
That sends the high voltage to your chest,
I have a sad unexplainable sensation
Running through my breast.

WALTERS (*screaming savagely*). I'm gonna come back and
haunt you, like a ghost, if ya don't shut up!

WERNER (*not even hearing him*).

When your time grows near . . . less than one hour,
And you get that reprieve of a *little* more rest.

KIRBY (*approving*). Now you're talkin' sense.

WERNER (*continuing*).

Why do they pull that black cap over your face,
And let it remain until you are dead?
Why? Because the high voltage of electricity
Will make your eyes pop out of your head!

WALTERS (*shrieking*). God, God, I'll go mad. Stop him
. . . somebody!

MEARS. Drake! Why the hell don't you stop him?

DRAKE. Stop him yerself. I like it.

MEARS (*contemptuously*). Bitch!

WERNER (*continuing*). When I'm speaking of the Midnight
Special . . .

DRAKE (*menacingly*). I'll bitch you . . .

WERNER (*continuing*). You probably don't understand what
I mean . . .

MEARS (*with withering contempt*). Ya yeller screw. Come
on, flatfoot.

DRAKE (*changing his mind and reseating himself*). Aw, pipe
down.

WALTERS (*pleading, piteously*). Eleven. Cut it out. Will
ya please?

WERNER (*not pausing*).

When the warden tightens the helmet
And places the sponge upon your head,
Then pulls the lever of injustice,
In one minute . . . you are dead . . .
  (*Pause*)
Hol——mes!

WALTERS (*exhausted*).   Christ!

[*Bell rings.   O'Flaherty, another guard, enters.*

O'FLAHERTY (*perfunctorily*).   How is it?

DRAKE.   Quiet.

O'FLAHERTY.   O.K.   (*O'Flaherty lets Drake out, then crosses to Walters*)   How you feel, Walters?

WALTERS.   All right, O'Flaherty, all right.

O'FLAHERTY.   That's good.   Better try an' take a nap. Through eating?   I'll save the coffee in case you want it later on.

WALTERS.   All right.

[*The lights suddenly grow dim, then brighten again.*

JACKSON (*savage, African, barbaric*).   Heya, Heya . . . Theah're testin' the Midnight Special for Number Seven!

WALTERS.   Jesus!

WERNER.

And when I see the bright lights grow dim,
In the 'lectric chair another soul is dead.
Look at those lights go dim!

MEARS (*between his teeth, with suppressed rage*).   They're playin' with that thing again.   Why do they have to play with it?   They're playin' with it all the goddam day. Do they think we got no nerves?

MAYOR.   We got more nerves than anybody else.

JACKSON.   We're the most nervous people in the world.

WALTERS (*shouting to those behind the green door*).   Hey, you goddam monkeys, get the hell out!   Jeez.   Ain't it bad enough?   Cut it out.   Christ, that makes me sick.

MAYOR.   I can't stand so much of this.   I'd rather be anywhere than here.

JACKSON. That talk foh me too.

WALTERS. That got me in the gut. It made a funny sensation then. Kind of burnin' like. . . .

KIRBY. It'll get worse, kid. I know. Wait'll it begins to tighten up real like a vise. (*Very slight pause*) Fellers, it's no joke. I'd like to be some place else now.

MAYOR. You'd have been some place else if you hadn't gotten that stay.

KIRBY (*sighing*). Huh! How well I know it. But honest, I hate like hell to be in here when a man is goin' to burn.

MEARS (*quietly*). You think you're the only one? You're lucky, Red. You got a smart Jew lawyer. You'll get some more stays maybe, and see a coupla more get the works.

[*Principal Keeper Frank Callahan and Guards Peddie and Harris enter with Tom D'Amoro, a young Italian-American. Harris unlocks Cell One. D'Amoro pauses in the cell door frame. He places his hands on the jambs and examines the interior with a feigned criticism. Harris and Peddie stand near him.*

PEDDIE. Come on . . . move in.

JACKSON. Say, Mister Callahan, didn't yuh promise me Numbah One cell?

CALLAHAN (*with O'Flaherty*). What? Oh, you? Don't you see how busy I am? This is no time to bother me.

JACKSON. But yuh . . . promised me.

CALLAHAN (*interrupting*). Didn't you understand me? I'm too busy now.

HARRIS (*to D'Amoro*). All right. This is yours. Come on. Get in.

D'AMORO. What's your hurry? I got plenty time. (*He reaches up as high as he can, with his hands on the jambs, then on his toes*) So this is the ice-box.

[*And he spits with gusto at the ceiling of the cell.*

PEDDIE (*as he slams door*). Use your handkerchief, wop!

JACKSON (*stubbornly*). But yuh did promise me.

CALLAHAN (*as he is leaving*). I'll put you in Number Seven later.

JACKSON (*sadly, slowly*). I won't be able to sleep in Seven. Gee, Boss. What's this pore nigger done to yuh?
[*Callahan exits.*

JACKSON. Say, fellers, how come they don't let us in them cells 'cross the way? How come?

MAYOR. So we don't see each other, Sunny. So we'll be more alone, so . . .

MEARS (*interrupting, to D'Amoro*). What's yer name, One?

D'AMORO. Tom D'Amoro.

MEARS (*taking in his breath, causing a whistle*). Oh, so you're the dago that croaked that cop.

D'AMORO (*with some bravado*). Yea, I'm the guy.

MEARS. My name is Mears, Cell Five.

MAYOR. Fred Mayor, Cell Three.

JACKSON. Vincent Jackson, in the *last* cell.

KIRBY. Red Kirby, Cell Nine.

D'AMORO. Pleased to meet you fellers. Who's goin' to burn to-night?

WALTERS (*suddenly hysterical*). Number Seven, Seven is gonna burn. . . . Richard Walters!

WERNER. Hol——mes!

D'AMORO. What the hell is that?

MAYOR. That's Ed Werner, Cell Eleven. He's gone nuts, so the Governor gave him a stay.

D'AMORO. Well, why don't they take him the hell out of here?

MEARS. They don't take him out. They leave him here, so that he can drive us all nuts.

MAYOR (*explaining*). They've got to keep him here for the Lunacy Commission. The regular doctors here can't touch him. Then the Commission makes its report direct to the Governor. Sometimes it takes three or four weeks to get a nut out.

KIRBY. He's a poet too. He'll drive you mad. But just don't listen to him, One.

WALTERS (*after a slight silence*). You're right about that chair makin' your stomach turn over, Red.

KIRBY. Lordy . . . don't I know! (*Slight pause*) Gonna tell the reporters anything, Seven?

WALTERS. They're expectin' me to tell 'em the whole story to-night. They're crazy. It wouldn't do me a damn bit of good! What good can it do me!

MAYOR. Seven, keep everybody out but the state witnesses. Don't let the rubbernecks in. I wouldn't if I were you.

WALTERS (*with forced bravado*). Aw, I don't care who sees it. (*Impulsively*) Say! Who am I gonna give this money to? (*Silence*) Well, say somethin', you damn guys.

JACKSON. Send dat money on down here, Boss, if it's botherin' yuh.

WALTERS (*passing it to Kirby who passes it on*). It's only a coupla dollars. Say, Red, do you remember when you sent me everything you had, money and all, when you were gettin' ready to go . . . and the Governor gave you the stay and I had to give you everything back again? I sure did cuss.

KIRBY. Yeah! Sure I remember.

JACKSON (*lightly — cheeringly*). I'll send yuh everything back to-morrow mornin', Seven.

WALTERS. All right, Sunny. Say, Three, do you want these cigarettes? I got four packs.

MAYOR. Keep 'em, Seven. You can smoke 'em to-morrow.

WALTERS (*fervently*). God, I hope so.

MEARS (*extending his hand*). Gimme a pack, Seven, I'm all run out.

[*Walters does so.*

WALTERS. What time is it, somebody?

MEARS. It's early, it's about half-past.

WALTERS (*getting excited*). Half-past what?

KIRBY (*consoling*). Nine, Kid, only half-past nine. You'll have that stay yet. See if you don't.

WERNER (*wailing*). Hol——mes!

D'AMORO.   What's that guy yellin'?
[*Pause.*
WERNER.   Hol——mes!
D'AMORO.   Hey, Guard, why the hell don't you stop him?
That sounds like the name of the cop I croaked.   His name
was Holman.   Sol Holman.
O'FLAHERTY.   Shut up, Werner.
D'AMORO (*without pausing*).   I couldn't help killin' him.
He shot at me on the roof and it was either me or him.
Now what could I do?   If a guy is pumpin' lead at you
and you hear the bulls and dicks blowin' their whistles
down below in the streets and people shoutin', and ya got
a gun, why ya just shoot back.   Ya can't help it.   Ya
gotta shoot back . . . ya gotta. . . .
MEARS.   Take it easy, One.
D'AMORO.   Jesus!
JACKSON (*singing*).
    It ain't what yuh eat
    Is gonna make yuh fat,
    It's what yuh reap, sweetheart.
    It ain't what yuh sow
    Is gonna make you weep,
    It's what . . .
    [*Bell.*
KIRBY (*to Walters, quietly*).   Say, Seven, here's the warden's
brother-in-law, with what looks like a telegram, — maybe
it's a stay.
[*Callahan crosses to Walters and shows him the telegram which
the convict reads.*
WALTERS (*as he finishes, suddenly*).   Hell, no!   (*Steps to rear
of cell, then returns and repeats*)   Tell 'em I said, Hell, no!
CALLAHAN.   Who are you yelling at?
WALTERS.   You, you!   Tell 'em I said Hell, no!
CALLAHAN (*as he exits*).   That's what the Governor said for
you, too.
WALTERS (*very short pause, then shouting after him*).   Huh?
What d' ya say?   Did ya hear what he said, fellers?

Didn't ya hear? Why don't you guys answer, dammit?
Answer me, somebody, for Christ's sake!

KIRBY. Don't listen to him, Seven. He's just that way.

JACKSON. He's a mean skunk jest like the warden. He's
lookin' foh to frighten you. That's all.

WALTERS. Huh! Did youse hear what I told him? Hell,
no! That was a telegram from the sheriff of some damn
county wantin' to know if he and some friend of his, a
justice of the peace, could get my permission to come and
see the electrocution. Say, if they get me sore I won't
let anyone in that the state gives me choice of keeping
out.

MAYOR. Don't let 'em in!

D'AMORO. Keep 'em out, Seven!

WALTERS. Ya heard me tell him what to say, didn't ya?

MAYOR. Sure we heard. (*Slight pause*) Which reporters
you lettin' in, Seven?

WALTERS. I don't know.

MAYOR. Let in the boys from the *Post* and the *News* if they
come. They're good fellows.

WALTERS. Yea, they're not so bad, I think.

MAYOR. They've treated us pretty white.

WALTERS. Ya see, the warden explained everything to me
last week. He gave me to understand that there would
be five witnesses for the state, and besides that, the guards.
And that I could have any five I wanted for my own
witnesses, but if I didn't want anybody for my witnesses,
I could keep 'em out, and only have the state's.
[*Bell.*

O'FLAHERTY. Howdo, Father?

O'CONNORS. How do you do, boys? (*Guard opens Cell
Seven, Priest enters*) Well, how do you feel, Walters?

WALTERS. All right.

O'CONNORS. That's the spirit, boy. Are you ready for me
now?

WALTERS. Yes. I finished reading the prayers. (*Points
to prayer book*) Up to here.

O'CONNORS. That's right. (*Points to script and places stole on his shoulders*) Now read that, Walters.

WALTERS (*reading*). I confess to Almighty God, to Blessed Mary ever Virgin . . . to Blessed Michael the Archangel . . . to Blessed John the Baptist, to the Holy Apostles, Peter and Paul, and to all the saints, and to you, Father, that I have sinned exceedingly in thought, word and deed, through my fault, through my fault, through my own grievous fault.

O'CONNORS. Sancti. Amen. Now, Walters, you believe in God?

WALTERS. I do, Father.

O'CONNORS. In His only Son, Our Lord . . .

MAYOR (*contemptuously*). Huh!

MEARS. Shh. . . . Keep quiet.

O'CONNORS (*continuing*). Forgiveness of sin through the resurrection of the body, and Life everlasting?

WALTERS. I do, Father.

O'CONNORS. Taken the name of God in vain?

WALTERS. I have.

O'CONNORS. Committed robbery or adultery?

WALTERS (*emphatically*). No, never, Father, never.

O'CONNORS. Procured, desired, or hastened the death of anyone?

WALTERS. Huh? What's that? What did you say?

O'CONNORS. Procured, desired, or hastened the death of anyone? (*Walters is still*) Well, have you?

WALTERS. I have, Father, but I didn't mean it. Honest! I didn't. It was all an accident. So help me Jesus. So help me. . . .

[*He commences to sob quietly but convulsively.*

O'CONNORS (*places his hand on his shoulder consolingly*). God is merciful, Walters, to those who have faith. Say a good act of contrition.

WALTERS (*pointing to page*). Here?

O'CONNORS. Yes, begin here.

WALTERS (*reads*). O my God, I am heartily sorry for having

offended Thee, and I detest all my sins, because I dread the
loss of Heaven and the pains of Hell, but most of all because
they offend Thee, my God, who art all, good and deserving
of all my love. I firmly resolve, with the help of Thy
grace, to confess my sins, to do penance, and to amend my
life. Amen.

o'connors (*as Walters reads*). Dominus noster Jesus Chris-
tus te absolvat; et ego, auctoritate ipsius, te absolvat (*In
decreasing tones*) ab omni vinculo excommunicationis, et in-
terdisti, inquintum possum, et tu indigues. Deinde ego
te absolve a peccatis tuis, in nomine Patris et Filii, et
Spiritus. Amen. All right. God bless you. I 'll see you
later, Walters. (*Exits cell, speaks to Mayor*) Well, boy,
how are you feeling?

[*Walters sits on his stool and reads prayers.*

mayor. Swell.

o'connors. I 've been praying for him. I think his soul is
at peace.

mayor (*sarcastically*). Yeah!

o'connors (*unmindful*). It is not possible for me to save
his life or body. The Governor has refused to grant a stay.
I 'm coming back presently to give him Holy Communion.
I 'll stay with him then to the end. It will calm him and
bring him nearer to God and Jesus. I always walk to the
chair with the man I prepare for death and administer the
last rites to. It helps them to go without fear.

mayor (*interrupting*). All right, all right. I 've got two
weeks yet. Do I have to go through this a million times?

o'connors (*smiling benignly*). I 'll speak to you again to-
night when I come back.

[*As he crosses right.*

mayor. Don't bother.

o'connors (*walking past Mayor stops by Mears . . . then
quietly*). That boy in there is hopeless.

mears (*wearily*). Uh-huh.

o'connors. Yes. (*In another tone*) You look fatigued —
John. You ought to go to bed.

MEARS. No. I don't want no sleep.

O'CONNORS. You need it.

MEARS. I don't need nothing.

O'CONNORS. Why, you haven't slept for nights.

MEARS. Well — what's the difference? (*Suddenly*) Why the hell don't you leave me alone, O'Connors?

O'CONNORS. I'm sorry. I was only trying —

MEARS (*interrupting*). I can't sleep, don't you see? I don't see him but I know what he looks like — I know what he's going through in there —

O'CONNORS. He's taking it like a man —

MEARS. The hell he is. Aw, you're like the rest of 'em. (*Slowly*) He's scared stiff, in there.

O'CONNORS. It seems to me he's very brave.

MEARS. Brave? Why — how the hell is he brave if I'm afraid to pukin'? How is he feeling if my belly is turning over with the idea?

O'CONNORS. He has faith. — John, he believes. I wish you would allow me to talk to you too about God — about —

MEARS. Listen here, O'Connors — I look at you and I can't make you out. You look like a fellow that's read books and always kept your eyes open. You talk like a three years old. You want me to believe — in what? In another world? So that I shouldn't fear to go on the week of the ninth? Eh? All right. What kind of a place is this next world of yours? What's in it? Did anyone ever see it? Where's your proof that it exists?

O'CONNORS (*silent for an instant, conscious of his impotence to answer*). I hoped you wouldn't talk that way, John — I —

MEARS. Well — what do you want then? You want me to take it all in, on your word? Who the hell are you? [*Slight pause.*

O'CONNORS. Why don't you let me —?

MEARS. Aw, crap!

O'CONNORS. You won't understand —

MEARS. Well — then make me understand!

O'CONNORS. You've got to have faith — in the Lord, and believe in His Son — the Christ — He promised — He died.

MEARS. That ain't faith. That's just closing your eyes and wishing. Say — I've been through too much. Maybe I never went to school. Maybe I never had no education, but I've thought a lot in my time. I had to, and I know this : I got to see it on black and white, I got to have two and two make four. I ain't talkin' myself into nothing. Say, don't you think I'd like to believe and so not be afraid of that in there — (*Gestures to door on right*) not to have to wait and worry and wait — and go nice and peaceful, and smiling and have faith? Why sure — you can talk that way — you don't have to go — you're not waiting — afraid — afraid —

O'CONNORS. I would have no fear.

MEARS. You wouldn't? —

O'CONNORS. I'm certain I wouldn't.

[*Two Guards enter, one of whom is also a barber. They unlock Walters' cell. O'Flaherty still remains at the door right. O'Connors nods to Mears and exits.*

DRAKE. Come out, Seven.

WALTERS. What for? It ain't time.

DRAKE. You're gonna be shaved. Open up, O'Flaherty.

WALTERS (*exits from cell into corridor. His hands hold a few oranges, a pipe, and book*). Here are some oranges I don't want. Can I give them to the boys?

O'FLAHERTY. Sure.

[*Walters distributes them to the various cells, while the guard Peddie arranges his shaving materials and Drake follows Walters about.*

MEARS (*taking an orange*). Say, Seven!

WALTERS. What?

MEARS. Stay with 'em.

WALTERS. I will, don't you worry. I'll be waitin' for you in hell on the fifteenth.

MAYOR (*as Walters gives him oranges and book*). Keep it up, Walters. It's better for all of us if you do. Ya see, if you go strong and don't break, why we're just ashamed, see, so —

WALTERS (*laughs*). Huh! It's a cinch.

DRAKE. Come on, come on. (*He sits down and Peddie shaves him*) What about his head, Peddie?

WALTERS. Say, nothin' doin'. I don't want my mother to pass out lookin' at me when I get home —

PEDDIE. The warden said all right; we don't have to do it to him, 'cause he spoke to Seven already.

DRAKE. All right, Seven, you're crazy, not me. But don't say later that I didn't warn you. You'll get twice as many shots of juice this way, cause the hair'll be in the way and should be shaved off.

[*Kneels and begins to slit Walters' right trouser-leg.*

WALTERS (*laconically*). This is my funeral, not yours. (*Slight pause*) I'll run it the way I like. Say, Sunny, sing somethin', will you?

JACKSON. What do you want to hear, Boss?

WALTERS. Any damn thing, so long as it's a song. (*The Guards commence to wash him*) Oh, boy, I'm gettin' to feel all tightened up. I'm gonna give up hope. What time you got there on your wrist, Guard?

PEDDIE (*looking at his wrist-watch*). Ten o'clock.

WALTERS. Ten o'clock?

[*Peddie is now shaving his leg.*

PEDDIE. Yea, just.

WALTERS (*whistles*). Whooie, my time is gettin' short. Why in hell don't you sing, Sunny?

WERNER. Hol——mes!

WALTERS. They're gonna fix that chair up for you right away, Thirteen.

JACKSON. No they ain't, Mister. Don't you be givin' me no jinx blues jest because I cain't sing now.

WALTERS. I'll be waitin' down below for you, Sunny. (*A Guard enters Cell Seven, and removes blanket, chair, and*

*pillow. Walters is then locked up in his bare cell. The
Guards now exit and only O'Flaherty is left. Pause)* I'm
sick in my stomach.

KIRBY. Take an orange. It'll do you good.

WALTERS. It ain't that, Red. You see, I just hate to go.
I didn't know I hated anything so bad in all my life. I
hate to leave you guys.

KIRBY. This old life isn't any good anyway, Kid. Let's
just hope you're goin' to a better one. Maybe there is a
better place somewhere. There oughta be.

[*O'Flaherty blows his nose suddenly.*

WALTERS (*mumbling to himself*). What if I shouldn't get
that stay? What —?

JACKSON. Keep standin' up, Boss.

MAYOR (*together with Jackson*). Don't let it get you, Walters.

WALTERS. What if I shouldn't get that stay, Red?

KIRBY (*consolingly*). You'll get it — Seven.

WALTERS (*a bit faster*). But what if I shouldn't?

KIRBY. But you will.

WALTERS (*louder and faster*). But what if I shouldn't?
What if I shouldn't?

KIRBY. I got one, and why should you be an exception?

WALTERS (*still louder*). But what if I shouldn't? (*Hysterically*) What if I shouldn't? —

[*Leaps to his feet and clutches bars insanely.*

MEARS. Stay there, Seven.

WALTERS (*speaks staccato, in jerks*). Well — just keep by
me — you damn guys, keep stickin' by me. I'll build me
an air-castle — or somethin', to get my mind off it, off the
chair. Hey, tell us how you slit his throat, Sunny. Tell
us how you ripped up that high yaller.

JACKSON. Lemme 'lone, white boy. Ah'm busy prayin' for
you.

WALTERS. Thanks. Keep it up. I'll pray for you later
on. Wish I had a drink.

O'FLAHERTY (*advances and offers him a pint-flask from his hip*).
It's against the rules; but take a slug o' this, Kid.

MEARS (*as Walters drinks*).   Watch it!
[*O'Flaherty takes flask and returns to door.   He then opens to show Guard and Evangelist.*
GUARD (*crosses to Seven*).   Right here, sir.   This is the fellow who goes to-night.
EVANGELIST (*advances to Seven*).   I sure am glad to know you, my son!
WALTERS (*quickly*).   Who are you?
EVANGELIST.   A friend of God, the same as you.   (*Effusively*) When I read of your impending execution, I just had to come and see you, and find out for the peace of my soul if you were saved in God's own true way, if you were ready to embrace the faith —
WALTERS (*dully*).   Yes, I'm ready, but I'm still hoping till the last second that my life will be spared —
EVANGELIST.   I'm very grateful to hear that you are ready to die in God's way, standing upright, and not as a heathen sinner —
MAYOR (*interrupting derisively*).   How does a sinner die, preacher?   On his behind?
EVANGELIST (*turning to Mayor truculently*).   What are you? A wise guy?   Think you know it all?   Don't you? Maybe that's why you're here, wise guy.
MAYOR (*making quite an expressive gesture, though rather vulgar*).   Aw, can that stuff, Aimee MacPherson.   Don't think you can make us believe you're a man by using slang.
EVANGELIST (*returning to Walters, comments*).   Wise guy!
WALTERS (*simply*).   Well, I certainly am glad I'm not leaving a wife and kids.   I'm glad I never married.   I'm glad now.
EVANGELIST.   Yes, it is easier, brother, where there is no one concerned but yourself.
WALTERS.   Not so much easier.   (*Slight pause*) I hate to leave Mother.   It hurts her, I know.
EVANGELIST.   It will be ever so much easier for her to bear, knowing that when her son went the way of all flesh, he

was all right with God; that all his accounts were settled
with our Friend up above, that his —

MAYOR (*shouting*). Oh, Jeez. Get the hell out of here.
Do I have to stand for all that crap too? Hey, screw!
Get this bastard out. Screw!

GUARD. All right. Let's go.

[*They exit.*

EVANGELIST (*to Walters, as he leaves*). Good-by. Meet
Him with a smile.

WALTERS. Yea! Good-by. (*Guard enters with coffee for
Seven. As he drinks, Guard exits*) Red, you were damned
lucky to get that thirty-five day stay. Boy, I wish I had
one. Looks like I ought to get one stay at least. Just one.

KIRBY (*sincerely*). Seven, if it was possible for me to do it,
I'd give you half of mine, and we'd both have seventeen
and a half days each. I wish I could do it.

WALTERS (*with intensity*). You wouldn't fool me, would
you, Red? This ain't no time to do that.

KIRBY (*emphatically*). Not right here in town with my shirt
on. Of course I got no way to prove my statement to you.
I can see why you find it hard to believe; but just the same
I would do it. I would. I wish it was only possible,
because I hate like hell to see you go, Seven.

WALTERS. I wish you could do it, Red. If you ain't kiddin'
me?

MAYOR. He ain't. He'd do it. I believe him.

WALTERS (*finding it very difficult to believe*). Ya all think so,
guys?

D'AMORO (*slowly*). Seven, we all think he means what he
says.

WALTERS (*extremely thankful*). Well, (*Breathing deeply*)
thanks a lot, Red.

[*Father O'Connors enters. O'Flaherty unlocks cell Number
Seven. O'Connors enters cell — places candles etc. on stool.*

MAYOR. Say, One. Did you say your name was (*Saying it
carefully*) D'Amoro?

D'AMORO. Sure, that's my name. Why?

MAYOR. Nothin'. Only your name D'Amoro sounds like a French word I know. *Amour.* It means — love.

D'AMORO. Same in Italian. Love.

MAYOR (*wistfully*). Hm. Love.

D'AMORO. Say, ain't that a funny word to say in this place and at this time?

MAYOR. Funny is right. (*Slight pause, during which the Priest's voice is heard murmuring*) Then —

O'CONNORS. Open up, Guard.

O'FLAHERTY. Yes, Father.

[*Does so.*

O'CONNORS. I'll be back.

[*Exits.*

MAYOR. What would ya say, One, if I told you that I was in love?

D'AMORO. Right now?

MAYOR. Right now.

D'AMORO. No kiddin'. Who with?

MAYOR. With a girl. What d' ya think? A fag?

D'AMORO. That's funny. What does she look like . . . ?

WALTERS (*as he interrupts, they stop conversing*). Light me a cigarette, Five. I'm afraid my head'll catch on fire with all this alcohol on it, if I get near a match.

O'FLAHERTY.

[*Takes cigarette from Mears who has lighted it and gives it to Walters.*

KIRBY (*with some conviction*). Seven, there must be somethin' for you to look forward to. It must be better than this life or it wouldn't be worth much. I don't think any of us is losin' much when we walk to that chair. Anyhow there's bound to be a heaven or somethin', and if there is somethin' or somebody like a God, everybody'll have the opportunity to get in right.

[*Bell rings — Drake enters with two Reporters and conducts them to Cell Seven.*

BROOKS. Hello — Walters.

WALTERS. Hello, fellers.

FROST. How do you feel?

WALTERS. Pretty well. Thanks.

BROOKS (*trying to put it delicately*). Feel like givin' us a little information?

WALTERS (*suspiciously*). Where ya from?

FROST. I'm from the *Post*. Brooks here is on the *News*. But he's all right.

MEARS. They're O.K., Seven.

BROOKS. How do, Killer?

MEARS. All right, Slim. O.K.

WALTERS (*slowly, undecided*). Yea, maybe I'll tell ya somethin'. I don't know, but, (*Reporters pay close attention*) she wasn't no kid, like the D.A. said she was. She was over sixteen. You seen her pictures. (*Pause*) I was makin' pretty good money. I was workin' then for the town gas company, as a meter-reader. I loved her —

FROST. You did? (*Walters nods*) You really loved her?

WALTERS (*slowly*). Yes, I did. I was crazy over her, I guess. I'd been pretty wild, ya see, and I liked her, so much, I guess, because she was so, so — clean, a virgin, and very pretty.

FROST. Then what?

WALTERS (*slight pause, as he speaks, he now and then wets his lips*). Well — I wanted to marry her — I asked her, ya might not believe me, but I did. I'd done everything for her, but she kidded me and teased me along, and I — I couldn't sleep nights. I wanted her so. Well, that day I took her riding, you won't believe me, but it's true — true as God. I took her ridin' to elope with her. She asked me where I was goin'. I said, 'Just ridin'.' And she says, 'It's time to go back,' and I laugh and say, 'Sure Ethel, sure. We'll go back, and how.' Well, she gets nervous. Ya see, she didn't give me much credit for honest intentions, and that was what — (*Catches himself*) well, I'll come to that, and here she is gettin' nervous — So I see she's gotta know and I drive into a side road, and

park under a tree near a little brook. Well very slow-like
I take out the diamond engagement ring I had bought for
her, and I tell her to shut her eyes. She does. I slip the
ring on her finger, now get this, cause you woulda done the
same, I take and I kiss her hand with the ring on it. She
opens her eyes and looks at me for a second, then she looks
at her hand and says softly — 'Oh' — Then I kiss her on
the mouth, and it was the first time, and — it was —
wonderful. It was a nice clear day, near about sunset.
She lets me kiss her, but suddenly she begins to squirm and
yell, 'No, no. I don't want to. Take me home. Let me
go, I tell you. Let me go. I hate you. I hate you.'
And she rips off the ring and throws it into the little brook
near us, right outa the car.

FROST (*makes a note*). A little brook, eh?

BROOKS (*aside to Frost*). Sh. Sh. Well, what happened?

WALTERS (*after a slight pause, speaking a bit faster*). I don't
know what. But I think to myself. Aw, what the hell.
I'll give her the works. I don't care. And besides, I was
sore. Jeez, figger throwin' away my ring, the ring that
would have made her my own wife. I was sore. I pulled
her out of the car and laid her on the grass and just —

FROST. Forced her?

WALTERS (*speaking quite rapidly now*). Yea. Then she
began to cry and yell. Then she said, 'I'll have you arrested. I'll have you put in jail.' And she called me all
kinds of dirty names. Well, I don't know, I was sore.
Now get this, cause you would have done the same, maybe.
I get peeved and I hit her. She goes down. (*Slight pause*)
I'm sure it was that sharp rock under her head that did the
killin', 'cause I couldn't hit hard enough to kill anybody,
although maybe I could, but anyway it wasn't like that
D.A. said, that I hit her with the rock, but I didn't mean
it, — honest, I didn't mean it —

[*Stops abruptly.*

BROOKS. Anything else? Any more?

WALTERS (*slowly, wearily*). Huh? More? No — buddy —

I'm tired. (*Apologetically*) I don't feel like goin' on. You guys know the rest.

BROOKS. Sure, we do, sure. Well, thanks. I'll do somethin' for you some day.

WALTERS. See what you can do for my mother. Will ya?

FROST. Sure we will. We'll run her a newspaper fund — O.K.?

WALTERS. Gee. Thanks.

FROST. Well, so long. Good luck.

WALTERS. So long, fellers. Thanks a lot for comin'.

BROOKS. So long.

[*Guard and Reporters exit.*

WALTERS (*in a hollow tone*). Say, boys, wouldn't I feel tickled to get a thirty day stay? I've got more hopes now than I had two hours ago. I was pretty low then, I guess. The warden's secretary promised me that he'd stand right near the telephone.

KIRBY. You'll get it, Seven.

WALTERS. I still got hopes.

[*Slight pause.*

JACKSON. What time is it, Nine?

KIRBY. Near to it, Sunny. Near to it. Pray hard.

JACKSON. Ah is, Red Boy. I'm praying hard as hell.

WALTERS. Say, I'm beginning to feel funny again in the belly. It's like a cramp and —

PRINCIPAL KEEPER (*enters*). I've got to read this.

[*Reads Death Warrant to Seven.*

DEATH WARRANT

People of the State of Oklahoma
                    Vs
Richard Walters

. . . .

State of Oklahoma
County of Elmira. . . . . . . .s. s.

To the Agents and Warden of the Keystone Prison at Keystone, Oklahoma.

WHEREAS: at a trial term of the County Court, held in and for the County of Elmira at the Elmira County Court House, in the village of Hutchinson, County of Elmira, State of Oklahoma, on the ninth day of April, 1929, and on the days following, Richard Walters was placed on trial for the murder of Ethel Wayne Simmons in the said County of Elmira on the fifteenth day of December, 1928; and upon said trial was found guilty of murder in the first degree for said killing and on the sixteenth day of April, 1929, and on the eighteenth day of April, 1929, was sentenced to be put to death in the manner provided by the law on some day in the week beginning the 26th day of May, 1929; now:

IT IS HEREBY ORDERED, that execution on the said sentence be done upon said Richard Walters by you, the said Agent and Warden of the Keystone Prison, in the manner provided by the law, on such day of the week beginning on the 26th day of May, 1929, as you shall determine, within the walls of your said prison, or the yard or enclosure thereto adjoining.

Witness my hand and seal at Hutchinson, County of Elmira, State of Oklahoma, aforesaid, this eighteenth day of April, 1929.

> *James Carney Leffingworth*
> County Judge of Elmira County,
> Oklahoma, Presiding.

Given under my hand
and seal and attested by the
said court this 18th day of
April, 1929.
Daniel Corrigan
Clerk

That's all, Seven. Anything you want to say, say now.

Your mother asked me to get your last words for her.

WALTERS. I'd send her a telegram if I had the money. But I gave it all away to Thirteen.

JACKSON. Here's some.

[*He extends a bill through the bars.*

WALTERS. Will you send it, Mr. Callahan?

[*Guard takes the bill, gives it to the Principal Keeper.*

CALLAHAN. What do you want to tell her?

WALTERS. Tell her I'm laughin', and jokin', and singin'.
Tell her I'm thinkin' of her. Tell her I'm all right. All
right. Got that? That my thoughts are all of her —

CALLAHAN. I'll do it now. Stay here, Harris.

[*Exits.*

WALTERS (*passing slippers*). Do ya want these slippers,
Red?

KIRBY. No, I gotta pair. I'll give 'em to Sunny.

WALTERS. All right.

JACKSON (*takes them from Guard, who took them from Kirby*).
Thanks, Boss. Ah'm still prayin' fo' yuh.

WALTERS. Uh-huh. Say, Guard, light me a cigarette, will ya.
(*Guard does so. Suddenly breaks into song, away off-key*)
"A little white light will lead you to my blue heaven.
A smiling face, a fire-place, a cozy room —"
[*Stops abruptly.*

KIRBY. Hold on, Seven. The Governor's liable to give you
that stay yet. I'll bet he's jest lettin' ya get up tight in
order to scare ya. Ya know the Legislature is in session
now, and he can't go to bed before midnight. He might
wire or phone any minute now.

WALTERS. All right. But, if I don't get that stay, I'm
going to try to set a good example here. They say that a
fellow has never died here who didn't show weakness.
I'm going to show them that I can go like a man. I can,
all right. I can. I can.

D'AMORO. I hate to see you go, buddy, but if ya have to go,
it's better to take it like a man. Don't weaken.

WALTERS. I — hate — to — go.

JACKSON. Here comes the keys.

[*Guard enters with the Priest who is let into Cell Seven.
There he administers the Holy Communion.*

O'CONNORS. Our Father who art in Heaven, hallowed be Thy Name. Thy Kingdom come. Thy will be done on earth as it is in Heaven. Give us this day our daily bread, and forgive us our trespasses, as we forgive those who trespass against us. And lead us not into temptation, but deliver us from evil. Amen. Read the prayer, Walters.

WALTERS (*swallowing*). Almighty God, unto whom all hearts are open, all desires known, and from whom no secrets are hid; cleanse the thoughts of our hearts by the inspiration of Thy Holy Spirit that we may perfectly love Thee, and worthily magnify Thy Holy Name; through Thy Christ, Our Lord; Amen.

O'CONNORS.
Lord, have mercy on us.
Christ, have mercy on us.
Lord, have mercy on us. (*He turns some pages*) Now read the other prayer.

WALTERS. O Lord Jesus, God of my heart, and Life of my soul, (*He breaks down and sobs*) O Jesus Christ, get me out of here, don't let me go, don't let me die. I'll do anything you say, only don't let me go, please Jesus, I'll cut my arm off, I'll cut my leg off, Jesus, don't let me —

O'CONNORS (*interrupting*). Calm yourself, boy, calm yourself. There, there. (*Pause*) Now repeat after me, O God, who has saved me and forgiven me.

WALTERS (*brokenly*). O God, who has saved me and forgiven me —

O'CONNORS. Hear my supplications —

WALTERS. Hear my supplications.

O'CONNORS. And take me unto thy eternal keeping —

WALTERS. And take me unto thy eternal keeping.

O'CONNORS. Amen. Domine, nostrum dignus, ut intres sub tectum meum set tautum dic verbo, et sanabitus anima mea. (*Repeat three times, then*) Corpus Domini nostri Jesus Christi custiodiat animam tuam in vitam æternam, Amen. Now Richard Walters, let us pray. (*Blesses him*)

Benedictio Dei Omnipotentis Patris et Filio. Et Spiritus
Sancti descendant super te, et maneat semper. Amen.
[*Exits from cell to green door and remains there reading
prayers.*

WALTERS (*as the Priest is let out of the cell*). I hate to go, but
it looks like it's gotta be done.
[*The Priest now stands near the green door reading quietly
from his book.*

KIRBY. Don't give up hope.

WALTERS. I still got hopes but they're gettin' weak.

WERNER. Hol——mes!

WALTERS. Light me a cigarette. (*There is a tense air of
expectancy that grows heavier and heavier. More and more
intense. One can almost feel it, touch it*) Let me out with
the boys, O'Flaherty, I wanna tell 'em all good-by.

O'FLAHERTY. I can't do it, Seven. I would if I could, but
it would be against the rules. I'm awfully sorry. I wish
I could.

WALTERS (*with attempted nonchalance*). Oh, I don't care.
'Sall right. (*He is given a lighted cigarette*) I'm not
takin' it as hard as I thought I'd be. I'm pretty nervous
though; I never had anything to do with electricity before.
Wonder how it feels? Wonder if a guy knows anything?
I hope it won't take long. They say Skippy Woodworth
turned all his insides red from the burning. His brain too.
Is that right about them keepin' the brains here in the
hospital for findin' out things? I don't think my insides'll
turn red. They got it perfected by now. Skippy was a
long time ago. I hope my insides don't turn red —

MAYOR. Aw, ya never know what hits ya. It's all over in a
few shakes. Brace up.

WALTERS (*speaking in a sort of strange monotone*). Ya know
it's funny. I was worse at my trial than I am now. I
almost broke down at my trial. I lost fifteen and a half
pounds, while the case was in court. (*Suddenly as if
in anguish*) Give me some more coffee, fer Christ's
sakes!

MAYOR. Oh, my God.

WALTERS (*as Guard gives him coffee*). Huh! Well, here's
to the old death house, boys!

CALLAHAN (*enters with more Guards. Cell Seven is unlocked
by the Principal Keeper*). All right, Seven. Let's go.
[*Seven exits cell slowly.*

WALTERS (*wavers, but the Guards hold him on either side.
Gulps and swallows with difficulty*). I wanna say good-by
to the boys.

CALLAHAN. All right. Start back there with the nigger.

WALTERS (*crosses to Thirteen; the Guards follow him, but have
released their hold on him*). Good-by, Sunny. I won't
shake hands. It's bad luck.

JACKSON. Good-by, Mister Walters. Ah hope mah prayahs
done yuh some good.

WALTERS (*crosses to Eleven*). Good-by, Eddie. I don't
know which of us is better off.

WERNER. Good-by, son. Farewell. (*Beckons to him with
finger to come closer*) If you should meet Louis there —
tell him that I —

WALTERS (*interrupts*). O.K., Eddie. I'll do it.

KIRBY. Good-by, kid. Stand right up.

WALTERS. Huh. I think I'm doin' about as well as you
would do.

KIRBY. I know you are.

WALTERS. Good-by.

KIRBY. S'long. Don't fergit to hold it.

WALTERS (*as he crosses slowly to Five, he looks down upon his
split trouser-leg*). Huh. They split my pants, and I don't
like it much. This is a new style, boys. How do you like
it? Hello, Five. Give me a drag, will ya? (*The Guards
seize him, as he bends over to take a puff*) Don't worry. I
ain't gonna run away.

MEARS. Good-by, Seven. Stay with 'em.

WALTERS. I'll make it. Good-by, Killer John Mears.

MEARS. Good-by, Richard Walters. Give 'em my best
regards. (*Laughs*) Laugh at 'em.

WALTERS. I will. I will. I can do it. Good-by, Freddie. I hope you get a stay.

MAYOR. Hope so. Good-by. I'll meet ya in two weeks. Wait for me.

WALTERS. Uh-huh. S'long. Glad I met ya, One.

D'AMORO. Likewise. Good-by.

[*Walters is now again held by the Guards. They hold him on either side, by wrist and shoulder.*

WALTERS. This is the last mile. (*He is now at the green door, the Principal Keeper Callahan behind him and the Priest and a Guard in front. The Guard unlocks the green door, yanks at it but it sticks. Almost hysterically*) Say, Five! They can't get that damned door open. What d' ya think of that?

MEARS. Take those keys and open it for them, Seven!

[*Laughs.*

WALTERS (*slowly*). I'd stay right here until next Christmas before I'd open it for them. (*The door is finally opened*) Well, it's open. I'll say good-by to everybody again. So long, everybody! (*Cries of "Good-by, So long," etc.*) I wish I'm the last one who ever sits in that goddam, bastard chair. . . .

[*He exits.*

The lights suddenly grow dim after a pause and the whine of the motor is heard. Pause. Lights go up. Mayor breaks down and sobs. Pause. Lights grow dim again.

MEARS (*as the lights go dim for the second time*). They're givin' him the juice again. (*Shouts in a terrible rage*) What the hell are they tryin' to do? Cook him?

CURTAIN

LAWD, DOES YOU UNDAHSTAN'?

ANN SEYMOUR

As the one-act play has come closer to the lives of many people, both to audience and to play-makers, its uses have multiplied. Always a means of entertainment, plays are sometimes sponsored by purposeful organizations to advance a law or a cause. "Lawd, Does You Undahstan'?" is one of these. It was awarded a prize offered by the Association of Southern Women for the Prevention of Lynching.

Ann Seymour, the author, was born in Strawn, Texas, in 1906, and still calls it " home." She attended Texas State College for Women, majored in Speech Arts and Dramatics, and received her degree in 1927. Since 1930 she has been teaching in the Junior High School at Palestine, Texas, which has a large negro population. She has also been active there in Little Theatre work.

Her two other one-act plays are "On the Other Side of the Moon" and "At the Foot of the Dump." For these she was awarded a literary prize and the Texas Intercollegiate Press Association prize.

LAWD, DOES YOU UNDAHSTAN'?

By ANN SEYMOUR

"Lawd, Does You Undahstan'?" was originally produced by the School of Dramatics at Paine College, Augusta, Georgia, on December 12, 1936.

Original Cast

AUNT DOADY	Lessie M. O. Snuggs
JIM	Joseph Lacy
LUCY	Anne Duren
EPSIE LEE	Thelma Perry
FRUIT CAKE	Warren Williams
TOM MOORE	Vanholt Blanchard
MILES	James Gaulden
MAN	Frank G. Yerby
TWO MINOR CHARACTERS	{ Jonathan Scarborough { John J. Hicks

Directed by Miss Emma C. W. Gray.

LAWD, DOES YOU UNDAHSTAN'?

SCENE. *The scene is laid in front of a negro cabin. The door is open, as is the one window. Through the door can be seen a table with a lamp on it; and through the window, a bed. Outside it is bright moonlight. To the right, under the window is a wash bench with wash pan, bucket and dipper, and fruit jar with some cyanide in the bottom of it. There is a small wood-pile to the extreme left and a wash pot down stage at the right. A cane-bottom chair leans against the house. The only lights are the yellow light of the lamp and the moonlight.*

Aunt Doady, an old negro woman, is sitting on the door-step, leaning forward, elbows resting on knees. Her black, wrinkled face has the rather mournful tranquillity found on so many black faces: a calm acceptance of fate.

The night is very still until from the shadowy woods close by a whippoorwill calls plaintively.

The dialect is only suggested. The voices are soft and melodious, and the vowels are much plainer than the consonants.

AUNT DOADY. Listen to dat bird! Soun' lak he heart done broke in two. (*The whippoorwill calls again*) What de mattah, whippoorwill? Why you cryin', hunh? Is youah wife done gone and left you, or is you jus' lone-some cause you ain' got no wife? Ain' no use takin' on lak dat.

[*A little negro boy runs on the stage. He has been running hard and is panting so that he finds it hard to speak. Aunt Doady peers at him.*

AUNT DOADY. Is dat you, Fruit Cake?

FRUIT CAKE. Yes 'm, Aunt Doady, I jus' been . . .

AUNT DOADY. Wheah 's youah ma?

FRUIT CAKE. She 's a-comin' up de road. I took a short cut through de woods an' when . . .

AUNT DOADY.   Who with yo' ma?

FRUIT CAKE.   Epsie Lee, pappy an' 'em. Dey's goin' to
church, and when I gits to dat ole dead tree stump down
in de slough, ole screech owl a-settin' up dere, jus' yell
lak evahthing. Hit scah me an' I run as hahd as I kin.
Bet I was goin' fastah'n anything. Bet I was goin'
fastah'n ole win' could go.

AUNT DOADY.   Boy, how many times dat owl screech?

FRUIT CAKE.   T'ree times, Aunt Doady.

AUNT DOADY.   Is you suah?

FRUIT CAKE.   Yes'm, I'se suah! T'ree times, jes' lak dis:
Hoo! Hoo! Hoo!

AUNT DOADY.   Hush yo' mouf! Dat's soun' I doan lak.
Screech owl mean death. Fruit Cake, you ain't got no
business comin' through dem woods. Ef'n you hadn',
you wouldn' a heard no screech owl.

[*From offstage at the right comes the sound of voices of negroes,
laughing and calling to each other, walking down the moonlit
road to church. Epsie Lee, a young negro girl, finely built,
with an intelligent, sympathetic face, enters a little ahead of
the others. Lucy, Fruit Cake's mother, follows closely.
She is good-natured and lazy, with an ever ready laugh.
Three men and two other women complete the group. They
seat themselves easily about the stage, Lucy dropping on
the wash bench at the right. One of the men sits on the
ground and leans against the wash bench, another sits on
the wood-pile at extreme left and faces the house; the other
man leans against the house in a cane-bottom chair, just to
the left of an overturned box where one of the women sits.
As they come in, they call greetings to Aunt Doady.*]

ALL.   Good evening, Aunt Doady.

AUNT DOADY.   I'se fine. How's you dis evenin'?

EPSIE LEE (*going toward the doorstep where Aunt Doady sits*).
M'hunh, cotch you a talkin' to youahself, didn' we,
Aunt Doady? Mighty good sign you's gittin' old.

AUNT DOADY.   What if I does talk to myself? I'se suah
somebody's listenin' den, and dat's mo' dan I kin say

ef'n I talks to somebody else. But I 'se been talkin' to Fruit Cake.

LUCY. He been heah, has he? I been wonderin' wheah dat chile shisted off to.

AUNT DOADY. He were heah jus' a moment ago. Fruit Cake, wheah you go? (*Fruit Cake, who hid in the wash pot when he first heard the voices, pops up his grinning head*) Git outa dat wash pot fo' I skin you. Lawd! You so black I cain' tell wheah you staht an' de wash pot leave off.

FRUIT CAKE (*hops out*). Aunt Doady, why I so black anyhow?

EPSIE LEE (*chanting*).
      "God made de dahkey
      Made him in de night
      Made him in a hurry
      And fo'got to paint him white!"

Dat 's what Aunt Doady use to tell me an' Jim. Who learn it to you, Aunt Doady?

AUNT DOADY. My ole mammy learn it to me. Dunno wheah she got it.

FRUIT CAKE. "God made de dahkey." What come nex', Epsie Lee?

EPSIE LEE. "Made him in de night."

FRUIT CAKE. "God made de dahkey,
      Made him in de night."

EPSIE LEE. "Made him in a hurry
      And fo'got to paint him white!"

FRUIT CAKE. "Made him in a hurry
      And fo'got to paint him white!"

LUCY. Night lak dis make me jes' want to sit an' sit.

AUNT DOADY. Seem lak any kin' night make you wan' to sit. Any kin' day, too.

LUCY (*she laughs with the others*). Reck'n you 's right about dat. But when I knows I oughta be up an' doin' sumpin', seem lak I cain' jus' sit without worryin' a mite.

LUCY'S HUSBAND. Worryin' ain't gonna tiah you out none.

EPSIE LEE. Look, ol' moon done got hisself hung in a tree.

FRUIT CAKE. Wan' a drink.

LUCY. Go lif' dat dippah an' git one den.

[*Fruit Cake goes to wash bench and gets a drink of water. After he drinks, he picks up the fruit jar on the bench.*

AUNT DOADY. Fruit Cake, put dat jah down! Take yo' han's of'n it, I say. Hit's pizen!

FRUIT CAKE. Pizen? Why's it pizen, Aunt Doady?

LUCY. Git away from dere, Fruit Cake! Does you wan' to drop dead?

ONE OF THE WOMEN. Lucy, ain' dat chile got anuthah name?

LUCY (*laughs*). Lawd, I doan know. Fruit Cake, is you got anuthah name?

FRUIT CAKE. No 'm, jes' Fruit Cake.

AUNT DOADY. Humph! Doan even know whethah youah own youngun got anuthah name.

LUCY. Reck'n we kinda run out when he come along. Aunt Doady, what you got pizen in dat jah for?

AUNT DOADY. Dat's wheah Jim keep he buttahflies and bugs. He jes' drop 'em in an' hit doan huht none. Dey jes' sorta goes to sleep.

EPSIE LEE. Jim, he couldn' stan' to huht nothin', not even a little bug.

ONE OF THE MEN. Mighty funny work fo' a man, catchin' 'em buttahflies.

ANOTHER. You ain' gonna catch dat Jim doin' no man's wuhk. He doan lak dat plowin' an' choppin' cotton. No suh! He gotta catch hisself some buttahflies.

EPSIE LEE (*heatedly*). Jim jus' smart, dat's all. He make a whole lot more money catchin' buttahflies an' sellin' 'em to Professah Brown, dan you does, Reely Watson.

AUNT DOADY. Hit's what he laks to do. Ef'n he'd ruthah catch bugs dan chop cotton, dat's he business, I reck'n. Evahbody be a sight happier ef'n he doin' what he laks.

REELY. What dey do with bugs, anyhow? Wish dey'd come and git some dem boll weevils off'n my cotton.

EPSIE LEE. Jim say Professah Brown stick pins in 'em and put 'em on a card. Dey use 'em in dey studies at de college.

REELY. Still say hit 's funny wuhk fo' a man!

EPSIE LEE. I ain' nevah notice you collapsin' from too much work!

REELY. Anyway ef'n I had a gran'son . . .

AUNT DOADY. Well, you ain' got one yet, an' Lawd pity him does you evah have one!

LUCY. Hol' youah mouths, all of you. Epsie Lee, sing somethin' fo' us: "Dat 's Why Darkeys Were Born."

AUNT DOADY. Dat 's white folks' song. Sing "The Old Hen Cackle."

[*Epsie Lee smiles and starts the familiar old song, moving down stage toward the wash pot. The other darkeys join in. Gradually they get up, and in response to the lively tune, that works into organic melody the notes of the hen cackling, pat their feet and sway their bodies. As the music grows faster, Fruit Cake breaks into a cake walk.*

THE OLD HEN CACKLE

The old hen she cackle, she cackle in the corn;
The next time she cackle, she cackle in the barn.

CHORUS

Well, the old hen she cackle, she sholy gwain to lay.

The old hen she cackle, she cackle in the loft;
The next time she cackle, she cackle further off.

CHORUS

Well, the old hen she cackle, she sholy must-a laid.

The old hen she cackle, she cackle in the lot;
Well, the next time she cackle, she 'll cackle in the pot.

CHORUS

The old hen she cackle, well, she sholy ought to lay.

[*At last, Lucy, the only one, besides Aunt Doady, who has remained seated, rises and interrupts the merriment.*

LUCY.   It's time we git to church, ef'n dey's gonna be any.

AUNT DOADY.   You's powerful late gittin' dere.

LUCY.   Brothah Hawkins went ovah to Stormy Hill fo' a funeral, so church is late to-night.   Bettah come along with us.

AUNT DOADY.   Nope.   I'se too old fo' dat shoutin' religion now.   When you gits as old as I is, an' has known God as long as I has, you doan have to go to church; you can jes' set on youah do'step an' talk to Him.   You doan have to say words even.   He jus' sorta knows what's on youah min'.

REELY (*facetiously*).   Wish I knowed I stood in with de Lawd lak dat.

LUCY.   Ef'n you'd been as good as Aunt Doady all youah life, you wouldn't have to worry no more than she do.

REELY.   I vow Aunt Doady's a good woman all right.   I ain' nevah knowed her to do nothin' that wasn't right, 'cept run off at de mouth powerful hahd.

EPSIE LEE.   Sometime I think Aunt Doady ain' quite lak de res' of us.   She's mo' lak a saint, dat's what!

AUNT DOADY.   Git out!   Doan be makin' no saint out of me.   It's jus' dat I'se lived my life, an' it's been a long one, an' in all dose yeahs I'se known de Lawd an' He's known me.   We jus' undahstan's each othah, dat's all. I ain' nevah stole, no' lied no mo' that I had to, nor killed nobody.   I'se kept as right as I could.   And now dat I'se almost ready to go, I feels kinda peaceful lak — without nothin' to worry about.

LUCY.   Come on, or we's gonna be late fo' meetin' sho.

[*Epsie Lee lags behind, as the others call good-bys and start off the stage at left.*

EPSIE LEE.   Aunt Doady, ain' Jim comin' to church to-night?

AUNT DOADY.   I'se jus' wonderin' wheah Jim at.   He stay gone mos' all day, catchin' bugs.   Den, dis evenin' jus' befo' suppah time, he go down to de Crossroad Store, an' he ain' come back yet. (*Aunt Doady gets up very slowly and walks to the right as though she is looking down the road*) I put his tuhnip greens and cawn bread on the back of de stove to wahm, but de stove gonna be stone cold fo' he gits heah, ef'n he doan hurry.

[*Epsie Lee follows her and then turns and goes to the left as she talks. Aunt Doady, listening to her, moves back to the wash bench, gets a drink of water, and then goes to the wood pile, and gathers a few chips, which she drops in her apron.*

EPSIE LEE. You know, Aunt Doady, it's funny how folks think Jim is lazy and sorta queer 'cause he doan git out and chop cotton or plow lak all de rest ob 'em does. Dere ain' a lazy bone in Jim's body. Us two, we know him; we's de only two what does, I reck'n. Jim, he's jus' different from de othah niggehs aroun' heah, dat's all. He stay in de woods cause he lak 'em. He lak de stillness, de trees, all de birds an' frogs. An' he learn me to like 'em too. I lissen to old bull bats all my life; but one evenin' Jim and me was watchin' 'em swoop around, and hollerin' ovah de lake, an' somehow, jus' de way Jim stood so still-like, a-lookin' at 'em, made me see 'em different; I doan know how. Now I allus gits a little shivery when I sees 'em, jus' lak I does when I sees de mist rise off de lake about sun-up, or de first dogwood in de spring, or heahs a mocking bird singing jus' like he gonna bus' hisself wide open!

AUNT DOADY. Yessuh, Epsie Lee, dere's a whole lot out dere (*She gestures vaguely toward the woods*) ef'n you can jus' stop to see it or lissen to it. Jim, he know how to do it.

[*From a distance Lucy calls Epsie Lee's name.*

EPSIE LEE. I'se comin'. Good night, Aunt Doady. See you in de mawnin'!

AUNT DOADY. Good night, Epsie Lee. Jim got hisself a mighty fine gal. (*Epsie Lee goes off, left, and Aunt Doady gathers chips. The whippoorwill calls, startlingly close*) Still grievin', is you? Body'd think you was mou'nin' fo' de whole worl'. (*She stops suddenly and peers to the right*) What's dat? Who dat out there?

[*Jim, a young negro, comes from the right hurriedly. He is nervous; but even the terror which he tries to hide cannot take away the simplicity and fineness that are naturally his. He tries to assume an air of indifference, even swaggering a little.*

JIM. It's me, Aunt Doady.

AUNT DOADY. How come you slip through de woods lak dat? You scah a body to death! I been listenin' fo' youah whistle fo' an houh. Come on while I gits youah suppah out fo' you.

JIM. No'm, I don' want it. I ain' got time!

AUNT DOADY. Ain't got time? (*She goes toward him and looks at him closely. His eyes evade hers*) Fo' why? What you gotta do? Wheah's you goin'? What's de mattah with you, Jim? You's powerful jumpy.

JIM. Ain' a thing, Aunt Doady. Honest!

AUNT DOADY. What you listenin' to?

[*Dogs bark in the distance. At the sound, Aunt Doady lets the chips drop from her lap, and stands still, suddenly fearful.*

AUNT DOADY. Ain' dem dawgs I heah?

JIM. Yes'm, reck'n so. Maybe dey's coon dawgs. Somebody huntin' coons, I reck'n, or maybe dey's fox houn's. White folks is a huntin' fox. Good night fo' fox huntin'. Scent easy to pick up.

[*The sound of the barking dogs grows louder.*

AUNT DOADY. Are you suah dem's fox houn's, Jim? (*Aunt Doady's voice is ominous*) Jim! Look at me! Dem ain' fox houn's; dem's blood houn's! Gawd! I cain' nebah fo'git dat soun'! De night dey come an' got yo' pappy. You could heah dem blood houn's, gittin' closuh, and closuh, an' closuh all de time. An' yo' pappy, he was gray as a grave stone. He didn't know what to do, wheah to go, thinkin' dey couldn' fin' him in de lof'. But when white folks staht out lynchin', dey ain' no hidin', no

runnin', no talkin' 'em out of it. Dey go up, and dey
drag him out, an' he scream! Gawd! I cain' nevah fo'git
his screams! (*She is living again the terrible night when
her son had been taken by a mob and lynched*) Dey didn'
say much. None o' 'em did, an' dey wouldn't let us.
Dey tie him onto a horse an' drag him, drag him ovah de
groun', ovah de rocks and weeds. Den dey hang him to a
tree an' dey shot him, shot him plum full o' holes! An'
dey wouldn' let me or youah mammy go neah him! Dey
wouldn' let us take him down! We, we could see him
up dere, dangling . . .

JIM. For God's sake, Aunt Doady, stop!

AUNT DOADY (*brokenly*). Jim, baby. Aunt Doady's sorry!
Only I wakes up at night sometime an' I heahs him sayin',
"I didn' mean to kill him, I jus' twisted he gun, so he
wouldn' shoot me!" An' he wouldn', Jim. Youah pappy
wouldn' ha haht nothin'! But de white folks, dey didn'
know dat . . .

JIM. I tell you, I can't stand it!

AUNT DOADY. Jim, who dey aftah, dem blood houn's?
(*Jim stares at her and the truth finally dawns on her*)
Dey's aftah you!

JIM. I ain' done nothin'! I sweahs I ain'! (*They listen
fearfully to the distant barking of the dogs*) I was comin'
along de road from de sto' when I sees Mr. Watkins a
layin' in a little huddle ovah to one side. I went ovah to
him, an' he was bleedin'. He'd been shot. I stahted runnin' off, an' dey take in aftah me. I knowed den dey
think I done it an' it scah me, Aunt Doady. It scah me
so I didn' know what I'se doin', so I jus' go fastah 'n evah!
I heahs one of 'em yell, "Catch him!" An' anothah one
say, "Who was it?" An' somebody else say, "I doan
know what niggeh it was!"

AUNT DOADY. Why didn' you stop an' tell 'em you ain' done
nothin'?

JIM. I'se scahed, I tell you! I couldn' think. I couldn'
do nothin' but run! I lights out to'd de ribbah bottom

an' dey chases me. Dey almos' had me once. I 'se hidin'
hin' a little holly tree, an' dey was as close as you is to me
now, so close I could ha' teched 'em. I couldn' even
breathe. I heahs one of 'em say he 'll go git de sheriff an'
blood houn's. I waits till dey leaves an' den I wades across
de ribbah wheah it 's shallow, so 's dey cain't fin' my trail.

AUNT DOADY. Jim baby, you 's all wet!

JIM. Ef'n I hurries, mebbe I kin make it to de Louisiana
bordah. I 'll stay till dey fin's who done it. I ain' gonna
face 'em now, Aunt Doady, I cain't!

AUNT DOADY. Yes, I knows, son. I rembah youah pappy.
He couldn' 'splain, he couldn' hide. Heah, go roun' an'
look undah dat rock by de hen house doah. I done put a
li'l buryin' money in a can dere. You take 'em. Spec
you 'll need 'em in Louisiana.

JIM. Thanks, Aunt Doady! I oughta git a lettah from
Professah Brown with some money fo' de bugs nex' week.
You jes open it an' keep dat.

AUNT DOADY. I go in an' fix a cup of coffee for you. You
gonna need it.

[*Jim goes around the house to the back and Aunt Doady
goes inside. You can hear her mumbling to herself as she
warms the coffee and pours it in a cup. The dogs get closer.
She comes to the door and listens; then gets the cup of coffee
and brings it outside.*

JIM (*coming around the house*). I foun' it. I kin cut through.

AUNT DOADY (*listening*). Jim, dey 's ovah dere too. Dey 's
split de pack! Listen to 'em, ovah dere, and ovah youn-
dah. Dey musta foun' out it was you, an' now dey 's all
aroun', and gittin' closeh.

[*They look at each other in terror.*

JIM. I gotta git out! I gotta hurry! I gotta make it!

AUNT DOADY. No, Jim! You cain' nevah git away from
'em! You cain' nevah now. Heah, run to de shed room
an' git de shot gun! (*He disappears into the house*) God,
dey cain't take my Jim! Dey cain't drag him ovah
de rocks and weeds, drag him till he 's skinned an' bleedin',

hang him, put a rope aroun' his neck and pull it till dey ain' no life lef' in 'em, see him danglin' from a tree! Jim, what's so gentle he wouldn' even huht a buttahfly! (*When she says "butterfly", she stands stock still, struck by a sudden thought. Then she moves slowly toward the wash bench and fearfully picks up the fruit jar containing cyanide. She puts it down quickly, but the dogs sound closer than ever; so hurriedly she takes the lid off the jar, empties some of the cyanide into the coffee, and replaces the jar on the bench*) Lawd, he say it doan huht de li'l wil' things. They just takes a sniff an' goes to sleep. Dey doan evah know what happen to 'em. But ef'n I gives him pizen, I kills him. I kills him myself. Blood on my soul! . . . An' ef'n I doan, dey git him. Dey drag him, dey hang him from a lim'. I goes to Hell, Lawd, not Jim, not Jim!

[*Jim returns carrying the gun.*

AUNT DOADY. Jim baby, you knows Aunt Doady loves you, doan you, son?

JIM. 'Cose I does, Aunt Doady. Why you ask dat? You been both mammy and pappy to me.

AUNT DOADY. Epsie Lee, she heah dis evenin'.

JIM. You tell Epsie Lee, Aunt Doady, tell huh why I didn' see huh befo' I lef', tell huh I be back fo' long.

AUNT DOADY. Sho, baby, you be back fo' long.

JIM. Lissen! Dey's comin' closuh! Dey's heah almos'. I'se goin', Aunt Doady. I'se gotta go!

AUNT DOADY (*talking almost to herself*). Hit's a terrible thing I'se doin'. De pearly gates is gittin' dimmah an' dimmah, furdah an' furdah away. But I'se got to! I'se got to do it fo' Jim!

JIM. What you say, Aunt Doady?

AUNT DOADY (*hands him the coffee*). Heah. Drink it down. It ain' so hot now. Drink it all at once!

[*Aunt Doady, with horror and misery written on her black face, watches him take a huge gulp of coffee, seeming to swallow most of it at once. He gasps and chokes.*

JIM. It tastes funny. Aunt Doady, I'se . . . sick.

AUNT DOADY. Hit's cause you'se upset an' nervous, Jim. Heah, come in an' lie down a minute fo' you goes.

[*Jim staggers into the house and drops on the bed. Aunt Doady stands in the door, stunned, looking at him. Then she moves the lamp to a table near the narrow bed so that the lamplight shines on him. You can see his body stretched out on the bed, through the window. She comes back to the door and drops on the doorstep. Her face is tragic in the realization of what she has done.*

AUNT DOADY. Lawd, I wondah, does you undahstan' . . .

[*The dogs are in the woods near at hand now and men are heard, trying to quiet them. One voice is heard above the others.*

VOICE. Circle the house and see that he don't slip out!

[*Two men enter from the right. Tom Moore is a stalwart, slow-moving, slow-talking man. Miles Chambers is a younger man, thoughtless and arrogant.*

TOM MOORE. Good evening, Aunt Doady.

AUNT DOADY (*answering as though she is in a stupor*). Awright, thank you. How's you?

TOM MOORE. Is Jim here?

AUNT DOADY. Yessuh, Jim's heah.

MILES CHAMBERS. Well, tell him to get himself out here and not try any funny business, or else he'll wish he hadn't.

AUNT DOADY. Musta been youah dogs I heahd bahkin' ovah dere. Is you been coon huntin'?

MILES CHAMBERS (*facetiously*). Oh, we're hunting coon right enough.

TOM MOORE. Aunt Doady, Jim just killed a white man and we're here to get him. You can't let niggers get away with things like that, and you'd better tell him not to try to run.

AUNT DOADY. No, suh, Mr. Moore, he won't run away.

MILES CHAMBERS. Well, stop palaverin' and tell us where he is.

[*He grabs Aunt Doady's shoulder and shakes her.*

TOM MOORE. Cut it out, Miles. Aunt Doady ain't done nothing.

MILES CHAMBERS. You 've got to put the fear of God in these damn niggers or they 'll take the country. Where is he?

AUNT DOADY (*pointing to window*). Dere he is. He 's daid.

MILES CHAMBERS. Well, I 'll be a. . . .

[*A man enters from the left. He has been running.*

MAN. Tom, you haven't done nothin' yet, have you?

TOM MOORE. No, why?

MAN. You 're on the wrong track! Jim didn't do it. Henry Watts' brother-in-law killed him. He went over to the county seat and turned himself in. The sheriff caught us at the Catfish Bridge.

TOM MOORE. His brother-in-law! Well! They 've been on bad terms for years.

MILES CHAMBERS. Well, old Jim here kicked the bucket before we got him anyway. Couldn't lynch a dead nigger.

TOM MOORE. Shut up, Miles! We 're sorry, Aunt Doady. We shouldn't have bothered you. I feel kinda bad about Jim. He allus seemed like a good nigger. He musta had a bad heart.

[*The men, greatly subdued, go quietly and rather awkwardly off the stage. Aunt Doady's face is pitiful to see as she realizes she has needlessly given him poison.*

AUNT DOADY. Dey wouldn' 'a' took him. Dey wouldn' ha' took him. Lawd, you gotta undahstan'. I didn' know it. I thought dey kill him. I thought dey hang 'em up on a tree lak dey done his pappy. Jesus, I done kill my own gran'son. De owl he hoot t'ree times! Wish it ud been me, Lawd, 'stead uh Jim!

[*Epsie Lee runs in from the left.*

EPSIE LEE. It ain' so, Aunt Doady. Jim ain' dead. Men down de road say Jim dead. Wheah is he, Aunt Doady?

AUNT DOADY (*motions toward window*). Dere he is.

EPSIE LEE. Oh, Lawd!

[*Epsie Lee goes into the house. You can see her standing,*

*looking at Jim for a few moments. Then she drops to her
knees and sobs.*

AUNT DOADY. He was standin' right dere talkin' to me
jus' a moment ago. An' now he's gone. He ain' heah.
I won' nevah heah him come whistlin' home in de evenin'.
His cawn bread an' tuhnip greens is still a settin' on de
back uh de stove a waitin' for 'em jus' wheah I put 'em
myself. Oh, God! Ef'n he could only git up and eat
'em! Dere's all his bugs jes' lak he lef' 'em. Ef'n it
hadn' been fo' de bugs, I never would a thought uh de
jah! Ef'n I only hadn' . . . God, I wondah why us
has to do such things! I lose my Jim . . . Won' nevah
know peace no mo'.

[*The whippoorwill calls, low and mournfully. Lucy and
the other negroes come from the left. They are silent and
sympathetic. Lucy goes to Aunt Doady. The others
stand about looking in the window, saying nothing. Fruit
Cake stays close to his mother, his eyes round with wonder
and fear.*

LUCY. Dere, Aunt Doady. Doan look lak dat. Ef'n you
could jus' break down, you feel so much bettah. What
happen', Aunt Doady? I see 'em dis mawnin' an' he
look jes' es peart, goin' along whis'lin'.

AUNT DOADY (*unaware that anyone has spoken to her*). He
was funny li'l boy. He wa'n't no mo' dan seben when
he went out an' catch a fish. He brung him home, dip
him in cawn meal, an' fry 'em, jes' so he could surprise me.
Bless his haht! He done fo'got to take de fish's insides
out . . . An' he brung me a new cap jes' las' week. Epsie
Lee! Come heah!

[*Lucy calls to Epsie Lee and the girl comes out. She drops
to the ground and puts her head in Aunt Doady's lap.*

AUNT DOADY. He say he sorry he couldn't see you fo' he
lef' . . . (*After a moment's silence*) You'se jus' gonna
miss him . . . Fo' God! Wish dat's all my mournin'
gonna be!

EPSIE LEE. Ain' it cruel, Aunt Doady? Ain' death cruel?

AUNT DOADY. They's things crueller than death, Epsie
Lee. They's things crueller than death.
[*The other negroes start singing very low at first, gradually
growing louder, the weird old song, "What Is Dis?"*

What is dis dat steals, dat steals
    Across my brow?
Is it death? Is it death?
What is dis dat steals
    My breath away?
Is it death? Is it death?

CHORUS

If dis is death, I soon shall be
From ebry pain an' trouble free.
I shall the King of Glory see,
All is well. All is well!

What is dis dat make, dat make
    My pulse beat feeble and slow?
Is it death? Is it death?
What is dis dat creeps, dat creeps
    Across my frame?
Is it death? Is it death?

THE CURTAIN FALLS.

TILL THE DAY I DIE

CLIFFORD ODETS

ONE cannot mention the name of Clifford Odets without speaking also of the proletarian movement in drama, of which he is the outstanding spokesman of the day.

The people's theatre movement, like the art theatre development, originated abroad, in the *Volksbühne* of the German Social-Democratic Party; in the workers' circles of Austria-Hungary, France, and the Scandinavian countries; among the Jews of Poland and the Czechs of the Hapsburg empire. Large numbers of these workers emigrated to America, and brought their traditions with them.

The Norwegians among them staged Ibsen in the original language in Montana; the Jewish needle-trades workers in the Labor Lyceums of New York's East Side staged him in Yiddish translations. Others gave Hauptmann in German, Gorky in Russian, and Shakespeare in all languages. They developed some outstanding production groups such as the Artef, the Jewish workers' theatre, and the Ukrainian Dramatic Circle. But until recently, the barriers of language kept these groups from commingling.

Then came the "Pageant of Labor", staged by Harvard's John Reed, the pageant of the "Paris Commune" at Madison Square Garden, and the Workers' Drama League of New York in 1926.

Finally, about 1930, the proletarian play found its organized audience — just as the art play, the psychological play, the folk play in the college proving-grounds, had done before it. The Workers Laboratory Theatre (now the Theatre of Action), an English-language group, became an organizing center in the presentation of labor emotions to worker audiences. In 1931 came the Group Theatre, sponsored at first by the Theatre Guild; in 1933 came the Theatre Union; and in 1935 the New Theatre League. It was the Group Theatre which introduced "Till the Day I Die" and Clifford Odets to American audiences.

Mr. Odets was born in Philadelphia, July 18, 1906. He graduated from public school in New York City, and spent two years in high school. From his public school days he has always been interested in acting, although, on occasions, he has tried writing poetry and short stories, clerking in a woollen house, and selling Fuller brushes.

He has written and directed plays for local radio stations, and has acted in stock in New York, Brooklyn, Philadelphia, and Camden. This experience led directly to work with the Theatre Guild, and then the Group Theatre, in which he was one of the original members.

His one-act plays are: "Waiting for Lefty" and "Till the Day I Die." His full-length plays are: "Awake and Sing", "Paradise Lost", and "The Silent Partner."

Since the year 1936 he has been on the Western coast, writing screen dialogue for Paramount.

But above all his work, his chief interest and greatest love is music, especially Beethoven.

TILL THE DAY I DIE

By CLIFFORD ODETS

"Till the Day I Die" was first presented by the Group Theatre at the Longacre Theatre on the evening of March 26th, 1935.

Original Cast

KARL TAUSIG	Walter Coy
BAUM	Elia Kazan
ERNST TAUSIG	Alexander Kirkland
TILLY	Margaret Barker
ZELDA	Eunice Stoddard
DETECTIVE POPPER	Lee J. Cobb
MARTIN, an orderly	Bob Lewis
ANOTHER ORDERLY	Harry Stone
CAPTAIN SCHLEGEL	Lewis Leverett
ADOLPH	Herbert Ratner
ZELTNER	David Kortchmar
SCHLUPP	Russell Collins
EDSEL PELTZ	William Challee
1ST STORM TROOPER	Samuel Roland
2ND STORM TROOPER	Harry Stone
3RD STORM TROOPER	Gerrit Kraber
4TH STORM TROOPER	Abner Biberman
BOY	Wendell Keith Phillips
OLD MAN	George Heller
OTHER PRISONERS	Elia Kazan, David Kortchmar, Paul Morrison
MAJOR DUHRING	Roman Bohnen
FRAU DUHRING	Dorothy Patten
1ST DETECTIVE	Gerrit Kraber
2ND DETECTIVE	David Kortchmar
SECRETARY	George Heller
ARNO	Samuel Roland

STIEGLITZ	. . . .	Lee Martin
JULIUS	. . . .	Bernard Zanville
WOMEN	. . . .	Ruth Nelson, Paula Miller

The action takes places in present-day Berlin.

" Till the Day I Die " was suggested by a letter from Germany printed in *The New Masses.*
The production was directed by Cheryl Crawford.
The scenery was designed by Alexander Chertoff from suggestions by Paul Morrison.

TILL THE DAY I DIE

SCENE I

SCENE. *A small room underground in Berlin to-day. A small man with a rueful face, named Baum, is silently operating a hectograph machine. Watching him are the two brothers, Ernst and Carl Tausig. Downstage at a long littered table sits an alert girl who is concentrated on work before her. Her name is Tilly Westermann. The two brothers watch the operating machine for quite some time. Carl finally picks up a leaflet which has just come from the machine. Scans it, replaces it finally.*

CARL. How long will this stencil hold out?

BAUM (*singing out the answer*). Another hundred.

ERNST. That's plenty. This particular leaflet's going to make some of our Nazi's friends perspire once it gets into the workers' hands. Workers might like to know the American embargo on German goods has increased fifty per cent in the last six months. They might like to know wages are down one third and vital foods are up seventy-five per cent.

TILLY (*without looking up*). Stop loafing, comrades.

ERNST (*humor ugly*). She says that to a man who hasn't slept for thirty hours.

CARL. Listen, Dodo, you better take care. Just out of a sick bed, and —

ERNST. Good as new. I could swing you around my finger.

CARL (*laughing*). Try it.

[*They spar with good nature.*

TILLY. Comrades! Stop loafing ⁝

CARL. That's right. (*Picks up leaflets*) How many of these do I take?

ERNST. Two hundred. Get them to Zeltner. He'll take care of distribution.

CARL. Listen, Ernst, I hate to say it, I don't trust Zeltner.

[*Tilly suddenly looks up, Baum turns his head.*

ERNST. Why don't you trust Zeltner?

CARL. He is too damn brave, too damn willing to die for what he calls "The Cause", too damn downright curious.

ERNST. In the last analysis maybe just romantic.

CARL. He wanted to know this address. Is that romantic?

ERNST. He asked?

CARL. This morning. I told him Berlin's a big city.

TILLY. Did he press the point?

CARL. No, but his knuckles went white around the pencil.

ERNST. We are prepared to move on a moment's notice. Baum's removing the machine as soon as he is finished. In the meantime deliver this package to Zeltner.

CARL. Why take a chance?

ERNST. When we see what he does with this package we'll know where we stand.

CARL (*seriously*). I see.

BAUM. I used to be a peaceful man who planted tulips.

ERNST. Get going, Carl, the back streets.

TILLY (*not looking up*). All Comrades to be referred to by first names. Please remember to spread the word.

BAUM (*sings*). "*Oh Tannenbaum.*"

CARL. I don't suppose you and Tilly could come to Frieda's to hear some Bach to-night.

ERNST. With all this work?

CARL. Do you know the trio hasn't met for five months?

BAUM (*sings*). My father hated music.

ERNST. My fingers are stiff as boards.

BAUM. The day he died a six-piece band accompanied him right to the cemetery.

ERNST. Not to have touched a violin for six months? Incredible!

CARL. See you to-morrow.

ERNST (*stopping him*). Wait a minute, Carl. I know what's

on your mind. Every time we say good-by we both think, "When will we meet again? . . . What will to-morrow bring? . . . Is this the last time together?"

CARL (*trying to jest*). Look, a mind-reader.

ERNST. You must be careful, Carl.

CARL. I know how you feel.

ERNST. You've got an awful hot head. You mustn't ever lose your temper when you find yourself in a jam.

CARL (*laughing*). Don't worry about your little brother; he is slippery as an eel.

BAUM. Did you ever eat a pickled eel?

ERNST. Be careful.

CARL. Sure. (*The brothers grip hands and look at each other*) Know what I do? When I walk in the streets I sing. That makes them say, "He's above board, he can't be doing underground work." But they don't know I'm singing because I know where we'll be some day. When I sing —

TILLY. You sing yourself right out of here, comrade. Right this minute.

CARL (*laughing*). Correctemente, as the Spaniards say. Adios.

ERNST. Adios.

TILLY. And pull the door tight.

BAUM. Don't take no wooden money.

[*Carl exits.*

ERNST. I wouldn't like to see him in a detention camp. Emil went yesterday. (*Walks up to Baum*) Will the rest take long?

BAUM. Yes. (*Counts deliberate turn of crank*) One, two, three. That's the whole run.

[*Stops.*

ERNST. Good.

BAUM. Oh, I'm a fast worker.

TILLY. Learn it from your father?

BAUM (*beginning to clean and pack up machine as Ernst takes printed sheets down to table and packs them*). My father?

You should have seen him. A dead ringer for Von Hindenburg. A Corporal of 1870. What would happen if he lived today? Some Nazi would say, "A war hero", tickle him under the arm — presto! The next day he would be wearing a brown shirt and killing workers a mile a minute. A real smoke.

ERNST. What's the time?

BAUM (*looking at watch*). Time for supper. Seven o'clock.

ERNST. Where's Zelda?

TILLY. Said she would be here at six.

ERNST. She is usually on time. Here is the last package to go.

TILLY. I hope Zelda won't crack. She hasn't heard from Hugo for three months.

BAUM (*seriously*). Hugo? He might be dead by now. Like the report on Schlegel yesterday. Trying to escape, they said. To fill a man's back full of lead like that. [*Puts on a ragged coat.*

ERNST. Take some money for your supper. (*Puts coins on table*) This much to spare.

BAUM (*shy as a young girl*). I don't like to take it, Ernst.

ERNST. Well, we're even — I don't like to give it. (*Indicates machine in box*) Mark it "glass."

BAUM. I used to be crazy on tulip bulbs. For years I spent my weekly salary on them.

TILLY. "Glass" in big letters!

BAUM (*doing so*). Do you spell glass with one "s" or two?

ERNST. Two.

TILLY (*laughing*). That's one your father didn't teach you.

BAUM. It's no joke. I'm getting dehydrated, that's what I am. Yep, the juices is going right outa me. (*Picks up package*) Well, don't take no wooden money. [*Exits.*

TILLY. I like him.

ERNST. He's a good worker. [*Suddenly shows faintness.*

TILLY (*up and to him*). What's the matter, Ernst?

ERNST (*sitting*). I guess I'm tired. Maybe the body doesn't throw off disease bugs as easy as I think.

TILLY. If I say you need a month's rest, you'll say, "Who does my work?" Is that right?

ERNST. Right!

TILLY. Dammit, I'll do your work.

ERNST. Alone?

TILLY. Why not?

ERNST. Tempting, but improbable.

TILLY. You and your male chauvinism!

ERNST (*with smiling protest*). No, Tilly, no.

TILLY. To-day I'm particularly concerned with you.

ERNST. You want to know a secret? There is something altogether lovely and birdlike about you. (*Knock on the door*) Zelda?

TILLY (*softly*). I'll see.

[*She goes, and for a brief moment, Ernst allows his real weariness to show, but straightens up as Tilly enters with Zelda.*

ERNST (*overbrightly*). Late, Zelda?

ZELDA. Yes, I — I —

[*Suddenly begins to cry, head in arms on table.*

ERNST. Dear Zelda, what happened?

TILLY (*framing name with lips*). Hugo.

[*Ernst goes behind Zelda as if to say some comforting thing but realizes better. Looks at Tilly and shakes his head pityingly. Zelda finally straightens up and dries her eyes.*

ZELDA. I got the news this morning. They say he jumped out the window. Hugo would do that! They sent the body to his mother. I'll spend the night with her. Is it all right?

ERNST. Sure it is.

ZELDA. I'll deliver the leaflets first. This package? (*Ernst nods. She takes it*) Tell the comrades to stay away from the funeral. They'll be watching.

[*Ernst embraces her, she exits.*

ERNST (*in a burst*).   Hell! I'd like to go and sit in a park somewhere!

TILLY.   They met in the park. She told me once. He was feeding pigeons. You and I met on the subway three years ago. To-day is an anniversary for us.

ERNST.   Really?

TILLY.   Zelda took the wind out of my lungs. I wanted to propose . . .

ERNST.   Something nice?

TILLY.   A walk in the park — a small supper — then we would walk home slowly, quietly. You'd let me hold your hand. . . . Poor Zelda.

ERNST.   My present dream of the world — I ask for happy laughing people everywhere. I ask for hope in eyes: for wonderful baby boys and girls I ask, growing up strong and prepared for a new world. I won't ever forget the first time we visited the nursery in Moscow. Such faces on those children! Future engineers, doctors; when I saw them I understood most deeply what the revolution meant.

TILLY.   Maybe we could have one like that, a baby I mean.

ERNST.   When the day comes that we don't have to live like rats in sewers —   Did I thank you for nursing me the past three weeks?

TILLY.   Not a word came out of that stingy mouth. (*He kisses her in thanks*)   Did I thank you for the birthday card?

ERNST.   Not a word came out of that stingy mouth. (*She kisses him in thanks*)   Did I thank you for the woolen socks?

TILLY.   Ingratitude! (*Kisses her again*)   And you, Comrade Tausig, I never thanked you just for living!

ERNST.   Ahhh. . . .

[*Kisses her fully this time. She finally breaks away.*

TILLY.   Stop loafing on my mouth, Comrade. (*Looking at papers on table*)   We have to finish this.

ERNST.   Getting tough again?

TILLY.   Seriously, I decoded the milk bill. There are nine

names and addresses of party officials to be memorized by your most excellent brain.

ERNST. Berlin?

TILLY. Look it over. The rest of the room's as clean as a plucked chicken. Not a suspicious word.

ERNST. Who's Spitzer?

[*Examines list.*

TILLY. Rosenfeld, I think.

ERNST. And Strasser?

TILLY. My brother, Hans.

ERNST. Chris' sake, when did you see him last?

TILLY. Four months ago.

ERNST. I think we — (*A low knock on the door stops him. Both freeze into position. From now on they whisper*) Did someone knock?

TILLY (*listening*). Just a minute.

[*Knock is louder.*

ERNST. Don't answer. (*Tears name list in half*) Memorize those. Quick!

VOICE (*outside*). Open the door!

ERNST. Sisst!

[*Both stand there memorizing.*

VOICE (*as knocking increases*). Open the door — Secret Police.

TILLY. The Gestapo!

ERNST. That bastard, Zeltner! (*Saying address aloud*) 783–783–783. . . . (*Finally the knocking stops*) Don't stop. (*Her lips move rapidly and silently*) All right?

TILLY. All right.

[*But she goes on. Knocking comes again and "Secret Police." Ernst lights end of his paper. Watches her while paper burns. Finally she nods her head and he touches lighted paper to hers. Both burn down and are stamped to dust on the floor.*

ERNST (*all in whispers*). You and I were here on the couch.

[*Puts coat and vest on back of chair.*

TILLY. An affair?

ERNST. You're in the business. Your room. (*Points to himself*) Your customer. Push your hair around.

[*She does so.*

TILLY. All ready.

[*Musses up couch.*

VOICE (*outside*). Open the door! This is the Secret Police.

SLOW FADEOUT

In the dark between this scene and the next the shrill sounds of a half dozen whistles, variously pitched, slowing with hysterical intensity.

This device to be carried throughout.

SCENE II

SCENE. *Office in a Nazi brown house. A fat detective in a trench coat and brown derby at telephone on desk which also holds typewriter. His name is Popper. Two Orderlies in Nazi uniform at the side sitting on a bench. They are counting from a list. To one side of the desk stands Ernst Tausig, a prisoner.*

POPPER (*excited and angry on phone*). I'm waiting for you. (*Waits, drums fingers, spits*) I'm waiting for you, I said. Mommer God! You think I've got all day.

ORDERLY (*begins to count aloud*). Thirty-seven, thirty-eight, thirty-nine —

POPPER (*yelling at them*). Dumbbells, can't you see I'm trying to work here. Mommer God, it's full of crazy people, the whole house. Hello! The one I mean is the Communist Ernst Tausig. Find the rest of the report and bring it to me on the third floor immediately. Captain Schlegel is waiting for the report. What? No, Schlegel, S as in Samuel. (*Hastily corrects himself*) No, I mean S as in Storm Trooper. Also you made a mistake on the first part of the report. Don't give me back talk, Dumbbell, the report is in front of my eyes here. His girl friend was released. A plain out and out whore. What? No, not war, whore. (*Turns to orderly, in desperation*) You tell him.

ORDERLY 1 (*immediately at phone*). W-h-o-r-e.

[*Retires primly.*

POPPER (*back at phone*). We brought him in yesterday. So look in the top file right away. (*Hangs up*) Imagine, that nobody tells me it's my fault; I'll poke my finger through his eye. Such confusion!

ORDERLY 1 (*sympathetically*). Terrible!

POPPER. The country is running over with those red ants. Such confusion.

ORDERLY 2. Terrible!

POPPER. Take the typewriter.

ORDERLY 2. Me?

POPPER. You.

ORDERLY 2. Yes, sir. (*Comes over to desk, a pleasant type*) Where will I take it?

POPPER. What's the matter with you? To type, to type.

ORDERLY 2. I can't type.

POPPER. You can't type?

ORDERLY 2. No, sir.

POPPER. Dumbbell.

ORDERLY 1. Terrible!

POPPER *to* ORDERLY 1. Can you type?

ORDERLY 1. No, sir.

POPPER. So shut up. Such disorder, such confusion. Every Brown house I was connected with in the past six months is like this. Mommer God, they'll say I'm inefficient, they'll kill me. (*Suddenly turning on Ernst*) You! You make trouble for Captain Schlegel and I'll — I don't know what I'll do to you. You know where you are?

ERNST. Yes.

POPPER. You know what happens in the Columbia Brown House to Communists?

ERNST. Yes.

POPPER. Why did you say you never lived in Linden Street?

ERNST. I never did.

POPPER *to* ORDERLIES. Did you hear that? He said he never lived there. (*To Ernst*) Never in possession of certain illegal materials in connection with the underground work?

ERNST. No.

POPPER (*shaking finger under Ernst's nose*). Listen, stinker, I — (*Controls himself, goes back to behind desk*) Write down the liar's answer. (*Writes it down himself*) You were last employed by the Musical Instrument Company, Eberhard?

ERNST. Yes.

POPPER. Write down he was last employed by that company. (*Writes it down himself. Trooper passes through, whispers,* "Courage" *to Ernst*) You know we have here enough information to burn you in hell. For three weeks we watched you, you red fox. Do you — (*Suddenly stops as Captain Schlegel enters, followed by an Orderly named Adolph. Popper continues, fawningly*) Good morning, Captain Schlegel.

SCHLEGEL (*a man like Goering*). Is this him?

POPPER. Yes, sir, this is the one, Captain Schlegel.

SCHLEGEL. Any illegal papers found on him?

POPPER. He got rid of them before the arrest, Captain.

SCHLEGEL. Red fighter?

POPPER. Without a doubt, Captain.

SCHLEGEL. Writer?

POPPER. Former editor of a unit paper, Captain.

SCHLEGEL (*to Ernst as he examines report from desk*). That so?

ERNST. Formerly so.

POPPER. Flat as the rug when you catch them. Otherwise burning Reichstags twice a day.

SCHLEGEL. Never mind. Where's the rest of the report?

POPPER. Begging your pardon, Captain, they can't find it downstairs.

SCHLEGEL. You'd better be careful, Popper. Such inefficiency will not be tolerated.

POPPER (*whining*). I do the best I can, Captain.

SCHLEGEL. Never mind, never mind. (*To Ernst*) How long have you belonged to the Communist Party?

ERNST. Since 1923.

SCHLEGEL. You deny belonging to the underground party at the present time?

ERNST. I do.

SCHLEGEL. You are on friendly terms with foreigners?

ERNST. No.

SCHLEGEL. You are not familiar with certain Bulgarian incendiaries?

ERNST. No.

SCHLEGEL. Married?

ERNST. No.

SCHLEGEL. Any children?

ERNST (*smiling*). No.

SCHLEGEL. What's funny?

ERNST. Nothing.

SCHLEGEL (*taking Ernst by his coat lapels*). Wipe off the smile. (*Releases Ernst and dusts off hands as if contaminated*) What unit did you work with?

ERNST. Unit Number twenty-fifteen.

SCHLEGEL. Who was the Unit organizer?

ERNST. A man named Hess.

SCHLEGEL. Where is he now?

ERNST. I saw him last one year ago.

POPPER (*until now holding back his eagerness*). Where does he live, huh?

[*Captain gives Popper a superior look. Popper fades apologetically.*

SCHLEGEL. You had charge of a secret printing press on Hartsheim Street?

ERNST. No.

SCHLEGEL. You insist you did not help organize the underground press in Berlin.

ERNST. I did not.

SCHLEGEL. No illegal leaflets?

ERNST. No.

SCHLEGEL (*goes over and takes rifle from Orderly. Taps twice on floor with butt of rifle, hands it back to Orderly, and returns to Ernst at the same time taking the report up from desk*). This report — all a tissue of lies you say?

ERNST. I cannot say.

[*A Man enters — wears mask — limps.*

SCHLEGEL (*turning to the man*). What's his name?

MAN. Ernst Tausig.

SCHLEGEL. His work?

MAN. The underground press.

SCHLEGEL. You may go, Zerrago.

[*Man goes.*

ERNST. We knew the rat as Zeltner.

[*Captain suddenly slaps him in the face.*

SCHLEGEL. Control your tongue. When you are asked you will speak, concerning three matters. A, identification of prisoners; B, names; C, addresses. Until then keep quiet.

[*Turns from him, walks directly away, but suddenly turns and throws the whole sheaf of paper in Ernst's face.*

POPPER. He thinks he's in kindergarten.

SCHLEGEL. You'll be in kindergarten, if you don't keep your face shut. (*Approaches Ernst, examines him from all sides*) I hear you're a musician of sorts.

ERNST. Yes.

SCHLEGEL. Play an instrument?

ERNST. Formerly the violin.

SCHLEGEL. Such sensitive hands. Hold them up. (*Ernst does so*) So filthy. Put them on the desk. (*Ernst does so*) So, a scraper of catgut. Now, what I have against the communists is — (*Holding and turning Ernst's jaw in his hand*) — the snout-like narrowness of their non-Nordic jaws. The nostrils display sensual and voluptuous self-indulgence, talking with the aid of hands and feet; non-Nordic characteristics.

[*Walking away from Ernst, wipes his hands on a handkerchief.*

ADOLPH. For every S.A. man killed in Berlin, Brandenburg, three communists will have to answer with their lives.

SCHLEGEL. A violin is an eloquent instrument. Perhaps you are familiar with Beethoven's Opus sixty-one, the violin concerto. Answer yes or no.

ERNST. Yes.

SCHLEGEL. In the key of D? (*Having taken rifle from Orderly's hand, he suddenly brings down the butt of it on Ernst's fingers, smashing them. Roars*) With the Joachim Cadenza? (*Ernst, writhing with pain, puts his smashed right hand under his left armpit and almost faints. Captain Schlegel now roars the rest*) And if you think that's the end, let me tell you by to-morrow you'll find your neck half broken instead of three lousy fingers!!! Stand up straight! Do you hear me? (*Ernst straightens up*) Put your hand down. Put it down!!! (*Ernst slowly does so*) In ten minutes your old slut of a mother won't know you. (*Suddenly, softly*) Unless you answer my questions. (*Waits*) You refuse . . .?

ERNST (*finally, controlling his pain*). I have nothing to say.

SCHLEGEL. Take him to the barrack rooms. Take him out of my sight.

ORDERLY 2. Yes, sir.

SCHLEGEL *to* ORDERLY 1. Get out.

ORDERLY 1. Yes, sir.

[*Exits quickly.*

SCHLEGEL. We've been too easy with that one.

POPPER. Yes, sir, he's a fresh guy.

SCHLEGEL. What the hell are they saving him for?

POPPER. I can't say. I seen the order myself signed by Major Duhring. Handle him with kid gloves, it says. He was in a position to know a big pile of names and addresses. Major Duhring is expected next week to personally question him.

SCHLEGEL (*bitterly*). Duhring? Duhring?

POPPER. He's soft as butter but he knows how to make them talk.

SCHLEGEL. Oh, I see, he can make them talk, but I can't.

POPPER. No, Captain, I only meant —

SCHLEGEL. Get out. You make me vomit.

POPPER. Yes, Captain.

[*Bows his way out backwards and bumps into chair. Exits.*

SCHLEGEL (*turning around the room in anger*). I think that Popper one must have Jewish blood. He hasn't the brains of a trained flea. What strikes you as being funny, Adolph?

ADOLPH. How that fat slob bowed his way out.

SCHLEGEL. I have seen you in a few peculiar positions at times. In fact, it might be much better for both of us if you weren't so graceful with those expressive hands of yours. Flitting around here like a soulful antelope. I'm lonely. I've got no one in the whole world.

ADOLPH. You've got me, Eric.

SCHLEGEL. Hitler is lonely too. So is God.

ADOLPH. I know.

SCHLEGEL. I lost my temper and smashed him against orders.

ADOLPH. You need a rest. You're nervous.

SCHLEGEL. Say it — nervous as a woman — say it! Yes, that's the third one in a week I haven't been able to get a word out of. All I need is for them to find out about us and I am through for good. My God, you don't know who to trust.

ADOLPH. Trust me.

SCHLEGEL (*examining Adolph's face between his hands*). You? You're as fickle as a girl. You know that song by Hugo Wolf, *I wish all your charm was painted.* It's written for you and me. Last night I heard a lieder concert. There weren't fifty people in the audience. The country is gripped by fear. Houses are locked by day and night.

ADOLPH. Please . . . I'm very fond of you.

SCHLEGEL. Fond? You probably carry tales. . . . I know, you love the Captain's uniform, not the man.

ADOLPH. You're hurting me.

SCHLEGEL. What does a child like you know?

ADOLPH. Please, I mean . . .

[*Suddenly begins to cry.*

SCHLEGEL. Sisst! You'll drive me crazy. Where do you think you are? Go out and wash your face. (*Looks at papers on desk*) Who's crazy, they or me? Saving a communist because they think he'll spill the beans. I thought I told you to go.

ADOLPH. Please.

SCHLEGEL. Get out of here, don't you hear me? Get out!

ADOLPH. Yes, sir.

[*Hurries out.*

SCHLEGEL (*looks at papers, scatters them around*). My God! My God! What's the world coming to? Where's it going? My God!

BLACKOUT

Whistles in the dark

SCENE III

SCENE. *The barracks room. Troopers playing pinochle. Drink beer. Guns and blackjacks on table. Five prisoners lined up against wall, backs to audience. Young Trooper marching back and forth behind them. Peltz and Weiner, two troopers, having a hot argument downstage.*

PELTZ. I'm always for the practical side of the thing.

WEINER. Was you ever in a school, if I'm not getting too personal?

PELTZ. I went to school.

WEINER. Where, if I'm not getting too personal?

PELTZ. Right here in Berlin. We learned all that stuff in school, Napoleon an' all that stuff, but it didn't help in business. Adages an' all that. They're for the idlers. When I was in business we didn't talk about Napoleon. We talked about how much.

WEINER. You are absolutely without doubt the most ignorant man I ever met.

PELTZ. I know, I know, we just don't agree.

WEINER. What made Von Hindenburg a great general?

PELTZ. There was other great generals besides him.

WEINER. There never was a greater one.

PELTZ. How about the few others who was great? Don't you know every generation must have its magnet? You don' see that!

WEINER. What's the use of arguing? It's like religion. Some say —

PELTZ. You got that student stuff, artistic. Me, I'm more for the practical side. But you are a good scholar. Yes, I can see that, Weiner. Was you always that way? More on the student side..

WEINER. What? What the hell are you talking about?

PELTZ. Now you know —

WEINER. You're so dumb!

[*Walks away. Peltz shrugs his shoulders, goes back to newspaper.*

YOUNG TROOPER (*to elderly man*). Can't you stand still when you're told to stand still!! (*Kicks him strongly; Man falls; trooper picks him up*) You weren't too old to be a Social-Democrat, were you!!

[*Shoves him back in line. Another brings in two more prisoners — One feebly attempts a Nazi salute, says, "Heil Hitler", but is shoved in line.*

TROOPER 1 (*at table*). The bastards think they'll save their skin like that!

[*Trooper 2 squirts beer from mouth at prisoner.*

YOUNG TROOPER. The old one wanted a good day's rest on the floor.

TROOPER 2. Which one?

[*Goes to him with bottle.*

YOUNG TROOPER. This one.

[*Trooper 2 fills mouth with beer, squirts it in old man's face. All roar with laughter.*

TROOPER 1 (*coming over*). Dammit! I know this one. You know where you are?

BOY. Yes, sir.

TROOPER 1 (*points to boy*). You was here before, wasn't you?

BOY. Yes, sir.

TROOPER 1. What was you arrested for that time?

BOY. I was accused of distributing pamphlets.

TROOPER 1. And what now?

TROOPER 5. Riding on a truck load of illegal literature.

TROOPER 1. Jesus, Mary, and Joseph!

BOY. He came up to me — the man. I was standing on the corner and he offered me five marks to help drive the load.

TROOPER 2. You didn't know what was in the boxes?

BOY. No, he didn't tell me that and I didn't ask questions.

TROOPER 1. This little one is telling fairy tales.

BOY. I was glad to earn the five marks.

TROOPER 3 (*at the table*). What did you do it for? They won't believe you now.

BOY. I didn't work since I left school. The labor camps won't accept me because I'm a Communist. What can I do?

TROOPER 1. What you can do? Eat floor wax! (*Hits him; the boy falls*) Good appetite!

TROOPER 3 (*coming forward*). Leave the boy alone, Max!

TROOPER 5. Look at these remarks. (*Reads from pamphlets*) "The Brutal Slaughter of Red Front Comrades by Hitler's Brown Murder-Hordes —"

TROOPER 1. Jesus, Mary, and Joseph!

[*Kicks the fallen boy.*

TROOPER 3. Leave the boy alone, Max.

[*Sorry for him.*

TROOPER 1. I'll leave him alone!

TROOPER 4 (*still at the table with handful of cards*). If you're playing cards, play.

TROOPER 3. Play cards, Max!

TROOPER 1. All right, Professor.

[*The game begins and presently Popper walks in with Ernst.*

POPPER. Over there. (*Ernst goes into line. Popper watches fallen boy get up into line*) What happened with him?

TROOPER 3. The thunderbolt made a visit.

[*Indicates Trooper 1.*

TROOPER 1 (*jumping up*). You are just too damn smart, Hassel!

POPPER. Silence!

[*Popper goes to them, whispers. They nod heads as they furtively look Ernst over. Popper says "Don't forget", and exits. Trooper 2 marches around Otto and examines him insolently. Goes back to seat and says to others:*

TROOPER 2. Not a blemish on the lily!

TROOPER 4. Are we playing cards or not?

TROOPER 1. I will say three fifty in spades.

TROOPER 2. You pay double if you lose.

TROOPER 1. Don't put no evil eye on me, Hassel!

TROOPER 2. Don't you act so mean, Herr Thunderbolt!

TROOPER 1. You wanna make something of it?

TROOPER 2. To me you can't talk like to your snotnose friends!

TROOPER 1. You must think —

TROOPER 3. Boys! Is this the trust the Leader puts in you — to start fights in the barracks with Jews and Bolsheviks watching you.

TROOPER 2. That's right!

TROOPER 4. Heil Hitler.

[*All salute as if toasting and all sit. Card improvisation. Trooper scene. Weiner edges his way over to Peltz.*

WEINER. What kind of education can you get from the newspapers?

PELTZ. I see how it is. You like to lay around in those cafés with all the Bohemians. See them lying around with frocks on — dreamers. They can't come to the front — just dreamers.

WEINER. Did you read what Thyssen said?

PELTZ. A big man, a big man.

WEINER. Success is ninety per cent luck, five per cent work, he said.

PELTZ. Exactly, exactly, an' don't any intelligent man say the same? The same thing, he says, the same.

WEINER. What?

PELTZ. That means something, don't it?

[Improvisation on pinochle game goes on in loud voices. The Old Man who has been swaying now falls again. The Young Trooper looking over a shoulder at the game finally turns and sees the fallen man.

YOUNG TROOPER. Look at him — can't stand no more. (*Examines him*) He's bleeding from the mouth.

TROOPER 3. Take him to the hospital. My trick.

TROOPER 1. He's been standing seven hours.

OLD MAN. Don't hit me, please don't hit me.

YOUNG TROOPER. No, just dusting you off.

[Hits hard.

OLD MAN. Please don't hit me. I was in the war. I was decorated for bravery. Von Macksen decorated me for merit.

YOUNG TROOPER. *General* Von Macksen.

OLD MAN. I swear. Don't hit me again. I swear I — Yes, I was — (*Now laughs and goes very hysterical*) . . . Please, please . . .

[The Thunderbolt runs over — hits the Old Man who crumples silently.

TROOPER 1. These Social-Democrats is a noisy bunch. (*Has retained hand of cards.   Starts back to table and on way says "The ace of diamonds", puts it on table, says to Young Trooper*) Courtplaster on his head, Fritz!

[The Young Trooper drags the Old Man out like a sack of sawdust.

TROOPER 4 (*as they play cards*). Your muscle's better than his.

TROOPER 1. Whose?

TROOPER 4. Tauchner in 120. He bets anything he can knock a man out in one blow — nine out of ten.

Why, yesterday he won fifteen marks and a smoking pipe.

TROOPER 2. That's scientific. Just how you hit them . . . like tearing telephone books.

TROOPER 1. I guess you can do it too!

TROOPER 2. If I want . . .

TROOPER 1. Only you don't want?

TROOPER 2. Maybe I'll show you and maybe I won't.

TROOPER 1. How about a bet — the pack of cards against my belt?

TROOPER 2. With the silver buckle?

[*A scream heard from below.*

TROOPER 1. Yeah.

TROOPER 2. You go first.

TROOPER 1. Then you go and if I don't do it, you go again.

TROOPER 2. That's right.

TROOPER 4. Hand over the bets. (*They do so*) Try the one Popper brought in. He's the biggest and freshest. (*Calls to Ernst*) Hey Blackhead! Fall out of line! (*Pulls him out by coat tail*) Stand there, pig.

[*Ernst stands in place. Trooper 3 stays at table. The others approach.*

TROOPER 2. Who takes this one?

TROOPER 1. You're his size. I'll take that boy. Hey —!

[*Pulls out Boy.*

TROOPER 4. I count three. You both hit together. Ready.

TROOPER 2 (*preparing for blow with other*). Yes, ready . . .

TROOPER 4. Gentlemen, one . . .

[*Trooper 1 spits on his fist. Trooper 2 stands motionless. The Boy at the count of two will cover his face with his hands.*

TROOPER 2. Remember, only in the head!

TROOPER 4. Gentlemen — two!

BOY (*covering face*). No.

TROOPER 1. Put your hands down, stinker! (*Boy refuses*) Put them down, bastard!!

[*Boy does so.*

TROOPER 4. Gentlemen — two and a half . . .

TROOPER 2. Just a minute.

TROOPER 1. What's the matter —

TROOPER 2. Yours is half fainting — a pushover —

TROOPER 1. Well, I'll take him. You!

[*Pulls another out — pushes Boy who falls sitting and cries monotonously.*

TROOPER 4. Now — 1 — 2 — 3 —!

[*Both Men let blows fly. The victim of No. 1 goes down in a heap. Ernst stands stunned. In disgust Trooper 2 goes back to seat.*

TROOPER 1 (*delighted*). Well, who is the big scientist now?

TROOPER 2. That was a pushover.

TROOPER 4. Max won the bet.

[*Hands over the prizes to Trooper 1.*

TROOPER 1. You wasn't so smart.

[*Suddenly Trooper 2 in a fury lets fly at Ernst who slowly crumples to his knees.*

TROOPER 2. Get back in the line, you louse!

[*Stalks back to table and sits moodily with chin on fist. Ernst slowly crawls back into line and rises painfully.*

TROOPER 3. Fritzie, get a bucket of water for the kid.

[*He laughs triumphantly.*

TROOPER 1. Ha, ha, Professor!

[*Laughs. Trooper scene. Peltz and Weiner have been arguing throughout this last scene.*

PELTZ. Oh, there's no question, no question. Then what's the use of cursing the world and blaming it on a handful of rich men?

WEINER (*disgusted completely*). I'm not cursing the world!

PELTZ. Now you was pretty strong there. Tell the truth, wasn't you, Weiner?

WEINER. All I said was —

PELTZ. I don't care what this one or that one says about the rich men. It really don't interest me. Or taxes or socialism. I don't listen to them artists. But just because there's a depression I wouldn't say, "Oh, the goddamn rich men."

WEINER. I didn't say the goddamn rich men.

PELTZ. Absolutely, absolutely . . .

WEINER. My God, you're dumb! If I'm not getting too personal.

PELTZ. I know, Weiner, I know. Naturally people ain't of the same temper-a-ment. Naturally . . . the practical side — like Herr Doctor Goebbels says here in the paper. (*Reads*) "The head of a prominent Jew must be displayed on every telegraph pole from Munich to Berlin." No dreamy stuff, Weiner. That's practical . . .
[*A scream heard from below.*

FADEOUT

SCENE IV

SCENE. *The same as 3. Nazi swastika flag as background. Orderlies 1 and 2 rediscovered, respectively Edsel and Martin.*

EDSEL. "What's the world comin' to," he says to poppa. Poppa began cryin'. My uncle said, "Don't cry 'cause it won't help nothin'." After all he didn't work for three years.

MARTIN. The leader has promised a job to every German.

EDSEL. Don't you think I said that? "Read the papers," I told him. "Plenty of work in Munich." So he laughs and says that he just came from Munich and not a job to be had there. But their papers say plenty of jobs in Berlin.

MARTIN. That sounds to me like red propaganda. Why didn't you arrest him?

EDSEL. My own uncle?

MARTIN. He told a lie, didn't he?

EDSEL. I don't know.

MARTIN. The Leader says there's jobs for everyone.

EDSEL. I know . . .

MARTIN. Government work on the roads.

EDSEL. Two and a half marks a week. Can a mouse live on it?

MARTIN. Is that a nice thing to say?

EDSEL. Well, can a mouse live on it?

MARTIN. I don't know. Dr. Goebbels spoke on the radio last night. He says we must be prepared for a war with them any day.

EDSEL. Momma said some Jews was very nice people.

MARTIN (*jumps up and goes away*). Say, you better be careful — saying things like that. I don't wanna even know you.

EDSEL. Oh, she says it. Of course I don't agree.

MARTIN. You better be careful. They're hot as hornets around here to-day. This morning they found the zoological garden plastered with red propaganda. They can't find out who done it. They cleaned them all away on one side and when they turned around it was all plastered up on the other side.

EDSEL. They will lose their heads, all them Communists.

MARTIN. Of course . . .

EDSEL. If they catch them.

MARTIN. The Major brought in some of the leaflets for examination. Right there on the desk.

[*Edsel backs away from desk as if stung.*

EDSEL. Those things there?

MARTIN. The tissue paper — they print it on tissue paper so the wind blows them all over. A certain lady on Friedrichstrasse, one flew right on her face and when she seen what it was she fainted dead away.

EDSEL (*craning his neck for a look at the desk*). Can you see what they say? Read what it says.

MARTIN. Say, read it yourself.

EDSEL. You're closer to the desk than me.

MARTIN (*they are whispering now*). It don't prove nothing 'cause I'm closer to the desk. (*Slowly edges over. Looks around. Finally whispers:*) "Workers of Germany!"

[*Springs away, amazed at his own audacity.*

EDSEL (*whispering*). What?

MARTIN. That's what it says . . .

EDSEL (*both whispering*). Read some more, Martin, shh.
[*Tiptoes to right side and watches out.*

MARTIN (*looks around and tiptoes to desk. Picks up slip nervously, clears throat, reads*). "The Krupp armament works ran at a loss until Hitler came into power. Now it announces a six per cent dividend —" (*Breaks off nervously*) Watch out, Edsel.

EDSEL. I'm watching.
[*Looks off left.*

MARTIN (*looks left, continues nervously, in a whisper*). "While five and a half million workers are unemployed, which, with their families, constitute one-third of the German working class, increased military forces are the basis of the Hitler economic . . ."
[*Paper drops out of his nervous hands.*

EDSEL. Pick it up.

MARTIN. I can't.

EDSEL (*comes over*). What are you so nervous for?

MARTIN (*chattering*). Who's nervous?

EDSEL (*himself shaking*). You're sweating.

MARTIN. It's a hot day.

EDSEL. Stand at the door. (*Martin does so. Edsel looks around, then picks up paper; reads:*) "In the meantime there is no bread, no milk. The Hitler-controlled newspapers print lies. The —"

MARTIN (*suddenly panic-struck*). The Major!
[*Edsel runs around not knowing where to put the slip. Tries to find a place. Suddenly puts it in his mouth and chews violently. As Major Duhring enters, ceases chewing and with Martin comes rigidly to attention. Major walks in, notices Edsel.*

MAJOR. What's wrong?

MARTIN. Beg pardon, sir?

MAJOR (*pointing to Edsel who has a mouthful*). You! (*Waits*) Can't talk?
[*Edsel finally swallows strongly*

EDSEL. Yes, sir?

MAJOR.   Why are you men loafing around here?

EDSEL.   Beg pardon, sir, we were assigned to this room.

MAJOR.   What room?

EDSEL.   To the examination room.

MAJOR.   Now boys, does this look like an examination room? Clear out before I lose my temper. (*They scramble out with heels clicking and salutes*)   All right, all right, get out. (*Laughs when they exit, a tired civilized man. Calls one back*)   You!

MARTIN (*badly scared*).   Yes, sir, this is not the examination room.

MAJOR.   Here, don't stand there like a whipped dog.   I'm not calling you down.   Inform them on the floor below to send up the Communist, Ernst Tausig.

BOTH (*bowing and scraping*).   Yes, sir.

[*Try to get out of door together and comic mixup, finally out.*

MAJOR (*shakes head with pity*).   Hmmm . . .   (*Picks up red leaflet*) "Workers of Germany . . ."   (*Puts down slip, shakes his head again.   Goes up to Nazi insignia, examines it reflectively, with bitterness.   Ernst is brought in.   His back still turned, says to Orderly*)   Leave us alone. (*Orderly clicks heels, salutes.   Major with back turned*) Sit down, Tausig.

[*Ernst, wearied, mistrustful, does not move.   Major slowly turns, handkerchief at lower portion of face.*

MAJOR.   What?   Another whipped and frightened dog? You may be seated . . .   (*Ernst looks at him a long time and finally sits*)   Cigarette? . . .   (*Ernst takes one, Major putting it in his mouth and lighting it.   Waits to see what Major has up his sleeve*)   You look different, Tausig, than when I saw you last — a meeting — in Charlottenburg.

ERNST.   I remember you — Duhring.

MAJOR.   What happened to your hand?

ERNST.   What happened to your "social ideals"?

MAJOR.   Why I am in a Nazi uniform happens to be unimportant.   A realistic necessity.   I am married into one of the finest old German families, Nordic from the year one. The work I do for the National Socialists harms no foe of the Nazi state; in fact I am inclined to believe that if the truth were known, my work may often be interpreted as a positive hindrance. (*Laughs, and then adds soberly*) Not for publication. Perhaps I don't care. . . . That's nearer the truth. I will not deny the justness of the scorn in your eyes. This may cost me my head . . . I'm not sure I care. (*Turns around room and comes back*) I want to warn you. . . . They'll get what they want out of you. Trust me to —

ERNST (*bitterly*). A man tortured by his conscience?

MAJOR. Call it what you will. Here they use — (*Voices heard without. Major harshly, tearing cigarette from Ernst's mouth*) Stand up! When these three questions are answered — (*Breaks off to greet a blonde woman escorted by Captain Schlegel*) Good afternoon, dear.

HEDVIG (*his wife, vacuous but energetic*). Ruppert, the handsome captain showed me the way. I had to ask your advice about an important matter.

MAJOR (*ironically to Captain*). Thank you, Captain.

SCHLEGEL (*with ironic courtesy himself*). You're welcome, Major. Your wife and I chatted pleasantly for ten minutes on the lower floor before I realized her identity.

HEDVIG. Yes, the place is full of nasty-mannered men. They kept me waiting ten minutes. (*Suddenly aware of Ernst*) Who is this?

MAJOR (*with ironic intent*). A Communist, Hedvig . . .

HEDVIG (*shrinking away to other side of desk, now protected by Captain*). Oh!

MAJOR (*smiling in spite of himself*). They don't bite.

SCHLEGEL. Only in the dark.

HEDVIG. Such dirty beasts. Don't they ever wash?

MAJOR. When they have the facilities.

HEDVIG. And these were the ones who were supposed to be masters of the coming new world. (*Slaps him with glove. Ernst stands unflinchingly. She drops her glove. Captain*

picks it up and proffers it to her)   Oh, no, I couldn't wear
it again.

[*Captain puts it on desk.   Major takes it up.*

MAJOR (*ironic*).   They're expensive gloves.   What was on
your mind, Hedvig?

HEDVIG.   About my broadcast speech.

[*Takes it from purse.*

MAJOR.   Did you write it yourself, Hedvig?

HEDVIG.   No, Poppa's secretary wrote it, but of course
I believe every word of it myself, so it's the same thing,
isn't it?

MAJOR.   I should think so, Hedvig.

[*With ironic seriousness.*

HEDVIG.   I wanted you to hear it before I broadcasted.
I don't have to tell you that at least a half million German
housewives —

MAJOR.   Will put down their housework to listen to Hedvig
von Barbossa explain their reason for existence.

HEDVIG.   Oh, you!   Always anticipating my next word!

MAJOR.   A perfect husband.   Don't you think so, Captain
Schlegel?

CAPTAIN (*ironic.   A constant fight goes on between the two men*).
By all means.

MAJOR.   Hedvig, we are having a very heavy day, here.

SCHLEGEL (*ironic*).   Oh, very heavy.

[*Major gives him a penetrating look — a slight duel goes on
between their eyes.*

MAJOR.   So I must ask you to merely give me the gist of the
speech, dear.   Suppose we say, merely the summation.

HEDVIG.   Oh you!   You just aren't interested in my
intellectual development.

SCHLEGEL (*ironic*).   Your husband is really the busiest
officer in our section.

MAJOR.   That answers you, my dear.   So merely the gist.

HEDVIG.   Well . . . I thought I would conclude as follows.
(*Reads speech*)   "Women must understand their part in
this moral renaissance of the German people.   Well has it

been said by our great leader, 'In eternal warfare mankind will become great. In eternal peace mankind would be ruined.' Yes, my dear friends, war alone puts the stamp of greatness on a people! Let women tend the home! Let women breed warriors! Let women forget the pursuit of culture! Germany must expand! Germany must push her frontiers east and west! Women of Germany, give your lives for this cause!" Is that all right, Ruppert?

MAJOR. Splendid — The whole theory of the fascist state in a paragraph. You might be one of our leading theoreticians one of these days.

HEDVIG. I told Poppa's secretary what to write, I truly did.

MAJOR. Yes, now you must run along, Hedvig. Leave us to our work. Good-by.

HEDVIG. And remember dinner at the Hauptmann's to-night.

MAJOR. I won't forget. Captain, please see my wife safely out.

SCHLEGEL. Yes, sir.

[*Goes with her.*

MAJOR (*to Ernst*). You see the sort of convenient marriages one can sometimes be forced to make.

ERNST. The captain is not your friend.

MAJOR. Nor yours. (*Indicating wife's glove in his hand*) The captain suspects me of leniency to prisoners. My lineage. (*In a sudden emotional outburst*) I tell you a civilized human can't stand it! A great sermon requiem is being played. It's a nightmare! (*Gets himself in control*) He holds his knowledge over my head like a sword — the captain, I mean. In turn I have collected certain data concerning the captain's private life and loves — enough to have him purged to a blood stain on the wall! We will duel ourselves to death, we two! This amuses you?

ERNST. Yes.

MAJOR. I can understand. Briefly, here is some information. (*Business-like, now*) You can take it or leave it, Tausig. Our side wants information from you. Addresses and names of party officials.

ERNST. Don't have them!

MAJOR. I'm not asking. They're sure you can identify prisoners. They mean to make you do it. You've been here three weeks. Until now they've been comparatively mild. They'll beat you to within an inch of death. You won't want to live. Then they'll nurse you back to health. This will happen several times.

ERNST. I will remember my proletarian task.

MAJOR. It's possible you may forget your proletarian task. Don't smile. A man's made of flesh and bone. They'll inform your comrades through subversive means that you've turned stool pigeon. Before you know it your own unit papers will be passing the word along. In a few months — no friends. No home. Only the new clothes and money in the pocket this side will furnish to keep up the fraud. You still smile? But suppose they put you next to the driver when they make raids? Suppose you are stood outside the courtroom where your comrades will be tried for treason? Will they understand the truth of your position? That's right — screw up your face . . .

ERNST. My hand hurts.

MAJOR. Get medical attention on the way out. I'll sign an order.

ERNST. On the way out?

MAJOR. On the way out! That's the first step. We're releasing you. You're expected to make contacts with other party members. You'll be followed every minute of the day and night. If you don't prove valuable — (*Hands over signed medical order*) — back you come . . . and then begins the breaking-down process. (*Stops*) Listen, take my advice. There is an easier way out . . .

ERNST. What is that?

MAJOR. Shoot yourself. There is peace and quiet in the grave. (*Quotes*) "So I returned and considered all the oppressions that are done under the sun . . . wherefore I praised the dead."

[*Schlegel enters.*

MAJOR. Very good.

SCHLEGEL. The compliments of General Goering and staff, who will pay us a visit this afternoon.

MAJOR (*wary*). Very good. You saw my wife safely to the door?

SCHLEGEL. To her car.

MAJOR. Very good.

SCHLEGEL. Our prisoner displays a most fraternal attitude. [*Nods towards seated Ernst.*

MAJOR. Judging from the success of the prisoner's political party in distributing illegal literature, it might be well to fraternize with them in order to learn the secrets of that success.

SCHLEGEL. I resent such remarks before a prisoner. Stand up, you!

[*Ernst stands.*

MAJOR. With both of us in one room I give orders. Remain seated.

[*Ernst sits.*

SCHLEGEL. Major, I regret to inform you as house captain that it is my duty to make various reports concerning —

MAJOR. Silence!

[*Furious.*

SCHLEGEL. Aside from your shoulder straps I am —

MAJOR. Goddamit! Silence!

SCHLEGEL (*turns and walks to door, white with inner rage. Stops, turns*). Jew!

MAJOR. What?

SCHLEGEL. You didn't think I knew that?

MAJOR. Come here.

[*Other slowly approaches.*

SCHLEGEL (*coolly*). What's on your mind?

[*They look at each other eye to eye.*

MAJOR (*finally*). What do you mean?

SCHLEGEL. Does your wife know that?

MAJOR. Know what?

SCHLEGEL. Obviously staff headquarters has never made a close examination of the Duhring family tree.

MAJOR. If I hear one more word out of your mouth —
[*Catches and twists his tunic.*

SCHLEGEL. You'll do that?

MAJOR. With my own hands.

SCHLEGEL (*with smiling insolence*). By gun or sword? Here is one of 38 caliber. (*Insolently hands over gun from his own holster*) The first instinct of the Jew is to run.
[*At this close range the Major suddenly pulls the gun trigger. The Captain gets the whole automatic charge in the belly. Grabs himself with both hands. Slowly crumples in a soft pile. Gets to desk — falls behind it. Major finally speaks in a soft voice.*

MAJOR. I didn't want to do it. He asked for it — (*Adolph runs in*) Wait outside. You will escort this prisoner to the street when he leaves the room.

ADOLPH (*seeing body*). Very good.
[*Exits smartly.*

ERNST (*finally*). You're in trouble.

MAJOR. It need not concern you. (*Eyes still on body*) One thing: see your girl if you like. She reported as a prostitute, not a party worker — which she is.

ERNST. You're mistaken.

MAJOR. I'm telling you! Not asking! See her — it's all right, she won't be molested. And for God's sake give some good girl a kiss for me. I am so slimed over with rottenness. . . . "Red Front" I can't say to you. . . . But "United Front" — I say that. In every capitalist country in the world this day let them work for the united front.

ERNST. I know.

MAJOR. Have the hand fixed. You have the pass. Good luck. . . . Just a second — cigarettes — (*Gives pack*) Say I am not despised. Please say it.

ERNST. No — really, you are not despised.

MAJOR. You are talking to a dying man.

ERNST. With so much work to do?

MAJOR. I did the work — like an embezzling bank teller — I destroyed three files of valuable information against your comrades this morning. With this murder on my hands, what is to be expected? You see, the contradictions of my own nature have backed up on me. Get out!

ERNST. Thanks.

[*He slowly goes. Major stands there. Looks at dead body. Goes back to desk. Sits jauntily on it. Whistles a snatch. Examines and twirls his own gun, thinks about and touches various vulnerable spots of his physiognomy, finally concentrates on one spot, places handkerchief over gun hand — stops. Suddenly puts gun on desk, looks at uniform, removes coat or Nazi arm band. Tears flag off wall . . . Picks up gun — puts muzzle in mouth.*
Simultaneously with Blackout there is a shot fired. Whistles in the dark.

SCENE V

SCENE. *In the dark, under the whistles we pick up on radio music, full and classical. With the lights fading up we see Tilly's small room. A rough cot. One window looking out on a world of clear light. A small bureau, wash basin and pitcher of water on it. A door. Tilly in an old bathrobe. Music coming from her little radio. Tilly dips a corner of a towel in the water, slowly wipes her face clean with it. She finishes. Turns down cot covers. Goes to window, raises shade — Blue night light comes in. She turns down lamp. Turns off radio, but puts it on again. Sits on bed and just as she bends to remove slippers there is a tap on her door. She stays in her bent position for a second, finally when a second knock comes — she slithers to the door. Listens. The knock again.*

TILLY (*in a faint whisper*). Who is it?

VOICE. Ernst. . . . (*Tilly does not believe it. Comes to center of room. Listens, looks around, finally in a full impulse goes to door. Throws it open. Ernst is there. She is away from door. He slowly comes in, closes door, stands against it. For a long time they look at each other silently, finally)* Ernst!

ERNST (*and they are in each other's arms*). Tilly!

TILLY. Alive!

ERNST. Alive!

TILLY. Please, sit here on the bed. (*She escorts him to the bed. He sits. She lowers shade. Turns on lamp. Turns and looks at him; is shocked by his appearance*) Dear. . . . (*She throws herself at his feet, on her knees, holds him as a mother might do with a child*) You're hurt. . . .

ERNST. Not as much as I might be. Only my back is raw . . . the shirt is stuck to it.

TILLY. Here, I'll fix it.

[*Goes to wet towel.*

ERNST. No, darling, if you touch me there I'll faint.

TILLY. Are you hungry?

ERNST. No, dear, no. Here, someone gave me cigarettes. We'll smoke and talk. Don't be excited. I want news. Here —

[*They light cigarettes. She gets a little ashtray — they sit together on cot.*

TILLY. News, what news? You've been released.

ERNST. They held me in the Columbia House since the arrest. I counted the days when I could remember — twenty-two. . . .

TILLY. Twenty-three, Ernst.

ERNST. You counted too.

TILLY. What then?

ERNST. You don't know what happens, you don't know. No one knows until he walks through that hell. . . .

TILLY. Why have they released you?

ERNST. I am being followed. I'm expected to make party contacts. Don't look out the window. Two of them in the grocery doorway. . . . I couldn't give them the slip. Maybe I shouldn't have come.

TILLY. A man must have some place.

ERNST. It won't harm. We fooled them about your identity. Where's Carl?

TILLY. Safe at work in the suburbs.

ERNST. Good.

TILLY. Were you afraid there?

ERNST. A man who knows that the world contains millions of brothers and sisters can't be afraid. Don't think I haven't screamed with pain — they have ways of arousing every corpuscle to pain — but you keep your mouth shut.

TILLY. Your hand . . .

ERNST (*wincing*). Don't touch it.

[*Gets up. Walks away.*

TILLY. Sit down again. Don't be afraid of softness, of sorrow. . . .

ERNST (*holds back his emotional impulse to cry on her shoulder. Finally*). What news of the others?

TILLY. Raff is dead.

ERNST (*deeply touched*). How?

TILLY. The report they gave out was that he jumped from a window. And Hans Mathieson. . . .

ERNST. The same?

TILLY. The same.

ERNST. Those brave fighters. . . .

TILLY. I'm glad you're living, Ernst.

ERNST (*suddenly crying out in protest*). Tilly, I must tell you. Tilly, for a week I have been chewing my heart to pieces. All the time I was in the Brown House they were offering me bribes, any inducements to turn informer. First a session of endearment. Then a session of torture. The human body is a tower of strength. After a while comes numbness, but the mind begins to wander. I'm afraid, Tilly — do you hear that, afraid! Something might happen. There is no rest, no possible contact with party members permitted. They will seize me again, return me to the same program. I'm afraid of what might happen. I ask for one hour of peace.

TILLY. Peace in this war?

ERNST. Yes, peace! In the cell there — I know I stayed alive because I knew my comrades were with me in the same pain and chaos. Yes, I know that till the day I die there is no peace for an honest worker in the whole world.

TILLY. Till the day we die there is steady work to do. Let us hope we will both live to see strange and wonderful things. Perhaps we will die before then. Our children will see it then. Ours!

ERNST (*bitterly*). Our children!

TILLY. I'm going to have a baby, Ernst. . . .

ERNST. Who is?

TILLY. I am.

ERNST. You mean it?

TILLY. Your baby.

[*Dawn — where even the teakettle sings from happiness.*

ERNST (*finally, after looking at her and not knowing what to say*). Please, allow me to change the subject. . . . Overgaard, I met him three streets away from here. I made signals with my eyes. He understood. Passed by like a stranger. (*Finally*) A baby?

TILLY. Yes.

ERNST (*walks to window*). It's almost morning. . . .

TILLY (*joining him*). Ernst, the tenderness I feel for you. . . . I don't know how to say. . . . Part of my deepest life came back to me when you walked in the door here. You keep coming up in my eyes like the sense of tears. . . .

ERNST. I understand.

TILLY. It is true our work comes before our personal happiness. But we must try to wrest some joy from life.

ERNST. How can that be when presently I shall be a decoy to trap other wild ducks?

TILLY. We'll manage. Escape is possible one way or another. Now I want you to undress and sleep.

ERNST. Sleep?

TILLY. Under the warm blankets.

ERNST. Sleep in your little bed? My sister, comrade . . . my wife. . . .

[*Sits on bed. She takes off his shoes. His coat. He winches as he stretches out.*

TILLY. It hurts?

ERNST. Yes.

TILLY. To-morrow we'll fix all these things. Sleep, Ernst, sleep. To-morrow you can read the full report on the united front. *L'Humanité* came through, several copies.

ERNST (*suddenly sitting up*). What united front?

TILLY. The united front in France.

ERNST. It has happened?

TILLY. I thought you knew?

ERNST. In France they have joined to make a solid front against the Fascists?

TILLY. Please don't get so excited, Ernst.

[*Tries to calm him.*

ERNST. Our work is bearing fruit? In that beautiful classic country. The united front? Oh Tilly, oh Tilly!!

[*And suddenly he is crying in the pillow, for all his pains and for the joy of this news. Tilly soothes him with understanding.*

TILLY. Yes, cry, cry. . . . (*She strokes him until the sobs become more quiet. Suddenly there is a knock on the door. Tilly whispers*) Quiet! You're sleeping. Don't move. (*He lies still. She stealthily goes to the door*) Who is it?

VOICE (*also whispering*). Open the door. . . .

TILLY. Who is it?

VOICE. Carl!

[*Tilly looks around at Ernst who raises himself on his hands. Tilly quickly opens the door, admits Carl, quickly closes door.*

TILLY. You're spotted! Get out quick!

CARL. Where?

TILLY. They must be right behind you. Watching the house.

[*Carl quickly goes over to the cot, touches Ernst. Starts for door again where Tilly has been listening.*

TILLY. They're coming! (*Suddenly in a loud voice which Carl immediately takes up*) I'm telling you to get out. What's the matter — can't a respectable girl entertain her boy friend?

CARL. You made a date with me.

[*Simulates a drunkard.*

TILLY. You're a liar. Now get out before I call the police.

CARL. Didn't you say it? In the Park didn't you tell me to come to-night? Why, for two marks —

[*Door is pushed open: two detectives in trench coats stand there.*

TILLY. My God! What's this, more customers?

DICK 1. Who's this?

TILLY. A fresh guy who pushed his way in. There's my boy friend, dead tired on the bed, fresh from the jug, and this garbage can won't let him rest.

CARL. Never mind that stuff! When I met her in the Kunzterplatz Tuesday she tells me to come up to-night. "I love you," she tells me.

TILLY. Yah, yah, yah!

DICK (*comes in and looks around. Assistant blocks the door*). Is this your boy friend?

TILLY. Yeah. He's dead tired. He was —

DICK. All right, all right! (*To Carl*) What do you wanna start up with this alley cat for? You know they do it for anyone.

CARL. Sure. . . . But the next time I meet you in that same place at lunch time —

TILLY. Yah, yah, yah, yah. . . . Thanks, officer — a real man!

[*Dick pushes out protesting Carl and looks superciliously at Tilly as he closes door. Tilly stands in her place for a second, listens, then turns down to Ernst.*

ERNST. Did he get away?

TILLY. They believed every word. (*Suddenly door pushed open. Dick stands there again*) What do you want? . . .

DICK (*advancing into room. Finally*). I forgot my glove,

cutie. (*Picks it up from table, goes back to door*) You
wanna be careful. Better girls than you are in the jails.

TILLY. All right.

DICK. Lemme know if anyone makes trouble. . . .

TILLY. All right.

DICK. Or if you're lonely some night.

TILLY. All right.

DICK (*winking. Taps his chest*). A real man, me . . .

TILLY (*first locking door*). Sleep, Ernst, sleep. . . .

[*But he is already asleep. She sits herself in window light
in profile as daylight comes fuller in the window.*

BLACKOUT

Whistles

SCENE VI

COMRADES' SCENE. *About a dozen party members seated
in a small locked room. The Secretary of the unit is finishing
a report. Carl sits downstage with back to audience. Tilly is
there. Also little Baum of the first scene. Sitting with a
woman holding his hand is a man with a fine looking head,
a famous theoretician, a shawl over his shoulders, gray-haired —
Stieglitz. Guard at door.*

SECRETARY (*reading*). Three new theater-of-action groups
have been formed in the last week. They are now func-
tioning regularly throughout the city. Three thousand
cheap jazz records have been distributed since the 10th.
These each end in one of our speeches. Since the first —
(*Stops to admonish a small man named Julius, who is wend-
ing his way through some seated comrades*) Will the comrades kindly remain seated until the reports are concluded.

JULIUS (*who is revealed to be wearing only one shoe*). I left my
shoe in the corner. My foot is cold.

SECRETARY (*continues*). Since the first, we have spent on
Hitler joke books and leaflets the sum of two hundred and

ten marks. (*Puts down report*) I suggest that since we are all agreed on the accuracy of the report that we do not waste time but go ahead to other business. Will someone ask the question?

VARIOUS. The question, etc.

SECRETARY. All in favor will please assent in the usual manner.

ARNO. Just a minute. This seems to me to be in a way like a little steam rolling.

SECRETARY. Does the comrade have any suggestions in reference —

ARNO. No, but it seems —

OTHERS. Sit down, Arno.

ARNO. What about Comrade Tausig?

SECRETARY. Next.

ARNO. How was I supposed to know —

SECRETARY. All in favor. (*The suggestion is passed. There is a slight respite. Improvisation*) We will now read the roll of honor.

COMRADE (*gets up and reads*). "Unit 2026 — Killed in carrying out their proletarian duties, on the 3rd, Friedrich Meyers, Elsa Schorr. On the 12th, George Pfitzner. (*In the background a woman suddenly sobs. She is comforted by another and soon stops*) Imprisoned or captured during this month, Paul Schnitzler, Ernst Tausig." [*Sits.*

SECRETARY. This is not time for sentiment, but it would not be wrong to stop for one minute to remark upon the fine qualities of those valiant fighters who are now lost to our cause, some forever. In the case of our slain fighters their merits are known to all of us. In the case of Ernst Tausig we must pause for serious consideration. It has been proposed by the unit functionaries that his name be added to the blacklist. But in accordance with usual procedure we have brought this matter to your attention in the hope of arriving at a wider understanding of the case. Comrade Tilly Westermann.

TILLY (*rises, wipes hands with small handkerchief*).   Since the
reports on Ernst Tausig come from reliable sources we
must give them strong credence.   Briefly he was first
arrested in March.   Three weeks later he was released.
(*Carl turns around and looks into the face of the audience*)
At that time he knew he was being followed.   They were
hoping he would contact party members.   This he positively did not do.   Four days later he was picked up again.
I saw him once after that in the hospital with his brother.
(*Lapsing for one line into a less official, less impersonal
attitude*)   I didn't recognize him.   He held my hand. . . .
We wanted —   (*Breaks off, stops for a minute, resumes the
impersonal tone*)   It's no secret to most of you that
I am bearing his child.   This fact will seem to make for
strong partiality on my part.   But I protest that because
Ernst Tausig was in a room when others identified prisoners
is no reason to assume that he has turned informer.   This
is not the Tausig whom most of us have known and worked
with in the last four years or more.

BAUM.   Right!

ARNO.   How about when Mickle saw him with the police
in the Herfheim Street raid?   Maybe he was just
knitting a muffler while he was sitting there next to the
driver!

SECRETARY.   The comrades will please ask permission for the
floor.   (*Arno raises his hand*)   Comrade Arno?

ARNO (*on his feet*).   Personally, I'm sorry for Tausig.   But
who can take a chance nowadays?   Even if he is not
guilty, who can take a chance when the secret police have
any connection with him?

SECRETARY.   Please be more specific.

ARNO.   I mean he must go on the blacklist.   Every unit
paper in the country must carry his name and description.
For our purposes he is deadly, dangerous.

SECRETARY (*recognizing Tilly*).   Comrade Westermann?

TILLY.   I can't disagree with what has just been said —

ARNO.   I should say not!

TILLY. But will the chair permit me to read a small note
I received from Ernst last week?

SECRETARY. Please read the note.

TILLY (*reads*). "They are taking my life by the inch. Day
and night they press me for an answer — identify prisoners
or be killed. I cannot last much longer. The terrible
truth is they do not kill me. I am enclosing money which
they handed over to me yesterday after forcing me to sit
beside their chauffeur when they made a street raid.
You may be sure I have kept my mouth shut. Love to
Carl and you."

[*The man with one shoe comes over and looks at the note.*

SECRETARY. Before we decide the action in this case would
any other comrade care to say something?

GIRL. Perhaps Comrade Stieglitz.

SECRETARY (*looking in his direction*). I don't think. . . .

[*Companion of Stieglitz whispers to him. He nods.*

ZELDA. He says he will say a few words about the case.

SECRETARY. Comrade Stieglitz has just come back to us
from three months in the Sonnenberg detention camp.
(*Pointedly*) I will ask you to listen carefully — to these
few remarks from one of our leading theoreticians.

[*Small bandage on head. All wait. The imposing looking
man gets up quietly and takes his place at the other side of the
room, next to the Secretary. He looks around him gently,
smiles softly at Tilly.*

STIEGLITZ. Always in such rare cases where there is a doubt
as to the accused one's guilt it is the custom to be careful
in consideration of the known facts. But a different face is
placed on the matter in times of stress and danger. Often
. . . (*He stops, thinks, continues*) Often the class struggle . . . it seems to me . . . it seems to me . . . (*He
stops, a little puzzled, plays with fringe of shawl*) I was
saying . . . (*Looks around helplessly. Walks over to his
female companion*) Where are we, Zelda?

ZELDA. With friends, Benno.

STIEGLITZ. What was I saying?

ZELDA. Please sit down, Benno.

STIEGLITZ. Take me home, Zelda. . . . (*Looks around helplessly*) Zelda . . .

SECRETARY (*into the breach*). I think it would be best if he were home.

ZELDA. Yes. We're going, Benno. I have your hat.

STIEGLITZ. I'll hold your hand. Good-by, my friends, good-by. You must come to my house for breakfast. We have the sunniest breakfast room. . . . Yes. . . . [*She leads him out. The door is locked behind him. She has been admonished first to be careful. Baum blows his nose vigorously.*

BAUM. So have the devils broken that noble mind!!

SECRETARY. Comrades, now is no time for sentiment. This is the hour of steel, when — No sentiment! [*But he himself has to hide his tear-filled eyes. Presently controls himself.*

JULIUS. It's a pretty kettle of fish, I must say.

CARL (*suddenly up*). I would like to say something in reference to my brother.

SECRETARY. Take the floor. [*Piano and violin duo begin downstairs.*

CARL. Comrades, you are wondering where the music comes from. This is the very same house in which my brother and myself were born and raised. My uncle and his old friend, Seligmann, are playing. The war, the revolution, the banishing of Jews from Germany have turned their poor old hearts to water. These days you will find them forever — the two of them playing their Mozart and Beethoven sonatas. The music they are playing now is Mozart, the andante of the C Major Sonata — C Major, my dear comrades, is a very wholesome beautiful key. You must excuse what may seem an irrelevant excursion into sentiment. But this is the first piece of Mozart my brother and I ever played together. When we came from school — I am surprised how fresh this dead life is in my memory — nineteen years back — but that's another story. (*Now suddenly turning hard*) But Mozart — is there time for music to-day? What are we fighting for? I need not answer the question. Yes, it is brother against brother. Many a comrade has found with deep realization that he has no home, no brother — even no mothers or fathers! What must we do here? Is this what you asked me? We must expose this one brother wherever he is met. Whosoever looks in his face is to point the finger. Children will jeer him in the darkest streets of his life! Yes, the brother, the erstwhile comrade cast out! There is no brother, no family, no deeper mother than the working class. Long live the struggle for true democracy! [*He sits now.*

The music finishes before anyone speaks.

The vote is called for. All raise their hands in assent except Tilly. She looks around at the others. One of the men is eating small nuts loudly. Her hand slowly comes up.

FADEOUT

SCENE VII

Scene. *Carl's room. Small. Only a door set up in center. In darkness we hear two typewriters. When lights fade up we see Carl and Tilly each at a typewriter. Typing. Tilly finally stops.*

TILLY. A few mistakes.

CARL (*older*). No matter.

TILLY. My heart hurts. Hurt me all day.

CARL. Take care. Lie down before we go.

TILLY. I can't rest.

[*Comes to him.*

TILLY. Carl, I want to ask you — are you ever afraid?

CARL. Sometimes.

TILLY. Now? Tell the truth.

CARL. Yes, if you want it. The place we're going to is

swarming with S.S. men. We might never come out alive.
I'm not so masculine that I won't admit I'm scared.

TILLY. All day I had this pain under the heart.

CARL. When will the baby be coming?

TILLY. A long time yet.

CARL (*in a low voice*). What will you call him?

TILLY. If it's a girl, I don't know. If it's a boy . . .

CARL. Not *his* name.

TILLY (*suddenly clutching him*). Tell me, how do you know?
What makes you so sure?

CARL. There's proof — plenty!

TILLY. You believe it?

CARL. In the beginning I didn't. Maybe the brown shirts
spread the tales themselves.

TILLY. They've done it before.

CARL. I don't say no. That's why I didn't believe a word
I heard at first.

TILLY. Now you believe it.

CARL. Yes. Too many reliable comrades have checked
on his activity.

TILLY. Maybe he's drugged. Maybe he walks in his sleep.
You know — yes, you know — he would have found some
way to do away with himself before he was forced to act
as a spy. You know that! You know you do!

CARL. Don't tear my shirt.
[*Trying to jest.*

TILLY (*persistently*). Answer the question!

CARL (*finally, in a burst*). Goddamit, I say he's guilty!

TILLY. If he came here, broken in mind and body, would
you refuse to see him? Can you stand there and tell me
you wouldn't even listen to what he had to say?

CARL. To me he has nothing to say!

TILLY. He's your brother.

CARL. That won't sell a postage stamp!

TILLY. Suppose he knocks on the door this minute!

CARL. You're in love.

TILLY. Answer what I ask!

CARL. What makes you think you're the only one? Maybe I slept better at night the last two months. Maybe I cried myself to sleep some nights. This big blustering idiot wept like a girl. (*Walks around*) Yes, yes, the whole thing funnels up in me like fever. My head'll bust a vein!

TILLY (*catching herself*). We're talking too loud.

CARL (*whispering, but with same intense flow*). Seeing him together at the hospital the last time — the picture follows me like a dog. I'm sick, I tell you I'm sick of the whole damn affair! (*Sitting*) Perhaps we ought to change — do our work apart. This way, this is a secret eating thing between us. Each reminds the other.

TILLY. We'll talk about it to-morrow. I want to find a glass of milk before we start to work.

CARL. We'll get some on the corner.

TILLY. The baby has to eat. . . .

[*He gets her coat. Smiles at its shabbiness.*

CARL. Nothing is too good for the proletariat.

TILLY. I had a nice coat once. I had a mother. I had a father. I was a little girl with pigtails and her face scrubbed every morning. I was a good child. I believed in God. In summer I ate mulberries from our own tree. In late summer the ground was rotten where they fell. (*Knock at the door*) Open the door. Don't ask who it is. It's Ernst, I know it is.

CARL (*looks at her, puzzled. Tilly goes to open door. He stops her. Whispering*). Are you crazy?

TILLY. I know it's him.

CARL. Let the door alone.

VOICE (*outside*). Carl . . .

CARL (*covers door*). You can't let him in.

TILLY. You can't keep him out. (*Waits*) He's waiting. . . .

CARL. He'll go away.

TILLY. Maybe he's sick.

CARL. And the others in detention camps, they're not sick?

TILLY. You might be wrong.

CARL. Then better one mistake like this than a thousand arrests and murders.

VOICE (*knocks without*). Carl. . . .

TILLY. He won't leave. (*After another knock*) Give me the key, Carl.

[*Carl looks at her. Puts key on table. Walks away. She opens door with it. Opens wide the door. There stands Ernst. Looks terrible. Wears a large velour hat, black, making his face look small. This man, sick, broken, alone, desperate, humble, something of amusement in him too. Has a handful of coins he plays with. Clothes are too big on him. Looks like a ghost.*

ERNST. Tilly. . . .

TILLY. Come in, Ernst.

ERNST. May I . . . ?

TILLY. Come in . . .

[*Carl on side, back turned. Tilly locks door. Retains key. She takes off his overcoat. He is revealed in a soiled shirt, tails out on one side. Takes off his hat while he plays with coins and looks at floor. His hair is streaked with white. He seems abstracted. Finally, becomes aware of room when coins drop out of his hand. He doesn't notice the coins.*

ERNST. Tilly. . . . Let me . . .

[*He slowly walks over to her, falls on his knees, kisses her hand. She draws her hand away.*

CARL (*turning*). Stand up. (*Ernst does so*) What do you want?

ERNST. I came —

CARL. To tell us lies.

TILLY. Let him talk. There are enough executioners in Germany without —

CARL. For the present I'm not used to one in my own room. For the present I —

ERNST (*in a violent burst*). No. Stop it. No!

CARL. What is "no"? Mickle saw you with the police. Arno saw you in the court. You give the secret police information!

TILLY. They'll hear you in the street!

ERNST. Listen to me — (*Carl makes a move for door. Ernst blocks it*) I came to have a talk.

CARL. Get out of my way.

ERNST. No!

CARL (*pushes him away, throws him to floor. Finds door locked. Turns to Tilly. She puts the table between them*). Give me the key.

TILLY. No.

[*Carl looks at Ernst. Picks him up from floor. Sits aside.*

ERNST. It's all right — I understand — you don't want to listen. It's all right — I'll talk to myself. It's a habit now. I talk to myself on the street, frighten children — frighten myself. Don't listen to me. I'll talk to the chair. Here — (*Turns chair around, addresses it as to a person*) Mr. Chair! First, we understand the situation. Second, the charges are listed in our minds. (*Tilly, out of pity and terror, removes the chair which he has been addressing very earnestly. Finally Ernst continues in a low, intense voice*) Now we must examine the living witness: what do you know of what happened? Who told you?

CARL (*jumping up fiercely*). I won't listen to you.

ERNST (*jumping up the same*). What am I asking of you? Pity? No! You must *know*, Tilly must know the accusations against me are untrue. I want you both to stand clear and proud in the world — not to think your brother and husband turned . . .

CARL. I don't care for the personal issues.

ERNST. Then I care! For my son I care. He need never be ashamed to bear my name.

CARL. Every unit paper in the country screams out you're a rat.

ERNST. And they know?

CARL. You're damn right they know.

ERNST. When I was released from the barracks in General Pape street — did they know then?

CARL. That's four months back.

ERNST. They left me free that time.

CARL. Because you were supposed to lead them to the comrades.

ERNST. But I didn't.

CARL. Because you couldn't walk.

ERNST. So far so good, no?

TILLY. Yes. . . .

ERNST. Then they picked me up again. The whole thing started fresh — questioned day and night. No let-up. Swollen, bleeding, the hospital again. What good was I to them dead? Suddenly you fall — a bucket of water — they stand you up — the lash — dig your nails into the wall to remain standing.

CARL. When did you make up your mind to tell?

ERNST. Not yet!

TILLY. Not yet?

ERNST. They tie your feet, seat you with the driver on the round-ups. This makes you seem a guide for them.

CARL. But you never sent a message, not a warning.

ERNST. Two dozen. Intercepted. You don't believe it?

CARL. No.

ERNST. You're made to stand outside the courtroom door where comrades pass.

CARL. We know all about it.

ERNST. Inside they say, "Don't make denials. Your former comrade told us everything." Some comrades believed that.

CARL. That explains the new clothes, money in your pocket?

ERNST. They dressed me up. That was the plan, to look like a paid stool pigeon. Then the first leaflet appears: "Ernst Tausig is a paid stool pigeon." Who printed them? Comrades? No, the Nazis. The comrades keep away. Out of the crowd some one hits me — it happens often. I turn around. Children hoot me on the street. All day and night the rank injustice freezes my heart to ice.

CARL. Why tell us, why —?

ERNST. They have a detective taking me home at nights.

I live in his house. I can't understand. They did something to me. Sulphur is running in my veins. At night I wake up perspiring. My tongue is thick, my eyes won't open.

TILLY. Ernst, what can we do?

ERNST. Nothing, nothing. Only I want you to believe me. I must have some one believing me. I'm not a traitor. I'm not so far gone I don't understand the position I'm in. I see what you must do to me. Warn all party members against me. You can't know the truth. Yes, what is one person like me against the whole enslaved German working class? I know I must be cast away. But you two can believe me. Yes, officially you need not believe — but yourselves. Carl, don't look at me that way!

CARL. What is that?

ERNST. What?

CARL. Perfume? You're using perfume? Ladyfingers and whipped cream for breakfast.

ERNST. No, you see how it was. They gave me money. It falls out of my hands. My mind wanders like smoke. I passed the store the other day and it was in the window. Perfumed soap. I bought some. A man must have something. It smells like flowers. (*Sits with abstracted quality. Finally says, after Carl removes leaflets on table from his sight*) Five weeks ago — I think it was the 8th of last month — I don't remember — the day we had the thunder shower — the hand was badly infected — it seems I knocked it against the wall or something — the 9th or 10th — they amputated it. We had that fine surgeon, D. B. Kellner. (*There is a luminous full pause. Yes, his hand has been removed and all this time he kept the stump in a pocket. Does not take it out now either. Tilly, unbearably moved, comes to him. He refuses her touch. Jumps up*) Don't touch me. No, it isn't so easy. Three months — it's not so easy. That's why I'm telling you. *You must know everything!* Last night I sat in my room and it came to me. I was thinking that when I went there the next day I would tell them everything. (*Laughs and changes voice to a whisper*) Do you know what you must do? I brought the whole thing with me. A gun, cleaned, oiled. This morning I did it. With one hand it isn't easy. Kill me!

CARL. What?

ERNST. Take the gun. Carl, you loved me once. Kill me. One day more and I'll stand there like an idiot identifying prisoners for them. I know so many. In all honor and courage you must pull the little trigger. I brought the money. Put it in the fighting fund. Maybe tell a few comrades the truth.

CARL. It is the truth?

ERNST. Yes.

TILLY. There must be no talk of dying.

ERNST. For me there's one thing, Tilly — nothing is left to do. Carl —?

CARL. They've killed you already.

ERNST. That's right. But you're alive. Other comrades are working. The day is coming and I'll be in the final result. That right can't be denied me. In that dizzy dazzling structure some part of me is built. You must understand. Take the gun, Carl.

CARL (*drawing hand away*). I won't do it.

ERNST. I couldn't do it myself. There isn't enough strength left. . . . Tilly, no tears! (*Smiles wearily*) Such bourgeois traits in a worker. . . . What is your answer, Carl?

CARL. That is what you must do. Do it yourself. Before you turn idiot. When you do that the world will know you were innocent. They'll see you came voluntarily, that . . . (*Suddenly*) Who am I to sit in judgment?

ERNST. These guns are complicated pieces of machinery. (*Has picked it up*) Our Germans make them like works of art. (*Weighs the gun in his hand*) Tilly, Carl, our agony is real. But we live in the joy of a great coming people! The animal kingdom is past. Day must follow the night.

Now we are ready : we have been steeled in a terrible fire, but soon all the desolate places of the world must flourish with human genius. Brothers will live in the soviets of the world! Yes, a world of security and freedom is waiting for all mankind! (*Looks at them both deeply. Walks to door to room* L.) Do your work, Comrades.

[*Exits.*

TILLY (*for a moment stands still. Then starts for room. Carl stops her*). Carl, stop him, stop him.

[*Carl holds her back.*

CARL. Let him die. . . .

TILLY. Carl. . . .

[*Shot heard within.*

CARL. Let him live. . . .

SLOW CURTAIN

AMERICA, AMERICA!

ALFRED KREYMBORG

ALFRED KREYMBORG is an author who has contributed some original techniques to the American theatre. In the first edition of this anthology, his "Lima Beans", a free-verse "scherzo-play", as he called it, drew some fire from the professional critics, but the play has proved its popularity time and again with producing groups. Recently, Kreymborg has allied himself with the proletarian thinkers, but his writing still demonstrates individuality of technique. "America, America!" is a "mass recital."

The first of the "agitprop" (agitation-and-propaganda) plays were introduced into America by a German-speaking labor group, known as the *Prolet-Bühne*, in the fall of 1930. They staged plays and mass recitations with very little scenery and with symbolical costumes, so as to draw the audience into the recitation, after the manner of the workers' theatres of Germany and the amateur theatres of the U. S. S. R. By 1935, the Theatre of Action had popularized the mass-recitation form in English, and Alfred Kreymborg, in "America, America!" had demonstrated in poetic terms the dynamic rhythm of such a harmonious interplay of acting forces.

Mr. Kreymborg was born in New York City, December 10, 1883. He was one of the early members of the Province-town Players, and wrote his first plays for them. He has directed various theatre groups, and during the last year has been with the Federal Theatre—first as director of the Poetic Theatre, and more recently as Managing Producer of the Manhattan and Bronx circuit, with eight touring companies.

He has published thirty-two books and written thirty-six plays; he is known as poet, playwright, editor, critic, anthologist, and for his tours of America in the rôle of troubadour and lecturer.

Most of his one-act plays have been published in four collections: *Puppet Plays* (preface by Gordon Craig), *Plays for Merry Andrews*, *Rocking Chairs*, and *How Do You Do, Sir?* Another collection, *The Dead Are Free*, is in preparation.

His full-length plays are: "There's a Moon To-night", "Money in Love", "Phyllis Ashley", and "Commencement."

All of Alfred Kreymborg's plays are a dramatic development of his feeling for music in life and human relations.

AMERICA, AMERICA!

By ALFRED KREYMBORG

"America, America!" was originally produced in New York by the Repertory Playhouse Associates.

Original Cast

AN ORATOR	Harold Baumstone
JACK, a rich boy	Colfax Sanderson
JILL, a rich girl	Theodosia Young
JIM, a poor husband	John O'Shaughnessy
JANE, a poor wife	Elizabeth Timberman
CHORUS OF UNEMPLOYED	

AMERICA, AMERICA!

SCENE. *This dramatic ode contains five principal characters and a background of street scenes, moving crowds. The main character is a soap-box orator who harangues a small gathering of workers and derelicts on some Union Square corner. At times the mob joins in on certain familiar lines. The refrain, "America, America", is spoken throughout by the orator, or by the chorus in growing unison, and from the loudest to the lowest pitch, in accordance with the mood. In Scene II, he speaks of two rich kids, Jack and Jill, and they enter — the girl's part in italics. In Scene III, the poor married pair, Jim and Jane, are revealed in their wretched home — the woman's part in italics. The final "America" is sounded in a threatening tone by the orator and crowd in a long and pregnant pianissimo.*

[*Before the curtain rises, we hear off-stage echoes of a patriotic past: "I pledge allegiance to my flag", spoken by school-children; Sousa's "Stars and Stripes Forever"; snatches of modern jazz. Then the light strikes the orator, the soap-box, the gathering mob. . . .*

SCENE I

What have you done with all your gold,
  America, America?
What have you bought and calmly sold
  of human flesh and misery:
What has it cost the growing poor
  to earn their cornered liberty:
  The right to live awhile and wed,
  the right to share a loaf of bread,
  the right to one dark room and bed,
  the right to love before they're dead,
  and all the children comforted —

Why are the children thin and cold,
    America?

What is it makes the young grow old,
    America:
The young who marry young, grow old,
caught in a daily strangle-hold:
    The man in a ditch,
    The woman a witch
    who swings a broom
    and makes a room
    shine as if the room were rich —
    only to drop her hands and weep
    as she sees her husband creep,
    every muscle uninspired,
    tired brain and body tired,
        up the stair,
        up the stair —
    every step a deadly echo:
    "I've been fired, fired."
What is it makes her run to him,
drag him in, what's left of him,
and hug and kiss him back to life?
    Doesn't she need him as well,
    weary of the wifely hell
    of doing things she's had to do
    to make one stipend carry two,
    and carry three and drag on four? —
    (God help them if there are more!)
Ah, but how she needs the man!
    Now he's holding her and she
    smiles upon him dreamily:
    He is up where he belongs,
    mumbling silly things and songs
    as the morrow in their lives
    gathers hope and love revives.

Shake them, wake them, make them rise,
  America, America,
   ere the animal arise,
   and the phallus and the womb
   one more child of theirs entomb!
    They were careless
    once before —
    twice before —
    slam the door —
Thank you for that shutter, Wind —
that was harsh and kind of you —
the poor are never blind to you —
  Slam the shutter — that 'll do!

What is it makes the pair go pale,
  America, America?
Why has their home become a jail
  where the wolves of poverty
  wall them in and lose the key —
What have they done — what crime is theirs —
  what do they see
  that makes them look,
  look as if their lives were done,
  lives the pair have scarce begun?

And what is the line along the street,
  a line a million lines repeat,
  where the most heroic feet
  join the zeros and the mob
  looking for a little job
  good enough — my God how good
  if it buy their women food!
What in God's name can it be,
  America, America,
   has robbed them of their liberty?

What do I see go rolling by,
   America, oh land of mine,
racing along and joy skyhigh,
boys and girls and all skyhigh,
    everyone drunk with youthful health,
    bedizened and mad with Daddy's wealth,
    sailing along in a blinding car,
    making the earth a dancing star,
    rending the day from moon to sun,
    their dizzy hearts a barrel of fun
    that doesn't give a damn for what we are,
    doesn't give a damn for what you are,
      oh land of mine,
      so long as they can sail and kiss,
      drink and kiss, kiss and love,
      the girl below, the boy above,
    drunk with each other
    and drunk for awhile
    with the world they own
      mile after mile,
    earth and air and underground
    where nobody dies while they're around!

Ah, what a joy-ride, boy-ride, girl-ride,
   girl-wide boy-ride,
   world-wide joy-ride!
Nothing in the world to worry about,
the old Harry's in and the old Harry's out,
nothing in the world to be sorry about —
"Who the hell cares what Mother'll say? —"
"*Daddy's got a bank and the bank will pay* —"
"Jesus Christ, I could almost pray —
Never knew a girl could be so gay!"
"*Never knew a boy, Jack* —" "Never knew a
   dame
Who'd go the whole hog and then not blame —"

"*I shoulda worn a wedding ring —*"
"Cut out the giggling — get up and sing —"
"*Turn on the radio — let's us dance —*"
"What have I done with my silly pants?"
"*My, you're naughty — my dress is gone —*"
"Why not dance in what you've got on?"
"*Turn on the light, Jack — isn't it late?*"
"Long after daylight — half past eight."
"*Mother'll throw a fit —*" "And Dad!
We'd have been good if we hadn't had —"
"*Let's have another drink —*" "Let's have
    two —"
"*I never knew what a drink could do —*"
"I never knew a girl I'd just met —"
"*A boy in respectable evening dress —*"
"Could bow like an iceberg and then let —"
"*You do what you did —*" "I did? —" "*Yes.*"
"What did I do that you didn't do?"
"*Come a little closer and I'll tell you.*"
"Jill — you're a lady — don't lie on your back —"
"*And you're no gentleman — Jack — oh, Jack!*"

SCENE III

"What have you got for dinner, Honey?"
"*Yesterday's soup — I'm out o' money —*"
    (America, America.)
"What'll we do when the rent comes round?"
"*Butter's gone up ten cents a pound.*"
"I've been all over — no job in sight."
"*Jim — you were awfully late to-night.*"
"Every bone o' mine's done in —"
"*Sit down now an' let's begin.*"
"Jane, I'm too tired — can't eat a mite —"
"*Jim, you're trembling — an' oh so white!*"
"I'd like to lay right down an' die —"
"*Don't wake the kids — you'll make 'em cry.*"

"I don't deserve a woman like you."
*"Don't say that after all you've been
         through —"*
"I'm not through yet — to-morrow I —
Christ Almighty ! —" *"Jim, don't cry —
Sit a little closer — poor old dear —"*
"You're tired too —" *"Not while you're near."*

"Blow out the lamp — I love the dark —"
    (America.)
"Remember how we first met in the park —"
    (America?)
"I sat beside you —" *"An' I beside you —"*
"An' you began —" *"You began, Howdoyou-
         do?"*
"Jane, you were flirting —" *"No, you were —"*
"Well, I was lonely —" *"So was I, sir."*
"You looked so cold there, sitting alone —
An' when I sat down you looked like a stone."
"It's not for a girl to encourage a man —"
"You coulda got up when I began —"
"I hadn't the strength or will, I suppose."
"An' how long we sat there nobody knows."
"It seems like a hundred years ago —"
    (America) —
"More than a thousand years and oh —"
"You kissed me before you knew my name —"
"An' you never stopped me, did you, Jane?"
"We got married an' the Five an' Ten —"
"Sold us a load o' funny stuff when
I had a job —" *"An' I had one too —"*
"An' we were so young an' happy you —"
"You, Jim —" "You, Jane —" *"You an' I —"*
    "Yes —"
"Jumped aboard a crazy express —"
"An' kids came out of our happiness !"

"Christ, I could smash such a lousy town —"
    (America!)
"*Don't get up, Jim — come back, sit down!*"
"Look at me, Jane — do I look like a slob? —
I tried an' I tried — not a goddamn job."
"*Be patient, Honey, don't get the blues —
Hundreds an' thousands are in our shoes.*"
"Where's all the money gone — who's to
        blame —"
    (America?) — "*Yes, who's to blame?*"
"Who owns the earth an' what have we got?
What right have they to make us rot?"
"*Please don't cry, dear —*" "I'm not cryin' —
I'm sick an' tired o' seein' you tryin'
To make one meal last a week or two —"
"*Don't you know I'm in love with you? —*"
"Don't tell me that —" "*But I will, I do —*"
"You're tearin' my heart out —" "*I don't care —
I work as you work, fair an' square.*"
"Work as I work? — I don't do a thing
But try great bastards, king after king,
Who tell me the whole wide world is poor,
Act down an' out an' show me the door.
Who wants a handout? — I wanta work —
There's not a job on earth I'd shirk.
Bring back my slavery — let me earn
Enough to come home an' see you turn
With the light of old — the light that stops —
Turns to other things — an' then drops!"

"*Never mind, Jim — to-morrow I'll
Hunt for a job —*" "Like hell you will!"
"*Jim, what's the matter? — don't look that
        way —
You look as if —*" "Will you be still?"
"*You'll wake the kids, dear — what did I say?*"
"Hell with the kids — to hell with it all —"

"*Honey — you're crazy — Honey —*" "Don't
   bawl!"
"*I'm not bawlin' — please come to bed —*"
"Not on your life — I'd sooner drop dead."
"*Jim — God in Heaven —*" "I've had my fill —"
"*You haven't eaten the soup or bread —*"
"Say one more word about bread an' I'll
   kill —"
"*Jim — let go o' me — what did I do?*"
"One more word an' I'm through — through."
"*Honey — I'm sorry — I musta meant —*"
"Butter's gone up — we can't raise the rent —"
"*No, Jim, never — I never said that —*"
"Christ, how I hate this lousy flat —
The table an' chairs — the sink an' stove —"
"*Jim — come back — you no longer love —*"
"Say one more word about love an' I'll —"
"*Take to the streets! —*" "Like hell you will!"

"*Oh, but we're mad, we're raving mad!*"
"Ah, my poor darling!" "*My starving lad!*"
"How could I turn on my girl, an' knife —"
"*Jim — you still love me —*" "Love you for
   life!"
"*Somebody — somebody —*" "Send us a job —"
"*Down on your knees, Jim — send us a job —*"
"Down on your knees, Jane — I've never
   prayed —"
"*Don't turn to God, Jim — I am afraid.*"
"Where is your hand, Jane — hold me tight —"
"*Christ save my lover — so thin an' white —*"
"Jane — what makes you shiver so cold? —"
"*What have they done with all the gold?*"
"Jane — they're killing you — where have you
   gone?"
"*Jim — they're killing you — what have we
   done?*"

"Why can't they give us a bite to live?"
"*The right to earn a loaf o' bread?*"
"The right to love before we're dead? —"
"*An' our poor children comforted?*"
"Up on your feet, Jane — up again now!
Now we'll start fighting —" "*How, dear,
    how?*"
"To-morrow I'll tear down the whole damn
    sky!"
"*An' we'll run beside you — the children an'
    I!*"
"To-morrow we'll start all over and ah —"
"*Die if we have to —*"   (America!)

BIBLIOGRAPHIES

1. REFERENCE READINGS

Archer, William. *Old Drama and the New, The.* Dodd, New York, 1936.
    Playmaking, A Manual of Craftsmanship. Dodd, New York, 1933.
Baker, George Pierce. *Dramatic Technique.* Houghton, Boston, 1919.
Blake, Ben. *Awakening of the American Theatre.* New Theatre, New York, 1935.
Bricker, Herschel L. *Our Theatre To-day.* French, New York, 1936.
Brown, John Mason. *Upstage.* Norton, New York, 1930.
Burleigh, Louise. *Community Theatre, The.* Little, Boston, 1917.
Carter, Jean, and Jess Ogden. *Play Book, The.* Harcourt, New York, 1937.
Cheney, Sheldon. *Art Theatre, The.* Knopf, New York, 1925.
    New Movement in the Theatre, The. Kennerly, New York, 1914.
    Stage Decoration. Day, New York, 1930.
    Theatre, The: 3000 Years of Drama, Acting, and Stagecraft. Longmans, New York, 1929.
Clark, Barrett H. *Eugene O'Neill.* McBride, New York, 1926.
    Hour of American Drama, An. Lippincott, Philadelphia, 1930.
    How to Produce Amateur Plays. Little, Boston, 1925.
    Paul Green. McBride, New York, 1928.
    Study of Modern Drama, The. Appleton, New York, 1928.
Collins, Lillian Foster. *Little Theatre in School, The.* Dodd, New York, 1930.
Dean, Alexander. *Little Theatre Organization and Management.* Appleton, New York, 1926.
DeGoveia, C. J. *Community Playhouse, The.* Viking, New York, 1923.
Deutsch, Helen, and Stella Hanau. *Provincetown Playhouse.* Farrar, New York, 1931.
Dickinson, Thomas H. *Insurgent Theatre, The.* Heubsch, New York, 1917.
    Playwrights of the New American Theatre. Macmillan, New York, 1925.
Eastman, Fred, and Louis Wilson. *Drama in the Church.* French, New York, 1933.
Eaton, Walter Prichard. *Theatre Guild, The.* Brentano, New York, 1929.
Fuerst, Walter René, and Samuel J. Hume. *Twentieth Century Stage Decoration,* 2 vols. Knopf, New York, 1929.

Gannon, Robert I. *Technique of the One-Act Play, The.* Fordham Univ. Press, New York, 1925.

Glaspell, Susan. *Road to the Temple, The.* Stokes, New York, 1927.

Hamilton, Clayton. *Conversations on Contemporary Drama.* New York, 1924.
  Problems of the Playwright. Holt, New York, 1917.
  So You're Writing a Play. Little, Boston, 1925.

Hillebrand, H. N. *Writing the One-Act Play.* Knopf, New York, 1925.

Hinsdell, Oliver. *Making the Little Theatre Pay.* French, New York, 1927.

Kreymborg, Alfred. *Troubadour.* Boni, New York, 1925.

Krows, Arthur Edwin. *Playwriting for Profit.* Longmans, New York, 1928.

Lawson, John Howard. *Theory and Technique of Playwriting.* Putnams, New York, 1936.

Lewis, B. R. *Technique of the One-Act Play, The.* Luce, Boston, 1918.

Macgowan, Kenneth. *Footlights Across America.* Harcourt, New York, 1929.
  Theatre of To-morrow, The. Boni, New York, 1921.

Mackay, Constance D'Arcy. *Little Theatre in the United States, The.* Holt, New York, 1917.

MacKaye, Percy. *Civic Theatre, The.* Kennerly, New York, 1912.
  Playhouse and the Play, The. Macmillan, New York, 1909.
  Community Drama. Houghton, Boston, 1917.

Mantle, Burns. *American Playwrights of To-day.* Dodd, New York, 1929.

Matthews, Brander. *Principles of Playmaking.* Scribner, New York, 1919.
  Study of the Drama. Houghton, Boston, 1910.

Mayorga, Margaret. *Short History of the American Drama, A.* Dodd, New York, 1932.

Moderwell, Hiram Kelly. *Theatre of To-day, The.* Dodd, New York, 1928.

Moses, Montrose J. *American Dramatist, The.* Little, Boston, 1925.

Nicoll, Allardyce. *Theory of Drama, The.* Harrap, London, 1931.

Playwriting, The Art of. Lectures. Univ. of Pennsylvania Press, Philadelphia, 1928.

Quinn, Arthur Hobson. *History of the American Drama, A.* Crofts, New York, 1936.

Rockwell, Ethel Theodora. *Study Course in American One-Act Plays.* Univ. of North Carolina Press, Chapel Hill, 1929.

Sayler, Oliver M. *Our American Theatre.* Brentano, New York, 1923.

Shipley, Joseph T. *Art of Eugene O'Neill, The.* Univ. of Washington Press, Seattle, 1928.

Skinner, Richard Dana. *Our Changing Theatre.* Longmans, New York, 1931.
  Eugene O'Neill, A Poet's Quest. Longmans, New York, 1935.

Stevens, Thomas Wood. *Theatre from Athens to Broadway, The.* Appleton, New York, 1932.

Swan, Mark. *How You Can Write Plays.* French, New York, 1927.

Walter, Eugene. *How to Write a Play.* French, New York, 1928.

White, A. F. *Plays of Eugene O'Neill.* Western Reserve Univ., Cleveland, 1923.

Wilde, Percival. *Craftsmanship of the One-Act Play.* Little, Boston, 1923.

Winther, Sophus Keith. *Eugene O'Neill: A Critical Study.* Univ. of Washington Press, Seattle, 1934.

2. GENERAL ANTHOLOGIES

Church, Virginia. *Curtain! A Book of Modern Plays.* Harper, New York, 1932.

Clark, Barrett H., and T. R. Cook. *One-Act Plays.* Heath, New York, 1929.

Clark, Barrett H., and Kenyon Nicholson. *American Scene, The.* Appleton, New York, 1930.

Cohen, Helen Louise. *More One-Act Plays by Modern Authors.* Harcourt, New York, 1927.

    One-Act Plays by Modern Authors. Harcourt, New York, revised 1934.

Dickinson, Asa Don. *Drama.* Doubleday, Garden City, 1922.

Goldstone, George A. *One-Act Plays.* Allyn, Boston, New York, 1926.

Hubbell, J. B., and J. O. Beaty. *Introduction to Drama, An.* Macmillan, New York, 1927.

Hughes, Glenn. *Short Plays for Modern Players.* Appleton, New York, 1931.

Isaacs, Edith J. *Plays of American Life and Fantasy.* Theatre Arts, New York, 1929.

Johnson, Theodore, and LeRoy Phillips. *Miniature Plays.* Baker, Boston (Series).

    Types of Modern Dramatic Composition. Baker, Boston, 1927.

Knickerbocker, Edwin VanBerghen. *Twelve Plays.* Holt, New York, 1931.

Law, Frederick Houk. *Modern Plays, Short and Long.* Century, New York, London, 1921.

Leonard, S. A. *Atlantic Book of Modern Plays, The.* Atlantic, Boston, 1921.

Lewis, Benjamin Roland. *Contemporary One-Act Plays.* Scribner, New York, Chicago, 1922.

Loving, Pierre. *Ten Minute Plays.* Brentano, New York, 1923.

Mayorga, Margaret. *Twenty Short Plays on a Royalty Holiday* (1937–1940). French, New York, 1937.

Nicholson, Kenyon. *Appleton Book of Short Plays.* Appleton, New York, 1926.

One-Act Plays for Stage and Study. French, New York (Series).

Pence, R. W. *Dramas by Present-Day Writers.* Scribner, New York, 1927.
Schafer, Barbara Louise. *Book of One-Act Plays, A.* Bobbs, Indianapolis, 1922.
Shay, Frank. *Contemporary One-Act Plays.* Appleton, New York, 1922.
    Fifty More Contemporary One-Act Plays. Appleton, New York, 1928.
    Plays for Strolling Mummers. Appleton, New York, 1926.
    Twenty Contemporary One-Act Plays. Appleton, New York, 1921.
    Twenty-Five Short Plays, International. Appleton, New York, 1925.
Shay, Frank, and Pierre Loving. *Fifty Contemporary One-Act Plays.* Appleton, New York, 1925.
Snook, Lee Owen. *Yearbook of Short Plays.* Row, Evanston (Series).
Tucker, S. M. *Twelve One-Act Plays for Study and Production.* Ginn, Boston, 1929.
Wilde, Percival. *Contemporary One-Act Plays from Nine Countries.* Little, Boston, 1936.

3. SPECIALIZED COLLECTIONS

(NOTE: *Other specialized collections are included under author classification, Section 4 of Bibliographies.*)

Baker, George Pierce. *Yale One-Act Plays.* French, New York, 1930.
Boston Theatre Guild Plays. Baker, Boston, 1924.
Clements, Colin C. *Sea Plays.* Small, Boston, 1925.
Cohen, Helen Louise. *Junior Play Book, The.* Harcourt, New York, 1923.
Dakota Playmakers Plays. Baker, Boston (Series).
Dean, Alexander. *Seven to Seventeen.* French, New York, 1931.
Drummond, A. M. *Cornell University Plays.* French, New York, 1932.
Eastman, Fred. *Plays of American Life.* French, New York, 1934.
    Modern Religious Dramas. Holt, New York, 1928.
Eaton, Walter Prichard. *Yale Plays.* French, New York, 1936.
Edmonds, Randolph. *Six Plays for a Negro Theatre.* Baker, Boston, 1934.
Forty-Minute Prize Plays from "Stage." Dodd, New York, 1936.
"Goin' Home" and Other Plays of the 1927 Contest. Longmans, New York, 1928.
Harvard Dramatic Club, Plays of the. Brentano, New York, 1918.
Hughes, Glenn. *University of Washington Plays.* French, New York (Series).
Indiana Prize Plays. Bobbs, Indianapolis, 1924.
Jagendorf, M. A. *One-Act Plays for Young Folks.* Coward, New York, 1924.
Jagendorf, M. A., and Nina B. Lamkin. *Around America with the Indian.* French, New York, 1933.
    Plays for Club, School, and Camp. French, New York, 1935.

Johnson, Theodore. *Prize Plays for Women and Girls.* Baker, Boston, 1936.
  Ten Fantasies for Stage and Study. Baker, Boston, 1932.
Keeley, Mary Paxton. *Christian College Plays.* Christian College, Columbia, Missouri, 1935.
Koch, Frederick. *Carolina Folk Plays.* Holt, New York (Series).
Ladies' Home Journal One-Act Plays. Doubleday, Garden City, 1925.
Lewis, Benjamin Roland. *University of Utah Plays.* Baker, Boston, 1928.
Locke, Alain, and M. Gregory. *Plays of Negro Life.* Harper, New York, 1927.
Moses, Montrose. *Another Treasury of Plays for Children.* Little, Boston, 1926.
  Ring Up the Curtain. Little, Boston, 1932.
  Treasury of Plays for Children, A. Little, Boston, 1921.
New Plays for Men and Boys. French, New York, 1935.
New Plays for Women and Girls. French, New York, 1932.
Nicholson, Kenyon. *Hollywood Plays.* French, New York, 1930.
O'Hara, Frank. *Plays, Skits, Lyrics.* University of Chicago Press, Chicago, 1936.
Oneal, B. *Prize-Winning One-Act Plays.* Southwest, Dallas, 1930.
Players' Book of One-Act Plays (Players of Detroit). McKee, New York, 1928.
Price, Olive. *Debutante Plays.* French, New York, 1936.
  Plays of Far Places. Baker, Boston (Series).
  Short Plays from American History and Literature. French, New York (Series).
Pride, Leo B. *Shadow of the Mine, The.* French, New York, 1929.
Provincetown Plays. Appleton, New York (Series).
Richardson, W., and M. Miller. *Negro History in Thirteen Plays.* Associated, Washington, D. C., 1935.
Robinson, Donald Fay. *Harvard Dramatic Club Miracle Plays, The.* French, New York, 1928.
Rowe, Kenneth Thorpe. *University of Michigan Plays.* Ann Arbor (Series).
Sanford, A. P. *Little Plays for Everybody.* Dodd, New York, 1932.
  One-Act Plays for Women. Dodd, New York, 1934.
  Outdoor Plays for Boys and Girls. Dodd, New York, 1930.
  Peace Plays. Dodd, New York, 1932.
Sanford, A. P., and R. H. Schauffler. *Little Plays for Little People.* Dodd, New York, 1932.
  Plays for Our American Holidays. Dodd, New York (Series).
Shay, Frank. *Appleton Book of Christmas Plays.* Appleton, New York, 1929.
  Appleton Book of Holiday Plays. Appleton, New York, 1930.
  Treasury of Plays for Men, A. Little, Boston, 1923.
  Treasury of Plays for Women, A. Little, Boston, 1930.

Simon, S. Sylvan. *Easily Staged Plays for Boys.* French, New York, 1936.

Smith, Addison Geery. *Ten Plays from O. Henry.* French, New York, 1936.

Thomas, Charles Swain. *Atlantic Book of Junior Plays, The.* Little, Boston, 1924.

Vagabond Plays. Norman Remington, Baltimore (Series).

Washington Square Plays. Doubleday, Garden City, 1925.

Webber, J. P., and H. H. Webster. *Short Plays for Young People.* Houghton, Boston, 1925.

Wisconsin Plays. Huebsch, New York (Series).

4. SELECTIVE LIST OF ONE–ACT PLAYS BY AMERICAN AUTHORS

(NOTE: * *designates plays available through Samuel French, Inc.* † *designates Collections listed in Sections 2 and 3 of Bibliographies.*)

Ade, George. * Marse Covington.

    * Mayor and the Manicure, The.

    * Nettie.

    * Speaking to Father.

Akins, Zoë. * Did It Really Happen? *Smart Set,* Vol. 52, 343. New York, 1917.

    Magical City, The. *Forum,* Vol. 55, 507. New York, 1916.

    Portrait of Tiero, The. *Theatre Arts,* Vol. 4, 316. New York, 1920.

    * Such a Charming Young Man.

Aldis, Mary. *Plays for Small Stages.* Duffield, New York, 1915.

    Contains Mrs. Pat and the Law, The Drama Class of Tankaha, Extreme Unction, The Letter, Temperament.

    Ten P.M. *Drama,* Vol. 11, 187. Mt. Morris, 1921.

Alexander, Hartley Burr. Carved Woman. † In Cohen, *More One-Act Plays.*

    Kills-with-Her-Man. † In Isaacs, *Plays.*

Allen, Gertrude. Grass Is Always Greener, The. Baker, Boston, 1935.

    Homespun. Baker, Boston, 1936.

    Paternity Case, A. † In Mayorga, *Twenty Short Plays.*

Anderson, Sherwood. Mother. † In Wilde, *Contemporary One-Act Plays.*

Atlas, Leopold Lawrence. L. † In Baker, *Yale One-Act Plays.*

    * So Long.

Ballard, Fred (in collaboration with Pearl Franklin). * Young America.

Beach, Lewis. * *Four One-Act Plays.*

    Contains The Clod, A Guest for Dinner, Love Among the Lions, Brothers.

    [" *The Clod*" *is reprinted in this volume.*]

Belasco, David. * Madame Butterfly.
Brown, Alice. * But an' Ben.
    One-Act Plays. Macmillan, New York, 1921.
        Contains The Hero, Doctor Auntie, The Crimson Lake, Milly
Dear, The Web, The Loving Cup, Joint Owners in Spain, The Sugar
House, A March Wind.
Bynner, Witter. *Book of Plays, A.* Knopf, New York, 1922.
        Contains The Little King, A Night Wind, Tiger, Cycle, Iphigenia
in Tauris.
    War. *Stratford Journal*, Vol. 6, 44. Boston, 1920.
Carpenter, Edward Childs. * Prairie Doll, The.
Clements, Colin. Across the Border. † In Clark and Nicholson, *American
    Scene.*
    * Boy Through the Window, The.
    * Curtain.
    * Job.
    * Just Women.
    * Love in a French Kitchen (in collaboration with John Monk Saunders).
    Modern Harlequinade. *Poet Lore*, Vol. 31, 579. Boston, 1920.
    * Pirates.
    Plays for a Folding Theatre. Appleton, New York [1923].
        Contains Pierrot in Paris, Columbine, The Return of Harlequin,
Three Lepers of Suk-el-Garab, The Desert, The Siege, Moontide.
    Plays for Pagans. Appleton, New York, 1924.
        Contains The Haiduc, Harlequin, Yesterday, Spring, Four Who
Were Blind.
    Seven Plays of Old Japan. *Poet Lore*, Vol. 31, 159. Boston, 1920.
        Includes The Cherry Blossom River, By the Sumida River, Grow-
ing Old Together, The Star Dust Path, The Father, A Man and His
Wife, Life Is a Dream.
    * You.
Clements, Colin, and Florence Ryerson. * *All on a Summer's Day, and
    Six Other Short Plays.*
        Contains All on a Summer's Day, On the Lot, Men Folk, Storm,
Letters, A Romantic Interval, Love Is Like That.
    * Hot Lemonade.
    Jilted. Baker, Boston, n. d.
    * Littlest Shepherd, The.
    Loop, The. *Emerson Quarterly*, Vol. 10, 15. Boston, 1930.
    On the Other Side of the Wall. † In Sanford, *Peace Plays.*
    * Perfect Ending.
    * Willow Plate, The.
Conkle, Ellsworth Prouty. * Chief Sittum Bull.
    * *Crick Bottom Plays.*

Contains Minnie Field, Warter Wucks, 'Lection, Things Is That-a-Way, Sparkin'.
[*"Sparkin'"* is reprinted in this volume.]
* Feller from Omaha, Th'.
* Juber Bird, The.
* *Loolie and Other Short Plays.*
Contains Loolie, Madge, Lace, The Owl and Two Young Men, P'taters in the Spring, Little Granny Graver.
* 'Nitiated, Th'.
Cook, George Cram. (*See* Susan Glaspell.)
Cowan, Sada. Auf Wiedersehen. † In Mayorga, *Twenty Short Plays.*
Pomp, and Other One-Act Plays. Brentano, New York, 1926.
Contains Pomp, As I Remember You, In the Morgue, The Ball and Chain, Sintram of Skagerrak, Collaboration, The State Forbids.
[*"Sintram of Skagerrak"* is reprinted in this volume.]
Moonlit Way, The. Baker, Boston, 1937.
Woman's Touch, A. Baker, Boston, 1934.
Crocker, Bosworth. Coquine. † In Mayorga, *Twenty Short Plays.*
Humble Folk. Appleton, New York, 1923.
Contains The Last Straw, The Baby Carriage, The Dog, The First Time, The Cost of a Hat.
[*"The Last Straw"* is reprinted in this volume.]
* Josephine.
Crothers, Rachel. * Rector, The.
Six One-Act Plays. Baker, Boston, 1925.
Contains The Importance of Being Clothed, The Importance of Being Nice, The Importance of Being Married, The Importance of Being a Woman, What They Think.
Culbertson, Ernest Howard. * Across the Jordan.
* Color in Court.
End of the Trail, The. † In Nicholson, *Appleton Book.*
Rackey. † In Locke, *Plays of Negro Life.*
Dargan, O. T. (and F. Peterson). *The Flutter of the Goldleaf and Other Plays.* Scribner, New York, 1922.
Contains The Flutter of the Goldleaf, The Journey, Everychild, Two Doctors of Akragas.
Woods of Ida. *Century,* Vol. 74, 590. New York, 1907.
Davies, Mary Caroline. * Cobweb Kings.
* Slave with Two Faces.
* Tables and Chairs.
Davis, Allen. On Vengeance Height (in collaboration with C. C. Vencill).
† In Knickerbocker, *Twelve Plays.*
* Wolves.

Davis, Richard Harding. *Farces.* Scribner, New York, 1906.
    Contains The Dictator, The Galloper, Miss Civilization.
    * Peace Manœuvres.
    * Zone Police, The.
Delano, Edith, and David Carb. Grandma Pulls the Strings. † In Phillips,
    Types.
    Lady of Pain, The. Baker, Boston, n. d.
Dix, Beulah Marie. Across the Border. Holt, New York, 1915.
    Allison's Lad, and Other Martial Interludes. Holt, New York, 1910.
    Contains Allison's Lad, The Hundredth Trick, The Weakest Link,
    The Snare and the Fowler, The Captain of the Gate, The Dark of
    the Dawn.
    Cicely's Cavalier. Baker, Boston, 1897.
    * Girl Comes Home, The.
Dransfield, Jane. Blood O' Kings. † In Shay, *Treasury.*
    * Joe.
Dreiser, Theodore. Dream, The. *Seven Arts*, Vol. 2, 319. New York,
    1917.
    Plays of the Natural and Supernatural. Lane, New York, 1916.
    Contains The Girl in the Coffin, The Blue Sphere, Laughing Gas,
    In the Dark, The Spring Recital, The Light in the Window, Old
    Rag-Picker.
Eaton, Walter Prichard. * Grandfather's Chair.
    * Grandma — Old Style.
    * Purple Door Knob, The.
Emery, Gilbert. Riches. Appleton, New York, n. d.
Erskine, John. Hearts Enduring. † In Cohen, *More One-Act Plays.*
Farrar, John. * Here Are Sailors.
    * Jack.
    Magic Sea Shell and Other Plays for Children. Doubleday, Garden
    City, 1923.
    * Nerves.
    * Wedding Rehearsal, The.
Ferber, Edna. The Eldest. Appleton, New York, n. d.
Field, Rachel L. * Bad Penny, The.
    * Cinderella Married.
    * Columbine in Business.
    Cross-Stitch Heart and Other Plays. Scribner, New York, 1927.
    Contains The Cross-Stitch Heart, Greasy Luck, The Nine Day's
    Queen, The Londonderry Air, At the Junction, Bargains in Cathay.
    Fifteenth Candle, The. † In Thomas, *Atlantic Book.*
    * Patchwork Quilt, The.
    * Polly Patchwork.
    * Rise Up, Jennie Smith.

    * Sentimental Scarecrow.

    * Three Pills in a Bottle.

    * Wisdom Teeth.

Flavin, Martin. * *Brains and Other One-Act Plays.*

    Contains Brains, Casualties, An Emergency Case, The Blind Man, A Question of Principle, Caleb Stone's Death Watch.

Flexner, Hortense. Faun, The. *Drama*, Vol. 11, 311. Mt. Morris, 1921.

    Voices. *Seven Arts*, Vol. 1, 135. New York, 1916.

Frank, Florence Kiper. Faith of Their Fathers, The. *Menorah Journal*, Vol. 11, 377. New York, 1925.

    Garden, The. *Drama*, Vol. 8, 471. Chicago, 1918.

    Over the Hills and Far Away. *Drama*, Vol. 11, 80. Chicago, 1920.

Galbraith, Esther. Brink of Silence, The. † In Clements, *Sea Plays.*

Gale, Zona. * Clouds, The.

    Evening Clothes. Baker, Boston, n. d.

    Neighbors, The. Huebsch, New York, 1920.

    Uncle Jimmy. Baker, Boston, 1922.

Garland, Robert. * At Night All Cats Are Gray.

    Double Miracle, The. † In *Vagabond Plays.*

    * Importance of Being a Roughneck, The.

Gerstenberg, Alice. *Comedies All.* Longmans, New York, 1930.

    Includes The Setback, Mere Man, The Menu, Facing Facts, Upstage, Rhythm, The Opera Matinée, At the Club, The Puppeteer, Latchkeys.

    Four Plays for Four Women. Brentano, New York, 1924.

    Includes Mah-Jongg, Their Husband, Ever Young, Seaweed.

    Patroness, The.

    Star Dust.

    Ten One-Act Plays. Brentano, New York, 1928.

    Includes The Unseen, Fourteen, Overtones, The Pot Boiler, Hearts, He Said and She Said, The Buffer, Illuminati in Drama Libre, Attuned, Beyond.

    Trap, The.

    Tuning In.

    [*" Tuning In"* is reprinted in this volume.]

Gillette, William. * Among Thieves.

    * How Well George Does It.

    * Red Owl, The.

Glaspell, Susan. *Plays.* Small, Boston, 1920.

    Contains Trifles, Close the Book, The Outside, The People, Woman's Honor; Suppressed Desires, and Tickless Time (in collaboration with George Cram Cook).

    [*" Suppressed Desires"* is reprinted in this volume.]

Glick, Carl.   * Fourth Mrs. Phillips, The.
    Immortal, The (in collaboration with B. Sobel).   *Poet Lore*, Vol. 32,
        441.   Boston, 1921.
    It Isn't Done.   † In Shay, *Treasury*.
    Outclassed.   † In Shay, *Treasury*.
    Prologue.   *Poet Lore*, Vol. 33, 553.   Boston, 1922.
    * Sun-Cold.
    * Ten Days Later.
Gold, Michael.   * Money.
Goodman, Kenneth Sawyer.   Dancing Dolls.   † In Shay, *Plays for Mum-
    mers*.
    Dust of the Road.   † In Goldstone, *One-Act Plays*.
    Game of Chess, A.   † In Knickerbocker, *Twelve Plays*.
    Green Scarf, The.
    Quick Curtains.   Stage Guild, Chicago, 1915.
        Contains Dust of the Road, The Game of Chess, Barbara, Ephraim
        and the Winged Bear, Back of the Yards, Dancing Dolls, A Man
        Can Only Do His Best.
Goodman, Kenneth Sawyer, and Ben Hecht.   *The Wonder Hat and Other
    One-Act Plays*.   Appleton, New York, 1925.
        Contains The Wonder Hat, The Two Lamps, An Idyll of the
        Shops, The Hand of Siva, The Hero of Santa Maria.
        [" *The Wonder Hat*" *is reprinted in this volume*.]
Goodman, Kenneth Sawyer, and Thomas Wood Stevens.   Holbein in
    Blackfriars.
    Ryland.
        [" *Ryland*" *is reprinted in this volume*.]
Goodman, Jules Eckert.   * Back to Your Knitting.
Green, Paul.   * Blue Thunder.
    Bread and Butter Come to Supper.   In *Wide Fields*, McBride,
        New York, 1927.
    * Fixin's.
    * Hymn to the Rising Sun.
    * *In the Valley and Other Carolina Plays*.
        Contains In the Valley, Quare Medicine, Supper for the Dead,
        Saturday Night, The Man Who Died at Twelve O'Clock, Unto
        Such Glory, The Man on the House, The Picnic, In Aunt Mahaly's
        Cabin, The Good-by, The No 'Count Boy.
        [" *Unto Such Glory*" *is reprinted in this volume*.]
    Lonesome Road, Six Plays for the Negro Theatre.   McBride, New
        York, 1927.
        Contains In Abraham's Bosom (one-act version), White Dresses,
        The Hot Iron, The Prayer Meeting (Granny Boling), The End of
        the Row, Your Fiery Furnace (Sam Tucker).

The Lord's Will and Other Carolina Plays. Holt, New York, 1925.

Contains The Lord's Will, Blackbeard, Old Wash Lucas (The Miser), The No 'Count Boy, The Old Man of Edenton, The Last of the Lowries.

Old Christmas. In *Wide Fields*, McBride, New York, 1927.

Hall, Holworthy, and Robert Middlemass. (*See* Middlemass.)

Halman, Doris. * How Not to Write a Play.

* It Behooves Us.

* Lenna Looks Down.

Set the Stage for Eight. Little, Boston, 1923.

Contains Lady Anne, Santa Claus, The Playroom, Famine and the Ghost, The Difficult Border, The Closet, The Dog, Will O' the Wisp.

["*Will O' the Wisp*" *is reprinted in this volume.*]

* Voice of the Snake, The.

Hecht, Ben. (*See* Goodman, Kenneth Sawyer.)

Helburn, Theresa. * Enter the Hero.

Hoffman, Phoebe. About Face.

* Advantages of Being Shy, The.

* In Mrs. Saturday's Shop.

* Lady of Destiny, The.

Man of the Moment, The. † In Johnson, *Ten Fantasies.*

Martha's Mourning. Baker, Boston, 1920.

* Mrs. Leicester's School.

Triumph of Mary, The. Baker, Boston, n. d.

* Undertones.

* Wedding Dress, The.

When It's Spring. Baker, Boston, 1924.

Hopkins, Arthur. * Moonshine.

Housum, Robert. * Corsican Lieutenant, The.

* Ellen's Elopement.

* Eligible Mr. Bangs, The.

Howard, Bronson. * Old Love Letters.

Howells, William Dean. * Albany Depot, The.

* Evening Dress.

* Five O'Clock Tea.

* Letter of Introduction, A.

* Likely Story, A.

* Mouse-Trap, The.

* Unexpected Guests, The.

Hudson, Holland. Action. † In Shay, *Treasury.*

* Kite, The.

Hughes, Babette. * Angelica.

Backstage. † In Clark and Cook, *One-Act Plays.*

* Bound for Mexico.

Calf That Laid the Golden Eggs, The. † In Hughes, *Short Plays*.

Columbine in the Country. Baker, Boston, n. d.

* First White Woman, The.

* Fit as a Fiddle.

* March Heir, The.

Money for Jam. Baker, Boston, n. d.

* Murder! Murder! Murder!

* No More Americans.

* One Egg.

Please Do Not Pick the Flowers. Row, Evanston, 1931.

Safety Pins First. Baker, Boston, n. d.

* Three Men and a Boat.

* Three Players, a Fop and a Duchess.

Hughes, Glenn. * Art and Mrs. Palmer.

* Babbitt's Boy.

* Barber-Shop Blues.

* Blue Sea and Red Rose.

Bottled in Bond. *Drama*, Vol. 13, 170. Mt. Morris, 1923.

Cloaks.

Columbine Madonna.

* Eve in Evelyn, The.

* For Love of Michael.

* Funny Business.

* Harlequinade in Green and Orange.

Heaven Will Protect the Working Girl. Baker, Boston, 1931.

Lace. Row, Evanston, 1931.

* Lady Fingers.

* Men Only.

Much Ado About Loving.

New Plays for Mummers. Univ. of Washington Press, Seattle, 1926.

Contains Manners and Manors, Life on the Steppes, Pretty Little Plum-Pit, Lucy the Farmer's Daughter, The Vengeance of Hello-Hello, The Heart of Old Kentucky, The Killing of Aaron Kale, Nell of the Golden West, Whittle, The Suspicious Drummer.

None Too Good for Dodo.

Pierrot's Mother. † In Nicholson, *Appleton Book*.

Purple Cottage.

Real Gloria.

* Red Carnations.

Hughes, Rupert. Ambush, The. † In Hughes, *Short Plays*.

On the Razor Edge. † In Nicholson, *Appleton Book*.

Jones, Howard Mumford. Fascinating Mr. Denby, The. Keddra. *Univ. of California Chronicle*, Vol. 23, 169. Berkeley, 1921.

Shadow, The. † In *Wisconsin Plays.*
Sundial, The. *Texas Review*, Vol. 5, 93. Austin, 1920.
Kaufman, George S. * If Men Played Cards as Women Do.
  * Pride of the Claghornes, The.
  * Still Alarm, The.
Kelly, George. Finders Keepers. † In Nicholson, *Appleton Book.*
  Flattering Word and Other One-Act Plays, The. Little, Boston, 1925.
  Contains The Flattering Word, Smarty's Party, The Weak Spot, Poor Aubrey.
  ["*Poor Aubrey*" *is reprinted in this volume.*]
  * One of Those Things.
Kemp, Harry. Boccaccio's Untold Tale. †In Johnson, T., *Miniature Plays.*
  Prodigal Son, The. *Smart Set*, Vol. 52, 83. New York, 1917.
  White Hawk, The. † In Goldstone, *One-Act Plays.*
Kennedy, Charles O'Brien. * And There Was Light.
  * Falling of an Apple, The.
  * Gift of Wisdom, The.
  * Kingdom of the Mind, The.
  Man with the Iron Jaw, The. Appleton, New York, n. d.
  * Men, Women, and Goats.
  * More in Sorrow than in Anger.
  * Natural Conclusion, A.
  * Romeo Passes By.
  * Some Words in Edgewise.
  * This Daring Young Man.
Kennedy, Charles Rann. Necessary Evil, The. Univ. of Chicago Press, 1930.
  Terrible Meek, The. Univ. of Chicago Press, 1930.
  ["*The Terrible Meek*" *is reprinted in this volume.*]
Kreymborg, Alfred. * How Do You Do, Sir?
  Contains I'm Not Complaining, How Do You Do, Sir?, Haverstraw Haircut, America! America!, Limping Along, Frank and Mr. Frankenstein, Nothing Ever Happens, Brother Bill, Good Story.
  ["*America! America!*" *is reprinted in this volume.*]
  * Jane, Jean, and John.
  * Lima Beans.
  * Maniken and Miniken.
  Plays for Merry Andrews. Sunwise Turn, New York, 1920.
  Contains Vote, The New Moon, At the Sign of the Thumb and Nose, Uneasy Street, The Silent Waiter, Monday.
  Puppet Plays. Secker, London, 1923.
  Contains When the Willow Nods, Blue and Green, Maniken and

Miniken, Jack's House, Lima Beans, People Who Die, Pianissimo.

* Queen's Gambit Declined.

* *Rocking Chairs and Other Comedies.*

Contains Rocking Chairs, Helpless Herberts, Adverbs, Trap Doors, Not Too Far from the Angels.

Kummer, Clare. * Bridges.

* Chinese Love.

* Choir Rehearsal, The.

* Papers.

* Robbery, The.

* So's Your Old Antique.

[*" The Robbery" is reprinted in this volume.*]

Langner, Lawrence. * Accidents Will Happen.

Broken Image, The.

Five One-Act Comedies. Appleton, New York [1922].

Contains Matinata, Another Way Out, The Family Exit, Pie, Licensed.

Patent Applied For.

Pyramid, The. *Guardian*, Vol. 1, 100. Philadelphia, 1925.

* Sire de Maletroit's Door, The.

Wedded. *Little Review*, Vol. 1, 8. Chicago, 1914.

Levinger, Elmer E. At the Gates. Union Hebrew Congregation, Cincinnati, 1925.

Burden, The. Baker, Boston, 1918.

Child of the Frontier, A. Appleton, New York, 1925.

Cow with Wings, The. † In Clark and Nicholson, *American Scene.*

Great Hope, The. *Stratford Journal*, Vol. 5, 231. Boston, 1919.

How Succoth Came to Chayim. Union Hebrew Congregation, Cincinnati, 1923.

Return of the Prodigal. Pilgrim, Boston, 1927.

Ruth of Moab. Union Hebrew Congregation, Cincinnati, 1923.

Silver Cup, The. Union Hebrew Congregation. Cincinnati, 1923.

Tenth Man, The. Baker, Boston, n. d.

Through the School Year. Baker, Boston, n. d.

Contains plays for the various holidays.

Loving, Pierre. Autumn. *Drama*, Vol. 13, 61. Mt. Morris, 1922.

Drift Flake. Bookfellows, Chicago, 1921.

Stick-Up, The. † In Shay, *Treasury.*

Macdonald, Zillah. Circumventin' Sandy. *Drama*, Vol. 16, 291. Mt. Morris, 1926.

Feather Fisher, The. *Touchstone*, Vol. 4, 120. New York, 1918.

Light Along the Rails. *Touchstone*, Vol. 3, 229. New York, 1918.

Long Box, The. *Drama*, Vol. 14, 180. Mt. Morris, 1924.

Markheim.

Mackay, Constance D'Arcy. *The Beau of Bath and Other One-Act Plays.* Holt, New York, 1915.

Contains The Beau of Bath, The Silver Lining, Ashes of Roses, Gretna Green, Counsel Retained, The Prince of Court Painters.

Benjamin Franklin. † In Law, *Modern Plays.*

Boston Tea Party, The. † In Webber and Webster, *Short Plays.*

* Christmas Guest.

The Forest Princess and Other Masques. Holt, New York, 1916.

* On Christmas Eve.

Plays of the Pioneers. Harper, New York, 1915.

Contains The Pioneers, The Fountain of Youth, May Day, The Vanishing Race, The Passing of Hiawatha, Dame Greel o' Portland Town.

Youth's Highway and Other Plays for Young People. Holt, New York, 1929.

MacKaye, Percy. * George Washington at the Delaware.

* *Kentucky Mountain Fantasies.*

Contains Napoleon Crossing the Rockies, The Funeralizing of Crickneck, Timber.

* Kinfolk of Robin Hood, The.

* Pilgrim and the Book, The.

Sphinx, The. Row, Evanston, 1929.

Two at Chateau Thierry. *New York Tribune,* Feb. 16, 1919.

* Washington and Betsy Ross.

* *Yankee Fantasies.*

Contains Chuck, Gettysburg, The Antick, The Cat Boat, Sam Average.

["*Sam Average*" *is reprinted in this volume.*]

* Young Washington at Mt. Vernon.

Macmillan, Mary. * Her Doll.

More Short Plays. Appleton, New York [1917].

Contains His Second Girl, At the Church Door, Honey, The Dress Rehearsal of Hamlet, The Pioneers, In Mendelesia, The Dryad.

Pan or Pierrot. Appleton, New York, 1924.

Plenty of Time. Appleton, New York, 1928.

Short Plays. Appleton, New York [1915].

Contains The Shadowed Star, The Ring, The Rose, Luck?, Entr'acte, A Woman's a Woman for A' That, A Fan and Two Candlesticks, A Modern Masque, The Futurists, The Gate of Wishes.

Third Book of Short Plays. Appleton, New York [1922].

Contains The Weak End, The Storm, In Heaven, When Two's Company, Peter Donelly, An Apocryphal Episode, Standing Moving.

Maltz, Albert. Private Hicks. New Theatre League, New York, 1935.

Manners, John Hartley. Day of Dupes, The. Dodd, New York, 1914.
God's Outcast.
* Hanging and Wiving.
Happiness. Dodd, New York, 1914.
Just As Well. Dodd, New York, 1914.
* Queen's Messenger, A.
* Woman Intervenes, The.
Mapes, Victor. * Flower of Yeddo, The.
* Mechanism Man, The.
Marks, Jeanette. *The Merry Merry Cuckoo and Other Welsh Plays.* Appleton, New York, 1927.
Contains The Merry Merry Cuckoo, The Deacon's Hat, Welsh Honeymoon, A Tress of Hair, Love Letters, Steppin' Westward, Look to the End.
[*"The Merry Merry Cuckoo" is reprinted in this volume.*]
Marquis, Don. Words and Thoughts. Appleton, New York, n. d.
McFadden, Elizabeth. * Boy Who Discovered Easter, The.
* Boy Who Found the King, The.
* Knights of the Silver Shield.
* Palace of Knossos, The.
* Tidings of Joy, The.
* Why the Chimes Rang.
Mellon, Evelyn Emig. *Two Prize Plays, and Four Others.* Baker, Boston, 1929.
Contains The China Pig, Mother and Son, The Old Order, Trains, Love! Love! Love!, Pen and Ink.
Middlemass, Robert, and Holworthy Hall. Under Dog, The. Longmans, New York, 1928.
Valiant, The. Baker, Boston, n. d.
Middleton, George. * Back of the Ballot.
Criminals. Huebsch, New York, 1915.
Embers and Other One-Act Plays. Holt, New York, 1911.
Contains Embers, The Failures, The Gargoyle, In His House, Madonna, The Man Masterful.
Masks and Other One-Act Plays. Holt, New York, 1920.
Contains Masks, Jim's Beast, Tides, Among the Lions, The Reason, The House.
Possession and Other One-Act Plays. Holt, New York, 1915.
Contains The Groove, The Unborn, Circles, A Good Woman, The Black Tie.
[*"A Good Woman" is reprinted in this volume.*]
Tradition and Other One-Act Plays. Holt, New York, 1913.
Contains Tradition, On Bail, Their Wife, Waiting, The Cheat of Pity, Mothers.

Millay, Edna St. Vincent. Princess Marries the Page, The. Harper, New
York, 1932.
> *Three Plays.* Harper, New York, 1926.
> Contains Two Slatterns and a King, Aria da Capo, The Lamp
> and the Bell.

Mitchell, Ronald Elwy. * Better Days.
> * Handful of Sheep, A.
> * Rocky Wooing, A.
> * Rogue in Bed, A.
> Royal Inn, The. Harrap, London, 1925.
> Skinflint. † In Mayorga, *Twenty Short Plays.*
> Way to London, The.

Moeller, Philip. *Five Somewhat Historical Plays.* Knopf, New York,
1918.
> Contains Helena's Husband, A Roadhouse in Arden, Sisters of
> Susannah, The Little Supper, Pokey.
> * Two Blind Beggars and One Less Blind.

Morley, Christopher. Good Theatre. † In Cohen, *More One-Act Plays.*
> In Modern Dress. Random House, New York, 1929.
> *One-Act Plays.* Doubleday, New York, 1924.
> Contains Thursday Evening, Rehearsal, Bedroom Suite, On the
> Shelf, Walt, East of Eden.
> Really, My Dear. † In Hughes, *Short Plays.*

Nicholson, Kenyon. * Bedside Manners (in collaboration with S. N. Behr-
man).
> * Bug Man, The.
> *Garden Varieties.* Appleton, New York, 1924.
> Contains White Elephants, The Bug Man, Confession, The Anony-
> mous Letter, The Casino Gardens, The Marriage of Little Eva, So
> This Is Paris Green.
> * Gentle Assassin.
> * Hint to Brides, A.
> * Meet the Mussus.
> Meet the Wife. *Smart Set*, Vol. 68, 85. New York, 1922.
> * Night's Work, A (in collaboration with S. N. Behrman).
> * Organ, The (in collaboration with G. Edward Pendray).
> Shame the Devil (in collaboration with A. DeSola). Appleton, New
> York, 1928.
> * Snake Eater, The.
> Wanderlust. † In Phillips and Johnson, *Types.*
> * Words and Music.

Nirdlinger, Charles Frederic. Feather's Honeymoon, The. Baker, Boston, 1925.
> *Four Short Plays.* Kennerly, New York, 1916.

Contains Look After Louise, Big Kate, The Real People, Aren't They Wonders?
 * Washington's First Defeat.
O'Brien, Seumas. * Black Bottle, The.
 * Christmas Eve.
 Duty and Other Irish Comedies. Little, Boston, 1916.
 Contains Duty, Jurisprudence, Magnanimity, Matchmakers, Retribution.
O'Dea, Mark. *Red Bud Women.* Appleton, New York, 1925.
 Contains The Song of Solomon, Shivaree, Miss Myrtle Says "Yes", Not in the Lessons.
Odets, Clifford. Till the Day I Die. Random House, New York, 1936.
 Waiting for Lefty. Random House, New York, 1936.
 [*" Till the Day I Die" is reprinted in this volume.*]
O'Neill, Eugene G. Before Breakfast. Appleton, New York [1916].
 Dreamy Kid, The. *Theatre Arts,* Vol. 4, 41. New York, 1920.
 Moon of the Caribbees, The, and Six Other Plays of the Sea. Boni, New York, 1919.
 Contains The Moon of the Caribbees, Bound East for Cardiff, The Long Voyage Home, In the Zone, 'Ile, Where the Cross Is Made, The Rope.
 [*"In the Zone" is reprinted in this volume.*]
 Thirst and Other One-Act Plays. Gorham, Boston, 1914.
 Contains Thirst, The Web, Warnings, Fog, Recklessness.
Peabody, Josephine Preston. *Collected Plays.* Houghton, Boston, 1927.
 Contains Fortune and Men's Eyes, The Wings.
Peterkin, Julia. * Boy-Chillen.
Pillot, Eugene. Gazing Globe, The.
 Hunger.
 * Just Two Men.
 * Little Red Geranium, The.
 * My Lady Dreams.
 * Sundial, The.
 Young Wonder, The. *Drama,* Vol. 11, 151. Mt. Morris, 1921.
Rice, Cale Young. *Collected Plays and Poems.* Doubleday, Garden City, 1915.
 Contains A Night in Avignon.
 Immortal Lure, The, and Other Poetic Dramas. Doubleday, Garden City, 1911.
 Contains Giorgione, Arduin, O-Umè's Gods, The Immortal Lure.
 Selected Plays and Poems. Century, New York, 1926.
Rice, Elmer. * Diadem of Snow, A.
 * Gay White Way, The.
 * Home of the Free, The.

* Passing of Chow Chow, The.

* Three Plays without Words.

Riggs, Lynn.   * Knives from Syria.

  * Reckless.

    ["*Reckless*" *is reprinted in this volume.*]

Riley, Alice C. D.   *Let's Pretend, Four Half-Hour Plays for Young People.*
    Baker, Boston, 1934.

  * Little New Moon.

    Mandarin Coat, The, and Five Other Plays.   Brentano, New York,
    1925.

    Contains Skim Milk, Their Anniversary, The Sponge, Radio,
    The Black Suit Case.

    Play Shop Plays.

    Rival Peach-Trees, The.   † In Dean, *Seven to Seventeen.*

  * Skim Milk.

  * Taxi.

    Ten Minutes by the Clock, and Three Other Children's Plays.   Baker,
    Boston, n. d.

  * Uplifting Sadie.

  * Weathervane Elopes, The.

Rogers, John William.   * Bumblepuppy.

  * Judge Lynch.

  * Mary Means What She Says.

  * Rescue of Cynthia Ann, The.

  * Saved.

  * Wedding Presents.

  * Westward People.

  * Women Folks.

Rogers, Robert Emmons.   Behind a Watteau Picture.   Baker, Boston, n. d.

Rostetter, Alice.   Queen's Lost Dignity, The.   † In Cohen, *Junior Play Book.*

  * Widow's Veil, The.

Ruthenberg, Grace Dorcas.   Alas, Dear Goliath.   † In Sanford, *Assembly
    Room Plays.*

    Death of Anulis, The.   † In Sanford, *One-Act Plays.*

  * Gooseberry Mandarin, The.

    Hans Bulow's Last Puppet.   † In Baker, *Yale One-Act Plays.*

    Moon for a Prince, The.   † In Dean, *Seven to Seventeen.*

  * Moses Was an Oysterman.

  * O Bright Flame Lifted.

  * Retreat.

Saunders, Louise.   Knave of Hearts, The.   † In Leonard, *Atlantic Book.*

    Magic Lanterns.   Scribner, New York, 1923.

    Contains Figureheads, Our Kind, Poor Maddalena, See-Saw,
    King and Commoner.

Seiler, Conrad. *Husband of Xanthippe and Other Short Plays.* Baker, Boston, 1929.

Contains The Husband of Xanthippe, In a Window, Matrimony, Box Seats, Eyes, The Lady in the Sack.

Mistress Shakespeare. *Poet Lore,* Vol. 43, 119. Boston, 1936.

Suicide and Other One-Act Comedies. T. Y. Crowell, New York, 1926.

Contains Suicide, Time Will Tell, Poets All, Crime, An Eye for an Eye, Fantasia.

Seymour, Ann. Lawd, Does You Undahstan'? † In Mayorga, *Twenty Short Plays.*

[*"Lawd, Does You Undahstan'?" is reprinted in this volume.*]

Shaw, Irwin. Bury the Dead. Random House, New York, 1936.

Sinclair, Upton. Indignant Subscriber, The. *Socialist Review,* Vol. 4, 389. London, 1910.

John D. *Socialist Review,* Vol. 4, 463. London, 1910.

Second Story Man, The. *Socialist Review,* Vol. 4, 91. London, 1910.

Steele, Wilbur Daniel. *Terrible Woman, The, and Other One-Act Plays.* Appleton, New York, 1925.

Includes The Terrible Woman, The Giants' Stair, Not Smart, Ropes.

Stevens, Thomas Wood. Gold Circle, The. † In Shay, *Treasury.*

Nursery Maid of Heaven, The, and Other Plays. Appleton, New York, 1926.

Contains The Nursery Maid of Heaven, Three Wishes, Highways Cross, The Triumph of Punchinello, Friend Mary, The Duquesne Christmas Mystery.

Three Wishes. † In Shay, *Treasury.*

Stevens, Thomas Wood, and Kenneth Sawyer Goodman. Holbein in Blackfriars.

Ryland.

[*"Ryland" is reprinted in this volume.*]

Stevens, Thomas Wood, and Wallace Rice. Chaplet of Pan.

Stone, Weldon. All Through the House. Row, Evanston, 1936.

Darksome Furriner, A. † In Mayorga, *Twenty Short Plays.*

Quarrytown. *Players,* Vol. 13, No. 1. Peru, Nebraska, 1936.

Strong, Austin. * Drums of Oude, The.

* Little Father of the Wilderness (in collaboration with L. Osbourne).

Tarkington, Booth. Beauty and the Jacobin. Harper, New York, 1912.

* Bimbo the Pirate.

* Ghost Story, The.

Help Each Other Club. Appleton, New York, 1934.

* Station YYYY.

* Travelers, The.
* Trysting Place, The.
Thomas, Augustus. * Constitutional Point, A.
   * Editha's Burglar.
   * Man Upstairs, The.
   * Proper Impropriety, A.
Tompkins, F. G. In Front of Potter's. † In Shay, *Treasury.*
   Letters, The. Appleton, New York [1923].
   Philanthropy. † In Loving, *Ten Minute Plays.*
   Sham. † In Dickinson, *Drama.*
Torrence, Ridgely. *Rider of Dreams, The, and Other One-Act Plays.*
   Macmillan, New York, 1917.
     Contains The Rider of Dreams, Granny Maumee, Simon the
   Cyrenian.
Totheroh, Dan. * One-Act Plays for Everyone.
     Contains The Stolen Prince, The Lost Princess, Good Vintage,
   In the Darkness, The Breaking of the Calm, Pearls, The Great Dark,
   While the Mushrooms Bubble, The Widdy's Mite, A Tune of a Tune,
   Mirthful Marionettes.
     [*"Good Vintage" is reprinted in this volume.*]
Walker, Stuart. King's Great Aunt Sits on the Floor, The. Appleton,
   New York, 1925.
   More Portmanteau Plays. Appleton, New York [1921].
     Contains The Birthday of the Infanta, The Very Naked Boy,
   Sir David Wears a Crown, Nellijumbo.
   Portmanteau Plays. Appleton, New York [1917].
     Contains The Trimplet, Nevertheless, The Medicine Show, Six
   Who Pass While the Lentils Boil.
   [*"Six Who Pass While the Lentils Boil" is reprinted in this volume.*]
Ware, Alice Holdship. Mighty Wind a' Blowin'. New Theatre League,
   New York, 1936.
Weaver. John V. A. So That's That. Appleton, New York, 1926.
Wellman, Rita. Dawn. *Drama,* Vol. 9, 89. Mt. Morris, 1919.
   Funiculi Funicula.
   Lady with the Mirror, The. *Drama,* Vol. 8, 299. Chicago, 1918.
Wentworth, Marion Craig. War Brides. Century, New York, 1915.
Wexley, John. Last Mile, The (one-act version).
     [*"The Last Mile" is reprinted in this volume.*]
Wiggin, Kate Douglas. * Old Peabody Pew, The.
Wilde, Percival. Alias Santa Claus. Baker, Boston, 1929.
   Comrades in Arms, and Other Plays for Little Theatres. Little,
   Boston, 1935.
     Contains Comrades in Arms, Over the Teacups, Glamour, A Bow
   to Lotta, An Affair of Dishonor, The Moving Finger.

Dawn, and Other One-Act Plays of Life To-day. Little, Boston, 1922.
Contains Dawn, The Noble Lord, The Traitor, A House of Cards, Playing with Fire, The Finger of God.
Eight Comedies for Little Theatres. Little, Boston, 1922.
Contains The Sequel, The Previous Engagement, The Dyspeptic Ogre, In the Net, A Wonderful Woman, Catesby, His Return, Embryo.
Enchanted Christmas Tree, The. Baker, Boston, 1927.
Inn of Discontent and Other Fantastic Plays, The. Little, Boston, 1924.
Contains The Inn of Discontent, Lady of Dreams, The Luck-Piece, Ashes of Romance, Nocturne.
Kings in Nomania. Baker, Boston, 1928.
Line of No Resistance, The. Baker, Boston, 1922.
Question of Morality and Other Plays, A. Little, Boston, 1922.
Contains Confessional, The Villain in the Piece, According to Darwin, A Question of Morality, The Beautiful Story.
Reckoning, The. Baker, Boston, 1924.
Reverie. Baker, Boston, 1924.
Ten Plays for Little Theatres. Little, Boston, 1931.
Contains Gadgets, Standish Pride, The Thing, The Lost Elevator, Lot's Wife, What Never Dies, The Short Cut, Vignette, Out of the Mouths of . . ., The Great American Drama.
Three-Minute Plays. Baker, Boston, 1935.
Contains Robert Burns, Ever Upwards!, The Great American Drama, The Meticulous Customer, Yashmak!, The Phial, The First Client, 'T was the Night Before, The Stork, The National Anthem, Duetto, Hush Money, Love Is Blind, Out of the Mouths of . . ., The Past Pluperfect, Costume de Rigueur, Con Amore, The Un-accepted Apology, The Facts, Vignette.
Toy-Shop, The. Baker, Boston, 1924.
Unseen Host and Other War Plays, The. Little, Boston, 1917.
Contains The Unseen Host, Mothers of Men, Pawns, In the Ravine, Valkyrie!
["*Pawns*" is reprinted in this volume.]
Wilder, Thornton. Angel on the Ship, The. † In Church, *Curtain.*
Long Christmas Dinner, The, and Other Plays in One Act. Coward, New York, 1931.
Contains The Long Christmas Dinner, Queens of France, Pullman Car Hiawatha, Love and How to Cure It, Such Things Only Happen in Books, The Happy Journey to Trenton and Camden.
* Love and How to Cure It.
Wolff, Oscar M. Where But in America. †In Knickerbocker, *Twelve Plays.*

Young, Stark.   King with the Iron Heart, The.   † In Moses, *Another Treas-*
     ury.
     Queen of Sheba, The.   In Isaacs, *Plays.*
     Rose Windows.   † In Isaacs, *Plays.*
     Three One-Act Plays.   Appleton, New York [1921].
       Contains Madretta, At the Shrine, Addio.
    * Twilight Saint, The.

DATE DUE
